CW01507515
1965
The JAM
66
Abbey Road Studios

Paul Weller
Dancing Through the Fire

THE AUTHORISED ORAL HISTORY
BY DAN JENNINGS

CONSTABLE

First published in Great Britain in 2025 by Constable

3 5 7 9 10 8 6 4

A CIP catalogue record for this book is available from the British Library.

ISBN: 978-1-40872-163-6 (hardback)
ISBN: 978-1-40872-162-9 (trade paperback)

Typeset in Sabon LT by Hewer Text UK Ltd, Edinburgh
Printed and bound in Great Britain by Clays Ltd, Elcograf S.p.A.

Papers used by Constable are from well-managed forests and other responsible sources.

Constable
An imprint of
Little, Brown Book Group
Carmelite House
50 Victoria Embankment
London EC4Y 0DZ

The authorised representative
in the EEA is
Hachette Ireland
8 Castlecourt Centre, Dublin 15,
D15 XTP3, Ireland
(email: info@hbgi.ie)

An Hachette UK Company
www.hachette.co.uk

www.littlebrown.co.uk

For Kate, Henry and Freddie –
thanks for the time, space and support to see this through.

Contents

Foreword

It's incredible to think that the podcast Dan started in lockdown as a hobby grew and grew to such a degree that he seems to have interviewed nearly everyone I know – and a lot of people I don't! The level of detail and research that Dan put into every episode is testament to how successful they became for him.

After he interviewed me for the final episode, we were chatting about 'what next', and I suggested he should turn the podcast into a book. How brilliant that he actually did! This is probably one of the most comprehensive books covering my career, mainly because of the scope of people that Dan interviewed: from family, friends, musicians I've worked with, photographers, film directors, my current team and music industry execs, amongst many, many more. I'm flattered that people had so much to say!

This book, as well as the podcast series, reflects the hard work put in by Dan, but also the fact that so many were happy to chat to him shows what a good bloke he is.

Paul Weller, July 2025

The Wellers of Woking

Ann Weller: I met John Weller at the Lion Works in Maybury in Woking. I was working in the filing office, typing and organising paperwork. He came in to tarmac the roads. Whenever we had to take papers across, all the blokes in them days would wolf whistle at us. John was so good looking. He could have been a bloody film star. The Lion Works had a social club, so you'd go dancing on a Friday and Saturday night. John was a brilliant jiver. John had boxed for the RAF, Southern Counties, and England, winning all his fights. He was Southern Counties champion, ABA champion, and services champion. We've still got all of his cups and trophies. He was going to turn professional, but he couldn't afford the bus fare to where he had to go.

Nicky Weller: Mum was besotted with him. She was only sixteen or seventeen. My dad was something like nine years older.

Ann Weller: John and I got married when I was seventeen in March 1957. I was eighteen when I had Paul, and Nicky was born four years later.

Paul Weller: It's funny to think I was only born thirteen years after the end of the Second World War. It's fucking bonkers in some ways.

Nicky Weller: In those days, you'd have to register them within a week at the hospital. Mum put his name down as John William Weller, which was a mix of names from both my dad and his dad.

Ann Weller: I didn't know what to call him. John came in and went, 'I want to call him Paul.' I said, 'That's the first time you've ever mentioned it!'

Nicky Weller: He was always known as Paul, but his actual birth certificate said 'John William'. In 1976, he officially changed it by deed poll. I never knew he wasn't anything other than Paul. When he came to have the papers signed, I remember him being a little shit, and saying, 'I'm changing my name to Sid Snot!' because the punk scene had come around. I was panicking, 'Mum, you can't let him call himself Sid Snot – it's ridiculous'.

Ann Weller: He's always been a little shit.

Nicky Weller: Mum and Dad both had strange childhoods, so they didn't want that for either of us. Even though we were pretty poor, living in an old council house in Stanley Road, they made sure we could do whatever we wanted to – I used to go ballroom dancing, karate, St John's Ambulance – across the road at the drill hall. They were totally different to most parents. They'd be like, 'Here's a letter, you're not going to school tomorrow. We're going to fucking Kingston. I've won loads of money on cards.' Paul's mates used to come around and say, 'I wish our parents were like this.' It was quite a mental childhood.

Paul Weller: We were just a regular working-class family really, like a lot of people at that time. We had great times me and him. I used to go out when he was on the cabs sometimes in Woking. There's a housing project just outside Woking. At the entrance to where this posh road, nice estate place was, there was new turfed roads. We used to have one of them big old-fashioned prams, probably for my sister. I was only a wee lad, tiny and [*laughs*] he dug up all these freshly laid turfs, cut them in squares, loaded the pram up, stuck me on top of it. And off we went back to our house and lo and behold by morning we had grassed a little garden – all freshly turfed.

Ann Weller: I used to get paid three pound a week to clean at Woking Mosque. I could take Paul with me, and they were lovely, lovely people. We went back recently with Paul. He said, 'There's the pond I fell in.' Well, all of us – Nicky, John – well, we've always worked. She had a job when she was twelve. Well, I like it anyway, I couldn't sit around all day.

Nicky Weller: As kids, Paul and his mates would all go over to the Indian cemetery. Their names are still carved in the bricks there. We took one of Paul's youngest kids over and walked along the canal, back past Boundary Road to Walton Terrace, where Mum and Dad had their first house – the one where Paul was born. Amazingly, that house is still standing, even though not much else around there is.

Ann Weller: I had to find jobs where I could take Paul with me, so got jobs at the school. That was quite good because the caretaker down Maybury school was really nice. He used to say, 'Right, girls, come in and work two days solid.' We had to wax the floors, and get paid by the council, but he used to let us off.

Nicky Weller: I remember my brother wanted to set up a football team, and Dad was like, 'OK, I'll look after you, I'll get the games.' They'd cover any kids who couldn't pay the subs, even though they didn't have any money themselves at the time.

Ann Weller: It was called Maybury Rovers. John knew someone at Chelsea, and they gave us the old strip. When the boys put the tops on, they were down past their shorts. After a while, we had to get rid of Paul because he was no good.

Nicky Weller: He was so crap at football that he was sitting on the sidelines and my dad was like, 'This is ridiculous, I don't mind having a football team but you're not even playing because you're so rubbish.'

Ann Weller: Nicky was a very good girl, yeah. What about Paul? We'll pass on that [*laughs*]. He was a nice little boy, wasn't he? Then he grew up . . .

Paul Weller: Yeah, a happy childhood, definitely. I was painfully shy. That's the only thing I'd say. I think I was happy anyway. I always felt there was something else. Not when I was a young kid, but the older I got, I just thought, *I gotta do something else. I gotta get out of this environment*. Not my family, but just Woking I suppose. My form of escape was to one day get to go to London. That's as far afield as I thought of. But, yeah, really happy. We were very lucky where we lived to be surrounded by this countryside, which is only a few miles from Woking. So, we'd just spend time, me and my mates, just riding our bikes and playing. Whatever we didn't have, we didn't know about, so it didn't really bother ya.

Nicky Weller: When Paul got into music, Dad was chuffed to bits because Paul really found his true vocation in life. Music was always part of our home. Dad had a shitty old upright piano under the stairs in Stanley Road that he nicked from somewhere. He was an amazing pianist. He had a real ear for music, and my brother took after him. Paul would be doing Beatles tunes on there, me doing classical and Dad doing his rock and roll.

Paul Weller: My dad wasn't a big music fan. He only liked Frank Sinatra and Nat King Cole really, but my mum was very young. She was only eighteen when she had me. She'd have the radio on, or we used to have one of them old radiograms, where you could stack all the singles up. She had a few singles that she bought. They were quite expensive at the time, in relative terms anyway, still a bit of a luxury item, but I would go and borrow records off my mum's friends.

Nicky Weller: We had a little black cat that we called Lindy Lollipop. Paul would be playing his guitar in his room, coming down to the loo, whatever, and this cat would just cling round my brother's neck. She loved him. She really loved the music, sitting on top of the piano with her little ears going. My mum used to go 'It's fucking Beethoven innit.' You know how eloquent my mum is. We thought she was Beethoven reincarnated.

Paul Weller: I've been a fan of The Beatles since seeing them on the Royal Command Performance in 1963. From a six-year-old to now. They've been such a massive part of my life. As much as my parents are, or my sister, or direct family. Even at that very, very young age, that's all I really thought about. I loved music and the whole culture that went with music. I thought that The Beatles were totally entwined – clothes, hair and attitudes – it was revolutionary, especially after we'd come out of such a bleak post-war time.

Nicky Weller: It was a fun-filled music house. Mum had a big Motown collection, and she'd always be singing around the house. Dad loved Nat King Cole, all that kind of stuff. My brother was into The Beatles. I loved Bowie, Roxy Music and T. Rex, that whole glam thing that was going on. I absolutely loved David Cassidy and David Essex.

Paul Weller: I don't know if music will ever have that same cultural importance again. Because it was such a pioneering time. There were so many barriers that were broken in the sixties, so many frontiers that were created and I don't know if it's even possible to do that again because we know so much. We've got fifty, sixty years of pop culture to refer to now as well. But I look at my kids . . . They love music and it's a big part of their lives but not in the same way.

Ann Weller: Paul has always been into the clothes since he was a kid. I love clothes and shoes too.

Nicky Weller: She's the Imelda Marcos of Surrey.

Paul Weller: Fashion was as important as music. My mum was very young, she didn't have much money, but she would always look nice and trendy. But I do think it was very much of that culture, of that time, in the sixties as well. It changes very slowly now, people are still wearing the same clothes they wore back in the early noughties, but fashion changed so quickly in the sixties. Every week was something different, even into the early seventies when I was a sort of suedehead, skinhead. You'd save up for what seemed like ages to buy an item, only to go to youth club or the disco on a Thursday and see that the faces are wearing something else already.

I got stuff on tick and then had a paper round and would save up and then bug Mum for the rest of it. *You must have this thing, must have that record, got to have that shirt, got to have them shoes*. They were important, cultural things.

Nicky Weller: If my dad couldn't work on the building site because it was fucking pissing with snow or something for six weeks, he'd go and nick coal or we'd go and break into old, empty houses to get copper, coal and lead. They'd have it away. Paul found some old tin signs that we sold at the top of the road.

Paul Weller: He used to be a hod carrier for a long time, which was a fucking tough job. But one way or the other he would make sure that he'd provide for us.

There used to be a lot of disused houses in Woking. He'd break into them looking for copper, whatever it may be. Anything that could be saleable. I remember him knocking off coal from the railyard down the bottom of Woking near Goldsworth Road. I was sitting in the car, and he's going, 'I won't be a minute.' The boot's gone up. He's fucking putting all this coal in for our fire. I could feel the seat of the car getting lower and lower.

Nicky Weller: You'd do whatever was needed to put food on the table. Plus, my dad's love of cards helped as well.

Paul Weller: I will always think of myself as being working class, and I'm very proud of that. I don't care how big my house is, or how much money I've earned, I will always have those values, and I will always think of myself as being working class. A friend of mine, I won't name who it is, texted me some time ago, and he said, 'Isn't it funny how we end up middle class?' I was like 'Speak for yourself, mate, because I fucking ain't!' I don't care about houses or money or whatever, I will always be working class, and I will always approach life from that point of view. I think it's very important to hang on to really and I've no wish to be middle class. So yeah, it is very important that, again, a very formative time. Me and my sister never struggled, right. We always had clean clothes, we always had food, but I could see it was a struggle for my mum and dad, as it was for a lot of families, and still is.

I also think with the working class of my youth, there was a very strong work ethic. *Everyone's got to work. You've got to pay your way. You've got to make money.* Being on the dole was a bit frowned upon. There was a pride value as well in that, that you worked and did your best. My old man was a hustler. Even though he worked his bollocks off as well, but he would still hustle, and a little bit light fingered at times as well, shall we say! But he did what he had to do for his family.

Nicky Weller: To get my brother his guitar, they'd have the phone or something else cut off that week.

Paul Weller: It'd be once a week almost, we'd hear the doorbell go or the knock on the door and me and my sis, and my mum, would go 'Get behind the settee.' They'd be peering in the window. That was quite a regular thing. We had a phone sometimes that worked and other times when they couldn't pay the bill . . . we got cut off. I'm sure my mum and dad went without, but me and my sister didn't. We always had food, we always had clean clothes. We always had laughs. It was all fun.

Roger Pilling: I first met Paul at Sheerwater County Secondary School in 1971. I was thirteen . . . He wasn't a child prodigy, only a few people knew that he even had a guitar. He wasn't constantly singing or tapping his desk to a beat. We had a little clique – me, Steve Baker, Pete Carver and Paul – we called ourselves 'The Clan'. At school, we had to wear a uniform, but Paul's was just slightly different. While most of the kids wore woollen blazers, he'd have a Trevira one, and while we were supposed to wear black trousers, his were grey. He always stood out. There was a sense that he was different to anybody else, but nobody could quite put their finger on it. You'd walk down the corridors and all the older kids lining the corridor walls, the skinheads, would all nod and speak to him, which was odd because he was a year younger. He commanded a sense of respect, for no real reason. No obvious talent and nothing was ever mentioned.

Paul Weller: We used to go to Woking Football Club disco on a Thursday night. They played a lot of Motown, soul and all the reggae tunes. That's all people listened to. You might hear Slade or T. Rex, maybe a couple of chart things of the time, but generally you wouldn't hear Led Zeppelin, man, or that sort of thing. That disco was another massive influence on me.

Roger Pilling: Soon after becoming friends, I was invited to Paul's house for tea. Stanley Road was a little terraced house. John would have been out at work. Ann was welcoming and easy-going. They were clearly proud of their son and had a friendship going too. There wasn't a hierarchy or a pecking order. It was a very nice thing.

My own bedroom was typical for a thirteen-year-old – minimalist with a football, boots, Subbuteo, casual clothes and school uniform. That was it. But Paul's room was full of posters of The Beatles, a record player, guitar and a prehistoric chest of drawers with Beatles albums that I'd never heard of, along with a massive collection of Beatles monthlies. It was so far removed from anybody else's bedroom . . . and he was telling me that when he left school, he was going to be in a band. I felt honoured that he told me that.

Paul Weller: There are core things that I've always loved, and I still love, and soul is a big part of that. I guess they're all the things that were my first formative influences. The Beatles and the whole sixties thing with The Kinks and Small Faces, but then also reggae and soul music and funk. I remember hearing James Brown's 'Sex Machine' at the disco, it was like it was being beamed in from somewhere else. What he was doing at the time was revolutionary, and it's only when you start back-tracking, and discovering more and more music as you go along, and you see the roots of James Brown comes from African music, you hear other African music and you think, *that's like James Brown, man*. Then you see the whole universal connection with this music, where it's from and its roots, and how it got to be where it is, and its influence. It's fascinating. I think that it's the heartbeat of the world and it shows how we're all really connected.

Forming the band

Nicky Weller: We were in Stanley Road when Paul got into music and, at the time, his best mate was Steve Brookes.

Roger Pilling: I introduced him to Paul, and they immediately hit it off. Steve had an interest in music. He had a few records and a guitar, which would have sparked some interest to Paul, and that friendship was well and truly cemented.

Steve Brookes: We got to know each other in November 1971, when I first attended Sheerwater School. We were both thirteen. He's a day older than me. His birthday is 25 May, mine's 26 May. I get to pull his leg about being younger than him.

Roger Pilling: There was a common bond, and they became best buddies. I did actually practise with them with an old guitar that I bought, but I was completely useless. Very soon I was either kicked out of the band or decided to go.

Ann Weller: Steve was at school with Paul and his mum and dad split up. He didn't want to go to where his dad was or where his mum was going, so he came to live with us. Because they were a bit posher than us, I said, 'If he wants to share a bed with Paul and live at Stanley Road, with no hot water and an outside loo, then he can come.'

Nicky Weller: It was supposed to be for a few months, but Steve was here for two years I reckon . . .

Ann Weller: Paul and Steve both took up the guitar and they would be up in their bedroom playing. I got this guy who worked in Woking record shop to teach them. They did two-for-one, because we couldn't afford it.

Steve Brookes: Once the new year got underway, Paul and I started kicking around and realised that we both wanted to do the same thing. I'd show him little things that I'd learned, and he'd do the same. We just bonded. I think his dad got us our first gig about six months later . . .

Paul Weller: At fourteen, I started taking music more seriously. Me and Steve had a few lessons with this guy called Smithy, who used to work in a music shop in Woking. We didn't last long, man, because it was so tedious. He was teaching us to read the dots and dashes, which we just couldn't get our heads around. We just wanted to be able to play a song. The thing we got from that was the little chord boxes that are on sheet music that show you how to play the chords. C. OK, yeah. G.

Nicky Weller: Two lessons and they decided that they were already The Beatles . . .

Paul Weller: By the time we learned three or four chords, we went off and did our own thing and started writing songs together. Daft little Beatles knockoffs. We developed like that. We'd both find a different chord. Brooksie would say, 'I've just found this chord. It's a D major seventh,' and we thought that was the greatest chord we'd ever heard, and would write five songs with this chord in. That's just how it went, learning more and more chords.

Ann Weller: They had a good music teacher at Sheerwater. Mr Avory. He was a bit more for the kids. Paul used to phone me up to bring his guitar down.

Steve Brookes: We started off as a duo. The first gig we ever did was one lunchtime at school. We had this microphone that was plugged in through the record player, which had a speaker in it. We were so nervous. Really bricking it and we just looked down the whole time. When we looked up, most of the audience was girls. We thought, yeah, this is a good job.

Ann Weller: Paul and Steve would play up in their room, so John went up one day and said, 'How long are you going to sit up here playing that bleeding guitar? Are you going to go and play out?'

Paul Weller: I remember telling my mum, 'I'm going to play next week.' She's like, 'Really?' and I stand up there and do it. It was only a Wednesday night at the Woking Working Men's Club, just me and Steve. Two little kids and seven old geezers with their pints. Totally disinterested.

Ann Weller: I couldn't get over that because Paul was always shy as a little boy. I thought, he's not going to get up in front of people and sing, he'd have his back to them. I couldn't see him as a front man. Brooksie was in your face, wasn't he? I suppose it was weird, but then you just get used to it.

Paul Weller: It was our introduction to it, or our induction to it, but I couldn't imagine it either. It's a weird thing, isn't it? I think there's quite a lot of artists, performers, whatever you want to call them, that are very shy really. But then when you get on them boards, you just change. Your personality changes, your thoughts change. Why that is . . . I don't know. It's just another side of me, that's all.

Roger Pilling: We had to go to the careers office one day. Paul was an impatient fella. He had no interest in school or anything to do with the working life. We were waiting and he said, 'You do realise that this is a complete waste of my time? I'm going to be in a band when I leave this fucking place' . . . Everybody knew that that was a possibility. How big it then got, nobody could have ever imagined that, but everybody knew that he wouldn't be doing the same as everybody else.

Paul Weller: I probably thought that when I was a kid, *I want to be a pop star*. I always felt we were working towards something, and I always thought we were going to go somewhere. I remember in the eighties people were saying how pretentious I'd got, but I always had those pretentions, depends how you look at them. When I was fourteen or fifteen, I thought we were going to make it, I always had my head in the clouds, in those terms anyway. I always felt something was going to happen.

Ann Weller: John started getting them little gigs in pubs. They only had about six songs that they could play, and they were all oldies, things like 'Johnny B. Goode'. All the sixties stuff.

Steve Brookes: The first lineup had a guy called Dave Waller playing rhythm guitar, and a couple of other drummers before Paul Buckler came along.

Rick Buckler: One way out of working-class life was football or music, so many people learned instruments. Mr Avory encouraged pupils to meet in the music room at lunch, there was a lot of album-swapping and muso talk. That's where I met Paul and Steve . . . I was drawn to the drums. I couldn't afford a brand new one, so I made my own, and borrowed a bass drum from Guildford YMCA. I don't think they ever got it back, actually! I practised on the end of my bed, which went through a lot of sheets and annoyed my mum.

Steve Brookes: He was the one that we gelled with and then it became a three-piece. That was when The Jam name came up. We never went out as anything other than The Jam. That was it. There was no name before that.

Roger Pilling: Paul became very friendly with Dave, who had moved down from London. He was into music and poetry and looked a little bit different with his tonic jacket, mass of curls and cockney accent. Paul found a bit of a kindred spirit, they connected more than he did with most others.

Paul Weller: Oh, we just loved it, man. That was all we wanted to do. We hated school. We hated any kind of system at all. We were trying to look at how can we live outside of all this bullshit, and we thought music was the way out . . . and luckily it was.

Rick Buckler: We couldn't have two Pauls in the band, so I changed to my middle name of Rick. Paul's real name is actually John but he's a fan of Paul McCartney, so that's why he's called Paul.

Steve Brookes: We used to play a very ropey version of 'I Saw Her Standing There', and 'Norwegian Wood' – things that weren't too complicated . . . We'd have a bit of rock and roll as well, Chuck Berry, but then The Beatles had done that too . . .

Rick Buckler: There was a guy called Dave Striker who ran the Sheerwater youth club who said, 'Why don't you come along and play?'

Roger Pilling: Paul's dad did building work, he was also an evening taxi driver who used to hustle. Just about everybody that got in his cab would have been told about his boy and if they had a connection with any function room, pub or club, he'd be asking for gigs. He was an extremely resourceful man, a very pushy man and if there was a chance of getting in somewhere, he would have found a way of getting in there for Paul.

Rick Buckler: Paul gave me a stack of Chuck Berry records to learn for covers of these rock and roll standards. Well, we learned the beginnings and then we made up the ends, so it was a bit of a hilarious show in that respect. A lot of winking and nudging going on about when we should finish playing, making this noise. But I suppose that was the start of it and it gave us a taste for doing more. Then we got a bit more serious and got a proper set together.

Steve Brookes: As soon as we started playing, we started writing songs. Our first recording was at Kingston. Recording studios were expensive in those days. You really had to be on the ball because you couldn't waste a minute once you got in there . . . We did a song called 'Blueberry Rock' and 'Taking My Love', which later became the *B*-side for 'In the City'. When we first did it, it was a swingy, rock and roll song . . . Paul carried on playing later on and pumped it up.

Rick Buckler: Paul and Steve had started writing songs, mostly love songs and not good ones! They were OK, but there was no real direction to the songwriting. We did a few recordings and got turned down by some of the best record companies in Britain.

Nicky Weller: They started to play Michael's Club, which was a bit of a plastic gangster's gaffe in Woking. They shouldn't have been playing there really because they were underage, but they got a Friday night residency. Then there was a shooting one night, the police turned up and it was shut down. That was mad.

Steve Brookes: It was great because a lot of John's mates used to come up and it was just like a little family meeting every week. We used to get about fifteen quid between the three of us, which in those days was all right. We started when we were fifteen, so we weren't really old enough to be in there, let alone actually providing the entertainment.

Rick Buckler: We turned up on time, packed away and behaved ourselves. We became quite reliable in that respect. I think our work ethic always was very good.

Ann Weller: John used to go out with his little book on a Thursday night to get them gigs. Sometimes they were booed off, sometimes it was all right, but they were getting better as they went along. We went out every Saturday night round the working men's club. John would go off with the van and the boys. Then me and Nicky would follow in our little 1100 cc later on. I'm not being horrible, they could have taken off without John, but I don't think so. You've got to have somebody that says, 'Come on, loves,' and gets on with it. There's also the fact that we knew everybody in Woking so they could always go round the club to rehearse.

Steve Brookes: You are entertainment. Make a noise for the first hour and a half, then they have bingo, and then a dance at the end when they're all lashed up.

Paul Weller: They were just there, man, on their Saturday-night piss up, cheap drink, and the band is a secondary thing. But that kept us playing and made us better musicians and got us pretty tight as a band, plus it earned us a few bob.

Nicky Weller: They'd have a little twenty-minute set and then the bingo would start so they'd have to stop, and then the cockle man would come round with his prawns and then they'd say, 'We've run out of songs, Dad,' and he'd say, 'Just play them again. They won't know.'

Steve Brookes: John was so encouraging and that encouraged us to try harder . . . He was like our mentor. Many years later, he said that when he was a youngster, he'd been a boxer and had a real chance with a big fight down in Brighton, and he went out on the lash the night before. When he turned up, his trainer looked at him and said, 'You're wasting your time, son,' and he said it stayed with him. Don't mess it up.

Ann Weller: I enjoyed those early days more than when they all got famous because we just had fun. You never knew from one day to the other if you were going to be all right or not. You get booed off or they liked you. Or they'd be fighting in the back of the van.

Paul Weller: I was always conscious that he was my dad as well, even though he was my best friend. But I don't know how far we would have got without Dad, to be honest.

Maybe it wouldn't have even happened. I have no idea. He was the one who would go and hustle the gigs, get a van from someone, whether it's beg, borrow . . . Not necessarily steal! But beg and borrow to get a van and our funny little equipment and all that. You've got to have someone who has got that drive. If you haven't got someone in the band that's got that drive to do that, to organise these things, you're fucked really, man. You need someone to pull these things together. We were really lucky, and I was extremely lucky to have a dad who was prepared to do that and actively encouraged it as well. I think he saw it as the way out for me, so I wouldn't have to go through what he went through, and I could maybe make it in music, or make a different living from making music.

Steve Brookes: It's funny, at one of our first gigs at Shearwater Youth Club, we tried to emulate the Faces and the Stones, with a little bar on the stage. They'd have paper cups and bottles of wine and bottles of Jack Daniel's, and we thought that was magic. So, we had the same thing with bottles of Blue Nun, Newcastle Brown and gawd knows what in the corner with the view of drinking it while we're on. But then something happened, and the PA didn't work so we just drank a lot, ended up slaughtered and then someone sorted out all of the sound gear and we had to go on. We were off our tits and John did his nut because it was a reflection of what had happened to him.

He said, 'I'm putting a lot of time into this, if you boys ain't going to take it seriously, then I'm out.'

Paul Weller: He wasn't like a showbiz dad or something. He wasn't like that at all, but I think he must have seen something in me. I don't know, I couldn't see anything apart from my little pipe dreams of one day making it. I had no idea how you'd actually do that, but he must have thought I had something, and we had something, and he was right.

Roger Pilling: I saw them play at Michael's a few times, the new go-to place in Woking, as well as Sheerwater Youth Club and the Labour Club at Walton Road, but then unfortunately, there was a parting of the ways. School ended, or rather, we all got expelled – no tearful farewells, we all just stopped going. I decided to spend the summer in Torquay with some other friends. Then got a job there and didn't come home for two years.

30 May 1974 – Bruce Foxton joins The Jam

Steve Brookes: Our lineup was just me, Paul, and Rick – two guitars and drums, no bass player. The plan was for Paul to switch to bass and bring in Bruce on rhythm guitar. He was a good singer too, so we thought he'd be perfect. Bruce came to a rehearsal, did a few songs, and sounded great, but he wasn't keen. He thought we were a bit *pony* for him – probably because we'd already started wearing white ties by then. His band were a bit more progressive, but they weren't gigging, whereas we were out playing a couple of nights a week, every weekend. He disappeared for a bit but eventually came back on the scene.

Rick Buckler: Bruce was a rhythm guitarist, and Paul wanted to play bass, but Bruce wasn't into our music. He said, 'All your stuff is dated. It's not modern, it's not going anywhere.'

Bruce Foxton: If anybody's seen any photos of me in the early seventies, I've got shoulder-length hair. It was partly their image that attracted me to The Jam, actually, not alienated me. But my band Rita weren't going anywhere . . . no one wanted to book us. So, what attracted me to The Jam was that they had work lined up, playing working men's clubs, and that's what I wanted – to perform.

Steve Brookes: Bruce came back on the scene, and we had our first rehearsal as a four-piece. The sound was gone – without Paul on rhythm guitar, the whole band didn't sound right. Paul struggled to sing and play bass at the same time. It got tense, and John suggested Paul return to guitar and Bruce try bass. Bruce wasn't keen but gave it a go and although he was playing quite rudimentary bass, it was just what it needed. Paul was back on the guitar. He had a very strong rhythmic feel to his playing.

Rick Buckler: Paul said to Bruce one day, if you want to stay in the band, you're going to have to give up rhythm guitar and take up bass. I don't think Bruce was particularly happy about that to start with and there was a bit of a transition period, but he took to it.

1975 – Mod discovery

Paul Weller: Before punk happened, I thought Dr Feelgood were one of the most exciting things around. Their first album, *Down by the Jetty* came out in early '75. Me and Brooksie went to see them, Guildford Civic, that was just incredible, man. Just the power and commitment of that band. The seventies felt desolate after the whole skinhead phase ended for me. I found it quite a boring period really. All those big, American stadium bands, I don't even know what a lot of them are called, but they all had big hair and big-sounding records. I didn't relate to any of that at all.

Roger Pilling: When I finally came back, I had a big argument with my mum. She said, 'Now you've got this out your system, you need to settle down – and tell that bloody Paul Weller to stop coming round on his scooter asking where you are.' By then, he was a proper little mod, buzzing around Woking on his scooter.

Paul Weller: Mod probably started for me, I'm going to say 1975, around that time. Bearing in mind that prior to that, from like 1970 to '72, I'd been into the whole suedehead thing, which really wasn't a million miles away, in my mind, to the mod thing. The skinhead thing might have been a little bit different, but there was a lot of very similar sources and influences, definitely with the clothing, but also with the music as well. Just instead of ska and early soul stuff, it was just a few years down the line.

I can't really think of the exact moment. Something crazy as just seeing a picture. I never heard the Who's music in the sixties as a kid, I don't know why . . . So I hadn't heard 'My Generation'. When I heard that on this compilation I bought, I just thought 'Fuck, that's just so amazing.' And at that time, right, some of the sixties records were still on catalogue. There used to be a little store called Rock On, Ted Carroll and Roger Armstrong used to run it, in Soho Market, where the fire station is now, right at the top of Piccadilly. I bought The Who album there, *My Generation* and the Artwoods album as well, so a few 'moddy' things. I just thought this is the most amazing sound. But it was the look more than anything. I saw something in *NME* or a magazine or whatever. 'That's fucking great, man!' It was probably in the back of my subconscious that recognised that look from years before, when I was a little kid, clocking it, without even thinking about it really. But it rung a bell with me anyway. I kind of know that look, but I don't know it. That was the start of it for me.

Bit by bit, I just tried to find photos, information, whatever. And then I got a scooter as well, and that was it for me, really. I've never looked back since. It would just be me driving around Woking town centre on my scooter, in my parka. I don't know what people thought. I didn't really care anyway. I managed to find some old stock Sta-Prest in the Co-op there, left over from the early seventies. My mum bought me a Brutus jumper she found like, again, old stock. So I would just try to, bit by bit, expand this thing, this idea. Probably getting it wrong compared to the original mods. But it didn't really matter to me. It was my interpretation of it really.

Steve Brookes: Unfortunately, Paul and I started drifting apart as friends. When we had got together, we were thirteen, and when I left the band, we were seventeen. We both changed. Paul wanted to do the mod thing with The Jam suits, the thing that they later became famous for. Either you're going to go and get one of these and be part of this new image that Paul wants to create or not. 'When are you going to go for your fitting?' – but I thought, 'No, I'm not doing it.'

Nicky Weller: My mum went and got the band these black suits from Burton's with the white shirts and ties and stuff. They'd come home from the gigs soaked to the skin. She would have to dry them out. Everyone thought it was a fashion statement when the trousers started getting shorter and shorter. It was because they'd been cleaned so many times that they'd actually shrunk.

Ann Weller: At first, we only had one lot. Couldn't afford more. They were ten pound each, had to pay weekly for them. It was great when they decided to have black suits and white shirts because Paul could use his school shirt. That was an easy thing to do.

Bruce Foxton: Yeah, it was what we wanted to wear. When we went into Burton's to say we wanted three mod suits, they looked at us as if we'd just come from Mars. They said, 'What? Narrow lapels? No, sir, you don't want that. You want wide lapels. No, no, no.' 'No, we want narrow lapels. Narrow trousers.' Eventually, they did what we wanted. We did get some strange looks, but it looked sharp, and it gave John Weller a vehicle of three smart-looking lads, *They must be respectable, they're wearing suits*. It enabled him to get us more work and we felt good. It's part of the gig. It's not just on stage, it's the build up to it and putting the suit on, you think, 'Let's go and get these guys.'

Steve Brookes: The style was always more Paul's thing than mine . . . It was just time for us to part . . . Paul even called once to say EMI had been sniffing around, but they wanted it as a four-piece. He asked if I'd give it another shot. So, I didn't just turn down The Jam once – I turned them down twice. Look, I didn't sit around wringing my hands and crying in my beer about it. But, yeah, you look at something like that and you think, maybe I should have knuckled down and just joined in with it. But being the individual that I am and Paul being the individual that he is, I probably wouldn't have lasted that long anyway. It was better that I went when I did. The testament to it is that since Paul and I re-established our friendship back in the nineties, we've been really good buddies and we now make music together.

Rick Buckler: There was an upside to this, though, that when Bruce plays bass, he plays it like a rhythm guitarist. So as a three-piece, it's ideal, we've got rhythm with bass. There was a couple of other changes. A guy called Dave Waller was involved for a bit and we tried getting a keyboard player. We were always looking for a fourth member. We could never find anybody who stuck around long enough. So, we started to form this core of the three-piece, while trying very hard to sound like a four-piece band. I think that helped develop the sound and the energy, and how we played and put songs together in the future.

1976 – Punk

Paul Weller: Our eye was always to try and get to London, on the pub circuit. At that time, you could play so many pubs in London. We used to play in the Fulham Palace Road – the Greyhound – it was a great boozer. The Scottish fella who ran it gave us a few shots. We started playing a few pubs in London, which was around '76. That was the way forward, because we were playing more to people our own age and people who actually come to see a band, not necessarily us, but they come to see a band because they know it's a live venue.

Rick Buckler: We'd been filling all these pubs and clubs for quite a while, and we weren't really getting anywhere . . . We were reading *NME* and *Sounds* and seeing all these other bands playing in London. That's only about thirty miles from Woking, so we told John we wanted to try gigs there. These shows didn't pay much, if anything, and John wasn't particularly chuffed about it. He thought we had a good thing going with the local clubs and moving into London would cost us money . . . We decided that if record companies wouldn't come to us, we'd go to them – they all seemed to hang around the London pub-rock scene. Once we got there, we started seeing other bands and realised there was an audience our age showing up.

Paul Weller: I was waiting, I didn't even know what shape or form it would take, but I was waiting for something new – *when was it going to be our time? When is it going to be my generation's time?*

Nicky Weller: We moved to Balmoral Drive in 1976, which was another council house. We had a massive 200-foot garden, and then at the other end of that was another 200-foot garden where the Carver family lived. My brother didn't stay that long in Balmoral Drive before he moved up to London.

Steve 'Tufty' Carver: The Wellers got kicked out of Stanley Road and relocated to our estate, which was named after royalty. I lived in Windsor Way and Paul lived in Balmoral Drive, but our back gardens touched each other. One day, I saw Paul mooching about in his new back garden and my brother Pete said, 'I went to school with that geezer.' Weirdly, I chose a different boozer that night. Paul was in there, and in my memory of it all, I said, 'Hello mate, you live at the back of my garden now,' and he went, 'Hello, nice to meet ya. Do you like the Sex Pistols?' . . . It was that quick. Literally bumped into him on a Saturday and by Tuesday we were seeing the Sex Pistols together. Then I jumped on a rollercoaster that lasted over forty-five years.

Paul Weller: Me and Tufty and a few other mates went up to see the Pistols. We had read the review in the *NME* by Neil Spencer. I think it was probably one of their first reviews of the Pistols at the Marquee, and we were like, 'Did you see that review? We've got to go and see them; we've got to see that band.' Took the train up to the Lyceum in the Strand and it was a Friday all-nighter. There was Supercharge, the Pretty Things were headlining, although I don't remember either of them, and the Pistols came on really late, like five in the morning or something like that. That was it, man. Ahh, this is it. This is the revolution . . .

Steve 'Tufty' Carver: My friends were playing dominoes, darts and cards and they were getting married. I was twenty. I thought, *I don't want to get married and play dominos. What the hell's going on here?* I walked into the Roxy and 100 Club. It was technicolour. Girls wearing bin liners with pink hair. I remember Rotten was strapped up in bondage, he couldn't move. Girls were hanging upside down crucifixes on him. He looked so weird. Purple ginger hair with safety pins and bondage and crucifixes . . . It was this mad youth club in London and as Paul would say, 'Everyone was twenty years old watching a group who were twenty years old playing music.'

On the day we saw the Sex Pistols, Paul's dad drove us, which is kind of weird, that your mate goes, 'Do you want to see the Sex Pistols?' and then he brings his dad along. When we got to the venue, it become evident very quickly that he was giving out phone numbers. *This is a bit weird, isn't it?* And then somewhere during that evening, Paul said to me, 'I'm in a band as well.'

Nicky Weller: Paul went to see the Pistols and he bought this workman's boiler suit and got Mum spray-painting it in the kitchen for him. That's what your trendy mum does in them days. I remember him coming back from there because, if you ever heard the demo for 'In the City', it's quite slow and then, suddenly, he went to see the Pistols and it was speeded up 100 miles an hour. It really opened his eyes and really changed his world.

Ann Weller: The boiler suit? Yeah. But Paul done things just to wind people up most of the time, didn't he? I won't tell you what John would say, but Paul is like that. I think he likes annoying people. He'll do something like that and then he'd start laughing, knowing that he's caught you out on something.

Bruce Foxton: I think we all got into it but Paul particularly. We went to see the Pistols. I think it was at 100 Club in Oxford Street and that just ignited Paul. He thought, *This is the way that I want to go with the band*, and Rick and myself were in agreement.

Nicky Weller: Punk was like anybody can get up and play, however crap they were . . . That's when my dad got them onto the London scene, as a new wave punk band. They weren't really punk; they were too smart to be punks, and they didn't like the gobbing.

Rick Buckler: When Paul saw the Pistols, I think it gave him a few pointers and a direction, which was brilliant. It opened his eyes to the possibilities of what you could do with songwriting. It wasn't just the traditional thing that had gone on in the early seventies. So, it all started to kick off quite quickly for us at that point. That's when you would recognise us as The Jam. After doing about three years around the clubs, we did a year and a half on the London pub scene and because we were getting audiences in these places, it started to attract the attention of the record companies.

In the early days, we didn't have a van, so we'd borrow one from anyone we could. There was this guy in Woking who owned a lioness. When we first saw it at Michael's Club, it was the size of a small dog, but it kept growing and eventually got too big for his house, tearing up the furniture. By the time it stood six or seven feet tall, he bought a Luton van and kept it in the back. If we borrowed the van, we had to take the lion with us to shows. People don't believe it, but it's absolutely true.

Paul Weller: Dad had this old beat-up, shitty old van which was used for the gigs. It's a van we had sometimes, and then sometimes we didn't, so I don't know what the deal was [*laughs*]. Occasionally, I'd help him on the site. On the trail, laying bricks or on the hod. I would've been fifteen, sixteen maybe.

One night after work, he was like 'Come here boy, come and help us with this.' Back doors are open, and he's loading an entire bathroom suite into the back of the van. The foreman comes up, and he's like, 'What are you doing with that? Where are you going with that?' He's going 'Oh fucking so-and-so says I've got to take it around the corner.' It was a big estate that they were building. He got away with it. I don't know how. Even as we're lifting, I was going, 'Are you sure this is all right?' He was like, 'Yeah, yeah, it's fine . . . just do it.' And then the next day, there's a knock on the door. I was at home on my own and the old bill were there, and they're going, 'Is your father in?' 'No, he's not in.' 'Do you ever help your dad with his work?' And I was like 'no, not really'. I could see him peering in the van. How he got away with it, I fucking don't know. He got away with loads of things. He wasn't the sort of tea leaf who would steal from you or your mum or someone in the street. It wasn't like that. But if it wasn't nailed down, he'd have it away, and sometimes that involved nefarious sort of methods. That's the way it was.

Ann Weller: I'd also make them jam sandwiches when they were first starting off, so they had something to eat when they come out from the gigs. The thing with Paul is he'd eat them before on the way there because Paul could eat for England. Then they'd have a fight in the back coming home.

Steve 'Tufty' Carver: John was driving us around for the gigs. He's probably forty and we're twenty. We were stupid and drunk, and there was a lot of spitting and farting. God bless him, he put up with all this . . . he must have really thought, *These boys are going somewhere.*

Paul Weller: I've been extremely blessed and lucky; I could think of loads of great times, but they were definitely amongst my favourite times, if not my favourite times, because I just loved that whole thing. We'd get in this battered old van with our equipment driving up and down the A3, all pissed in the back of this van . . . having a laugh.

Roger Armstrong: I had a record stall in Soho Market called Rock On and Paul would regularly come to buy records. I had an idea that he was in a band, but at this point the three of them were an unknown entity . . . It was a Saturday lunchtime. October 1976, I remember his dad John came in and handed me a three-pin plug and said, 'Roger, could you plug this in for us? We're going to try and do a gig outside.' I said, 'No, John, everything we've got runs off the light socket.' I shot round to the little electrical shop around the corner and bought one of those things you plug into a light bulb to run the power off the bayonet, and I rewired his three-pin into the two-pin. It's a miracle they survived and weren't electrocuted to death. It didn't last long. The police came along and moved them on.

Adrian Thrills: I got totally immersed in the very early London punk scene . . . I made a few mates there, Shane MacGowan being one of them. We heard about this band called The Jam who were dressed in mod gear but were playing with the energy of punk. We noticed they were supporting a pub rock band called Roogalator at the 100 Club. I went along with Shane and a couple of others, and we were just blown away by their energy and by Weller's intensity on stage.

Dan Adler [Roogalator]: I was in the dressing room warming up on my Fender Jazzmaster, when this large rather formidable gentleman knocked and came in. He immediately put me at my ease when he shook my hand and introduced himself as Paul Weller's dad . . . He was holding a raggedy Rickenbacker guitar, which was strung up like a train wreck, and he was very concerned. Senior Weller said, 'Here, Dan, is there any way that you can fix our kid's guitar? It's in a terrible state.' . . . After perusing Paul's spaghetti-mess Rickenbacker, I took my wire cutter and chopped off all the strings and installed a complete set of brand-new strings which I wound on properly, stretched them out and tuned up. After I tweaked the bridge a bit, that Rickenbacker turned out to be a respectable little guitar and not a minute too soon . . . they were due on stage right away.

Sam Molnar: John bowled into the Princess of Wales pub in Woking and said, 'Right, you lot, Paul's playing Ronnie Scott's on Tuesday night, the coach will be here to pick you up.' A few days later, we all piled on this coach and went up to Ronnie Scott's. Walked in. Free concert. All these soul boys turned up, who got in because John was walking around Soho, which was his way of filling out the crowd.

Adrian Thrills: It was November 1976. Upstairs at Ronnie's. They weren't big enough to play the hallowed downstairs. Paul was on fire and smashed up a guitar on stage, emulating Pete Townshend, I guess. I remember walking out with Shane MacGowan and him saying 'That was just so inspiring – seeing him smashing that guitar.'

Paul Weller: As that went on and we got more and more shows, and we played the Hope & Anchor and the Red Cow in Hammersmith and all that, it just changed us all. I went to see the Pistols and The Clash as well at the 100 Club, and then my writing changed. I was probably just trying to mimic what I was hearing. Things like 'In the City' was the first big tune for me. I can distinctly remember us rehearsing that song in Sheerwater Youth Club. I'd just written it, and we rehearsed it and thought, *This is so good!* And then it was, *This is our new direction now.*

1977 – Signing with Polydor

Peter Wilson: I had joined Polydor in '75 . . . They were busy with things like the Bee Gees, *Saturday Night Fever*, but towards the end of '76, punk started happening in London, the 100 Club and so on. The A&R department then started to sniff at this because it was pretty tiny, but record companies really want to sign the next big thing and sign it up early because it's cheaper. In particular, Chris Parry, the A&R man, was checking out bands.

Chris Parry: I got parachuted in as the token A&R guy with this very early punk movement and over time I started to get quite passionate about it. I was concerned that as a label, Polydor was going to miss out on punk . . . I could see quite clearly it wasn't going to just stop with the Pistols and The Clash. . . . It went from being underground, with just a few people I could talk to and bounce ideas off, to exploding into the mainstream. At first, a lot of the journalists didn't get it, either. But by late November that changed. The *NME*, *Sounds*, all the papers, went from dismissing it as 'crap' to calling it the 'new thing'. I was very much in on that scene, which eventually led to me knowing about The Jam . . . I'd had a pretty grim Christmas period because none of the signings that I wanted came through. I was not very happy.

Steve 'Tufty' Carver: Shane MacGowan was in our gang . . . He was one of the first people all over this scene. He was saying to the record company people, 'Sign the Banshees, sign The Jam, sign whoever.'

Chris Parry: I found out about The Jam through Shane. He was a number one Sex Pistols fan. I was the only guy hanging around that had an expense account, so I was ripping into the bar tab, but it cost me a few bob. I was at Chelsea Town Hall, I'm buying some beers and Shane came over, he said, ''Ere, Chris, there's this band playing on Saturday night at the Marquee called The Jam. You want to go and check them out.' If it was a tip from Shane, I thought it was worth doing, so that's exactly what I did.

Chris Difford: The Jam supported Squeeze at the Marquee. Their energy and their assault on stage was just genius. It was like seeing The Who or the Small Faces. And it was a band that I wanted to be in . . . Paul's dad accused us of nicking his mic stands and the microphones, which we didn't do. I am a bit of a tea leaf, and I would have nicked them back in the day, but I wouldn't have nicked them from The Jam because they were so brilliant.

Adrian Thrills: I remember the famous gig at the Marquee where The Jam were supporting Bearded Lady. Back then, as a hang-over from the hippie and the progressive rock thing, people would sit down cross legged on the floor. So, the Bearded Lady fans, they came in and did that as The Jam were cranking out these mod-punk anthems at 100 miles an hour. Paul got increasingly frustrated and invited Shane, me and another early Jam fan, Claudio Magnani, on stage to gyrate with The Jam, much to the disgust of the Marquee hippies. We were pogoing and doing a bit of mod dancing, to try and liven up the crowd, and get some reaction.

Chris Parry: The Jam presented themselves slightly differently because they weren't a punk band as such, they were coming through that kind of idea. It was all part of a new wave of music. I first met Paul backstage at the Marquee and said I was with Polydor. He picked up immediately on that. He's definitely into his music background and history of recorded music and everything. But he also liked soul and the Stax/Volt label . . . and clearly, he was massively influenced in his early days by the Who. He was very keen on that, which made my job easier to explore signing to Polydor before anybody else.

Roger Armstrong: I was seeing lots of bands with one of my business partners, Ted Carroll. We had our own label, Chiswick Records, and we negotiated with John to sign the band for a single. I'm sure we had issued contracts, and John had taken them away and everything had been agreed. Ted had a flat above Rock On, and John and Paul, probably the whole band, were coming up to sign the contract. Ted put up the *Ready Steady Who* EP, Motown stuff and pictures and decorated the flat for the occasion. Then the day before, John rang up and said, 'Sorry, Polydor have offered us a deal.' Chris Parry had caught wind of it and offered John a deal. The story I got was that he was high and dry because the Pistols, The Clash and Buzzcocks weren't available. I think his view was *I need one of these bands* and so he rang John. It was a no-brainer for them to go with Polydor and not us at the time. We had actually picked 'In the City' as the obvious single. It would have been nice if we'd just done the first single. I'm sure they would have moved on to somebody else after that.

Chris Parry: We were talking about things and hadn't quite done the deal but had got some initial demos done just off Wardour Street somewhere and then we did some at Polydor with Vic Smith [Coppersmith-Heaven]. We were about ready to sign, but in the meantime, I would be seeing them, keeping tabs with them and everything. It was at a very well-known drinking hole called the Lamb & Flag just off Oxford Street that Paul told me how he saw himself. He wasn't boasting. It was quite impressive really, this young guy saying, 'Well, I'm going to be some force in this country musically, as it happens.'

Vic Coppersmith-Heaven: In 1977, I was employed as an audio engineer at Polydor. One day I was called in by the A&R team and presented with a challenge; three artists were being invited to the studio to lay down tracks for a hopeful record contract. It was up to me to demo several tracks from each musical group; they were Billy Idol, The Clash and The Jam – what a task and what results, they were all great and inspiring. How indeed, I thought, could the label decide to sign only one band amongst such talent? . . . I decided to see my favourite band live at the Half Moon at Putney. Very few people turned up, but The Jam's set was electric, and I could feel that a collaboration with them in the studio would be musically exciting and a challenge.

Chas de Whalley: I first saw The Jam on Wednesday 9 February 1977, in the Nashville, which was a big pub in west London . . . For a band that I'd never heard of, it was packed, half the A&R men in London were there . . . I reviewed it for *Sounds*. They were awesome. I was blown away [but] I thought they had the wrong lead singer. Bruce Foxton had the much better voice, or so I thought at the time. I was saying to people that Weller's good, but Bruce Foxton has got the voice.

I used to think that I'd written the very first review of The Jam, but it turns out that John Tobler beat me to it, but I certainly wrote the first feature on them . . . I went back to *Sounds* to the editor, Alan Lewis, and said, 'We really need to be on this one.' He said, 'Well, go and see them again and see whether it's as good the second time.' Friday evening at the Roxy Club . . . I was very impressed because at the end of their set they came off stage, went back to the dressing rooms and ran round to the back of the crowd to start screaming for their own encore, pushing people forward.

Adrian Thrills: I started a fanzine called *48 Thrills*, which was one of the original punk fanzines ... It was dedicated to The Clash and The Jam. I did one of the first ever Jam interviews, again with Shane MacGowan in tow. We interviewed Paul at the 100 Club. Even then, he had his own take on punk. Some of those bands were becoming stars and he didn't like that. I think Pete Townshend said later that he's never known a musician as hung up on their credibility as Paul. He was so vehemently against what he would see as a sellout.

Barry Cain: I joined *Record Mirror* in November 1976 ... The first time I met them was at a party. This lovely Canadian guy called Geoff Deane was the PR at Polydor. He used to have parties and this particular evening, we're all having a nice time, when suddenly, these three guys came in. All dressed quite smartly, but all a bit pissed. Geoff said, 'This is the band that we're just about to sign at Polydor.' They told me their name and I thought, *What a shit name, The Jam.* We've had Marmalade and now we've got The Jam. No chance. They came in empty handed and then proceeded to drink everything around them. I'd brought a nice bottle of wine with me. That went, they drank the lot. They got even more pissed. Then they all went. I thought, *What obnoxious bastards. Horrible buggers.*

Jim Cook: By the time we signed The Jam, I'd been in the job two years ... We got them for a very good, very, very cheap deal. It was very much a development deal. We were going to put them in our studio to make their records and see how it went ... Most of the big acts we signed in the late seventies for Polydor started off with singles deals. I remember the signing very well.

It was in Chris's office. It was about seven o'clock at night. Welcome to Polydor. It wasn't anything big. A little toast, probably not champagne because that wouldn't have been the idea, would it? They wouldn't have been too impressed if we'd bought a bottle of champagne. Probably had a few cans of lager.

Chris Parry: John said, 'What's this?' I said, 'It's a cheque, John.' He said, 'I don't want a cheque.' So, we went across the road to Polydor's bank at the time at Oxford Street. Someone phoned up Lloyd's to say that I'd be coming by with a Polydor cheque and it was OK to cash it for six thousand readies. It came in a big envelope. John just looked at it, grabbed it and disappeared down the bloody escalator as quick as a rat down a drainpipe.

Nicky Weller: When they got signed, I remember Dad going to do the signing at Polydor and they were like, 'We've got this big lunch,' and he was, 'No, I don't want your lunches, I've just come to get the money, come to collect our dough and then we'll sign the thing and we're off.' I remember when they first got signed, they were trying to get rid of my dad and talk the boys into having a proper manager and Paul was like, 'Well, no, I'm not signing then, we're not doing it without my dad. This is where he's got us so far.'

Ann Weller: We had people being horrible to John, going, 'What? You've got them a record deal? Really? You?' In the end, I had to swear and say, 'Yes, he did.' Just because John worked on the building sites, and was rough and ready, a jack of all trades, in a sense. Polydor wanted to get rid of him and put some suited-booted person in, but the band said, 'No, He's staying.' He was a really good manager. In fact, in the end, he had so many people wanting him to be their manager.

Nicky Weller: From somebody that had gone from the building site, never knew a thing about it, he competed with all these manager moguls and all these other people that have ripped people off. My dad was the fairest person ever and a very clever man. He got everything they wanted, and he would negotiate. He always said that I could actually sell snow to the Eskimos, and I think I probably run in my dad's footsteps more than anything else. That's what he was like. He lived off his wits. No nonsense. It was all black and white.

Jim Cook: We had a small sixteen-track studio in the building next to our offices, which was quite fun sometimes because people would turn the volume up too much and you couldn't do any work at all . . . but it was fine for The Jam because they were a three-piece.

Vic Coppersmith-Heaven: The studio was built within its office walls, which only had minimal audio construction, with damping, meaning that it was lifeless. It still makes me wonder how we managed to create the sound of the first Jam songs in such a flat, non-acoustic environment, but we did manage to achieve it, and it has really stood the test of time.

Ann Weller: All the girls at Polydor liked John. They said, 'He calls me a babe.' I thought he calls everybody a babe because he can't remember their name . . . 'Right, babe, couldn't do this for me, could you? Won't take you long.' He was a ducker and diver, weren't he?

Barry Cain: About two months after that party, Geoff said, 'We've signed this band, come and see them at the Hope & Anchor.' So, I went and there must have been thirty people, forty people maximum there, and they'd just signed them. I thought, *Oh dear, there's not many people here, this could be a bit of a bad signing.* And then they played, and from that moment I just fell in love with them.

Steve 'Tufty' Carver: They had badges by now. Jam at the Red Cow, Jam at the Marquee, Jam at the 100 Club, and kids were starting to collect them ... it was a month of Tuesdays or something. So, if thirty people went to the Red Cow on the first night, they told their mates, and then the next night was 100. By the fourth night, it was rammed. I can remember the last night, everyone in the audience bouncing up and down, pogo-ing and when they all left, me, Nicky and my brother Pete picked up all the money off the floor and had enough money for beer.

Mick Talbot: I first saw The Jam very early 1977 during their residency at the Red Cow in Hammersmith ... and there was a queue going around the block. I was a big fan of Dr Feelgood, and my friend pointed out that The Jam had a similar vision image, the energy, rhythm-and-blues roots. Paul's about five months older than me, and to see someone of your own generation doing that was really refreshing. The Jam didn't deny their musical past. Everyone else was trying to make out that like 1977 was year zero and people had just been left here by a spaceship [but] all of their set that night was covers. The Who, Lee Dorsey, 'In the Midnight Hour'. They did play 'In the City', they were quite proud of that one – they played it twice! They really connected and there was an honesty about them compared to some of the other bands that they came up with.

Chris Parry: The Jam gigged a lot, so I got them working with an agency called Cow Bell and a guy called Martin Hopewell. This is no disrespect to John, he knew that he loved the band and he wanted to be with them and take them around all the places, but really all the stuff that was going on was way beyond his ability as a manager.

Martin Hopewell: Chris Parry teamed up with chap called Bryan Morrison to form a publishing company, And Son Limited. Bryan was a great character ... a cigar-chewing Eastender, already a millionaire. I got a call from Chris and Bryan, insisting that I see this band at the Red Cow in Hammersmith. Now, given that I was a bit of a little tosser back in the day and a bit full of myself, I dutifully turned up and found about sixty in the audience bouncing up and down and these three guys on the stage with suits that looked as if they'd been bought five years earlier because they didn't quite fit, also bouncing up and down to the *Batman* theme. I thought, *You're having a laugh. This is just silly.* I should say that I came to like those suits. A lot of people would say they saw them and it was like this blinding light, and they knew they were going to be immense. I didn't. Chris and Bryan took me to a local hamburger joint and persuaded me to start getting them a few gigs. A couple of months later, after it had all suddenly taken off, I was pursuing John and the three lads around the Royal College of Art, frantically trying to hand out contracts for them all to sign.

Bob Manton: The first time I saw The Jam, they were supporting the Troggs and Meal Ticket at the Imperial College of Art ... The adrenaline was like having a cattle prod to the chest. This would be March 1977. Then the three of us from our band, Purple Hearts, started to go to see them straight from school on a 25-pence Red Bus Rover single ticket.

Jeff Shadbolt: We went from school in Romford, wearing our school uniforms, all the way to the Red Cow in Hammersmith. They'd just finished their sound check and we thought we'd missed the actual gig. We sat down and started talking to some of the cool Southend mods, then Paul, Bruce and Rick come over and start talking and said, 'Oh, we thought you was a couple of mods.' We was like, 'Yeah, we are.'

Bob Manton: We were thinking, this stuff is great, this is better than the punk rock we're listening to. It really speaks to us. It came from that British Invasion type, the *Quadrophenia* booklet and David Bowie, with all those sixties covers on *Pin Ups*. There was a lot of mod influence in the punk movement.

Dylan Jones: They were quite separate from the orthodox punk triumvirate. A lot of the early punks were quite dismissive of The Jam and there was a war of attrition between both the groups and their followers, and The Jam and their followers. Right from the beginning I think that they were particular and separate, and it was no surprise that they wanted to move on quite quickly.

Steve 'Tufty' Carver: We went to see them at Hastings Pier and Johnny Thunder's Heartbreakers had pulled out. They were a leather-clad biker, heroin junkie punk thing with Hell's Angels fans to match. On the door, people were offered their money back or could see The Jam. John offered to play it for fifty quid. All these rockers are stood there, and these three lads come on stage with white socks and black suits, *1-2-3-4, bam bam*. They just stood there saying to people not to dance, and, in my stupid, drunken, ignorance, I thought, *This is my favourite band – I'm going to dance.* I can only do the pogo. These Hell's Angels are looking at me, going, 'You got a kangaroo in your pocket, boy?'

It was a shit gig and in the dressing room afterwards Bruce threw a beer bottle at the wall, and it stuck, which seemed like a great thing to do. We all joined in, the dressing room was completely wrecked. Then the promoter come in to pay John his fifty quid and went 'What the fuck has gone on in here?' and one of us, quick as a flash, went, 'All them Hell's Angels came in and started throwing bottles about.'

29 April 1977 – 'In the City' (debut single, no. 40)

Vic Coppersmith-Heaven: Previously I had had a lot of training at the Decca studios, working fast to achieve the recording of ten bands, and some thirty songs in a day, so I was quite used to capturing the energy and excitement of The Jam through this training, which was pretty much the recording of their live gig. Once their first single hit the charts, I followed The Jam to all their promotional radio and TV shows, to help mix the sound, which also helped me understand their live set and prepare for our future developments of our work together.

Adrian Thrills: In issue three of *48 Thrills*, I reviewed The Jam's first single. I had asked Paul for some lyrics, and he wrote out a couple of songs for me, including 'In the City' . . . That was always going to be the debut single. Paul was always a good letter writer. I'd send him a copy of the magazine and he'd write a letter back, almost critiquing that issue. 'Liven up yourself, Adrian. This was a crap issue.'

Steve 'Tufty' Carver: Kid Jensen promised that he'd play it. It was a Saturday lunchtime. Mrs Weller would always make cheese and tomato sandwiches. She said, 'Let's all sit around the kitchen table, he's going to play it on the radio.' The Jam were an unknown quantity, and he played out with it at the end. We sat there for two whole hours to get 'Here's an up-and-coming band . . . anyway that's the end of that.'

Ann Weller: We knew quite a few of them . . . Tony Blackburn and John Peel. He was really good, helping them at the right time.

Billy Bragg: They were really the first of those punk bands that truly made sense to me and my mates. We were a bit suspicious of the Sex Pistols and The Clash – they seemed a bit art school. We were working-class lads living in the suburbs and The Jam had a dynamic that related to the things that we were interested in: early albums by the Stones, Small Faces and the Who. We were really into that hardcore beat group thing, so The Jam fitted right in as a modern iteration of that idea. The Feelgoods were part of it as well, but they were a bit older than us, whereas The Jam were the same age.

Chris Pope: John Peel was very influential. He was no musical snob. It was genuine. If he liked it, he'd play it. He showed that anything can happen if people make their own music.

Billy Bragg: After 'In the City' came out, we saw The Jam at the Nashville Rooms, a key venue on the punk scene, where bands like the Pistols had played . . . I remember joking that the grey-haired old geezer who came on and fixed their amps and set up the mics was probably their dad, only to realise years later when I met him that it *was* their dad. Then they announced their next London show would be at the Rainbow Theatre . . . The Jam were second on the bill to The Clash, and to be honest, they didn't quite have the energy that they had at the Nashville. They were really good at playing pubs and places like the Marquee, but their leaping, highly sprung energy dissipated in the room there. They'd not worked out how to play an auditorium like they had worked out how to play a pub.

Sodge Adams: I was there for that 'White Riot' tour when The Clash headlined at the Rainbow and The Jam were the first or second band. I always remember John Weller used to come out in front and he'd go 'On your feet, but not on the seats for The Jam.' We jumped on the seats, and it was them with their little amps and speakers and the whole of the space on stage and Paul and Bruce jumping around, Paul really working that guitar. 'In the City', what a song. The first time I ever spoke to them, I remember sharing a joint at the 100 Club and Paul being interested in anarchy because we had little anarchy symbols on our shirts. A *Vive l'anarchie* T-shirt. He was inquisitive about it because, of course, The Jam got taken slightly wrong. They had the Union Jacks. There was a slight dichotomy then anyway, because punk, to begin with, was just do what you want to do and then it divided a little bit and some went slightly to the right and more anarchy as well.

Jill Furmanovsky: I first photographed The Jam at the Marquee or some pub like the Hope & Anchor, and in Tower Hamlets, they were wearing those suits that had a reddish tinge to them, they looked like two-tone suits. We knew who they were, but they weren't typically punk. I was involved with Mark Perry and Harry Murlowski who started the fanzine *Sniffin' Glue* and they liked The Jam. So that was good, because if they hadn't, they would tend to be down on bands. You're either in or out, but they were accepting of The Jam.

Gary Crowley: There was one interview which the band did with that famous Pennie Smith *NME* front cover where they're on Oxford Street and the three of them have got the suits on. Paul namechecked The Beatles and talked about his love of Motown. It quickly dawned on me that The Jam was the band for me.

Paul Weller: I'd spent all those years, including in the sixties, religiously watching *Top of the Pops*, man. That was the only show really and you think, *I'm going to be on there one day. I'm going to get on that show*, and then getting on it, it's actually, fucking rubbish!

We did 'In the City' on *Top of the Pops*. We were like, 'Oh, fucking hell, is this it? Jesus!' Didn't like it whatsoever. I thought it's so fake and so phony, and all the crappy DJs they had on there, and all the floor managers telling the kids to clap, and when to clap, and when not to clap. And miming as well. Not playing live, that was so weird. Lip-syncing and all that shite. And in them days as well you had to sometimes actually re-record the track in a few hours. Sometimes later, we would just fake it and bung the geezer a little drink and he'd fuck off to the pub and swap the tapes and that. But to be on national TV for the first time was a bit of a milestone for us, I guess.

Bruce Foxton: On signing to Polydor, I thought we'd made it. When you're on *Top of the Pops* for the very first time and the next day your mates and their mums are saying, 'Saw you on the telly the other night, it was really cool.' That convinced my mum that I'm on to a winner because she didn't want me to leave work, basically. Getting the seven-inch piece of plastic in your hand, the 45 of 'In the City', and going to your local pub and mates putting it on and on, to the point where it got to be embarrassing, really. But it's great that it was on the jukebox in your own pub, your home pub. Very exciting. I didn't take it for granted, didn't plan it. The songs spoke for themselves, I suppose.

Gary Crowley: The great thing about The Jam was that you could attain that early look that we saw on TV, with those suits. All I had was my school uniform so that became my Jam suit – it looked like an ill-fitting Norman Wisdom, but I thought I looked the part.

Steve 'Tufty' Carver: That first time, I watched with my mum, dad and brothers and I just thought, *Wow, my mates have just been on* Top of the Pops, *I should really go down the pub and celebrate*. I'm on my second pint and Paul come running in and went 'Well, thanks for fucking coming round for me.' I went, 'Well you were on *Top of the Pops*!' and he went, 'That was recorded yesterday!'

Nicky Weller: Dad was brilliant. He'd say, 'Don't go to school today, babe. We're going to do *Top of the Pops*.' I'd be like, 'No, I've got to go to school.' He's like, 'No, come to *Top of the Pops*.'

Bruce Foxton: We were just pleased to be on *Top of the Pops*. If you look at the recordings Paul probably wasn't pleased to be there and promote the song, but it was crazy, really. We couldn't tour places like Scotland every week, so I saw it as vehicle for our fans, to see and hear the band without us actually being there and without having to wait six months to a year to see us once.

Ann Weller: We'd sit down as a family to watch *Top of the Pops* together. And we'd criticise. 'Paul should have polished his shoes,' or he should have done that. I don't think Paul ever watched himself on *Top of the Pops*. Nicky was still at school, because she had a lot of flak from kids going 'We don't like your brother.' And she said, 'Well, I don't care if you do or not,' but they gave her a really hard time at school. A few years later, oh, it's different then. 'Can you put us on the guestlist?' The guestlist used to be more than the people that were paying to get in.

Jim Cook: I would see John Weller if we had meetings, usually about money. The managing director, Tony Morris, would also be there because The Jam were becoming a very important act for us. We suggested that John hire John Cohen as his lawyer, as I don't think he had one initially . . . we thought it was a smart move for them to have somebody who we couldn't be accused of ripping off later. John became their lawyer, and things became much more organised.

John Cohen: After The Jam's first single was a success and got into the charts, they needed a proper deal. They had initially signed a one-page agreement with Polydor for that single. Chris Parry suggested me, and I'm very grateful to him for that. I met Paul and the other members of the band – and John, of course – and we negotiated with Polydor who had their own lawyer in-house, possibly Clive Fisher, though Jim Cook was around too. John needed his hand held quite a lot and was very happy to have it held. I represented artists, did their record negotiations and publishing negotiations and management negotiations, although there certainly wasn't one of those with The Jam. I was looking for a good advance in the first instance, because at that stage they didn't have any money. Secondly, a good royalty rate and good terms. It's more sophisticated these days but back then we were talking about vinyl records, albums and singles. The record company has the option to pick up albums, but if they fail, then the record company can let them go.

20 May 1977 – *In the City* (debut album, no. 20)

Paul Weller: I was just bluffing it really. Copying other people. The first album is almost a rewrite of The Who's *My Generation*. I hadn't really found my own voice, not at all. I was still copying things and the words and all that. Shocking really, man, looking back on it. But then I was eighteen. That's my only excuse, really.

Chris Parry: Vic Coppersmith-Heaven co-produced the first album with me, and it took a while to get the studio sound right. We recorded it in the Polydor Studios, which was on the A&R floor – quite funky and cool. You'd walk out of the studio and see my boss, Jim Cook. He was quite a square pants.

The music that he liked was all that American twangy rock stuff and hi-fi, and that's why I called him the Bang & Olufsen Set. He did have ears but in a funny way. He just didn't really get any of the stuff. Vic and I would go there, try and mix and then we'd play it on his AR5 speakers and Jim would stroke his beard and go, 'Neh, neh, neh, don't think so, neh,' and Vic and I would look at each other and say, 'It's not right.'

In the City was the album that we really struggled with. I'm pretty sure we had the recordings, but it was getting the right mixes where we struggled. If I remember right, there's some slight slap back returning, pulsing echo on one or two things that just gave it the kick it needed. It really had to sound like that sense of going out and something exciting was going to happen. There had to be that sense of that teenage rush, and that album does have it.

Vic Coppersmith-Heaven: I was to produce the first album as well as to engineer, and Chris joined me for the first album. Recording sessions were difficult initially to get a good sound, as acoustically the recording room had no reverberation or live atmosphere, but we got there. Instruments were hit hard, to create the excitement of the music, and there became a lot of tuning problems, so many hours were also spent retuning instruments in the workshop, but it was all part of the job at the time. Chris seemed to spend a lot of time inspiring the band, madly gesticulating like a conductor in the studio, while I recorded in the control room, which I thought was odd, but he was inspiring performance, and it worked. Not sure what the band thought about it at the time, as we did not discuss, it just became part of the team project.

Bill Smith: I was a junior art director at Polydor when Chris Parry said, 'We've just signed this band called The Jam. They're playing at Fulham Greyhound. Why don't you go and see them, see what you think about them, because I want you to work on the sleeve covers?' From the moment I saw them, I knew I wanted a black and white press, 'now', feel for the cover, which caused problems with Polydor. *Why was I not wanting to use a full colour picture of this band?* They were a new wave band, not part of the London punk scene, so I had the idea of the band being chased into an underground toilet by rival fans or some irate punk band that they'd been better than. They're waiting for things to calm down, then leave their mark with graffiti of their name. 'The Jam was here.' That image came to me immediately when I saw the band. I commissioned a photographer called Martyn Goddard.

Martyn Goddard: They let us get away with all sorts of things. We were off the radar . . . I did eight shoots starting on 2 March 1977, which was the *In the City* album cover. I said to Bill, 'This is crazy. They're a young band. We're going to go out at night and photograph these guys spraying public toilets or subways with graffiti. They're going to want to look good in their suits. This is lunacy. It ain't going to work.' I persuaded him to build the set inside, which paid dividends because Bill was able to spray that logo with one hit. He wasn't worrying about the local police apprehending him for criminal damage.

Bill Smith: My career as a record sleeve designer all started with The Jam and that graffiti logo. That was completely improvised. It was in my head before I even knew what I wanted to do.

On the morning of the shoot, we had a couple of six by three flat boards which we tiled. That was my first art direction job, basically tiling a wall. It looked really good, like black and white graph paper, almost like a drawing. I liked the whole graphic approach to it.

The band came in, put their suits on, and we sat them in place. Martyn did some lighting, did a couple of Polaroids. Everybody looked great. Fantastic. They stepped out, had a cup of tea and I stepped in with a black can of spray paint and sprayed the logo. I'd never sprayed anything before. It was the first go, and luckily all the planets were inline.

They stepped back in and we shot three rolls of film with them against the tiled wall. I said, 'It'd be really great if the band have left the toilet, but someone's come in and gone, "Oh, I hate The Jam" and has started smashing it up', so I took a hammer to the tiled wall and started smashing it up and then sprayed 'In the City' underneath. That was what we put together for the album cover and we'd used some for the first single bag.

They then said, 'Oh, we're doing some gigs with The Clash. Could you respray the logo on a white backdrop so that we can hang it behind us?' so I had to go and do a huge great version of it. It was a really simple logo – very graphic, black and white, very hard edge – I suppose it's a good logo because it's lasted and it says what it is. People drew the logo on their pencil cases and the backs of exercise books. Even today you still see people using that logo. Somebody said to me once, 200,000 pin badges have been sold of The Jam logo on a little one-inch pin badge and I just thought, *Well it'd be really nice if I'd got a penny for each one.*

David Lines: I loved *In the City*. It took me years to realise that they were in an underground station. I thought they were all in a shower together!

Chas de Whalley: I reviewed the first album for *Sounds* with the headline 'Flamin' Groovies Weybridge style'. The first thing that Paul's mother said to me, 'Oi, we're not from Weybridge, we're from Woking.' Clearly, I have blind spots about finer detail. It was a four-star review and picking out all the really good stuff on it. But, in those days, as a music critic, you had a duty to dig down a bit and put it into context and impart some extra wisdom if you thought they needed it. I remember feeling that these are great songs, it's a great band, but if they sounded a bit more polished, like Thin Lizzy, they'd really go somewhere. I've since realised that trying to judge them by conventional rock standards was missing the point. They were such a good band. Mind you, I gave the second album five and everybody else loathed it.

Barry Cain: They did manage to capture that energy on that album. It was raw and rough, but in a good way. They were using punk as a springboard, even though they were around long before all those bands were themselves. Because of his love for The Beatles and quite a lot of music, he had that melody in him. He wasn't a punk writer, he was a songwriter and that came through. So even though they had to give it some balls, to put some bollocks into the sound, something like 'Away from the Numbers' on that album is such a classic song. It's complex and they were coming out with interesting melodies. The lyrics were not like a lot of the other punk lyrics which were *destroy this* or, *bang, bang, bang*. There was some tenderness in it as well. There was feeling, hatred and despair. This was a poetic soul here. It was something different that I'd never heard before.

Nick Heyward: 'Away from the Numbers' really resonated with me – that's where I fell in love with The Jam. It's such a soft moment for them, like the strawberry jam in a doughnut, especially on an album with tracks that went like the clappers, like 'Art School' and 'Batman' . . . it was pop art at its best.

Adrian Thrills: I was living in Stevenage . . . Paul was in Woking; we were classic suburban kids. On that first Jam album, you had 'Sounds from the Street' and the lyrics, 'I know I come from Woking, and you say I'm a fraud' . . . One of The Jam's great strengths was that they spoke to those kids in suburban towns. I think Paul felt slightly apart from the London punk scene, even though the bands themselves really liked The Jam . . . They had a strange relationship with punk, and in the long term, that probably suited Weller because he never really has been that comfortable at being pigeonholed. He never really wanted to be an orthodox punk.

Steve 'Tufty' Carver: The Jam were getting better and better. I heard 'Away from the Numbers' when they played one afternoon in the 100 Club and as usual, we went to the pub after. I said to Paul, 'You've just gone up a level.' A proper song, wasn't it?

Barry Cain: I did the first interview with The Jam for *Record Mirror*. We got them these Union Jack jackets from a boutique in Carnaby Street. That's an iconic photo now. We toured London in a cab – Buckingham Palace, Houses of Parliament in Westminster – for the shoot. I always thought they'd hired the jackets for the day, but I spoke to Rick Buckler recently and he told me they actually kept them. They must be worth a fortune these days. I did this first interview with them, and it was really funny. You could see that Paul was the main man, even though he was young, but it was fascinating because he was still unsure of his opinions . . . He wasn't a loudmouth or anything. You'd see he was thinking about things . . . If you know what his background was, you thought, *Well, when did he think?*, because he did shit at school. He wasn't interested.

June–July 1977 – First nationwide tour

Barry Cain: The Queen's Jubilee was the opening night of The Jam's first nationwide tour, 7 June 1977, at Barbarella's in Birmingham . . . I went backstage, and the band just came off stage and Rick Buckler downed two bottles of Bull's Blood, the Hungarian red wine. That was their first headline tour gig. Amazing. That just shows you the pressure. Mind you, they were a band for drinking. They weren't a druggie band like a lot of the others were with speed, but Paul loved a drink, he really did.

Chas de Whalley: In those days in the journalism circles the coveted thing was for the band and the record company to say, 'We'll take you on the road with the band for a couple of days . . .' and so I went on that first nationwide tour. They weren't really hideously hedonistic but there was a lot of drinking . . . There could have been a bit of speed, bit of amphetamine, but it wasn't as if everybody was really going for it or was completely off their faces all the time. I do believe that Paul gave up drinking fairly quickly or gave up heavy, heavy intoxicants – at least while on tour – quite early on. I suspect he might have had a couple of bad experiences and thought, *Hang about, if I want to do this properly, I can't do it this way.*

I remember the Holiday Inn, Birmingham, when they threw me in the bath. I said, 'Not my cowboy boots, please.' So, they took them off before they put me in the bath. What lovely boys!

Debsey Wykes: Without realising it, we were all just getting really bored. Everything was old and a bit dusty and then all this great music came out. Because we lived in Cambridge, we were a bit behind really. But then 1977, it was our time and we went to everything we could. The Jam played Cambridge Corn Exchange. Really inspiring times. I liked the way people sounded and looked. It was sharp, it was loud, it was everything.

Lawrence Watson: I was a youngster, thirteen or fourteen probably, bunking into the Rainbow with all my mates at secondary school . . . The Jam spoke to us a lot. It was that punk ethos. The idea that you could go out and do and be whatever you wanted to be in life. We were scruffy herberts from council estates aspiring to that idea that you can be a musician, you could be this, you could be that – and lo and behold, I became a photographer.

Richard Houghton: The lyrics clearly spoke to an audience and when you went to a Jam gig, you weren't suddenly disabused. What Paul said in his songs wasn't something that he just said. He actually lived it. The band themselves lived it. They were nice people who would talk to the fans, make time for the fans, give them autographs.

Gary Crowley: I think that first gig always stays with you. I can almost see it like a film unfolding. Battersea Town Hall and The Boys were supporting. We got there at six o'clock. I remember my dad winding me up, saying, 'You better bring some cotton wool, because you'll go deaf you will. It's going to be so loud, it's going to be so noisy.' So, I walked into this very, very cool gig with cotton wool hanging out of both ears.

I remember the doors opening, rushing right down to the front, and not long after the Boys came on stage. Then the anticipation builds for the Woking Wonders. Them rushing out on stage and picking up those gleaming red and white Rickenbacker guitars. Paul and Bruce and Rick at the back, I think he was still wearing the shades then, keeping that steady beat and straight into 'Art School'. The energy was electric

– visceral and so vital. Paul and Bruce were darting around the stage, like demented rabbits, pogoing and running around. You didn't know where to look. I already knew the songs inside out – I'd played the album to death – but seeing it live was something else entirely. I think it's fair to say that night changed my life.

Paul Weller: Yeah, it was mental ... incredible ... pure energy from start to finish, and we were very young. I was three years younger than the other two, but our audience were even younger and the bigger we got, the more that permeated to younger kids like a school-playground band. People would chat about us after Thursday's *Top of the Pops*. So, there's a lot of teenage angst going on there.

Nick Heyward: The Jam were a kind of three-headed thing, weren't they? Wow. Position one, position two, back centre. So powerful. It's like a pitchfork and they're digging around the punk haystack.

Bruce Foxton: Yeah, I've always looked at it that it was always a three piece. I think Paul did too really. Although he had the bulk of the initial ideas, we all contributed to it. I would say that my bass playing wasn't fantastic, but it just worked. It was the right time. It worked with Rick's style of drumming and Paul's songwriting and his guitar and his vocal – Paul made it work and made it sound special. Each individual element was good but maybe wasn't going to set the world on fire. But when it came together, it was fantastic.

Shaun Hand: There is this school of thought that it was all Paul Weller, and they were just bumbling sidekicks, but I think anyone who knows about music and how it's played, particularly drums and bass, would listen to what Bruce and Rick do and will say, 'Jesus, they were good' ... there are certain things that are going on that are really advanced. You only have to look at them playing live to see Bruce Foxton and Rick Buckler always just going for it.

Nick Heyward: I stood. I pogoed, I was in the audience watching and mythologising it. It was the dream. Standing in the audience of the Greyhound, looking at The Jam, sweating as they did. I thought, I want to be on stage sweating like that.

Gary Crowley: After that Battersea gig, I vividly remember taking two buses back to where we lived, talking about how can we get involved and the fanzine thing seemed like the way to go. We had this phone box right outside our school which became my office at lunchtimes.

I saw a fact file in *Melody Maker* which actually had John Weller's contact number on there – Maybury 64717. I decided to give it a whirl and Paul's mum, Ann, answered the phone. I had my routine perfected, 'I'm Gary Crowley and we love The Jam and we're going to call our fanzine *The Modern World* . . .' She was like, 'Calm down, dear, calm down, hold on, hold on . . . Paul, Paul,' and then he came on and, bless his cottons, 'What are you doing tomorrow afternoon? Can you get up to Stratford Place?'

Me and my mate Mark got the bus early and then Paul rocked up with his girlfriend, Gill. We were with him for an hour and a half, and do you know what? He hasn't changed that much. He was fascinated about what we were listening to and what our thoughts were. He had a bag of reggae records from one of the reggae shops in Soho and was talking me through his bag of records. I've got the cassette somewhere, and one day maybe I'll have the chutzpah to play it to people, but if you can imagine a cave boy with a very, very high-pitched voice: 'Hello, Paul. What's your favourite colour?'

July–October 1977 – 'All Around the World' (no. 13) / 'The Modern World' (no. 36)

Rick Buckler: From the moment we got signed, it became serious. It wasn't the weekend job that it was before and if we wanted to stay there, we had to not only prove ourselves to the audience and build a fanbase, but we had to also prove ourselves to the record company that we were worth spending money on.

Chris Parry: Things were moving fast. This was a great opportunity because there was a hunger. Young people wanted stuff, and The Jam's music was visceral and quite high energy and was an extra dimension or another channel off the core punk idea, so it was important to catch that wave. When I heard them play 'All Around the World' live, I said, 'We've got to get that out quickly,' because we had Hammersmith Odeon coming up, which was a big jump up so we needed something fresh for the radio. We managed to get them to do this recording *el rápido* and had contacts at the factory to turn it around quickly. We got it out within a few weeks, and it came out the week before the show. That gig was an important step and as a follow up to *In the City* it was a strong single and it reconfirmed them further along.

Martyn Goddard: We did the photo shoot for 'All Around the World' on 1 June 1977. A veritable production line really in that period. If spraying the logo on the tiles was dodgy, the yellow plastic was even dodgier because it was affected by the paint. If you look at the pictures, all the plastic is creasing and crinkling up because the chemicals in the paint were doing funny things to the chemicals in the plastic. That could have been a total disaster with a yellow pile dripping . . .

Trevor Neal: The first time I saw The Jam was on the Marc Bolan show . . . 'All Around the World', although I'd heard them on

John Peel. They're playing it live and you're just waiting for the final chord and Rick Buckler throws his stick, but it flies away, and so you can see Paul scowling, and then turn his back as the song fizzles out. I wouldn't like to have been in the dressing room after that one.

Chris Parry: 'All Around the World' was weird because it was done . . . two, three, four, bang . . . and for some reason they put six beats in there and I just couldn't get my head around that . . . Because I have a drumming background, I pulled Rick back to something much stronger and more delivered. He was totally Keith Moon, splashing around. Rick and Bruce were a great rhythm section but, at first, they were a bit ragged. That song was fun. Very old school, old-fashioned way of doing things. But of all the records that I've made, the singles and quick turnarounds and had success, that's up there with them.

1977 – Live

Rick Buckler: We had this almost ridiculous ethic that if you offered us a gig, we'd do it. There was no, 'Well, what show is it, how much money they're being paid?' or anything like that. 'Yeah, we'll do it!' Sometimes you'd do two shows a day and it was crazy stuff. The first UK tour that Polydor set up for us was just enormously long. It just kept growing with more dates being added. The pressure started to take its toll – the constant travelling, doing ridiculous long hours during the day. Don't forget, we only had one suit, our stage suit, that used to come out every night, irrespective.

Martin Hopewell: At first, we were booking them in to colleges and clubs, as many gigs as they could possibly fit in. Sometimes we'd double up and would do one show in London, for example, early evening, then race off to University of London Union or something for a late-night gig. They worked like troopers. Unbelievable. Just work, work, work.

I should mention Mont-de-Marsan Festival du Punk with The Jam, The Stranglers, the Damned on the bill . . . and me, which was a huge mistake. Don't ever, ever go on a trip with a band who are on a jet that's been chartered for a whole load of punk bands and everyone's travelling together. I arrived at the airport with my nice jacket, briefcase and neatly pressed jeans, only to be greeted by a plane full of herberts all piled onto this charter jet. Two minutes after take-off somebody was pissed and was insistent on flying the plane. When they hand the food out, it's just all over the walls and all over everybody. I'm ducking, trying to stay out of the way. The Jam were very well behaved – it was the others.

At the other end, a coach takes all the bands to Mont-de-Marsan, this sleepy French village. I'm keeping a low profile but see this liquid trickling down between my legs – someone's had a slash further up the bus. Rat Scabies, drummer from the Damned, turns up, and says to the boys in The Jam, 'Who's this geezer?' and they very politely said, 'Well, he's our agent.' He said, 'I'm going to bite his fucking leg,' and if you have ever seen his teeth, it's not a pretty sight. The next thing this guy sunk into my thigh and stayed there. He didn't move.

We arrive in this village, with its medieval buildings and a tiny square with a fountain. The Jam were the last ones to be dropped off, and by then they've had too much to drink. They headed straight into the fountain, fully dressed. A minute later you hear police sirens and two minutes after that, the lads have been packed into the back of a French police van with the corrugated iron sides, which roars off down the road with John Weller and me chasing after them. At the gendarmerie, I had to then drag out my schoolboy French to say, '*Pardon monsieur, nous sommes désolés*' and explain who they were. They're sat there looking like three little drowned rats, with Rick Buckler's black hair dye running down his face. It was a sorry sight.

Paul Weller: Furthest I'd ever been was Wales to visit my relations. First time I ever flew was when I was eighteen. That was going to Mont-de-Marsan, which was a festival we were going to play out there. Which we never played in the end anyway. I don't know why we didn't play. We spent two or three days just getting drunk. But that was the first time I flew, and I had to get a passport for that. That was the first passport I ever had. So, any thought of travelling was out of our reach. I remember my mum and dad went on a Spanish holiday, early seventies, and that was a big deal. Came back with castanets and stupid plates, and all that crap. It was like, 'oooh, they've gone abroad'. Just the two of them. Not us.

Sodge Adams: There was a big concert in the south of France, Mont-de-Marsan, and The Clash, The Jam, the Damned all played with some French bands. We printed up a load of T-shirts. Stole some images. Patti Smith, *Vive L'anarchie*. Johnny Rotten heads. The Clash, just taken out of *NME*. Jill Furmanovsky didn't seem to mind. We had quite a funny time down there.

It was alcohol, dope and speed. The three of those would just knock you sideways, dangerous combination. After seeing the Damned on a stretcher, I ended up round the back with the French Red Cross passed out. The Clash came on stage and one of the founders of the T-shirt company came, propped me up and he's shovelling sulphate up my nose. There were a lot of people on heroin there, but I just jumped up and ran down the front, climbed on the barrier, and there was Paul Simonon and 'Clash City Rockers' with their brilliant visual backdrops. Just unbelievable. The Jam didn't play. They had an argument. But fortunately, we saw the Damned and The Clash. The weird thing is, we didn't stay for Lou Reed on the last day. That was a bit passé. We'd taken so much sulphate by then and needed to head home.

Martin Hopewell: Of course, as the history books now show, The Jam didn't actually end up playing it. Somebody had decided to change the running order. John didn't like that, and I was sent to tell the promoter we weren't going to play, but still wanted our money in cash. At the time it was scary stuff – all flick knives and a bunch of heavies. I'm in my early twenties going, 'Excuse me, we're not playing but can we have our money please?' . . . Maybe they took pity on me or I was too little to beat up but we got it.

Barry Cain: I'd also been on the road with The Jam that year, for the German tour. It was a funny tour. I got to Stuttgart the day before the first gig, and they cancelled. Couldn't sell a ticket. One man and his dog. I suppose they just weren't that well known then. The next gig was in Munich, but we had a day to spare so we went to Dachau, the concentration camp, which had quite a profound effect on Paul. He wrote 'Ghosts of Dachau' years later. I vividly remember walking around the camp with Paul and peering into the ovens. It sent shivers down his spine. It was terrifying. Paul wandered off on his own for a while. Very pensive. It really had an effect on us . . . Paul was very quiet for the rest of the time I was there on that tour. I think it really did affect him.

Jim Cook: They didn't sell over there. They sold a bit in France, quickly found a good market in Italy. Breaking America was a total disaster because Paul didn't want to commit to the 150-date tours needed to succeed there . . . It did frustrate us, but America was a difficult country then. British record companies weren't selling much there. It didn't start up again until the early eighties with Duran Duran and Culture Club. Suddenly there was another British invasion. But when I was doing things in the late seventies, America was like another world really. We couldn't get interest.

Paul Weller: With America. I think I was too stubborn, too young and too stupid to really realise what was going on there. I found it really old-fashioned when we first went there, because we had this whole punk revolt thing going on. Then we went to America, and everyone was still wearing double denim and taking quaaludes and whatever. And it was like fucking hell, it's like going back to the sixties. But there are so many people now that I meet when I play America who were at those gigs, and it meant so much to them. I was too stupid to realise that.

I think we probably could have cracked America if we'd have continued. But it wasn't top of my list. I never saw that 'You have to make it in America to really make it.' I mean that's a financial thing obviously. But I remember talking to this MD, arrogant twat, probably in '77, and he was going, 'You gotta be over here for six months. You gotta tour every place for six months, maybe come and live here for a bit.' As he was speaking, I was just thinking, *I'm not fucking doing that. I'm not leaving home for six months and schlepping around in a fucking bus.* So it was never top of my list. And whether that's good or bad, I don't know. It is what it is.

Rick Buckler: The first time we went to the States we did four towns, two shows a night, two nights in each town. Sixteen shows over ten days, starting off in Los Angeles, San Francisco, Boston, then New York. By the time we got to New York, the show could have been done by the suits on their own! It was no fun putting them on, because they were still wet from the night before, soaked in sweat and stuff. It was all pretty dreadful. That might have added to a certain flavour of the band. *Look at these guys and the suits they're wearing.* I've got fond memories of those things, even though it was no fun, really. They were good days.

Bruce Foxton: We played CBGB's, which was the club to play in New York for upcoming bands. We were doing two shows a day – a matinee and then the main show . . . We only had one suit each for the whole tour. They were minging. I've still got some of those suits and can't even get my wrist in the leg hole. I don't think I'm too bad now for me age, but, boy, those suits were tight.

1977 – The Jam fan club begins

Ann Weller: We started a fan club. Oh, that was a laugh. Nicky started it and then, being a teenager, she wanted to go out, so I used to help her. In Balmoral Drive, you had your front door, and then next door you had the coal shed with a door. But John, being a builder, knocked it down, brought a window home and made it into a little office.

Nicky Weller: I had joined the David Essex Fan Club and when I look at what I got for a fiver a year, it was crap compared to The Jam one. We ran it ourselves and for five quid you'd get these special things – letters, badges, priority to gigs and flexi discs at Christmas. One year we did a little book of matches. People still write to me to say, 'I've still got this bloody thing from all those years ago.'

Ann Weller: We put our home address on the fan club. I know . . . Well, we didn't know. You know, when you're green, you don't think. Our postman would bring all the letters down in a van on their own. There were so many of them. We'd all sit around with the neighbours, having cups of tea going through them. You put shitty ones in one pile and ones you had to reply to in another.

Nicky Weller: Sacks full of it . . . It was quite stressful at times, especially in the early days when you had to get the neighbours to come and write envelopes out by hand, because you didn't have printers. We had five or six old ladies churning out thousands and thousands of envelopes and labels, writing them out of a big book. Four times a year. We had 11,000 members in the Fan Club.

Ann Weller: All me and Nicky ever did was fill bleeding envelopes.

Nicky Weller: I got paid five quid a week doing that.

Rick Buckler: I used to hate doing them things, because I never could really think of an answer. I'd just say any old shit really.

Nicky Weller: They were pretty good boys. But I've got to say my brother was probably the best. 'You've got to do something. Write a letter or include a doodle or something.' We always had competitions where the fans could win stage clothes. Trying to keep that all together was quite tough, but good fun. They were away on tour so often that I'd have a stack of stuff to get signed when they got back. 'You're not going anywhere. You sit down. Sign this lot, and they did.'

Claire Mahoney: The Jam fan club was amazing, getting your little card saying that you were a member of this special club. I would pore over the letters and Paul's beautiful handwriting. Of course, he had to have beautiful handwriting, that was no surprise. I remember he used to sign off some of the letters with 'Stay Cool, Clean and Hard' . . . I thought, *I've got to try and use that* . . . As a woman, it's a weird thing to say, but there you go, I've said it and I have tried to live by that mantra ever since I first read that.

Ann Weller: These three girls turned up at our house from Japan. *What the bloody hell am I going to give them?* So, I gave them

John's dinner. *I thought I could cook him egg and bacon or something when he comes home.* There was one guy later who came from America that stayed for three days. The fans just used to turn up and all I ever did was make tea. It was hilarious. But if you think about it, all those people are still friends with us. The fans loved John. He used to call them little cockers. 'Get in here, little cockers, don't stand out there. Have you got enough money to get home?' They loved him.

18 November 1977 – *This Is the Modern World* (no. 22)

Paul Weller: There was a couple of good songs in those early days. 'In the City' is a good little single and there might be one off *Modern World*, I don't know, I've not heard it since the time it was made. But I didn't take myself seriously as a writer until *All Mod Cons*.

Dennis Munday: I was Polydor's jazz A&R manager. I went into the office and the guys were in there, in their black mohair suits . . . It reminded me of when I was a mod, and it shook me a bit because I looked at them and thought, *That was me, ten or fifteen years ago*. The record business was totally against punk and hoped it would burn out. They saw the bands as short term, make-money-quick acts, before they disappeared. That's why The Jam were forced to do the second album. Back then, you usually did one album every year. The second album is the hardest – your first is easy, because it's what you've been playing live. But *Modern World* is a lot better than people give it credit for. It does stand up . . . for a songwriter to have done two albums in one year is phenomenal.

Vic Coppersmith-Heaven: I was called into the record company offices to discuss The Jam's second album project, as I was only signed up for the first album. Polydor seemed pleased that the first single had entered the charts at number forty, but we began disagreeing at the meeting, as the record company wanted to offer me 25 per cent less wages to produce the second album and they did not want to move from that position. Maybe they only had a short-term vision for the band then . . . We were at a stalemate in the meeting, so I said, 'OK, give me less cash to live on but I want a higher percentage of sales as a producer,' which they then simply agreed to. Looking back now, after forty-plus years of continuous sales, I bet they wished they had not made that decision.

Contract settled, we moved over to Notting Hill Gate's Basing Street Studios, which was also the home to Island Records. At this time, it was the beginning of us all working out songs in the studio. I was actually not really that happy with the studio choice after we began the recording, as it was not confined enough for the three-piece band, but as we had started recording there, we were committed to carry on to meet record company demands to complete in time for the band going on tour in order to maximise sales.

Paul Weller: Some people really love *This Is the Modern World*. I've no idea how. That record nearly finished us off. It was Chris Parry's idea – he said, 'The Beatles used to put two albums out a year. You should do another one.' I thought, *Fuck! It's already taken me a good two years to write* In the City, *and that was a fucking slog! What do you mean I've got to do it again?* Now it's different. Yeah, now I might rise to the challenge, but I didn't have that . . . I don't think I've ever been a natural talent. I've had to work at it, and it's taken a long time to become anything really, in my estimation.

Jim Cook: We never had a situation where The Jam had a writing block, whereas other bands ... you know, when Sham 69 needed to do the first album, they only had seven songs as the gigs used to turn into fights after that.

The Jam started spending more money on studios and that freaked them a bit because they realised that they had to pay for it [*laughs*] – it was all advanced against royalties. The first album cost bugger all. The second one cost a bit more and then suddenly boom, they would have started experimenting a bit and it was costing a fortune.

Nicky Weller: Paul would have moved to London with his girlfriend by then, so he was a little bit more separated from us. But with Dad as his manager, you heard about things that had happened. They worked their socks off. If they weren't touring, they're in the studio, and if they weren't in the studio, Paul was writing new material. It was a rollercoaster like that. He must have felt pressurised.

Vic Coppersmith-Heaven: Sometimes you do get surprised during a recording and not sure where a particular sound disappeared to. We were in full recording mode in Basing Street Studios when a big chunk of the sound disappeared from the mix during a live recording with the band. I was checking everything, and then caught a glimpse of a guitar flying through the air in the studio below the control room. Paul had disconnected his guitar, which if I remember correctly was due to endless tuning problems, and the instrument headed skywards and fell to end as a heap on the floor.

Steve 'Tufty' Carver: I remember being around Paul's house with his mum and dad and Paul left the room the minute that The Jam come on *Top of the Pops* to perform 'Modern World'. When he come back, I stupidly went, you just missed yourself on telly and he went, 'Oh, I don't think much of that song anyway.'

David Cracknell: 'The Combine' on the *Modern World*, references to news quite a lot in Paul's songs: *Sunday papers and the dailies/Ena Sharples/Page Three Girls/News at Ten/War in Rhodesia far away in a distant land.* He was quite a foreign correspondent even at that age. He read the papers. He's a knowledgeable man.

Neil Sheasby: *This Is the Modern World*. There they were. These three guys looking cool. The guy in his own homemade jumper with tacked on arrows that I thought was fascinating. Then on the back that motion action picture of them playing live where Bruce is midair. I thought, *Wow, what's this?* Put it on and just fell in love with it. It transpired that was the weakest album. That's up for debate.

Gary Crowley: I loved the album from the moment I got my hands on it. The dreamlike quality of 'Life from a Window'. That metaphor for life. It's a great, great song. I'm trying to think of the opening line now. 'Looking from a hilltop. Sometimes it don't look nice, but that's OK.'

Rick Buckler: Any one of The Jam songs could have been a single. There are some gems hidden on albums, things like 'Life from a Window', that was a fabulous song. A lot of the stuff on the *Modern World* album got passed over a bit too quickly.

Vic Coppersmith-Heaven: The poet shines through and creates a vision that maybe we can all relate to or imagine, in that life from a window can inspire us, relax and focus the mind, create visions . . . Whenever I think of catching up on a Jam track, I often relate to this title, music and lyric. And then there is the performance, and how three people orchestrated songs and made them become a kind of musical dynamic poetry with an edge. It's OK to just play your instrument to accompany a song, but there is an art to actually playing the song, and that made The Jam so special.

Shaun Hand: That album is almost like a first draft of *All Mod Cons* in a way because you get lines and themes in 'The Combine' that later pop up on 'In the Crowd'. I don't think it suffers so much in terms of songwriting as production, and you can tell it's rushed. Some of it feels quite first take. When you listen to the live versions later on, from that Reading Uni gig on *Fire and Skill* and bootlegs, things like 'Here Comes the Weekend' and 'In the Street Today' sound a lot better because they've been playing them for eighteen months by then, so they're played in and tight. I really like it and can always listen to it. I can't quite bring myself to like 'London Traffic'. With the best will in the world that's not one of the better songs . . . But then it's that thing where I've listened to them that many times that I almost don't have an opinion on it. It's just in the bloodstream.

Bob Manton: I wish I could write something as poetic and as romantic as 'Tonight at Noon'. Most of my songs are me whining about how fucked up I am. I've tried to write thematically like Paul, but he's got a lot more poetry to what he does because he was influenced by Adrian Henri and the Liverpool poets school and all that.

Adrian Thrills: When Paul started getting into reading, he started devouring books. Really early on he gave me a copy of *One Flew Over the Cuckoo's Nest* in paperback, which I've still got. He goes, 'You've got to read this.' It was around the time they were doing the second album. It's all about songs like 'The Combine' and 'Standards', which had that slight dystopian feel to it. We were young and discovering stuff. Paul had a massive interest in poetry and started publishing young poets a bit later on. He's a great songwriter but it's always been a coalescence of influence, isn't it? There's poems, artwork, there's pop art, there's fashion.

Bill Smith: The first album didn't perform as well as hoped, but a couple of singles did OK, so they wanted to get another album out. It was a singles-driven industry, with picture sleeves being new and everything focused on image. For *This Is the Modern World*, I took a postmodernist approach. I visited the band during demos and recordings, which has always been crucial for my design process. Hearing the music helps convey what the band is trying to say. *In the City* had staked their claim – this is who and what we are. On *Modern World*, I wanted to find a place that was post-modernist. We found a nice spot under the Westway – I liked the tower blocks in the distance and the angles that the overpass created. I used a photographer called Gered Mankowitz, who goes back a long way, shooting The Rolling Stones and Small Faces back in the sixties and seventies. Paul was jumping for joy knowing that.

Gered Mankowitz: Paul had a deep love for the sixties, especially the Small Faces, who I'd worked with a lot, but the band weren't particularly communicative. They had a reserve and independence, and I think they saw me a bit as an outsider. They were tight as a unit, not especially friendly or welcoming, they weren't really going to let anybody in, and it was quite an edgy session.

The shot under the Westway was technically challenging. We chose the location because it epitomised visually aspects of the modern world that the band were referencing. I used a mixed-light technique, balancing flash with daylight to get an exposure in the distance of the tower blocks and the sky. Back then, this wasn't easy. I sensed the band would have preferred a looser, more spontaneous approach – not as tightly controlled as I needed them to be.

It's a great shot, and I'm proud of it. Album covers were a thrill to shoot – twelve inches square is a significant canvas. My generation pushed for photos shot specifically for albums, not just repurposed images, and that *Modern World* cover reflects that. Of course, there was also the incident with Paul's jumper . . .

Bill Smith: The band turned up, not wearing their black and white suits, but very much in civies. Gered was underwhelmed as Paul was just wearing a grey-ish jumper. I asked Paul if had anything else and he said, 'No, but I've seen a picture where Pete Townshend was wearing a jacket with arrows on it.' I grabbed the gaffer tape and added arrows – one up, one down – a bit postmodernist – *Direction, Creation, Reaction*.

Gered Mankowitz: My memory is that the sweater Paul wore might have been a very, very cool piece of fashion, but it was a bit dull. Paul was in the foreground, and I wanted it to say something. The others looked a bit funkier, and Paul was wearing this grey schoolboy sweater. We plucked up the courage to say, 'Hey, Paul, anything we can do about the sweater? It's a bit boring.' My memory is that he grabbed some black gaffer tape and put on these two arrows himself – he just did it. It was a moment of genius. It worked perfect.

Paul looks pissed off in the shot. They were smoking, as everybody did back then, and I think they were generally irritated. I don't remember any good vibes from the session or how they felt about the cover. But I thought it was a really powerful image.

Conny Jude: I was commissioned by Bill Smith to do some drawings for the inside sleeve. I had just left the Royal College of

Art. I met Paul in Bill's office and he seemed quiet and shy. I took my inspiration from the lyrics of the songs. Luckily, I must have got it right because my first drawings were all accepted except for my 'London Girl' illustration. So I drew it again, the second attempt was accepted. I was happy because that is a drawing of me! Immortalised forever on their inner sleeve. I met and saw The Jam perform later that year at the 100 Club on Oxford Street. I was in my late twenties, much older than most of the audience of what seemed to be young boy fans, dressed in various versions of school uniforms. I remember, to my surprise, one fan asked me for permission if he could stand on the table next to me. Laughing, of course I said yes, and so he did and then suddenly dived into the mosh pit . . . never to be seen again!

Bill Smith: The back cover featured that fantastic shot of Paul jumping up in the air, Pete Townshend-like, showing their energy and musicianship. The contrasting covers, with a new logo and look, pushed me creatively as an art director and challenged the band to evolve, something Paul always demanded. Every Jam album had a distinct identity, and this one was no exception.

Barry Cain: I got a review copy of the *Modern World* album, and I looked at the back. It says *Mister B. Cain, Teenage Blue*. I was shocked. He used the phrase in the lyrics for 'Life from a Window' too. Paul never gave me any royalties. He must owe me a fortune! I got such a kick out of that. My name there on a Jam album. It's an honour. He would have put Barry, but he forgot my first name.

Jonathan Ross: The first album was great although I always thought the photographs on it were a bit shit. I didn't like the cover for the second album. It was like they needed to spend a day shopping. They always struggled with their covers. I don't think they had one good album cover that I really liked.

There was that interesting period when punk shifted and it became the people who didn't really have what it took trying to churn out the same old shit, the same three chords nonsense, where the others went into slightly more interesting, challenging areas. Weller being one of them. I got the feeling that he wanted to explore other things. You can tell that even from the second album onwards when there's tracks like 'Tonight at Noon' that are so clearly not in the punk mould. That second album was really a tremendous album. You could see that Weller had been reading Beat poetry and was trying to do that stuff. There was that thing of growing up together that you got with bands that were smart. Whereas even though I love Generation X, they tried to do a sub-Springsteen thing on one of the albums, but they were always going to be a disposable band. But when you saw a band like The Clash, they were going to try and stretch themselves. Look at what Lydon did with Public Image, which was an extraordinary leap that the Pistols probably wouldn't have been able to be comfortable making with him. Weller is interesting because he did a lot of those movements while he stayed in The Jam.

November–December 1977 – *Modern World*, UK tour

Chas de Whalley: There was a press trip to Newcastle for the second night of the *Modern World* tour, arranged by Polydor's press office to thank a few journalists who'd been really keen on The Jam. We arrived late at the Mayfair to find the doors effectively closed. The place was packed and there was a whole bunch of kids outside, really pissed off because they couldn't get in. When we showed up – this bunch of southerners – going, 'Excuse me, we're the press,' they weren't having it and set about us. Steve Clarke from *NME* got punched out . . . This was November 1977. Punk inherently had this skeleton of violence within it. You'd get situations where there'd be massive stage invasions. It could get a bit nasty.

Jonathan Ross: I saw The Jam in Canterbury. Me and my friend who was the only other punk in Leytonstone hitchhiked there. He'd started spitting at gigs. For a brief period that was a thing. We got right to the front and this idiot next to me was pogoing and he spat. He got Foxton right in the face. He leaned down furiously, understandably, but thought it was me. He wanted to beat me up and I was going, 'It wasn't me. I don't spit!'

Chas de Whalley: I did an article at the end of '77 and went down to the family home in Woking. They were a very entrepreneurial, enterprising family. John had been a builder for years; his sister ran the fan club, and his mother did the merchandise. I think that they were one of those families for whom their son was the focus of all the family activities. In the same way as you get families with the Olympics and the son is a great swimmer and so the whole family's routine begins to focus in on making sure he can get to training at five o'clock in the morning . . . John said that once Paul was writing songs, 'It was like having a little jukebox all of our own in the house,' so from very early days they spotted that, not to say there was a living to be made out of Paul, but that there was a living for them all and they were all in it together.

I think Paul, Bruce and Rick were friends. They weren't best friends, but they were friends. They were having a laugh and enjoying this experience together. I can't remember witnessing any obvious animosities happening or cracks opening up in their relationships. I spent more time with Paul than I did with the other two. When I started working at CBS, he was at Polydor with Pete Wilson in their little studio doing demos. We'd have lunch in some little pub or café, and then he'd ask if I could get him things like the Bob Dylan catalogue . . . I gave him the opportunity of plugging all sorts of gaps in his collection. I remember being very impressed that he was talking about albums he'd got, Small Faces B-sides and stuff. He was genuinely searching stuff out. He knew his stuff and that informed his own work.

January–March 1978 – 'London Blitz' tour and 'News of the World' (no. 27)

Nicky Weller: My dad had meetings with all the Polydor chiefs in New York in 1978. He said to me, 'You're not going to school for a couple of days. We're going to take a trip.' He took me on Concorde to New York. Fucking amazing. There was a lovely girl that worked at Polydor in New York called Leigh Ellen. She did all the sightseeing stuff with us, horse drawn carriages, up the Trade Center, Staten Island, Statue of Liberty. We even went to see Adam and the Ants at the town hall. She said, 'John, I doubt if you want to come, do you?' He went, 'Fucking right I do.' When it came to the gig, my dad was like, 'What we doing standing in this queue?' She went, 'Oh, this is the guest-list queue,' and he went, 'Fuck that,' went straight to the front, bunged somebody at the door, and we were straight into the gig.

Barry Cain: He was good at bunging people.

Nicky Weller: He was always a chancer. For example, Polydor headquarters in London was a beautiful building. There was a lovely old fella on the door called Charlie. Dad would go up there once a week and commandeer an office. No one from Polydor knew this, except for Charlie . . . 'Number six office is empty, John.' Then he'd say to me, 'Don't go to school, babe. Come up and photocopy all the fan-club stuff for free.' Polydor would then come around and go, 'John, we've signed the band. We haven't signed you. You're not allowed to just commandeer an office.' 'I won't do it again.' Of course, the next week, Charlie let him in again. He ended up staying in my mum and dad's caravan, so he was well in with them.

Chris Parry: In early 1978, there was pressure coming from John to get another album because they made another payment . . . But I was unsure. I knew that Paul had this new girlfriend, Gill Price, and was getting a bit moody, and things were getting tetchy. John was complaining that he wasn't the same boy any more. I could see that Paul was distancing himself from the whole thing. It was just a reaction to the fact that they toured a lot, and it was all getting a bit challenging.

Jim Cook: When John ran out of money, he'd come to us and say, 'I could do with some cash,' and you'd say, 'What do you want, John?' 'I could do with twenty grand' or whatever. 'All right, John. We'll give you a twenty grand advance,' because we knew we had plenty of stuff coming in from various places, and it was never a difficult negotiation at that point in time with The Jam. Then you'd say, well, give us an extra album, John, tag another album on the end.

Peter Button: I don't think there was a lot of renegotiations of the terms, but there were some additional payments. Lump sum payments. Because of the success that they had, Polydor wanted to keep the band happy. So, they would give them some extra money. Always recoupable. But they didn't necessarily ask for additional albums.

John Cohen: Advances from record companies and publishers were not paid in cash. They were all dealt with formally and were recoupable from royalties. He didn't walk out with his pocket stuffed.

John was wonderful. I mean, he was the best manager of any band because he was so loyal, would fight to the end of time for his artists. I don't want to upset Paul . . . but [John] had no experience in the business. He needed us to help him but there were certain battles with John that I had to try and make him understand things which he didn't. Some of the times that was not to the benefit of the band, not to the benefit of Paul, but entirely in good faith. He just misunderstood things.

Rick Buckler: When we first signed, the record company recommended the publisher, agent and solicitors, because we knew nothing about running a band professionally, John included. He was great in the early days, driving us around to the clubs and making sure we got our twenty-five quid, but as soon as you step into the professional world, and especially in the way that the band suddenly took off and went global, we were all completely inexperienced.

Chris Parry: I put Paul in the studio to do a few demos, just to see what we had. After hearing them, I thought, *Well, this is going to be an awful conversation*. This could be the end of my relationship with the band. I was going to have to say to Paul that until you really give this thing attention, and you write the songs, it ain't going to happen. Paul said, 'What do you mean?' 'Well, you won't be recording.'

It was tough, it was pretty damning to Bruce as he'd written some songs too. He'd done the single 'News of the World', which did OK, but I could sense there was a little bit of tension between Paul and Bruce. It was clear that someone had to say something. 'If Paul's not writing, there ain't no Jam. Forget it.' . . . I wasn't here to just drop into another album. The second album had been done under extreme pressure . . . They had to come out with a third album which was superior, by a long chalk, to *This Is the Modern World*.

Adrian Thrills: I don't think *Modern World* is as bad as it's sometimes painted, but it feels like a hurried record, and then there was the infamous album that was scrapped between *Modern World* and *All Mod Cons*, where Chris Parry told him these songs aren't good enough. I talked to Paul about that. There was a song called 'I Want to Paint'.

Shaun Hand: Paul seemed to be writing songs about the same lyrical theme: Gill Price. There was one called 'She's Got Everything' . . . There was 'On Sunday Morning'. It was a pretty low period. It does seem like Weller was actually writing songs, it's just he wasn't writing particularly good ones, or if he was, he just couldn't focus it enough until whoever it was said, no, this is shit, go away and rethink it, and he got a kick up the arse.

Dennis Munday: They delivered some demos, most of them Bruce's, and that's when Chris came in and said, 'Go back and start again.' The stories were that they delivered an album that was rejected. They didn't. I've been through Paul's archives and have never found anything that warranted that at all.

Chris Parry: I can't tell you the track titles of what ended up in the bin, but there wasn't much that was particularly good. There was some contribution from Rick Buckler, but it was very minor. One or two songs from Bruce. There was a Paul song in there, but it wasn't a particularly impressive song . . . certainly not an album and there was no lost record, that's just a musical myth.

Dennis Munday: That's when it all kicked off. Chris had turned all the demos down. It was not a particularly pleasant time. He was quite rude about Bruce. 'Go back and play the bass. You're not a songwriter.' It was very heavy at the time. I had been promoted to be The Jam's product manager. John had called a meeting to discuss the fifth single and third album, and I remember walking out of the first meeting, thinking, *I don't know if I want to do this*. It was that heavy. As I left, I remember Bruce said, 'Are you Jim Cook's spy?'

Jim Cook: They initially thought I put Dennis in to get all the dirt, but that wasn't the case. Paul was doing his own thing, and Dennis became their man. He was doing all the liaison. Chris Parry was a Simon Cowell-type figure in his own way – he was good, and knew what he wanted, but he did break a few rules and caused a few problems, but those were the types of guys who did well.

Bruce Foxton: They were probably right – we needed to stop and rethink. They sent us off to a caravan in Aylesbury to write to order, but it didn't work; you can't force it. Paul had a rethink, and we came up with *All Mod Cons*. It was a pivotal moment and make-or-break for staying with Polydor. It had to be good, and successful. That was the big turning point.

Chris Parry: It was a bit of a bruising thing. They went away, licked their wounds, and then Paul got started. There was tension between him and the others and, in a way, I was putting him in the position that he needed to be in, and he responded heroically. But of course, Rick, and particularly Bruce, were very unhappy about it. We started to do some studio stuff, but I couldn't get Bruce to listen particularly. He wasn't unpleasant but you could tell there was some stuff going on. John Weller said, 'I don't think the band want you to go in today,' so, we sat down with Paul, Vic and Bruce himself, and decided to call it a day. If they didn't want me, then I didn't want to be there.

Vic Coppersmith-Heaven: Co-production was not really a positive idea to continue with. Chris would often come to me with suggestions of individual sounds, like 'Please recreate Charlie Watts's snare sound', which is not the way that I felt to go about creativity at all, as you work on the projects to recreate the original sound. Chris would often turn up at RAK Studios in the evening and want to change many of the creative decisions that we had made during the day. His main commitment was A&R director at the record company, so he was responsible for the future of many artists, and while the collaboration did work well for a while, it came to a point where eventually we chose to part company and The Jam chose me to continue, which pretty much allowed us to focus the new direction and refine the sound for the *All Mod Cons* album.

Dennis Munday: Chris's relationship with the band broke up and he only produced five tracks on the album. They decided they wanted to go with Vic on his own.

Chris Parry: Paul was sad about it, but it was pretty clear that [Vic] had control of the desk. Paul had got a lot of really good tunes, so they were a team ready to go and my withdrawing, in some respects, put down a benchmark. *OK, you guys better deliver.* I was still the A&R boss and have to say that they did exactly that.

I do wonder if Paul went into those demo studios with the third album in mind, having got all these other songs and was hiding them in his little schoolbag because he just wanted to get this thing sorted out? There's then no more arguments about who's writing the songs.

Paul Weller: No! Sadly, no! I didn't have anything to bring to the table when we did those demos, and anything I did have, we demoed, and it was shocking. Dreadful. Bruce, bless him, man, tried to step up and write a few, but it wasn't happening. Chris, thank God, came round my little flat in Baker Street and said, 'I've got to have a chat with you. This is just shit. These songs are shit, all of them, and you've got to start again or it's not going to happen.' He was the first person to say that. No one else in our team was saying that at all. That's what made me sit up and think, *OK, right, let's get fucking serious about this now.* He said it from a good place, and he was absolutely right. It wasn't just him doing a heavy-handed record company thing. He was right in what he said. If we'd gone down that road – even if the record company had released it, maybe they would, maybe they wouldn't – that would have been a nail in the coffin, after *Modern World*. Thank goodness he did say that. It made me sit up and listen.

March–August 1978 – US and UK tours

Mark Cooper: The first gig I reviewed was the Sex Pistols in Winterland, San Francisco, in January '78. Then very shortly after that, I saw The Jam again, at the Starwood in LA . . . I found the review. It was a great subject, because it was about the collision between the new energy coming out of the UK and a California scene that was dominated by Supertramp, Fleetwood Mac, Journey, and a very small emerging club scene in LA that had its own punk thing going but was still aping the UK . . . As a Brit abroad, I had a sense of the world The Jam were coming from, what they represented, and how novel and fresh they seemed.

Martin Hopewell: I don't think the Americans ever really got The Jam. I hate to use the word 'punk', but their idea of punk was not ours. Our idea of punk was something far harder-edged, not just sticking make-up on and prancing around with long hair and tight trousers.

Nicky Weller: The Jam did end up doing a lot of US trips. I don't think people realised how much they did. They didn't like it. The politics didn't agree with Paul.

Ann Weller: He'd say, 'I'm fucking off home.'

Nicky Weller: It was one of them things where he wouldn't put up with stuff if he didn't agree on something. He was very young. He was just a really angry little person, wasn't he?

Bruce Foxton: East and West Coast were pretty good for The Jam. We went out there to support Blue Öyster Cult in spring '78.

Nicky Weller: That was the most ridiculous support ever.

Bruce Foxton: The management over there thought that if you're playing in front of 20,000 people and win over a thousand, it's better than doing the club dates where you're playing to 300, 400, 500 max. It just didn't work. We went out into a big old auditorium and they're all Blue Öyster Cult band fans and we had 20,000 people booing us. It completely backfired and pissed us off. Understandably. It didn't sound right in the first place when they said about Blue Öyster Cult band, but that's the trouble when you put something in the hands of someone else, they go off in their own direction and it didn't work. It was a disaster.

Chas de Whalley: The Americans didn't know what they were talking about. I can well imagine that the US didn't get it because it wasn't polished enough. I interviewed Be Bop Deluxe once who almost made it really big. They actually did that same tour with The Jam. They toured the US thinking, 'We're going to appear in suits, this will be a really different image'. This was about 1976, and the Americans went, 'Fuck off. These guys in suits. What's this all about?' It killed them dead. Flamin' Groovies never got big in America, they were only ever a cult band, and they wore sixties suits and ties . . . Those suits didn't work for Americans.

Steve Hinders: I saw them in April '78 when they came to a small club called Bogart's in Cincinnati, Ohio. We'd gone in early and met John, who was as nice as can be, his silver hair was swept back so beautifully. Bruce and Rick were very friendly, but a little bit on edge because they had a show coming up. Paul was very open, very friendly. We talked about The Beatles, the Who, about what The Jam were going to be, what other areas in the United States they were going to visit. They did a sound check and then that night, I was right down front. They were pinballing against each other. Bruce and Paul would hit their backs together, then spring out. They had the Union Jacks on their Vox amps. They were very, very loud and it was one of the most exciting moments of my life. To see The Jam up close, ten feet away, oh my God, they were on fire.

18 August 1978 – 'David Watts' / '"A" Bomb in Wardour Street' (double A-side, no. 25)

Rick Buckler: It was obvious that we had no direction, with the record company and agent setting the agenda for recording, releases and tours. They pretty much managed the band, and they wanted their pound of flesh. You'd do a tour of Europe, and would come back and record another single, and then go and record an album, release that and promote it, and then go to the States or Japan. We just did it. The record company dictated nearly all of that.

It was great that we had a record company that was behind us but, on the other hand, their agenda was slightly different from ours. They wanted to sell units and that was their prime goal. It's a business. There were occasions when they would say, 'We want another single,' and Paul didn't like writing to order. He never did. Not many people do. So it was nice to say, we'll do a cover version. We did 'David Watts' as a single, which was a great song. It was not a particularly well-known Kinks number, and a lot of people still think that The Jam wrote that. It was nice to have that to draw upon when we were under pressure for releases.

Vic Coppersmith-Heaven: There were lots of different aspects of keeping musicians and bands happy in the production role. I remember meeting Paul at the Marquee Club in Wardour Street where we were watching another band performing, and I asked him how the vinyl cut of our latest single release sounded on his 45 rpm player, and his instant reaction was 'Not loud enough!' which would sometimes mean a complete remix of the track or an audio frequency engineer in the vinyl cutting room who would rearrange the frequencies to give the impact of the audio signal jumping out at the loudest volume on a record player. Sound impact had to be instant in those days.

Adrian Thrills: I remember interviewing Paul in *ZigZag* and he was talking about how serious he took it. *We're not like the Boomtown Rats who are just having a laugh. I think it's important for bands to take themselves seriously*. He might have had a few beers in the coach coming back from the gig and he was just shooting from the hip. Sometimes he'd just say things. I spoke to him a few weeks after 'David Watts' came out, and he felt he overstepped the mark and didn't like reading back what he'd said. I've interviewed him so many times over the years and he's very honest. He'll speak his mind.

25 August 1978 – Reading Festival

Steve Barron: I left school early and worked as a camera assistant and tea boy on some big films like *A Bridge Too Far* and *Superman* . . . In 1978, someone said we should shoot Reading Rock Festival, which was headlined by The Jam on Friday, Status Quo on Saturday, and Patti Smith on the Sunday with loads of great bands. I was cajoled along to believe this guy had the money to pay for all this. So, I got out my notebook and hired people I'd been working with – professional camera people and crew. I had this horrific experience because he kept saying the money's coming to pay them and on the Friday it still hadn't come, and this guy suddenly stopped answering his phone and disappeared, and I realised it was all a big fraud. We had sixty crew there in the tent and I told them that the money hadn't come through. They got together, had a meeting, and said, 'We're here, so we'll film this night for you, you can take it and try and raise the money.' . . . We produced a fifty-minute film, *Kids Like Me and You*, and got a deal with John Weller for The Jam, who said we could sell it to raise money.

Chas de Whalley: I was really there for The Jam, and that was the gig with Sham 69, where there was a huge, massive stage invasion . . . John Peel was the DJ on stage, and he was in tears over the way that the crowd had completely taken over proceedings.

Steve Barron: There was a lot of aggro that night. Music was at a real crossroads and the lineup had rock and roll, punk, new wave, mods, skinheads, Sham 69, Penetration, the Pirates, Ultravox and The Jam. Everyone was around just not liking each other's music and yet they're all on the same bill. When Sham came on there was a big invasion of the stage. Our cameras were suddenly ripped off their tripods. There's footage of Jimmy Pursey breaking down, screaming out 'If the Kids Are United'. Paul Weller and the guys had a rough night, he was quite flustered.

Chas de Whalley: It was very emotionally charged that evening, there was needles in the air. I watched the gig from backstage and it felt like I was somehow looking after Paul's girlfriend, Gill. We accidentally ended up out into the crowd and I was remonstrating with the guard on the gate to let us back in. Paul got wind of this and was really angry with me. I don't think he can have thought I was running off with her, but clearly I'm at fault for the whole situation . . . I had heard about Paul having a temper on occasion but that was the only time that I saw him at his wits' end. I don't know whether he wanted to stick one on me or not . . . but it wasn't nice for either of us.

13 October 1978 – 'Down in the Tube Station at Midnight' (no. 15)

Nicky Weller: I still get goosebumps on the back of my neck when I hear 'Down in the Tube Station at Midnight'.

Vic Coppersmith-Heaven: The concept of recording was changing a lot now, as rehearsing new songs was now being undertaken in the studio, whereas the first album was a fully rehearsed live set that had been played many times on stage. We were developing ideas as we recorded them. This was one of the reasons that 'Down in the Tube Station' didn't work initially. Arrangement ideas were being kicked around but didn't seem to gel. I was in the control room, listening to developments and rehearsal ideas which halted when parts did not work, but Paul was strumming his guitar, and there was the time when he said, 'Fuck it!' and I saw him screwing up a piece of paper and chucking it into a wastepaper bin in the studio, followed by a silence from everyone.

Paul Weller: I had a little hissy fit with Vic Smith and chucked it in the bin. 'Fuck it, it's rubbish,' and Vic, bless his heart, said, 'This is good. You should carry on working on this. We've got to see it through.' That's the way you know you've got a good producer – someone who encourages you. Luckily, we did that. Same with 'English Rose'. I didn't want to do that, and it was only Vic that talked me round.

Vic Coppersmith-Heaven: I left the control room into the studio and chatted with Paul about next plans and asked him what was in the bin. I checked it out and it was the lyrics of 'Tube Station'. It was removed from the bin and I read it. I thought that they were great lyrics, so we all revisited the song, changed tack, bounced ideas and worked on it together, and it developed into one of The Jam's most exciting songs.

But it was missing something initially. The icing on the cake. Then I had the idea to record an underground train at St John's Wood station, which was close to the studio. I recorded the sound of the train emerging from the tunnel on a mobile quarter-inch-tape magnetic recorder. It worked perfectly to introduce the track.

Sodge Adams: We had to take T-shirt samples for the tour down to show the band. They were rehearsing at Easy Hire in Market Road, up from Caledonian Road. I arrived with this kid who worked for us who was literally a school dropout and a mad,

mad Jam fan. Paul was there in bare feet and said, 'Sit down. Listen to this. What do you think?' We sat down on this mouldy old couch and the three of them went into 'Down in the Tube Station at Midnight'. Never heard it before in my life. That was a real seminal moment . . . It was like hairs standing up on the back of your neck.

Stuart Deabill: It wasn't the type of song you heard on the radio. It had a bit of menace, tension, and an almost otherworldly feel.

Andy Rosen: That was the great thing about that era – everyone wanted to be original . . . Paul's songwriting resonated the most, they just connected. 'Down in the Tube Station at Midnight'. 'Takeaway curry'. We've all done that. He was an incredible songwriter . . . I photographed them a lot – Paul gritting his teeth, the amount of guitar strings they went through and the energy was just incredible.

Ian Stone: The depiction of London, the storytelling – it's a story in a visual song. You could question why you would buy a takeaway curry and then get on the Tube, instead of going to a curry house closer to home. I love the confidence, the imagery of 'pubs, Wormwood Scrubs, too many right-wing meetings', all of that.

Bruce Foxton: Some songs like 'Tube Station' just pop into your head and you immediately think 'Wow, that works.' They don't have to be complicated to be good.

Steve 'Tufty' Carver: Paul obviously wasn't listening to the same teachers as me because he come up with a line, 'Jesus saves, painted by an atheist nutter'. To me, that's beyond genius.

Any other songwriter would have gone with 'religious nutter', but Paul, being awkward, chose 'atheist nutter'.

Chris Pope: Paul's connection to Ray Davies and Pete Townshend is clear but Paul was original with what he did, especially 'Tube Station', taking something of the past and you're making it in the present . . . I thought, *That is a cut above the rest.* The imagery about something that's happening on the streets of London.

Trevor Neal: It hinted at where The Jam were heading. They'd taken punk and they were going somewhere else now. They told stories with more control and subtlety than much of the punk stuff.

Paul Barry: I'd never heard anything like that before. A murder in a tube station turned into art. Weller can have one phrase like, 'the distant echo of faraway voices', and you're there. He can set a scene with minimal language. It's so powerful, the toffee wrappers, and the guy lying there dying, thinking 'cause they took the keys, and she'll think it's me'. He takes you to the darkest place in a beautiful song.

Steve 'Tufty' Carver: I remember Mike Read moaning about the violence of it and you just think, *what can't you hear?* I remember Dennis Munday telling me, 'It's got too many words in it', and I went, 'What are you talking about? Tell that to a Jam audience who sing every syllable of every word.'

Dennis Munday: It was a great song, but it wasn't going to give them a top ten hit. The lyrics were too violent for daytime radio.

Martyn Goddard: We had no permission for the 'Tube Station' photo shoot, so I couldn't use a flash. When I reviewed the contact sheets, only one frame could be used – the moment a train came in and broke up the black of the tunnel. It was the perfect picture. We kept looking behind us all the time, waiting to get caught by the transport police. At one point, we were waiting so long for a train that Rick started doing press ups.

Barry Cain: That song came out the blue. I never expected that from them. It was so claustrophobic and frightening, and yet it had that beat to it. Phenomenal ... For me, that is the best thing Paul Weller has ever written. He's created wonderful things, but that stands out. It took my breath away.

3 November 1978 – *All Mod Cons* (no. 6)

Paul Weller: *All Mod Cons* was the moment for me when I started to take it more seriously. Songs like 'Down in the Tube Station' and 'English Rose' broke out of that punk thing, becoming more musical and more our own sound. People liked it too, it got good reviews and so it felt like people took us a bit more seriously and then consequently I took it more seriously as well.

John Wilson: Paul was writing what you'd call the quintessential English lyric – suburbia, character studies, vignettes, and small-town dramas revealing bigger truths. Where does that come from in a twenty-year-old who wasn't academic, enjoyed English but little else, and didn't grow up with a library or tutor? Paul just had an astonishing way with words.

Daniel Rachel: He's got an instinctive intelligence. It doesn't matter if he's well read or not well read. It's just the ability to be able to put your thoughts and ideas into a song, and he can do that.

Adrian Thrills: Paul said that he wasn't particularly academic or much of a reader, but these lyrics are so poetic and evocative. I asked him where it came from and the only thing he could pinpoint was listening to early Pink Floyd, Traffic and The

Beatles – wistful English psychedelia that sparked his imagination and fed into these lyrics.

Paul Weller: I wasn't reaching for the thesaurus to look up words and things. I wouldn't even be able to spell it! I didn't go anywhere near anything like that. I honestly don't know where it comes from and I don't care either, because I know this is something I can do, and I'm happy with that.

Bill Smith: Up until *All Mod Cons*, we hadn't really done a studio shoot for the album cover. I love the simplicity of the three of them in the room, not altogether, holding hands and arms, round shoulders, like a normal band shot would be, but slightly separated. Three individuals, but in this great band. The new Jam logo was Paul's idea. He liked the Immediate Records label and wanted to use the lettering but the word Immediate . . . was only ever written in that particular font style, so I had to create it to make 'The Jam' and then 'All Mod Cons'. Paul was also very strong about wanting a collage of his favourite things on the inside of that album sleeve, like that whole mod thing with the exploded diagram of how to mend a scooter.

Alan McGee: If it wasn't for Paul putting the Creation on a fucking sleeve, I wouldn't have known about that band. I then went and bought their records and got into the Creation. That totally influenced where we started from.

Andy Lewis: The inner sleeve of *All Mod Cons* became a guidebook for me. He also started namechecking bands like the Zombies or the Action, and because of that I started digging even deeper into old sixties freakbeat, soul and obscure psychedelia.

Bill Smith: Of course, there was the single, with the arrows, again. Paul said to me, 'Creation Reaction, Direction'. That came from those arrows on *Modern World* – there is method in some of this madness.

Keiko Egawa: I loved 'English Rose'. I used to think, *Why aren't I English?* Lyrics were so important. I said to Paul one time . . . 'What do you think about all these Japanese fans? A lot of them don't understand your lyrics,' and he said, 'It's just music, they don't have to understand lyrics. I mean it's better if you understand lyrics, but music is so important.'

Dylan Jones: In the early punk days, melody was perceived to be old school. There's the famous 'English Rose' story that Paul was embarrassed to write something that was that intricate, that melodic and perhaps that personal and that soft. In the first couple of years of punk, everything had to be hard with a hard edge, and everyone was angry. That was part of the excitement, but to deny melody, craftsmanship and the art of songwriting quite soon seemed to be a bit bonkers.

Dennis Munday: That was written during that disastrous American tour where they supported Blue Öyster Cult. You can hear how lonely he was when he wrote it. We had already printed the album sleeve, but Paul said, 'I want it on,' so it's like a secret track when you listen.

Vic Coppersmith-Heaven: I'll never forget being at RAK and witnessing that magical moment of Paul sitting alone in the studio performing one of his latest compositions, 'English Rose'. It would not work with a three-piece band arrangement, so we had to work out how to fit that into the album concept as it was such a good song. I imagined a magical mystical setting, and so I went out and purchased a BBC sound effects album and extracted the wind and other effects, like sounds of the ocean and mixed them into the track to help follow the song's lyric.

Shaun Hand: They were going to have excerpts of conversation between the tunes on that album. They recorded chats with some mods to intersperse between the tracks. It might have thrown it off balance because it's a very coherent album.

Suggs: Paul's evolution has always been an inspiration. He's always taken risks and that is part of why I think we're still here. I was one of the one million people who went to the Red Cow and I've still got the badge upstairs somewhere. Our keyboard player, Mike, said he wasn't mad on punk and all that, but apparently there's this mob and they're doing a bit of Motown, which is what we loved . . . Then, funnily enough, I've seen him supporting Slade at Wembley Arena at the end of '78. Talk about the last cross of the two generations, but it kind of worked.

Kenny Wheeler: I didn't like The Jam when I first saw them. I weren't really into what they'd done but I hadn't really listened to it properly . . . I was short of work and doing this Mel Bush thing at Wembley. He done these rock and roll events, with six bands on in one day. The Jam were on with Slade and it was all kicking off. John said afterwards, 'Come and see me. We've got a job for you', and that was it . . . As you can see, I'm a big lad and I was even bigger then. I'm no heavyweight boxer, but John said just be about, carry the bags and that's how it started.

1– 29 November 1978 – UK 'Apocalypse' tour

Chris Bostock: I saw The Jam on that 'Apocalypse' tour at the Bristol Colston Hall. It was spine-tingling, unlike anything else I've experienced. Paul had that Pete Townshend vibe – slightly aggressive, bashing the guitar, he was on the edge of smashing it. The tension was electrifying. He was one of the first angry young men.

Derek D'Souza: The gigs were crazy. They were quite violent and scary at times. You get knocked about and would be standing in one place and five seconds later you were thirty feet away and had no choice in the matter! You'd know the songs but there were times when you'd have to choose between singing along and just breathing!

Ian Stone: My first Jam gig was 21 December 1978 at the Music Machine, Camden High Street. We'd broken up from Jewish Free School, went home, got changed and headed out – me and my friends, Simon and Robert. We were only fourteen or fifteen . . . It was a much more laissez-faire attitude to children and alcohol back then, and we weren't the youngest either . . . The support bands were Jab Jab, who were a rock reggae band, Gang of Four, who had a song, something about a tourist, and Shane MacGowan – his band were called Nipple Erectors. Shane was wearing a tutu and looked like he'd possibly had a drink . . . the roadies came on and cleared the stage until it was just a couple of microphones and the drum kit and then The Jam sign behind them . . . Then Paul Weller's dad walks on and shouts, 'Please welcome the best fucking band in the world: The Jam.' They came on and started playing 'It's Too Bad'. I was ten foot away, and that blew my tiny mind.

Chris Parry: The Jam were great, but I had the sense that I wanted to do more. The Jam didn't travel very well. I guess that's why they're so entrenched and so loved in the British culture because they were very much lovers of all things British. I came from New Zealand, and I wanted to go everywhere . . . This band were not going to exotic places all around the world . . . I thought, what if I just form my own label and I could find bands to take around the world and have a bit of laugh? I also wanted to do my own damn thing, and I didn't really want too many people to get in the way of it. It all got a little bit weird with The Jam. I'd burned a few bridges for creative reasons, I had no problems with it. You have to break it from time to time.

Dennis Munday: When Chris Parry left to form Fiction Records with the Cure, Polydor got a new A&R man in, but he came to me and said, 'Look, I can't deal with it. The band don't want to talk to me,' so my boss said, 'You have to do both jobs. You are now the A&R man and the product manager.' They didn't pay me any extra.

Jim Cook: *All Mod Cons* was a great album, but it didn't sell that great – getting out to around 60,000 copies in the UK. But it was seeing them live on that tour in Reading when I realised that The Jam were going to be a massive band. It was just a question of when and with the right record. That's when Dennis started playing a bigger role. His background was jazz, but he was very interested in the more modern stuff as well, so, he started getting more involved. The big bug bear around *All Mod Cons* and its singles was the promotion – we weren't getting enough Radio 1 airplay. We had guys working the country around all of the local radio stations, but we could have a thousand plays a week on local and it wouldn't have sold any records. To break a record in the late seventies, you needed to be on the first sheet of the Radio 1 playlist, getting eighteen to twenty plays a week and prime slots like breakfast, but The Jam were getting evenings.

Vic Coppersmith-Heaven: It was great for me towards the end of *All Mod Cons* to be totally involved in production of future recordings; sometimes I was titled producer, sometimes co-producer with Paul, Bruce and Rick, and sometimes I was co-arranger with the band and other times I was engineer, mixer.

Dennis Munday: After *All Mod Cons*, management wanted to get rid of Vic Smith. We had a guy called Tony Bramwell working at Polydor, who'd worked with The Beatles for ten, eleven years. He knew everyone in the business and wanted to get George Martin as producer. I argued that Vic did a great job on *All Mod Cons*. He had pulled it together and I can't fault the production of it. You don't change a winning horse and jockey. George Martin wasn't right for The Jam. He was my father's generation. He didn't like punk, so I couldn't see that working and also his diary would have been full; we would have needed another album in '79 and I doubt that he would have had the time.

Vic Coppersmith-Heaven: It was unbalancing for me to hear that Polydor record company individuals talked of replacing me with an American producer, which record companies seemed to find fashionable at the time, probably for marketing opportunities, but such activity seemed to be very short-sighted in their thinking. I will always be thankful for the support of the band and John Weller, who continued to support my production work with The Jam and to work on the next two album projects. John was great enthusiastic company in the recording studio, and we understood each other well. As we moved forward, you could hear a real progressive development in the sound and our musical relationship together.

Jim Cook: People didn't believe that Vic existed at one point. They thought he was a pseudonym for Paul because it's such a weird name. I've got a picture from *NME* where somebody's saying 'Who is Vic Coppersmith-Heaven, does he actually exist?' They showed a picture of him with The Jam, so, yes, he was a real person.

9 March 1979 – 'Strange Town' (no. 15)

Vic Coppersmith-Heaven: Jam recording sessions were on occasions interrupted by fans storming the studio, as they spent time outside waiting to speak with the band, and on one occasion Paul let them in to the control room to see the action; there were about thirty of them sitting behind me unknowingly, but it was a great atmosphere and a real treat for them to see recording in process.

Dennis Munday: I used to know their names. I mean they were nice lads, and they always behaved themselves. I don't think Vic was too happy about it, but if they turned up, then they got let in.

Stuart Deabill: I started buying singles with 'Strange Town' in '79. It was Weller's post-punk mini opera. Them singles just meant everything and it was like a calling . . . The youth of them, they weren't that much older than us . . . You can't relate to geezers with long hair in Supertramp or Pink Floyd.

Adrian Thrills: 'Butterfly Collector' – the B-side on 'Strange Town' – in anyone else's hands, it's one of your very best songs, and it's just a B-side.

Dylan Jones: I played that Jam B-side to death. It is a great performance and very evocative of that period.

Steve Barron: We got the gig to create the music promotional film for 'Strange Town'. There wasn't really a big brief; a bit of chat and had a meeting. Paul said he felt it was the sort of music where they could be running through Soho, a bit like The Beatles, and then a bit of live, and that was it. It rained that morning so Paul said to forget the running stuff. The budget was £2,500, which gets you pretty much nothing, but it was my first commission as a producer/director, with our little company, in a time when I was suddenly very much in debt . . . cos of what we owed for the Reading Festival disaster.

We screened it at a Thursday mod night in Charing Cross, borrowing a projector to show 'Strange Town' on repeat on the club wall, while setting up a 'Strange Town café' to earn some extra cash. Loads of kids started asking us to play it again . . . so we showed this three-minute video over and over, even though the music downstairs was drowning out the sound of it, but it was just cool. I don't know what happened, the word got out, if you get a burger at the 'Strange Town café', you're in. Suddenly we had a queue of about fifty kids wanting a burger and we had to look in the very bottom of our grungy old freezer to find anything left because we weren't prepared for it.

April 1979 – Third US tour and first Canada dates

Steve Hinders: April 1979, The Jam came over for their third American tour. Agora Ballroom in Cleveland, Ohio. That's when we became pen pals after I asked Paul 'How about I write you?' 'Sure, that sounds really good.' Gill wrote their address on a drinks napkin, which I still have, and I've still got all my letters from Paul. I would lay my feelings on the line. What I liked about a lot of music, what I didn't like about some American music, or politics, touched upon different things. Books, magazines. We had talked about James Jamerson, who was the great session player in those Motown songs, so I sent him a book about him. These letters that I got from Paul were very personal. There was humour, decency, and there was kindness. When he wrote that letter, he was focused on writing that letter . . . That went on probably until 1982.

Mark Cooper: I saw a gig in Oakland, and in my memory, they were on with The Ramones, which seems slightly incredible ... those gigs at the Whisky and the Starwood were quite well attended, because there was a little nascent English scene ... English-loving hipsters. There'd always been a small scene in LA like that. They just didn't get very much beyond that, because American AOR rock was very overblown, very melodic, full of grand gestures, and The Jam felt like the opposite of that, they were a short, sharp shock in contrast, so while I think the scenesters were fascinated, the broader radio landscape didn't make any sense of The Jam, despite the fact they kept coming back.

May 1979 – 'Jam Pact' UK tour

Kenny Wheeler: It started to get chaotic at that point. We used to call the fans the Muppets, like *The Muppet Show* ain't it? ... It weren't meant in that way, but like Muppets ... chaotic. John always liked a nice hotel but you used to have to watch where you stayed because there was one hotel we stayed at in Sheffield, a place called the Rutlands. We was listening at breakfast to the hotel staff saying, 'I thought we only had about eight or nine people in?' and she said, 'Well, we have.' 'But we've done thirty-odd breakfasts.' The Muppets used to follow us back to the hotels, get in the cupboards and sleep there.

Paul Weller: It was crazy back in the day, man. The soundcheck was like a matinee show. There'd be hundreds of kids who would come in to watch the soundcheck. We'd let them in, which is quite mad thinking about it now. Then we stayed behind. I'd stay for a couple of hours sometimes, just chatting and signing shit for people and whatever. Fortunately, no one had a phone in them days doing the selfie thing, so it was more just chatting with people. That was interesting to do that. I was young, but they were like twelve or thirteen or something.

Ann Weller: John used to let them all in. If you think about it, Paul and John were novices, weren't they? They didn't know what was going on. You were just making it up as you go along.

Kenny Wheeler: It started before I was with them. John and Paul went, 'Let 'em in, let 'em in.' It had started off with a few kids, but we was doing Newcastle City Hall, and the security guy there come running up and said, 'There's three hundred effin' kids in here. How are we going to get them out?' I said, 'Don't worry about it. We'll get them out.' I just said, 'Time to go now,' and they all file out through the doors. Sometimes it would get out of hand when they haven't got tickets and they'd go and hide, but the band liked doing it.

Bruce Foxton: It turned into us almost doing extra performances; fifty to a hundred people there watching the soundcheck. For that to happen, it was pretty unique I think. They couldn't do it now with security, etc. It was good times, and it was nice. After all, they paid their money and put us there. It's something that we felt we were almost repaying them by; this doesn't happen every day of the week, so enjoy it.

Ian Stone: The band and John looked after us. Being outside the Rainbow Theatre, all waiting in the cold about four o'clock in the afternoon. John Weller comes out and makes us a cup of tea. He lets us come in, and I'm fairly certain that it was the first time we heard 'Eton Rifles', in that soundcheck. About 150 of us standing there and then Bruce Foxton wanders out. 'Hello, lads.' It's surreal to think about it. That's a very real connection that you have and Paul was always very aware of that.

Chris Pope: We formed The Chords in January '78 and started playing the local pubs in Deptford doing covers of The Beatles, Who, Jam, Clash. We started writing our own stuff in late September. Paul turned up to one of the gigs and said that we were really good. It was our eighth or ninth gig and he offered us a support slot. It was ridiculous. It happened so quick. When you play a big gig like that as one of your first ever gigs, you shit yourself. I do remember that we went into The Jam's dressing room and John went to us, 'You can stay if you behave.' I think we got drunk.

Richard Houghton: It was May 1979 when The Jam came to play at Loughborough University in the brand-new student union building ... I will never forget when they finished with '"A" Bomb in Wardour Street' and the pyrotechnics went off. The lighting rig was shaking backwards and forwards. I thought it was going to collapse. I mentioned that to Rick years later and he said that was a common problem – they overdid the explosives.

David Lines: It's amazing that three men could produce so much raw power. Jesus Christ, that drumming! And that driving bass. Bruce was a really sensitive bass player. All three of them were naturally gifted musicians ... When you saw that band live, it was like some sort of vortex. It took you to a completely different level. It energised, transfixed and mesmerised you ... I'm sure that people leave bits of their soul in a gig.

Bruce Foxton: I'd say Ringo Starr seems to be underrated and perhaps Rick is as well. His style was different. On his own, maybe it wouldn't sound that great, but when you put him in the mix with me – bass and drums go together – it was fantastic.

Virginia Turbett: I met Gary Bushell, who had just started on *Sounds*. He asked me to take pictures with him as he covered emerging new bands from little towns and villages all over the country. One of the first big gigs I did was The Jam at Sheffield University in 1979. I was living in Dalston, which was really poor, all rented housing, sweatshops and everything. Polydor Records sent a limo to pick me up at about six o'clock in the morning. It drove us to meet The Jam coach somewhere and we went up to Sheffield. We were talking with Paul on the coach and there were these kids in parkas walking over the bridge. They were eating chips and Paul stopped the coach, went down to the door and waved them to come on the coach. These kids just chucked their hard-earned chips over the bridge and came on the coach with Weller.

17 August 1979 – 'When You're Young' (no. 17)

Adrian Thrills: By the time we get to 'When You're Young', Paul was incredibly confident as a songwriter. He was confident in that wall of sound of that production that Vic Smith had helped them create and those lyrics, 'Why the world is your oyster but your future's a clam' and 'think you're king but you're really a pawn'. It's quite a depressing song when you listen to the lyrics, but it's also fired with this romantic idealism. Paul is a really good social commentator and chronicler . . . But I think he's even better writing about a more romantic view of life. That song just encapsulated it, and like a lot of these songs, it ebbs and flows . . . He'd mastered the art of crafting brilliant three-minute pop songs by that point.

Vic Coppersmith-Heaven: We had moved to Richard Branson's Virgin Townhouse Studios by then, where we found a favourite recording space in Studio 1. Rick had his own glass drum room. The atmosphere of the studio complex was excellent. Queen were recording down the hall in Studio 4, Peter Gabriel was completing a new album in Studio 2. It was a very relaxed, homely atmosphere and designed as a real dynamic recording space. New solid state logic mixing consoles with computer tracking devices were also installed at this time, so it was a super creative space. Our studio was built with glass, wood and stone, together with some absorbent sections, all well thought out by the genius Japanese designer Sam Toyoshima. But it did require a truckload of corrugated iron at one point with lots of microphones around Paul's amplifier to achieve a few nasty but jagged guitar sounds.

Shane Juson: My first single was 'When You're Young'. I passed a record shop, saw the single sleeve in the window and thought, *Bloody hell, that's a good image*, with Paul Weller's turn-ups and paisley shirt. So I bought it on that. I had just turned thirteen and 1979 is when mods all kicked off again, so I did get myself a parka. I was wearing suits and polka-dot shirts to school, getting pulled up by the headmaster for having a Union Jack on the back of my parka.

Steve Barron: That music video . . . was in the little bandstand in Queen's Park. It was just a place of convenience for us all to descend on for a few hours. The Jam had that style, so you just found the best thing was to shoot it and let it be what it was. They were very cool. At that point, I don't think anything had gone top twenty yet. They weren't massive but they were the cool ones coming up. But nothing had exploded yet by any means.

Dennis Munday: 'When You're Young' was a standalone release and a real step up from all the other singles because they bought in that reggae riff and I thought, *Wow, this is it. People* *can't complain about this because it's hard or about the lyrics.* I really thought that this would be the big hit, but it only got to 17 in the charts. It sold around 150,000 copies. I was really mad with Polydor when it didn't happen. I wrote a letter to everybody, the board of directors, castigating them. When I came back from lunch my secretary said, 'You can't send this.' I said, 'OK,' but then went, 'Fuck it, send it, whatever happens, happens.' My boss came in steaming, throwing the memo on the table and said, 'When the shit goes down,' meaning punk, 'it'll go down with all the bands.' In the letter, I explained that if you look at the history of music, every decade you get two or three acts that go on to have a career of three or four decades. I went back to the thirties, Bing Crosby, Frank Sinatra, right to The Beatles, The Rolling Stones. They were still relevant then. I said that The Jam will be one of those bands.

Jim Cook: Dennis in those days was quite a spiky character so he made his views known around the place. He thought the promotion department didn't like the band or they weren't doing what they should have done for the band. He really wanted a change for the next record.

Steve Hinders: September 1979, I travelled to the UK. I wanted to see Woking . . . What did they see when they walked out of their homes? I nodded off in that boulevard and then an elderly woman, eighty years old, tapped me on the shoulder because I'm wearing my white and black pointed Jam shoes. She told me that she was Paul's nan, Mrs Milton, and she mentioned that her daughter Ann, Paul's mother, was across the street. She was going to make some sandwiches. Would I like to come in? It was such a shock.

So, I'm invited in and Nicky Weller, Ann Weller, Steve Carver, great friends of the family – all come over. Neighbours come over. We're sitting out in the back garden and Nicky asked,

'Why would you come all the way here to see my brother?' And I said, 'Well, because it's Paul Weller and I just wanted to get a flavour for the neighbourhood.' . . . John Weller came home about six o'clock. We then started drinking Scotch, sat around listening to music. John said, 'Hey I'm going to play something for you out in the car.' He puts in a cassette of Paul, and it had to be when he was about fourteen. Paul was on guitar, singing these really melodic Gerry and the Pacemaker-style tunes, little Beatley, really pretty and melancholy at the same time.

We had a bite to eat and then I said that I was going to go back up to London because I had a little hotel there. They said, 'No, no, we can't do that. Stay here.' John gets on the phone to Paul and tells him that I'm there, and Paul invites me up to Townhouse studios for the recording of *Setting Sons*.

26 October 1979 – 'The Eton Rifles' (no. 3)

Vic Coppersmith-Heaven: The tailor would turn up out of the blue and measure the guys for their suits for their next live shows in the middle of a recording. It all added to the atmosphere – I loved it. Through this studio chaos, really creative song developments were evolving from Paul, both musically and lyrically, like 'Eton Rifles', which after completing the recording was actually mixed in only five minutes. We then moved to Studio 2 to overdub some Jam fans singing the chorus of 'Eton Rifles' in the Toyoshima stone room where Phil Collins captured his dynamic drum sound. It was built out of rugged stone, so not to produce any standing waves of sound. That original mix had all the atmosphere of the recording but technically missed many important sounds of the track, such as bass, organ, guitar licks and vocals. I had many attempts at remixing the song as I felt it failed to capture the excitement of the track.

I ended up returning to RAK Studios to manually synchronise the twenty-four-track master with the rough stereo quarter-inch analogue mix from the Townhouse. I then manually copied and inserted snippets of sound, which produced about fifty edits in the whole track. That was a real surprise for the playback engineer in the vinyl cutting room. He was cutting the master of the single, watching edit after edit of white sticky tape passing the playback heads.

Jim Cook: By the time that we got to 'Eton Rifles', we had Tony Branwell running the product and promotion department. Tony was Brian Epstein's man with The Beatles. A real character. He had really good contacts, but by then there was a big thing in the company. Dennis was very anti the fact that they hadn't got as much airplay as he thought they should have done, and he pushed for Clive Banks to get involved. That caused a bit of friction because we gave The Jam to Clive on a nice deal and, of course, the promotion department weren't very happy about that. Clive got major airplay on 'Eton Rifles'. But I think anyone probably could have got airplay on 'Eton Rifles' because it was a great record, and the band was really bubbling under at that point in time. A lot of Radio 1 people must have seen that they would be a big band.

Dennis Munday: What really pissed me off was that the company went off the boil because they saw *All Mod Cons* as the apex. Listen to the bloody songwriting, it's not the apex. This is the beginning. It's the transition from the young man writing 'In the City' to suddenly being a serious songwriter. There was the line in 'Eton Rifles', 'Then went to bed with a charming young thing', and the one thing about promo guys is they're always looking for a way out, reasons why you don't get the record played, and I thought, *Well, I know what the Polydor lot are going to say. They're going to come back to me and say, the BBC won't play it.* I met with the band, told them what was happening, and John said, 'Something's got to happen about Tony.' They wanted to change.

Noel Gallagher: I remember seeing them on the TV, doing 'Eton Rifles'. I was at that age where you're getting into music. There was nothing else for me. Thank the fucking Lord, there was nothing else: music, and music programmes, and the radio, and seven inches was everything. Punk was blended into new wave and I just thought, *Fucking hell!* Even then, at that age, you knew what a good song was, and what was good and what was not. It's difficult to explain to people now how big The Jam were. They were huge. They were the most important band in the country . . . And to me, they've gone on now to be as important as The Beatles.

Peter Watts: I'm a bit of a socialist, and that song captures something that I feel about privilege exceptionally well in a way that I don't think any other song has ever come close to doing since. Paul was so young yet incredibly wise. Despite his success, he sometimes downplays his intelligence. He's got that working-class attitude of being a little bit embarrassed about being bright. Sometimes when you interview him, you can see he's almost dumbing down a little bit. You don't normally think about someone like Paul Weller as being vulnerable, but I think there is a little bit of vulnerability there. He doesn't want to be seen as a nerd. But the mind that can write those lyrics is so bright. I wish he'd be more proud of that.

Simon Napier-Bell: The Jam's music was incredibly well produced, and every time I heard it, I thought, *God, it's so perfectly balanced* . . . I like the fact that Paul genuinely seemed to come from a working-class background where very few other groups had done . . . even the previously angry groups like The Rolling Stones and The Who, none of them really came from a working-class background. They were all pretty well educated and middle class and put on a bit of a down-market accent, you know, and Paul wasn't. That made me more interested in his lyrics than say, The Clash. Because if you came from Paul's background, as he developed, as he got hits and as he became established, he was learning that you can't make money in the music business without moving into a middle-class life. It's one of the things which happens to all working-class people when they make money . . . And Paul must have gone through that same thing.

Trevor Neal: He was reaching a huge audience, which was so brave with those lyrics. So many lines in those songs set an agenda. That put me on a political track that I've never left, really. It still makes me angry and there's a relevance to it.

Dennis Munday: 'Eton Rifles' was the first record that John Peel didn't get the first play on. We got two acetates – one for Peely and one for Mike Read, who did the Radio 1 breakfast show. He was always a fan anyway. He gave it a big blast and it made a big difference. Radio 1 had a tremendous amount of power. Well, it could blow a single . . . literally.

Clive Banks was very positive, and he delivered. He also understood dealing with Paul. He didn't get uptight if Paul said, 'I don't want to do this,' he just moved on.

Nigel 'Spanner' Sweeney: Clive was very well respected, so I felt in great company. Paul Weller never gave me his phone number because he didn't want me ringing up every five minutes, but I would get a message to him through John or through Dennis or whatever. You have a relationship with these people, but it's not a 'go out at dinner with them every night', but they like to know you're there. Dennis was the contact during The Jam and probably too much if I was honest about it. Probably too much. If you look back on those situations. They needed a different opinion every so often to challenge, because at that point The Jam were almighty.

Pete Paphides: 'The Eton Rifles' captured a way of looking at the world and it had this chippiness, which was really important, to feel that someone could occupy their space from your social class in such an assured way. Lyrically, 'Sup up your beer and collect your fags, there's a row going on down near Slough' is probably the greatest opening line gambit of all time.

November 1979 – Secret gigs

Debsey Wykes: I went to the Marquee when The Jam were doing a secret gig as 'John's Boys' . . . I hadn't realised that they were so good. We were close-up and it was really powerful.

Eddie Piller: I saw The Jam 52 times, I saw John's Boys once . . . The thing about 1979, 1980, was if you were a mod, you could go and see a different mod band twenty times a week. We trawled *Sounds* and the *NME*, the small ads, looking for where our bands were going to play. I was fifteen years old and when you saw John's Boys were playing the Nashville and you thought, *What? John's Boys?* Gary Crowley was a mate quite early doors and he was a good friend of Paul. So, if we wanted to confirm anything, we'd get hold of Crowley.

Andy Rosen: I got asked to take some pictures of The Jam at the Rainbow and from there, I became their go-to photographer for a lot of live stuff. It was just mobbed. When you're a photographer, you have to be at the front. You were in the orchestra pit when shit got out of hand, things flying, ripping out the seats, and you get hit with all kinds of stuff and people gobbing. That was the worst part of it . . .

Some of the bands had real thugs as security and roadies but having John around kept this band quite special. There were crazy times, and Paul would get into it and have drinks and I always remember that he would go missing after the gig. There was always this frantic thing with everyone running around, 'Where's Paul?' and someone would say, 'Oh, I saw him go out the back door.' 'Oh, fuck, we'd better go find him.' He's going to get into trouble, drink too much or get in a fight, or skinheads are going to corner him, and there was this mass panic. That was the difference between The Jam and a lot of other bands. I don't remember The Clash having any father figures around.

Rhoda Dakar: Our friend Gill was following a band called The Jam. She was mates with Siouxsie Sioux, Steve Severin and Tracie O'Keefe, so was our lead into punk. She had a friend called Pauline who was the only girl who was allowed to see The Jam with Gill. We were all banned from going, so I never saw The Jam because it was just too much aggro. Eventually, I went to see them as John's Boys at the Marquee. It was so funny to see her face. 'Oh my God. What are you doing here?' It was literally like that. I just thought, hang on a minute, I was banned for years and technically this isn't The Jam, so I am allowed to come. Her rules were strict . . . Why weren't we allowed? Well, I mean, use your imagination. I wasn't allowed to come just in case . . . So there was no competition.

16 November 1979 – *Setting Sons* (no. 4)

Paul Weller: In my mind, around that time, a lot of those songs were little *Play for Today*-type things. I could see 'em as like a little programme or something. Little films. I don't know [where it came from]. Definitely not from school. There wasn't the English teacher who inspired me. Mr Fucking . . . whatever his name was. None of that. I don't know, I suppose people like Ray Davies, John and Paul obviously. Ray's songs were very . . . like little mini plays in a way, weren't they? A lot of them, anyway. Maybe people like that. I honestly don't know. And I don't care either, because I know this is something I can do, and I'm happy with that.

Peter Wilson: They would come into the studio to demo songs or rehearse, and Paul would often come in on his own to work on new tracks. He'd knock them down, demo them to see how they sounded, and would share with the rest of the band to hear them. I was on quite a few of those sessions from *Setting Sons* onwards.

Vic Coppersmith-Heaven: We worked hard on the *Setting Sons* album and to meet these important record company deadlines for an album release, again to tie in with tour dates. There was no gap allowed between completing all the tracks for the album and going straight into the final mix. We mixed for about ten days, put the tracks into the final running order and, once the band and I signed off after many playbacks, the final part was to cut the vinyl master disc. Only problem was, that it was now 7 in the morning and my vinyl-cutting session was in two hours' time at 9 a.m. I crashed out on the sofa in Studio 1 and was gracefully awoken by the cleaners with their hoover at 9.15 a.m. I attended the cutting session, which took all of the day, then headed home for a proper sleep.

Polydor confirmed to me the next day that the factory had received the master discs and a test pressing would soon be available for review and sign-off for manufacture. I was now fully rested, and my ears had woken up after the long process of recording and mixing. I put the test pressing on the player at home and from the first track I was shocked: it all sounded compressed, tinny and generally over equalised; it sounded terrible. The record company called me for approval and without question I rejected the pressing, disagreements followed, because of timing, but Polydor could not move forward without my technical approval, so we agreed that I recut the album and we then proceeded to album release.

Three months later, Polydor unbelievably sent me an invoice for the full price of the *Setting Sons* recut and furthermore deducted the total sum from monies they owed me . . . it was outrageous when all I was doing was to protect the artist and the company from the release of an inferior product. Sometimes with companies, it's just all about the money and not much respect for artist integrity.

Dennis Munday: One thing that I really liked about the way Paul drove The Jam was that every album was different. You can see the step up to *All Mod Cons* from *In the City* and *The Modern World* and then another really big step to the album *Setting Sons*. That has got a lot of great songs on it.

Jim Cook: The *Setting Sons* album just went berserk, which is what happens with bands when they break. I remember Dennis meeting me on the stairs saying, 'We're going to press another 100,000.' We'd never got an album past 60,000 with them before and suddenly we were selling 160,000 upwards, and then of course the overseas thing became a big thing because that wasn't doing very well. Only a few countries embraced The Jam in a big way, which caused us problems. Polygram is a Dutch and German company – the goal wasn't for the UK to make the money but to produce acts that they could sell around the world.

John Wilson: The complexity of *Setting Sons* was totally different to anything else. I've discussed this with Paul, and lyrically it's so dense with these vivid character studies. He started off with this idea of a concept album and the loose idea of a journey of letting go of your past, framed within this notional civil war, and three mates who were thrown together and then went their separate ways. I think at the heart there was the sense of Paul being very different to a lot of his mates and making a leap from where he came to where he was heading to, and he knew he was having to change all the time and let go of the past. I think you hear that. 'Thick as Thieves' in particular – the density, complexity and the poetry of that lyric is still astonishing to me.

Shaun Hand: If you look at the songs that are part of the concept, you've got one of my favourite ever Jam songs – 'Wasteland', as well as 'Burning Sky', 'Little Boy Soldiers', 'Thick as Thieves' and 'Eton Rifles'. Imagine if they hadn't rushed to meet the deadline and had created a whole album of that standard of lyricism quality, playing and arrangements. That would blow *All Mod Cons* out of the water. The industry was still in that mode where they wanted an album every Christmas, three or four singles, and you've gotta tour, so they were under pressure. But then even when you're rushing to finish an album, you come up with 'Private Hell'. Incredible.

Bruce Foxton: As a songwriter, I have my moments. Every now and again I come up with something that is good and worthwhile as far as I am concerned. I was very proud of 'Smithers-Jones'. It's a song about my dad. Loyal to the company that he was working for twenty or thirty years, and then when circumstances change, they just disregard you, throw you away and there's no taking into account your loyalty to the business. It was happening a lot, and it still happens now, that people just get used, basically. It was the B-side for 'When You're Young' and then I think it was probably Vic Smith's idea to add the orchestration to make it worthwhile putting it on the album. He worked out the score for it and it just sounded lovely. I've got an old jukebox these days and when my granddaughter comes over, she puts it on every time.

Vic Coppersmith-Heaven: We recorded 'Smithers-Jones' a few times with the band, but we could not make it fit into the album project, so, inspired by what George Martin created for 'Eleanor Rigby', I hired a string quartet and a music arranger, and gave the arranger the brief to listen carefully to the band's bass, drums and guitar parts and rescore the rhythm, notes and dynamics of each instrument as much as possible, into the final music score for the string quartet. This brief made the string backing still representative of the feel of the instrumentation. It was a good moment when this just worked, and the new version of the song made its way back onto the album.

Mick Talbot: The band I was in, The Merton Parkas, used to play at the Two Brewers in Clapham . . . There was a rumour that Bruce came down the Two Brewers and crept in the back. A few months later, we played a gig upstairs at Ronnie Scott's, and Rick was in the crowd. Someone talked him into getting up with us for an encore of 'In the Midnight Hour'. Our drummer had to play a tambourine because, by that time, Rick was rock and roll royalty.

I don't think I was in the same room with Paul until late '79, but he'd met my brother, who was also in the band, a few times . . . Paul said, 'Yeah, I've heard of you.' Apparently, he'd got a copy of our single. He didn't like it, but he bothered to listen to the B-side. There's a piano solo on it, and he just thought there was something in my playing. That's how I got booked to play on the track 'Heat Wave', which was the closing track on the *Setting Sons* album.

I think '79 was a key year for them. They'd been working really hard for two years. And something really clicked with the *Setting Sons* album. They gained mainstream acceptance. They could now get on Radio 1 during the day, not just on John Peel. They'd definitely arrived, but they weren't full of it. They were all quite down to earth.

Bill Smith: I've done hundreds of sleeves, and I think collaboration is so important. From *Setting Sons* onwards, Paul started to share his ideas and then I'd come up with something and it would be, 'Yeah, that's not bad, but I like this.' So, it became, *Well look, I'm Paul Weller and this is my band, and this is the way I want us to go*, which is fair enough, that's cool, so with *Setting Sons*, he gave me the back cover and said, 'I've been working with these other designers and illustrators and this is what they come up with. It's a sort of a concept album, about Britain and the war and this band of brothers.' He couldn't think of anything to go with the front cover.

Andrew Douglas and I talked about something from the war, maybe a statue, and in the end, Andrew found this lovely little statuette through the Imperial War Museum, which was only about twelve or thirteen inches high. Combining Paul's vision, listening to some of the music, and input from others, and then it's my job, as the designer, to put it together in a way that will make a passerby go into a record store, pick up the album and, if they didn't know The Jam, we'd draw them into their world.

Andy Rosen: The dog in that photo on the back is actually a boxer, not a British bulldog, but no one notices because it's so iconic. Robin Richards, the art director at Fifth Column, he's left a trail of great early punk designs that still stand up today. The plan was to use a British bulldog. We booked one that was getting paid a lot more than me. Paul used to say, 'Just charge them double. Fuck the record company, I don't care.' We booked the job, but the guy never turned up. We didn't have cell phones back then; I couldn't track him down. I could only find one other dog, so I thought, *Fuck it, I'll take the boxer.*

We headed to Brighton beach, set everything up, and stapled a silk-screened design to the deckchair, and then brought the dog out. The moment he was loose, he was gone. Out of the beach, gone. We spent about an hour chasing him. When we finally got him back, we had to tie him down to get the photo – he was definitely not a photo dog.

Claire Mahoney: I became obsessed, bought everything, and covered my walls with posters. My bedroom walls were Artex, and you could see little indentations on Paul's mouth where I kissed him goodnight. I hoped nobody noticed, but they were there!

Den Davis: If I got front row tickets, I'd spend one night in front of Paul, one night in front of Bruce. It wasn't the Paul Weller show – it was a band. Nobody said, 'I'm going to see Paul Weller,' but over time you could see how the press started focusing more on Paul as the face of the band, almost like they knew it was going to shift that way.

John Wilson: I made a programme for Radio 4 about English pop lyricists, drawing a line from Ray Davies through Paul, Damon Albarn and Alex Turner . . . I spoke to Simon Armitage, who's now been Poet Laureate. I quoted 'Thick as Thieves' and said, 'I still think about "We stole the burning sun in the open sky, the twinkling . . ."' and he carried that line on, 'Twinkling stars in the black night. We stole the green belt fields that made us believe, we stole everything that we can see. But something came along and changes our minds. I don't know what and I don't know why . . .' We both went, 'Oh, my God! Wow!' He just had a way with words. and it's really astonishing.

Claire Mahoney: 'Wasteland' takes me back to the railway embankment with rope on the trees to make swings. It's personal for a lot of people and how many artists can do that? That's the mark of a truly great songwriter. They can take you on a journey. That's why it's so special for everybody and it never leaves you.

John Wilson: At school, we were asked to bring in a poem for English class, and I brought in 'Wasteland'. The teacher said it didn't count, that I was cheating. 'That's not a poem.' I think a lot of his songs were written as poems. I suspect that one was because there is a bit more of a free-form structure to it. Just beautiful imagery. That's the weird thing about a lot of those lyrics. They lodge their way in, and I sometimes see them rather than remember them as lines. These days every song has to be visualised, but with most of those songs you could create your own films in your head with scenes and images based on the lyrics.

Billy Bragg: I wouldn't say *Setting Sons* directly influenced me to join the army, but it certainly put me in that mindset. As Thatcher came into power in '79, the Cold War was getting stoked up, and it seemed that the ideals of sixties and seventies – ideas like the common good and collective responsibility – were being rejected. The clouds were darkening. My little band had split up and I'd run out of things to do.

1979–80 – *Setting Sons* tour

Tim Parsons: Mel Bush had promoted The Jam's first big headline show at Hammersmith Odeon, but for some reason, John and Mel hadn't made a relationship or a connection and as a result, they were looking for a new promoter. Martin Hopewell came to us at MCP and asked if we wanted to promote The Jam, and of course we bit his hand off. Our job was very simple: put the tickets on sale, market the show, manage the show and hopefully make money and move on to the next one.

We were promoting The Jam during the time they transitioned from playing small venues to city hall theatres. Those were wonderful days, incredible days. It was also lovely working with record company executives who genuinely loved the band. Dennis had a huge love of music, and I wouldn't say The Jam was necessarily within the genre he really liked, I think he's more of a jazz guy, but he had a really nice way about him, which probably endeared himself to John, who was this ducker and diver.

Dennis Munday: From the *Setting Sons* tour, I started to get my own tour jackets that John used to give me. I would give away most of my gear to fans.

David Lines: Those Jam gigs were like being in a war zone . . . The weirdest Jam gig I ever saw was on the Setting Sons tour. They gave away album sleeves on the way in and I don't know why, but the support act was this skinhead poet called Seething Wells . . . It was just a rant. You had this sea of Jam fans, baying for Paul, Bruce and Rick to come on. I can see it now. There's only one thing three thousand people waiting for The Jam want to do with 3,000 empty album sleeves of *Setting Sons* and that's set fire to them and hurl them like flaming frisbees onto the stage to burn Seething Wells down and get The Jam on. It's a miracle that we didn't burn down Bridlington Spa Pavilion.

Den Davies: When it got to November '79 and the *Setting Sons* tour, I persuaded my brother to take me. The crowd was intense – squashed, ribs crushing, lungs giving way and you're sweating – but it's such an experience that you've got to do it over and over again. That's what set me on the journey of being in the front row.

Keiko Egawa: I asked my parents if I could study English in England, because in Japan they teach American English more than British English. I wanted to learn British English so that I could understand what The Jam were singing about. Woolworths and bingo accents.

December 1979, I saw The Jam at the Rainbow Theatre. I felt something from the band straight to my soul, and I was hooked. It was so special. I couldn't stand the thought of going back to Japan and waiting for a year to be able to see them again. That was seven, eight months before they did their first Japan tour, so I extended my visa. Then in 1980, they announced the Japan tour, I told my parents, 'I'm coming back to see you.'

Andy Miller: I was sixteen and still at school. Our form tutor, Mr Jones, was a massive music fan, seeing Sex Pistols, Stranglers, Ruts at Brunel University. He had to arrange the school trips and asked where we wanted to go. One of my mates said, 'See The Jam at the Rainbow, sir!' He got a cheer from a few of us and it was agreed that our school trip would be to see The Jam on the *Setting Sons* tour. We got fifty tickets, all dressed in our finest attire trying to look cool. John Weller introduced 'The best band in the fucking world' and they launched into 'Girl on the Phone'. It was like a religious experience.

Roger Pilling: I moved to Hull in 1979 . . . I hadn't seen Paul during that period because I'd gone AWOL . . . They were playing at Bridlington Spa on the North Yorkshire coast, so I went. After a couple of numbers, Paul spotted me in the audience and said something like, 'This is for my mate Roger Pilling' and played 'Thick as Thieves' . . . The first person I saw backstage was Pete Carver. I hadn't seen him since school and he was one of the road crew, and everything just clicked back into place seamlessly. Had a really good chat with Paul, went back to his hotel. We all got pissed, because in those days, it was a big drinking culture. All the band were there. Paul always kept the same road crew, with people like Kenny Wheeler with him for years . . . We were great pals and we always have been. I was very privileged to go to the shows, backstage, and to see it all unfolding. All the drunken nights in the hotels.

Virginia Turbett: Everyone sang every word to every song at a Jam gig. I loved it down the front. I even loved to take pictures down the front. I would go in the pit or the front if there wasn't one, with all my cameras, getting gobbed on. You've got to be down the front, otherwise you might as well be at home. I don't miss the gobbing.

Neil Sheasby: Youth culture was happening everywhere. We were all clambering to get dodgy VHS copies of *Quadrophenia* because we're too young to get into the cinema. The mod revival thing exploded and it was insanely exciting – even in a small town like mine. That's how big The Jam were. Their influence really touched all the provinces.

Kenny Wheeler: It was great to see how The Jam progressed and got stronger. Audiences were fired up by the three of them, it was full-on energy. When we were in the States, early in 1980, we had kids from England coming out, travelling all over to follow the band.

I remember one kid, Bradley, who used to turn up everywhere. He got his money together and went out on tour in the States and followed us everywhere. We still see some of the old faces now and again. A few years ago, Paul bumped into a cab driver that we used to throw out of gigs.

Dennis Munday: The biggest problem with America was that Paul never wanted to commit to a long tour, which is essential. To really make it, you need to spend nine months to a year there. Paul would play half-a-dozen dates each coast but what about the middle?

Martin Hopewell: It's fair to say that throughout The Jam's career there was always this lingering thing from critics that it was too English. That didn't stop the band from doing really well in a lot of places that weren't English, but I think that was probably the problem with America. I'm not one to comment on who Paul Weller is, although I have my own view of it, but American society is not Paul Weller. That's not what he's about. It was never about 'We've got to break America to get bigger.' Paul wasn't bothered about that.

Paul Weller: In America, at that time, you were expected to compromise so much to make it there. Talking to these twatty DJs when they used to take us around these radio stations. Some were great, but there was a lot of knob-ends, who didn't really get it at all. I just thought, *I'm not doing this,* and we were very rude at times and that didn't go down well with the record company. That probably didn't help us either. I never wanted to play the game. There was a lot of pressure within the band, especially from my dad, for us to compromise and, whatever anyone else says, it was only me that stopped it from happening. It's just like, *no, we're not doing that. We're not going down that road.* I remember me old man saying, 'you should get some interviews with some of the dailies, you could be as big as The Police', and it's like, *I don't want to be as big as The Police.* It doesn't interest me one bit. I wanted to be left alone to do my own thing or our own thing and be in control of it.

Jim Cook: A lot of people wanted Paul to have a manager rather than John. There was this feeling that John could not do what was needed, which was a bit mean, really. The idea of The Jam with some fancy American manager who was going to get them sorted out with a big deal in America was just ridiculous. It wouldn't have happened. Paul put his foot down right at the beginning – his dad was his manager, end of story.

Dennis Munday: John was very important. He gets a lot of stick, which is unwarranted, particularly from the record company. There was a time when they actually wanted to replace him. They tried to get what they saw as a typical record business manager. I remember one guy said, 'I could really do a job on them, get them into America.' I said, 'You can't. You're a great guy and a great manager, but within five minutes either Paul or Bruce would give you a smack in the mouth.'

Barry Cain: The Jam were too English for America. They're always compared with the Who, but they were an international, big, heavy metal kind of band. The Jam weren't. They don't go on and do long guitar solos. They weren't punk. They wore suits. The Americans couldn't categorise them, they really couldn't understand where this was coming from . . . They weren't going to crack that market.

Rick Buckler: It moved on at pace. We came out of the clubs to the smaller venues, then going on tour, being signed, moving up to bigger venues, being paid a little bit more money. We could afford better hotels, better transport. Then you start doing other things, other territories. You're going to Europe and Japan and the odd foray into America. So it just kept moving. The scenery changed, but we were still doing the same thing. We were still planning ahead with what we enjoyed doing.

10 March 1980 – 'Going Underground' / 'Dreams of Children' (double A-side, no. 1)

Vic Coppersmith-Heaven: 'Going Underground' was an exciting track to build on. Paul Bruce and Rick were totally in rhythmic command now and producing some exciting sounds and rhythms together. When completed and on playback it certainly sounded like the next single, but to mix it was an effort. I could not get the vocal to sit comfortably with the track. So maybe now is a good time for me to apologise to Paul for repeatedly luring him back in the studio from the canteen to re-vocal sections of the track. I think he really got pissed off with me at one point and could not see what I was looking for to complete the track, but as we worked further together, Paul's vocal just hit the right tone and energy, which matched the energy of the track, and the result then became a dream to mix.

Jim Cook: It became a big thing for record companies to have a strike force, besides the usual sales teams handling the catalogue and new releases. But people suddenly realised that only about 100 shops really mattered because they were the chart return shops. You had to find and know the chart return shops and get people in there every week pushing your records. A guy called John Pearson ran our strike force and they really tucked it up. That was why we got the number ones. It was funny because Slade had been number one three times five years earlier on Polydor, so there was a pressure to replicate that. Then 'Going Underground' went straight to number one in its first week.

Dennis Munday: The sales guys did a fantastic marketing job. That hadn't been done before because we used to release a single on a Friday, but the factory would start work, pick, packing, posting on the Monday before to get to the shops by the weekend. On this one our sales guys decided that they would go in on Saturday, Sunday, pick, pack and start posting directly. They had the shops flooded and our sales team also carried a bigger quantity than they usually would. I couldn't remember anyone doing it before that. All the record companies would have what they called their singles strike forces. Their job was only working on singles. As far as I know, certainly at Polydor, we'd never done it before – obviously it's expensive because if you're going in Saturday and Sunday, you're paying everyone time and a half and double time for Sunday. I don't know what the big wigs said because that wasn't my decision, but that's really what did it. It was a unified effort. The song itself was great. I think it would have gone to number one regardless but whether it would have gone in at the top with the old sales service, I don't know. They did a fantastic job.

Bruce Foxton: I'm fortunate enough to have a lot of memorable moments. That was a proud moment. The amount of records you had to sell in those days was unbelievable. We were doing something like 60,000 singles a day and now I'm saying it to you, I can't visualise that amount of people going into all their record stores and buying 'Going Underground'.

Nigel 'Spanner' Sweeney: That was the first record I promoted, and it was just phenomenal. I remember doing Radio Luxembourg with them for the interview, premiering it, and then all of a sudden it goes straight in at number one. That's probably what addicted me to it. This was a buzz.

Dennis Munday: That was a tremendous feeling. There was a lot of hard work from everyone. From when I started, I honestly thought that some of the singles before could have done better, but they weren't in the same class as 'Going Underground'. When I heard it had gone straight in at number one, I leaped up, punched the air and hit my head on the door bar. I really did head it hard.

Jim Cook: If you had a 200,000-plus-selling single then you made money . . . The strike forces became crazy after a couple of years. Labels started giving away promotional items to the dealers to make sure they put them in the book . . . Promotion items had to be related to the artist, so, you could put another single in, which we did with 'Going Underground' with the special second single in the pack. We did about 20,000. What you weren't supposed to do was give away bottles of whisky with a sticker on it saying, 'The Jam, In the City'. That's what a lot of companies started doing. Unrelated items like bottles of whisky with Rod Stewart on the front . . . All the way through The Jam's life, it was about getting the records into the chart return shops and getting the chart return shops to sell them, and if they didn't sell them then maybe put a few ticks down for us anyway.

Suggs: The charts was something else in them days, but I couldn't quite understand how The Jam always went straight to number one. They had some sort of trick, how they built it up and they released just at the last minute and get to number one even if it didn't stay there for very long . . . I liked 'em from the beginning and bought their records. There was no jealousy, just a healthy competition. There was correlation with 2-Tone, us,

The Specials and Selecter, the rude boy thing with the mod thing, cos we come out of punk where everyone wanted to tear their clothes up and spit at each other, and that isn't what working-class people from my generation wanted to do. I remember crossing the road and a geezer shouted out the cab, 'Just like Paul Weller, cool, clean and hard.'

Nicky Weller: They were on tour in America and went to number one, Dad was like, 'Fuck this, let's just get Concorde home.' They flew back to do *Top of the Pops*.

Paul Weller: If we did go back on Concorde, I don't remember it, because we were in Los Angeles. I'm pretty sure the Concorde didn't fly there. But yeah, we went home the next day.

Bruce Foxton: I've still got the luggage tag on my suitcase.

Jim Cook: That was the week I got married. We watched them at number one on *Top of the Pops* as part of my wedding reception. It was great. After that first time, it was like, 'Oh, now we've got to do it again.'

Lenny Henry: I saw them on the telly when 'Going Underground' was number one and if there was something that was going to get your attention, it was that. Such a brash, funky, but propulsive song, where you went, this is actually a great record, it means something and it's powerful but it's also got that R&B thing, which I like. Paul was this young, charismatic and quite cross-looking guy saying things that were important about our society and about race and about class, and writing things in a very cinematic way that meant something to people.

David Lines: When you bought into The Jam, it wasn't just about Paul, Bruce and Rick – it was the whole look. I remember seeing a bloke at a gig who had Jam bowling shoes but mismatched them: a blue shoe with a white stripe on one foot and a red one from another pair with a white stripe on the other. I was so impressed – he'd taken that look and made it his own.

Adrian Thrills: It was their moment. They were the biggest band in Britain, not just in the *NME*, their singles were going straight to number one. It was their imperial phase, producing incredible records with Vic Coppersmith-Heaven and they'd found a real sound. They were on a roll. Even the non-album singles like 'Strange Town', 'When You're Young', 'Going Underground' . . . It was a bit like The Clash – these bands were just chucking out this stuff. Nowadays, any one of those tracks would be the lead track on an album but in those days, they were just stopgap non-album singles.

Tim Parsons: Vic always used to hang around. He was this very, very quiet individual who had a huge amount to do with The Jam sound and the interpretation of what Paul had in mind.

Pat Gilbert: The Jam's sound had a lot of attack – both in the guitars and the vocal delivery – while their records showed real craft. Vic Coppersmith-Heaven was very clever at channelling all that live energy into a polished record. You hear it on 'Going Underground'. The compression on those guitars is just amazing.

Tracie Young: A lot of my friends were mods and into The Jam. I remember being at school and the chart was Tuesday lunchtime so that was a big day for us all hanging out in B-16 with our packed lunches. There was a huge buzz – not just at school but on the news too – about The Jam, possibly going straight in at number one, which was so rare back then. When the announcement came, everybody exploded. I liked the song and was so happy, but that was nothing compared to the atmosphere around me. It was like New Year's Eve, things being thrown in the air, cheering. It was crazy.

Paul Dowling: I loved the video, and that intro was tight as fuck. The opening lyric just grabs you by the balls straight away. I think it's the best fuck-you song ever written, even to this day. That can come on the radio now and I turn the volume up to 100, I start driving fast and just think, *Fuck yeah. How good is this song?* Lyrical genius.

Steve Barron: We hadn't done many music videos beyond The Jam – just a few, like Secret Affair. This was our first number one, and being a double A-side with 'Dreams of Children' made it tricky with two videos to shoot. Still, I was excited to work in a studio for the first time, moving towards a more filmic approach. We couldn't afford a full set but managed a white cyclorama, which was close. Paul had clear ideas, like the shots of prime ministers and the hand mushing them away. I definitely wasn't a political beast at that time, but Paul was. While we likely discussed those concepts, they were entirely his vision.

Dennis Munday: They used to sell 250,000 in the first two or three weeks, which meant that whatever chart position they went to, it wouldn't last long because they would probably sell 60 per cent of their sales in those two weeks whereas other bands would take five, six, seven weeks and once they got to number one would stay longer. But with The Jam . . . the fans just went out and bought them en masse.

Nigel 'Spanner' Sweeney: It would often fall flat the next week because 200,000 Jam kids had gone out and bought it. I had a good reputation as a young plugger . . . In the case of The Jam, you needed to get on the radio, get the video on the TV and you get it to number one and then hopefully you hold it there.

But unfortunately, The Jam used to drop like a rock the following week – 29, 39 the next week. It was just the way it was.

Steve Barron: That video started appearing on many shows, though the BBC banned parts of it, even re-editing Thatcher's face. They didn't like any politics.

Nigel 'Spanner' Sweeney: I got a call from the lovely Kenny Wheeler, who used to frighten me. He said, 'Spanner, Paul wants to do *Tiswas*.' This is Sally James, Chris Tarrant, Spit the Dog, Bob Carolgees. Of course, Paul turned up very well dressed so I warned Kenny, 'They're going to get absolutely hammered with the gunge.' He'd gone out and bought three decorators' outfits.

It was live TV so The Jam fans knew exactly where we were. We go for a drink afterwards in the bar on the twelfth floor with Sally and Chris because it's a major thing. The Jam were huge. The most exciting band for that era. But then we suddenly realised that all the mods had surrounded the building with their scooters, creating a circle of Lambrettas. Shit. Suddenly there's a problem. Kenny and John were going, 'This is serious.' We got taken to ATV Studios holding bay, put into three taxis and driven out. When 3,000 kids are rocking your taxi, trying to get hold of somebody, they'll get them. I've never been so frightened in my life.

Russell Hastings: Back then, we always wondered, where did they go when they left the stage? That was it, until you saw them on telly again, like on *Tiswas* months later. You didn't know where they went. I spent many a time asking Rick and Bruce, where did you go after so and so? I found out. It wasn't so much of a mystery. 'We went home.'

April–June 1980 – UK and Europe tour

Simon Napier-Bell: I had set up Nomis Studios in 1977 . . . Every group that was anybody rehearsed there. You'd go in the canteen any day of the week and it would be Tina Turner and Mick Jagger queuing up to get a bacon sandwich along with a group of eighteen-year-olds who had come down from Wigan for the day . . . In among that we had about ten offices to let and John Weller rented one of those offices. He was a very, very pleasant, affable man . . . he came to see us because we could make tea, and he couldn't. People often talk about him, 'He's a bit of a rough diamond.' I just found him delightful and funny and amusing. I don't think I ever heard a cross word from him. He was a wonderful man.

Paul used to leave his scooter there in the storage facilities. I think amps were thrown out on the road and the scooter was carefully kept in there, pristine condition . . . Paul would wander in, sometimes in a terrible mood and sometimes in a good mood . . . Paul in a bad mood was pretty bad, and Paul in a good mood was delightful. It's like anyone else but just more extreme. But the artists are always more extreme so that's totally understandable.

Mick Talbot: I never went on tour with The Jam, but I did do a couple of live things. There was the Rainbow in 1980, where they got a Hammond organ. That was really enjoyable. I had to go to rehearsals for that at Nomis. Bruce and Rick went to lunch, but Paul didn't. We were jamming soul tunes with one of his road crew, Dave Liddle – Booker T and Stax numbers – there was a real connection with just the three of us. I was playing the Hammond, Paul was alternating between guitar and drums, and Dave was playing a bass, and they were swapping instruments. I think that's probably when we gelled a bit more, but then I didn't see him for quite a while. It was a couple of years before I got contacted by Paul about a new project, but that had been a turning point in our musical connection.

Eddie Piller: I've known Paul properly since 1980, when I got the chance to interview him for a fanzine. Ray Margetson from *Patriotic* and I were both trying to interview Paul. He said, 'You might as well come and do it together.' I think, by then, he was dismissive of the mod revival, but he was never dismissive of the kids that had embraced the way of life that he created. In '78 and '79, he hadn't been dismissive at all. He gave breaks to The Chords and got Purple Hearts record deals by introducing them. He was massively part of it. But at some point, he must have thought, 'Oh my God, what have I done? I didn't want this.' It was like Frankenstein realising the monster he's created has cognitive thought and isn't going to do exactly what he wants. He must have been in a real dilemma. *I don't want people walking about dressing like me and copying me, but on the other hand, I've created them, so I feel a responsibility to look after them, show them the way.*

He was recording the *Sound Affects* album but gave us half a day to hang out in the studio. I dressed in my best mod clothes. It was incredible that someone charting records and recording an album would give his time to a couple of teenagers. Adrian Thrills told me that Paul and Bruce helped him staple up fanzines during the actual takes of 'In the Crowd'. Fuck me if he's got time to do that.

Ian Stone: I went up to the Loch Lomond festival, my first time in Scotland ... Youth culture was tribal – Teds, mods, punks, skins, rockers. There was a lot of fighting. If you saw a leather jacket, you're having a pop at them and if they're seeing a Harrington, they're like, 'We're not having that.' The festival was quite violent . . . That was also the first time I heard The Jam play 'Start!'

Rick Buckler: It was more than gigs – it was a cultural community. People used to come to shows, they would meet people, make friends, see familiar faces. Some people met their future partners. We used to talk to the fans after the show, we didn't shut ourselves off. There was no 'us and them' . . . It was mutual: they valued us and we valued them.

Eddie Piller: Simone Linch, another mod, was still at school like me. Her dad, a self-employed coach driver with a fifty-two-seater coach, became our secret weapon. I said, 'Can you get your dad to drive us somewhere cool to see The Jam'? I then spoke to Nicky Weller, 'Could you get us fifty tickets for Brighton?' So, fifty of us, all under seventeen, piled on Simone's dad's coach to see The Jam . . . but soon everyone's going, 'Let's go to Holland, let's go to France.' These completely unauthorised Jam tours became our thing. Our parents let us go because Simone's dad was there. God, if they knew about the fights, the drugs, everything else we got up to.

We went all over Europe . . . Holland was the best. The Dutch mods made us really welcome. I'll never forget Rick Buckler hopping onto the bus after a gig in Amsterdam, 'What the hell are you lot doing here? How come your parents let you come?' Everybody had just said, 'I'm staying at a mate's house tonight.'

Rick Buckler: Drinking became our hobby as a band, because it was the easiest thing to do. We always met in the hotel bar to let off steam. We probably drank far too much. People used to warn 'Don't go out with those guys. You'll regret it' Most of the time, they weren't up to our standards.

Our tour rider reflected our habits. Paul got two bottles of vodka on every show, Bruce used to have two bottles of

Bacardi, and I'd have two bottles of red wine – Bull's Blood, recommended by Dickie Bell, our tour manager. Dickie was brilliant, doing most of the groundwork on the day-to-day running of a tour. Before he worked with us, he'd done world tours with Iron Maiden, so he knew his stuff. I got on like a house on fire with him.

You can't drink two bottles a day – well, you can but you'd not have a liver. I was taking a rest, so they piled up in a cupboard. The night before going to Pink Pop Festival in Holland, Dickie stayed at mine, opened up the cupboard and said, 'Ooh, you've got fourteen bottles of red wine here.' So, we drank the lot. In the morning my missus came downstairs to go to work to find us still on the floor finishing off the last bottle as the taxi turned up to take us to the airport. We missed the flight, spent another two hours in the bar drinking in the airport. We eventually made it to Pink Pop and by this time we were fighting in front of The Kinks, and somebody found John and said, 'Your tour manager and drummer have arrived.'

Bruce Foxton: One Christmas at the end of a Jam tour, I took home twenty-one unopened bottles of Bacardi. I'm not leaving those behind.

Rick Buckler: I didn't drink during the day, because I can't play drunk. Paul used to drink all day, right from the early hours. Bruce started at midday. Crates of beer leftover from the previous night's rider would get loaded onto the bus, and by ten, eleven o'clock in the morning, you'd hear the bottles start to open. Paul was often physically sick before a show because he drank too much. That became a bit of a mess really. You can't keep that going for long.

July 1980 – First Japanese tour

Keiko Egawa: The Jam first went over to Japan in July 1980. The concerts were all-seated and the audiences were very quiet and polite. Me and my friend were the only ones who were standing and shouting. They played in this 2,000-capacity plaza hall, and while a lot of people had started liking Western music, including new wave, it wasn't really that popular at the time. I remember Paul introducing 'Pretty Green' by saying, 'The next one is all about yen.' Nobody understood the joke, so it all went completely silent.

Nicky Weller: I came across postcards that Paul sent me and Mum during his first trips to Japan. He wrote, 'The food's a bit funny'!

Keiko Egawa: I went to the hotel to get an autograph . . . After ten minutes, Gill came over and said, 'Paul wants to chat with you.' I didn't understand what 'chat' meant, so she said, 'Talk,' and added, 'Cup of tea?' I said, 'Yes please.' I was lucky. We went to the hotel's tearoom – me, my friend and Paul and Gill. It was quite funny because I was wearing punk clothes, and Paul asked, 'Where did you get that?' So I said in 'Shibuya. There's one punk clothing shop there.' Then he asked, 'How do you say "excuse me" in Japanese?' I taught him *sumimasen* and he repeated it over and over, 'Sumimasen, sumimasen, sumimasen.' But when the waiter came along, he just said, 'Excuse me,' in English!

Dennis Munday: During the summer, around August, Paul told me he didn't want to finish the next album as he didn't have the songs. I said, 'Fine, let's not push it.' I went up and told the old man, A. J. [Tony Morris], 'He's having problems. He's genuine. I don't think he's mucking about.' He wasn't one of those petulant artists. We had signed Godley and Creme to Polydor, and he suggested they could write songs and help to finish the album. I just did not know what to say. He's the MD, I can't say fuck off! So I said, 'They're brilliant, great songwriters, great producers, but I think the fans will know the difference.' He said, 'They can do it, you know, they can do it,' and I said, 'Well, maybe, but no.'

9 August 1980 – Turku Rock Festival, Finland

Paul Du Noyer: Paul came into the *NME* office quite a lot around that time and I ended up being sent on the road with The Jam for my first interview with him. They were playing a big music festival in Finland. They were finishing off the *Sound Affects* album and 'Start!' was the new single. Paul was clearly going through a 1966 phase, wearing silk cravats and a stylish sixties dark suit. I always admired his dress sense – it was brilliant. From hearing the *Sound Affects* demos it was clear he was really pushing the boundaries of what he'd achieved with The Jam previously.

I'd very much liked Paul on a personal level, though he was a bugger about doing interviews. He was like that for years. He wasn't standoffish or surly; he was pretty friendly. He just didn't want me to sit down, turn on that tape recorder and do a formal interview. He kept putting it off until the last minute. The interview wasn't the greatest, but it was a great experience for me.

We were all staying in a hotel in a provincial town in Finland somewhere and a bizarre thing happened. People were having drinks and dinner, and then the lights went down and a stripper came on ... The theme tune to

Clockwork Orange played, really icy, chilly, synth music by Wendy Carlos, as this stripper was doing a slow routine to this spine-chilling piece of music. Paul was quite a serious young man and he didn't like this turn of events at all. He was sitting there with Gill, and they exchanged glances, shook their heads and left. I probably stayed for the novelty and sheer strangeness of it all, but Paul didn't approve of it at all and quite rightly so.

11 August 1980 – 'Start!' (no. 1)

Dennis Munday: We had two sleeves done because we had 'Pretty Green' as a possible A-side along with 'Start!' and there was a lot of debate over that. In fact, the majority wanted to go with 'Pretty Green', but I didn't really see that because that was very similar to other Jam singles, whereas 'Start!' would open them up to a whole new audience.

Vic Coppersmith-Heaven: I always thought that 'Pretty Green' should have been a single. I think it would have reached a much wider audience for The Jam; it was very catchy as a lyric statement and popular piece of music writing and still relates to today.

Dennis Munday: I gave Paul some time to make the decision and we discussed it. I said that we should go with 'Start!' because it's radically different. Even after we picked it, people were saying to me, 'Are you sure you've got that right?' I said, 'Look, "Pretty Green" will get us the top five record, but it ain't going to go to number one.' It wasn't. It's a great song but I don't think it's a single. It's a great album track. The airplay that 'Start!' got was phenomenal.

Jonathan Ross: I remember when 'Start!' came out and even though we all know there's a heavy Beatles – 'Taxman' – riff in there, it seemed revolutionary. It carried the same authentic voice and stance that the early Jam had, but it had matured, becoming more sophisticated and interesting. I love how Paul progressed like that – wanting to move in other directions. After a while, you must get tired of being tied to the same people.

Bruce Foxton: You said 'Taxman', not me – oh no, now I've said it. You get inspiration. That came about because we were in the States and things weren't going terribly well, but we were playing *Revolver* a lot and maybe I was brainwashed or something. Then we got home and came up with 'Start!'

Dennis Munday: Because everyone was going on about the 'Taxman' bassline, when I first heard it, I actually went into the studio with the multi-track, turned all the vocals down and tried to sing 'Taxman' to it. And I couldn't, I really couldn't do that. I didn't see a problem. There isn't anyone that doesn't nick something, whether it's a bassline, a riff or whatever. The Beatles did it. The Beatles were probably the worst. Paul McCartney admitted that.

Tracie Young: I did an interview with Paul much later and we talked a lot about sampling and how back in The Jam days, he'd been accused of ripping off certain things. He talked about it as live sampling. It's not a rip-off. It's just incorporating another artist's work as a way of almost flattering and including it as inspiration . . . For example, the whole 'Start!'/'Taxman' thing.

28 November 1980 – *Sound Affects* (no. 2)

Graham Coxon: I was twelve when I first heard about The Jam, and I was soon obsessed. My dad taught sax to this boy called Paul Thompson, who'd turn up on his Lambretta scooter, with mirrors and lights on it, and his alto sax strapped to the back. He wore a parka with 'The Jam' written on it, white jeans and desert boots. He looked so cool. I was like, 'The Jam?' and he said, 'Yeah, I'll get you a cassette.' He gave me *Sound Affects*, which I played non-stop . . . I remember then getting *Setting Sons* and playing 'Girl on the Phone' to my mum and dad's friends, Chris and Lloyd, and Chris said, 'The size of my cock?' I was like, *Oh, no, she heard that lyric. Shit!*

The Jam made me feel superior to everyone else at school, not in a bad way, but because they represented something I identified with. I didn't have a proper American parka, but I had one of those German ones. I wore desert boots and bowling shoes to school when I was thirteen. I'd listen to The Jam and there was something so great, rhythmic, snappy and exciting about how it all sounded. I liked the imperfections in his voice – he could sing so prettily, but it was never posh pretty. There was something quietly emotional about how he sang. It was intelligent. His insight about stuff that was beyond his years. I love this anti-cynicism that he used to have. He was romantic and that has always stuck with me. He wasn't ashamed to be sentimental. These things are feelings, and that cynicism is the enemy. That really influenced me in my everyday life.

Dennis Munday: I remember talking to Paul during the summer of 1980, while he was demoing *Sound Affects* in Polydor's studio . . . and he said something that stuck with me. He told me that that he didn't want The Jam to become like The Rolling

Stones and other bands, constantly touring and playing the same hits. He said, 'I want The Jam to mean something. I don't want to end up on the "chicken in a basket" tour,' just regurgitating all the hits. I remember driving home thinking, *That's a very odd thing to say*, because the group were really happening by then.

Paul Weller: I thought that 'Going Underground' was the pinnacle of that sound, of what people call now 'The Jam sound'. We probably could have carried on cutting tunes like that, but I just thought we really need a change. I think we all felt that. So, *Sound Affects* was a result of us trying to do something different.

Rick Buckler: We didn't want to become boring. You can see the band's progression – from the raw energy of *In the City*, to being slicker or more studio savvy by the time *Sound Affects* comes out. We were trying to be intelligent about it, moving on and evolving. 'What can we do with a three-piece band that we haven't done before?' We never wanted to rest on our laurels.

Dennis Munday: There was talk of wanting to do a spontaneous album. Vic decided to do a 'lockout', which means that you have the studio for twenty-four/seven, instead of the usual twelve-hour slots. But that doubles the cost. They ended up with a bill for £120,000. I would have been OK with fifty or sixty. That still would have been excessive.

I found a two-inch master tape, and the whole thing was Paul having a conversation with the trumpet player. I think everyone was to blame. Vic could have been harder on them, and I should have kept an eye on it. It got to a point where the bosses were coming to me saying, 'Have you seen the bill?' and I said, 'We've got to get the record out. Let's just run with it and see what occurs.' The lockout wasn't necessary.

Jim Cook: I remember the Townhouse bill was a bit large. They were going all over the place and forgetting that they had to pay for it in the end. So that caused a few rucks at the time. I think that's why Vic got fired after. He spent too much on that one.

Bill Smith: *Sound Affects* was the last Jam album cover that I worked on. I went to the studio and Paul gave me this BBC *Sound Effects* record – albums used by radio programmes with honking horns or grass being cut. He'd scribbled out BBC, and said, 'I want that to be "The Jam" and "Sound Affects" instead of "Effects"' – fantastic wordplay. 'I want the cover like this.' I asked for song titles and lyrical content to build the concept. That's the collaboration.

Martyn Goddard: Bill said we needed a series of images, like the BBC *Sound Effects* album covers – intentionally quite boring and almost abstract. The sort of thing the BBC would have shot at the time, which would have been rubbish.

Bill Smith: Martyn shot some images, and we created that iconic photo montage for the cover.

Andy Rosen: I got involved with *Sound Affects*, 'Start!' and did the single cover for 'Town Called Malice', along with a few other things along the way, posters, bits and pieces. The family thing also made it different. His father, his mother, girlfriend, everything was run by that, so I suppose that made it a bit more laid back. 'Andy, do you want to come down and take a picture of the gig?' I wasn't really dealing with the record company.

Danny Eccleston: When *Sound Affects* came out, I was twelve – the classic age for getting into The Jam. Paul Weller once told me, 'We were a real playground band. There was us, Madness,

The Specials and a couple others.' As soon as he said it, all these memories came flooding back of kids turning their school ties so the thin bit showed, trying to get your mum to take in your school trousers and cutting lapels off jackets. Anything to make you a bit more Jam-friendly.

Rod Argent: I didn't like the punk movement at all, but the one band that I did really, really like was The Jam; hearing 'Start!' and thinking, 'My God! He's hitting with all the energy of someone who's just come onto the scene.' The band were all great players and hugely original with their own stamp. It embraced the early parts of the sixties that I loved.

Shaun Hand: On the lyric sheet for 'Scrape Away', it says 'French by Laurent'. I thought he was some like old French poet but it turns out he was a French fan called Laurent who was in the studio while they were recording the song. Weller goes to him. 'How'd you say this in French?' Laurent told him, and Paul said, 'You record it then.' That's how it ended up on the track. It's actually one of the more advanced pieces of French I know.

What's interesting is how some songs, like 'Dreamtime', seemed so central at the time. It opened almost every date on the *Sound Affects* tour and then they never played it again. Whereas 'Scrape Away', even in mid '82, when Weller was on his big soul-boy kick, they're still playing something as angry and angular as that.

John Harris: 'Monday' from *Sound Affects* is Paul channelling the Mersey poets, Adrian Henri, Roger McGough and Brian Patten. The poetry and fascination of the ordinary and the everyday. That song is a brilliant example of it. I love 'Man in the Corner Shop'. Those lyrics all ring true still. Only no one goes to church any more.

Daniel Rachel: 'Man in the Corner Shop'. I love the idea of the chain of events of, the one person's looking up to the other person, who's looking up to the other person is looking up to the other person. Lyrically it's brilliant and melodically, it's beautiful.

Pete Paphides: With *Sound Affects*, Paul really noticed the details of suburban life – the expectations that society and your family have for you in a working-class or low-middle class existence. That can be a frustrating thing, but in that quite straightened existence there are moments of beauty and magic that you could never really explain to one of the posh kids in 'Eton Rifles', but you wouldn't want to anyway.

Songs like 'That's Entertainment' and 'A Town Called Malice' capture that perfectly. There's a magic in things that a lot of people would find ugly. I really related to that. Long summer days spent in anonymous conurbations, hanging around by the big industrial planters next to the new estate, talking about nothing. Girls going to work at Woolworths, in their shop uniforms with their name badges on. They looked like they could be in a band because it was the early eighties, and the girls all looked like a member of Bananarama. Paul was seeing the world just like me, my brother and our friends did.

Tim Parsons: At this point, The Jam are huge so selling tickets for their tours was never an issue. The real difficulty was the process of working on the road, especially with Kenny and his security team, who thought they knew better than the people that had worked a venue for decades. John didn't like cameras or people bootlegging, which made it more difficult. The start of shows go mental so you're trying to control that and you've got John in your ear because somebody is doing a bootleg or has a camera.

Martin Hopewell: As it was getting bigger, we found ourselves scouting the countryside for big venues. The big arenas that people now see big bands in weren't there. We'd put on gigs in equestrian centres or ice rinks, whatever you could board over to do a gig in. It was all pretty exciting.

Tim Parsons: The biggest challenge was finding standing venues because they didn't like playing seated gigs . . . In that process we found loads of venues for The Jam and they were the first band to go in, which then became standards for other bands. Places like Queens Hall in Leeds, Bingley Hall in Birmingham . . . I'm from Newcastle, so a gig at Whitley Bay Ice Rink was a big deal for me. Tyne Tees TV filmed the soundcheck, and it turned into more of a song creation session. It was fascinating. The news presenter, Tom Coyne, a wise old sage, said at the end of it, 'I wonder if The Jam are earning frozen assets from that concert?'

Martin Hopewell: I still prefer the days of gigs with sticky beer-soaked carpets, sweat dripping off the ceiling and smoke everywhere. Now it's all immaculate, modern, American-built arenas where you can't smoke . . . We were just winging it. With The Jam, we were heading off to Scandinavia with a year's supply of baked beans because I didn't know what the food was going to be like.

Steve 'Tufty' Carver: The dole office called me in, saying they didn't think I was trying hard enough to get a job. They were going to cut my dole money, so I got a job at a Woking factory called EMI. I really didn't want a job, so I went to the pub to drown my sorrows. Then I hear beep-beep: 'Tufty!' It was John Weller. 'Got a job yet?' I said, 'No.' He asked if I wanted to join the tour for a month selling T-shirts. I thought, *Fucking hell, I'm meant to be starting work on Monday.* I said, 'Yeah, all right, John. I'll do that.'

I told my dad, 'I got a job today, but I'm not taking it, I'm going to sell T-shirts for a month instead.' My dad said, 'You bloody idiot. A job for a month or a job for life?' I still think I made the right decision.

Keiko Egawa: I started my first job in London in 1980, working sixteen-hour days, six days a week, to save up for their tours. I didn't have any social life, just worked to follow them around the country. For the *Sound Affects* tour I booked a B&B. After the gig, John Weller invited me to say hello to Paul. Back at the hotel, John said, 'Rick's gone home, his room is empty, stay here. We'll get your luggage.' He always looked after me, making sure I was OK. He'd say, 'You pay for the hotel and travel, so I give you a pass.'

Debsey Wykes: We supported The Jam as Dolly Mixture at Hammersmith Odeon in December 1980. That was a pinnacle – 5,000 people. It felt enormous. It was less intimidating than being on stage with Bad Manners, who we also supported, where people would literally *Sieg heil* and spit at us. With The Jam, we didn't need to think, *Fuck you, we're going to annoy you . . .*

We felt that Paul's parents were taking us under their wing. I guess maybe we wanted them as our parents and to look after us. Ann Weller always said, 'I'll do anything I can.' It felt like a safe house – we'd finally got somewhere. Nothing ever stays like that, but it was a great feeling that you were on your way.

Steve 'Tufty' Carver: The tour ended at Hammersmith Odeon at Christmas. I was on about 100 quid a week. John said, 'The boys want to give you a Christmas bonus – 100 quid,' which was a lot of money in the 1980s. I was getting paid to watch the best band in the world play every night. Ridiculous. Me and Gill, Paul's girlfriend, handled merchandise, selling T-shirts.

There'd be 200 kids wanting a shirt, and when we heard John come on stage, we'd shut the case. These kids would go, 'I want a T-shirt'. We'd go, 'No, you don't buy T-shirts when this group is on stage – go away.' I remember promoters asking how much we made. 'Two thousand quid.' They said, 'Iron Maiden make 8,000 quid on T-shirts'. I replied, 'Yeah, but we're not here to sell T-shirts. This is a group.' Iron Maiden sell leather jackets with studs in. Who wants one of them?

Dennis Munday: We used to throw a Christmas party for The Jam, and then in 1980, John said to me, 'We don't want just a DJ. Can we have a band on?' So I got my mate's band to do it. They were a really good covers band doing Motown stuff. They did their set, and John said to me, 'Get the boys up, because their families are there, they'll love it.' We called them the Greyhound All Stars – The Jam, Dolly Mixture and Shane MacGowan. I've never forgotten it because my mate said, 'He looks like a Morris Minor with the doors open.'

7 December 1980 – *Alright Now*

Malcolm Gerrie: In the late seventies, I worked as a TV researcher at Tyne Tees television in darkest Newcastle. The first music show I produced was *Alright Now*. One of the delightful surprises of making music shows was meeting record companies' pluggers – people whose job was to get bands on TV or radio. There was one guy called Clive Banks, who was instrumental in introducing me to Paul and The Jam, and became hugely important as part of the story of *The Tube* later on. He looked after the Who, Pretenders, Elvis Costello, Secret Affair and The Jam, all these really great bands. Clive just had that seal of quality.

I vividly remember him coming to see me and said, 'Have a listen to this.' It was The Jam. It blew me away. 'There's only three of them, Malcolm, so it's not going to be expensive for you to put them on the show!' I was like 'You don't need to do that. I've heard the music, I love it' . . . One of the producers, Chris Cowey, listened and went 'Whoa, that's really great.' Immediately, it reminded us of the Small Faces, and Paul had that thing that Steve Marriott had of almost spitting into the microphone, guitar slung around. There was so much soul and heart in the lyrics and especially in the presentation. And then I found out that Paul was a mega fan of the Small Faces.

December 1980 – 'Pop Art Poem' for *Flexipop*

Barry Cain: I left *Record Mirror*, did some PR before going freelance. I had a drink with Tim Loss, who was still on *Record Mirror*, and had always dreamed of doing a magazine. We came up with the *Flexipop* idea. We had contacts in the business, so could get exclusive records supplied by everyone . . . The second issue was a game-changer. We did The Jam. Paul recorded 'Pop Art Poem' for *Flexipop*, along with a remix of 'Boy about Town' that everyone says was better than the original. We sold about 65,000 copies.

Shaun Hand: 'Pop Art Poem' is another of those unusual songs that I'm a big fan of that other people go, *What the bloody hell is this? Stick 'Going Underground' on will you?* If you read the lyrics to 'Pretty Green', it's a Pop Art poem. Their lyrics set them apart from a lot of other bands. The lyrics are so good and still are.

7 February 1981 – 'That's Entertainment' (import single, no. 21)

Jim Cook: I loved 'That's Entertainment', but that was another disaster. When we first heard it, we said, 'That's another number one record.' We took it to Radio 1 and they said, 'No, the lyrics aren't suitable. We can't play it.' All because it had had the phrase 'kick in the balls' in it. So, of course, we go back to Paul to ask if he'd change the lyric. Paul said, 'Go fuck yourself' [*laughs*]. So we had to come up with another scheme on that. We got Metronome in Germany to press up 15,000 copies and we imported them and sold it on that basis, which made it a hit but it wasn't the big hit that it should have been. They then had to play it when it went top forty, but they never changed their minds. I mean, the BBC's policies on lyrics have always been totally ridiculous. They allowed about fifty drug songs to hit number one. The import was a way of trying to make it a bit special and therefore make the fans go out and buy it.

Peter Wilson: We did the demo for 'That's Entertainment' and it was pretty well-formed. Paul had written all the lyrics, played it with an acoustic guitar and added bass and another guitar on top. We'd regularly do demos with Paul and his roadie, Dave Liddle. When Paul ran out of songs, we'd have maybe a spare afternoon or day in the studio, so we'd muck about with covers, like The Kinks, Sandie Shaw or Beatles. We did 'And Your Bird Can Sing' from *Revolver*, which I put organ onto, and that Beatles B-side called 'Rain' when I played drums. That was just low-pressure fun.

Kenny Wheeler: Paul gave me a little cassette in a cab going down to Heathrow, and that's when I first heard that demo. That was just Paul, and the others weren't on it yet. Sometimes it's frustrating, because you hear something start off in one way and by time it's finished, it's slightly different, or a lot different, and sometimes you liked the demo more. It's great that way.

Billy Bragg: I spoke to Paul about 'That's Entertainment' early in our relationship. He was very dismissive of it. He was like 'wrote it in ten minutes'. He did his whole thing about how much better the demo was and eventually when I heard the demo, I was like, 'You don't know what you're talking about. That's such bullshit.'

Vic Coppersmith-Heaven: We had a lot of fun on those sessions, plenty of time to hang out in the studio after hours with Rick and Bruce, trying new sounds, new overdubs, like the cardboard box that Rick played on for 'That's Entertainment', which is a great song, and the version we created was perfect for the album. Paul thought that we never caught the magic of his initial demo, but that happens . . . the first time you lay down a song as a writer, there can be a kind of magic in parts that sometimes cannot be repeated on a re-recording. But new angles on further recordings can increase the overall vision of the song and particularly if it's not a standalone song, but has to fit into an album project.

Billy Bragg: You have got to respect any songwriter who has the balls to put 'Two lovers missing the tranquillity of solitude' into a song. That's such a great line. And in that song too, which is a really gritty urban song. The reason I love it is it really reminds me of my world in the mid-seventies. The concrete, sirens, smell of piss, rotten beer, power cuts, it's like, 'That's Entertainment', it's all there. But then suddenly out of that comes this line, 'Two lovers missing the tranquillity of solitude.' It's like Shakespeare. What are you doing here? Go and get a proper job. It's like finding a diamond in a gasometer. Really beautiful. As soon as I hear those strummed chords, it has everything that a great Jam song does. The Jam were a great working-class British band for expressing working-class sentiments. Those songs really spoke to me of my youth.

David F. Ross: Those lyrics captured exactly what life is like, the joys and the frustrations and the boredom of growing up in backward-looking towns and that's not in any way being disrespectful to the place you grow up. There's maybe a lack of excitement, it's not a big city and bands and music that you want to go and see don't ever come and play there, so you always have to go somewhere else.

Ian Snowball: On my eleventh birthday, 'That's Entertainment' had just come out and I was given some money, and I have such a vivid memory of walking down to Woolworths on a Saturday morning with 50p and buying a copy with the picture sleeve. The first seven-inch I ever bought. Racing home, up to my bedroom, dropping to my knees, putting on the record player, taking it out of the sleeve only to discover that it didn't have that little bit in the middle, so I couldn't play it. I had to rush back to get one.

February–May 1981 – British Rock & Pop Awards and touring

Nicky Weller: I remember going to the British Rock and Pop Awards. February 1981. The Jam won best single for 'Going Underground'. Now, the reason that sticks in my mind is not because of The Jam. I remember sitting in the audience thinking, *Oh my God, there's David Bowie and there's David Essex and Roxy Music.* And as we went backstage, I got to meet David Bowie, and I was speechless. He had this blue suit on and I was like, *Oh my God, I've just met my hero.* My brother didn't get out of his seat to collect his award. Bruce and Rick went up and got it.

Bob Manton: We started Purple Hearts in 1977. When you've got a band like The Jam, who are successful with a mod image, then it doesn't seem such a silly thing to do it yourself.

Jeff Shadbolt: For me, mod is a state of mind and feeling part of something. It doesn't matter what you wear – a patched-up parka or a Savile Row suit. The press turned 'Mod' into a dirty word but it's never gone away for us. I'm not a musician in a mod band; I'm a mod in a band.

I was in my mum's garage working on a scooter, when she came out and said, 'Someone's on the phone.' I asked who, and she came back saying, 'It's Paul.' I assumed it was a chap called Paul who was the manager of a clothes shop in Romford called Mints and Davis, so I said 'What, Paul from Mints?' She went back to check and then said, 'No, it's Paul from The Jam.' He'd arranged a couple of days for us in his studio.

Bob Manton: He got a good couple of tracks out of us. Paul played piano on 'Concrete Mixer' and 'Plane Crash' and offered to release it on his Respond label, but I think us being arrogant and up ourselves, we just used it as a demo to take around other companies and then didn't get it out. More fool us. Paul also brought a lot of records in and made us a tape each. John's Children, early Pink Floyd, The Creation, The Action, The Eyes. It was freakbeat basically and a lot of stuff we'd never have known. A C90 cassette each.

Jeff Shadbolt: We then supported The Jam in Brighton, Crawley and the Woking Youth Club secret gig in February 1981. At the time, we didn't grasp the enormity of it and just took it in our stride. Looking back, I just wish now we had more photos. It's a pinch-me moment. Did it really happen? People keep reminding us that they were there but it's still a blur.

Steve 'Tufty' Carver: At the height of their career, The Jam played three times in one weekend in Woking – a youth club, a pub and the YMCA. I kept a notepad by Mum's phone, writing down all these secret gigs. 'Tufty, you've got to come to this. It's called The English Roses or The Eton Rifles or John's Boys.' There was one at the Wheatsheaf in Woking, which turned into an absolute riot. It was called The Jam's Road Crew. This pub was absolutely heaving with people. It wasn't The Jam's Road Crew – it was The Jam, and it turned into a massive fight. These things always do.

Derek D'Souza: I popped into the snooker club and my dad said, 'Some Weller woman rung for you about a photo shoot. She'll call back.' It was so strange, because he never normally would say that – usually it'd be Mrs Weller or Ann Weller. I ran home but no call came. I stayed in all week waiting, until Sunday night, when Ann finally called. 'I'm so sorry. I lost your number. We really like your pictures and want to talk about doing a photo session for the band.'

I couldn't believe it. Ann met me at Woking station and took me to their house. She'd just got a new car, and when we went to leave, she couldn't work out how to turn the lights on, so she took John's Mercedes and dropped me back to Woking station so I could get a train home. They were wonderful. I went another time, and I hadn't eaten after work, so Ann did me some dinner. Cup of tea in hand, thinking *I can't believe I'm in the house, with Paul's parents.*

Steve 'Tufty' Carver: The only time John gave me a bollocking was when they played at the YMCA during *Sound Affects*. We'd spent all day drinking in a beer garden near Ripley. Paul was meant to be playing that night, and we were absolutely bolloxed when we started trying to walk back home. Halfway, I said to Paul, 'We're not even going to make the gig.' I swear this is true. My brother was a dust cart driver, and he tooted and picked us up. We arrived at the gig in a dust cart, but we were still pissed.

The next day, The Jam were playing Sheerwater Youth Club. I went round for Paul, and we were all looking at our feet because of what happened. I was meant to go to Paris with them a week later, and John went, 'By the way, you ain't coming to Paris.' I got blamed for that one.

Martin Hopewell: That period is the one I remember the clearest. It was very vivid. When you talk about Paul Weller, certainly through my experience of working with him, it's all about the work ethic. Paul didn't want to piss about – you clock in, do your time and clock out late. Work, work, work. The sheer volume of shows that The Jam did was phenomenal.

When we ran out of places that were big enough to play in one night, we'd play two, hitting weird places like Birmingham's Bingley Hall, Deeside Leisure Centre and that Equestrian Centre in Braintree. Touring would normally be in the spring and in the autumn. Then they wanted to do the seaside tours, which were bloody hilarious. Wigan Pier sounded like a seaside resort, and we all know that Wigan is quite a long way away from the sea, right? Swindon Oasis, which sounded seaside-y but obviously not. For a laugh, to see if anybody was paying any attention to all the verbiage I was putting into contracts, I wrote a clause to say, very officially, 'it was agreed and understood that the promoter will arrange for all of the taps in the venue to be turned on at least forty-eight hours prior to the performance, and twenty-seven tonnes of sharp sand deposited in front of the venue to create a seaside atmosphere.' Nobody even questioned it. They didn't do it, of course, but nobody called me and went 'Oi, what's this?

There were so many wonderful characters involved. It wasn't just Paul, Rick, Bruce, John, Ann, Nicky and Kenny. But also people like Tony Gibney, aka Mono, who was deaf in one ear, and you had the wonderful Joe Awome – I think he was a Commonwealth gold heavyweight boxer. John was quite keen on recruiting people by the pound, so you had these rather large, lovely, and really funny people.

Chris Green: My first ever gig . . . The Jam at Stafford Bingley Hall . . . pogoing nonstop, elbows in the face, no one wanting to hurt anybody, but just this explosion of passion and desire and letting it all out. I remember that it went a bit quiet when they were swapping guitars over and Paul said, 'Any requests?' My mate meant to shout, 'That's Entertainment!' but instead shouted, 'That's Education!' It went completely quiet and we all looked at him like, *Uh Oh*.

David F. Ross: I met Paul in June 1981, 'The Bucket and Spade Tour', playing Irvine Magnum Centre. At the time, John Weller put a note in *NME* for local bands to send a cassette, and they'd consider putting them on the bill. My mate and I were helping a local band and DJing for them, so we sent in a tape. Dale, the singer, wrote to John saying, 'You're coming to Irvine, any chance we could get on the bill?' He wrote back and said yes.

The night before the gig, The Jam were up in Kilmarnock. The band was invited to meet them at the curry house, and we went along as their 'roadies'. There was a girl sat in the corner; I've seen her since and she said that when they all left, she asked the barman for the pint glass that Paul Weller had been drinking from. She still has it.

It was such a weird thing. They'd just released *Sound Affects*, they're the biggest band in the UK and they're sitting in a curry house with eight hangers-on from a local band.

Virginia Turbett: Guildford was my home turf. It was a really hot day. Bruce wore the shortest shorts, like people used to in the seventies. During the gig, Weller took his top off. I remember Wendy O. Williams of the Plasmatics did that and put black tape on her nipples. Weller had thought about this in advance, because he took his top off and there are his black-taped nipples.

Helen Jones: I went to that gig with my friends, Dawn and Paul. When we arrived, everyone was outside soaking up the sun. After a while, John opened the side doors and let us all in for soundcheck, which was an unexpected bonus. The gig was amazing, we had standing tickets the first night and seated the second night.

We were fan club members, so knew the Weller family home was at Balmoral Drive. It was on the letters. On the second day we went to see it. There's a green area in front of the little crescent where number 45 is, and as Dawn drove up, I nearly fainted – Paul was standing on the green leaning on a skip with a mug of tea talking to a builder. I was freaking out saying 'Don't stop, don't stop.' Paul clocked us and half smiled, probably expecting us to stop. To this day, I don't know why they listened to me. He would have probably got us a cuppa.

Later that day, everyone was euphoric having seen them play and that second night was the black tape on the nipples. So funny. After the show everyone was hanging about hoping to see the boys come out. After a few hours nothing was happening, so I wandered around the side of the building alone, and to my amazement the door opened, and Paul came down the steps on his own. We chatted, he asked where I was from, and I asked when he was coming to Wales next. Paul was pretty trolleyed, and after a few minutes he fell over the low hedge we were standing by! It wasn't long before a man came along, yanked him back over the hedge, 'C'mon, Paul, this way.' It was Kenny of course.

Tim Parsons: Kenny was great fun to be around – just a natural, normal, lovely guy. Dave Liddle, the guitar tech, was a bit of a likable buffoon. Everyone took the piss out of him. Ian Harvey, the production manager, was the stereotypical Scot – hard-working and dedicated. Ray Salter, known as Rat, was on the monitor desk, and played a huge part in the sound. A really important role. There were loads of fantastic people that you came across within The Jam camp. But we were all naive, innocent and in our early twenties, apart from John and a few of the road crew . . . Working with The Jam taught me a lot about working with other bands. The Police benefited from us working with The Jam because they played a lot of the venues that we'd already found with them. The Clash is another example. A difficult manager, Bernard Rhodes, with a so-called difficult band wanting to do weird and wonderful things, like the 'Casbah Club' tour. But because we had experience with The Jam, it was no big deal.

Ian Stone: I remember being at the soundcheck, and one of the guys there, called Kenny, was talking to a mate. Both had roll-up cigarettes going, big fellas in standard roadie gear – T-shirt, jeans, humping stuff about for a living. They made sure the fans didn't get too close unless Paul and the boys were OK with it. Swearing at each other in the most beautiful, colourful way. I'm fourteen, so I've heard a fair bit of swearing but not like this. It was really impressive. The sound desk – they called it the 'sound fucking desk', and I thought, *Is there any real need for an expletive between 'sound' and 'desk'?* I just loved all that. 'Where the fuck are you going with those cables?' 'Never mind what that cunt told you to do. Leave those fucking cables there and give me a fucking hand lifting this fucking sound fucking desk onto the fucking stage.' It was Olympic-level swearing and even as a fourteen-year-old, who was at school and did swear on occasion, it was very impressive. It felt very grown up.

29 May 1981 – 'Funeral Pyre' (no. 4)

Vic Coppersmith-Heaven: I was not expecting my Jam story to end, and when Paul phoned me and said he would like to continue with the band on his own, I was gutted, but, on reflection, I had been with them for almost five years and devoted a lot of time to The Jam in and out of the studio, which also included mixing live gigs . . . it was quite an experience to record tracks in the studio, then mixing them again at a live concert and also have that live ambience and fan atmospheric support around you.

Paul had been demoing new songs with another producer after we had completed *Sound Affects* and you can get attached to that way of working, simple demos recorded straight off the drawing board, and a light relief maybe to work on with someone who might not be as critical as me, so all understandable.

Dennis Munday: If you look at 1981, that's when I started to see what would happen with The Jam. You have the two singles, 'Funeral Pyre' and 'Absolute Beginners'. When 'Funeral Pyre' came out, I thought, *That's standing still, that's not going forward.* With every other single, there was a step forward. Sometimes a small step, sometimes a big step, but that song could have come out in 1978, 1979 or 1980, but then you get to 'Absolute Beginners' and that's completely unexpected, totally out of leftfield. That was where Paul was going and that was the future.

Peter Wilson: When they wanted to split with their producer after *Sound Affects*, they first asked me to do a couple of singles, which were 'Funeral Pyre' and 'Absolute Beginners', which then led on to the next album. It was awesome because they were huge then. They'd done 'Down in the Tube Station at Midnight', 'Going Underground' and 'Start!', and they had a fanatical following; they were on *Top of the Pops*. They were big time. So even though I'd produced some records that had gone top ten, it was still an exciting challenge. So, I took them to AIR Studios, which was then in Oxford Circus, George Martin's place, great studio and nicely placed for Soho in the West End, and we did most of our recording there.

Derek D'Souza: They arranged a day for me to meet the band at AIR Studios . . . But the night before, I got arrested. I'd been out with some friends in London and saw a plastic traffic cone on the side of the pavement. I flicked it with my foot, and it just wobbled, didn't even fall over. I then heard a voice: 'You're nicked for being drunk and disorderly. You've got to go Horseferry Road Magistrates Court in the morning.' I said, 'I can't do tomorrow morning, I'm meeting The Jam in the studio!' And the bloke was like, 'I don't care what your plans are. You're going to court.'

I thought *Pay the money and go*. Then I jumped in a cab and as I went into the building, the lift door opened, and George Martin walked out of the lift. I've gone 'Hi, George!' He said, 'Hello, young man!'

I went up to meet the band. I was really nervous. They were recording 'Absolute Beginners' and 'Tales from the Riverbank'. At one point, I'm sitting on an amp just watching Paul, who was about three foot away, doing his guitar parts. Then he said. 'We'll have a break. Do you fancy a game of pool? We'll play doubles against Joe and Kenny,' the minders. We won two–one!

Adrian Thrills: Paul's a musical fanatic and around the time of 'Funeral Pyre', he was really taken with that post-punk angular sound, especially northern bands, Gang of Four and the Mekons. That was a single where you could hear a little bit of that jagged guitar influence. It was an avenue that they could have gone down a lot more. In some ways, Paul did revisit it years later on albums like *Sonik Kicks*, using motorik beats and other elements. It probably took thirty years for that particular influence to come to fruition. Listen to Gang of Four's Andy Gill – his aggressive, jagged, trebly guitar sound – you could hear elements of Wilco Johnson, which you can also hear in Paul's rhythm guitar playing. There's a clear common ground. It is an oft-neglected back portal of The Jam, where they went a bit post-punk.

Dylan Jones: There were periods when Paul was more into the sound, the sonic. When The Jam went through their Gang of Four period, he was taking that idea of modernism in a very particular way. The art and the craft of writing – not just songwriting, but writing – is very important to Paul, and he developed a way to channel that into pop, and when it really works, like in any great pop medium, the great pop single, the great pop song, is when those two things fuse together.

Robert Howard: I loved 'Funeral Pyre'. The tune, the noise and the energy, and I wondered who produced it. *Oh, Pete Wilson.* When I went to RCA, they asked who I wanted to produce me, so I said, 'Pete Wilson.' Of course, 'Funeral Pyre' really doesn't have anything to do with Pete Wilson. It's to do with Paul. His guitar sound and then the drums are great on top.

16 October 1981 – 'Absolute Beginners' (no. 4)

Shaun Hand: One of my favourite periods of The Jam is 1981, when they didn't release an album. Despite only two singles, developmentally for Weller it seems like it was a very important year. He launched his record labels, Respond and Jamming, started writing essays, becoming more politically active and that's where he likely began to grow away from the group and The Jam thing. 'Funeral Pyre' was followed four months later by 'Absolute Beginners' and 'Tales from the Riverbank' – my favourite Jam song. That B-side version, not the one with the horns. It has to be the trippy, faded-up version.

David F. Ross: I read and loved Colin MacInnes's *Absolute Beginners* book. I would have discovered it through that song and reading about its connection to the literature. His writing, particularly about London, is so central to mod philosophy and iconography, that if it had become part of a song that I was really interested in, then I would have wanted to read that. I don't really recall reading much as a child until I found influences from musicians that I liked. My discovery through that song sparked an interest in working-class or urban literature and stories about how young people lived their lives, connected and took advantage of opportunities.

Rick Buckler: I'm particularly proud of 'Absolute Beginners' and 'Riverbank' because often people would listen to that and not realise it's The Jam. It was a real exploration for us.

Steve 'Tufty' Carver: I'd wait for a new single and sometimes they were disappointments. I'll be honest, when they did 'Absolute Beginners', I didn't think, *That's fucking brilliant.* Paul once said to me, down the pub, 'You've always been a punk, Tufty,' and he wasn't wrong. I do love one, two, three, four – Bam! Hearing them tear through 'Slow Down' at 180 miles an hour is The Jam to me. Sweat, spittle, blood and speed – that's how I remember them.

John Wilson: Looking at what The Beatles did, you would buy 'We Can Work It Out' and have 'Day Tripper' on the other side, 'Paperback Writer' with 'Rain' – B-sides as brilliant as the A-sides. Paul applies that same quality control and logic in The Jam. 'Dreams of Children', technically a double A-side with 'Going Underground', but that could have been a huge single on its own. 'Tales from the Riverbank', which he still plays, was the B-side to 'Absolute Beginners'. A song like 'Liza Radley' you could regard as a throwaway song, but it's a beautifully rendered sketch of small-town loneliness and the outsider, which is a recurring character in a lot of his songs. The outsider. Somebody who doesn't quite fit. Psychoanalyse Mr Weller and you realise he's that young man sitting in the corner of the pub that produces 'Away from the Numbers'. That person who he identifies with. It's the artistic experience.

Noel Gallagher: Two of the most important bands in my musical life are The Smiths and The Jam and both had incredible B-sides. It wasn't a thing that I designed for Oasis, I didn't write B-sides, I just wrote songs. With those two bands, it's not just about the singles and the art, there's a whole other thing going on. It's no coincidence why Oasis are as revered as they are. Let's say, a kid is getting into it today, of course, his dad buys him *Morning Glory* and then *Definitely Maybe*. There's then another five years working out 'What the fucking hell's all this other shit?' Which are equally as good or even better than what was done on the album.

Gered Mankowitz: Bill Smith and I stupidly got involved in shooting a video for 'Absolute Beginners', which was a total disaster. We had joined forces to shoot promotional videos and came up with an idea, very illustrative of the song. Created complicated storyboards and laid out exactly how we saw it. Everybody seemed excited, but when they actually arrived for the shoot, they were so uncommitted. Everything felt like a surprise to them and they weren't really interested in doing it. It was an awful shoot.

The cameraman was telling us that it was great, but we didn't have any way of seeing it until the next day. When we saw the rushes, it was horrible. The band was out of focus. I was so disappointed. It came together in the editing room, and then we showed it. The record company and band rejected it immediately. As an experience it was horrible.

Derek D'Souza: That single sleeve was my very first photoshoot. We went to Chiswick Park in London, and I was really nervous. The band were patient with me and really relaxed, trying anything. We spent two or three hours walking around and shooting. Paul was trying to find the tree that The Beatles sat in, though he never mentioned it at the time. I saw him on tour in 2015 and asked if he'd known about The Beatles connection, 'Of course, I fucking did!' Those was his exact words. Any excuse to shoot where the Fabs had been photographed.

I remember Ann telling me Paul once bought a stack of Beatles magazines from a charity shop. When he got home, he emptied a drawer of his clothes, put them on the floor, and replaced them with the magazines because they were more important.

The photo that I did with them behind the bars is now in the National Portrait Gallery. It was my idea – I thought the gate looked interesting. People will look at it and say Paul's slightly further away from the other two, and did he feel trapped in the band? No, they were just three guys standing behind a gate while I took a picture. Sorry to shatter any illusions.

Alan McGee: When I was about nineteen or twenty, I'd started writing songs and wrote to Paul. He'd just started his own label Respond, and he wrote back . . . I've never told him this – I don't see him very often, I don't hang out with Paul Weller. When I like people that much, I don't really want to become their friend, you know what I mean? He does respect me, which is lovely . . . I like it the way it is, that he's one of my idols, my heroes, and I don't want to get on with him too well . . .

It was 1981, and he wrote back a few times and liked my songs, which was unbelievable. My band was just me really, it was called Soul Organisation or some fucking weird name.

I'd love to pull out those letters next time that I run into him. 'Guess what? You nearly signed me!' Just for the craic.

Simon Halfon: I started working as an assistant to Neville Brody; he designed *The Face* magazine, among other things. He was a big influence on how I approached design. Around that time, I started seeing Paul socially. We'd meet at the Barley Mow, a pub near Selfridges off Oxford Street. I was still a bit in awe of him. It was Paul, Paolo Hewitt, a writer for *Melody Maker*, and Gary Crowley. We'd go for a beer. I didn't even drink – I'd sit with a big pint glass of lemonade. We all got on but I was still very much a fanboy.

At one meeting, Paul said, 'I'm doing this Small Faces book for my publishing company, Riot Stories. Do you want to design it?' I jumped at the chance, although I didn't really know what I was doing.

November 1981 – Respond record label begins

Debsey Wykes: Paul spoke to us at the Hammersmith Odeon before he had Respond, said he wished he had his own label as there were so many good bands about, but he didn't feel he had the time. A few months later, Respond was set up and he signed our band Dolly Mixture. We mostly dealt with his dad, but Paul came along to a few meetings.

There was one meeting about the contract, we were the only ones who'd actually read it. We were basically saying *It's really shit*, and then Paul realised it was shit and told his dad it was shit. Good on him. Good bloke.

We were quite shy with Paul, and he was quite shy with us. I think he got on with The Questions really well, they were very tight, chatting about records, clothes and hairstyles or something. I don't think he knew what to say to us very much. We did two singles, and he came to the studio when Captain Sensible and Paul Gray were producing. They all stood around chatting, which was interesting to watch . . . we didn't see him much after that.

Paul Barry: When we were getting songs together as The Questions, John Robinson sent a tape to Paul. Not only did he reply – not many people would do that – he said he loved the songs and even made suggestions. That's Weller, his advice always has merit. Then he said, 'We're playing Edinburgh, do you want to support us?'

Meeting him, and then signing for Respond, was amazing. I've never met anyone so unaffected. He's the same now as he was then. I met him at eighteen and we're still in touch. I was working with him a few years back, we did a song for James Morrison. Paul still sends me new songs or records, asking 'What do you think?'

October–December 1981 – London gigs

Annajoy David: I have to be honest – I didn't know much about Paul. I was aware of The Jam, but I wasn't big into music. I'd helped set up the youth wing of the Campaign for Nuclear Disarmament, which was a significant movement from the late seventies into the eighties. It collided with the Thatcher years and was the start of a cultural shift for two generations in the UK. Paul heard me speak at a rally with Lord Fenner Brockway and Bruce Kent, got in touch and said, 'I'd like to help.' I quickly got familiar with The Jam and really liked him. He was completely genuine, down to earth and his motives were really straightforward. He wasn't complicated to deal with at all. It was a pleasure. We formed this great friendship and working relationship which endured over a decade.

Our first thing together, that's not often noted or recorded, was putting The Jam on the back of a loader at a CND rally. They played as over 250,000 people marched through London to protest over the siting of nuclear missiles in the UK. That was impromptu, a spontaneous thing that they did.

Robert Howard: Weirdly, I only saw The Jam once. It was at a CND festival on the back of a truck near Temple Station. I went around the corner, and there they were, playing a song called 'Desdemona', by a band called John's Children – a Marc Bolan song. I swear I didn't imagine this. I think that's the only time they ever played it. They finished. I only ever saw the one song [*laughs*].

John Wilson: I saw them two nights in a row at the Michael Sobell Sports Centre at the end of 1981. Those gigs were part of four CND benefit gigs. They previewed songs from their next album. It wasn't out yet, but something had changed – the sound had a real soul vibe.

Tim Parsons: Adding the brass players to The Jam was the insight into where Paul was going musically.

Steve Rapport: I took pictures of The Jam at that legendary Christmas gig, when there were pitch battles in the street with all the skinheads from the gig at the Rainbow just around the corner. It was Bananarama, Department S and The Jam at the Michael Sobell Sports Centre. It was skinheads and mods fighting in the snow and ice outside, like a *Game of Thrones* battle.

Steve Nichols: Michael Sobell was an intense atmosphere. My first major show playing in The Jam. We get out on stage and there were 150,000 skinheads rushing towards you. Quite nerve-wracking. Not so much for us but for his warm-up act, Bananarama. That was a real experience live.

John Wilson: Paul billed it as his version of a Stax revue show. There would always be a local band supporting The Jam on every leg of a gig. I remember Bananarama came on – nobody knew who they were. They got booed and bottled off.

Paul Moody: They played 'Town Called Malice' to complete silence because no one had ever heard it.

Russell Hastings: The hall was dead silent. Paul would go, 'Here's another new one' and he played 'Precious'. People were looking, there were a few nods and that, and then it went dead silent, which was something that you never had at a Jam concert. If you're going to go and do that, bring yourself a good shovel because you better start digging.

Steve Nichols: Every show was different. Sometimes there'd be fights at the front, sometimes fights at the back! After the first show and seeing that situation, I just thought, this is what's going to happen, I better get used to it. The gobbing still went on. That was always there.

Bruno Gallone: They were massive when [Reaction] supported them at Hammersmith. They announced 'Town Called Malice' as their next single. John Weller told us to turn up at four, but we got there really early. The Jam were already set up from the night before, Paul was playing cards with Kenny and the roadies. They had a DJ at that gig because Paul wanted an immersive experience for that run. We were chatting and suddenly he said, 'Don't you think you should get ready?' – Oh yeah, I was playing . . .

John Weller was great. We got paid forty quid, but he gave us fifty: 'You were all right, guys, get yourself some chips on the way home.'

Our sound was fast and furious, moddy-punk, a bit New Wave. When it finished, everybody went off on a buzz, but I stood back a little bit behind the monitors and just looked back and wanted to just take that moment in. I was quickly knocked back by Kenny saying, 'No, effing encore,' and I went, 'Oh, no, I just want to take in this moment.' 'You've had your effing moment.'

Adrian Thrills: I stayed friends with Paul, but the relationship between the journalist and the band obviously changes. I went on to write for the *NME* and you have to be slightly more detached, more critical. There were moments where we'd disagree over a review. There was a period where he didn't take too kindly to the new romantic scene, and thought that the *NME* had strayed a little bit too much into that. He chastised me and other *NME* writers from the stage at the Sobell Centre as 'the *NME* cocktail set'. That ruffled a few feathers. I'd also reviewed a 1981 Rainbow show where I said, 'The Jam are in a rut and it's going to take all of Weller's flair to get them out of it. In retrospect . . . I think I was wrong.

29 January 1982 – 'Town Called Malice' / 'Precious' (double A-side, no. 1)

Dennis Munday: I remember them going into the studio at the beginning of 1982 to finish off the next album. Paul had told the press that he wanted to make the greatest Jam album ever. You can't say that. You cannot. What you can say is 'I'm going to go in and try' but when you go in and do that, I think that you are setting yourself up for a disappointment.

Steve Nichols: We were at AIR Studios, George Martin's place. It was strange because we're up there playing pool, and Paul McCartney walked in, and immediately Paul dropped his cue stick and went over to Paul to say hello.

Virginia Turbett: I was there waiting to photograph Weller for a *Smash Hits* feature. Paul McCartney comes in this little side room and does a 'Sieg heil' to Thatcher, who is on the telly. We're in the same room; I've got all my cameras and I'm a rock photographer. There is one of The Beatles, one of the most famous recognisable people in the world in the twentieth century, and do I take a photo of Paul McCartney? No, I didn't even think about it. I just thought, *You're just being a bit of a tosser.*

Bruce Foxton: We'd finished for the day, and I came down in the lift. In front of me were a couple of girls walking towards me. I'm thinking, *I've been in the studio all day, the weather is miserable, I want to get home, I don't want to be caught chatting and signing autographs now, I'm knackered.* So I'm walking towards them, ready with my pen in my hand and they went straight past me. I turned around to have a look where they were going, and Paul McCartney was coming out of the lift. Fair enough. He was doing *Tug of War* up there. Linda

McCartney was taking photographs of various people, and she took a shot of me. I'm pleased with it because I look so good in it [*laughs*], probably at my peak.

Peter Wilson: The making of *The Gift* was stressful – the record company circus, as I call it. You make an album, release singles, tour to promote it, then the label wants another album with twelve new songs and the whole thing starts again. It's gruelling, especially after five years of such intensity. I think The Beatles found something similar. Their touring career was very short because of it. At this point with The Jam there was tension and difficulty, and a lot of pressure on Paul to come up with the songs.

As I recall the record company wanted the album out by Christmas 1981, which is a great marketing idea if you're a high-end big-selling artist, if you're major league; it's a huge market and you want your product to be out there. Well, it didn't happen.

My job was to listen to what the band and the songwriter wanted to do and support that direction constructively, unless it was a bad one, but it wasn't.

Andy Rosen: One of my favourite shots of Paul was taken at AIR Studios. He was always there early in the morning, knocking out Beatle songs on the piano in the hallway or the foyer. I'd arrive early to scout locations for photographs, and one day I noticed the sun coming out, which is rare in England. I saw the perfect reflection for a great photo. Paul, however, was late. This was a moment where I thought, *Shit, if the clouds come by, I'm going to lose this shot and it's meaningless.* I'm waiting and then just as he turns up, the fucking sun goes down or the clouds come over. I asked him to go back and carry on recording and the moment the sun comes up again, I'd run up and get the shot, which I did, and got this shot, which I'm glad that I did. I've got my own personal favourites, but out of all my portraits, I don't know why, this one just really resonates with me.

Steve Nichols: I went to the College for Young Musicians at thirteen, and by sixteen, I was playing in the London School Symphony Orchestra. By eighteen, I was principal trumpet and toured around the world, so I was quite used to that level, but going into the studio with Paul and The Jam was exhilarating. Paul always pushed for more intensity and fire. I was sweating! It was quite an intense ride. No two days were the same.

The brass arrangements were often created on the spot. You had to have your wits about you and think on a slightly different level – almost like improvisation. You'd do a riff and then try to remember it. Paul wanted a different sound – a bigger, Motown-inspired brass sound. That's the way I felt it was going. Bruce and Rick were involved, but Paul was the main person behind everything.

Neil 'Twink' Tinning: The songwriting coming out of Paul at that point in his life was amazing. When you look back, where did he get that from? I know he's always influenced by other bands and still has a huge record collection. They did one song, 'Precious', that was a bit like 'Papa's Got a Brand New Pig Bag'. When I was asked my opinion, which wasn't very often, I used to say, oh, well, that sounds like such and such. When they were recording 'Town Called Malice', the producer, Pete Wilson, was saying 'You can smell the gold on this one. Smell the gold, boys.'

Peter Wilson: To be honest, to me, 'Town Called Malice' didn't stand out as a big, big hit. John Weller was mad about it. 'That's the single! That's the single!' And he was right.

Steve Nichols: Pete Wilson, the engineer, came up with the idea for the melody on keys and played it on the record. I just emulated it on the music video. That was quite strange because Paul said to me, 'I've got this idea. Why don't you put a white glove on?' So, I put on this one white glove and played the melody.

Neil 'Twink' Tinning: The front-of-house sound guy, Mike Brady, wanted to get into video. They were getting charged quite a lot of money for videoing in a recording studio. They did two tracks for the double A-side. I did the video stills. I also got the job to go and get the McDonald's at lunch. Oh, the glamour of it. Paul Weller would only eat chips from McDonald's. He was vegetarian.

Dennis Munday: He put too much pressure on himself with that album. I remember we had an album playback meeting for *The Gift* at George Martin's studios. We sat there and I could see that Paul wasn't 100 per cent happy. His body language, everything. It's an album that didn't really work. When it worked, it worked, but when it didn't, it didn't. It's got some great songs on. You can hear where The Jam are standing still, but Paul's moving away. He wanted to control his career and to control the music he was recording, which he couldn't do in The Jam because it's 'democracy rules'. What's the point of writing songs, recording them, then you think, well, that's not what I want? You can't do that. There are several tracks on the album that just don't work.

Vic Coppersmith-Heaven: Paul probably made the best decision to change me as producer, as I would have waited for more songs from Paul to develop the album, but I have to say that I would have loved to have produced 'Town Called Malice' and got that tight, driving, biting bass and drum drive that worked so well with Bruce and Rick on 'Tube Station', 'David Watts' and 'Start!'

Simon Halfon: I started in the post room at Stiff Records and after a few months they moved me to being a plugger, taking records to radio stations, and I was the junior plugger, so I'd end up with the real crap. You'd see them putting the needle on the thing for a few seconds to then reject it. I hated going up to Radio 1. It got to the point where I'd go back to Stiff and I'd say that no one was in because I didn't have the heart to go through it. Occasionally, I'd hear The Jam were recording, so instead of going to Radio 1, I'd walk a bit further up and pop into AIR Studios to see Paul. I remember coming back to Stiff having to explain how I'd been to Radio 1 but had come back with a white label of 'Town Called Malice'.

Chris Parry: 'Town Called Malice' . . . says a lot about Paul's ability to write a brilliant lyric that really has got a huge amount of social context to it. Still angry, in a sense, and that guitar is pushed very hard, but it's also sort of sweet.

Dean Rudland: I remember buying 'Town Called Malice', playing it non-stop, carrying it around with me everywhere in school and snapping the record, because obviously you shouldn't carry a seven-inch 45 around with you all the time.

Nigel 'Spanner' Sweeney: There was one moment I was very proud of, and Paul was too. Michael Hurle, a very grumpy but great producer at *Top of the Pops*, called me about the double A-side 'Town Called Malice' and 'Precious'. He said, 'Will it go in at number one?' I said, 'It will.' He suggested playing both songs on the programme.

I was good at saying yes, when I knew it would be right for the artist. This was right for the artist, right for The Jam, right for the record company to sell more records, and right for me as a promo man. It was a Yes. But I hadn't asked Paul at this point. There was a slight danger because Paul might have gone, *Nah, I ain't doing that*, but he didn't.

The only other people that had done it before were The Beatles with 'Penny Lane' / 'Strawberry Fields', but those were music videos. Paul was quite proud of this fact. To play two songs in the studio on *Top of the Pops* on the same week was a badge of honour for him. The Jam went on there and performed both songs and it was fucking genius, because when the album came out we were on a roll.

Steve Nichols: We actually only found out on the day that *Top of the Pops* wanted us to do two songs. The programme director turned around and said, 'We want both songs.' It's quite a small room, it's just the way they show you on the camera angles that makes it look bigger. The sound is terrible. It's quite shite.

12 March 1982 – *The Gift* (no. 1) / 11 June 1982 – 'Just Who Is the 5 O'Clock Hero?' (import single, no. 8)

Neil 'Twink' Tinning: By January, Paul came up to me and asked if I wanted to do the photos for the album cover. I said, 'I'd love to.' The picture on the back is from their performance at the Michael Sobell Centre, which I personally hated, but Paul really loved it. It was his album, so fair enough. For the front cover, Paul wanted pictures of the band running on the spot after the song. We did it at the top of AIR Studios, with each member running on the spot for thirty-six frames on motor wind. Bruce didn't like the colour of the pants that he was wearing that day, so we had to have a reshoot with different-coloured trousers.

When I was doing The Jam, I worked in a graphic design studio and their trainees were called Winkles. I don't know why. I was close with Rick Buckler's twin brother Pete, and somehow 'Winkle' turned into 'Twinkle'. When the credit appeared on *The Gift* album cover, it just said, 'Photographed by Twink', which I found devastating. It was an inside joke, and I didn't think anyone would understand who it was. I assume Paul Weller added 'Twink' as the credit.

John Lewis: It's probably my favourite album, partly because it was the gateway to what came next. That post-punk era is one of my favourites, where punk, which is very, very reductive, started to take on lots of other influences. There was this art-school edge, with people blending funk, African music, world music, reggae, and integrating that into a much spikier and more experimental form of music. I suppose nobody would have called The Jam post punk in the way that you would describe Gang of Four or something like that, but they were certainly part of that wave of groups who started to really embrace Black American music, which I found fascinating.

I remember hearing 'Precious' on the radio when that came out and being absolutely astonished. The Jam doing this intelligent embrace of American funk, and they're doing it really, really well. They were able to play with non-rock influences. That's what I really admire about Paul Weller, he was pushing his band in these directions that they probably didn't want to go and getting in these horn players and session musicians, and also probably alienating his audience who just wanted another 'Going Underground'.

Trevor Neal: I thought *The Gift* was a great album. I remember at the time some Jam fans were less enthusiastic about it, but I loved it. All that gradual soul stuff that was coming into it, the brass section, the horns and everything, I always enjoyed that side of that journey.

Graham Coxon: The sound of *The Gift* is just crazy. The production on that is insane. If I have to be quite persuasive to my partner, Rose, and other people about The Jam . . . then I'll play 'Trans-Global Express'. 'Listen to this,' and they're like, 'What the fuck! Jesus, this is fucking amazing.'

John Lewis: He was unafraid to push in interesting directions that amused him. I really admire that, and I suppose that's what I like about that album. I interviewed Julian Cope, and he had this slightly paranoid belief that The Jam started using a horn section because they'd seen the success of Teardrop Explodes using one on 'Reward'. I asked Paul about this, and he said, 'With respect to dear old Julian Cope, I think I'd heard of a fucking trumpet before The Teardrop Explodes existed'.

Peter Wilson: You're supposed to be producing good-quality stuff, but you get squeezed between tours. High pressure. So that was the last album, and I think Paul was feeling that then. There were some frictions, which you get in any band, but I suppose in retrospect, Paul had the whip hand. He was the songwriter, so if he said this is it, this is the end, there's nothing others could do about it except try and persuade him. But I think he made his mind up by the end of the album.

Paul Weller: I like that record. Maybe not everything on it, but most of it. Some great tunes, so it wasn't like we were going downhill or anything like that. Quite the opposite. There were some great songs on it. 'Precious' and 'Malice', obviously, but also 'Carnation', 'Five O'Clock Hero'. So, we probably had another good album left in us, if not more. But, during '82, after making *The Gift*, I think possibly after the album came out, I just had a change of heart.

Mark Cooper: I reviewed *The Gift* for *Record Mirror* and did an interview around that time as well . . . it was called 'One man and his misery. Paul Weller of The Jam' . . . Paul was a hero of mine, but there was a real sense of a man drowning in . . . I won't say depression, but misery, you know, and struggling for the music to mean as much to him. I guess ultimately feeling very frustrated by The Jam's audiences, that he couldn't expand

and change that. People booing the support act or chanting for The Jam the whole way through.

I think he'd started to feel very constrained. I suspect he'd found an earnestness in himself, which I quizzed him and teased him about. To my shame I used the expression 'His heart's as big as a gasworks'. It was slightly taking the piss, because I think Paul was just drowning in his own puritan drive. I think he himself knew he needed a new aesthetic, and he has the courage to do something about it in a way, in a very Neil Young like way, to strike out on his own and a completely new path. You could feel somebody reaching a dead end.

1982 – 'Trans-Global Express' tour

Tim Parsons: Dear God, the number of live shows they did in 1982. You forget. Plus, just how big they were! I do think that John was in a relentless touring mode, either because he knew where Paul's head was at or his inexperience meant that he went where the immediate money was – touring, merchandise – because, even then, I cannot imagine huge sums were coming through the record/publishing system.

Neil 'Twink' Tinning: After I got the album gig, they asked if I fancied doing some photographs for the 'Trans-Global Express' 1982 tour. The first date was in Portsmouth. I did all those venues taking pictures of the performances and got a message back after the gig saying we don't want you to do what other people can do. We're giving you access to the backstage stuff. That's what we want. I was pally with them, I used to point a camera at Paul Weller, he'd always pull this stupid grin. He was really quite accommodating and loved the idea of having a photographer on the road. I was twenty-one, travelling around in a big, fancy, tour bus with a stereo and a television, it was just unreal.

Paul Barry: That tour was brilliant, though it wasn't all good. We got a lot of coins, shoes, and spit. We had to get pretty good at dodging around this big stage. Our drummer, Frank, tilted his cymbals to avoid being hit by the coins. Our roadie, Derek, would collect them at the end of gigs, which usually meant drinks were sorted for the night. We struggled at times with our white-boy soul, blue-eyed soul, whatever you want to call it. That didn't go down well with everyone, but we eventually won over a certain audience. It was a bit hairy for a while. One gig in Leeds had 7,000 people vibrating with hate – something I'd never experienced before in one place. The PA broke down, and John, in his wisdom, said, 'Are you waiting for someone? Well, you can effing wait.' The police wanted to arrest us backstage for inciting a riot.

Den Davis: Paul and I met after a while and I pitched him the idea of recording tapes from the crowd so people could relive the experience of the show – the noise, the singing along, all of it. At first, he wasn't keen. Polydor recorded all the gigs, so he didn't see the need. I explained that bootleggers charged a fiver, but I wanted to do it as a service for just a couple of quid. And thinking about it, he agreed, saying, 'Well, if you can do it for a couple of quid, then do it.' I was always at the front, hiding the tape recorder, getting a great sound.

Kenny Wheeler: I've been told all sorts of things by the Muppets to try and get into gigs. 'Paul's put me on the list and they're not there.' The weirdest thing I've ever heard was from a guy called Crank, who used to follow us. I've thrown Crank out of gigs before. He turned up at the stage door. 'Kenny, Kenny, let me in.' I said, 'Why ain't you got a ticket?' He said, 'I had a ticket, but my nan got buried today and the ticket was in her coat pocket!' 'Come on in.'

Steve Nichols: We were on tour in Europe, and you could sense a divide between what Rick wanted to do, what Bruce wanted to do, and what Paul wanted to do. There were intense things going on behind the scenes. I did hear rumours that Paul wanted to move on . . .

Neil 'Twink' Tinning: I took a picture of Paul and his girlfriend looking out of the window on the tour bus when they'd had an argument. The rest of the guys, you can see in their eyes, *Has he got the bollocks to go to the front of the bus and take a picture?* Weller used to always take the piss out of me. He'd say, 'See if you can go and sell these outside,' and he'd give me his dirty underpants from the gig.

Steve Nichols: The audience in Japan was, how can I put it, very stiff. They were very, very silent. They were told not to clap, not to jump up until each song was finished. During one of the shows, Paul leaped out to the audience and said, 'For God's effing sake. Clap. Jump, do something!' He really wanted them to have a bit more life.

We'd have the setlist, written in English, taped to our monitors. On the final night of the tour, they changed our setlists into Japanese. It was complete wind up. I picked up my trumpet to play, and all my valves were turned the wrong way around. They'd put talcum powder down Keith's saxophone. When we went to play, nothing was coming out. It took us about three songs into the show before they could actually hear us.

During the day, Paul was hinting that he might want a break. The other two were huffing and puffing. You could see on the horizon that something was up.

Paul Weller: I just wanted to move on. I just thought I can't keep doing this. Or at least I wanted to see what else was out there for me. I was only twenty-three or twenty-four, so in one shape or form I'd been with The Jam since I was fourteen. I just thought, all I know is this world that we've created, which is great, but I need to see what else is out there, what else I could be? So it was partly musical, but more personal really.

Neil 'Twink' Tinning: Most successful bands tend to be on the verge of splitting up at any particular time and that's what I thought made the energy of The Jam so relevant because there's only three members. Yeah, they were mates, but they were in a successful band and that keeps you together for quite a long time until someone says I've had enough.

Chris Catchpole: Paul comes off the tour, takes a holiday, with his then-girlfriend, during which he reads *Absolute Beginners* and explored European modernist roots. That is a pivotal moment. There's an idea of a mod being like, having a feather haircut and a parka, and listening to The Who and driving a scooter. That trip was a real eureka moment for him, discovering modernism's deeper meaning – an attitude, the aesthetics and approach that has since defined him as a human being, as an artist, as a person.

Paul Weller: I think it was probably the first fucking holiday I ever had. Because when everyone else had a bit of holiday time, I'd have to be writing songs. So, that was the first holiday abroad, and I read *Absolute Beginners*. That had a profound effect on me in terms of modernism, and the whole cultural thing shifted in me. It scared me the thought of probably doing this for another five, ten years. I just thought I'd be thirty by that time or thirty-five. I don't know if I want to do that. And that was it.

1982 – The split

Nicky Weller: I remember Paul coming to the house in Balmoral Drive to tell my dad that he was splitting The Jam and Dad said, 'Are you mental?'

Ann Weller: I can't repeat what John said . . . I mean, The Jam were at the top of their game.

Nicky Weller: The air was blue. Dad was gutted. He was absolutely devastated. But if Paul's made his mind up that's it. There's no changing his mind on anything. I remember Bruce coming to our house crying.

Ann Weller: It was a big shock to Rick and Bruce, really, wasn't it? It was like the end of your life, really, for them, weren't it? Because Paul was the songwriter. He had this plan to go on . . . He'd just had enough.

Dennis Munday: John and Polydor wanted to keep the split secret from Rick and Bruce. It was silly really. There was this huge tour booked and they were worried that Bruce might not do it. In fact, he did walk out, which is understandable, it was a shock. I was there when he was told, and it was a shock. We went round the pub, I'm feeding him beer and trying to tell him that it's one of those things, there's nothing to be done if that's what Paul wants.

Bruce Foxton: It's all right, I've got my tissues ready. Difficult. Mixed emotions. At the time, I didn't really understand why Paul wanted to leave the band. He leaves the band, and it's finished as far as we were concerned, or so we thought. It was very emotional.

Rick Buckler: I think the point is that we weren't being managed properly. We didn't have anybody to turn around and say,

'We've established ourselves, we can call the shots now about how much workload we take on, where we go and what releases we do.' I think that pressure started to really build, and I think Paul started to feel that more than me and Bruce did, although we all felt it too. I think Paul just reacted to it a lot more badly than myself and Bruce did. Which led to, I suppose you could say, Paul burning out really, but nobody actually said, right, OK, stop. Let's take six months out, let's just take control and get our own career back online.

Paul Weller: I saw something recently, and I'm not saying this in any bad way at all, with Rick saying that he thought that the breakup was more down to John talking me into it. 'Go on your own. Go on your own'. But it wasn't at all, and Rick was saying it's more over money and all that. But I don't remember any of that stuff going on and in fact, when I told me old man, he was just like, 'Are you fucking mad!' So he definitely wouldn't have been for that at all. So, there was no one in my ear saying 'you should go solo' or whatever. Not at all. And everyone thought I was fucking mental for leaving.

Bruce Foxton: It was hard initially. I thought, I can't do this farewell tour. I can't possibly go on, but in the end got talked round. I was sold it on the basis of giving the fans the last opportunity to see the band live. And obviously, financially it helps as well, because I don't know what I'm going to be doing after this tour. So, yeah, it was difficult.

Rick Buckler: I think the only way that Paul could see of getting out was to break the band up. That's the most logical thing in his mind that he felt he could do. And despite everything from us and John and record companies, saying, 'You really should think about this, don't throw the baby out with the bathwater,' it just didn't come up on his radar at all, which was unfortunate.

But on the other hand, there's five years of very intense work and we did a lot, all of us. We all worked really hard and we achieved a great deal, which is great to look back on.

Paul Weller: You can look at it two ways. It's either a very selfish move, because of all these other people that rely on you, or you can look upon it that I've just followed my own instinct, whatever way. Probably a mixture of both. But I thought for my own peace of mind and personal preservation, I really need to move on and try something else, see what else I could do or not do.

Dennis Munday: I wasn't devastated. I remember at the time going down Le Beat Route club with Paul and it was very strange, because I didn't think he'd like that stuff and he was getting into stuff like Spandau Ballet, and he was broadening his horizons, which was an influence. He'd gone from being influenced by The Kinks, The Beatles, The Who and now there was other things coming in. He was listening to a lot of different stuff and he was channelling that through, as any great songwriter does. I'm not saying I expected it, but it wasn't unexpected. You can't go on being the angry young man. I mean, I've tried it long enough, even I had to give it up.

Jim Cook: Dennis must have told me that they were going to split. But it's weird, really, because it was quite seamless in a lot of ways. For all that by then Bruce and Rick were part of the whole thing, nobody ever thought that they would be the ones to go on having careers. The thing was that Paul was by then so much in charge of it and so much calling the shots, that as long as he had plans then we'd be with him.

Peter Wilson: I didn't know about it before the band members were told. That wouldn't have been a nice thing. Fortunately, I was left out of that conversation, and it was just a fait accompli by the time I knew about it, which was fine.

Steve 'Tufty' Carver: My brother Pete was working as John and Paul's driver. He'd pick John up at Balmoral Drive, and then Paul, and would take him to the recording studios. One of them weird things that everyone thinks, *Wow, what a glamorous job*. You take Paul and John Weller to a recording studio. Fair play, you do hear the songs being made, but when you're doing that every day, you're hearing the same song over and over. It's not all glamour. Pete's taking John and Paul home every day. He heard 'knocking it on the head' and all that. Yeah, I was in the know really early. Me and Pete had a couple of dogs. We used to take them for long walks every day. It was just 'No, he's knocking it on the head. He's calling it a day,' which I thought was mental. John said, 'You're off your fucking rocker, mate.'

Gary Crowley: It was kept very close to the immediate band and very close friends like Tufty. I don't remember any heads up. Somebody might have said something just before the music press announced it and, like everybody, I had mixed emotions. They were the biggest band in the country. The only band that I can remember who was alongside them, at the time, as far as popularity was concerned, was probably The Police. In 1982, they were enormous, so it was an incredibly brave decision. I can't think of many bands that have gone out at the top like that, but I think that's why we look back at it with such fondness because it was never soiled in any way. It was so fresh and still so vital.

Martin Hopewell: Shock and horror, really. It was at the peak of The Jam success, and suddenly I found out that this was going to be the last tour we were doing.

Tim Parsons: This is an undisciplined business. You don't put The Jam on your balance sheet because their tours or albums aren't guaranteed. Everybody was employed for Paul. It was the Paul and John show. Nothing wrong with that particularly, but John wasn't looking out specifically for Rick or Bruce, and I don't say that in a bad way, because whatever he was doing for Paul as The Jam was very, very good for Rick and for Bruce because they shared in the benefit of it.

When they announced The Jam split, it did come as a surprise, but it's part of the business we're in. Bands break up. Band members die – these things continue to happen. That is a far more shocking thing to deal with than it is to deal with a band splitting up.

I was really sad for Bruce and Rick because they'd had this phenomenal five, six years, these three boys from Woking with John, going from making a bit of fun to making a significant income and enjoying a good life. I knew that Paul gave The Jam up to do something else, not to quit.

Neil 'Twink' Tinning: Around June, I came back down to the south from Newcastle. They were struggling to record 'Pity Poor Alfie' – I think that had three re-records. Rick pulled me aside and said, 'You can't tell anyone, but the band is going to split.' I was shocked. They put lots of options to Paul, like have a year off, reconsider in a couple of years, but Paul was having none of it. He was set on moving on to do other things. That was the end of it.

Rick Buckler: At that point, everything was going well – selling records, big tours, the shows are great. There just seemed no reason for it at all. Bruce and I noticed later on that the reasons we were given in the summer of '82 were totally different from the reasons that came out in the press in early '83. That made us think, 'Well hang on a minute, why did you really do this?' It just seemed ridiculous.

I thought that Paul would change his mind, because we were having such a great time. It just seemed crazy to us. *What are you going to do?* The Jam was the reason for getting out of bed for ten years, and all of a sudden it was suddenly not there. It's worse than being made redundant. You don't have a purpose in life. You've put your heart and soul into it, and everything – girlfriends, holidays, jobs, whatever – all came second to the band. All of us had that ethic. It was a kick in the teeth, especially because we weren't even consulted about it. It was just, right, that's what's going to happen. You simply have to deal with it and that's that.

John Cohen: I remember Bruce and Rick coming to see me and feeling very hard done by, but I had to tell them that Paul was perfectly entitled to carry on as a Polydor artist. He wasn't doing it as The Jam, he was doing it as himself or under another name. I'm just telling them, sadly, they have no rights. They have no rights to join in the new deal. Paul has made that decision.

Jim Cook: I remember Dennis saying to me, 'Don't worry about it. I've heard the first two singles that Paul's going to put out on his own. They're fantastic. Don't worry about it.' And that's the way it worked.

In those days, you signed a band, you signed them all. If one of them wanted to leave, then you had the chance to go on with them. I can't remember whether we had to do a big renegotiation with Paul, we must have done, but at that point in time, we all knew that we weren't going to sign Bruce as a solo artist and we weren't going to sign Rick. So, it was a question of sorting out Paul, and I don't remember it being a big problem.

We knew in November that we were going to have the last Jam single, and we were going to really push it and go mad with it. Then in February, we'd have the first Paul single. It was seamless, really.

Kenny Wheeler: I knew what was going to happen. Paul just asked me, 'What are you going to do?' I said, 'I'm with you and your dad.' I love John to bits, and Paul was always great – that's where my loyalty lay.

Nicky Weller: I just knew that Paul would go on and do something else because that's how he is. He never looks back. He always looks forward. He was already going in another direction by adding the brass section, which was a big change on everything. He'd already written a few songs that were going to be the next thing. It was just a progression. I think he had enough of The Jam and doing everything.

September–October 1982 – The 'Oh Gawd, Not Another Tour'

Jamie Telford: The Jam were looking for a keyboard player, and Martin Hopewell and Bryan Morrison knew that I played. The Jam's split wasn't mentioned to me at first, but it soon became evident they weren't getting on. I think it was just the fact they'd been together a long time – you can be in the same room as some people too long and all the weaknesses and problems come up and you could see that happening to them.

It wasn't a case of them not being up to scratch musically. Bruce was a strong bass player and part frontman, and Rick was a pretty good drummer. Paul just wanted a new direction and more control.

It was the biggest tour I'd ever done, and still is. There was a lot of strife, but I got on well with Paul – I liked him. He was clever, driven and pretty focused, for somebody that was very young at the time.

Dean Standerwick: I'm fifteen, sat on the organised concert charabanc from Bristol to Shepton Mallet. Beyond excited. The venue was just a glorified cowshed, to be honest. It was really loud, football-terrace-style motion forwards and backwards in the crowd with the heat clouds rising. They opened with 'Strange Town', played 'Butterfly Collector', 'Private Hell' and new songs, 'Running on the Spot', 'Ghosts' with mind-blowing strobe lights.

Jamie Telford: John thought that they were like boxers and would always have towels and drinks after the show ready for them, come off stage, you have a dressing gown ... *Fuck me, where did I see this before? Oh, yeah, boxing ring*. They didn't bother about me and any backing singers.

The Jam were right at the peak of their fame and really they hadn't broken in America, because at the time, I remember Paul saying, 'I fucking hate Americans.' I asked him about Steve Winwood. 'Yeah, I met him. He's the same as all the other Americans' [*laughs*]. Of course, he wasn't American at all.

I remember playing a gig at the Royal Court in Liverpool and the fans were exceedingly intense. A Liverpool fan had earwigged me in the bar and was saying, 'I liked it much better before they got fucking keyboards involved.' Thanks a lot, mate.

The fans would drive them insane. They always called them the 'fucking Muppets'. There was a lot of that slightly chippy banter and the card school and the making money.

There was a gig at Leeds in a bus shed. The whole stage was bouncing up and down. Every time Paul played a chord, he went up in the air and then he came down for the next chord. It was ridiculous. Bizarre. Like you've been dropped into an alien life situation.

Paul got shingles on that tour. I remember backstage at one gig he was getting treated by a doctor that they roped in from somewhere.

Dennis Munday: John had these metal briefcases with all of the tour per diems in it, and it was a lot of money. He said 'Den, look after that for me.' I'm trudging around with it, and I finally got fed up and I said to Mike Bucket, who was the coach driver, 'can we put this in the coach, lock it in the toilet, then lock the bus?' John turned up and said, 'Where's the case?' I said, 'I don't know, I gave it back to you.' He was running round frantically looking for them.

Jim Cook: John absolutely loved cash. That's why he loved the live gigs more, because he could flog the merchandise and then it was in the back pocket. When they were selling out Wembley, they were still doing the cash for the merchandising. They would sit down afterwards and the roadies would come in with all the cash and they would divvy it all up. John loved money, because he'd never had much, you know.

Jamie Telford: The merch was where they made a lot of money. John had this guy, a mate of his from Walthamstow, who sold T-shirts at the gigs. This is before merch became the thing … Sometimes in your life you're not very aware of money. Not switched on to the idea that there's money involved and you're not even sure what to do with the money if you've got it. I was a bit like that and I think probably Paul was too. But the dad was completely switched on to the idea of money. 'Fucking hell. We sold a thousand T-shirts. Fucking great.' Paul's going, 'Yeah. OK, I've got an idea for a song.' I'm thinking, *This is a bit odd, isn't it? Having a brickie in charge of the management.*

He was a character, to say the least. I played cards with him once and started winning, and they didn't like it, so I really had to stop or start losing. It was him and Kenny. I don't know if he was a roadie so much as a tour manager, but he was a big, heavy character. It's a bit like the Led Zeppelin manager that they had, Peter Grant, he was from the same school of *Fuck off, mate, where's me money?*

Ann Weller: It used to be a lot of money going up. John was brilliant, but he didn't cheat. He just watched. He knew the cards. It seems if he was a card cheat, but he wasn't. He was just really good at watching. He knew everybody else's cards . . . We got a photo somewhere. 'This man is dangerous. Do not play cards with him.'

Bruce Foxton: No. I didn't play because I wanted to go home with some money in my back pocket. I think if you ask Kenny Wheeler, he usually goes home with nothing. John's there with this big pot of money on the table in the bus. I didn't risk it.

Tim Parsons: I did manage to get into the card school and escape with my winnings. I bought my first ever SLR camera on the basis of winning £300 in the card school at the end of a tour in Glasgow. I only ever played on the last day of the tour because they didn't expect me to get in on the next day and lose it all.

Nigel 'Spanner' Sweeney: Is Paul still upset with me for hiding in the toilet after I'd won a game of poker with John Weller, him and Kenny Wheeler, on a train, and I hid in the toilet until it got into the station because I'd won 200 quid? They were addicted to it. The money went from Paul to John to John to Kenny, from Kenny to Paul. Suddenly there's this young whipper snapper Spanner coming in there, putting money down that they want. They were very good at the poker, but they used to play blind all the time. How can you put 50 quid on a blind bet? Oh, my good God. So, when I won a hand, I've got in a toilet, and I stayed there until the train rolled into its destination.

Paul Weller: I don't remember that! He was very tight, man. I'll say that about Spanner anyway!

Steve Nichols: We got stuck one night at Glasgow Airport. Paul got the cards out to play with John and Bruce. Then Keith and I joined in. Little did we know that the other three had this little system going. They let us win to start with. So, I was up about £120, and then next thing I know, I'm down £120. I ended up losing quite a bit that night. They were all in on this little scam so let us win a bit first. I was out after that.

6 September 1982 – 'The Bitterest Pill (I Ever Had to Swallow)' (no. 2)

Peter Wilson: With 'The Bitterest Pill' – I think Paul's inspiration was from sixties songs, northern soul and big production ballads. Although there's gritty guitar and beefy drums, it does seem some distance from what The Jam were known for, although I think it's very successful.

Dennis Munday: The fans didn't know about the split when that song came out. It was a strange record for Paul to come up with. Not that you could ever say that Paul would always write a certain kind of song. I've got six or seven copies of that song where they recorded the backing track, and he wasn't completely happy with it even at the end.

Peter Wilson: We recorded at AIR Studios in Oxford Street where we also recorded *The Gift* album. Their Studio 1 had a lovely Bösendorfer grand piano and is a great room for recording a string section. Paul had a good idea what he wanted the strings to do and the style to be captured, so I wrote out a complete arrangement for the strings.

Dennis Munday: They recorded the actual single twice. The first time, I remember, because Pete Wilson did the strings on a Sunday, which really pissed me off because you had to pay all of the string section double bubble. I sat there and thought, *Why can't you do it on a Monday?* Paul came in a couple of days after and wanted to scrap it and start again. I thought he meant scrap the strings, but he meant all of it. He had a cod break in it, as I remember. He took that out and added another verse.

Peter Wilson: Jenny McKeown from the Belle Stars came in on harmony vocals which worked well.

Junior Giscombe: I always liked the energy and the urgency of The Jam, and the lyrical flow, the way Paul constructs the songs . . . 'Bitterest Pill', what he was saying in that song really grabbed me: *Wait a minute, this guy's actually talking to a whole generation here.* It wasn't like he was just a good writer. He was a part of a generation and a movement through that generation at that time that he was talking to them. He was talking to kids his age, slightly older and younger, who could understand where he was coming from, what was going on in London at that time, what was going on his head at that time, what he was seeing. He was like a sponge. Every time you hear Paul, it would be something different, but it would be on point.

Dennis Munday: By the time we did the video, Bruce and Rick knew The Jam were ending, and unfortunately the video took ages. I had to stand in for Bruce. Just dancing with this girl, but you only see the back of my head. A lot of people said that he threw a wobbler. He didn't. I mean, I really was getting frustrated with this director because everything was taking a long time to set up to shoot and he kept disappearing. Now, I don't know what he was doing. I can guess, maybe, I don't know, but he kept coming back eventually.

The second day, I got up early because I had to pick up the girl who was in the video and we got to the embankment at two o'clock in the morning and he'd disappeared again. Finally, I said to the guy setting it up, if he's not back by half past two then I'll direct it. That bit was only ten seconds. It wasn't long. I'm there thinking, I want to go to bed now, I don't care any more. I understood what Bruce was going through. and he was still coming to terms with it . . . If you look at it, it's just me dancing with her. You see her face. Originally you would have seen Bruce's face. But then obviously they can't show my face because everyone would go, *Who the fuck is he?*

30 October 1982 – The Jam split leaked to the press/5 November 1982 – *The Tube* (final live TV performance)

Malcolm Gerrie: I got in touch with Clive Banks and said, 'I need to speak to Paul. We've got this huge new show on Channel 4. It's live, an hour and forty-five minutes, fully networked. I'd love to put The Jam on at some point'. Clive said, 'You'll need to speak to his manager, John. Just to give you the heads up, Malcolm. He's not your normal kind of manager. Firstly, he's Paul's dad, and secondly, he'll call a spade a spade.'

John and I just clicked immediately. In our very first conversation, he said, 'I love Geordies, me! Geordies and cockneys. Two peas in a pod! Tell me about the show, Malcolm.' I explained the show's format – it's live, similar to *Alright Now*, but bigger, with three stages and films from around the country. The band would need to be there for soundcheck most of Thursday. John said, 'Yeah, don't worry about the plumbing.

We'll be there,' and then he said, 'But has Clive given you the heads up?' and I said, 'No.' He said, 'Oh, no, don't worry then. Don't worry.' It was like, *What the fuck?*

Nigel 'Spanner' Sweeney: We looked after lots of very credible artists and ended up doing loads with *The Tube*. We had booked The Who on that first programme . . . All of a sudden, The Who have a biff up. Daltrey and Townshend are not speaking . . . but Clive turned it into a Jam booking. So that was the first programme, and I got to look after it.

Malcolm Gerrie: I spoke to Clive who said, 'How did you get on with John?' I said, 'Great. What a diamond geezer, but he mentioned something at the end' . . . 'Ah, did he? Well, I don't know how you're going to react to this, Malcolm. I hope you're going to think it's a good thing. But I've got to swear you to a confidence. The band are going to split up.'

Immediately I thought, *I'm not going to get them*. I wanted them right at the top of the series, because I knew they'd be dynamite in the studio, Paul just loves playing live and they're a brilliant live band. And he said, 'I've been talking to Paul about this, and what about if we gave you the exclusive news and the last ever performance of the band on show one?' I could have just burst into tears! He said, 'It'll be a story.' I said, 'Yeah, I've already thought about that, but will John and Paul want to do this?' He said, 'Oh yeah. They're really up for it, Malcolm. But we'll have to keep it absolutely top secret and keep the lid on this.'

Nigel 'Spanner' Sweeney: We had a soundcheck on the Thursday, with the show live on the Friday, so we went up the day before and stayed in the five-star Gosforth Park Hotel. We're having dinner, the night before the programme, and there's a little band playing lift music in the lounge where we were eating.

Paul went, 'Should we get up and play?' So, Paul, Bruce and Rick got on the guitars and drums and The Jam was the lounge entertainment. This band are at the top of the tree, having number ones and now they're playing the bloody Gosforth Park Hotel lounge. It was a blast.

Malcolm Gerrie: Pete Townshend said he couldn't perform because The Who are all over the place. He also said, 'If The Jam are on there, I ain't doing anything. I just want to sit and enjoy it. I wouldn't miss it for anything.' Pete didn't know what Paul was going to say, so he was in tears, man. Really upset. 'Fuck. You can't do this.'

It was just sensational. Everybody went berserk. It was in all the red tops, in the broadsheets, big splashes in the music show press. It sadly leaked beforehand, but it was just the biggest gift, as a TV producer, that anybody could possibly give you. Here was one of the biggest bands in the country, giving the exclusive news that they were going to break up, and that was probably going to be their last ever live TV performance, on my show. This is just a gift from the gods. Thank you! And, of course, they delivered just an amazing, amazing performance.

I've seen Paul socially, many, many times since then, and we always have a little laugh about that. You know what Paul's like. He's so droll. He said, 'Yeah, did the trick, mate, didn't it? Did the trick.'

Tim Burgess: I was watching *The Tube*, and they said, 'Paul Weller has got an announcement to make,' and he was talking about the break-up of The Jam as if it was a really positive thing, it's come to an end. This is it. How can you get any better than this? I was quite gutted, but that really made me excited. That was a remarkable thing. Then I read somewhere that his dad was upset about it and I thought that was even better.

Malcolm Gerrie: When Paul split The Jam up and went in a completely different musical trajectory, it was because he wanted to do it. He wasn't thinking that it was going to make him a millionaire or it would get him extra column inches, quite the opposite. The artists who genuinely follow their heart and soul are the ones that you truly believe in. Like John Lennon – he was so loved, and so credible, because he spoke exactly what he felt, and it came from the heart. The same goes for Paul.

Neil 'Twink' Tinning: Somebody leaked it to the press. I don't know who, but somebody did. Everybody was under suspicion, who leaked the news – the fact that the band was splitting? It wasn't me. I've got no reason to do it. I was just getting to a point of working for the biggest band in the land, having exclusive access and Paul wanted to pull the plug.

Noel Gallagher: I will never forget it. I was in the final year of school, and we got off the number 50 bus outside the Mauldeth pub . . . A guy who'd left school the year before, who was our mate, was waiting at the bus stop and he was a little mod dude with the shoes on, parka, shirt and tie . . . The first thing he said was 'The Jam are split up.' And we were like 'What? The Jam are split up?' 'It's just been announced on the radio.'

It was on *Nationwide* that night – the famous interview in Brighton where he said, 'I don't want to go on until I'm twenty-five and mean nothing.' I didn't get a record deal until I was twenty-seven, so that blows that fucking theory out of the water for a start.

Paul Dowling: You could usually sense when a band was in trouble. You'd hear of tantrums on tour or issues with writing and credits. But with The Jam, it happened so fast. I picked up *NME* one day, saw the split on the front page. I was absolutely gutted.

Their music was evolving and they were getting better and better. Paul was maturing in his songwriting, as I was as a teenager, so I was connecting more with his lyrics. They're still with me now. Absolute poetry. The Jam split at their peak. It wasn't just me, every Jam fan and the UK music industry was in shock.

Adrian Thrills: Paul was twenty-four when The Jam split up. I still find it mind boggling that George Harrison was twenty-seven when The Beatles split up. To have completed The Jam by the age of twenty-four is quite astonishing.

Paul Du Noyer: Most of us think of The Jam as being a very short-lived phenomenon but they had a long pre-career. They were kicking around for quite a long time before they became The Jam that we knew of. So, in that sense they probably did have a lifespan roughly equivalent to The Beatles.

Mark Cooper: They were in such a unique position. They were the number one British band and had this heavy responsibility, in a way. The only band who'd really survived the punk period with their integrity and politics intact. But, I think that became a really heavy weight for Paul, it became like a duty and a responsibility, rather than being about the music. I think he felt enclosed by his audience.

Trevor Neal: I could see it coming. I thought there was a hint with *The Gift*. There was a softer side to things and with songs like 'Precious', he was exploring dance music and funkier basslines, so it wasn't a big surprise.

Tim Parsons: Paul went from doing everything he wanted really, really well to being expected to do something he no longer loved, and I don't know what that tipping point moment was – a song, a gig, an argument – but it'd be absolutely fascinating to understand. He's a very brave individual musically, and to sacrifice whatever they were, for a musical ideal that nobody understood, was a very, very brave decision. It must have been something deep. He didn't wake up one day, start cutting his nails thinking, *The Jam, no, thanks.*

Shane Juson: I was coming back on the train ... and saw the news. It just said 'Jam split' and I thought, *Shit.* I went back into the train carriage and all my mates from college were there and they were all taking the piss out of me crying on the train. [*Starts crying*] Sorry. Look what you've done. I'm going to get so much shit for this again.

I remember the last Birmingham gig I went to in December. I was lucky enough to get backstage after the gig. I was sat talking to Paul and said, 'Do you know what you're going to do yet, Paul?' He said, 'I haven't got a clue yet.' As if he was going to give a sixteen-year-old kid a world exclusive about what Paul Weller is going to do after The Jam.

Keiko Egawa: I was actually in Japan at my parents' house and Paul sent me a letter. He didn't talk about the split at the time, but said, 'This is going to be The Jam's last single.' I thought, *What's he talking about?* Then I got myself *NME* and saw the split. I was crying for three days. I felt lost.

Jonathan Ross: I wasn't overly upset. The Jam split felt big, but part of me was pleased because it reminds me of why punk was so attractive – bands had gotten too big and out of touch with their fans. The Jam never lost that connection, but by the time they got so big, they felt like they were living a totally different life and like they'd become one of those bands. It's much more exciting to have a new sound, to restart and start small again. I still love that now.

Steve Hinders: I was in a San Francisco record shop when a girl told me The Jam were breaking up. She said they might still do some shows, but it was over. He'd mentioned that pressure cooker in his recent letters. 'God, I've now got to come up with another batch of songs.' Who knows what was going on in his mind . . . but I think Weller's thinking, *I've got to get out of this. Got to have some freedom here* . . . I was disappointed, but it's a pretty cool, brave move.

Jill Webb: Gutted. I didn't believe it. We went on that final tour, and it was the most amazing gig, but there was this deep feeling of sadness . . . I started a petition for them to reform. That's how serious it was.

Paul Moody: By then, I was part of the mod scene, and nobody really knew where to go. Without The Jam's leadership, everything felt scattered. A whole generation had to figure out a way forward. There's a famous Steve Pyke photo of Paul coming out of a pub in Oxford, surrounded by mods. He's wearing Italian designer clothes, houndstooth coat and loafers, and those young mods are still wearing the parkas. That picture is so telling, it's part admiration, but they can't quite figure out what to do. He's clearly not doing what they thought he was going to do. That's always been Paul's modus operandi, but I think there was a definite sense of loss there.

Neil 'Twink' Tinning: There was a lot of emotional distress. Lots of people went to Paul Weller's mother's house, trying to get her to persuade Paul to reconsider. In hindsight, we're only interested in The Jam because they did split and cemented themselves in history. If they'd been like The Stranglers who went on and on, they wouldn't have the same loyalty and lasting connection fans still have with The Jam today.

Ann Weller: We had fans coming round crying their eyes out. 'You've got to tell him to go back.' For about a month all I did was make tea and hand out tissues.

Steve 'Tufty' Carver: For six years of my life, there was always a single, a video, a gig, an LP, a party, and then someone told me, 'This is all coming to an end.' Someone said to me the other day, 'What do you think Paul would have done if he wasn't Paul Weller?' I went, 'Fuck Paul. What would I have done?'

Paul Du Noyer: Imagine walking away from that band at the absolute peak of their success. The bottle required to make a career decision like that. One of the things I rate him so highly for is he had that bravery that The Beatles had, and Bowie had, and Dylan has had. They will always drop everything that they're known for and their success has been based upon to do something utterly new the next time. It's as if they're willing to risk everything, to alienate all their fans. The Beatles would always get away with it, less so Bowie and Dylan. Paul didn't entirely get away with it all the time. It was very hard to keep up with Paul after The Jam, and with each twist and turn that he took creatively, he wasn't going to bring everybody along with him,

Claire Mahoney: I think I heard it on Radio 1 . . . I thought I was having a heart attack. My world just fell apart. Seeing Paul do that fateful interview on Brighton Pier, with his blinking chewing gum. I was so angry at him, and it took a long time. I was one of those bitter Jam fans for a while. I was totally crushed by it because they were the soundtrack to everything. They were the thing that I'd put on in the morning and listen to. They got me through school. I hated school. I was the only mod, and my best friend was the only punk. I just couldn't imagine life without them. It was my first major loss, which sounds ridiculous, but it was, and it was really hard.

David Quantick: I'd loved *All Mod Cons*. I love the singles, but then to me, they started to go a bit gammy. I thought 'Funeral

Pyre' was crap. 'Precious' was just 'Papa's Got a Brand New Pig Bag'. That last album, *The Gift*, was dreadful, apart from 'Carnation', which was a really nice song, and I was just bored of The Jam, and they were very popular and had started to get this lad following, like Oasis did later. It was this interesting contrast, as the fans got more and more 'meat and potatoes', Paul Weller was getting more and more unusual. I enjoyed 'Beat Surrender', even though it's not really a song, it's a collection of catchphrases, and I went, 'Oh, great, The Jam split up. That's a nice record. Never mind.'

Barry Cain: When The Jam split up, we did the final interview in *Flexipop* ... Bruce didn't turn up for that interview. He was very upset about the whole affair. He really was choked. Well, they all were. But it was all down to Paul. It was his decision.

Rick Buckler: Bruce wanted to leave the band there and then when Paul told us in the summer. He said, 'Well, bollocks to this. I'm off,' and we had to persuade him not to do that, because Paul could always change his mind and just stick with it.

Barry Cain: Paul and Rick have spoken once since they split up. The last time Paul spoke to Rick, he didn't have any kids, and now Paul's got eight. Imagine that was the last time you spoke to someone. Paul's actual words to me were, 'I think in all the time we were in The Jam, Rick and I probably only had three conversations. We had nothing in common.' Funny, innit?

Rat Scabies said to me, 'The Jam were from Woking and my parents were from Redhill, so I knew that Surrey belt mentality. The Jam were the classic example of a band formed by geography. I have come up with a theory over the years. A bloke who starts out in suburbia and wants to form a band is very limited to the amount of musicians he can unearth, so if he finds someone who's the same kind of age, who's got a bass or a drum kit, then they'll be in the band automatically, even if they don't really cover the same musical ground. That's why a band like The Jam split up. But it's also what makes a band great because they don't have that personal empathy. If you all agree, then it sucks. Rick Buckler wasn't as interested in being a mod as Weller, but he went along with it because it was more interesting than being a minicab driver.'

24 November 1982 – 'Beat Surrender' (The Jam's final single, no. 1)

Gary Crowley: Just after I first started on the radio, the announcement was made that The Jam was splitting up. So, the only single of theirs that I got to play on the radio when it came out was 'Beat Surrender'. Paul has got a memory like a fricking elephant. What was I thinking? The very first publicity photo that I had done, I had this little bow tie on, *circa* Haircut 100, ABC and he always brings that up, 'Have you still got that little bow tie?'

Adrian Thrills: I made 'Beat Surrender' the single of the week in *NME*. Around that time Paul had sensed that as a vehicle for his songwriting, he'd taken The Jam as far as he could and you could see it in that single.

Bruce Foxton: That song is a real 'tie your fingers up in knots' bassline. I don't know why I came up with it in the first place, but that was over forty years ago. I was a bit more nimble then.

Tracie Young: I responded to an advert in *Smash Hits*. 'Paul Weller's Respond label are looking for a female singer to record.' I got an audition. Pete Wilson played some tunes at the piano. Me and Paul had a little sing-song. From there it was, 'OK, here's a song, "The House that Jack Built". Go away and learn it. I'll be in touch.' I don't think there was ever a moment where he said, 'Yes, you're the one.' It was just a rolling conversation that never ended.

I heard that The Jam had split, and called Paul to ask how it affected me. He said it didn't but he wanted to send me another song called 'Solid Bond in Your Heart'. I had to learn some harmonies and come up with ideas for backing vocals.

Later, he told me that it would be the band's last single, and he wanted me on it to create a bit of a buzz. People would wonder who I was when they saw me with them on *Top of the Pops*.

About a week before, the rug was pulled out from under me when he changed the song to 'Beat Surrender'. It wasn't as instant, but I do love it. He said, 'You haven't got to do all of the backing vocals. We've got some other girls doing some parts.' The next thing I knew, I'm at AIR Studios. It was very weird. That was the first time that I met Bruce and Rick, recording the song.

Dennis Munday: When you get to the end, it was the choice of 'Beat Surrender' or 'Solid Bond'. The tour was called 'Solid Bond' so that was going to be the final single and then Paul came in and said, 'No, I don't want to do that, I want to save it, we'll go with "Beat Surrender".'

Jamie Telford: Paul said to me about two days before, 'Do you want to play on this next single?' He never played the fucking thing to me. I got hauled into AIR Studios and, luckily, I'm quite good at improvising. I think I did quite well on it because the most prominent thing on the bloody record is the piano. It was very much a kind of, I'm just going to see if you're any good. They liked it straight away. I remember the engineer enthusing madly about it.

Shaun Hand: I love 'Shopping' [B-side]. Given that the school of thought is that Bruce and Rick couldn't play a certain style, they played that jazzy style really well. They possibly could have gone off into another direction if they had wanted to. They weren't dunderheaded rock musicians. They were good and adaptable.

Steve Cradock: My sister did a cassette of the tune, 'Bitterest Pill', which she taped off the telly and then I saw 'Beat Surrender' on *Top of the Pops*. So, it was the last two singles that I was aware of The Jam. I was twelve years old, so I think at that age you're ready to be told or ready to be informed. You're at that time when you're looking for that life change, I just thought they looked incredible, and I thought the song was really powerful.

Peter Gordon: So much changed so quickly ... Suddenly, the 'Trans-Global Express' Tour came around, the split was announced in October 1982. Paul got his hair cut really short, did the tour, 'Bitterest Pill' came out, and 'Beat Surrender', that wonderful EP that also had things like 'Stoned Out of My Mind' on it and 'Move on Up' . . . and it was done. It was gone.

Tracie Young: That was indeed me, performing with The Jam on *Top of the Pops*. Me and Paul next to each other at the back. Rick was at the front, it's on TV all the time . . . We did a little rehearsal where Paul said, 'I want us to do a little dance, so we just need to be in sync with each other' – that was his favourite thing. 'You do it, and I'll follow.' Didn't take me long to suss that that wasn't true.

He was very interested in styling me at that time, and wanted me to wear ski pants, which was something I already wore anyway, and then he got it in his head that there was a lot of skiwear around at that time. We went to C&A, me and Paul, and bought this ski jumper. It had goggles and he wanted me to wear those as well. I didn't know him very well and I was only seventeen, but I was quite gobby, 'Are you taking the piss?' He went, 'People will be talking about it, it'd be great, really funny.' I said, 'Do you really want them to be asking, who's the nutty bird with ski goggles on? Is that really the buzz that you want to create?' 'It'll be hilarious.' Can you imagine watching *Top of the Pops,* people are all emotional. The Jam has split up. Here they are, number one. And in the background, there's this big distraction. This lunatic young girl wearing ski goggles.

He's a bit of a wind-up merchant. That was one of the first things that I discovered about him. He's a lot funnier and more mischievous than you might think. I had been very much under the impression that he was a bit of a misery guts before that, very serious and actually quite a negative, down person, who was angry about everything. He's really not. He's very funny.

November–December 1982 – The farewell 'Beat Surrender '82' tour

Rick Buckler: We had all put so much work into The Jam – myself, Bruce and Paul and all the people around us, the record company, the agents, and to build something like that and have that success is rare. A lot of bands don't survive very long, so to cut it short early seemed strange.

We still had commitments to tour, which, to my memory, were really good shows. We still put plenty into it. We didn't get down in the mouth. I always thought that Paul would change his mind.

Jamie Telford: They should have continued. It was stupidity, really, and not just from the financial point of view; they should have been big worldwide because they were great . . . I mean, if Bruce and him could have reconciled the differences, they would have gone a long way, but I think there might have been a bit of jealousy with Bruce. It's difficult for me to say anything, but I think Bruce, at the time, wasn't as concentrated on the art as Paul was, and I can see why that would be a problem, because, despite everything about Paul, he's actually a really brilliant songwriter and he knocks it out the park every time.

Claire Mahoney: I was fourteen years old. 29 November 1982, Port Talbot, Afan Lido. My first Jam gig. I had to get on a coach, me in my little boating blazer with my ski pants on and my really hideous white towelling socks. I don't know why we thought that was a good mod look.

It's the greatest experience of my young life. That just set the tone for everything. The whole energy of that night was really hot, sweaty and smelly. The crowd seemed to move as one. I was off my feet for most of the night, bouncing up and down. I've seen a lot of live bands, and I've never experienced anything like that since.

Bruce Foxton: We did five nights at Wembley, and we kept to what we liked doing every night. Going out, meeting the fans, signing whatever they had to be signed. But, of course, every punter was like, 'Why are you splitting up?' I don't know, maybe I sounded a bit stupid, saying . . . time and time again, 'We don't know' or 'Yes, it is a shame' and 'We're gutted, but we've got to respect Paul's decision.'

Neil 'Twink' Tinning: I had moved back up north because I didn't really like living in London, particularly with the band splitting up. There was no reason to be there then. I was unemployed and Rick said come down for the five Wembley gigs. It was a very bittersweet experience because the band were playing so well, but this thing was hanging over them. I did the Wembley shows and the final gig in Brighton. There was a guy called Dave Liddle, who was Paul's guitar roadie, and because it was the end of the tour, the rest of the crew decided that he should be strung up from his feet upside down on one of the lighting trusses.

John Wilson: I saw them three nights running at Wembley Arena. Those gigs were quite joyous. They had always come on at nine o'clock at gigs before but, on the first night, they came on early; I remember being caught out in the bar. Wembley Arena is a great big, cavernous place, and suddenly I'm hearing this very echoey, big booming sound of 'Start!' 'What? They're on!' It was half past eight, and, of course, they were going to do a longer two-hour show.

There was something wrong as soon as I walked in, they sounded different. I realised that Bruce wasn't playing a Fender Precision. It was an Aria Pro or something, which hasn't got that depth, that grunt or that distinctive thing which drove so much of The Jam. It was, in a weird way, more of a refined sound. They had the horns and backing singers, and, now in retrospect, you can see it was moving towards where Paul was then headed to. It was the musical stepping stone.

The shows felt like celebrations of everything. They'd go from doing quite complex versions of 'In the Crowd' to a really punky version of 'In the City', but they were fast and lean and it felt really good.

Johnny Chandler: Wembley was bittersweet – emotional and a little odd. When you've followed a band for five or six years, it's a big chunk of your life. The thought of not heading to the record shop for the new single or album, so I'm going to miss that. But, there was also optimism, that something else was coming.

Wembley can be an unforgiving place but it was brilliant. They weren't treading water – they were on fire, playing older tracks they hadn't touched in a while, alongside their newer material.

Jamie Telford: It was the third night at Wembley, and Paul suddenly dropped this one on me. 'Right, "That's Entertainment". Come on then,' and I'm going, *Fuck, I don't know this one. I have not got a clue*. I had a go and, of course, got the chords completely wrong. I'm playing the organ while turning it down, meanwhile, the guy in the mixing desk is turning it up as loud as possible because I've disappeared. I'm going, *Jesus, what's happening?* So, the next time I come in, I put it back up to the normal level, play the wrong chords – wrrrrr!

Weller turns around and goes, 'Fuck me, Hamish. What's going on?' in his cockney idiom. He was quite right – I didn't have a clue.

Virginia Turbett: That was a sad thing. There were people from all over the world there. Paul was in a really good mood at Wembley. There was a big backstage. Bruce and Rick were 'What the fuck are we going to do? This is terrible,' and I've never seen Paul so happy as he was at Wembley. He was charming, he was lovely, he was bright, he was really, really smiling. He was obviously very excited about what he was going to do next, whereas the atmosphere elsewhere in the room wasn't quite so positive. But Brighton was great. I went down, didn't have a ticket, but like lots of other people just knocked on the back door and John let us in, and then pushed my way right down the front and stood at the front singing every single song.

Steve Trigg: I went into a complete and utter sulk. The last night at Wembley, when they took the final bow and went off, I stood there and just stared into space. It was like somebody had died.

I flatly refused to have anything to do with what came next out of complete bloody-mindedness. I didn't like it, I wasn't going to listen to it, I wasn't going to entertain it. For a while, I wasn't having any of it from Paul at all.

Derek D'Souza: Sometimes a great camera shot can be a really blurry shot. It hasn't got to be technically good. There was one shot I got at the penultimate gig in Guildford. Paul jumping in the air and he's just a blur. He had the black Fred Perry on, playing a black Rickenbacker with the 'W' sticker on the red background, under the strings. And red and black bowling shoes on. It was a lot of red and black in this picture and he's in front of Rick, and it's just a blur. The last song was 'The Gift'. The last shot I took was Bruce jumping in the air, the very last shot, as Rick's about to hit the cymbals.

Alan McGee: I mean, could you imagine being in The Jam, for fuck's sake man. How wild would that have been. I'm friends with Bruce and I get him to tell me shit at times. That was like a fucking youth club band that went and ended up at Wembley.

Gary Crowley: Thinking back to those final gigs in Guildford and Brighton, it was very, very blokey. I remember coming away from Brighton and feeling a little bit depressed about it because it was like a football crowd. I was one of that dance troupe who went on. Honestly, I saw my life flash before my eyes that evening.

Jamie Telford: It felt a bit weird and anticlimactic, as if we should all be going on to something else. I felt, I'm just getting going here. I'm enjoying this. Touring, the high life, living in nice hotels and having good fun. This could go on for a long time, as far as I'm concerned.

Martin Hopewell: The tour ended at Brighton Conference Centre, which was a weird night . . . The whole venue was surrounded by fans at every entrance. I was at the back, being polite, trying to work out how to get in, when suddenly this great big hand seemed to reach over the heads of all the people and picked me up, felt like by the neck and lifted me over it all. It was Joe Awome. Picked me up, pulled me off the ground and carried me into the venue like I weighed nothing.

What stuck with me most happened after the gig. The band come off stage, we were on this staircase. The expressions on their faces said it all: *That's it, then.* It was sad, because we had no idea what was going to happen next. As far as we were concerned, that was the end of it.

To be honest, nobody, myself included, knew whether it would be Paul or Rick or Bruce who managed to do anything else afterwards.

Rick Buckler: On the last show, I remember thinking, well, that's the last time we'll ever play that song and that thought came every single time we finished a song. I'd look down and see what was next and think this is the last time doing this. It's difficult to explain the emotion of it, but I could see it in the faces of the people in the front row. I knew that they probably felt the same way that I did. I bet you Bruce and Paul felt the same way as well. These people had supported us, come to the shows and bought the records, and they're into the same thing that we were; we belong to them and vice versa. It was a bit of a teary experience. I mean it was a bit strange, to come to a stop like that, for no justifiable reason. None of us had died. It wasn't like we weren't selling records or selling tours or all the usual things that you see when bands come to a demise. It's quite novel in that respect.

Steve 'Tufty' Carver: I said to my brother a few years ago, 'Did we go to Brighton?' and he went, 'Course we did.' I think I've erased it from my memory because it was so traumatic. All I can remember is a girl at a petrol station saying to me, 'Well, what are you going to do now, Tufty?' and I went, 'I haven't got a fucking clue.'

Keiko Egawa: My friend, Akiko, lived in Japan at the time but wanted to go to the final tour with me. 'All of them?' 'Yeah. Why not?' Oh my God, it was so sad. After the final gig, me and Akiko were crying and Kenny Wheeler came over to us and said, 'Come on, no time to cry. Come and have a drink with us.' Which we did and I was still crying. In the bar, John came up to me, said, 'What are you crying for? Paul's got new material, why don't you look forward to that?'

Kenny Wheeler: At the last gig in Brighton, John was great. We knew touts were going to be about, and he got a load of tickets left over and handed them out. I had to drag him in the door because he nearly got lynched. People were going mad to get these tickets.

Andy Rosen: I got a phone call from Paul or John: 'You've done so many pictures; why don't you come down and cover the band?' It was at the Brighton Convention Centre. I thought long and hard. I'm only going to get one chance to get an iconic shot.

It was quite mad. I got behind the drum kit and waited there the whole time. If I was out front, I would find it difficult, even with my passes, to get back at the right moment. I waited until they'd finished and got the last ever shot. Them saying goodbye.

Look at Paul and how he stands back. I wouldn't call him grumpy. He was always the thinker. The lead singer of a top band with a lot of responsibilities. It can't be easy to keep churning out the songs that he was.

Look at this shot. No one's ever seen this before. John Weller. Anyone that was around The Jam, that was close to them from the beginning to the end, he was always there. He was obviously not the typical music business manager, but he was a great guy. Very normal, very approachable.

I remember being in the office talking to him and he'd stand up. He'd pull his trousers down to tuck his shirt in. He'd be standing there in his underpants. Do you remember that people used to do that, when they would tuck their shirt in like your father did? He was this father figure that was always there. This shot was the last shot. Everyone's gone. Paul's probably out partying or whatever, and I just thought, *This is him, the father, realising that it's the end of an incredible era* . . . To me, this shot is really powerful. A lot of people don't know who he is or whatever, but I think anybody around The Jam would find that interesting.

That's their last ever journey from the stage.

The Jam – legacy

Steve Brookes: Paul is immensely gifted, don't get me wrong. He has a gift, and he's very aware of that, but he does work very hard with that gift, which is the two sides of the coin.

Chris Parry: Looking back on it all, there was a certain longevity about The Jam. It's a very visceral, stripped-down, high-energy sound that excites young people. If you listen to all their recordings, there are some reflective songs. 'English Rose', 'That's Entertainment', which is fantastic. Paul's a very clever writer and a good lyricist as well. There are those things. A lot of the things are touching on British subjects. 'Eton Rifles' and all that stuff and 'Going Underground'. Very English-city stuff. You can relate a lot to them. There's the cultural relationship that they had with their audience, which put them in a very strong position, in much the same way Springsteen related to that Rust Belt group of rockers in America.

Nicky Weller: We've been lucky that he's always moved forward, so he's always gone with the flow and changed direction every time. I don't know how he does that, but it's really clever.

Ann Weller: I mean, his fans have been so loyal, haven't they? He's very lucky to have that.

Kenny Wheeler: I don't think Paul gets the credit that he should do. He is one of the best songwriters in this country, and one of the most consistent. I don't know anybody who writes songs like him with his back catalogue and what he writes.

Whenever The Jam got knocked in any of the music papers, they would get slaughtered the next week with mail. The kids would be on to them. I don't think you see that now. The whole business has changed. But the only thing that hasn't changed is going out and playing live.

Bruce Foxton: It was good to go out at the top, album wise and single wise. I can appreciate that. I felt that we had more to offer still. Don't ask me what because I don't know, but I didn't think we'd run our course. But Paul wanted to change direction, something that I wouldn't have been happy with anyway. It's a shame. There you are.

Rick Buckler: It's a difficult one when you were standing in the middle of it, because our perspective on it was different from everybody else's. I like the idea that we did move on, we didn't become boring, and the songs have lasted the test of time. They still stand up, lyrically as well as musically. So that's always a nice thing to look back on.

We were so wrapped up in the creative side of it and the performance side of it that we didn't look back too much at that time. We were all constantly looking forward and how can we reinvent ourselves all the time.

Paul has obviously taken his own decisions and that's fine. I think everybody's happy with that, really. So yeah, I just . . . Ask him if he wants to come down the pub sometime? He doesn't drink any more though, does he? I'll buy him an orange juice.

Noel Gallagher: Every band has a magic five-year period. The Jam had it, The Smiths had it, Stone Roses had it, The Mondays had it. All the bands that have shaped the fabric of the musical furniture. All the cool bands, they have that five-year thing. Now, whether you go on after that is irrelevant. You have this period where you make your mark. It's no coincidence the Pistols split up after a few years. The story of The Jam is perfect. They started as, you know, youth . . . I won't say angry, but, punk, new wave, and developed all the way through to 'Beat Surrender' at an extraordinary fucking pace. Then they were gone . . . The way it should be.

I still listen to them today. In fact, I'm doing a tune right now for what will be my next record, which is very reminiscent of The Jam. He's gonna be fucking livid when he hears it!

Steve 'Tufty' Carver: I always say if I changed Paul Weller to Elton John, you won't believe this. I'll say it again, mate. I will never, ever say it was nothing. Really. It was everything. Life-changing moments. Paul Weller moved into a house in the bottom of my garden. What are the actual chances? I'll say it again, guess who lives in the bottom of my garden now? Elton John. Fuck off. Did he? No one believes this shit. No one believes this shit. But it happened. It actually happened. People say to me now, they should make a film of it. No one will believe it. Talk to Nicky about taking lions for walks around Woking. No one will believe this shit. But it happened, man.

Paul Weller: It was exciting. I think there was a point I really enjoyed it up until about 1980. Before it went really, really big, I liked it when it was a little bit more contained. But then I'm always like that. I don't like anything when it gets too mass and too big . . . I was never really interested in being the biggest band in the world. I just wanted us to make it in terms of being recognised, our music being recognised and being allowed to make records and continue. It wasn't world domination. Not for me anyway. I wasn't interested.

1983 – The Style Council starts

Mick Talbot: Late summer 1982, Paul called me and said, 'I want to meet you up the West End. I've got something in mind . . . a project.' I didn't think it was a long-running permanent thing or a band thing, but he said, 'Look, keep it under your hat. I'm knocking The Jam on the head, and I've got this idea for a sort of band but more of a floating line up,' and that was the germ of the idea that became The Style Council.

In that meeting, I thought, *He's got so many ideas, and he seems so focused and driven, if it's half as good as he thinks it's going to be, it'll be a laugh anyway. It'll be great.* It just seemed there was so much liberation and, also, he had a profile and a reputation, but he didn't rest on his laurels. I didn't have anything to lose. He had plenty to lose. I'm so fortunate that he was brave enough to take it somewhere completely different.

I think it's probably late August when I first was aware that they were going to split up. He did say there aren't that many people that knew at that moment, and news didn't travel quite as fast as it might do now with the internet. So, if the cat did get out of the bag, there are only so many people that the finger could be pointed at. I was thinking, well, better keep this under my hat, proper. It was quite funny from my end of things, trying to keep a lid on that, because it sounded exciting, and I probably wanted to tell the world. But I couldn't tell anyone. I swore my mum and dad to secrecy, and I think they're the only people I told.

Peter Anderson: I was asked by *NME* to photograph Paul Weller for a special Christmas colour edition. This wasn't a story where it was following a new release or news of what the band were up to because The Jam was gone. I think it was also a slight manipulation by the PR officer at Polydor, who suggested maybe it would be good for me to meet Paul. A test to see if I could make photographs when The Style Council thing happened.

Paul had this fun idea that we should parody *The Avengers*, John Steed. He'd already got the props. We improvised all these photographs of him with his partner Gill ambushing round corners. I'd sneak around making quick snaps as they dashed from one imaginary scenario to another. We did photographs at the Barbara Hepworth statue by Victoria as Paul posed with a bowler hat and an umbrella. We then went back to an office and got the bottle of champagne thrown down on the table, with the hat and bunches of flowers. It was all a big spoof, fun thing. Paul's idea. I didn't think to ask why.

Mick Talbot: Paul and I come from a similar background. We're both suburban from the south side of London. I suppose I'm a bit closer to the middle than he was, but we both had to pay our dues at working men's clubs, where you're fourth on the bill, underneath the raffle, the bingo, the pie man, the fish man. You've got to announce all these people because you got a microphone. But it holds you in good stead when you're having a rough night in Dundee and the crowd turns nasty. If you've experienced Colliers Wood Constitutional Club or Fry's Metal Foundry Club, it tests your mettle.

I seemed to have gone through a band a year that had been signed to labels and dropped. The Merton Parkas and my next band, The Bureau, had come to an end. I was at a point where I thought, *Maybe the game's up and it's time to go out into the real world.* I was twenty-three and on the dole. Then in the nick of time, Paul came in and I didn't have to leave the circus.

Simon Halfon: I did a book of poetry for *Riot Stories* for Paul and the news came out that he was splitting The Jam. I knew about it but it was hush-hush, because the story hadn't broken yet. I got a call from Paul. 'Do you want to come down to the studio tomorrow?' This was in Marble Arch. It wasn't called Solid Bond Studios yet, but it was his studio. I went down the next morning, he said, 'Do you want a cup of coffee?' He's boiling the kettle. 'Listen, I'm starting this new band. Do you want to do the sleeve covers? . . . I'm calling it The Style Council. What do you think?' And so I jumped at it. From that moment onwards, he really made you feel part of the team. It was an exciting time because I would have been twenty-two.

Dennis Munday: We signed Paul Weller. He finished up The Jam contract. They had to give us a live album, *Dig the New Breed*, and what they termed as the 'Greatest Hits', which I compiled, called *Snap!* Then Paul signed as a solo artist. Mick was in the group, but Paul signed as a solo act.

Jim Cook: Funnily enough, Dennis knew Mick. He came from the same area in south London and knew him from his jazz stuff. We signed Paul and whoever he wanted, which is what happened with Sting when he went out on his own. No one cared who he played with any more. It was Sting. The actual name of The Style Council, some people thought it was a bit arty-farty and we're going to have a problem with this, and I suppose we did in a way. It was difficult to push around the world. It was difficult because in some ways they all knew who The Jam were and knew Paul as the main person of The Jam, but the way he went about the visuals of The Style Council was a bit different, wasn't it? It was all a bit cooler.

Mick Talbot: The Style Council was just a convenient title. We liked band names like Chairman of the Board. It alluded to that, but it wasn't specifically about clothes. I like to think it's about all things. It was us trying not to stick to one genre of music in some ways, if you look at it from a musical perspective. We liked our clothes, but . . . we weren't really dressing like a lot of the bands in the eighties. There was bit of a homogenised look, and a lot of the bands had stylists. We never had stylists. We just knew what we liked.

Steve Rapport: Between The Jam and The Style Council was the ICA gig. Somehow, I got to photograph that. Paul played with Everything But the Girl, and I love Tracey Thorn and Ben Watt – I worked with them quite a bit back in the day. It turns out that he just cold-called them and they were still at university. I think they were recording, and he heard their stuff and asked to come and do a gig with him. I love those pictures. He looks so sharp in those pictures, and it really is transitional because you know what he looks like in The Jam, you don't know what's next. I just remember how vibrant it was and how free he seemed. He clearly didn't know what to do next, but he thought, let's have a bit of fun in the meantime. That's the link between the two eras.

Kenny Wheeler: Nobody knew what was going to happen. We'd done the last Jam dates, and in the January Style Council started in the studio. He never had a band, just him and Mick. Started off in the studio, then doing some interviews.

Chris Difford: I don't really write lyrics for a lot of people outside of Squeeze, but when I get asked, I think about it, and I generally accept if I think it's going to be a very good project. In fact, Paul did ask me to write for him once. Would have been after The Jam, but before The Style Council. I went to Solid Bond Studios, and we sat around for a couple of hours, and he played me a couple of demos and songs that he had on the boil. Then he gave me a cassette of maybe six songs and said, 'If you come up with anything, let me know.' He was very open about it. I did come up with some ideas and sent them to him, but we didn't really expand upon it. I think I was a little bit too floral for him at the time.

Peter Anderson: An entourage of us then went to France for some photographs that we made up as we went along. I hadn't heard any of the music at that point. It was end of January. We're somewhere near Boulogne. Winter. Cold, grey and miserable and the day didn't last very long. The idea was to be doing something different. To not be in London. It was to be European. No distractions. Just to go and make photographs. Quite a few people went. There was Paul and Mick, Simon the designer, Paul's girlfriend and a few people from the record company.

I loved the idea of capturing a moment of people so while we did definite photo sessions for marketing, I also took imagery of Paul and Mick at pinball machines and in a café along with photographs of French locals at the bar. I would get Paul to lean in with a cup of coffee talking to the guys behind the bar with a French newspaper or sitting in the corner of the café.

Adrian Thrills: Paul and I had kept in touch. I went down to Solid Bond. I didn't have quite the same connection that we did in The Jam era. They made some great music and you could see his songwriting developed and the range of influences, some serious, some not so serious. The French, Italian shtick and the Gauloises and cappuccinos and stuff like that, was all a bit of fun, really, but underneath it there was still the songwriting, which is what you always come back to with Paul. He is one of the great British songwriters and the body of work he's produced over, getting on for fifty years now, is pretty breathtaking.

Simon Halfon: Our days would revolve around us meeting at a coffee shop called the St George's, which was just outside Polydor on the corner of Hannibal Square and St George's Street. We'd go and have a cappuccino in the morning. Paul would rock up with his *Paris Match* rolled up in his coat pocket and his Gitanes, because everything was about being European, and we'd just sit there, chew the fat, we'd go into Polydor and have a giggle with someone in there or annoy someone. It became our little routine for what seemed a very, very long time. It was just good fun.

Nicky Weller: Dad and Paul bought the studio and office from Polydor and called it Solid Bond. Just opposite Bond Street tube station. That's where the old Polydor used to be. To have that studio at the end of Marble Arch was pretty convenient for them.

Simon Halfon: It was a bit like a clubhouse, really. If you were in town, you popped in. You didn't have to wait to be invited. They were always there, doing something, because they owned the studio.

Mick Talbot: If we weren't on tour, we'd go there Monday to Friday. Start in the morning and often not go home at normal time, because if you're on the cusp of something that's really creative, you just go right through until you've got it. We were there all the time. It was a lovely work environment because of

John Weller's influence over everything. I'd been in three signed bands by the time I got together with Paul, so I was used to a lot of music business clichés and things. But this was really refreshing because it was like a family business and you wouldn't have known there was a studio the other side of the wall from the offices, you wouldn't have guessed it, other than the gold discs on the wall. John could have been running a building company or something and it would have been the same atmosphere. The fact that the meter was off because Paul owned Solid Bond was always a big help, and it stopped the red-light fever when you're recording. Otherwise, you're aware time is money and we must get this in the first take, whereas you want a chance to really pursue these things. Paul is a person who really sparks best when it's spontaneous.

Nicky Weller: I started off as the receptionist when I was about twenty. Paul's girlfriend, Gill, was the office manager and then later, when they split up, I jumped in and became the office manager. We used to have loads of different bands recording. People used to come in and do jingles. David Essex walked in one day. Oh my God, my idol has just walked in to record something in our studio.

It was a proper nine-to-five job. Even Paul's structure of recording in the studio was nine to five, with a stop for lunch. I used to call them school dinners. We had a menu up and you could have your one veggie on your dinner for the day. Paul and Mick would come down from the studio, have lunch in the kitchen then go back to work. It was quite a structured day like that.

Ann Weller: All the people that were Jam fans were gutted, weren't they? And I think people didn't think The Style Council were going to take off. It was totally opposite from The Jam. You couldn't have two more different groups.

11 March 1983 – 'Speak Like a Child' (no. 4)

Paul Weller: I just wanted to make singles for a bit. I didn't want the pressure of making an album. Single was always my favourite format. So, I guess that there was a kind of plan for it. One was just no set lineup, and we'd always try different styles of music. No one single would be the same as the next one. I had the MD of Polydor come down in '83 almost like, 'Can you make an album this year?' I think they must have not done very well that year. Almost begging. 'Please'. It's like, *no, I'm not doing that, I don't want to do one. I'm not ready yet.* So, it didn't go down well with a lot of people. Not only some ex-Jam fans but also a lot of people in the industry and around us. They all thought it was a weird move.

Gary Crowley: The early eighties was a very, very exciting time. When you think about punk, it was about going to gigs, and fast forward to the eighties and the dancefloor became very, very important. It wasn't so much about going to gigs, it was records, and could you dance to it? The Style Council, like a lot of those great post-punk pop-funk bands, were very much a part of that. The thing that really came across right at the beginning was that with this band, it was going to be about the songs and bringing in who was going to be right for that specific song.

Mick Talbot: Pretension is never far away from the surface with The Style Council, but it's part and parcel of our humour. I used to liken each song to being like a screenplay and you're casting for it. On some tracks, I'm not on it and Paul's not on it, but we're directing things and we're using the best people to get the job done and trying to put the song above anyone's personal ego, because we've both been in bands where, I don't know, the harmonica player just always says the harmonica needs to be twice as loud whenever you're mixing, and you just think, *Hang on, just ease up a bit, mate.* I likened it to someone like Orson Welles, who had the Mercury Players, and you see a lot of his classic films, the same half-dozen people turn up but then there's new people as well.

John Lewis: It's a really interesting point. You look at other bands like Big Audio Dynamite, Fun Boy Three. Big stars, big singers from bands of that era who split up and then try and go through their next phase. Style Council are influential in that form. Second-wave bands coming off those big punk-era bands, The Specials, The Clash, etc. You could see that Paul provided a template for Terry Hall and Mick Jones and suchlike.

Mick Talbot: Dennis Munday helped to steer us towards quite a lot of people that we didn't know. That also comes from Paul. When I first worked with him, he's very trusting. If he thinks you can do something, he's got a lot of enthusiasm about it and he trusts you to do it. We were fortunate that, more times than not, it worked. For instance, we only worked with Zeke Manyika for a couple of days in that first session but three of the first four singles came out of that. Those early Style Council sessions were great.

Zeke Manyika: When Orange Juice got signed to Polydor, Paul and I started bumping into each other at the offices. Then he heard my drumming and really liked that, so he asked me to play on the very first Style Council single, which was a serious honour.

I think he had a rough idea what he wanted to do towards the end of The Jam. The whole burden of being a spokesman for the youth was too much for him really. He loves music so much and he's so versatile. He listens to all sorts and The

Jam was a bit of a straitjacket towards the end. He couldn't really express himself in other ways because he's a damn good soul singer. I think he was quite ready because when we went in the studio, he knew exactly what he wanted to do. It was very quick. He wasn't precious about anything. You could sense that there was a lot of relief in him. It was time to have some fun.

Peter Wilson: I was really enthusiastic about that song early on. We'd done the demo, and I thought this was a good song. It came out really well. Zeke was great playing drums.

Zeke Manyika: Paul knew, lyrically and melodically and stylistically, what he wanted to do. He always does. There was a lot of air you could breathe creatively. So that was quite interesting. The songs – 'Speak Like a Child', 'Party Chambers' and 'Solid Bond in Your Heart' – had formed already, and we just elaborated on that.

Kenny Wheeler: It has got special memories for me from when we done the video. It was the first one, and it was so different from The Jam stuff. That was the bus in the Malvern Hills . . . it was a Tim Pope thing.

Nicky Weller: I'm in the 'Speak Like a Child' video. I've got a blonde wig on and a pink poncho. It was hilarious. Paul and Mick's ideas of fun. We were dressed as hippies, and everyone thought we were on rag week, and they were throwing things at us on this big double-decker bus. It was freezing up there. Three days we were up there filming that. I'd love to see the outtakes because we did some crazy things. We actually took a double bed out of one of the bedrooms and took it out on the snow and all got on it; Tracie Young and all of us used it as a sleigh down the side of the hill. The hotel were going mental at us, but none of that made the cut somehow.

Tim Pope: It was January. It was very cold. It was shiitake time, if you know what I mean, and I just remember being on the top of that bus and nearly killing you lot.

Mick Talbot: There was a man at the back of the bus who was in charge of telling us when to duck because there were quite low trees. It nearly took my head off and I went, 'Where's the geezer telling us to duck?' and he'd been hit by the tree and was on the floor.

Tracie Young: That was my first ever experience of making a music video. It was so cold. It just wasn't fun, but there was fun within it. I was still getting to know Paul and his sense of humour around that time.

Claire Mahoney: When I first saw that open-top bus, I was not happy. It was such a shock seeing Paul without a guitar, for a start. It looked like he didn't know what to do with himself. He looked really uncomfortable. He always came across as really shy. Whenever he was interviewed, you'd be cringing thinking, *This is the coolest man in the world, why does he seem uncomfortable?* There he was on this bus wearing a mac and he just looks uncomfortable with all the people doing their dancing. It's just awful. I was like, *Why is the man from The Merton Parkas with Paul Weller?* And to this day, I do not like that single, it makes me feel a bit queasy because it reminds me of that time.

Jonathan Ross: When Paul started The Style Council, I initially, like most people, mocked it because suddenly they were wearing this Italian elegant clothing. But that was mainly because we'd come from that punk background where you mocked everything. You had to pretend everything was shit, unless the *NME* had told you it was OK. So I was into that sort of idiocy, but I love The Style Council. I think I prefer The Style Council to The Jam.

Dean Rudland: 'Speak Like a Child' sums up the excitement I felt around the launch of The Style Council, and the feeling that if you weren't quite old enough to be into The Jam properly, it could be your thing. I always loved the cussedness, the determination not to do what you should do, that The Style Council represented, and everything about it . . . Not doing an album, doing all those different versions of the songs, it's just an extreme level of Modernism, if you ask me.

Mick Talbot: I think we were fortunate that Simon Halfon understood what we were doing and Peter Anderson, the photographer, we used on a lot of the earlier stuff, and we liked quite a lot of sleeve notes – that may have been on the back of the Blue Note influence. We quite liked humorous sleeve notes. Hence the Cappuccino Kid. Some of the language was influenced by Colin McInnes, but also a little bit by early Rolling Stones albums . . . The Cappuccino Kid was an amalgam of many things, and I don't say that me and Paul sat by the typewriter, but we had an influence and so did Simon Halfon, but largely the person who was left to do it was Paolo Hewitt, who was a journalist and a friend of the band.

Simon Halfon: Some of those sleeves you look back on and you think, *Oh, Jesus*, and then other ones you think, *Oh, actually still looks pretty good.* I was young when I started and I had no training, so some things that I did when I was twenty-one, twenty-two, it's just like, *Oh my God, what was I thinking?* We were learning and discovering stuff as we went through it, so there was no reference points other than physically seeing those references. There was no books to flick through, so it was a journey of discovery for us all.

Peter Anderson: 'Speak Like a Child' single cover was very intentional. It was going to be a low-key single. I would meet up with Paul and we'd talk about it. I also worked closely with Simon, and I would give him all these photographs to take and then he had to try and work out how he would use them. I think that he found it quite difficult, the idea it was just going to be a non-image for The Style Council when there was all these photographs. So they decided to put one on the back of the sleeve, which is quite good. That was one photograph which I really liked and for me it was something different. The whole idea of the long lens and making Paul walk down the street makes it difficult because it's movement and focus and dark ... I think it stands up as a slightly fashion-type photograph.

Nigel 'Spanner' Sweeney: Yes. I don't know how it happened, but together with Clive and Crowley, I just fell into the job with plugging The Style Council.

Simon Halfon: I went down to Paul with a typeface book, and he said, 'I really like that one. Let's just do the sleeve black and make the wording orange.' 'Oh, OK.' That was done. That's where that 'Keep on Burning' logo was first introduced. Like a northern soul reference, I guess. It wasn't like it was given a huge amount of thought. It was a huge amount of enthusiasm, but not a huge amount of thought. The picture on the back was fantastic. I would have used that picture on the front if it was down to me. It's such a great evocative picture. Peter Anderson did a fantastic job as being our go-to guy for those early singles. Lovely guy as well. It wasn't *Sgt Pepper* that sleeve, but I guess if you look back now, maybe the thinking was, *Right, this is a new artist. It's a new venture, so it's like a clean slate.* It's not saying anything in many ways.

Tracie Young: The first tour I did was a promotional tour for 'Speak Like a Child'. TV shows and bits and pieces with Paul and Mick and me. Paul had all these pinstripe suits made for us. Paul and Mick's were trouser suits, double-breasted, black . . . Mine was a skirt. The only time I ever wore it outside of that tour was on *Top of the Pops* for 'The House That Jack Built'. We went to Europe and did all this TV, including . . . that one with the hotel room, where we're all singing a cappella. Paul and Nicky's mum was in it. I think completely by accident Ann walked in with a tray of tea, bless her. We had such a laugh, honestly.

Ann Weller: Like Julie Walters as Mrs Overall, 'Would you like a nice cup of my acorn coffee?'

Dennis Munday: I remember when I started, I said I'd worked with all these jazz guys, and Paul just said, 'That's a load of fucking crap.' Which was very typical of the youth. Even when I was listening to jazz, a lot of my mates weren't interested. We used to go up west on Saturday night, past Ronnie Scott's, and I'd say, 'Come on, let's go.' 'No, we're going to the Flamingo and the Whiskey. We don't want to listen to that. You go on your own.'

Jill Furmanovsky: Nick Logan commissioned me to photograph Paul for *The Face*. That was really the first time I got to really chat to Paul and work with him. I wish I'd been a better photographer then. I must admit that I was winging it when I started in the studio as well. I hadn't been trained.

It wasn't like he came with an entourage of hair, make-up and stylists. He was just wearing his normal clothes, but they were all immaculate – I don't know who was ironing his shirts – and everything was on a hanger nicely . . . He was so neat and tidy, and he had a beautiful physique as well. He took his shirt off at one point and he had a beautiful chest. He was just a lovely looking guy.

Also, one thing about him, that was there from the first moment I had met him as a punk, was that he was serious. He wasn't mucking about. He was a man absolutely driven and I think it's the same to this day. It's like he was born to do it and that is quite rare in my experience. It wasn't that he wasn't funny or amusing or all the rest, but something must have driven that kid and, by the time he came to my studio, he was in his mid-twenties, and he was on his way to fuck knows where but he was going, he was there. He had his suits and his clothes and he knew what he was doing.

His relationship with Mick, who I think came to that shoot as well, was also quite funny. It was like almost Mick was Mr Ordinary in a strange kind of way. He didn't look like a rock person and so they were a funny couple, those two. Obviously great mates.

5 May 1983 – David 'Kid' Jenson Radio 1 session

Mick Talbot: We worked with drummer Zeke Manyika on the first recording session . . . but he was an important part of Orange Juice and he didn't want to leave them, so we knew we had to look around for someone else.

Dennis Munday: Paul phoned me up when they had to finish recording for the first album. 'I haven't got time. Can you find me a young drummer that can play everything?' I put the phone down and thought, *Fucking hell!* I'm not a great lover of wanting to listen to fifty, sixty drummers. Polydor had a soul band who had been auditioning drummers and I said, 'Look, I'm looking for a young drummer who must be able to play jazz.' He gave me two names. The first one I phoned up, I can't remember his name, but he didn't come across. And then I phoned Steve up. He's a southeast London boy like me . . . I went to the same school as him. He told me that Bill Bruford gave him lessons. Bruford only gave lessons to people that he wanted to give lessons to. He had to be good, so I set up the audition and that was it.

Kenny Wheeler: We'd already got a drummer from Brockwell Park. When Steve turned up, I said to him, 'We've got a drummer.' He said, 'I spent me last £1.80 getting over here, can I go and see Paul?' So, I give him a tenner, and he went in. When I walked in there, he's on the kit playing. I thought, *Fucking hell!* I think he was sixteen. He's on the kit playing and Paul said, 'What you doing Thursday?' He then came down and did a Kid Jensen radio session, that's how it started . . . No one was specifically in the band. Paul would pull different people in. He knew who he'd want and then we built up that way. He'd talk to someone, then have ideas, and that was it.

Nigel 'Spanner' Sweeney: I booked a Kid Jensen session in Maida Vale studios. Bands and artists were always up for it because it was good PR. We were at Nomis rehearsal studios, and they'd got a drummer that Kenny had sorted. Then this other young chap turned up called Steve White. He came in and did what I would have done, which is he pushed himself. I heard him say to Paul, 'Listen, I've got my sticks, can I play something to you?' Paul: 'Very well.' Took that on board and fell for a young kid that's saying, 'Can I just show you?'

Dennis Munday: He was seventeen, I think. His mum rang me back to check that it was legit. 'I hope you're not fucking about!' The funny thing is that after I got to know him, I met his uncle and his dad. I used to go around his house, and they started talking about his dad's brother, Maurice White, and I said I knew a Maurice White as Mojo. They said, 'Yeah, Mojo.' He used to DJ at Charlton Football Club, and when we were mods, we used to knock about together with him.

Mick Talbot: Steve was an unusual drummer. Very versatile. He had played with a lot of older people and did a dance band thing, which harked back to a lot of techniques that a lot of people his age would have dismissed and thought that's hackneyed or old hat. But he had a broad spectrum, so we were fortunate. That was something to build on. When I first met Steve, I was in the Bureau, and we were at the Albany Theatre in Deptford, south London. Him and his mate, Gary Wallace, who did do a bit of percussion work with us, were little drum spivs. They had a secret source of drumsticks and every band that turned up to load in, they'd just go like Flash Harry in *St Trinian's*. Open up their coat, going, 'Want to buy some cheap drumsticks?' That was him when he was about sixteen. We were doing a CND thing at Brixton, which is the first full lineup live gig we did. We had to scramble that band together because we'd done one benefit with tapes in Liverpool about five days before and we really needed a band. We'd had a long day when we saw Steve and we'd seen a lot of people. I'm not sure anyone was particularly right, but someone was right enough for Brixton, and it may have been testing our patience, but Steve's exuberance and endurance, he's pleading to say, 'Listen, just give me a listen, because I've come here,' and it's fair enough. He spoke up for himself and he let his drums do the talking.

He did that Kid Jensen radio session with just about twelve hours' notice, really. We just went in, and Paul had only just written 'Paris Match', so it was pretty new to me, let alone Steve. We said, 'We've got to check the mics and run through some things. We'll just play you this one,' and that's probably the strongest song of the session. Steve's just playing it blind, and he just did a good job. Those songs were just sketches and I barely knew them any better than Steve and he'd never heard them. At the time, you didn't think about the magnitude of how many millions that show reached. You just thought, this is the new song and we're eager to play it and however it comes out, that's how we're going to do it. Steve showed nerves of steel and just got on with it and did his thing and we liked what we heard and so we knew there was a future there.

7 May 1983 – Youth CND 'Festival for Peace'

Annajoy David: I organised Brockwell Park and Paul headlined that. We had John Peel DJ and Madness there and about 300,000 people. I had no idea how many people would turn up or what would happen. I was only seventeen myself, but I just knew that there had to be an alliance with popular culture and young people to represent a different view of Britain that I was clear about from quite a young age. Brockwell Park was a huge success, but I don't think any of us went into it understanding how big it would be.

Tom Sheehan: I didn't go out front because I can't stand crowds. Get a bit claustro in them. So I was just doing a load of photos backstage. Stuff of each of the bands that were on and Style Council went on and all the mad Jam supporters that thought they owned him and the band started pelting him with tufts of grass and earth.

Keiko Egawa: I first saw The Style Council in Brockwell Park . . . From The Jam to Style Council, some fans said they used to hate it, but I loved it straight away. That was a CND March. I used to think about it a lot because, obviously, I'm from Japan. Hiroshima and Nagasaki's problem. So I used to think, *Oh, CND. Yes, definitely*. I couldn't quite understand about miners and so on. But I still went.

Alan McGee: I was there, I was at the first Style Council gig. 'Speak Like a Child'. What a fucking tune, genius tune, man, genius. And then there was 'Money Go Round' after that. I must have been twenty-one or something like that. Just brilliant.

Annajoy David: I don't think anyone can underestimate the importance of the start of that cultural movement. It wasn't just a political movement. Off the back of it, Tony Blair was elected, we were all his children. We brought a different civil and social agenda through that cultural view of what Britain could look like. So, these things are all joined up. Live Aid wouldn't have happened without it. The Nelson Mandela concerts that we did with Jerry Dammers wouldn't have happened without it. The early Glastonburys that I was so proud to be involved with wouldn't have happened without it. People shouldn't underestimate the important and crucial role that Paul Weller played in spurring a whole generation to look at Britain and represent Britain in a very different way, while still being very patriotic and loving very much the country that we are and who we wanted to become. I don't think that people should underestimate the hope and ambition and can-do attitude of young people at that time. I completely reject the idea that it was all doom and gloom. I think it was a very gloomy environment with massive industrial changes and upheavals going on, with a very hopeful can-do generation that was very much culturally represented by Paul.

20 May 1983 – 'Money Go Round' (no. 11)

Dee C. Lee: I was working with Wham! and even though they were high profile, I was still at that time on the circuit as a session vocalist. Like a temp working in different jobs. At the same time, I was working with bands, Animal Nightlife and Jimmy the Hoover. These were all bands that were signed to Innervision, which was the label that Wham! were signed to, and that's how I met them. I remember my mum left a message saying a guy called Paul Weller called, 'He wants to offer you a job.' I called him back and he was talking about having been in one band and starting a new band with a different vibe, with a more soulful vibe, and he was looking for vocalists, would I be interested? So, I was like, yeah, absolutely. And over the phone we made plans for me to come down to meet him at Solid Bond. I turned up and it was a very relaxed, chilled atmosphere. It wasn't your audition in the way that I was used to doing it. After a cup of tea and a little bit of banter, they played me the track they were working on. They said, 'What do you think of this track?' And while I was listening, I was getting the ideas, and Paul was singing ideas of what he thought would be a BV thing. I got in with that. We connected very quickly musically, and I was like, 'Yeah, I totally know what you want. I can totally hear it.' So, we started jamming and I didn't even know the song. But on the day, the vibe that we jammed out, that's what went down on the record for 'Money Go Round' with a bit of polishing up with production. I remember us then going off and getting a pint, or in my case a glass of wine. It was quite fun.

Mick Talbot: 'Money Go Round' wasn't even planned. It was just a jam between takes. We were fortunate that Pete Wilson put the tape on. He had the fortitude to think this sounds quite good, I'll press record. Paul had this great notebook with all these stanzas of things, and he just said, 'I think this might work with that jam, if we edit it up a bit.' So that was very fortunate. Zeke's a tremendously talented person, and he was just very quick, and he had a nice feel.

Zeke Manyika: I loved the idea of being asked to mark the beginning of a new chapter for such an iconic artist, that was really special. Paul's just lovely to be around. There's no weirdness to him. He's a very clean spirit. Everything is straightforward. 'Money Go Round' was really just a jam session. They were checking sound and I could see that there was a lot of activity in the control room, so I just kept playing it. They actually cut it all up together when I wasn't there and made it into 'Money Go Round', which was a lovely surprise.

Peter Wilson: After extensive editing by me, that jam became 'Money Go Round'. *There's a verse that'll do and there's a chorus that'll do, OK, but it's got to come again after the second verse, so I'll copy that over there.* This is all razor blade and magnetic tape. There's no digital editing. This is tape on the floor, keep track of the bits, writing on the back of it with chinagraph and sticky tape to put it back together. It wasn't usually that complicated, but that one was.

Dee C. Lee: Paul was really very much into the collaboration of working with other musicians. With no disrespect to them, The Jam were a pop jammy band, you know, like *rah!* and all that. But I think Paul's musician feelers came in more. Because of the nature of the way that Paul wanted to do it, I think he'd already had enough of the band in that old way. Most musicians just want to do new, get better, experiment, and hopefully while you're doing that, the people listening to what you do will enjoy it too, and go with you, and sometimes they don't . . . you have to be true to yourself. There's no point in trying to follow trends. There's no point in the record company telling you that, oh, somebody's making a record like this, you should do it. But sometimes as musicians, you make music that you enjoy, doesn't necessarily mean that your public are going to enjoy it.

Guy Barker: I can remember the studio. I can remember how it looked. I remember where we set up . . . I can see the office where Paul's dad was, and the guy who was a tour manager, Kenny Wheeler, which was funny, because, of course, there's Kenny Wheeler, the famous jazz trumpet player. I always remember when they said to me, 'Oh, you'll speak to Ken Wheeler.' I went, 'Oh, really? Ken Wheeler. Wow, that's amazing.' And then this guy came in who wasn't the guy, but he was lovely as well.

Paul Barry: Kenny was working in a slightly different capacity then. He was larger than life, as he always has been, and he didn't take no shit. He always raised the mood of the room. Kenny was always a bright spark.

Keiko Egawa: Paul invited me to go to the studio. I took my Japanese friend at the time, Yasko. They were recording 'Money Go Round'. It was the last stage of recording. Paul was doing the vocals and then, after a while, Paul said, 'Will you do me a favour?' I thought he was going to say, *Go home!* but he said, 'will you make us some teas?' I said, 'Yeah, of course.' Then he showed me to the kitchen, and we made five or six, seven teas. Then went back to the studio. I was carrying a big, heavy tray. My friend opened the door for me. Both of us didn't realise there was a red light above the door, and we went in. The crew was, 'Oh, my God. What do you think you're doing?' and shouting. Paul was just laughing, laughing, laughing. 'I'm so sorry.' He said, 'Don't worry about it. We'll just have to do it again.'

Dee C. Lee: We were really getting on because the music's going on. So after all this tea, I've gone to the bathroom . . . and, just saw all these pictures of this band that were called The Jam . . . I really didn't recognise him at the time as the person who I was talking to in the studio. On the way back I said, 'That looks great, who are all these on the wall?' and Paul said, 'Oh, some shit group who recorded here.' And the rest of them all started laughing . . . Didn't think nothing of it.

A few days later I'm walking down the road and another muso friend of mine, he said to me, 'Dee, what are you working on?' I said, 'I've just started working with these people. His name is Paul Weller, he's starting a new band called The Style Council,' and the guy dropped his bass, and went, 'You're working with Paul Weller?' and I was like, 'Yeah. What? Why? What?' He went, 'He was from The Jam, and they were massive.' Then things started clicking. I was going, *Oh, God, the pictures in the hallway* . . . I went back and punched him in the arm.

Bill Wheeler: First actual memories . . . it's a mixture between going to either gigs at the Albert Hall, which are Style Council shows, or it was just going into work with my old man at Solid Bond, up at Marble Arch, and just hanging out with him and John, Tanya, and I used to get on really well with Arthur. If I got bored, Arthur was kicking about in the kitchen or whatever. I still swear down to this day, he used to make the best toast, but I think it was basically, he just put a load of salted butter on it. That's the reason I was a morbidly obese child!

Dee C. Lee: Little Arthur, just looking after us all. Our little tinned soup and our little cheese toasties. Oh, it was wonderful. The very best job I've ever had in my life, and I've had a few, I can tell you. Paul's mum was always on the scene. Paul's sister was always in the studio running things. It was very, very much a family affair. And the fact that, you see, I never saw anything awful because basically Paul . . . surrounded himself with really talented people. So, in the studio and even rehearsals, the vibe was always very complimentary to each other because everybody was at the same level and the vibe-ing as musicians . . . when you vibe and you're making music, you just become family forever.

John just ran it as a business and he knew that, firstly, his son was madly talented, and two, the people working with his son were good people and quite talented too. So he was very no-nonsense . . . Very fair, but no messing about.

Mick Talbot: The only thing that Paul really stipulated in the first year was that he didn't want to do an album too soon. He wanted to do a lot of singles. He was happy to do EPs. We were planning to do EPs in different locations around the world, but we only got as far as one, which was *À Paris*. We got a bit diverted from that . . . Some of the twelves had three tracks on them. The EP had four tracks. If we did a seven and a twelve, we didn't always have the same B-side on. We tried to give something unique to each. The first year's singles weren't part-and-parcel of the first album either. We were trying to give people value for money. I think it reflected our respect for singles. This just comes back to the power of the B-side. Paul and I had many long, probably boring conversations to an outsider about B-sides of things. We talk about classic records, yes, *but do you know the B-side?* Because quite often bands will try things that they might not try.

Peter Anderson: The photo on that sleeve was taken in the grounds of a stately home that was used for a TV programme. The idea was to do something light-hearted and fun. The idea relates back to the John Steed photograph shoot, *The Avengers*. There are other shots where they're sneaking around behind hedges and poking out and chasing each other and running up steps of the grounds of the garden. They're just all fun. The other thing is that to me, it was always quite apparent that in the media, with The Jam, it was a bit po-faced and serious, and Paul was very serious. But it was just brilliant with all these Style Council photographs that it was so much fun and light-hearted and tongue-in-cheek all the time.

July 1983 – Tracie and the Soul Squad

Chris Free: Lucy Barron and I recorded some demos and sent them to Respond. I remember getting the first call from Weller. The phone goes, it's about midnight, and I'm lying on the landing, that's where the phone was, on the ground, and I pick up the phone . . . 'Hello, it's Paul here. I've heard your demos. I'm really excited by them. Do you want to come into Solid Bond?' And I'm going, 'Who's this?' 'Paul Weller . . .' and at first, I thought, 'God, this is a wind up. It's midnight, what's going on?' But it turned out to be real.

We went down to Solid Bond and met Paul. Then the next week, we went in with the song 'Give It Some Emotion', and he said, 'I'd really like to give this to Tracie, what would you think about that?' and we go, 'OK, yeah . . .' And somewhere around there, we must have signed to Respond.

Tracie Young: When I walked in and heard 'Give It Some Emotion', I absolutely hated what he'd done to it. I had no idea when I turned up at the first recording session that he was already going to have spent so much time on the backing track. I thought we'd be starting from scratch, and I was going to have total input. Not to be. I turned up and he'd already laid down most of the backing track with this awful drum machine track that I hated. I had chosen a bunch of demos by Chris Free and Lucy Barron, A-Craze. This one song, it just really spoke to me, and I loved it. The lyrics were weird and dark and sadistic, almost, but the tune was so light and breezy, and the jangly guitar was just lovely . . . Wasn't something that I would ever have imagined myself doing . . . I was somebody who saw myself as a real soul girl. And then to walk into the studio and find that it had been, for want of a better word, butchered. I was really, really upset. Absolutely hated it. I cannot give enough emphasis to the loathing I had for what I heard when he played it to me that morning. That was a bit explosive.

Kevin Miller: I was obviously aware of The Jam situation, their last single, which Tracie sang on and knew who Tracie was when she had the single out, 'House That Jack Built'. She had an assistant called Hilary that worked for the record company, Polydor, at the time. Hilary used to go drinking in my local pub in Enfield in north London. Tracie was in the pub one evening on a Sunday and we just got chatting and she was looking to put a band together, and I said, 'I'd really be interested in being your bass player.' I wasn't doing anything at the time. One thing led to another, and she invited me down to Solid Bond to meet 'The Gaffer' as it were. There was a bass there and Paul said, 'Can you play the bass line to "Give It Some Emotion"?' which she had just released. I'd only heard it on the radio a couple of times, but it wasn't particularly tricky. I played that and he said 'Yeah, fine, you'll do!' I guess I was the founder member of Tracie's band, the Soul Squad.

Steve Sidelnyk: I was part of the Soul Squad. Awesome. I impressed because I had some really cool Adidas trainers that were light blue and bright orange. I was really into running, so I turned up in all this bizarre-looking gear.

John and Ann Weller with baby Paul, born 25 May 1958. *(Weller Family Archive)*

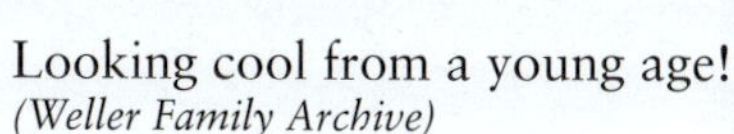

Looking cool from a young age! *(Weller Family Archive)*

Rockstar in waiting. *(Weller Family Archive)*

Early line up of The Jam (Steve Brookes, Rick Buckler, Paul) play Michael's Club in Woking, January 1975. *(Weller Family Archive)*

The Jam as a four piece with Bruce Foxton added to the mix. The Winning Post in Whitton, 16 December 1975. *(Steve Brookes Family Archive)*

The Jam. First shot taken on the 'In the City' shoot in Kensington Church Street, London, 2 March 1977. Complete with Bill's one-take graffiti logo! *(Photographer: Martyn Goddard; Art Director: Bill Smith)*

Breakfast at Frank's Café, 45 Lexington St, Soho, after the 'News of the World' shoot, 9 February 1978. *(Martyn Goddard)*

Jam Pact tour at Sheffield University on 4 May 1979. *(Virginia Turbett/ Getty Images)*

The Rainbow Theatre soundcheck on 15 November 1980. 'John Weller let a few fans in for the soundcheck and I got a few shots ... I was hooked!' *(Derek D'Souza)*

(left) Paul doing his Wendy O. Williams of the Plasmatics impression ... The Jam, Bucket and Spade tour, at Guildford Civic Hall on 8 July 1981. *(Virginia Turbett)*

(above) A game of pool, Paul and Kenny Wheeler, AIR Studios, 24 August 1981. *(Derek D'Souza – who teamed up with Paul against and Kenny and Joe)*

Brixton Fair Deal, 15 March 1982. *(Steve Rapport/Getty Images)*

Paul and John Weller on final night of five at Wembley Arena, 5 December 1982. *(Virginia Turbett)*

The final concert in Brighton, 11 December 1982. *(Mirrorpix/Getty Images)*

Post-The Jam/ pre-The Style Council ... Photoshoot for the *NME* Christmas double special, published 25 December 1982.
(Peter Anderson)

January 1983. Paul, Mick and others head to northern France for a pre-Style Council reveal photoshoot.
(Peter Anderson)

Photoshoot à Paris ... Summer 1983.
(Peter Anderson)

Paul and Mick enjoy a 'Long Hot Summer', August 1983. *((Steve Rapport/ Getty Images)*

(above) Photo taken on the 'Solid Bond in Your Heart' video shoot, 23 September 1983. *(Peter Anderson)*

(right) Mono (Tony Gibney), John, Paul and Kenny … WINNING! *(Jaye Ella-Ruth)*

The Live Aid finale, 13 July 1985. George Michael, Bob Geldof, (a bit of) Paul McCartney and Bono. *(Duncan Raban/ Getty Images)*

The Style Council, video shoot for 'The Lodgers', 1985. *(Steve Rapport/ Getty Images)*

The Red Wedge tour, De Montfort Hall, Leicester, 28 January 1986. Paul with Chas Smash, Billy Bragg, Junior Giscombe, Sarah Jane Morris and Jimmy Somerville. *(Steve Rapport/ Getty Images)*

Kevin Miller: We'd get our brown paper envelope at the end of the week, with 'Kevin' on it. That's when Nicky was basically the office manager, and she ran the show, more or less. It was like going into the office every day in Solid Bond. It was great. Steve Sidelnyk . . . we auditioned him at Clink Studios, it was actually on the site of Clink Prison. He was eighteen, fresh faced, straight down from Bradford, and he was a great guy. He became the drummer and played all the drums on *Far from the Hurting Kind* too.

Steve Sidelnyk: It was exactly like a youth club. Plus, we got paid, which I'd never really got before. We got paid to work all the time, which was amazing, and when you went to Solid Bond, it was like none of us really had anything else apart from that. You'd go in, have a cup of tea and toast with the studio maintenance guy, Arthur, then John would come in. You'd either be rehearsing or playing there a lot. Everybody that came in just mucked in, which is like a youth culture, but a little bit older.

Peter Anderson: There was definitely feelings, which had passed down through Paul and through Simon, the designer, and feelings I would have, and we really liked things like the images on Blue Note Records, where they're just everyday scenes or street scenes. It's like lots of acts just in a street or running. There's a brilliant photograph of Al Green running across a field. So, I made a whole lot of photographs with Tracie in Hyde Park with lots of pigeons round about her, and that was quite fun to do and it's very much a London image . . . Taking that feel of Blue Note Records, which is very American, and making that London like, and then Simon would design the records a bit like Blue Note Records.

Tracie Young: I remember Paul's face looking at me like I was from another planet when I happened to mention that I like the Eagles one day – you had to be careful what you mentioned around Paul. If it wasn't cool, it could make him look at you in a way that questioned your very being. I didn't really care. He could wither you with a kind of a look and a *why?* Don't care. I still like a lot of the stuff the Eagles did.

When I first met Paul, I was seventeen. I had a boyfriend ... and Paul did actually say to me, 'Probably not a good idea to talk about having a boyfriend in the press ... a boyfriend can make you seem unattainable' ... As it happens, we split up soon after so it wasn't an issue. But wow, Mr Weller, that's so non-PC!

5 August 1983 – *À Paris* (EP, no. 3)

Peter Wilson: I think Paul and maybe the rest of The Jam had always had this attitude that singles shouldn't be on the albums. The justification for that view was that normally a record company would put out a single for radio play. Maybe it would climb the charts, and the band would do *Top of the Pops*. Then they put out the album and the public rush out and buy the album. So, they're paying twice for something and it's ripping off the fans.

Mick Talbot: The *À Paris* EP was a pivotal point in our first year where we showed our versatility and four different strands that we would follow. Without that EP, there wouldn't have been *Café Bleu*. I think you can align a lot of our best stuff to one of those four things. There's a jazzy instrumental, or there's a plaintive piano piece, which is almost like soundtracky. There's a torch song that could almost be a jazz standard with the voicings of the chords with 'Paris Match', and there's a song that embraces vintage and contemporary soul as a very strong influence. So those four tunes and that EP, and the week that we spent making it, and the fun and frivolity, and the serious nature of the sounds that went into the grooves . . . I'm a bit biased, but that would be my favourite record.

Peter Anderson: We did a lot of photographs in Paris over a very short time spell. A morning, afternoon and at night. It was up to me try to do things that showed they were different, and they were The Style Council, and they were in Paris. Images of the Eiffel Tower out of focus trying to make something different. That was probably one of my favourite photographs, which were used as one of the large fly posters, which were around at the time. Record companies put out fly posters all the time, and they wouldn't put the names on them because I think they were illegal. There was a really big fly poster, with the Eiffel Tower in the background and Paul's shoe in the foreground and his hand beside his shoe with his bracelet. You knew exactly that was Paul Weller. I loved the ideas of the fashion photographers like Irving Penn or William Klein, who are not traditional fashion photographers, but they made amazing fashion photographs, and that's what inspired me. We did these other sleeves in Paris, the idea of being at the Arc de Triomphe at night and that feel of something European.

Peter Wilson: *Mais oui. Certainement.* Yes, we went to Paris. John Weller said to me, I've got a studio in Paris booked. Can you go and check it out? So I got on the plane . . . There was some Polydor guy the other end who was very kind to me and took the day off to take me around and the studio was crap. It was some demo studio, and I thought, *This is no good, we can't record here. What else is there?* So, he took me to this nice studio called Studio Grande Armée. It's down near the end of Champs-Élysées up past the Arc de Triomphe. Nice location, good studio, and they were available, so we went back there for a week.

We did the 'Long Hot Summer' backing track and 'Paris Match' with a fabulous Parisian accordionist who played in ten minutes, he just knocked off a great track. Then there's some lovely singing by a woman in French: 'The match that started my fire . . . L'allumette qui portait ma flamme.' She was actually American, but she lived in Paris and was a session musician. Then we took the tracks back to London and finished them off.

Chris Free: I get a late-night call from Pete Wilson, 'Chris, come to the studio, get a cab down, come to Marble Arch. You've got to tell Paul he can sing this song, do this vocal.' It was about midnight, getting the cab from Kilburn. There's just the Weller fella and Pete Wilson, and he's doing the vocals to 'Long Hot Summer', and 'Paris Match' . . . not thinking he can sing it, which, I think, is why he had Tracey Thorn come and do it, and Dee C. Lee did a version. This went on for quite a time. I remember him going, 'What do you think should be the single out of the two?' and I was going, '"Paris Match", it's got to be "Paris Match",' and of course it was 'Long Hot Summer'!

Jonathan Ross: 'Long Hot Summer' . . . My favourite period of his career probably, just because I like all the sounds around it. I like the look as well, pictures of him. Although Mick never looked comfortable in that gear, because Mick's got a bit of a kind of a snouty face . . . Paul looked like he could be in a café in Italy, whereas Mick always looked like he'd been dropped in from fucking Deptford . . . I love the way they were produced and the sound with the brass and the jazzy overtones, sometimes the piano up front, and sometimes quite sparse, but in a very tuneful way.

John Harris: I remember asking Paul about recording the *À Paris* EP in Paris, and he said every day him and Mick would get up and go to the same café, have croissants and coffee. It was like being on holiday. Now, that's quite innocuous, but I like that as an image, right? I think they were having such fun and realising all the possibilities around.

Peter Wilson: Those drums were my Oberheim DMX machine. Then add a bit of bongos and shakers and things on, which transforms it. When I hear some of the stuff from the eighties on Radio 2 with brash drum machines, it's a thin, metallic sound to everything, which we didn't get on that, did we?

Ted Kessler: I could not believe that he came back with *À Paris*. It was like 'I'm in Paris. You want to come to Paris? I'm here. I'm here in Paris!' The things that he was romanticising was just what I was starting to do on my own, with girls and stuff. I was going to cafés in the centre of Paris . . .

The early Style Council look was absolutely perfect. It's still my favourite Weller look. I love that white mac and the tailored trousers and the little polo shirts. I absolutely loved the thing he had going on. So I was totally on board. And I really liked the music too.

Dennis Munday: Talking about Paul changing. I remember when we did the Paris photo session for 'Long Hot Summer'. Peter Anderson and myself were late . . . I said, 'Polydor's paying. There's a really good restaurant, good wine' . . . The session was for midnight at the Arc de Triomphe. So, we arrived maybe five minutes late.

Peter Anderson: So, Dennis Munday made me late.

Dennis Munday: Kenny Wheeler went into one. Paul just turned around and said, 'For fuck's sake, Kenny. It's not The Jam. It's not important.' That's exactly . . . when I come back to why I think he had to leave The Jam, to get away from that constant pressure.

Simon Halfon: We just had so much fun with that stuff, and no one had to sign off on it. We just delivered the artwork and if it upset people, then so be it . . . you could never do that now. We would put out a single and the poster, for example, 'Long Hot Summer'. The *À Paris* thing was the two boys at the fountain on the single sleeve, and then the poster was just Paul's shoe with the Eiffel Tower in the background. Now, they'd be saying, 'Well hold on, where's the pack shot? How are people going to know that it's Paul?' but in those days, you got away with experimenting . . . You did what you enjoyed and what you felt was right for the record, and Paul was very up for anything . . . Paul always had the idea for the sleeves before he had recorded anything or written anything sometimes.

We started going to learn Italian together. Me, Paul and Paolo Hewitt. We did a term at Victoria, an adult learning institute. None of us did our homework. It was a nice try, but yeah, we loved all those things.

David Quantick: I absolutely love 'Long Hot Summer' because it achieves its ambition of sounding like the summer. It's languid and hot and sticky . . . It felt like Paul Weller had gone from 'Funeral Pyre' to 'Long Hot Summer' in the space of about an hour.

John Wilson: I love that very stripped-down Parisian version of 'Paris Match', where Paul sings in French . . . it's the sound of freedom and it's the sound of taking chances and there's something very romantic about it. People forget that Paul Weller is an absolute romantic at heart. You hear that in so many of the songs.

Mick Talbot: We packed a lot in, especially in that first year and we didn't really do much in the way of live work. I look back on it now and just think, wow, we were doing so much. We got a lot of shopping in, we did some photos, and occasionally we ate. At the time, it didn't seem unusual, and there was momentum to it and a lot of things were really clicking. We were fortunate as Paul had such a lot of material, and it was just a joy to be able to express yourself on that. That's the beauty of Paul as well, if he thinks he's got the right team around him, he's happy for them to do what they instinctively think. It's not a session where you're in a straitjacket and he wants one thing and only one thing. He doesn't narrow your path down like that. You got the liberation to express exactly what you felt about it and, fortunately, that all gelled.

Gary Crowley: I saw a lot more of Paul round about that time because there was a little gang of us who lived in the centre of town, Me, Paul, Paolo Hewitt and Simon, who was doing the artwork. We would go for drinks and socialise as well. I've got some good memories of going to see things like Brass Construction at the Venue in Victoria.

I was starting to be offered DJ stints and got given Tuesday nights at a club in South Harrow called Bogarts . . . George and Andrew from Wham! lived around the corner, so they would swing by . . . Rocksteady Crew came and did a PA . . . Paul and Mick came and did one, which was unheard of. My memory is that they did 'Long Hot Summer', which was a big record for us at the club. There are photos where they're drunkenly ricocheting around the stage. I always remember Paul saying to me that night, 'This is our audience. This is the audience that we want,' because it was that mix of girls and boys and a young up-for-it crowd.

Mick Talbot: We had a laugh, but we were serious about the music, and tackled some quite serious topics in the lyrical content of some of the songs. They were saying something quite pertinent to the times we were living in. The eighties were a time of quite extreme political change. So, on the one hand, there's that. On the other hand, come on, we all know this is a facade. We just go out and play this little game that we have to. We found that video was a powerful promotional tool for music we believed in, but we thought there's a lot of hanging about, surely we can invent some stupid storyline where we dress up in something even stupider than the last one . . . and do something a bit far-fetched or pretend that we're international milk race champions or we're a couple of Cambridge dons or punting up the Cam and things that were quite extremely away from what we really were.

Ann Weller: That was the music video when they were on the bloody River Cam. I just laughed. But John was old school. He come from a different generation . . .

Tim Pope: I can't remember who started stroking whose ear first.

Mick Talbot: Our heads weren't close enough.

Tim Pope: I was saying, closer, closer, closer.

Mick Talbot: I said to Paul, 'You know what this looks like?' and he went, 'Yeah, I know.' We started stroking each other's ears and you just kept the camera running and there became a myth.

Tim Pope: As they say, a myth is as good as a mile.

Mick Talbot: It wasn't in the script.

Tim Pope: It got to Monday morning and I'd cut the film together and Paul's dad John phoned up. And John was not a person to really cross, was he? I didn't realise he was a boxer, but now,

Jesus Christ, I remember the phone rang and that video had a slight gay connotation, maybe . . . John cuts straight to the chase. 'What have you done to my boy?' I said, 'I've done nothing!'

Steve Rapport: 'Long Hot Summer', that was one of my best days as a photographer. It was just a gorgeous day on the river in Cambridge, and everyone was really chill. Tim Pope was a crazy genius, and Paul was just in that playful mood. Everyone was really chill. A great bunch of blokes, just hanging out on the river and getting to take pictures of Paul Weller – it's a photographer's dream and a kid's dream and a student's dream and a Jam and Style Council fan's dream.

Simon Halfon: Neil Tennant was a journalist at *Smash Hits* and interviewed Paul around the time of 'Long Hot Summer'. I bumped into him recently and he summed it up perfectly. He says before The Style Council, it was just called *frothy coffee*. People didn't know about cappuccinos.

The whole thing from an aesthetic point of view was that we loved the Blue Note thing. The Beatles were still looming large as well as a reference point, but it was all that Ivy League, Brooks Brothers shirts. These are things that you can get easily today, a button-down shirt, a paisley tie or a pair of loafers. Back then we used to do our little jaunt. Cappuccino, Polydor, and then we'd take a wander over to Covent Garden to John Simon's, that was the Ivy League shop. It still exists in Chiltern Street. We used to go just to see what they had. He'd import stuff from the US. There was no Blue Note Records books, you'd have to go to record shops. I was lucky enough to go to New York a lot back then because my brother lived there. I'd come back with carrier bags full of Blue Note records because they were still reasonably priced. That became the blueprint for The Style Council's look.

October 1983 – The Style Council – 5 Nuits En Europe

Martin Hopewell: It was a question of starting all over again with The Style Council. We started the live stuff very cautiously because nobody had any expectations that Paul Weller with The Style Council would be instantly as big as The Jam. We thought the opposite would be true, so we better start carefully, do some trial gigs out of the way, and whatever we did in the UK, would err on the small side and build it up again. The Jam went from The Red Cow to playing the biggest venues that then existed in the UK inside a couple of years, and the same thing happened with The Style Council. It became pretty clear what was going to happen. It was a funny thing, because I think some people might see it as being this massive transition from the style of The Jam, you think about the early days, they were very raw, very punk, lots of gobbing and bouncing up and down and stuff, and then you think of The Style Council with the white trousers and the jumpers over the shoulders and everything else. It wasn't really like that, because at the end of The Jam, brass sections were coming in and stuff like that, and so moving on to The Style Council, it was a shift, but it wasn't as massive a gulf between the two as people would imagine.

Mick Talbot: The further we got down the line in '83, there was a looming thought of, *Let's get out and play some stuff live.* Steve White was appointed to the drum position for the live thing and we really got on well with Dee C. Lee. She came in and clicked really quickly . . . they would be pretty permanent, because it made sense when we were trying to put a live band together. The first time we went out live, it was very interesting because we had as many girls as men in the band, and it was an eight piece. Both the horns were girls. We didn't feel that girls just do backing vocals. So that was different as well. I think Anthony Harty was sixteen when he come on the road with us. He was a good year and a half younger than Steve White . . . and Steve Sidelnyk, who played percussion with us for quite a while, he was only about a year older than Steve. Yeah, it's like Paul said, it was like a youth club, really.

Anthony Harty: I started playing bass when I was fourteen. When I came to leave school, I said to this guy that I wanted to be a professional musician, but I didn't know how to go about it. Half-jokingly, he said, 'Why don't you write to Paul?' I took him at his word. 'Speak Like a Child' had just come out . . . I learned the bassline, played along, stuck that onto a cassette, and sent it off with a letter. Incredibly, I got a reply back in a couple of weeks. Just bonkers, really. Paul said, thanks for getting in touch. They were looking for a bass player and asked what other music I was into. I didn't really know, so asked my mate what Weller was into! Turns out it was Blue Note, John Coltrane, Miles Davis. *Who are these people?*

I then went down to London for auditions. My mum wouldn't let me go down on my own. Dave Liddle, the old stage manager, told me afterwards that there was another guy who thought of exactly the same thing at exactly the same time. They saw more potential in me, so they gave me the gig. They stuck me in a bed and breakfast opposite the studio at Stanhope Place and started rehearsing in September '83.

Hilary Seabrook: There are a number of us who played with The Style Council who weren't members of the band. People who were there for more than just one session or one gig or whatever, and we're quite a little family. When The Jam was happening, I was discovering music and very much going down the jazz route. I was classically trained and when I went sideways, I didn't go to pop, I went to jazz . . . I loved the freedom of it. I did know about The Jam, I just didn't listen to their music, but that bassline on 'Long Hot Summer', that was the musical motif that piqued my interest. Suddenly, I was like, *OK, I don't know what this is, but I really like it.*

Barbara Snow: I studied classically, and I live in a bubble with the things that I'm doing so I was just aware of the things that I was involved in. I was listening to classical music in my teens and pop music as well. I loved Tamla Motown, but I wasn't really aware of Paul Weller at all and it was only when they rang me . . . it was a slightly embarrassing memory. 'Would you like to play with Paul Weller?' and I didn't know who he was.

Hilary Seabrook: I played in the National Youth Jazz Orchestra. Bill Ashton, the director of NYJO, had a phone call from John Weller or Nicky or somebody from the office saying, 'NYJO, you're a breeding ground for young jazz musicians. We're after a sax player. Who can you suggest?' And he suggested me!

Barbara Snow: I don't know how they found me . . . They obviously wanted females . . . I was involved with this horn section called the Kick Horns who played with loads of people like The Who . . . I only worked with Hilary when we did The Style Council.

Hilary Seabrook: The phone call was about three or four in the afternoon, and the audition was at eleven o'clock the following morning. So, I ran down into Hitchin, where I lived, and an amazing music shop called John Myatt Woodwind. John had been my clarinet teacher when I was at school. I said, 'I've been given this audition. I need a tenor sax. Can I have a brand new one out of the box to borrow for twenty-four hours? If I get the gig, I'll buy it with the money I make, and if I don't get the gig, I'll just bring it back.' And he went, 'Yeah, that's fine.'

I spent the whole of that evening practising and trying to work out what Paul might want to hear. Because I was in

NYJO, Paul knew that I was going to be able to play and it was more about whether I could fit in with the band, him and Mick and the other guys at Solid Bond. I've got a vague recollection that they played me a track and asked me to play along with it.

'Get your sax out, play a bit,' and then it was, 'Right, OK, these are the dates' . . . At that stage, it was just to do the European tour.

Anthony Harty: It was surreal because I still had Jam posters on my wall. But there was a separation between the Paul that I worked with and the Paul that was on my wall. It was like two different people. When you're a kid, you never assume that you'll work with these guys or you'll know them or anything like that so I there's that altered thing that your mind does where he's one person, he's another. He was just so on it, and he knew exactly what he wanted to do and was totally in control and well beyond his years really, knocking out songs left, right and centre.

Kenny Wheeler: It was weird because we never done any real live dates at that time. I think the first thing we done live was Brockwell Park, that was a strange one. The first tour was in Europe. Paul wanted to break the stuff in over there, try and do something different. We had too many people with us. Back with The Jam, the most we had, might have been six, including a couple of brass players and little Jamie Telford, keyboard player. All of a sudden The Style Council involved a large number of people, which was crazy sometimes . . . some of the people you wonder what's between their heads. Putting it politely.

Dee C. Lee: I did personal appearance-type of performances touring with Wham! around big cities and nightclubs in the very early days before they blew up. The first tour I ever did was probably with the likes of Animal Nightlife. I found that quite distressing and quite hard work, but it also brings something out of you. You become a professional by doing this ... But when I got on tour with The Style Council, well, it was like going on a big school trip because we were very well looked after ... and sometimes sent to bed at a certain time. Maybe it was just me, because I'd get drunk or something ... And we had Kenny Wheeler, the most infamous tour manager ever, who would scream and shout at us, other than Paul ... So, we'd all gang up on him like naughty school kids. And we'd do silly things like knock at his door at night and run off. Really pathetic ...

Peter Wilson: Mick had the keyboard chops and was a fantastic collaborator. Steve White reminds me of Tony Williams, the jazz drummer, when he first played with Miles Davis ... Dee C. Lee. It was quite an awesome lineup.

Eddie Piller: I've known Dee since we were kids. She has the most beautiful voice. It's a very unusual long vibrato, which is difficult to control in the way that Dee does.

Dee C. Lee: Yeah, apparently it is, that's what I found out. Every time I was doing a vocal training and all the rest of it, they were like, *Oh, you have a very natural, long vibrato*. The hardest thing for me to do is actually hold a note without the vibrato in, but that I also can do. I don't even know what key I sing in. I sing in whatever I feel and whatever I hear.

Hilary Seabrook: She has got something special. The four of them – Paul, Mick, Steve and Dee – worked so well together, and it was obvious that the rest of us were contributing, but we were only contributing, whereas with the four of them, it was during that European tour that they started to kind of go 'OK, we're here now, and this is who we are.'

Dee C. Lee: And there was a lot of freedom too, because I just felt a lot of things. Paul would have the vibe, he'd also start something, and I could pick it up and finish it. He'd have a loop of an idea of a vocal, and I could always hear where he was trying to go. So he just used to let me be free, and it just worked.

Dennis Munday: With The Jam we had what we called the 'A Team', which was me, Bruce and a couple of roadies. That was heavy. You were first at the bar and the last to bed, and The Style Council was pretty much the same. Although Paul went in and out, sometimes he was drinking, sometimes not, but Mick and I were. I remember on one tour, in Scandinavia, we did three days of drinking. In the very early days, the very first unofficial European tour, in Brussels, I didn't actually use the bed in the hotel. I'd come back at five in the morning, showered, changed clothes, got on the bus.

Mick Talbot: There was less resistance in Europe. They seemed more open to us. It's not unusual in some respects because The Jam were the biggest band around, and they were very intrinsically British. Paul realised that he wanted to broaden his outlook and influences, and that may have helped us translate to Europe. It may have helped us translate to women as well, because that was another thing that Paul noticed when we first started playing live. He was astonished at the number of girls or women.

Anthony Harty: There was a real family environment within the band. You had Auntie Hilary, not Hilary the sax player, but one of the girls that used to work in the office. She used to come out on the road, do your ironing, and Uncle Dave used to look after you. It was a good environment to be in. Paul called the tour bus a youth club. It was a good place to be.

Hilary Seabrook: Steve White turned eighteen just before the European tour, which was why he was able to come . . . I think otherwise they would have had to have his mum coming along or something!

Tracie Young: I had just turned eighteen . . . I don't think I'd even reached my twenties throughout most of my time on Respond, it was bizarre. That's what being young's about, but the worst thing is Paul didn't drink in those days. He was in one of his teetotal phases . . . It was hilarious years later when there were stories and things in the paper showing him absolutely bladdered out in the street, caught by the press, and I'm like, no way! If I had two glasses of wine, I got judgemental looks from him.

Hilary Seabrook: October 1983, we started in Zurich, the world premiere of The Style Council live . . . Vaughn Toulouse went on first. He was a DJ. One of the nicest guys you could ever hope to meet. I'm getting chills thinking about him, because he died of AIDS some years later. He got everything warmed up and he was just amazing . . .

The one thing that I remember more than anything, they were shouting out names of songs that I'd never heard of. They were Jam songs, that's what they wanted to hear. It did actually wind Paul up. He really didn't like it.

Barbara Snow: I remember in Zurich people being really hostile in the audience because they were all Jam fans. That sticks in my memory. To just totally change your style and then have that backlash going on is a bit like Miles Davis trying different avenues, different styles, which you've got to say is very admirable.

Hilary Seabrook: Having said that, the audiences loved what we did, because Paul is still Paul. Don't forget. It's still Paul Weller standing up there. It might not be The Jam, but it's still Paul.

Mick Talbot: There was plenty of partying, but it had a different atmosphere to a lot of bands. I'm not saying we were choir boys or anything, but I could liken the typical evening after a gig to like being at a cousin's twenty-first birthday, and it's a really good do. That was the atmosphere. You've got different generations and there's a family vibe and it's a laugh. It's not like the last days of Rome or anything, but it had its moments.

Anthony Harty: We were in Brussels, and I hadn't really drunk before then . . . one of the first hotels we were in, John was going, 'Right, I'm getting them in. Who wants what?' I remember Mick going, 'I'll have a vodka and pineapple,' and I went, 'I'll have one of them.' . . . Didn't know what it was!

Barbara Snow: We even wore ski gear on stage in Zurich. I got this really nice ski jumper and white tracksuit bottoms. It was a little bit hot for stage though.

Hilary Seabrook: It was mad! . . . We thought we were entering into the spirit of where we were. There was a real sense of humour about everything. I mean, we worked our socks off, we did work hard, but there was a sense of humour about everything.

Anthony Harty: Paul didn't want session guys coming in, that just looked like it was another day at the office. He wanted enthusiasm and he wanted people around him who wanted to do it and wanted to prove themselves. Luckily, we gelled.

Barbara Snow: There were a lot of vegetarians in the band. There was an awful lot of chips and beans and eggs because they didn't really cater for those things in those days. I remember Paul always having to have these really dodgy-looking meals.

11 November 1983 – 'A Solid Bond in Your Heart' (no. 11)

Dennis Munday: 'Solid Bond in Your Heart' was going to be the final song from The Jam. Since that time I have fished that out and put it out on various compilations, three different versions. The very first version had a bridge in it. Paul took the bridge out and put it in 'Beat Surrender', so it left 'Solid Bond' as just verse, verse, verse, chorus, and I think to some extent it didn't work. It revs up, starts up and goes and it finishes. That's it. If you listen to it with the original bridge in, it becomes a slightly different song.

Eddie Piller: At this time, I was running the biggest mod club in London and the home counties. We started off with revival music and punk rock, but by 1983, when The Style Council made their first couple of releases, we discovered the concept of suedeheads – reggae, rare soul . . . Gary Crowley phoned me up and said, Paul's looking for some suedeheads for the music video . . . I told him, 'Well, not really, but we could do it!' because we all had windowpane-checked shirts, Fair Isle yoke jumpers, braces and brogues. We got a group together . . .

At the shoot, Tim Pope, the director, pointed at me and said, 'You . . . who's your girlfriend? Get over here.' My girlfriend Michelle . . . she had the perfect look with a three-quarter-length tonic jacket, big Essex-style hair, didn't have a suedehead or a skinhead girl haircut, but she had the right jacket. Tim Pope said, 'Right, Mick Talbot is going to nick your girlfriend. You're going to get angry, push him, and there's going to be a bit of argy-bargy, and then we're going to film him kissing her outside.' I don't know how I feel about this, but OK, we'll give it a go. After three takes of my wooden acting, Tim shouts, 'Cut! Get that fucking idiot in the blue suit out of shot now. Get rid of him. Get him out.' . . . They cut out the whole scene because I wasn't a good enough actor.

Paul 'Smiler' Anderson: Paul's dancing . . . When you watch 'Solid Bond in Your Heart', it looks so piss poor. What are they doing? Wouldn't you shoot that again? It's all misjudged, isn't it?

Eddie Piller: My favourite bit is that opening scene where Paul comes down the hill on the Lambretta, and Mick gets out of the Mark 1 Ford Cortina. They filmed that five or six times and the director kept going, 'No, do it again,' so by the end of it, Paul just got off the bike and it crashed into the side of the car, so we didn't have to do it again.

Peter Anderson: The set was set up as a club with an invited audience and there was dancing and a scenario outside with cars and scooters. My part of it was to make some photographs in between takes. There are some photographs that were made in the car park of Paul and Mick leaning over a car and it's like a spoof of *Minder*. I took a strange panoramic camera with me, which gave a wide-angle panoramic image without distortion. It becomes quite an abstract shot which, as a record sleeve, is quite intriguing. Simon chose to have that image as the sleeve, and you have to open it up to see it fully.

Mick Talbot: The B-side, 'It Just Came to Pieces in My Hands', had barbershop-style harmonies with just me and Paul – two of me and two of Paul. I'm the highest, and the lowest, and he's the two in the middle . . . We used to do it live as an a cappella, with just a bit of organ. I was happiest when we were experimenting with harmonies. I wasn't worried about doing lead vocals. I really enjoyed doing things like 'Long Hot Summer', where I'm the very highest voice with a bit of falsetto.

David F. Ross: 'It Just Came to Pieces in My Hands' captures what I really like about Weller. That song is a real distant cousin of 'To Be Someone' from *All Mod Cons*, and it identifies Weller as someone who's self-aware about the problems of fame and becoming a celebrity and acknowledging that those things can change the kind of person you are. I love the fact that someone quite young, involved in the music industry, has got the self-awareness to understand that it's quite shallow and fake. If you're aware of that and can write articulately about that, then you're likely to be able to avoid that.

18 November 1983 – *The Tube*

Malcolm Gerrie: The thing about artists like Paul is it's all about authenticity and being true to themselves and that is such an infectious thing as an artist. Audiences aren't stupid. You can smell it a mile off if somebody's not authentic and I always think the same thing about TV shows. Nothing gives me greater joy than watching Paul. I saw The Style Council live, and on other TV shows as well, but I've never seen him enjoy himself, or seem to enjoy himself as much as he did. He took some of those songs and added an extra bit of edge to it and I'm sure it was because we had a really lively audience. It was just like a gig. This is a man who's not renowned for smiling a lot! People used to take the piss out of him for not smiling and he's having a ball. I think that's the key, because if you can capture that on TV, then you've got something really special.

Hilary Seabrook: *The Tube* was live. In the early eighties, TV companies, for technical reasons, often wanted everything to be pre-recorded and mimed. Musicians wanted to perform live. As a result, there was a mixture of both approaches, but things were starting to change. *The Tube* being completely live made it so much fun.

Anthony Harty: It was after we'd done the first tour that we did the first *Tube* and then we did the second *Tube* a little later. The first one was rabbit in the headlights and the other one looking like I had been on stage for twenty years. Cocky bloke, chewing gum on stage. It was in at the deep end in the biggest sense of the word. We jumped in with both feet.

Hilary Seabrook: It was a big TV show, but there was also a sense that you were just performing to a room full of people. The fact that there were other people watching on TV . . . If I'd known that forty, however many, years later, people would still be asking me about what I was wearing and whatever, I think I might have given it some more thought than I did.

Simon Napier-Bell: You see him on stage. Look at those performances and his whole body language has changed. He's discovered a different life, a different self . . . I mean, he has a confidence. In The Jam, there was never confidence. He was throwing out a 'fuck-you attitude' and in The Style Council he was the lad.

Billy Bragg: It was late 1983 when Paul and I first connected, somewhere on the South Bank. The Young Trade Unionists had set up a little stage there and I was playing, and he came down . . . He borrowed my guitar to play, which was so cool. I managed to temper my fanboy instincts then, but he must have seen something in that because shortly after I was invited to open on The Style Council's first UK tour in 1984: 'Council Meetings Part 1'.

10 February 1984 – 'My Ever Changing Moods' (no. 5)

Richard Ogden: I arrived as head of international marketing at Polydor Records, working for a gentleman, ex-army officer, called A. J. Tony Morris who was a highly unlikely record company managing director . . . He was quite unusual, but he was a lovely man.

My job was to exploit the artists that we had on the label outside the UK and Style Council was very much an act as far as I was concerned . . . You couldn't really call The Jam an internationally successful band. They'd scratched the surface in America on Polydor . . . Australia, New Zealand, Canada, Holland, Sweden, the usual suspects, heavily influenced by the UK market, but other than that nothing, and in none of those places were they a giant band at all . . .

I remember doing my research and realising, here's a guy who in five years has had eighteen hit singles – some of them number ones. That is phenomenal success. So, I made it my business when The Style Council got going to get to know them, to go places where they went and to get the local affiliates to work on them. I spent a fair amount of time in foreign parts with the Wellers. I had a kind of love–hate relationship with dad. Sometimes he used to really like me and other times he used to complain about me. He actually complained about me to A. J. Morris once, for being too present or something. I remember being in Japan with them and playing poker and winning. And after I got about fifty quid up, I said, 'Well, I'm going to bed.' That went down really badly.

Mick Talbot: We had two different approaches to 'My Ever Changing Moods'. It came out as a full band version before the piano version was around but actually they weren't released as they were recorded. We did the piano and voice version first. Simply me and Paul . . . in a room . . . just doing it. No click track, there's no drummer. There's no one else. I'm doing the music and he's singing. You've got to lock into each other's brains a lot more than you would in a bigger lineup. You've just got to be quite intuitive . . . lot of listening . . . feel each other in a way.

We always fancied to try it as a full band, so we demoed it. Paul played guitar, Pete Wilson played synth bass and Steve was playing drums. I was playing an electric piano sound and the demo was really good. It was feeding off a lot of different influences . . . Curtis Mayfield, Isley Brothers . . . which made it quite a bit different to the piano and voice version that came out on the album.

Hilary Seabrook: I don't think when we recorded 'My Ever Changing Moods' we were sure whether it was going to be a single or not. On the way back from the Europe tour, we were sitting on the bus and Paul just turned around and said, 'We're going to start to do some recording next week, do you want to come in?'

I did a lot of sessions where you didn't have this sense of experimentation and creativity that Paul had with The Style Council. I think it's because it was his own studio, he could do whatever he liked. If it took three days to record a track, it didn't matter so much . . . There was a creativity and a freedom and a sense of working on a project that was interesting.

Mick Talbot: We worked hard on what we did, but I don't think we overdid it. Particularly from a point of view of recording things. If things took too long, I don't think Paul's patience level was there to pursue things endlessly. We'd just move on. but we tried to have fun. I also think if we had the right lineup and people had learned the songs pretty much, then we gave people room to express themselves as well.

Nicky Weller: I was in the video for 'My Ever Changing Moods', dressed up as a wood nymph. My brother wanted us to just wear very scantily clad stuff, and we were like, 'No, it's bloody freezing.' So, we had a bit of an in-between. It was him, me, his girlfriend Gill, and Tim Pope's girlfriend, Neve.

Peter Anderson: Was it Norwich? . . . I think one of the things that was quite inspiring about it was that it was going to be the cycling video. There was a typical stately home with the tree-lined avenue. Looking like the Tour de France going up through the trees in the French countryside. It was freezing cold, and it was wet and windy. Paul and Mick totally professional. I was commissioned to go along and sneak photographs in between the takes. The cycling bit was quite sneakily done because the bikes had the front wheels taken off and the forks were bolted onto a trailer behind the car.

Mick Talbot: A lot of the wacky ideas were certainly Paul's. It's just that I was up for them. It's not me coming in and going, *Hang on, I'm the joker, here we go. Stop me if you've heard this one before*, and all that. A lot of it was coming from him and he's saying, 'Are you up for this? Are you up for that?' 'Yeah OK, let's hire some mad outfits from wherever and let's go for it and do it.'

Nicky Weller: Mick is bloody hilarious. Bloody funny sense of humour. It's who you bounce off innit? . . . If he wasn't in a band, he'd be on stage . . . He says something and it's so droll, and it just cracks you up. You couldn't be miserable around Mick. He really brought out the best in my brother. Paul said it was fun, and you don't really hear that a lot out of my brother's mouth.

Dee C. Lee: *[laughs]* That's so true. I mean that's who I met when I met him. From the minute he left The Jam, he was probably a happier person – I mean, this is what I was told and I was happy that I was a part of that . . . he was happy, everybody else was happy and the making of music, it was a wonderful time and we didn't realise, I didn't actually realise, how lucky we were . . . It was ridiculous how much fun we had.

1984 – *NME*, 'Long Hot Summit'

Paul Du Noyer: Early 1984, Paul decided he would be interviewed by the *NME*, but it was going to be done as a board meeting. He wanted to be interviewed by four different journalists at once, and everybody had to wear a suit, or a shirt and tie, and we'd sit around a boardroom table. I did have a suit somewhere in the back of my wardrobe but then my wife went into labour on the day I was due to go and interview Paul, so I didn't do it. Tony Parsons went along. That was Paul just trying to set the terms of the engagement in his own way for once. He was very, very suspicious back then, and I think he thought it was all a game that was being framed and not in his favour.

Nick Knight: In the 1980s, three magazines stood out for their music imagery: *The Face*, *i-D* and *Blitz* – the latter being the slightly weirder, little brother of the other two. My first connection with Paul came through a photo portrait session for *Blitz*, then I did another for *i-D*, which then led to record covers later on.

Paul was such an interesting man to photograph. The Style Council were appropriately named. He had such a great look to him. There's very seldom when you see somebody that manages to make things look right and you just think, *Christ, that kid or that bloke knows how to dress* . . . Paul managed to take elements of mod, skinhead, but then weave them together in such an interesting and stylish way. That really sets him aside from so many people in this business, who just wholesale re-create a look from another time. I think what Paul did, especially when I was photographing him earlier on, you felt that he was pulling on elements, just like he was sonically, and combining them to make a new sound or a new vision within a certain genre.

Fashion isn't just putting the clothes on, it's how you put them on. What you put together, all the small details, every half-inch change in a shirt stand or a cuff length or all the fractional details . . . It's a real art form. Paul was one of those kids that knew how to dress, and where you are getting an innate sense of style from, God only knows.

March 1984 – 'Council Meetings Part 1' tour

Dee C. Lee: Off the back of Wham! I had been offered a recording deal with CBS . . . I took four songs to them to show them my writing skills. I brought them 'Selena Wow Wow' . . . 'See the Day' and two other songs . . . The label really did not like 'See the Day'. I was gutted that they thought it was a bit meh . . . They took the 'Selena Wow Wow' situation and I went and followed their lead, but I was much more of a singer than that song was about . . . They just locked on the pop thing and saw me as a Black Bananarama and that was it. So, they were pushing me down one channel and I was pushing to go another way, so we hit a proper big stalemate . . . I couldn't get off this deal. I couldn't go and work with anybody else as a solo artist. So, while I was working out what to do, I still needed to make money, and I was working with different bands.

Mick Talbot: There was quite a lot of tension about The Jam splitting. A lot of people were quite disappointed. I can understand that. I'm still getting over Ronnie Wood leaving The Faces, and that was 1975 . . . So, we never did play in the UK until '84, when Jaye Williamson [now Jaye Ella Ruth] was on board . . .

Jaye Ella Ruth: I had joined the Black Theatre Cooperative and ended up meeting Yvonne French, who was a presenter of a TV show called *Switch*. She came to see the play I was in and came up to me after to say, 'I'm really good friends with Dee C. Lee and she's in this band called The Style Council and she's leaving, and Paul's looking for a singer. Do you want to audition?'

Paul called my house a few days later. 'Can I speak to Jaye please? It's Paul Weller.' Now, I know who Paul Weller is. I've read interviews where Dee said she hadn't really heard of The Jam, and I'm like, *What? How can you never have heard of The Jam? They were fricking massive* . . . I loved, loved The Jam, but I was so busy with this little acting role, I hadn't really taken much notice of who or what The Style Council were . . . So, when the phone rang, I thought it was one of the guys from the band taking the mickey out of me because they knew that I'd given a tape to Paul Weller. He's like, 'All right, Jaye? This is Paul,' and I'm like, 'Yeah, right. Who is this? Is it you, Nat? Fuck off.' And it was actually really Paul.

Dee C. Lee: She filled in for me because I think I was still working with Animal Nightlife and . . . had some other recording commitments which clashed with the timing of The Style Council tour, and I couldn't do it. Once you've agreed to work with somebody, it's not cool to just let them down. So Jaye did my bit for me and as soon as I was able to, I came back. I was a bit like, *I wish I could be there, that's my spot, and don't get too popular there, girl, because that's my band,* but no, it was all good. We always had a lot of Honorary Councillors, so that was always wonderful too.

Mick Talbot: When we happened to go live, I was very fortunate that we met Helen Turner, who played second keyboards, because there's a lot of keyboards on most Style Council things and that can essentially mean there's three of me, so I need someone else to be one and a half of me when we go live. She was really good at picking it up quickly and very versatile – a great backing vocalist.

Helen Turner: It was really exciting. An Honorary Councillor? Yes. I got a wage from John [*laughs*]. I went to Dennis Munday's office on Oxford Street ... There was Paul and Mick, and I'd learned 'Mick's Up' and that's what I did. The next thing they said, 'Yep, fine, good.' Then I didn't hear anything for about three months and wondered what the hell was going on and then there it was, straight into rehearsals and off on tour.

Jaye Ella Ruth: Paul said, 'I'll send a tape round. Can you learn these songs?' I can't even tell you the type of butterflies I had. I had two days to learn 'Money Go Round' and two other tracks.

When I auditioned, I was shaking so badly ... We do the first number and Paul was just standing there watching me. Then he went, 'Great, now let's do "Money Go Round".' And I was like, *oh, my God*. This is the one that I really don't like singing because it's really high and I don't know how to sing properly yet. But I sung it anyway. When I finished, Paul said, 'Yeah, all right, great. I'm going to have a word with my dad.'

I found my 1984 diary recently. It says 'Monday 30 January 1984. Guess who is Paul Weller's new vocal backist?' Vocal backist! I don't even know the real words. I was so green around the gills. It was all a bit of a blur, but I did manage to get some of this in my diary at the time. Paul came back and said '*Jaye, go in the office, see me dad*'. John said '*Alright, Jaye, how much do you want? A ton, or something like that?*' and I'm like ... '*What? Who?*' We shook hands and that was it.

Mick Talbot: The horn section changed for that UK tour with Billy Chapman, Stewart Prosser and Chris Lawrence coming in ...

Hilary Seabrook: I have a lot of respect for Paul and always will have. And he decided that he was going to be the one to tell me that I wasn't going to do the next tour. I cried . . . It wasn't that they were dissatisfied with me, it was that Billy was available, and he would probably have always been their first-choice sax player . . . Billy was playing with Animal Nightlife, and as soon as they split up, Paul went 'Right, let's get Billy in.' Billy and I are good friends. We don't hate each other or anything. The fact that Paul showed me the respect of taking me to one side on my own and just saying, 'Right, this is what's going to happen . . .' Yes, that was my last day, but it wasn't my last day of contact . . . There's a little group of us who are friends because we have been Honorary Councillors.

Mick Talbot: The first concert was a televised one. Why not jump in the deep end? I don't know if we were ever very calculated or sensible about any of that sort of thing, but it's just like, well, it's got to happen at some time. Why not make it the beginning and build on that?

You're doing your first gig. It's Chippenham Gold Diggers and it's being filmed, and you're thinking, *Why didn't we do a warm-up tour before we decided to let cameras in?*

Jaye Ella Ruth: That was my first gig with The Style Council, and we were still rehearsing. Paul just sprung that on us, and I'm like, 'What? I've not learned all the songs yet and I don't know what to wear.'

Mick Talbot: I think it's important to have the right spirit, really. When I listen back to *Café Bleu*, now, at times I think maybe what I was trying to do then, I could do better now, but it wouldn't have half the spirit and that was the essence to putting the live band together as well.

Helen Turner: It was like a family. I was probably the latest to join. I definitely felt a new girl, but it was a real experience as to how all this worked. I used to call it a licensed school outing every time we went on tour [*laughs*]. When I think of the first tour, I was one of the older ones, but there were some really young people. All thinking that the minibar was free.

Stewart Prosser: It all went by in a blink of an eye, but looking back, the things we did, the camaraderie in the band, the energy, and the excitement – it was something special. We were really young musicians, eager to do something interesting, and it just all seemed to work. Thinking about it now, it must have been quite a risk for Paul. He could have easily gone out and hired session players right from the start, told them what to wear and play. But there was something organic about the way he brought the musicians together. We were all feeling our way through this massive new thing, and so it pulled us together as a unit. That was a really smart move, psychologically. It made us rely on each other, especially in the early days when it was such a small, tight operation with those very first shows.

Billy Bragg: My early 1984 was a run of benefit gigs interspersed with The Style Council tour . . . John Weller was a figure that I was very familiar with growing up. Mr Weller, the builder. My manager, Peter Jenner, who'd managed Pink Floyd, The Clash, Ian Dury and the Blockheads, had been to public school. He wasn't the kind of character I ever really met in life . . . Whereas John, as soon as I met him, I knew exactly from the working-class background I came from . . . He was probably a working-class Tory. I don't know that at all, but he respected what Paul was doing. But he was also very sceptical about the politics of it all when we were doing Red Wedge later on, but Paul was to some extent as well, so I respected that.

Stewart Prosser: I got a phone call out of the blue from Dennis Munday asking if I fancied doing a tour with The Style Council. I immediately dug out every single Weller-related piece of music that I could find and tried to learn everything. As long as I can play all this stuff,

I should be right. Got hold of The Jam singles that had brass on, any Style Council stuff that was around. Learned every single note.

So, I turn up at the studio and met Paul and Mick and Dennis. I went with Mick into the main body of Solid Bond and Paul and Dennis stayed in the control room. Mick asked me the one question I hadn't prepared for. He said, 'So what do you want to play?' I was about to say something, and he went 'How about we just do a blues?' I then had to change my head completely. We ended up doing a bit of Kenny Wheeler . . . For those jazz fans out there.

Mick Talbot: Not the tour manager Kenny Wheeler! You wouldn't want him blowing down anything!

Stewart Prosser: So, we did a blues jam thing. I just noodled around over it, and it sounded OK and I must have looked the part and that was it.

Billy Chapman: I think Paul believed in my ability and I felt very complimented and very proud to be part of that very early set up . . . We did the rehearsals which were really experimental. I didn't know how to handle half of it because it was on a bigger scale than I had ever experienced before. You suddenly realised that this is the guy from The Jam. You forget that when you're talking in normal ways about music and getting on with it. It had a nice, relaxed feel about the whole thing.

Stewart Prosser: We put some miles in for rehearsals. Mick and Paul then said they wanted to put an instrumental melody over 'Le Départ'. Could I give it a go? . . . we ran through it a couple of times and then literally a couple of days later, we got our first gig and it's in this place in Chippenham and, 'Oh, by the way, it's live on BBC Two.' I was absolutely petrified . . . The lights dimmed, it all went very quiet and I had to do this flugelhorn solo, just me and Mick, which was terrifying. But once we'd done that gig, we were ready for whatever came next.

Jaye Ella Ruth: I had nothing to wear. I think the skirt I had was my Post Office skirt and my tights were my mum's – in those days, you only had three shades of tights for Black girls, so I had my mum's burnt sienna tights on and some heels I couldn't walk in. I remember shaking so hard, and I think that's where my IBS started! *[Laughs]*

Stewart Prosser: Chris Lawrence and I were in this Rye and Quarterboys band when I first moved to London, and immediately found a soulmate musically. There was this joy and pleasure in playing with him. I introduced Billy to Chris, they got on. I said to Paul, 'Would you fancy adding a trombones and horn section?' And he said, 'Yeah, it could be interesting.' I ended up bunking with Chris and spent a lot of time with him. He was a troubled individual. He had had quite a difficult childhood, and that represented itself in different ways over the years, and he struggled with drinking and drugs later on, but he was just this superbly talented, energetic, focused musician. When he was on, no one could touch him, really. He was either full on or full off. I loved him, he was not an easy person, but we were friends for a long time.

Billy Bragg: The Style Council opened those shows, which was really impressive. They went out and played 'Meeting Over Yonder' by the Impressions to kick things off and get everybody in the auditorium, so that when I went on stage there was people there.

Paul Barry: The Style Council gigs were really good. It was an amazing thing for the Questions to be in the middle of a show, that was brilliant and so cool.

Tracie Young: I'd forgotten that. Yeah, Paul used to split his set in two, didn't he? and we'd come on in the middle. He is very experimental, but that is a lot of pressure.

Steve 'Tufty' Carver: It took me a while to get The Style Council. I'm not going to lie. I remember asking Gina Giraffe, 'Did you go to the first Style Council gig?' and she said, 'No. I was heartbroken.' I did feel like that. It took me a long time. The first time I saw The Style Council, John knocked on the door and went, 'Tufty, you coming to see Paul's new band?' Off I went, Dominion, Tottenham Court Road, and there's Paul without a guitar, singing songs that I'd never heard in my life and my brain's going ... *This guy used to be in The Jam*, and I went back to the dressing room and John come over and went, 'What do you think of it, Tufty?' and I just went, 'I don't know, John. I really don't know.' John, bless him, went 'Paul, Tufty fucking hates it!' Cheers, John.

So next day, John knocks on the door again, 'Are you coming tonight?' 'Yeah. Go on, I'll give it another go' ... Paul had changed out of a suit and he had a Pringle jumper on, and he looked much more relaxed and guess what? ... I thought, *Yeah, look, I like that one, I like that one, I like that one.* Went back to the dressing room, walked in, picked up a beer. Paul walked over me, he put his face right there into mine and went, 'You fucking come back for more though, didn't ya?'

Darren Fletcher: The first time I saw the Council was '84 at the Dominion. They really became my band. The look, the sound, Paul's swagger with it and the way they went about things really caught my attention big time. Fast forward to 2013 and I'm getting a few musicians and creating the world's first Style Council tribute band.

David Rowe: We went to every gig on those tours. We used to see Brian Hawkins, the merchandise guy, before the gigs. If it was raining, I'd help him in with boxes. They also did a sort of informal meet and greet thing after gigs where a small band of people would end up forming around the front of the stage and Chris, the security guy, would come and march you backstage. Paul and Mick would be sat there in the dressing room, and you would go through, get your autographs, have a chat, take photos. At the Glasgow Apollo gig, Paul said, 'I remember you from the Gold Diggers gig. You were down in the hall when we were doing the interview. I nearly came down because I really liked the pink Lacoste cardigan you were wearing.'

Billy Bragg: We played Glasgow Apollo ... I was with Andy Kershaw at the time. We decided to go and watch The Style Council's first bit from the audience that night. The noise that the audience made when they came on was a noise akin to Concorde taking off. I'd never heard anything like it before. The noise the audiences make when they like you is the same noise that other audiences make when they're going to kill you. I learned not to be put off when they really, really go off like a rocket because they're really into what you're doing.

That was my introduction to the fan mania. There was still a lot of Jam fans in those audiences, and they still had that 'Paul belongs to us' attitude. People hadn't got bored of that then. So, watching Paul deal with it and how he approached the idea of connecting with the fans and what he was doing was really great for me.

16 March 1984 – *Café Bleu* (no. 2)

Paul Weller: It was an exciting time because, for me, it was like wiping the board clean and starting again. Just doing whatever come in my head. Pretty much anyway and changing the style.

Every single was different or trying to be a little bit different. I don't think we could have done that with The Jam. I don't think our fans would have gone with that personally or even maybe us as a band would have been into that. I wanted that freedom to do that, and mad things, right? Like on the first Style Council album, where I think I only sing on three or four songs. We got different singers in and some instrumental tracks, and it's fucking try everything. Try whatever you got in your head. Just try it and see what happens. Some of it's successful, some of it not. I had the opportunity to do that and through those things, you find yourself as well, I think, sometimes if you're lucky.

Mick Talbot: We started with an instrumental and finished with instrumental. Almost treating that like credit music if it was a film, as you're finding your seat, you're hearing 'Mick's Blessings', and as you're leaving the theatre, you'll be hearing 'Council Meetin''. It's either filmic or theatrical, where you get your overtures at the beginning and closing credits.

Peter Anderson: The Style Council photographs were very much improvised, but they all had a starting point, and that was probably a meeting in a café with Paul and Paolo Hewitt and Simon Halfon. Quite often the conversation didn't need to go very far. 'All right, we're doing it this way,' then we'd do it. The results are that there's a lot of photographs of The Style Council in that first two years of their existence, and they were used so well, all over the place. Large fly posters, flyers, adverts and magazines. Special editions of records and marketing that went to Japan quite a lot. It was not always worked out that a specific photo session was for a record. It was often quite loose.

Peter Wilson: *Café Bleu* is a real ragbag of an album. Is that unfair? A real diverse range of styles. Yes. You might say some are more successful than others. One that I don't think was so successful was . . . 'Me Ship Came In!' Paul was listening to a lot of Blue Note Records and so was Mick. The jazz stuff, Herbie Hancock, Wayne Shorter and Cannonball Adderley, and wanted to emulate that. It's hard to do that . . . Wasn't there even that rap?

Mick Talbot: I wrote 'Mick's Blessings'. Some of the other stuff we co-wrote, and some Paul wrote on his own. 'Mick's Blessings' was just something I used to vamp a lot, and Paul asked, 'What's that?' It's very short and sweet – it does the job of setting the thing up, I suppose. We didn't really deliberate too much over it.

The first track I did was 'Mick's Up', which appeared on the B-side of the 'Money Go Round' twelve-inch. That track got a fair bit of attention, even from people who wouldn't normally like us. It was the first time we got a mention in *Blues and Soul*. They could be a bit elitist, but they liked it. The *NME* also picked up on it. X. Moore, a journalist who later formed the band The Redskins, made a big deal about it too. That seemed to have something special. Some people said it had a loose northern soul feel. It was just me playing piano with a Hammond organ layered over it. There wasn't a bassline or a drum kit – it was quite unconventional. But it had an atmosphere. It was just a laugh, we tried something, and it worked.

Dennis Munday: 'The Whole Point of No Return' is such a great song. It's political, it's sharp – a waspish record without the wasp, if you understand me. Just sitting there with an acoustic guitar, but it's absolutely the fire.

Dylan Jones: Writing about politics can be tricky, particularly when done from a place of privilege, as it can sometimes feel lacking in authenticity. But those are rebel songs, those are protest songs, and they remain as important and as hard-edged as they were in the early eighties.

Chris Bostock: They were aiming for the same thing we were – funky soul town, northern soul kind of direction. You can hear all the influences in there. Paul Weller was a huge fan of soul singles, as were we. We were in the charts at the same time but there wasn't rivalry at all. It was great to be part of a scene where others are doing similar things. It keeps you going.

We'd been on a crash course to meet way before *Café Bleu*. Back in 1981 we ran Club Left in Soho's Whiskey A Go Go, before it became known as the Wag. We were the house band for various singers, and everything we did was in the style of *Café Bleu*. So, when I finally got the call to play on that album, it didn't seem like a huge surprise.

For that new version of 'Paris Match', Paul said, 'I heard you can play some double bass. Want to give it a go?' . . . I've lost track of the number of people I've bumped into who've said it's the best Style Council track ever ... that particular version . . . There's a haunting ghostliness to it, a bit of danger.

Peter Wilson: 'Ever Changing Moods' started as piano and vocal. and then Paul had this idea of doing an up-tempo one for the single, which came together quickly in the studio. I grabbed a bass synthesiser and played a bassline to it. Put the horns on and a bit more bongo and redid the vocals.

Mick Talbot: 'Dropping Bombs on the Whitehouse' was to try and make a clumsy pun on Steve's name and create a little controversy. 'Dropping Bombs' is a term that jazz drummers use for a certain thing they do. Usually if you get a jazz-style drum solo, they'll be 'dropping bombs' at certain points. It's a punctuation thing. That's what it was alluding to, and it was just a bit of fun.

Anthony Harty: One thing that always sticks in my mind is Marilyn, the singer, who was working on a few tracks with

Boy George. There was this little green in front of the studio. I was just walking over from the B&B to the studio. I had no idea they were there. Suddenly, what came into my vision was Boy George and Marilyn having actual fisticuffs on the lawn. The most bizarre sight you could ever be confronted with!

Boy George: We used to have fights everywhere. Marilyn always wanted everyone to himself, so he couldn't share Paul. He was very jealous. If you ever want to have a lunatic interview with anyone, try interviewing Marilyn about Paul Weller. I mean it's so funny. I don't think any of it's true. It's fucking entertaining. Like, oh, really? Marilyn insisted that he slept with Paul. He used to say it all the time. And there was this great interview where the journalist said to Paul Weller, *did you go out with Marilyn?* And Paul said, '*well, if he said I did then I must have done*'. Which I thought was the fucking coolest thing. Talk about shut down a question. I thought it was so cool. More people should be like that. He was like, *'I don't know, maybe'*.

Chris Bostock: When I arrived, there was this patch of lawn outside the studio, and Paul was lying there, sunning himself. He played me a track – 'Here's One That Got Away'. He wanted it to be like a walking, skipping northern soul bass. He knew I did a lot of walking bass, so I immediately thought of Spiral Staircase's 'More Today Than Yesterday', one of my favourite northern soul songs. I got into that groove for the verse. For the chorus, I thought of 'I Can't Help Myself' by The Four Tops, but instead of sticking to straight northern soul beats, I locked the two parts together.

Paul seems like a workaholic to me. He wanted to have fun, but he always knew exactly what he wanted. At the same time, I can't imagine him having a big belly laugh. He's a pretty serious guy. At his core, he's still an angry young man, isn't he?

Hilary Seabrook: I loved 'Headstart for Happiness' from the moment we recorded it. It's so catchy, and it really resonated with me personally. My name is Hilary, and that name ties directly to happiness – Hilary, hilarious, hilarity – it all connects to being joyful. I feel like I had a head start to happiness because of my name.

Russell Hastings: That chord structure is out of this world. The rundown on it is mental. That's Paul's pure nuts-and-bolts talent on that . . . I think it's one of the most beautifully written songs that he's ever done.

Dennis Munday: I think the company expected an album full of 'Speak Like a Child', 'Long Hot Summer'. I would never let anyone hear anything when they were recording so they had no inkling of what the album was going to be like. I thought, *If they even get a whisper of this, I'll be up on the naughty chair again.*

Hilary Seabrook: I think that there was a sense everywhere . . . with the label, with the music press, with the radio and everything, that this was a bit odd. And you either thought it was good because it was a bit odd, or you thought it was bad because it was a bit odd. I love the fact that he gets his inspiration from loads of different places, literature, art and life in general and the news, and he's very aware of the world.

Martin Hopewell: It was a very strange time. Paul invited me down to the studio to hear the new album, and Paul could be an intimidating fucker. He'd sit right next to you to make sure you were paying attention to every single song, then ask, 'What do you think? Don't hold back, say exactly what's on your mind.' And you'd think, *Bloody hell,* and would try to come up with something, but I'm not a music critic. 'I don't know, it sounded very nice.' Luckily, it was really good, but I couldn't sit there again. Maybe some people can hear a piece of music and think, *Yeah, that's going to be huge*, but I never could . . .

It was the same back in the days of The Jam, when John would come around with a cassette and put it in the office stereo to play me the new single. Each one seemed to get more and more unpalatable, to the point where he played me one and I just thought, *Wow, this has gone too far. There's no way this is going to happen. How can you have a song called 'Eton Rifles'?*

Peter Gordon: I know opinions are mixed, but the range of material in such a short time and the eclectic, slightly erratic nature of *Café Bleu* was unique. Paul's writing during that period was cutting edge – political, observational, and sharp. I was sad about The Jam, but I got into The Style Council quickly. I liked the style and the tongue-in-cheek feel, which I understood, even if some missed the point. They were doing something no one else was, taking the mick out of everyone, including themselves.

Richard Ogden: My job was to try and get them international success. This was the point where in America they left Polydor and went to Geffen. I was very much involved with finding and making that deal – that was my responsibility.

Ed Rosenblatt was the head of the label, and one of the areas of stress with the Wellers was that Geffen wanted ... better production, and I would stand by that. I don't think The Style Council or The Jam records were very well produced. It's very much a garage-type approach. That was one of the things that John Weller didn't appreciate about me. I would just say what I thought.

John Cohen: The album that Paul delivered to Geffen was called *Dropping Bombs on the Whitehouse*, and the label felt that was not exactly a tactful title to deliver to the American company.

Peter Button: John wouldn't have given any thought about the record company's view on the album name. For him, it was simply, 'Well, it's what my boy wants.'

John Cohen: Which was great, but not always ideal. Maybe the boy needs some guidance and advice – *Don't do that, it won't help your career*. But John wasn't really that kind of manager.

Richard Ogden: There were many great advantages for Paul to be managed by his dad, but the old chap didn't have a view, he didn't have a vision. So, it was all on Paul. 'I'm going to do what I'm going to do.' I always remember somebody telling me once that all the money he'd ever made up until the mid-eighties he had in the Nationwide Building Society. If that was true, it kind of fits with the whole thing that we're king of this castle, which is in England, and it's fine for us . . . We don't want to go and conquer the rest of the world. It was just that mindset, I think.

March–April 1984 – Europe tour

Ann Weller: It was brilliant. We had such good times. The songs were totally different from The Jam, weren't they? I like the energy of The Jam because you got that 'argh' three minutes . . . and then I like the melodic lovely things of The Style Council.

Nicky Weller: We started another fan club for The Style Council. The Torch Society. It had over 7,000 members. Before it had all been quite male orientated and, suddenly, we're going to gigs and seeing girls turning up. It was a totally different vibe. That's got to be the best job I ever had. Working with The Style Council. Loved the music. People couldn't really get their head around it, a lot of The Jam fans, but they came round again at the end of it. Some of them might have departed, but most of them started following The Style Council.

Steve Sidelnyk: There was a European tour when *Café Bleu* came out. I was playing drums with Tracie. I don't think I had deodorant, but if I had some, I'd use some, as I'd get changed and go and play with The Style Council. I was young and I needed to be occupied, so it suited me down to the ground.

Jaye Ella Ruth: I got more confident over time, but I do remember John Weller not wanting me to sing any differently than Dee. We had this ongoing little feud – bless him. He'd say, ''Ere, Jaye, I want you to sing it like Dee.' I'd reply, 'But I'm not Dee. Look at me.' I was cocky with John, funnily enough – not with the boss.

On stage, I used to focus so much on getting it right. I thought in my little brain that if I sang one note wrong, Paul would sack me. I don't know where that came from, but he seemed to be a perfectionist. I saw him early on in rehearsals get a bit moody if something wasn't right, and I recognised that in myself . . . I remember one night singing one bum note during a gig. Paul was playing guitar, and he shot a look at me. I shot a look back and carried on singing, thinking that I was going to faint. *That's it. He's going to sack me.* It was that important to me. It was that intense.

Ted Kessler: I saw them in Paris in '84 . . . The Style Council was fresh and open. Everyone was dancing. It was mostly mods up front, and I'd never seen so many mods in Paris! . . . It was the total opposite of when a bunch of English fans came over for The Jam in '82 – lots of fighting . . . They were probably similar people, but the look and mood were different. I think Paul did exactly the right thing splitting them up because he popped that mania around The Jam and let everything bubble up more gently.

Kevin Miller: We were on tour in Europe and stopped at a service station. Paul was just larking about, which was nothing unusual, and chasing one of the backing singers around the car park . . .

Jaye Ella Ruth: I was talking to Paul about how fast a runner I was at school and that my hundred metres record was unbroken. He challenged me to a race to the tour bus. He was really fast. I had to make some effort, bearing in mind I'm a little girl and he's a tall guy with longer legs. We were neck and neck, maybe I was a nose in front and Paul don't like to lose . . . He took a dive for the door and a tumble, and I was just laughing because I thought nothing of it.

Stewart Prosser: East Germany in this bleak, austere, drab petrol station. All the food had been there for six months. We all got out because it had been a long day, and it was quite snowy. Paul slipped on something. Everybody just thought, *Oh wow.* Apart from worrying about him healthwise, *What are you going to do now then? Without the front man?*

Kevin Miller: He slipped and landed awkwardly, and they took him to the hospital. When we got to the hotel, about half past six, somebody said, 'Have you heard about Paul? He's broken his arm.' There was a gig that night. Anthony knew most of the set on guitar so I stay in the reception working out the basslines for The Style Council stuff, so I could stand in for that night, and Paul could do the gig in a sling.

Mick Talbot: We had to change things around. The actual date of this was April Fool's Day, and very sadly, news was coming through that Marvin Gaye had died as well. We got the show together, it was all hands-on deck, and we rejigged things. Anthony Harty said he could play the guitar, so we transferred him from bass to guitar. Dave Liddle played bass for most of that gig. Paul was in a sling, and we carried on like that.

Stewart Prosser: Paul did the gig and got Robbie the guitar tech to come out and play some of the parts. That was a punchy gig – there was so much tension in the band – concern for Paul and what would this mean. Paul was pissed off because it's not what he wanted. A really fiery, fiery gig. I remember, after gigs we'd always take turns to put what was left from the rider into a plastic sack and onto the coach. Everyone was very tired and emotional, but Chris got to the point where he figured it was Paul's turn to do that. Paul figured it wasn't. It was an edgy night.

Mick Talbot: Songs evolve on the road. Some really took off live. The instrumentals gave us a chance to give people a bit more time to extemporise, people like Steve White, Stewart and the horn players – like the flugelhorn version of 'Le Départ', which we only recorded live. It was also an opportunity to see what tunes worked, like 'Strength of Your Nature'. We used to dove-tail with another tune. The songs took on a different energy live. 'Headstart for Happiness' really took off live.

Nicky Weller: I was in the card school. My dad taught me everything I know about that. We used to count cards. When you first join as a member of the crew or band or whatever, you get, literally, 'Come on, card school.' You've all got to play. It's an initiation thing. You lose your first week's wages, you never fucking play again, let me tell you. The only people that ever used to win from that was probably my dad, me, Kenny. Kenny used to cry a lot. It was fun. I used to come home with not just my wages, but my card winnings.

Mick Talbot: I did join the card school very briefly. We were in Germany and had a bit of time on our hands. I was not that well versed in cards, but I did quite well in a game with Kenny and John and it shocked me. I went and spent all my winnings on a smoking jacket that I'm wearing on the 'Walls Come Tumbling Down' cover. Kenny said, 'What are you all done up like a ten-bob ham bone?' I just went, 'It's me winnings innit,' and he went, 'You're not supposed to spend it. Get back to the table and lose it.' I went, 'You know what? You're so angry. I'm retiring from the card school.'

Kevin Miller: During those days, it was like a big club really. The whole Respond, The Questions thing . . . because Paul hated flying we never flew anywhere. It was always driving on the coach, like a great big school outing.

Jaye Ella Ruth: *A Clockwork Orange* on The Style Council tour bus . . . I'll tell you what, I didn't sleep for about a week. It's a fricking frightening movie. I remember thinking at the time, *But Paul and Mick are such lovely guys. I don't understand why they would watch such awful, evil stuff.*

Stewart Prosser: We had watched about three-quarters of *A Clockwork Orange* when we got to the gig in the coach. We did the gig, and the first thing everybody wanted to do was get out of the gig, back onto the coach to watch the rest of the film. It's like, 'Great to see you all. Thanks for coming. Good night. Right. *Clockwork Orange*.'

Jaye Ella Ruth: It's the first time away from my mum. Even though she was really shocked and upset that I left the Post Office, she liked Paul Weller because I used to play The Jam in my little record player in my bedroom . . . my mum passed four years ago and her photo albums had all my Style Council pictures in there and she's written captions . . .

I used to follow Mick round a fair bit, like a little puppy, because he's so funny. My mum bought me a fake fur coat for my nineteenth birthday and there's a picture of Mick in my coat with my cousin's college scarf, doing a Noël Coward impression. It was just a lot of warm laughs. I couldn't talk to Paul very much because I just didn't know what to say. I was a bit tongue tied, because he was from The Jam.

April–May 1984 – Japan and US tour

Nicky Weller: We weren't used to flying in those early days and none of us really liked it. I remember us all having diazepam or something and falling into oblivion.

Mick Talbot: Japan was nuts. It was the closest I've ever felt to experiencing something like Beatlemania. When we arrived in Tokyo, there was such a frenzy – I don't think it was unique to us; fans there just have this extreme appreciation for artists who visit. We were never the kind of band to attract Beatles-level hysteria, but for a moment, you could imagine what that might have been like. It was mad.

Anthony Harty: I spent my seventeenth birthday flying to Japan and because of the time difference, it was during the second half of the flight. Back then, you had to go via Anchorage because of the no-fly zone over Russia. After we got back on the plane, the crew dressed in kimonos, brought out a little birthday cake, and handed me a card. Everyone sang 'Happy Birthday' in wonderfully bad Japanese English.

Steve Sidelnyk: Jazz music is massive in Japan – absolutely huge. Artists like Jaco Pastorius and Miles Davis would play stadiums there, it was a very different kind of thing. We'd always go record shopping because you could find things that weren't available anywhere else – only on Japanese pressings. The white Levis thing, it wasn't expensive. It was a very modernist style, and I think the Japanese really identified with that.

Stewart Prosser: Going to Japan was the most exciting thing – I was effectively being paid to go there, working. On the plane over, we were all so hyped that no one slept, so by the time we arrived, we were completely knackered and jetlagged. The first show wasn't the best that we'd ever played, and we got an absolute roasting from John. I'll let you use your imagination to fill in the expletives. The gist was, *Get your act together before tomorrow night, or we're all going home.* We were knackered. We were young. The next night we were on it.

Keiko Egawa: I saw The Style Council about sixty times, including in Japan. Why not? Flight is expensive, so I figured I'd meet my parents and go to the gigs at the same time. I loved the brass, and I'd started listening to jazz around then, so those influences in their music really appealed to me. I loved the music – from slow tracks like 'The Paris Match' to uplifting ones like 'Headstart for Happiness'. The Jam had meant absolutely everything to me, but I was always so uptight about seeing them, like I *had* to go. With The Style Council, it was different. The music made me feel more relaxed, and I even started dancing at gigs.

Anthony Harty: From the moment we got off the plane, it was insane. Girls camped outside the hotels, in the corridors, following you into the lifts. I'll never forget being in a lift with Paul one morning. He'd used one of those awful hotel razors, and his face was cut to ribbons and all these girls are snapping pictures of him. If you didn't stop for photos or autographs, they'd walk off in tears, and you'd feel really guilty.

Stewart Prosser: We had some of that in the UK with people being around the hotels we stayed at, but Japan was a whole other level. If I went into town with Chris, we'd be followed by people. It's like we're the horn section. Don't bother the bloke whose name is on the front. It was an intense tour and there wasn't a lot of let up. I've never been a pop star and had that constant attention and hassle I'm sure Paul gets, but I got a bit of a flavour of it then, and it's odd, not really my thing.

Mick Talbot: Paul had been there a few times with The Jam, and he said, 'When you go there, you'll start nodding to everyone,' and I go, 'No, I won't do that. I respect their thing.' But you can't help it. It's part of the way you speak to people, when it's polite. Back then, early eighties, it did seem like a different planet. I've been there since and it's a shame that it seems to be getting more and more Westernised. It did have its own thing, a unique little place. Tokyo was a bit like turning up in *Blade Runner*.

Martin Hopewell: The Style Council were playing a blistering show in Osaka, Japan. At the time, the security barrier was just a rope, with a bloke at each end, and the Japanese audience did not cross it. You couldn't even get them to stand up. They'd stay seated and clap politely. But during the show, you could see the audience was standing up and the promoter was saying to me this is getting a bit dangerous.

Steve Sidelnyk: Usually when you do a show in Japan, it's at six thirty in the evening, and then you're done by nine o'clock. Sit-down venues. It was always quite subdued. Bit of clapping at the end. But someone whipped them up into a bit of a frenzy and they started getting on stage. There was nothing violent about it.

Mick Talbot: I do remember the Osaka riots . . . That gig turned into something a bit mad.

Jaye Ella Ruth: In the encore, I grabbed Helen's hand and we jumped into the pit to dance with the people, and they surged forward. They were shaking my hand. 'Arigato, Arigato.' It was just a happy thing. Then I heard some noise, people surging forward. I remember looking up and people jumping from the balcony, us having to leg it. Apparently they, like, tore the place up. Beat these poor kids. I think the promoter was put in jail . . . It wasn't just a little selfish Jaye thing, I thought it was in the spirit of The Style Council, *Let's just party.* I used to get so lost in the joy of it. The band were like, 'Oh, Jaye, you're in trouble.' I was so scared, I can't tell you. I can actually remember the tingling fear. I've got a picture of John Weller leaning on the side of the stage with his fist clenched going, 'Oh, my God.'

Kevin Miller: The Style Council went off, came back on, did an encore and then all the lights came up and everyone was thinking it was the end. But then Paul decided to come back on and do another song and was encouraging everyone to stand up, let loose a little, and it more or less ended up in a riot. He stoked the crowd, but yeah, it was a crazy tour.

Mick Talbot: The security seemed to be getting a bit heavy-handed with some girls who wanted to dance. Paul saw it and told our team, 'Don't let that happen. This is mad.' It looked like a kung-fu expert squaring up to a little fourteen-year-old girl. We just said, 'If you want to dance, you can dance.' Before we knew it, half the crowd was on stage dancing. It had gone from one extreme to another. When we left, we thought, *These people are spirited in a way that's different from Tokyo.* We even joked about twinning Osaka with Glasgow because it felt like a similar vibe – if they want to dance, they'll dance.

Helen Turner: The security guys had batons, and they were actually whacking people. It was a real traditional theatre in the Western sense, with everything going up to the balconies, up to the gods, and it was like watching a human avalanche slowly come down. Eventually they were all on stage, and I think we were playing 'My Ever Changing Moods'. We played for as long as possible and then made a break for it, though we were barricaded in the dressing room for a bit and banned from playing there, apparently, ever again.

Stewart Prosser: The promoter came out and tried to tell us not to provoke this wild behaviour in these young people of Japan, morally reprehensible band that we were. That didn't go down too well, and there was a bit of argy-bargy ... The next day we're given a police escort to the station in Osaka and kept in a locker room until the train arrived and they could sort of hustle us out of town.

Jeff Slate: We hitch-hiked to see The Style Council here in New York in '84 ... It was a really small gig, and The Style Council were so 'not a thing' here. We thought there'd be scalpers. There were none. Nobody cared about this gig! That was another depressing thing.

Jaye Ella Ruth: The Style Council was, without a doubt, the best career experience of my life. It's where I cut my teeth and learned how to be a professional singer and how to get on with people. It's the strangest thing. I was with them for six months; I didn't know in what capacity – I didn't know I was a temporary replacement because there was no real dialogue. I thought I was in the band. So, all of sudden, when I wasn't, I was heartbroken, but I soon understood why. I love when people are in love [Paul and Dee]. I'm a soppy sort, and I could see the journey to each other from a distance. So, it made sense to me.

That time also helped me to become the real Jaye because, in my family, I had to diminish who I was, but with the band, I learned how a family works properly. I was in awe of Paul and John, watching how they interacted, their family dynamics. That experience enhanced so many aspects of my life. Leaving the band was devastating because I loved it so much. It took me quite a while to get over that. But I'm a grown woman now, and it was fucking fantastic!

There was supposed to be a gig that I assumed I'd be part of, but no one called. Later, I heard that they did it with Dee. I didn't say anything to anybody. I just thought someone could have called me or said 'Bye', but it's the industry – you learn tough lessons.

But I want to say this, and I've been thinking about this recently. Paul saw something in me that I didn't see in myself and for that, I just love that guy.

18 May 1984 – 'You're the Best Thing' (no. 5)

Dennis Munday: *Smash Hits* used to reprint lyrics, and I got a call saying, 'We get to the bridge on "You're the Best Thing" and can't understand what Paul's singing.' He did have a habit of mumbling – if he wasn't totally happy with something, he'd just give it a 'mmuurrah'. So, I pulled the twenty-four-track master tape and isolated the vocals. I wrote down what I thought he was singing and sent it off without a second thought.

Paul called me up and said, 'I've just read *Smash Hits*. I'm coming in to see you.' I had no idea what was wrong. When he walked in, he said, 'No, they're good. What I wrote was fucking shit. I'm going to use those.'

Jaye Ella Ruth: 'Big Boss Groove' [B-side] – how cool is that? I'm at Solid Bond Studios, just to hang out, and Paul goes, 'Oi, Jaye, come and sing on this.' Dee doubled, Mick sang a verse, and I doubled too . . . Then came the music video. Breakdancing was new-ish at the time, so we were mucking around, pretending to do it, spinning around, being daft. We were calling Dennis's efforts 'Break Wind Dancing'. At the start, there's a scene where Paul walks past me and Dee, and as Paul walks past, the director said, 'Just go qwoar.' Me being the actor, I really went for it. Paul walks past, slaps five to Dee, slaps five to me and as he walks past, I really theatrically, over-the-top went 'QWOAR,' with the arm and everything. Looking back now, I'm like, *Oh my God, so embarrassing.*

Dennis Munday: Paul said, 'I want to get shots of everybody dancing' so we all did it and before I left, I told the director, you're not to put any of that in. The night the director cut it, I went down, Paul and Mick were there, and they played it to me and there was about five seconds of me in it, and they promised they just did it as a joke and they weren't going to put it in. We went out that night, and when I went to work the next day, I had a huge hangover. I got a call from our PR guys saying, Paul and everyone is down here and they're going to play us the new video. It was John, Kenny, and all the top brass of Polydor and I'm sitting there and because my head was really woolly, I'm thinking, *What's going on?* We sit down, play the video, and then suddenly I pop up breakdancing, and it wasn't just for a few seconds. I even came up again at the end. I couldn't do that now. Looking back now it's really hilarious.

June 1984 – Tracie, *Far from the Hurting Kind*

Tracie Young: Paul's whole idea with Respond was to create a Motown environment with a house band, in-house writers and singers. Artists weren't expected to write their own songs or play instruments because the infrastructure was there to support them. The plan was good, but there wasn't enough to fill the pool.

Chris Free: Respond had a lot of diversity. It was all getting pigeonholed into like Paul's plaything, and it wasn't getting a fair hearing. Pressure started to build, and while there were some standout releases – like [The Questions'] 'Tuesday Sunshine' was out of this world, 'Everything and More' by Dolly Mixture, Tracie's stuff, and Vaughn Toulouse . . . nothing really took off. There was a real reticence in the industry to fully support Respond.

Tracie Young: I had already started recording songs for the second album but that was when Paul decided to no longer continue. I'm surmising here but things were said at the time which led me to believe that Polydor actually weren't that into it but did it because Paul was one of their biggest tickets . . . But I did end up owning the rights to all of that stuff. Paul sold it all to me for a pound . . . He let me type up an agreement, he signed it and sent it back. So, I own it all, and it cost me a quid.

7 September 1984 – Miners' benefit at Royal Albert Hall

Kevin Miller: The Style Council did a show for the miners at the Royal Festival Hall. Paul asked me to play the bass. Wham! shared the bill. They came on in all their white T-shirts, 'Choose Life'. But they just mimed. The headline in *Melody Maker* was 'Mimers' Benefit'.

Simon Halfon: In the eighties, Paul didn't get on with anyone in other bands. There was a whole hoo-hah with Wham! because they did the miners' benefit, but they mimed, and instead of people saying, *Wasn't it great that they did the miners' benefit because they're this teeny-bopper pop act that were all over the papers?*, they were just criticised because they didn't play live. Does anyone give a fuck? Really, that's not the issue . . .

I remember we'd gone out one night and it's Paul, Paolo and myself, and then George turned up in this little club and he'd just got back off the Wham! America tour . . . Then George said, 'I'm going back to Paul's flat. He wants to talk to me' . . . there was something in the paper where George did an interview with Julie Burchill, where he mentioned Paul showing him around his 'very small flat'. So, from that point onwards, that became 'Your fucking mate, George . . .'

Simon Napier-Bell: I was managing Wham! . . . I never talked to George about The Style Council, but the influence they had must have been a major influence on Wham! or at least on George post-Wham! I don't know if Paul was aware of that. I'm sure he was. Even the sound of Paul's voice on certain Style Council records is incredibly close to George's style and phrasing. I've gone back recently and checked the dates of records and thought, *Who was influencing who?*

Helen Turner: There was all that goaded rivalry between Wham! and Style Council. There wasn't any contest. They were completely different things. I'm sorry, but as far as I remember, most people playing with Wham! were session blokes. Nothing wrong with that, but Paul put a band together with women and very young people – very talented, but very young people.

Simon Napier-Bell: It's very similar melodies. Very similar sound to the voice. George obviously much more smoothed out, particularly if you're talking about George's solo records rather than Wham! ones. But it's very nice the way that Paul managed to sing this, what I would call smooth soul music, but . . . keep that slightly amateur quality. He never polished it up and made it sound like the pro singer. Usually when you do that, that's when you begin to lose personality, and George got around losing personality by making a very distinctive, polished, professional sound, which you knew was George and no one else could do it that way. And Paul got around it by not going for that and just being himself, but his singing improved incredibly, didn't it? If you just look at the quality of his singing as a singer and the range, and being able to hold open his breathing, between the beginning of The Jam and the end of Style Council, he'd really become a singer which was extraordinary.

Simon Halfon: I remember later on, I was living and working out of a small flat. I was finishing off a design on *Listen Without Prejudice*, and George had come over to see the artwork . . . then all of a sudden, the buzzer goes, 'Hello, it's me, Paul.' I thought, *Oh, this is going to be fun. Just the three of us together.* I said to George, 'That's Paul, you might want to leave.' He replied, 'I was going anyway'. They brushed past each other on the stairs and that was the end of that . . . once Paul makes his mind up about people – his mind is made up.

5 October 1984 – 'Shout to the Top!' (no. 7)

Mick Talbot: That song has got real impact. The strings help. Because of the arrangement and the percussive peaks and troughs, it stands up on its own without the vocal in a way. It's almost quite cinematic. When it came to the 12-inch version, we were pleased with how it sounded instrumentally without the vocals on and used part of that in the second mix. It's quite handy for people that want to do karaoke . . . they can do it on the original track.

Dennis Munday: Paul decided to produce himself on that song and that was something I wasn't overly keen on because my view, even to this day, is if The Beatles needed a producer, everybody else does. At the time, I wasn't convinced that you can be objective about what you're doing. But he bought in Jay Mark who worked out of Sigma Sound Studios, which was one of the studios in New York . . . he was really good, a lovely guy and a very, very, very good engineer.

Paul asked me to get Ian Levine, who was the man at the time for soul strings, but Ian couldn't do it so he recommended Johnny Mealing. Johnny had done a lot of TV themes and jingles. I thought, *Well that's good because you've got to say a lot in thirty seconds*.

Kevin Miller: Paul said, 'I've got something I'm working on. I'd like you to try out a bassline to it – see what comes out.' The original feel was very different from how it ended up . . . The same happened with 'Everything to Lose'. Paul had an idea for a fretless bass, and I had just coincidentally taken delivery of a new bass with a fretless neck.

Dennis Munday: I've got to say I still to this day think that it could have been better. I had the demo, and this final cut is not that different. I remember Kevin Miller put a funkier bassline on it and Paul said, 'No, no, no, take it off and go back to my bassline.'

Well, if you listen to it, everyone is playing the same thing. It's all point, it's all melody, there's no counter melody in. The same with the strings, until you get to the end, and Johnny said, 'I couldn't just carry on. I had to put some thrills on the end.' It sounds good but he wanted to bring violas and cellos in so as to underpin the strings as, if you listen to the Philadelphia studios, they had a really big string orchestra, and I just think that maybe it might have done better. I still think lyrics-wise it's one of his best songs.

John Mealing: Paul knew exactly what he wanted for the song, and I found him very easy to work with. It turned out to be a dynamite single.

Dennis Munday: Jay Mark went back to America and did a mix at Sigma Sound, and when we got it back, Paul listened and he said, 'Well, it sounds American to me.' I thought, *Well, yeah, what else would it be?* I don't think we ever used it. It's in the vault somewhere.

October–November 1984 – 'Council Meetings Part 2' tour

Tim Parsons: As a promoter, The Style Council tour felt a bit like doing a theatre tour with Jasper Carrott, with respect – there were no issues with damage, the theatres were nice, and the vibe was relaxed. It was a lovely show, and we all went home. Soundchecks, which were such a big deal with The Jam, weren't a thing with The Style Council. If the audience profile changed, so did the number of people outside the stage door.

From a security point of view, my life became immeasurably easier, but I still struggled with how many people were on the security team. The influence they believed they could have with me was something I had difficulty with. I respected Kenny and his role, as well as his relationship with John and Paul. But the others, hired hands, were a different matter. Being told by one of them that I didn't know what I was doing was not something I took kindly to. It's fair to say that as The Style Council came together, my relationship with John and Kenny soured. I was becoming more confident, both as a promoter and an organiser, and I didn't take kindly to being disrespected or treated with contempt, which I felt some of the sidekicks were doing.

David Rowe: We got to know Gill Price and Brian Hawkins, and Nicky Weller was often working on the merchandise as well. One day we went back to get our bag and Brian said, 'Oh, would you mind, selling a few programmes?' He had money belts ready, so we whipped them on. I went by one of the doors and Jo went to the other door, and we just shouted 'PROGRAMMES, PROGRAMMES'. It's amazing how many we sold as the hall emptied at the end of the gig. From then on, we started doing that at gigs and it became more and more regular.

David Quantick: When I became an *NME* journalist, one of the first things I wrote was a review of The Style Council's show at St David's Hall in Cardiff . . . At a drinks do, Paolo Hewitt, who worked for *Melody Maker*, came up to me and said, 'Paul wants to talk to you.' That happened a lot back then, especially with Paul Weller. I was like, *Oh crap* . . . Then Paul came over and asked, 'What do you mean by that review?' I tried to explain, but he just went 'Uh' and walked off. I was quite scared, but also impressed that someone was actually interested in what a journalist had to say. Instead of whining on about how they're always misrepresented in the press, Paul genuinely wanted to know.

Martin Speake: I briefly did that Council tour. At the time, I was in a saxophone quartet called Itchy Fingers . . . I was twenty-six. The experience was amazing in some ways, but disappointing in others. I knew lots of jazz musicians and horn who played with pop bands that had horn sections, like people who played with Elton John, and knew that the money was so much better. So, there was an issue with that. My memories of Paul was always fine, apart from little things like that or turning up really late for the rehearsals, and the usual rock and roll antics. He pretended he didn't know anything about the money. He didn't deal with it.

So, Paul's dad, John Weller . . . We sold out two nights at the Albert Hall, which should be decent money. He said a bizarre thing just to the horn section . . . 'It's 100 quid each for the two gigs.' The horn players, me, Chris and Stewart, said, 'That's terrible money,' and he said, 'All right then, 150 quid each for the two nights but keep it under your hat.'

We were also sharing rooms . . . We should have been treated better financially, like having our own rooms. They were a huge band. They're millionaires. They had the money . . . Thinking about it now, there were things that I like about Paul. At the time, I was very socialist, the old Labour type of socialist, and Paul came across as sharing that mindset. He also liked jazz. Those two things were attractive to me about him. That's why the money situation was disappointing.

Tim Parsons: We fell out on a tour that ended up at the Royal Albert Hall. It wasn't a case of 'I hate your fucking guts.' Business relationships have a time span. You can work well with people, but circumstances change and you move on. When I was told I wasn't doing the next Style Council tour, it wasn't a big surprise. If they thought I was a pain, then so be it.

Martin Hopewell: Oh shit, I was so naive. As an agent, you're trying to say *I'm here*, but really, you're a complete hanger-on. Most of the work is done months in advance, so by the time the gig rolls around, you're just a spare part, hanging around backstage with a laminate around your neck, trying to look important with nothing to do. I thought, *I'll invite everyone back to my place for a drink* and they cleaned out the minibar – completely. Left me with a bill that would be thousands today. It was messy . . . take it that alcohol played a fair part in a lot of what was going on. No naughtiness like throwing televisions out of windows, but a lot of bars in a lot of towns around the world, and some very funny stuff happened as a result – probably things I shouldn't go into.

19 October 1984 – *The Tube*

Malcolm Gerrie: Paul returned to *The Tube* towards the end of 1984 with a huge performance. 'A Man of Great Promise',

'Shout to the Top!', 'Strength of Your Nature' and a cover of 'Razor's Edge'. I always loved that about Paul. He was never afraid to explore different avenues. If you dive into his cultural influences, you'll find figures like Curtis Mayfield, Small Faces, massively influenced by Black music, but also people like Scott Walker.

Martin Speake: I do remember bits about that experience with *The Tube* and that was a little bit shocking. There was a rehearsal in the afternoon, and Paul had this beautiful guitar. A semi-acoustic jazz guitar, and he suddenly got really pissed off that it was out of tune and threw it across the stage in the soundcheck. It was a real rock and roll thing. 'This fucking thing's out of tune.' He can tune it himself, can't he? The roadie, long-haired hippie-type guy, David Liddle, came scurrying across the stage. It was horrible to see, to be honest. I didn't like that, that vibe.

Anthony Harty: My favourite guitar. It was the second *Tube*. Paul had this beautiful Aria – a big semi-acoustic Herb Ellis. It's on lots of photos in the studio and *Café Bleu* time. We were sound-checking for over an hour. They had some technical problem. Paul just completely lost it and got fed up. We played 'Shout to the Top!' about thirty times. He grabbed the guitar from around his neck and just chucked it. I saw it in slow motion, heading down towards the bit where the people stand, and the neck just snapped. I actually felt tears come into my eyes.

Malcolm Gerrie: We had two incredible stage managers, Colin and Big Clive, who came from the live touring business, not television. We had all sorts of moments in soundchecks, as you do on any normal gig. I've been asked in interviews, 'Oh, Paul. He was a real grumpy sod, wasn't he, in his early days? And didn't like television, and we had problems with him.' These are other producers that I've met in the dreaded Groucho Club or Soho House or wherever. My answer is always 'No!' Any frustration he had was more with his own thing than with the crew. It shocked everyone because we hadn't seen that side of him before.

November–December 1984 – Band Aid, 'Do They Know It's Christmas?' (no. 1)

Nigel 'Spanner' Sweeney: There are two stories that were important to me, and I think important to Paul at the time.

The first goes back a few years before, when Paul had a major argument with the Boomtown Rats in Belgium. It all started over a crate of beer. One band got, let's call it twelve crates, the other didn't, but one band nicked the beer, so of course the other band had the bloody hump with them, and they fell out.

Fast forward to 1984, and the Band Aid project comes up. And at this point, Paul Weller is pretty famous. Bob Geldof called me. 'Did you see the Michael Buerk report on telly last night? We're making a record on Sunday, get your people, get Bono and get Paul Weller.' But of course, Paul Weller's fallen out with him and memories of this crate of beer go long, right? But in my opinion, and I would also say Geldof's too, Paul was an absolute diamond. He walked in, looking very smart with a cane and everything. Turned up at Sarm Studios, which was, I bet, full of all these people that Paul didn't like. Duran Duran, Paul would have given them a hoisting, right? But they're all in the same place, in the same twenty by thirty room and drinking coffee.

Kenny Wheeler: I saw someone talking about that on a documentary the other day, saying they should have been as shrewd as

Paul Weller was when he got his driver to drop him off around the corner. That's bullshit. Paul just walked there. Me and John didn't even know he'd gone in and done it at the time. We only knew about Band Aid later on.

Nigel 'Spanner' Sweeney: What had also happened, that isn't common knowledge, is that Paul had phoned Geldof the day before and said, 'I'll come, just in case you need some guitar.' He sat there all of Saturday, six, seven hours, doing nothing, just to be there for Bob in case he needed him, which I thought was brilliant.

I think I was one of only five people there that weren't singing on the record. To see Geldof phone up Boy George and giving him a larapping over the phone, 'You're supposed to fucking be here, get on fucking Concorde now. You've got time,' and to see Phil Collins play the drums was incredible. We didn't know at the time, but that day would lead to that huge event – Live Aid – which also featured Paul.

Dee C. Lee: Around about the time that they were recording for Band Aid, as well as the live appearances, that was when Paul and I were really, sort of, together but there had been feelings, but nothing was actually happening. I was very, very, very hesitant. We were working together so I wasn't really crazy about that either, and I wanted us to keep it to ourselves because if it didn't work out, it didn't work out.

In between being a performer and all the rest of it, all my life I've always been somebody who's quite private about personal things. I don't feel the need to go on to the public about my personal life . . . I learned very early on, especially being around Wham!, how important it is to keep a little bit of something to yourself, otherwise people are just in your business, and it makes things messy and, yeah, it's just not fun.

14 December 1984 – The Council Collective, 'Soul Deep' (no. 24)

Dennis Munday: John Weller was very important to Paul all the way through it. I come back to why he split The Jam up, so he could control everything. I don't mean that negatively or big-headedly. He suddenly decided 'This is what I want to do' and he had his father behind him. Now, other managers might have said all sorts of things. I mean, if you look at some of the records The Style Council made, like the miners record or 'Money Go Round', now, your typical record business management would say, 'Oh, you can't make that.' Very few people at that time wanted to make that sort of thing. I can tell you that John was a much better manager than people give him credit for. He had the best lawyers. Their promoter was one of the best. He always had people there who were the best. He was surrounded by a team. The biggest decisions a group makes is the music and a manager's got very little sway over that. Paul would say 'I want to do this' and John didn't try and fight it, whereas other people may have.

I don't think the record company were that keen on 'Soul Deep'. Paul actually came in to see me very early one morning. He didn't usually do that just to chew the fat. He said, 'I want to make this record, and I really don't care what people think.' We sat down and discussed it and I said, 'The only thing is you're not going to get airplay. BBC Radio won't touch it with a barge pole.'

I loved it because I couldn't stand Thatcher. My politics are along the lines of Paul, always have been. I'm centre left and I hated Thatcher and some of the things that she came out with in that era. I thought it was good. Paul got everybody together. Martyn Ware from Human League and Heaven 17 produced it.

Junior Giscombe: I got a phone call from Paul. 'I want to make this song for the miners.' There was so much energy and power in what we were saying. We came up with a great little record. A lot of people don't even know it. Sometimes I would say about doing 'Soul Deep', and people will be like, you've worked with Paul Weller? It's like 'Yeah.' 'Billy Bragg?' 'Yeah.' 'Tom Robinson?' 'Yeah.' 'Nah, you're lying.' 'I'm telling you the truth.' 'Why would you go from soul music to making that kind of music?' And I'm like, 'You're not getting it.' Where I come from, good music stands. I don't have this whole thing of it is rock and roll or it's pop. These are labels given to our music. I know there were clubs, Black clubs, that would not usually play that kind of music, but they were playing it because of what it was saying. That was top notch for me.

Dennis Munday: Junior was the last one to do his vocals. Paul gave him the lyrics to sing and he just went in and blasted it out and it was fabulous. He'd never seen the lyrics before. He just went in and did it first take. Fantastic. He came out and then at least two of the others went back and redid their vocals after hearing him. Several people thought, *Wait a second . . .*

They did that live on *The Tube*, which was fantastic, but the whole thing was a bit hairy when the taxi driver got killed by miners when they chucked the rock or the boulder over the motorway and the record company really didn't want to put it out. I just said, 'Look, I'm not going to say anything to Paul. As far as I'm concerned, we go ahead but if you really want to then the record company has to pull it.' They have to take the blame for it because his credibility would have been shot.

The strange thing is that A. J., the managing director, came down to see me after the single was released and he said, 'Oh, the money really is going to the miners' wives and children.' I said, 'Yeah, I told you it was.' He said, 'I checked it out.' I'm sure these people don't believe now that Paul has done the concert for Gaza – 'That money's going to go to the terrorists or whatever' – because they want to believe it, you know.

Ernie McKone: One Paul Weller song that I love. You're going to be shocked by this. 'Soul Deep' . . . with Junior and Jimmy Ruffin. I was coming up at that time, getting into electro music, I was into soul, and I was like, *Who are these boys?* I know it's controversial, but it had a big influence on me.

Boy George: Geminis . . . we're very socially aware, we're very passionate, but also we're always in two minds about everything. I feel like, like myself, Paul has got much calmer as he's got older. There's still that essence of who he is, but he's more chilled now. There's a kind of wiseness. He knows what to get upset about and what not to.

I interviewed him for *Number One* magazine. The one where I've got a fur coat on. I put makeup on him. And his mum went, who put that on your face? It was so funny. I was like . . . me! I was writing an article; I suppose I was trying to be intellectual. I don't really know the ins and outs of what Paul thinks or doesn't think. But I've always liked him. I've always just thought, *He's not hard work*.

January 1985 – International Youth Year, *The Tube* and Lenny Henry

Annajoy David: International Youth Year, I went to work for the British Youth Council heading up their development efforts. It felt like the perfect opportunity to involve people like Paul Weller and Julie Walters . . . Our goal was to shine a torch on the work and hopes of young people, particularly in Britain, and advocate for greater accessibility. It was definitely the start of a very strong working relationship for me and Paul.

Malcolm Gerrie: The jacuzzi interview with Paul Weller at the beginning of '85 was one of those wonderfully surreal moments that we had on *The Tube*. Jools Holland was a huge fan of Paul and came up with the idea to 'debunk' Paul's image as aloof, grumpy and unsociable. Back then, Paul was slightly uncomfortable in interviews, so Jools suggested doing something completely different: an interview in the jacuzzi at Gosforth Park, this posh hotel in Newcastle . . . I thought, *God, this is not gonna work*. It turned out to be a chance to highlight a side of Paul that you didn't see much in the early eighties. His sense of humour, which I've always been able to enjoy. He's really sharp, so fast. He'll catch you unawares.

Lenny Henry: I never saw The Jam live, but I always thought there was something about this guy. There's more to him than that and when they broke up, I was sad – The Jam was a major brand in British culture. Kids knew who they were. People knew the band; they loved the music and nobody likes change. Suddenly here's this other band, The Style Council, with a manifesto, it's political, they've got something to say, a sense of humour about themselves. How great to see Paul smiling. It was also incredibly soulful, leaning into that soulful, R&B vibe.

So, I'm doing *Saturday Night Live* and Style Council are on and Paul says, 'Does Lenny want to sing with us?' 'You do know I'm a comedian and I sing for joke purposes, don't you?' They wanted me to rehearse 'You're the Best Thing'. I thought, *Well if this is shit, I'll just cover my head with a newspaper and leave*. I thought I'd be dismissed from that room where these real musicians and real singers are. But they didn't dismiss me . . . I'd been doing Theophilus P. Wildebeeste and been singing a bit and people knew that I could do it a bit. I even ad-libbed a thing at the end, which Paul liked it and kept in.

Wow, I'm actually singing live with The Style Council on Channel 4. That is up there as an event in my life. It was a huge honour to be allowed to do that. I'll never forget it. He wouldn't mind me saying this, but he's quite hard to know but he was respectful that I'd come there saying, 'Look, I don't know anything. What do you need me to do?' And then, I'm on the second album [*laughs*].

3 May 1985 – 'Walls Come Tumbling Down!' (no. 6)

Dee C. Lee: Just very hyper and a beautiful, beautiful song and I like the way our vocals play in that song. I've got to say, I was always, always blown away by the ease in which Paul used to come up with the different songs and how prolific he always was for writing. Even when we were together. There was always a song in his head. We would be somewhere, and he'd just be scribbling them down, non-stop, and always really good ones as well. I always thought that his writing, and his song producing and whatever, just got better and better.

Gary Crowley: Paul and Mick came on my Capital Radio show for an interview, and it was . . . let's just say, very in-jokey. I don't think anyone listening would have understood it really – they were definitely playing up. We all went for a coffee after, and Paul sensed that I was pissed off and he was mulling this over. It was like that scene in 'The Bitterest Pill' video when he slams his hand down on the table and the cups go flying. He said, 'If I didn't fucking like you so much, Crowley, I'd knock your head off' and then he flounced out of the coffee shop. I was like, 'What was that all about? Where did that come from?' Bless him, he called me later to apologise. 'Sorry, Knobbly. I was a little out of order there.' He always called me Knobbly – 'GC the Knobby Knee' – my rap name alter ego. It was always, 'Yeah alright Knobbly.'

Helen Turner: 'Walls Come Tumbling Down!' – well, all I know is I can't play it now. It was so fast! Paul wanted a slight gospel feel and it to be a live ensemble take. We rehearsed in the middle of winter with a bloody great big industrial blow heater to keep the ice off us . . .

For live performances, Paul wanted something at the start, so I came up with that intro, completely mixing up my popular modern classical music stuff. It wasn't polished, but it worked – with varying degrees of success. Sometimes I'd do a nice rundown, reasonably flawless, and then another time might be a bit of a crash. I'd be thinking, *Please let it work*.

One show, somewhere in Europe, at a big venue, we were all waiting backstage for the encore. Paul said, 'You go on first, Helen.' I asked, 'What do you mean?' 'Well, you start it off, don't you? You go on first and we'll be right behind you.' That old chestnut.

So, on I went, played the notes on the piano . . . and nothing. Nobody. Not a soul. I was playing this piece by ear, and there was only so far I could go with that . . . I was about to fall off the stool and faint. Then suddenly I heard this . . . dah-dah-dah-dah-dah . . . Whitey on drums. I'll never forgive them.

Tim Pope: I don't think that music video is the best, to be honest. I think I heard the word *walls* and I'd never been to Poland and the Berlin Wall was up. All I really remember is a geezer in the street with cheap vodka. We filmed in this jazz club, with a big, oppressive Russian building and the most unenlightened audience. Just trying to get them to tap their feet.

Helen Turner: It rained the entire time. It was miserable. Everything looked as though it needed a coat of paint, which it did, of course, although people said that if you went into people's homes, it was a different matter there. We did the video in this club. It was quite strange in some ways. The audience seemed hard to read, almost non-plussed. There was this young guy who clearly fancied himself as a bit of a gangster. He had Levi's on, an American leather jacket – a real biker thing – strutting around. We were all quite intrigued by him. He seemed to be the one in charge of the contraband – or at least that's what he wanted everyone to think. It was a funny one that. It could just have easily been Birmingham on a rainy Monday.

Simon Napier-Bell: 'Walls Come Tumbling Down!' is one of my favourite pop records of all time. What they're singing is intense and political, but they're singing it in a style of just being a casual jokey thing, which, apart from anything else, makes it wonderfully interesting. Dee sings with a lot of attitude and quite an angry look in her face. The sound which is coming out is chirpy and happy, and the look on her face is the opposite.

David Cracknell: I appreciated those lyrics from an early age – songs like 'Walls Come Tumbling Down!' and the references to the miners' strike. The messages were very powerful. Nobody else was being that overtly political and they got away with it wrapped up in such wonderful tunes. Lines like 'From family trees, the dukes do swing'.

Mick Talbot: What's surprising is that we were half the age that we are now when we put that single out, and how little things have changed. It's daunting. Things don't change that much. I don't know if it was designed to be prophetic, or we had hoped it was just reflecting the times we were in, but times haven't changed as much as people might like you to think.

31 May 1985 – *Our Favourite Shop* (no. 1)

Paul Weller: I like the idea we were just a singles band. But like all things, they change in time. It became a bit more settled by *Our Favourite Shop*. I love that record; I thought it was a great record and then it kind of went downhill after that.

Olly Ball: It never occurred to me that so many people would be so obsessed with my cover, but that's great. I used to work for women's magazines, mostly accessories – shoes, bags and catalogue work. My big break was the Habitat catalogue. Simon Halfon called me about an album cover and wouldn't say who it was for. I did it cheaply because I really wanted the job once I found out.

Paul turned up in the big Mercedes with his dad and these boxes of records and clothes, and we spent a few hours putting it all together. Paul was very serious, no chat, just business. Mick was a little lighter. Most of the stuff on the walls is theirs, some of mine. Marlene Dietrich, Johnny Hallyday, Bardot next to *Another Country*, Natalie Wood, Jessica Lange's next to The Beatles, the Hancock thing on the shelf. There's quite a sordid illustration of Paul and Mick, done by a mate.

Dean Rudland: I can tell that's *Introducing Kenny Burrell* on the front cover of *Our Favourite Shop*. I spoke to Marco Nelson from Young Disciples, and he told me how he and Paul would have competitions about who could buy the best Blue Notes – and who could buy the most. This was in the late eighties, and as Marco said, 'I always lost. Paul always had a deeper pocket than I did.'

Paul Moody: What happened to the boombox on the front of *Our Favourite Shop*? That album cover was like a metaphor, really, wasn't it? It felt like Paul was saying, *I'm now going to embrace everything available to me.* Mod's a church, but it became a prison for some ... It was about freedom. Also, the guy looks impeccable throughout. Not a single bad photo. He looks phenomenal. A classic, classic record. That still stands up. I don't know where we'd be culturally without him, with all the access to this other stuff.

Jeff Slate: You see Georgie Best, Lennon and McCartney, *A Clockwork Orange* and think, *I'm already on the train. I'm already part of the club. So, what are these other things going to make me? Even cooler.*

Paul 'Smiler' Anderson: I think *Our Favourite Shop* gives the biggest insight into both Paul and Mick Talbot's mindset at the time. Paul is really anti-retro; he doesn't dwell on the past. But what's strange is that, in all those situations, it was his idea – *Our Favourite Shop*, *All Mod Cons*, and even later on with *Stanley Road* – they're all collages of his influences.

Peter Wilson: The music direction of *Our Favourite Shop* was more solidified, though it still has a lot of diversity. It's a great album, and yeah, I'm not as attached to the later ones. I'm not an impartial observer, so I can't give you a neutral answer, but I do think all the songs on *Our Favourite Shop* work really well, though they're diverse.

Lenny Henry: I knew Paul by then, and they used to rehearse at Nomis Studios, where I also worked. I'd go there to practise my act. I discovered that if you practise, you get better! So, I'd be at Nomis in Shepherd's Bush, running through the show with my musician, writer and band. Meanwhile, people like Wham! would rehearse in other studios. One day, Paul was there ... He says, 'I've got this thing called "The Stand-Up Comic's Instructions". Do you want to do it for me?' I said, 'Yeah, sure. What's it about?' and he explained that it's about working men's clubs and how sexist, racist and homophobic comedy prevails. I went, 'Why are you doing that?' He said, 'I just wrote it and thought we should do it.'

It didn't take very long to record ... 'All right, lad. Do this and do that, try this' – I did a kind of northern club comedian voice on *The Lenny Henry Show* – Englishman, Irishman, Scotsman jokes – that kind of thing. I thought, *Yeah, I can do that.* It took about twenty minutes. It was really a poem with a groove underneath.

Simon O'Brien: When *Our Favourite Shop* came out, I could relate to every song and lyric on there. I was quite active around the miners' strike of '84 when I was a second-year apprentice. I went on a lot of marches supporting the miners. I donated five pounds a week from my wages to help the miners' families with food. I remember seeing the band on *The Lenny Henry Show* doing 'You're the Best Thing', and they all had 'Coal Not Dole' stickers on, which I had on at the time. I thought, *Wow, they're not flying around in helicopters or riding in big limousines.* They were standing for the people. To see a band wearing those stickers and supporting the working class – that nailed it for me.

Jeremy Murray-Wakefield: How I got involved with The Style Council was a series of completely random events. I was an average teenager from a random town. I'd done a couple of weekends of work experience at a studio, and it was something I wanted to pursue. So, one day, I took time off work and walked from one end of Oxford Street to the other, popping in to recording studios with my CV. The last stop of the day was Solid Bond, and by a wonderful coincidence, the big fella guarding the front door had gone to the toilet, so I walked straight in. Gold discs on the wall. Nobody around. I just heard a man shouting down the phone at somebody, who turned out to be Paul's dad, John Weller. At the time, I had no idea who he was. I told him I was looking for a job in a studio, and he asked if I'd heard of The Style Council?' I said no, which probably worked in my favour. He handed me his card and told me to call him back in a couple of weeks.

I called him back, and he said 'Ah, Jerry,' which was funny. He never got my name right during the whole time that I knew him. He said, 'I've been meaning to speak to you. Have you done this sort of thing before?' and I said, 'Yes.' He said 'All right, you start a week Monday.' That was it. That was the entire job interview.

Mick Talbot: 'Homebreakers' is the only song where I sang lead all the way through. I did sing a little bit on 'Man of Great Promise', as well, on some of the bridge. I also took a verse in the second version of 'Headstart for Happiness'. I have the opening verse, Paul has the second, and Dee has the third. Like a relay race. We harmonised in a three-part arrangement near the end.

I had most of the music for 'Homebreakers' and Paul wrote the lyrics. They were very pertinent to the plight my dad and my youngest brother were in. It's about unemployment, people being made redundant, and the unions being smashed in the mid-eighties. My dad wasn't a miner, but it was happening in the print union too. They were both part of SOGAT [Society of Graphical and Allied Trades]. So Paul felt the lyrics echoed some of the things he'd overheard me saying about my family. My dad had worked the same job from leaving school at fifteen to fifty, and then suddenly that went up the wall. Those lyrics are quite personal to me, and Paul said, 'I think you should sing it.' It gives it a different character.

John Mealing: The album was different to 'Shout to the Top!' because all the songs are so varied. The first one I scored was 'Come to Milton Keynes', which was great fun because it's just a crazy, crazy track. It was a blast doing that. We had the string quartet arrangement for 'Stone's Throw Away' on that album, which is a great song. His lyrics are so perceptive. I'm much more centre ground than Paul, probably left of centre, whereas Paul is very left wing, but he's very genuine about it and he puts his money where his mouth is with everything. He's not an armchair socialist. We weren't on track together politically, but we got on great.

Darren Fletcher: The storytelling and the message behind these songs is so clever, the way he interweaves the words with a melody. If you read them on a page, some of them don't rhyme, it's more like a poem than a song. His melodies are so strong, and you don't often find that with other bands . . . Paul's got this enviable ability to sing such a strong melody and get a strong message across in such a clever way.

Tracie Young: I sang backing vocals on 'Boy Who Cried Wolf' . . . I always liked the sound of mine and Paul's voices together. I wish we got to do it a bit more, really.

Jeremy Murray-Wakefield: They were finishing off *Our Favourite Shop* when I came in, but there were still a few things missing. The very first thing you hear on that album is me standing at Waterloo station. It was when digital recording first came out, so they sent me down there with a Betamax video recorder over one arm, a digital processor on the other, and two expensive mics I'd borrowed from the cupboard. I spent the morning recording sounds in different places, and that ended up being used for the intro.

Another sound on that album was at the start of 'A Man of Great Promise' – the church bells. That was recorded at my local church in Welwyn Village, where I was still living with my parents. It took us ages to find a section of the bells ringing that was in time. Paul had his head in his hands, he was shaking his head, saying, 'What is this, jazz timing or something? This is ridiculous.' But then we found one little section that we ended up using in the song.

Stewart Prosser: I played trumpet on 'Man of Great Promise'. It's always been my go-to second instrument, and I always carry it with me. Most gigs I do, it ends up coming out at some point. I think Paul liked that slightly darker, warmer sound. It's not quite as percussive as the French horn, but it has that warmth, which I think suited the track perfectly.

Dee C. Lee: When Paul wrote that song, 'Down in the Seine', I remember, like, what an unusual thing. I hadn't worked with anybody like that. I really enjoyed the different styles of writing in a different way that he would come up with. Just the lyrics and the stories that he could tell. That in itself is a really, really, special gift.

Anthony Harty: I was learning quickly, but not quickly enough, because I didn't have much studio experience. So, they brought Camelle Hinds in, and he was a stunning player. The ball was in his court after that. I do remember a time in rehearsals, maybe for 'Down in the Seine' or 'Piccadilly Trail', when Paul, Mick and Steve stayed behind. They played me a track and asked me to come up with something. I got about two minutes, and then they said, 'Oh, OK.' I don't want to sound ungrateful, but I don't think I was given as good a crack of the whip in the studio, like Steve White was. Steve started in the studio; I started in rehearsals. So, I was just playing my interpretation of what was already laid down.

Mick Talbot: Cam was a big part of the Brit-funk movement. One of the founding fathers. I remember him in his little mac, doing 'Beggar and Co.' on *Top of the Pops* with some wonderful moves as well.

Camelle Hinds: In August 1984, my band Central Line split up, and it felt like the end of a love affair. I was thinking, *Oh man, what am I going to do?* Rather than mope, I went through my A to Z . . . Then, the first ever message on my new answer machine was from Paul Weller. 'Would you like to come and play on my new album?' I thought, *You've got to be kidding, man.* He'd already done *Café Bleu*, which I thought was amazing. I love Tracey Thorn's 'Paris Match'; that still blows my mind to this day. He was doing the new album, *Our Favourite Shop*, and asked if I'd like to come down the studio. I knew that Mickey Talbot, Steve White, Helen Turner and Dee C. Lee were already on board, so I was like, *Yeah, I'll have some of that.*

Jeremy Murray-Wakefield: Solid Bond was a fascinating building with a rich history. Paul had inherited the lease, and it had been modified over the years. Back when the record company had offices upstairs, they actually had a viewing gallery, where execs and their guests could watch people like Dusty Springfield while they were recording . . . 'Here's our latest recording artist performing her new single – hope it'll be a hit!'

The building had other quirks. The canteen area was built under the next road and always leaking ooze and gunge. There was a basement flat at 16A in Stanhope Place, which served as Paul's crash pad when he was working late. A really nicely decked-out bedsit, where he could stay over. Through the kitchen there was stalactites and stalagmites and old tape stores with eight-tracks of Val Doonican and old classical recordings with water dripping off the ceiling. Underneath the studio, 12 Connaught Place, there was what looked like a torture chamber – a tiny, tiled prison. It was actually a reverb room. The process involved placing a loudspeaker and a couple of microphones in there to create echo effects.

Paul wanted to try it and had this crazy idea to take Mick's Leslie cabinet from the Hammond organ down to that chamber to see how it sounded. We got Dave Liddle and Kenny Wheeler to lug this massive thing down a very narrow basement staircase. We set it all up, ran a specially made cable all the way back to the studio, to where Mick was playing, and directed it to the speakers. It sounded awful! 'All right. Bring it back up.' Dave and Kenny are giving me these black looks, 'You're having a laugh.' 'It sounds shit. We don't want it. Take it back up.' It would have given us an authentic old mono sound, but it wasn't really what we were shooting for.

Peter Wilson: John Mealing did a fantastic arrangement for 'Come to Milton Keynes' . . . It has this sort of fantastical quality. I know some people in Milton Keynes gave Paul a bit of flak for it, feeling it was unfairly dissing their town. But in Paul's mind, it represented an alienating environment where dreams are sold to the people living there. The orchestration, with the harp, is really clever. We recorded the strings for the album at Pye Studios in Marble Arch, down in the basement, with the Central Line underneath. If you're recording a rock band, it's fine, but if you're recording a string quartet, every four minutes, you'd hear a tube train going past with a low-frequency rumble. We had to find ways to work around that.

Stewart Prosser: The album was really sophisticated in its thinking and arrangements. What John Mealing had written for the strings and other parts was just inspired . . . At that point, Polydor was standing behind Paul and funding the project. We were also touring a lot, so there was money coming in from that as well. Economically, I think it stood up. It was a number one album in the UK, and clearly generating solid returns for the record company. I'd imagine they were pretty happy with it at the time.

Stuart Deabill: It's important to talk about politics in the context of the band's story, as it was a big part of my perspective. My dad was a trade unionist, a shop steward, so I come from that background. Socialism wasn't drummed into me, but it doesn't take long to work out who's got the money and who ain't. You saw that with Thatcherism and what she was doing, and then the miners' strike came along, which really polarized. With all that happening and with that band being at the forefront of reflecting the mood through Weller's clever lyrics, it really pulled me into that world.

Steve Rapport: The Style Council was a revolutionary band. They had revolutionary lyrics, packed with politics, yet wrapped in a dance band format that crossed genres – jazz, funk, fusion, pop.

At the time, we didn't notice how powerful the lyrics were. He got a lot of shit for 'Come to Milton Keynes' when it came out, but when you listen to it now, it's hard not to be struck by that line, 'We used to chase dreams, now we chase the dragon.' I hope kids today understand what that means, because it's really a dagger to the heart of Thatcher's Britain.

Sarah Jane Morris: By listening to people like Paul, I learned that rather than knock people over the head with your politics, you wrap it up with a beautiful melody and it's there if people choose to take it to pieces and look at the lyrics later, but it's not the first thing they hear. First thing they hear is this incredibly catchy, beautiful tune.

Peter Wilson: That's part of the genius of it. Take 'A Stone's Throw Away', for example – it's about the miners but wrapped up in a quick, sweet song, a bittersweet song. John Mealing's string quartet arrangement was a lovely idea. Paul was inspired by 'Eleanor Rigby', the McCartney song, and it really works.

Mick Talbot: It was something that we liked doing, something like 'All Gone Away'. Musically, it has this samba influence, very bright and breezy but the lyrics tell a different story. We liked that contrast, that juxtaposition in a lot of those tunes.

Paul Weller: Whether we lost people through that, I'm sure we did. A few people were put off by the political side of it. But then The Jam had that as well, so I don't know why they would have been put off. When people have asked me in the past why don't I write any more political songs? What would I say? Sadly, a lot of those things are still exactly the same. 'Eton Rifles': that's just Boris and all these Bullingdon Club boys, isn't it? To me anyway.

Dee C. Lee: Paul was somebody who was very, very interested in what's going on in the world. If we were singing about things I didn't believe, then I'd have to say, 'Look, I'll have to step back and I might not sing on this,' but everything I was singing I agreed with, I would sing it and be a part of it, but I'm not somebody who likes to sit up and discuss politics with people who I don't know. I keep that for friends and the dinner table.

Adrian Thrills: There was definitely more levity in much of what The Style Council did, even though some of the songs had more social realism and politics. As a concept, The Style Council felt a bit more frivolous compared to The Jam.

Simon Halfon: The first record I ever got given by my grandparents when I was a kid was *Beatles for Sale* . . . It's a gatefold, but the record goes inside rather than outside, and that stayed with me. Paul and I used it a couple of times, firstly on *Our Favourite Shop* . . . then we did it again on *Stanley Road*. So, from being literally a toddler and having that record sleeve, it manifested itself all the way through to the eighties and nineties . . . obviously Paul was fully aware of that. One of the things that bound Paul and I together all those years was our love for The Beatles, so he was up for that immediately.

Nick Knight: If you're working with Paul Weller, it's a privilege and a joy because the man's got such insight, and if you don't listen to what he's saying it's such a waste. I guess that we worked together enough times to develop some sort of bond, and some sort of mutual understanding of what the visuals should be.

With the photo that I did of Paul and Mick for the inside of *Our Favourite Shop* there's a little bit of a nod and a wink, probably quite a big nod and a wink, to David Bailey in the sixties portraits. Lennon and McCartney, Mick Jagger and the Kray twins, and those half-a-dozen portraits that he created which became iconic versions of stylish portraiture.

I think with Paul, there are influences that are just like musical influences. You don't take them and just have them exact. You need to tweak them; you need to make them feel contemporary. You need to see them again, just like he does in his music.

Mick Talbot: There's only about four or five months between Paul and me, so we have a similar vintage and recall certain things the same way. We see eye to eye and lose track of time when we talk about it. We went on holiday together once, and both our partners got bored with us talking about it all the way to the Caribbean. 'You two have been talking about trousers for seven hours. It's pathetic!' But when you have a bond with someone like that, it stays with you and follows through.

Nick Knight: Paul was often quite surprising at what he'd want to look like. I remember one of the moments where I just thought to myself *Yes!* is when he wanted to wear the jacket that I was wearing for the photoshoot. Back in the early eighties, I had a pale blue cord jacket, which I got from a French brand called Chipie, which are probably dreadful now, or closed. But at the time they felt great. I remember Paul seeing that going, 'Ah, Nick, can I just put that jacket on?' and I said, 'Yes, at last!' Stylistic recognition from one of the greats. Paul's an easy man to photograph because he knew how to perform, and he was up for it. He knew how to stand and how to work everything; he could throw it all together. And he was surrounded by some pretty authentic-looking people. Mick Talbot and Dee, and everybody. They also knew how to put it together. I'm sure Paul had a lot to do with art directing the style of the rest of the band. As you can tell from all that . . . those white Levi's. They took it well and you had to wear it.

Dee C. Lee: Paul was really into the Levi look, so we were all in the white Levi's. This is a good look. Different little thing . . . for a little short while, it was our uniform, and then we'd change it up again.

Mick Talbot: Nowadays, you can get anything without leaving the country, but back then white Levi's were hard to come by. We'd be in Rome, and you just knew they were going to have a lot of them there, so we'd make it a mission to hit the shops. Paul used to describe me and him as like 'two old girls at a jumble sale' when we were on a quest for clothes. Paris was good for that too – they seemed to have more than we did. Occasionally, you'd hear about a shop in London that had some white Levi's, so it became a bit of a thing, and it became infectious through the band. Helen Turner remembers people just shouting, 'Hang on, I think I saw a shop with white Levi's – stop the coach!'

Peter Wilson: *Our Favourite Shop* was the last time I worked with The Style Council. I'm not sure Paul was learning to produce from me – he wouldn't say that. I mean, I was learning from him. But he did tend to follow his heart and his nose, so having someone a bit more dispassionate to keep track of everything else was useful. I did relish the opportunity to arrange for strings or horns or to play the occasional instrument. It was a collaborative process, and that was a lot of fun.

Jeremy Murray-Wakefield: I was really lucky because the thing about Paul was that he knew I was smart, but he also knew that I was quite vulnerable and quite young. I suffered a lot from being an Aspie teenager back then, so I was quite awkward still. He was protective towards me and always listened to my suggestions. To put that into context, many people my age working in other studios were exploited – not getting paid and even being given time off to sign on at the job centre. That's how some studios were operating. Some were regularly subjected to physical abuse, which seems unimaginable now, but back then the industry was a bit of a Wild West operation. I landed with the Weller family, and because it was a family-run business, they really took care of me with kindness and support.

Camelle Hinds: From then on, I was recruited to join the band. *Our Favourite Shop* went straight to number one on our first gig at Brixton Academy. It was like, *Blimey, man.*

Olly Ball: I was made up when *Our Favourite Shop* went to number one. I once found a bootleg poster of the cover at Dingwalls market and just bought it. I didn't even bother telling him it was mine – just thought, *I'll have that!* That was a real kick, seeing it go straight to number one. That's the only cover I ever did. The only album cover I ever shot.

Richard Ogden: There had been a big change in management of Polydor. A. J. Morris had retired and was succeeded by John Preston ... And they got a new chief executive, Maurice Oberstein, the 'legend' from CBS Records. He and John Preston didn't get on. John then left to run RCA and out of the blue, much to my surprise, I was appointed managing director of Polydor Records: 1985, I was thirty-five years old, and the youngest managing director.

I didn't know why I'd been given this job, and I didn't know what the job was and didn't know how to do it. But it dawned on me quite quickly that I'd been given this job because I was the only person in the company that had a personal relationship with the artists who were now out of contract. Paul Weller, Bryan Ferry and Roxy Music, Level 42, Andrew Lloyd-Webber, who we'd made millions out of because we had *Cats*, and The Cure. They were all out of deals ... that was the point when I had to re-sign Style Council. *Our Favourite Shop* was a number one album. I believe I'm right in saying that I then paid an advance of a million pounds for what came next.

June 1985 – 'Internationalists' UK tour

Mick Talbot: The Honorary Councillor thing, at some point it became apparent that Steve and Dee were really important to what we were doing. I suppose they were less 'honorary' and more permanent after a while. By the time we got to *Our Favourite Shop*, we had formulated things more, but we still wanted to have the liberation to bring in people just specifically for things. But we were building more of a core, and that's bound to happen once you go onto a live forum.

Camelle Hinds: Joining the live band in '85 was like joining a family. The camaraderie was beautiful. Solid Bond was an exceptional organisation with Paul, John and Kenny at the helm. Their management taught me so much. We didn't have to lift a finger until we got into soundcheck or got on stage – everything was taken care of. They knew that we had to be at our top to deliver. We were in a position whereby if we didn't deliver, we'd be out. There's no pressure, apart from having to deliver in your role to make this the best show possible. It wasn't always easy. Sometimes, you'd think you've done a great gig, and Paul would come off and say, 'That was rubbish.'

Mick Talbot: We were one of the last bands to play at the Apollo before it got knocked down. The whole crowd were singing, 'It's coming down on Tuesday, la-la-la-la!' The great thing about Glasgow is that they either love you, or they want to kill you. If you're appreciated there then it certainly is genuine.

David F. Ross: I've seen them live quite a lot of times, but the two that stand out the most are Manchester Apollo one night and Glasgow Apollo the following night. They always went away from that conventional thing of an unknown support act on for twenty minutes, a slightly better-known support act on for half an hour and then the main band come on just before nine for a couple of hours. You had circumstances where Weller would be on first for fifteen minutes and then there would be a break, and your man Vaughn Toulouse was the DJ and Junior Giscombe. It was like a revue thing. Sometimes it worked, sometimes it didn't. Glasgow audiences famously are difficult, particularly the Apollo ones, but that night with Style Council, everything clicked. The structure of it, the songs, the sequencing of everything, even the guests that they had on.

Dee C. Lee: John Weller very much became the dad that I didn't have. We were very, very close. But yeah, it really was a motley crew of the weirdest people. But I loved it because sitting around a table whenever we had to eat or travel together . . . You get quite close . . . my whole life was being involved in music, writing music or performing music. I didn't need much else of a life and, I didn't realise at the time, but I didn't actually have one. So, your inner circle, when you spend that much time with people, like at work or something, then some intense relationships can start!

22 June 1985 – Glastonbury Festival

Mick Talbot: We got to Glastonbury Festival early on the coach, and it was three or four feet of mud. We definitely didn't think that through – we were wearing white shoes and white trousers. Glastonbury back then was a lot messier, too. It wasn't as corporate or organised backstage as it is these days . . . Now, it's a bit more forgiving on your clothes. But there's no escaping the fact you're in the middle of a cow field, and if it's been raining, it's going to get boggy. Still, that doesn't mean you should drop your standards. Just because it's muddy doesn't mean we have to turn up looking like we're about to fix your drains!

Dee C. Lee: We all had the white Levi's on . . . I'd never done anything like that before. So, we all turned up in our whites, *Yeah, we're The Style Council.* We get there, we just see fields of mud and people covered in mud. I was already going 'Oh no, oh no, no, no. Turn back to London, please . . .' People started giving me drinks already on the bus, going, 'Oh God, shut her up' . . . I hate dirt and mud and especially if you're not dressed for it . . . I think we might have got over the white Levi's after Glastonbury!

Camelle Hinds: We had time to kill, so we got plastered. By the time we got on stage, I was a mess. Mick's Pro-One analogue synthesiser overheated and went badly out of tune, but we were too drunk to care. We were falling over risers, and the next day's paper had photos of us looking up at the sky. All good fun!

Mick Talbot: Pernod was mostly to blame, and with the rain, it felt like a scene from *MASH*. I think the crowd stuck with us because of the weather, especially when we opened with 'Long Hot Summer'.

Helen Turner: The crew had bin liners on their legs, and we were carried around like royalty – until I forgot and jumped off the back of the stage, straight into the mud up to my knees.

Dee C. Lee: They got us there at something like one in the afternoon . . . by the time we went on stage at about fricking twelve o'clock at night. Think I drank myself sober . . . I kept drinking, I got sober again and then got drunk again. It was that crazy.

I just remember us all sounding like a bunch of football hooligans and also giggling and laughing all the way through the set. Paul fell over backwards and was playing guitar on the floor with his legs sticking up in the air . . . Mick's all pie-eyed doing the keyboards. It was just so funny . . . I remember hearing [*shouts*] 'You're the best thing.' I was like, *That can't be me. Is that me? That's actually coming out of my mouth, isn't it?* . . . After that I don't remember anything.

Helen Turner: The bus driver was apoplectic as we climbed back on, completely covered in mud. Quite a day – I won't forget it!

Dennis Munday: Glastonbury was my last gig before leaving Polydor. Steve White announced on stage, 'Dennis is having a leaving do next week at the Lamb & Flag on James Street,' and, surprisingly, two lads actually turned up! I have no regrets about leaving. People told me it was stupid for my career, but I said, 'That's not what I'm about. You've only got one life' – if you're not getting something meaningful out of what you're doing, move on.

Mick Talbot: Dennis Munday was very helpful to our first three years. He fought our corner. There was quite a lot of chin stroking and muttering about a lot of things we did, but he was our bridge to the label. He spoke our language, and we were very fortunate to have him as an A&R man.

Richard Ogden: Maybe the artist thought that Dennis played an important role. But within the company, everybody thought he was just twiddling his thumbs because Polydor had no influence over Paul Weller. Not really. No influence at all. So, if Geffen Records think that Paul Weller should be working with Phil Ramone, then that was Dennis Munday's job to sell that. Did he? No, of course he didn't. I believe to this day that Paul Weller is a sufficiently great talent that he should have been a worldwide star. But he held himself back. I got into conflict with them about that when I was MD of Polydor. My view was 'I believe in you, but I think you need to open your minds to the fact there's a big world out there that are making more sophisticated music, are making it better, making it sound more expensive, you know, why don't you give it a try?' And they never would. Dennis worked for me: that should have been his job as Style Council's A&R man.

Dennis Munday: A year earlier, Polydor's management changed, bringing in younger people who I thought might be an improvement. However, it turned out to be worse. The new team wanted to make the company more upmarket and trendy, but I told them it wouldn't work as long as they were selling artists like James Last and Andrew Lloyd-Webber. Polydor's strength was its bands. Labels like Virgin and Stiff were focused on their brands, Polydor should have been about the music and the artists. When I felt my position was at risk, I knew it was time to leave. By 1985, I was fed up with the constant meetings and pointless arguments. I spoke with the MD, agreed on a package, and left. I was glad I did, especially since *Our Favourite Shop* was number one when I left, and Live Aid was the following day.

28 June 1985 – 'Come to Milton Keynes' (no. 23)

13 July 1985 – Live Aid

Mick Talbot: That day was such a whirlwind – four different things happened just that day, never mind the rest of the week.

Nigel 'Spanner' Sweeney: Paul got hoisted onto the Live Aid list. I felt he could have been higher up the bill. They were second on the bill after Status Quo, which was the perfect starter, 'Rocking All Over the World'. On the day, typical bloody plugger, I had also booked Paul on a TV programme in Maidstone singing 'Come to Milton Keynes'. Paul really loved the fact he was doing Live Aid and the TV programme. We went back to the stadium, and he sang the final bits at the end.

Dee C. Lee: Except for me. After all that buzz, I just had to go home and watch the rest of it on telly. They were very tight with it and only the very important people like . . . they only wanted

Paul. Nobody else. They wanted George Michael. Nobody else. It was a bit like that. So yeah, the rest of us were not invited . . . We had started the day after Status Quo, and the thing had been going on, I was watching it for the rest of the night going, I can't believe I was there and I performed there . . . so it's just like I was part of this history, which is so amazing.

Dylan Jones: One thing that stands out is how the so-called legacy performers, probably only in their thirties and forties at the time, really benefited from the event. While the newer acts like Spandau, Sade, Style Council and Adam and the Ants were at the front, I didn't think they suited the large-scale environment. They were better suited to smaller venues. As the day went on and the sun came down and you had rather more dramatic lighting, it was those older artists – The Who, Queen, McCartney, Bowie – who really benefited. After that, there was a surge, a global reacquaintance with acts like that and everybody wanted to play stadia.

Camelle Hinds: I was playing keyboard bass on 'You're the Best Thing'. I'm confident with a four-string bass . . . but playing keyboard bass made me nervous in case I hit a wrong note. Those analogue keyboards went out of tune in the heat . . . it's in front of the whole world, if I hit a wrong note then I'll be toast for the rest of my life. Backside, roadie Dave Liddle was winding me up, telling me that it had gone out of tune again. I panicked, but when I hit the first note, it was perfectly in tune. Relief! After that, I relaxed, put my bass on, and really enjoyed the performance.

Dee C. Lee: Before we went on, Steve White was going, 'Do you know how many people are out there?' I was like this is such a big deal. But come on, I'm a professional. Nothing's gonna faze me. I'm fine. Got all my make-up done. Then Steve White went,

'Go and look behind the curtain. Look at the audience.' I was like no, no, no. There's no point in doing that. It's gonna make me nervous. He said, 'Go have a look.' I had a look. It was bad enough . . . Then he said, 'and it's being televised all round the world.' I said, 'Shut up, Steve,' and had to run back and throw up . . . So, I went on stage with dark glasses on because I didn't have time to redo my eye makeup . . . I just look like a Black Alice Cooper joined The Style Council.

Mick Talbot: Yeah, it was nerve wracking. The more you thought about it, the worse it got. I'm quite pleased that we were on early and didn't really mess up too much and just did what we had to do. It was more about what it stood for. Love him or loathe him, it was a phenomenal achievement by Bob Geldof.

David F. Ross: I don't think there's any circumstance under which Weller was ever really comfortable with that level of fame. You can see it in moments like Live Aid and Band Aid – great causes, but he didn't want the baggage of it all. You can see he's not really part of that, and uncomfortable with the association of how many of the other acts that day reacted. There's a desire to have things that are valuable to him and a set of values that there's not with a lot of musicians.

August 1985 – Japan and Australia tour

Steve Sidelnyk: After Live Aid, we went to Japan, and at that time, you had to go through Anchorage due to Russian restrictions. There was a four-hour delay, and this woman recognised us from Live Aid. That's when you knew the massiveness of all that.

Nicky Weller: Japan was a massive bill. Boy George was on the lineup. I remember seeing the poster from Osaka. It was a festival of different people including The Style Council. The auditorium was absolutely massive.

Boy George: I remember having a massive mad time in Japan with The Style Council, Go West, and then Billy McKenzie was there. Jocelyn Brown was singing backing vocals for us. There was this mad moment where we got Billy to come on and sing with us, and he just went off on this insane tangent, screaming like a crazy person. I remember Jocelyn looking at me going, *Huh?*

Richard Ogden: I went to Japan with them and then Tony Morris told me, 'You need to go to Australia for a conference.' It dawned on me, about five hours across the South China Sea. 'Holy shit, I'm supposed to have a visa.' When I got to Australia, I got arrested, put in a little room by this appalling Australian policeman, who had khaki shorts and long white socks, and said things like, 'Yeah, you Pommies all think you still own this place, don't you?' And then the head of Polydor had to come bail me out.

Helen Turner: I came down with an all-over body rash, so I didn't have the greatest fun. I was confined to my room when I wasn't on the stage. It was very, very, very hot and humid that time in Japan. Imagine a mild drizzle about fifty degrees or something. Then we flew to Australia, and it was like 'phew'.

Dee C. Lee: We got really looked after. Like when everybody got ill, and John had to get a private doctor in. We all got B6 shots . . . touring, big bands and bad weather and immune systems get run down. And the next thing you know, everybody's got a tummy bug and one person gets it, the whole bang . . . John running backwards and forwards to different rooms. 'Are they OK? Is Dee OK?' Taking over hotels. Yeah, it was sweet and very funny and we just took it in our stride at the time. Every time I think about it, they were such wonderful times.

Nicky Weller: No, I would never go to Australia. I've turned down so many tours because of the spiders. I'm not joking.

Ann Weller: And I wouldn't go because of the snakes.

Steve Sidelnyk: Style Council were so huge in Australia . . . They even televised the Melbourne show. Of course, it's hard to get around because it's such a huge country.

Martin Hopewell: Flying was never very popular with any incarnations of Weller. Somehow, they managed to get themselves by plane down to Australia but arrived with blankets over their heads and really not wanting to see any of it, didn't like it. We had to go from Melbourne to Sydney and I tried to explain that the plane would be the same type they'd arrived on – not the bush doctor with goggles, but a 747. But no, they wouldn't have it, so they insisted on getting a train.

They arranged three special Pullman carriages for us on this train that wound its way through the outback from Melbourne to Sydney. A 1960s thing with nice big armchairs. One carriage was devoted to be a jamming space with a drum kit, tambourines, maracas, guitars and stuff – like something out of *A Hard Day's Night*. We sat on this bloody train for about nineteen hours, watching nothing of interest outside, sitting there playing appallingly badly in this makeshift music carriage.

Mick Talbot: We could go there and jam with an electric piano, drum kit and amps set up – it was surreal – like an episode of *The Monkees*. That killed a few hours. But Paul had probably got used to the faster bullet trains in Japan.

Paul Du Noyer: *The Hit* magazine sent me to Australia after Paul and The Style Council had finished in Japan. I spent a week with them, and it was nice hanging out with Paul, Mick and Steve White. His relationship with Dee C. Lee was coming together. The Style Council were pretty much at their peak. They had just about won everybody over at that stage.

Dee C. Lee: I think Ann and John were quite instrumental in maybe getting us together because I think they really, really liked us as a couple, and they saw something before we even saw something, looking back. So, yeah, got them to blame! But we just eased into it and didn't make a big deal because it's not really anybody's business as such.

Tracie Young: There was a jingle writer called Eamon who used Solid Bond, and he wrote a song for Eurovision. He'd approached John to ask if I'd be interested in recording this and submitting it to the *Song for Europe*. And John, I can hear him to this day, 'Fink about it, babe. Millions of people all around the world. It'll be fucking amazing. Fucking amazing'. I'm a massive Eurovision fan but even I knew that doing it would be career suicide at that time. I said, 'I don't think it'd be a good idea, honestly, but why don't you run it past Paul and then tell me what Paul said?' Needless to say, it went nowhere, but I can still hear him to this day. 'Millions of people all around the fucking world. It'd be fucking amazing. You'll sell fucking millions of records, babe.'

John was my manager. Just a lovely, lovely, warm person . . . The other week was the first time I've seen Nicky Weller in a while. She said to me, 'You sound a lot posher than I remember, is that because of presenting on radio?' and I said, 'Partly, but it wasn't a conscious effort. It's been a number of things. Partly living in different geographical areas around the country, kind of refining how I speak. But honestly, if I'm truthful, a lot of it comes from not just going fuckin' this and fuckin' that, and that's from not being around your brother and your father twenty-four/seven. I was hanging around with these guys from Woking, Kenny Wheeler and Dave Liddle and all these people, and every other word was 'fuck' pronounced 'faak'.

20 September 1985 – 'The Lodgers' (no. 13)

Dee C. Lee: I remember saying to Paul, your music is really changing a lot. I'm loving it.

Guy Barker: I got a call to go and play in the brass section at Solid Bond. John Mealing did all the brass and string charts. He was a proper old-school arranger, wrote everything out beautifully.

John Mealing: The horn section I booked, they were great musicians. They were doing it for more or less straight session fees, which was really wow . . . Once you start doing the arranging, you find out who are the guys with the right attitude in the studio, who can cut the mustard.

Ashley Slater: I discovered the trombone when I was about twelve. Absolutely adored it. We all suffer a little bit from impostor syndrome, and I did really suffer from that. With The Style Council, I'm certain that somebody else that they would rather have used wasn't able to do it . . . I'd say my USP is that I'm really good at doing one thing, and that's being Ashley Slater.

Guy Barker: There was a really nice energy being in the studio with Paul and Mick. A vibe where this music was hip and modern, but you could hear where it drew its influences from. Jazz and blues were in there, as well as the rock and the pop. I remember thinking it was very sophisticated.

Ashley Slater: When we did those sessions, Paul's dad was running things and did a great job too. I think Paul would happily admit that his dad really helped him out, focused his career. He was a cool guy and those sessions were really lovely. The charts are written out, sat down, friendly vibe, get it done. But it's weird when you're a session musician, I'm not so much any more, but you don't really think about what you're doing. What you're doing is earning 135 quid that day. The end. Sure, I'm playing with Paul Weller. You don't think about it. You turn up and do your best and you're just like, *Thank God I've got work today.*

October 1985 – Dee C. Lee, 'See the Day'

Dee C. Lee: I kept being offered more Style Council tours and I was going, 'I love working with you guys but I'm not going to do this tour.' Why? 'I need to concentrate on what the hell I'm doing because I'm just stuck in this stalemate with my record label and I need to do whatever it is I need to do, just to make the ball roll, so that I'm not just stuck here.' And then John was like, 'You do this tour, and we'll help you out' . . . So, I did the tour, I was very happy to do that and we started doing 'See the Day' as part of The Style Council set and the band learned it like that [*clicks fingers*] . . . Those guys, Paul especially, were like, 'No, you get up there.' I'd say, 'You're just going on to have a fag break.' But it did me the world of good and I'll be forever grateful always, because I really did perfect my stage presence, if you like, by working with The Style Council.

My record company wouldn't do the song, so the Wellers paid for it to be recorded, mastered, paid for the strings to come in and we put it out as a single ourselves. It did so well, it got to number three. There was a few, I wouldn't say red faces, but I scored one little point. It was like, *I did know what I was talking about.*

December 1985 – UK tour and Wembley Arena

Stewart Prosser: There were times when the band went out without a horn section, like Glastonbury and Live Aid . . . Once a tour ended, you'd go to the after-party and say, 'See you soon,' and really have no idea. It could be days, weeks, months, never.

After the big tours, I'd do session work, but it wasn't a lifestyle I enjoyed, sitting, waiting by the phone. I like to be active, structured, pushing ahead on things. So, I'd got a job at Chase Manhattan Bank as a financial analyst. A few weeks in, I got a call from Kenny Wheeler about a UK tour. 'I know you got this straight gig. Could you do it so you wouldn't need to do the rehearsals? Do one maybe?'

Mick Talbot: When we got to play Wembley at the end of 1985, the lineup was really bolstered with additional strings and brass. The staging was arranged to accommodate cameras, with rostrums and space between the band sections for better shots. In some ways, the Wembley gig was a compromise, as we knew the performance was being filmed. I respect the punter in the room with you at the time. I think if the film can happen, then that's a bonus; when you start compromising it, I'm in two minds then, but you've got to work out somehow how to do it.

Stewart Prosser: We ended up doing three nights at Wembley and the *Showbiz* film. Guy Barker and I were playing horns and that was just phenomenal.

My new boss had asked if music was out of my system. Desperate for a job and money, I said 'Yes, of course it is.' Two weeks later, I asked for annual leave, left the office on Friday, did rehearsals, played Wembley, and went to the after-party. The next day, I was back at work. My brain hadn't landed and this guy walks in the office and just points at me and I'm like, what? He said, 'I saw you last night.' I was thinking, *Where was I? Oh, you played at Wembley.* 'Keep your voice down.' No one knew apart from that one guy. I told him to shut up. My boss didn't find out.

Those gigs were very different. In the early days, it felt like a really tight club-band unit. Gigs in small places in Germany where the horn section was in line with Paul and Mick. Come the Wembley shows, at the very end of my time, we were four miles back on a podium at the car park. A very different experience . . . I've got slightly mixed memories. I was torn between wanting to do this all the time, but I also need to earn all the time.

Camelle Hinds: Going into rehearsals with Paul is no joke. It's like going to war sometimes. Seriously, it really is. When you come out the other side, you can play on any stage around the world and bring it on as good as anybody out there. He's got an astonishing work ethic. To this day, that's my model of operation in the industry . . . Before any Style Council tours, we'd do a good month of rehearsals, five days a week.

Guy Barker: I loved working with The Style Council. We didn't have any spitting or anything! . . . At the time I had a massive collection of Warner Bros cartoons on video, and I used to put them on the band bus and make them all watch them . . . You see, that's the thing. Most of the time, where the rock and roll actually happens isn't like rock and roll. That happens with the crowd and the media but not the band.

Junior Giscombe: Paul rang me up and said to me, 'Listen, you got to come down. We're doing Wembley. I want you to come on stage. I want you to sing.' I'm like 'What?' I did the three nights, and did 'Move on Up' each night with them. That was awesome, man.

Stewart Prosser: The Style Council was probably the most important, most influential musical experience of my life. I learned a lot from it. John's anecdotes. I learned phrases like 'it's not a problem, son, it's a situation'. That's really held me in good stead for years and years.

Billy Chapman: When things get to a scale of success, you don't fully grasp its place in the timeline until you look back on it. That period was definitely a peak of a moment – everyone was on point . . . Can you imagine standing behind Paul Weller during 'Long Hot Summer', watching him play the Moog synth, essentially playing the bassline? . . . Looking back now, it's one of the greatest moments ever.

Guy Barker: There was always a great consistency, we'd done a lot of rehearsals with The Style Council. Suddenly things slot into place very easily. I remember walking down to play the solo. It was just an immense occasion and it's six or seven thousand people. We were so high up at the back, and you could see Paul and Mick and Dee C. Lee down there. It was good fun. After that, there were a few other situations that I played in where I saw that kind of reaction, like doing the Sinatra tour, 25,000 people every night, and there's nothing quite like the roar that a crowd makes, and it's quite overwhelming. The Style Council was early days for me with those things.

Steve Sidelnyk: As you get older, you realise how many people were deeply influenced by that era and what we did. It's pretty immense, and definitely not something to brush under the carpet.

Stewart Prosser: After reaching that level of orchestral and sonic grandeur, there's not much space left to explore. Paul's the kind of writer who hears both the full sound and the spaces between it. We talked about that later, and I think he felt that at the time, that big sound was what he wanted to project. Big show. But it wasn't something he repeated – very quickly after that, he took it back down to the basics.

January 1986 – Red Wedge tour

Ann Weller: I'm a Conservative and Paul is whatever he is, and he said to me, 'Why are you Conservative?' 'Because I've always been a Conservative. I just have. Don't ask me why I've always been a Conservative.' I didn't take any notice of him. 'But you live in a *council house*.' It doesn't matter. The state of the bloody Labour lot. Bloody hell.

Dee C. Lee: Musicians write about whatever they feel and what is their thing. I personally am not crazy about putting my politics into music, but The Style Council wasn't my band. I was part of that band, and I was very proud to be part of it and whatever it stands for, I was happy for that too. So, I agreed with everything. I wouldn't have done it if I didn't. I was a working-class girl myself, but I was never as vocal about these things. That's not to say that I didn't think about them, so I was quite happy and proud for him to speak on our behalf.

Billy Bragg: The basic idea about Red Wedge wasn't that we were all diehard fans of the Labour Party. I was a member of the Labour Party because I believed in fully engaging with them. But what bound us together on Red Wedge was our opposition to Margaret Thatcher. That was the thing that we were all agreed on.

Paul Weller: I thought the intention of the artists was good, but the fact that we got roped into Red Wedge, and with the

Labour Party, I thought that was, in retrospect, a mistake. Even at the time I was not sure, but I went along with it, which I wouldn't now . . . to affiliate myself with anyone from any party. I think Red Wedge was helped along by the Labour Party because at the time they were trying to run down the Young Socialists, which was the younger wing of the Labour Party. They were trying to get rid of them because they were too radical for them. That's what I've heard anyway. Red Wedge was like this other thing. It really came from Billy Bragg. He's the one who came down to my studio at the time and, Bill's a very persuasive person, and he's right as well. He was right. Got to try and do something. And this was still just after the miners' strike.

Annajoy David: The face of Britain was changed. You can't underestimate that. If you take three hundred years of industrial evolution and dismantle it in just thirty years, you are going to get massive payback. You'll get chaos – the loss of community, loss of identity, and a disconnection from the pathways of how you live your life, not just economically, but socially, culturally . . . We came into the midst of that to say, 'Hang on a minute, there's a better way.' Through culture, we represented an alternative side to Britain that hadn't yet been created, but we were at the start of it.

Billy Bragg: The only viable vehicle for defeating Margaret Thatcher was the Labour Party in the 1987 election. Neil Kinnock was absolutely crucial, but Paul Weller really was the absolute crucial aspect of it because otherwise it would have been Billy Bragg and a load of little lefty herberts. I think I'm right in saying Weller was the only artist who did miners' benefits and Live Aid . . . and he was huge at the time, *Our Favourite Shop* had just been massive . . . In many ways, he had the most to lose in terms of his career if it all went tits up, but he committed himself to it 100 per cent and made the whole Style Council infrastructure available to us.

The first time I went to meet him at Solid Bond to talk about Red Wedge . . . we sat in an office there and while I chatted to him, he was cutting out his press for the week . . . the fact that Paul did it himself said something to me like, *This is an authentic guy . . . He's one of the biggest pop stars in Britain today and he's bought the music papers, is cutting out his press and putting it in a folder.* That was a key moment of bonding with me and Paul . . . when I was looking to find if Paul Weller was real or just a completely made-up construct like Boy George, Paul was real and he still is real. Trust me. To hold on to your authenticity is not easy and it's respectable because he's managed to do it over five decades now.

Lucy Hooberman: I read about this thing called Red Wedge being launched in one of the Sunday papers. Labour Party, music, young people. I phoned up the Labour Party, and they tried to put me through to about a million people. Eventually, someone told me where there was going to be a meeting, so I just pitched up. I was an aspiring filmmaker at the time; I'd always been interested in culture as a means of change.

At that first meeting, they were talking about the tour, so I asked, 'Is anyone planning to make a film?' I'd been inspired by the miners' strike, where local collectives had made powerful films about their communities. I thought: we're going to youth engagement events along the way, let's work with local groups rather than just show up with a big London crew. It felt important that we gave young people in those areas a chance to contribute.

Robert Howard: The first time I actually met Paul would have been when we were recording our first album, *Limping for a Generation* . . . Pete Wilson produced our first album, so Paul was always hanging around and we got to know each other, gently. I loved the idea of Red Wedge . . . Luckily, we had a hit with 'Digging Your Scene'. That was suddenly exploding and so I felt that, OK, we can do it now, because I didn't want to jump on some bandwagon to make it look like we were looking for help . . . we did the second Red Wedge tour . . . The Style Council hosted the whole thing. Kenny Wheeler was running it, and John, although I don't know whether their politics were the same as mine. Paul's definitely was. We'd use their backline and then we'd all get together and do something at the end of the night, 'Move on Up' usually . . . I made friends on that tour, Paul, Mick Talbot, Rhoda Dakar, Dee C. Lee, that I've kept for forty years.

Steve Rapport: I took pictures of Paul a whole shit ton of times. He was very expressive on stage and in his lyrics, but he was shy and really kept to himself, even on the Red Wedge tour in '86. He believed what he believed. He didn't want to be part of the party stuff. Billy was much more hard hitting. He was the driving force. It really was Billy and Paul that were the founders of Red Wedge and John Weller didn't like that. I think John was pretty conservative and had tried to talk Paul out of it, and I feel like me and John bumped heads a few times because he felt like I was one of those lefties that was corrupting his son.

Annajoy David: The impact of that period and its role in reshaping Britain can't be overstated. The success we saw later, particularly during the Blair years, was a result of the narrative we helped define. While others delivered it, we set the agenda, especially in terms of social change, like civil partnerships and LGBT rights. Paul Weller, Jerry Dammers, The Communards and Madness played key roles in that. Our cultural contributions and political ideas helped shape a more confident and progressive Britain, which ultimately influenced the policies of the 1997 Labour government. I'm incredibly proud of that legacy.

Billy Bragg: We had our own manifesto, which was signed off by Neil Kinnock, which touched on so many issues that are still current today: the climate, LGBTQI rights, although the alphabet didn't go that far in those days. Those issues that have always engaged young people. We were pushing hard to get those in there.

Robert Howard: I think it was music that politicised me. Paul and Strummer, some of those journalists that were writing about it, especially during the time when Neil Spencer was editor of the *NME*, really led me into places that opened my mind . . . this endless gruelling era of Thatcherism, which had decimated working-class communities, decimated the manufacturing base of the UK. We're still paying the price for that. The mantra of 'The market will decide', the way things have gone, and still are going.

Sarah Jane Morris: I met Paul at Artists Against Apartheid meetings. He was just a bit too cool . . . and I didn't have the confidence that I have now, hadn't worked out who I was. I was in the Communards by then, with Jimmy and Richard, it was before we'd had our hit, and we were there with our drum machine and our backing tracks and doing our songs. Paul and Billy and Junior were, in my eyes, leading the Red Wedge tour. They were the ones that had the confidence to talk to the press, along with Rhoda Dakar, who was brilliant . . . Billy Bragg had worked out who he was from a very early age, as had Paul, so I was a bit in awe of them.

Junior Giscombe: It seemed to me that Paul was always experimenting, having a good time with it, doing it all in a different way. He was challenging things with those gigs, the borders that he was prepared to kick down, I like that energy. I always did. For us to get together with Red Wedge was a phone call from him, and then Billy, Paul and myself got together and talked about what we were trying to achieve at the time, which was wanting young people to actually be aware of politics.

Billy Bragg: Annajoy was crucial because otherwise it would have just been a series of gigs. Rather than allow politicians to give speeches, we would introduce the local Labour politicians to the audience at the beginning of the gig and then send them to talk to people in the foyer. I remember one gig where we had finished, unloaded, got on the bus and the local MP, Clare Short, is still standing there with her back against the pole that's holding up the balcony, surrounded by spiky punks, still debating politics, smoking a cigar, and I was like, *That's my kind of politician.*

Daniel Rachel: Paul was a number one artist. Can you imagine Adele going with Skepta and Alex Turner, at three o'clock, down to the village hall to have a debate about the political situation and how things could change if you registered to vote and thought about different ideas? That's madness. Just that alone is incredible, but then you go to a gig on the night. Forget the politics, just enjoy some music.

Annajoy David: John Weller and Kenny Wheeler, Paul's tour manager, were brilliant. Without his team and infrastructure, a lot of it wouldn't happen . . . Paul would introduce me at the beginning of each gig, and I'd go out and say a few words about why we were there, what we were doing, what I thought our agenda should be, and then the guys would go on. Began to get a really big following of young people and community groups around the country. It was almost like an alternative youth parliament by default, by accident, of people contacting us. I remember one day, John Weller saying to me, when I went into Solid Bond Studios, 'I'll set you up an office over there because we've got so much post now, you actually have to start dealing with it.'

Billy Bragg: The Style Council were the backing band for everybody on the tour. The ability of people to come in and play was predicated on The Style Council opening their operation to everybody who wanted to come because, beyond the initial hardcore of the tour, which was The Styleys, The Communards, myself, Junior Giscombe and Lorna G, people would turn up and want to play. Johnny Marr . . . some of the guys from Madness . . . Tom Robinson would come along and guest and by the time we got to Newcastle, the entire Smiths had turned up.

Tom Robinson: Peter Jenner called me up and said, 'Get out the studio, come out and rock.' So that was the call to arms. I was making an album at the time, and I just did get out and pick up an acoustic guitar and drive out and join them. That was my first real close exposure to Paul Weller and his work. I knew the records, but I didn't have a sense of the man, who he was or what his ethos was until the Red Wedge tour . . . he was so fucking impressive . . . Style Council was still huge. So wherever Paul walked in and sat down and started eating, from nowhere, fourteen-year-old girls in pink mohair jumpers would materialise with autograph books. Everywhere he went. He would put down his knife and fork, turn to them, 'What's your name?', sign it for them. There you go. No hint of annoyance . . . over the last forty-five years, I haven't actually seen any star of that magnitude who handled themselves as unassumingly and unegotistically as Paul Weller did.

Lucy Hooberman: In Newcastle, we went to the young people's event in a community centre, and the audience was getting very riled up because Paul wasn't there, and the big names weren't there. Billy was there, and they were getting very impatient, and he took to the stage and had to answer their questions. Paul and some others had gone to *The Tube* for an interview. Elvis Costello had turned up, and he did a set for us. He sang 'Shipbuilding' in Newcastle. I hadn't really been prepared for that. I found that very, very moving – totally political – in a different way.

Nigel 'Spanner' Sweeney: I'm not the greatest politics person. I don't really understand it. I don't get all jumpy whether I'm this party or that party, Paul would have a go at me. 'You bloody support Maggie bloody Thatcher, you do.' We did the Red Wedge Day, and they played, and still, you've got big echoes of The Jam going on, and Paul Weller's in a place where the fans all know where he's going to be. So, you get all the mods turning up . . . there's a kid on a radio mast, swinging backwards and forwards trying to get near Paul Weller. They did the song, and we came out, Kenny got the bus that we were travelling on back to London . . . you look behind the coach and there's 600 people following us, running down the road, in cars, on motorbikes, on cycles, on Lambrettas, the whole lot. There is a tsunami of people coming along trying to get to the bus . . . and just get sight of Paul. It was nuts.

Junior Giscombe: My record company and even my co-writer, Bob, tried to talk me out of it. Everyone thought getting involved would ruin my career. I was seen as a pop artist with mainstream success, and they feared this would hurt my reputation. But I didn't care – I'm coming from around the corner in Brixton. It's been hell for years, so a bit more hell didn't really bother me. I was getting criticism from all sides, *What's he trying to jump on the Paul Weller bandwagon for?* But I used that as motivation, not something to hold me back.

Rhoda Dakar: I don't think it was a risk for the rest of us – it was really a risk for Paul. He truly believed in it. His record company was probably going crazy trying to stop him. I don't know how much John Weller was really behind it, but if Paul wanted it, then John would support him.

Annajoy David: That is why he deserves in the history books the utmost respect. Let's be honest, from a commercial point of view, he had the most to lose. He completely stood by who he was, but in a very accessible and open way. He never ever threw politics down people's throats. If some of his fans weren't into it and just said, concentrate on the music, he'd say, fair enough. He was always delightful to everybody.

Richard Ogden: I had no problem with it. That's what artists are meant to do. They're meant to have political views and there was a lot to stand up for . . . I can't claim to be a working-class boy from the industrial north, but I can claim to come from a steel, coal, iron town and know exactly what was happening and how society was being reshaped and why you would want to protest against it. I never had a problem with it. I didn't agree with it, because I was with Mrs Thatcher – Britain had to change. But Paul was with the miners – Britain didn't have to change. So, good for him. That never affected my feelings about him.

Rhoda Dakar: I was just a special guest, and I'd already had my time with skinheads and their sieg-heiling. What you have to remember with The Style Council is that a lot of those white boys just wanted The Jam back. They didn't want this new music with different people – women, Black women. The mod scene wasn't really mixed; it was very white, very suburban, and it still is. People didn't want that world disturbed. They had their own view of how the sixties had been, and they just wanted to replay it in their little world.

Tom Robinson: When we played Liverpool, some dickhead gave Junior some racist abuse when he went on. Billy just went out and said, 'Stop, hold on.' Just talked to this bloke and just put him straight. Got a huge cheer off the audience, the bloke completely crushed. Then Junior gets on and finishes his set. It was a great moment.

Junior Giscombe: They were chanting racist things. I stopped the show, 'Hold on a minute. This is supposed to be about all of us coming together. How come I've got racists inside here? What's going on?' That's what was happening on the tour. You'd get the hecklers, you'd get the chants of 'colour' this and 'colour' that, 'Black' this, and whatever else. It threw me.

Steve Rapport: Billy and Paul were the ones who brought it all together. I was involved early on and part of those formative meetings in a pub on the Old Kent Road. I remember Tim Roth being there a few times . . . It was an amazing experiment and experience. My role was mainly to take photos and to get people involved, like asking Gary Kemp to join. I think I approached Lloyd Cole, Dr Robert and Tom Robinson too. Phill Jupitus – Porky the Poet – and Joe Norris were involved.

Sarah Jane Morris: The tour was a highlight of my career. It was the first time I played to such big audiences. I loved it. My favourite part of each of the concerts was at the end, where we would all sing 'Move on Up' together. You'd have Madness on stage. Morrissey came once. I remember Jimmy and Richard just thinking it was so cool that Morrissey was in the next room.

Billy Bragg: Whatever people say about the politics on reflection, the tour was just absolutely brilliant. It had that feel of the Motown revue tours or the Stax revue with loads of bands playing together. Another thing crucial about it was, when you think of that initial lineup, so Paul, Jimmy, Junior and me, we're all soul boys, and Lorna Gee came from a reggae thing . . . It really felt like we were the unity that we sang about. We were embodying it and the audiences lapped it up.

Mick Talbot: It felt like there was a certain amount of manipulation by some politicians, I think, and it's a tricky one . . . you're getting behind one specific cause that's a little less complex than being loosely affiliated to someone like the Labour Party, where you've got misgivings about maybe half of what they've got to say . . . We were all young and quite naive, but it was a time to stand up and be counted.

Paul Weller: We were doing more before and, if anything, it just put me off doing that. We'd meet all these tossers along the way. Can't think of any exception, sadly, from the Labour Party. They'd come to the gig sometimes, and they were fake. Really fake. They weren't like us, and that put me off. I didn't expect it to be any different, because I always had a very low opinion of politicians. That's when I realised, we're being used a bit. I felt we had more to say on our own terms, when we were just doing it ourselves.

Steve Rapport: Paul didn't like getting railroaded. He didn't like groupthink or the organised part of it, the Labour Party or the idea that we were supporting the Labour Party.

Suggs: We'd always been Labour Party supporters . . . We'd done quite a lot of stuff for the miners. Jerry Dammers was doing the ANC and anti-racism stuff. Paul, I think, was just working-class people having a say. I can't remember exactly how it started, but yeah, it was a very nice thing to be involved in. Until Neil Kinnock slipped over on the beach.

Lenny Henry: That was also a connection with me and Paul. There was a Comedy Red Wedge, which might have come from Paul, actually. It was all about Neil Kinnock then, because we all thought he was going to win, and so me and Ben Elton and various other people just decided to do the Red Wedge tour and not get paid. Ridiculous, but our hearts were on our sleeves and we wanted something to happen, and Paul was the same and it was great. I loved it. But in the end, it didn't work.

Tom Robinson: Then of course, Thatcher got in the following year, leading to another ten years of Tory rule that we all had to put up with until 1997.

Billy Bragg: Kenny would fine people who were late on the bus and he would fine us a fiver. It was like herding cats, the Red Wedge tour, and it was his job. Unfortunately, I think the Red Wedge ensemble was less familiar with him than The Style Council lot.

Tom Robinson: Kenny was God. If Kenny said jump, you jumped. He just had natural authority. You didn't mess with him. He was really, really good at his job, and it was down to you to try and be as good at your job as he was at his. Fair play to him.

Billy Bragg: Kenny was actually late for the bus and so we fined him.

Kenny Wheeler: He fined me ten quid for losing my pass. It's a Scottish £10 note and I've still got it in a frame.

Billy Bragg: But that wasn't his greatest faux pas. He made an even better one . . . We all get back on the bus and after about half an hour on the road, someone says, 'Where's Mick Talbot?'

Kenny Wheeler: I used to fine people for losing their passes . . . So, at the end of the tour, I bought myself a bottle of champagne with the money and I got pissed! The last night was at a place called Lumley Castle. We left this hotel, and I had a hangover . . . Everybody had gone into the services and come out. We got on the bus and I'd usually physically walk down the bus and count everybody. I didn't. Instead of counting myself I said, 'Is everybody on?' and a guy called Mono who used to work for us went 'Yeah.' They reckon Mick was chasing the bus down the ramp. Everybody thinks I've done it deliberate . . . No, I didn't.

Mick Talbot: It was like Norman Wisdom. I'm screaming 'Mr Grimsdale!' but I'm really screaming 'Kenny!' and I'm saying, 'All right, it's not funny any more!' But I couldn't really keep up. No one did see me.

Rhoda Dakar: I wasn't on the bus . . . So I came back in the crew bus and they dropped me off at Leicester Forest services because I lived just over the back . . . I was like, 'Mick, what are you doing here?' and he went, 'They went without me.' I was like, 'Oh, wait a minute. There's a bus outside.' My seat on the crew bus. I ran outside and flagged them down so they didn't leave. He got the bus that I'd been on and went back to London with them.

Kenny Wheeler: I got grief for that for a few weeks. I walked in the office on the Monday and there was a picture of Mick on the wall, and it says, 'Has anybody seen this man?'

Billy Bragg: I think the defeat in '87 knocked the wind out of Red Wedge, which is bound to happen, because that was what our focus was. There were other initiatives that carried on, but Paul afterwards never was quite as engaged as he had been during the election campaign. When I read about him saying, 'I was very sceptical about the politicians. They were just using us,' I mean, he was saying that at the time, so I've got no counter to that. All I can say was, 'Respect, mate.' Because despite that, you still put your career on the line for us.

Paul Weller: Sadly, no progress. Well, the only progress I do think, is as people, as English people, British people. I think we've changed, and I think we've made progress. But politically and, in terms of government and all that, it's the same bullshit.

28 March 1986 – 'Have You Ever Had It Blue' (no. 14)

Chris Bangs: My first big introduction to Paul came with 'Have You Ever Had It Blue' . . . I used to DJ a lot with Gilles Peterson, who's a well-known jazz DJ . . . We used to ring up each other several times a week and go, 'Yeah, what you got? What's new? What you heard?' Because he's another inveterate digger. We both got sent that and said, 'We can play that, can't we? Yeah, let's play it, let's play it.'

David Quantick: The Style Council tried to do anything that wasn't The Jam – no loud guitars – people had gone off guitars in the mid-eighties. They had ambition, experimenting with genres like jazz and even rap. Listening to 'In the City', you'd never guess Paul would be playing jazz six years later. When you listen to something like one of my favourites on the *Absolute Beginners* soundtrack, 'Have You Ever Had It Blue', that's an amazing song. While it didn't always work – I don't think he's the best rapper in the world – it was the ambition, it was not trying too hard, it was going outside your boundaries, not staying in your lane. That made it exciting.

Paul 'Smiler' Anderson: On the mod scene, all we'd ever heard jazz-wise was maybe a bit of Jimmy Smith, old organ jazz. There was always talk about *Absolute Beginners*. I'd read the book, then me and my mate Millett went to see the film, and I remember walking away so disappointed. It felt futile – like, *Is this how we're seen?* Even Weller's 'Have You Ever Had It Blue' song was cut from the movie. Bowie looks brilliant and was amazing but as a film, it just lost the plot and had nothing to do with the book. That said, the jazz clubs in the eighties was incredible. You had Paul Murphy, Baz Fe Jazz and Gilles Peterson's nights as a great alternative to the mod scene. Paul Weller was digging jazz around that time too, and it might have been through him that I got into it. I'd read him saying 'Jazz is the way' or something, and that was it – Bang, I'm gone.

9 January 1987 – 'It Didn't Matter' (no. 9)

Ted Kessler: I liked *Our Favourite Shop*, but it then got to the point where I found the politics a bit exhausting. It was imbalanced. I found it slightly too hectoring. Maybe it was my own age. I just felt like I could make my own mind up about some things, and it just felt a bit 'stop lecturing me, man!' and I probably think that it was wearing him down a little bit doing that too. Deciding to be the spokesman for a generation, it's a full-time, exhausting job but it's quite hard to give that up. I remember buying 'It Didn't Matter' by The Style Council . . . I think that was it, though. I then got into other things.

Nick Knight: That photoshoot was one of the most terrifying moments. A little-known fact: I nearly killed Paul on that shoot. It was taking place in a recording studio where he was shooting a video. To get the shot that we wanted, I had to go up into the gantry above the band and look straight down on them. It was really hot up there and, in those days, cameras were big. My assistant, Andy Knight, passed me a lens for the

Hasselblad to swap, and I fumbled it. By sheer luck, it slipped back into Andy's grasp. A couple of inches either way and it could have been catastrophic. For the grace of God, I didn't kill him. I don't know if he even knows that.

6 February 1987 – *The Cost of Loving* (no. 2)

Mick Talbot: The Style Council was a game of two halves, and the first half of it was just more appreciated by the crowd at the time. You're following your nose and doing what you think you should do and enjoy. There was no magic formula and when it clicked, it clicked, and when it didn't, it didn't. You tried to do what you did and moved on. It's about being true to yourself. We could have played it safe and made *Our Favourite Shop (Part Two)*. It would have made twice as much money probably. It's not what it's about. It's trying to go somewhere new and fresh.

Richard Ogden: You have to remember what comes into play with that kind of deal is that we had his catalogue. In my mind, Paul Weller was Polydor's equivalent of Bruce Springsteen. He's an artist that, as far as I was concerned, should be allowed to do what he wanted because he'd been that important to the label and he was that important to the future of the label. As the new managing director of Polydor, I thought, *I know this guy's going off in a rather odd direction, but having an artist like that, that all other British artists respect, what more do you want on a label?* That's what I thought about Paul Weller. I wasn't bullshitting anybody.

Dennis Munday: I was working on the back catalogue at the time, and I went to see Paul at Nomis and he told me they'd offered him three million for three albums with no option. Now, normally the deal is the three albums and an option between each for the record company to pick it up. But instead, it meant they had to give him three million over the next three years. They *had* to give it to him. Now, Paul said to me, 'I can't turn that money down.' I would have loved to have seen John's face. Christmas, Easter, everything had come at once. It was a dumb deal to do. You can't blame the band and John for taking it. It's like if you're a plumber and you price a job at £5,000, and they come in and say, 'Well, I'm going to give you £25,000.' You're not going to say no, but my view on advances, and the problem with that, is for every pound you get, you've got to sell a record. So, if you're getting a million pounds, you've got to sell a million records. I think *Our Favourite Shop* sold 350,000. Now, overseas is a bonus, so if you can sell a million, including all your overseas territory, that's great. But *Our Favourite Shop* didn't because it never really took off in America.

Richard Ogden: *The Cost of Loving* album was a disaster, but so what? Everybody's allowed to have a disaster or two if they have a proper long career.

Nigel 'Spanner' Sweeney: When we were plugging The Style Council we had, excuse my French, such a fucking run of it. It was fucking immense right from the beginning but then it just fell away a little bit, and of course if you've not got the relationship with the record company, then the leaves start falling off the tree.

The immediacy, which he had with The Jam, was still there when you came to The Style Council. But when they came out with the third album *Cost of Loving*, that's where it started waning. It wasn't as good, and I think Paul was having a bit of a battle with the record company because I think they told him this is not as good and so he got the hump, and I think that's where things start getting a little bit all over the place.

Jeremy Murray-Wakefield: I was changing role to chief engineer. I was a little bit concerned, because it was a huge step up for me, so I asked Paul to agree to getting in some additional help. A friend of mine, Alan Leeming, was an engineer from PRT Studios, a classic recording studio on the other side of Edgware Road. He came in as a freelance engineer. He had been around for years, done all kinds of music for a very, very long time, just so I could have some confidence and a bit of support if I'd got myself into a difficult situation. Worked out reasonably well. I remember there was a time when Paul got quite frustrated because Alan was giving his benefit of experience, Paul would suggest something, and Alan would say, 'I can tell you that'd never work.' Paul would say, 'Can you tell him this is my studio, and if I want to do something, I would at least like to try without somebody telling me it can't be done?' Often, we'd try things, and they would work and then Alan would have to say 'Well, that's surprising. Yes, OK. Mmm, mmm, you learn something new every day.'

Dylan Jones: You only have to look at the template of The Beatles to understand that almost none of their records were similar to the ones that preceded them. Perhaps for the first couple of years, but after that there was a deliberate policy to confound people. *Why don't we do X?* And that ambition is no different from what Paul was doing with The Style Council in the eighties. I'm sure that lots of people, myself included, said wouldn't it be great to have an album that sounded like that Isley Brothers / 'Long Hot Summer' period, but why should he?

John Mealing: Paul was a dream to work with. He's got this image that you think he's going to be tough and a bit moody and all that. He's not like that at all. Funnily enough . . . he called the house a couple of times when I wasn't there and my wife said that he was the most polite person she's ever met in the music business . . .

I wasn't a great fan of English pop music in the eighties. I've always listened more to American music anyway. But the thing about Paul is you'd got all these influences coming in and The Style Council was one of the eighties English bands that I really enjoyed, so it was great being able to work with him. Lots of different influences and ideas.

Steve Sidelnyk: For me, it was a natural progression. Paul, and Mick at that point, they were accomplished writers, and I think he could do anything. He always wanted to try new things. He could have stuck to a formula, but he didn't. He went and tried something else that was in his repertoire.

Robert Howard: I went to see Curtis Mayfield at Dingwalls, went backstage and found out where he was staying . . . he's in this little hotel room, writing a song called 'Homeless'. He's sitting on the bed like some kind of guru, and he is a guru, and so he puts headphones on and while he's listening there's a knock at the door. I open the door . . . It's Paul! 'Oh! All right mate?' He had come to see Curtis because he was getting Curtis to do some mixes on *The Cost of Loving* album. So, it was me and Paul and Curtis sitting on the bed in Curtis's hotel room!

John Mealing: If I remember correctly, *The Cost of Loving* album didn't do quite so well sales wise. But I thought it was a good album, actually. I put strings on 'Heavens Above' and 'Fairy Tales'. Guy Barker does a lovely solo on 'Walking the Night'. Guy's a big cheese now, a household name. He was one of the top jazz trumpet players and session players back then. He was on flugel on that and it's bloody marvellous.

Ashley Slater: I'd compare Paul to somebody like Miles Davis . . . that thing of always wanting to stretch out a little bit. It's not rare, but it is rare to do it successfully. He has the musical, intellectual and emotional resources to continue to grow and expand as a musician.

Simon Halfon: For Paul, the record sleeve, and even down to the way it's manufactured, the way it was laminated, was super important. I remember on one Style Council sleeve – 'It Didn't Matter', or whatever the single was – it was a black and white photo, and we wanted the picture printed in full colour, black and white, which gives it a richness, but they just printed it in straight black and white, and the sleeves came in and it's like uh-oh, so they all had to be scrapped. If it wasn't right, it doesn't get through. Paul had a very high bar for what was good and what wasn't good.

We had some fun with it. When *The Cost of Loving* album came out . . . and it was just orange. I had people saying to me, 'Bloody hell, have you seen that? What's he doing? What's going on?' They thought we'd lost the plot at that point in time. I think maybe we had, maybe we took the in-joke too far, but that was really just done as an homage to the White Album. You just thought, *Well, The Style Council's colour is orange, let's just do it orange.* There genuinely was outrage about that. I don't know why. I think it was cited as the beginning of the end with Paul's relationship with Polydor. I don't think the album performed particularly well. It wasn't particularly critically well received, and I think the writing was on the wall. There was a new MD as well, who I don't think got on particularly well with Paul.

Richard Ogden: I'm sure we had conversations about that cover and that the music wasn't good enough and wasn't going to be successful, but we were also committed to the deal. It's the rough and the smooth. I had a dialogue with them. Not that I could ever say I influenced them.

I have no real recollection of that record at all, apart from the feeling of despair when it was delivered and an absolute company-wide 'Oh God, this is awful.' Then we had to make that bloody documentary about it as well. Everybody was looking at me like I must be mad spending all this money on Paul Weller, who's delivering this unmarketable, unsellable, music. Anyway, shortly afterwards, I got head-hunted by the McCartney organisation, and I left. So, what the hell.

Steve Sidelnyk: I was shocked when I saw the cover. I love it. It's just orange and it just made sense. I love orange. Even the fact they did the sleeve like that just shows you he was like, *OK, well, it's about the music, right?* That's what I felt about the whole thing. It was like, yeah, it's a progression. It's a different thing, but it's great.

Jeremy Murray-Wakefield: It was absolutely a Spinal Tap thing. At the time when we did it, Paul was saying, 'I want this to be really classy.' Then I think about three years later, he hated it. He said, 'I was so stupid. Nobody knows what it is in the record shop. They just flick straight past it. What was I thinking?'

Mick Talbot: There are some songs that work. I tend to agree it's possibly our weakest album. I think we put more into the production of it than the actual songs.

Dee C. Lee: I was hearing things, like we'd be sitting around, hear what reviews were, and some people were going with the flow, and a lot were, *Bloody hell, what the hell's he doing?* I asked Paul, 'Does it upset you?' He goes, 'It upsets me a little bit . . . but not really,' because he knows that he's just trying to make music and move on.

I always thought he was quite brave, really, because it's quite hard, if you've got that level of fans, of that level of people on you for what you do and really giving you their opinion all the time, and you being brave enough to go, *I'm sorry, guys, I'm just going to carry on.*

Danny Eccleston: As a fan, I have to say that *The Cost of Loving* was definitely a disconnect for me. It's not that I hadn't appreciated that eighties techno soul stuff . . . Arif Mardin productions . . . Scritti Politti . . . that kind of thing. But I didn't want that from The Style Council.

John Harris: I noticed people in my extended circle dropping off when The Style Council got too far out for them. But that made it even more worthwhile hanging in there and I honestly thought they could do no wrong.

Mick Talbot: In hindsight, I think that we were so clearly trying not to follow *Our Favourite Shop* up with something very similar. We tried to take it somewhere else by embracing contemporary soul influences, whereas I think looking back on it, we always had a bit of that, but we kept our own thing about it. So, a track like 'Long Hot Summer' had drum machine, synth bass, it wasn't very retro, it was quite of its time, yet it had Hammond organ, and it had a few classic things as well and it was very us. It was very influenced by music we grew up with in the early seventies, like The Delfonics, from the vocal harmony approach. But it was also influenced by records that had come out only a few months before we made it, with the way we programmed the drum machine and used the synth bass. We were already there in our own way and then with the Orange album, we were trying to get into that American contemporary soul production ethic that was around at that time and we lost some of our own identity in a way. That's only apparent to me many years later, but I do think that album did divide a lot of people that were into us. But all we were doing was following our nose and that's all we'd ever done really. I'd say that we were fortunate it had clicked up until that point.

February 1987 – *JerUSAlem*

Mick Talbot: For each single, there was a set budget for a promo video. We wanted to pool those funds into one project. We did an advert for BASF, a cassette company in Japan, and got additional money through that. We combined that with Polydor's budget for three promos over the next year and asked to make a short film instead. That's how *JerUSAlem* came about. As a bonus, we all got Equity cards out of it, which I suppose means we can act – or maybe it means we can't!

Lucy Hooberman: I was an aspiring filmmaker at the beginning of Red Wedge . . . *Days Like These*, our Red Wedge documentary, it's a charming film, and it's got little things in it that are quite priceless now. In interview terms, Paul was young and awkward. I can't say we had masses of conversations, because it was so busy . . . The thing he wanted to do was make a film that he and Paolo Hewitt had written. I think he must have got all that sorted out with Polydor, and they said fine. I've never talked about it since, but I think that led him to what was a question with him then, and probably is still now. A good question. Which is, 'Who can I work with who I trust?' That leads me on to the story of *JerUSAlem*.

I'm particularly sensitive about *JerUSAlem* because it was so harshly panned originally by most people. I think the budget was about £240,000, but it included four potential videos in the film's structure. Polydor's only firm instruction was 'four, possibly releasable, videos'. Looking at it that way, apart from the scripted narrative, it delivered good value – two of those videos were released with singles. Back then, labels were throwing silly money at standalone videos.

I was hired as the producer, and then I had to find the director, cast, crew and the locations . . . Normally, as producer, you'd sit down with a writer and director to refine the script – question whether certain parts needed reworking or simplifying. But we didn't have that opportunity. We were told it was like a non-negotiable script . . . I don't take any flak for the script, thank you very much, although I don't really think anybody should because it was unbelievably funny. It was a bit complex, and against the grain of what people were expecting from The Style Council at the time . . . We were not followers of Maggie Thatcher. So to be in opposition and to make something oppositional was fairly standard but I think the film did it in quite a clever way.

Nicky Weller: It was an incredibly funny time. Look at *JerUSAlem*. I mean, no one got that at all, but some of the scenes in that were just hysterical. It was a little bit of a cult movie.

Paul Weller: Fucking hilarious. It was just fun. I don't know how long it took. Wasn't long, but maybe we were out for a week, going to all these different little places, staying in hotels, and it was just fucking funny. How good the film is is anyone's guess. There were some good points made in it, but it went down like a lead balloon.

Dee C. Lee: I always was somebody who just went with the flow. *Oh, that's what we're doing now. OK then. Oh, we're acting now. OK then. And what's my part? You're the ditzy one. Oh, that's great, because I've always fancied doing a bit of acting.* We are so terrible. But it was very self-indulgent and very, very funny . . . For us. Maybe not for everybody else, but for us it was hilarious.

Annajoy David: Paul was really pushing boundaries. *JerUSAlem* was drawing from William Blake, whom I'm a massive fan of. Paul and I would talk about what his contribution was in terms of a very early message about injustice and building fairer societies – which is essentially what the film was about. It felt like a post-Beatles expression of creativity in the 1980s, and the whole project was so much fun to work on.

Lucy Hooberman: Paul played it as an opening act for some of his appearances . . . it may have been booed, or people didn't like it . . . I feel Paul might say now that it wasn't really worth doing.

Paul Weller: We had a screen come down and they showed the film [*laughs*] and after the film finished, it was just, what the fuck? [*laughs*] and then we came on and did stuff from *The Cost of Loving*, which everyone hated as well. Which is fair enough . . . but that was the beginning of the end.

Dee C. Lee: What can I say? It's crazy. I have no idea what the hell that video is about. Don't ask me. All I know is that we just managed to get a bunch of songs that were on an album in the middle of this crazy video, which included some very talented friends. Half the time I'd be sitting watching the scenes going, *er?* . . . Mick would be reading these things in this voice and Paul would be doing his thing and Steve. What am I? I'm just being a ditzy lady with the crazy make-up and the rolling of the eyes. It was basically a big piss up. It was a very, very funny thing and the reactions were very odd.

Brenda Taylor: I bloody loved it. I thought it was hilarious. It was on just before they came on for the live shows. Me and Karen used to go along and after a while we'd know it word for word. I showed it to other people and they're like, 'What a pile of poo.' We were like, 'No, you just don't get it.' It was very tongue in cheek, and I loved it.

Karen McBride: That was their warmup bit, so we must have seen it about a million times. Everything about it I love.

Mick Talbot: Did Paul ever put anything to me where I just went 'hang on a minute?' I don't think he ever did. I think it only encouraged me. I just thought, this is great. The more you can disguise yourself, the more you lose your inhibitions and, in a way, playing in a band is a bit like an act. I've been trying to act as if I know what I'm doing on keyboards for a long time, and sometimes I can convince people, when other times I can't, so you're not that far away from being a mainstream showbiz luvvie. We were just dabbling in that, and we thought we might be able to do something that was loosely satirical and make a few points. Some of it's very bizarre and then there's points made about race and class and unfair division and haves and have nots which are like a political cartoon.

Some of the things that were driving it are quite ahead of its time. We've got a Queen of England of colour in the eighties. We're trying to make some ham-fisted points, and some of them are serious. It's smothered in vague humour, but if I'm really under the microscope about people asking me what *JerUSAlem* is about, I usually say it's about thirty-five minutes.

Lucy Hooberman: The film was a cross between Voltaire's *Candide* and a road movie. You didn't really need fully rounded characters, but there were some nice cameos. Quite a lot of people who've become quite famous. The director, Richard Belfield ... was a documentary filmmaker and had been a newsperson. Originally, they wanted this *vérité* feel, which they got at the beginning. Black and white sequences of The Style Council running away. Their idea that a lot of this was social commentary. I think he did it very well, because as director, you're really handling the talent and I did feel, in those days, that a bloke would be better for them. I don't know what you think of the acting ... I don't think we're here to discuss their acting, really!

Danny Eccleston: Paul has become more and more open to taking the mickey out of himself, which may not always have been the case, or indeed, when it was the case, it might have been misunderstood in the past. A lot of the humour in The Style Council, they are fond of saying, was missed or misconstrued. Maybe the problem there was making *JerUSAlem*, which was perhaps giving sense of humour a bad name.

Lucy Hooberman: It was pretty early days for Paul and Dee, they were together, and I've got some lovely photographs of them walking across the fields together. They adopted a kitten or two from one of the little places they stayed in.

It was Mick's birthday on the shoot, somebody made him a birthday cake. We served it up to him in the windmill. So, it did feel quite . . . I can't say ordinary [but on] a lot of shoots, stuff happens, people have arguments, people walk out, you have to find a replacement. There was honestly nothing.

Jeremy Murray-Wakefield: I did say to Paul once, 'I need to ask you this, because it's going to hit me sometime sooner or later, what do you do when you achieve your life's ambition?' He thought about it, shrugged his shoulders and said, 'Well, just find another one, I guess!'

February 1987 – 'General Election' tour

David Rowe: That was the first tour that we had our access-all-area laminates. My partner Jo and I had been helping Brian with merchandise. He would send me backstage to wind Kenny up by filling up an ice bucket for a bottle of champagne. We'd have a bottle on the merchandise stand, which was probably not a good look. On that tour, we had quite a few incidents with touts. They would be pretty aggressive, coming into the foyer, trying to sell, making people think they were official.

They did four nights at the Albert Hall. There was a real change in the merchandising thing where you handed it over to them to sell and just did a deal where they took a cut. Brian didn't get a good deal with them, so we ended up selling the merchandise from a portacabin outside and he hired a couple of security guys with a dog to keep the touts away. We then spent all afternoon pairing up the General Election socks.

6 March 1987 – 'Waiting' (no. 52)

July 1987 – Paul and Dee C. Lee marry

October 1987 – 'Wanted' (no. 20) / 'Renaissance' tour

John Harris: There was a weird tour called *Renaissance* towards the end of 1987, which came after *Cost of Loving*. The support act was Phill Jupitus, who was then called Porky the Poet. He came on and did his rhymes about the youth training scheme and how awful Mrs Thatcher was and all that. We all cheered along, and then he went off and The Style Council came on and played . . . it was quite confrontational. After the first song, Paul leans into the microphone and said we've got the Edge from U2 coming along later to play some guitar. A lot of the audience like U2, and I was only fifteen, I didn't know my arse from my elbow. So we all cheer. Yeah, the Edge . . . He's saying that to gauge how many rockist throwbacks there are in the audience and what he's up against. There was this interesting dialogue going on and various resentments.

Steve Cradock: I loved The Style Council; I was seventeen when I saw them at the NEC '87. The Orange album. Yeah, they showed *JerUSAlem* at the beginning. I thought having a Black Queen and loads of scooters was enough for a pass from me . . . Around that time, I went down to Solid Bond . . . Nicky was outside with a little pet rabbit. I just wanted to meet him and say hello and then go home happy. We had a cup of tea. I played him some demos that I had, and I had an acoustic guitar as well. He had a little play of the guitar and that was it. Then we formed Ocean Colour Scene two years later.

I think I did get thrown out by Kenny though. He asked me to leave because, I don't know, I guess that's what Kenny did.

1988

Peter Button: As part of the renegotiations, the advances on the options always increase because the band has become more successful. The record company has to commit more financially and, suddenly, with all that extra money, they get to the stage when they're spending a lot of money, and don't like what they're hearing.

John Cohen: We were having a meeting with David Munns, who was running Polydor, just John and me. I don't know what it is we wanted, but we wanted something extra, and Munns was refusing to do it. John eventually lost his cool, got up, went round the desk to David Munns, picked him up by his lapels and held him high against the wall and said, 'If you don't do this, I'll make sure things happen in your life,' and put him down again.

Simon Napier-Bell: John Weller loved our office – he'd come in when there was a high or low point to tell us what was going right or what was going wrong and then we calmed it down for whatever he needed doing. I was aware there were problems. I was managing groups . . . Doesn't really help much, but we were able to cry on each other's shoulders. The groups were terrible things, and we couldn't imagine why we go on being managers, but we both did. I was very circumspect. I was somebody who always tried to find a compromise and John wasn't so good at that. He'd ask me sometimes, 'What should I do?' And I said, 'Well, have you thought to try to find a compromise?' 'What? Fuck that.'

February 1988 – Red Wedge club night

Billy Bragg: The last Red Wedge event that we did with Paul . . . Was it at the Town and Country Club? Me, Paul and Norman Cook. A club night in February 1988. Tell you what was funny about that night is we all took turns in DJing. We weren't really paying much attention. We were all in the backstage dressing room where the drinks were free. I spoke to someone afterwards who said, 'Every thirty minutes we had to listen to "The Revolution Will Not Be Televised" by Gil Scott Heron, because everybody played it.' We didn't realise. The first three times is fine, but after about the sixth time, everyone's like, *Not again!*

May 1988 – Nathaniel Weller born (first child with Dee C. Lee)

Dee C. Lee: No matter how successful you are as a musician or whatever, nothing really sets you up for when you have a baby. You can be poor, you can have money, but the fact of the matter is your body's changing. You're producing another human being out of your body. It does a lot of stuff to the mind, and it puts a lot of strain on relationships, because I think, still, it's always going to be really difficult for a man to really understand what women go through . . . Hindsight is great, but when you're in it, you know, it's a different thing. I think we all started growing up, basically. Mike and Shaney had Gene around that time too and I think we started growing up and everybody started having different values, other than the band.

We'd enjoyed it so much and then we were getting attacked a lot and then it was like, *Oh, you know what? We've got lives, man. You know, maybe we should think about different things. We don't need this.*

20 May 1988 – 'Life at a Top People's Health Club Farm' (no. 28)

24 June 1988 – *Confessions of a Pop Group* (no. 15)

John Williams: I was senior A&R manager at Chrysalis . . . and got noticed by Polydor as a guy who was making hits and signing hit bands, and they offered me the position of head of A&R . . . That's when I first met Paul Weller, by which point The Style Council had released three albums – two have been number two, one has been number one . . . with *Confessions of a Pop Group* due for release in June 1988.

Mick Talbot: Everything that we did in the first three years, people seemed to get and appreciate and then something happened with the Orange album. Quite often a largely derided album can still ride that storm, and it's the one that follows that will suffer. So, I think people weren't even interested in hearing *Confessions of a Pop Group*. They felt that the Orange album had let them down. A lot of people didn't want to hear it. But it's got its moments.

We'd lost quite a large section of our following and people's patience had been worn out by us. I think we were out of step.

Jeremy Murray-Wakefield: It became clear pretty quickly that it was going to be a very different album to what we had done before. There's a lot more personal stuff on there that's built into the tracks. When we recorded the song 'Confessions 1, 2 & 3', I was listening to the lyrics, and I couldn't really make sense of what it was about. Paul explained to me that what that is really about is how all of us that have been in relationships, you say things, you promise things to your partner and you really mean them at the time, but when you're somebody in the public eye, and you go through separations and everything else, often you get called to account for promises you made at that moment.

Mick Talbot: Brad Pitt is apparently quite an expert on that album. It sounds like a joke. Paul rang me up after meeting him at a radio show for Paul McCartney. Brad had said that he was one of three friends at college and The Style Council were their secret love. *Confessions* was their favourite album. Paul even said he knew a couple of the things that I did, like 'Little Boy in a Castle', just a solo piano piece, and Brad said, 'I've shared that with my wife,' and that was Angelina Jolie at the time. When you're making music like that, at the time you don't know how far reaching these things are or what this little college student, who's no one at the time, is going to become. It's funny how things can touch people. It's mad.

John Mealing: I thought it was a great, great album and so eclectic with the different influences. Paul was very into his Debussy and the Romantics at that time, but I don't think he managed to take the pop people with him. It was also a funny old time with English music then. I couldn't stand the bloody new romantic thing, and that was very big. Then we were getting Stock, Aitken and Waterman. Maybe it just didn't chime commercially at the time, but I thought it was a very interesting album.

That was an interesting album to do, particularly on 'The Gardener of Eden' because they had already pre-recorded bits of it. It was a bit of arranging, like a jigsaw puzzle, a very unusual way of coming at it. Of course it had the Swingle Singers on that album. That was funny, the way that came about, because at the same time I was doing the album with Paul, I was also working with them. They wanted a rhythm section, so I did that as a session player and then I did a live album at Ronnie Scott's and some vocal arrangements for a few songs. I mentioned this to Paul at the time and when it came to 'The Story of Someone's Shoe' he thought of them. I did the vocal arrangement for that. Paul often has these quirky ideas which are just brilliant.

Jeremy Murray-Wakefield: I remember Paul came in one day, said, 'Oh, Jezar, I've got this great idea. I want to do this track with the Swingle Singers'. I had no idea who he meant, so I just gave him this blank look. 'It's an a capella group . . .'

I got out a stereo microphone, the Swingle Singers came in, I double-tracked it so it sounds like there's twice as many of them. There were no lyrics at this point. It was just the 'duh-duh-du-ba-de-duh' background going on and then Paul came in a couple of days later, sort of waving a sheet, said, 'I've got the lyrics, we're going to sing this song.'

I switched off all the lights in the studio, put a spotlight on him and a little bit of light above the mixing desk. At that moment, I became intensely aware that I was the first person ever to hear this song. This is the moment. So, I hit record, and he sung the first take end to end, took his headphones off and he said, 'OK, I want to come in and listen to that.' And I said, 'No, you need to do another one.' He said, 'Really? I thought that was fine.' I said, 'No, you need to do another one.' He said, 'OK, if you say so.' So, he did another one. But actually, I lied. There was nothing wrong with the first take, but I didn't want him to see me crying . . . I needed him to just do a second take so that I could get my professional face back on. When he walked through the door I said, 'I think you're right, it's the first take.'

John Williams: Every group has its moment, and The Style Council had their time. I saw them playing Sheffield and they were great, but there were other things starting to happen musically and I think that Paul was tied to a unit that perhaps he couldn't express himself in so well any more. Although he didn't say that, but it was slightly tired, although still brilliant.

John Reed: Paul had started to drift off in the last couple of records; he was obviously less involved or less connected by his own admission . . . I struggle with the Orange album, but I think *Confessions* is a really intriguing record. I think it would have made a great six-track EP.

Lawrence Watson: What happened with me and The Style Council was fortuitous. I was in the dark room at London Weekend Television and there was a young lady up there, lovely Shane Chapman, who's Mick Talbot's partner, and she was in the press office. She knew that I was a big fan of The Jam and The Clash, and she said, 'Paul's doing a recording. I'll ask if you can go along with your camera.' He was doing a video shoot on three stages for *Confessions of a Pop Group*. I went along and shot, came back and processed all that film, and lo and behold, Paul wanted to put one on the cover of the album.

Dee was pregnant with Natty, probably about eight or nine months pregnant, hence hiding behind the piano. There are pictures where she isn't behind the piano, but Paul picked that one with Dee sat behind the piano.

Dee C. Lee: I hid behind because I was just so big. I was finding it difficult to sing because every time I hit high notes the baby was just not having it. I'd have to change the note. It was just getting harder and harder and . . . as you can probably see, I just blew up everywhere, so I was very, very self-conscious and I don't want to be in front of people. But when we were doing that, obviously I was pregnant and starting to change and my values at that time were becoming so not interested in music right now. Just nesting and doing what women do when you're pregnant and expecting babies. So, my brain started going off into a different scenario which, looking back, I could already see the beginnings of the end now, in hindsight.

It was difficult. We loved making music. It was great when it was just us and we could work, you know. I mean home and work, it's not always a good thing. But sometimes it is. And like I said, values started changing . . . it's only when you get old you see it all the time with young people, when kids turn up, it does put quite a strain on relationships, and if you don't work it out or deal with it quite soon, you'll find it's yet another couple separating. So, I had a lot of things on my mind around about that time of the album . . . I was enjoying it, but not as much as I had been, to be honest.

David Lines: Jesus Christ, there was a new depth to The Style Council. Those suites that they did, 'The Story of Someone's Shoe', man alive. You got Debussy in there. The music led you in a completely different direction.

Gary Crowley: That's my favourite Style Council album . . . I love 'Life at a Top People's Health Farm'. I remember saying to Paul, 'This is your "Penny Lane". This is going to be it' . . . He released it as a single and it only got to the dizzy heights of twenty-eight or something and then it started going down . . . 'Last fucking time I listen to you.'

Rhoda Dakar: They had the Swingle Singers doing backing vocals or something. That was the joke. *Weller Fitzgerald*. Not mine. I think that was his joke.

John Harris: Back in 1988, I thought that *Confessions of a Pop Group* was a masterpiece and I still do. It has great lines in it. *Too busy recreating the past to think about the future*. All that shitty plastic prefab town . . . All those great lines, they endure. It depresses me to say that vision of England hasn't changed that much. I personally didn't have a sense of The Style Council tailing off. I loved it and immersed myself in it throughout.

John Lewis: I bought that album the week it came out and listened to it, thinking, *Fucking hell. Surely the last vestige of any Jam loyalist who stayed with The Style Council will put on the first side of this and just throw it across the room. Take it to a charity shop immediately.* I admire that wilful alienation in pursuit of something you want to do. It had nothing in common with what was going on. That's the weird thing, looking back on it, it was kind of twenty years behind its time, but it's also ten, fifteen years ahead of its time. It's the kind of thing that lots of American indie bands were doing in the early 2000s, Beach Boys harmonies and big Brian Wilson-type orchestral arrangements.

Dylan Jones: I first interviewed him when the album came out for *The Face*. I've said to Paul since, you were so bloody difficult, you really were, you were a git. Absolute git. Because he didn't want to be interviewed. Mick didn't want to be interviewed either. I walked back to *The Face* office, about a fifteen-, twenty-minute walk from Solid Bond, and Nick Logan asked, 'How was it?' I said, 'It was difficult.' He said, 'Well, you can make it shorter if you want.' I said, 'No, I'm going to write this,' because, the thing is, I loved the record. I loved the whole idea of the record. I loved The Style Council, and I had respect for Paul and Mick. It was quite a generic piece in the end, because, you know, how many journalists have been to interview Paul Weller, Van Morrison or Lou Reed and come back and said, fuck, he's difficult? But that's fine. I know why. I respect him for it. I have a wry smile when I think about that interview.

Paul Lester: I remember the review where Allan Jones of *Melody Maker* dismissed Weller and Mick as 'the Don Estelle and Windsor Davis of supine albino funk', but I love that album. I think that's the truest reflection of the Weller personality – the suburban kid in love with contemporary American funk and disco, but with a penchant for aching Gallic chord sequences. It was such an unlikely Weller thing that, to me, it was the most Weller thing that album.

Tom Sheehan: Jonesy would sharpen his knife when there was a Style Council album coming out and give it almighty stick. Fuck knows why, but he did. I remember walking down Notting Hill once and I'm on the blower to Jonesy . . . 'Oh, hang on, is your mate walking towards me?' He goes, 'Who's that?' I go, 'Paul Weller.' He says, 'Oh, my God. I'll sign off then' . . . and Weller goes, 'Tommy, is that Jonesy?' and starts swearing down the phone as I'm trying to put it in my pocket.

Dee C. Lee: The press were very, very vicious, very bitchy, and we were just like . . . *OK, they've all got their minds set now, this is how they're going to be. We don't really need to do this. We can chill, everybody can start chilling. There's different things.* And all of us knew that getting slagged off by the press is not going to be something that's going to ruin our lives. We're all musicians who can work and we do work and we're still working and that's what we do. Paul's still working, Mick's still working, Steve's working and I'm still working. It's what we do.

Jo Ruocco: In the credits on the album, they put me down as Little Jo because, at the time, I thought I was Little Jo. I was four years old when I started drumming and it just was natural. By the age of ten, I had my drum kit, and by thirteen, I was doing my first showcase with Mr Ellington, and Ella Fitzgerald came out and was the guest singer . . .

I came home one day to a message on the answering machine. ''Ello. This is Paul. Yeah, Paul Weller. I'm doing this album right now and I don't have a drummer, and I need a drummer and percussion. I heard you, and I'd really like you to finish the album. Come down to Solid Bond.' I had to play that back so many times. Is this a nutter or is this real? I looked up to Paul, I really loved The Jam and everything he did, so I had to pinch myself . . . When do I call him back? Now? Or do I call him back on Monday? So, I called him on Monday at eleven o'clock and it was him. He says, 'Yeah, that was me.' I said, 'I'm really sorry I was delayed, but I didn't know if it was a nutter or if it really was you.'

Jeremy Murray-Wakefield: If you listen to the middle section of 'It's a Very Deep Sea', there is a bubbling sound that pans from left to right and that is the sound of Paul blowing bubbles into a McDonald's cola that we'd bought just before lunchtime.

Jo Ruocco: I have to admit, I had a crush on him. I never told him that. I just thought he was so cool and suave and the way he put himself together. The Style Council was all about image and sound . . . so when we did live stuff or television, we was very conscientious of how we appeared and the way to dress. I remember going in the drum booth and adding the bits that need to be added. I looked in the control room and I see Paul and Mick dancing, going crazy. I said, 'Is that all right?' 'Yeah! Keep going, keep going.'

Jeremy Murray-Wakefield: One of the challenges was balancing Paul's creative needs with external pressures to make the studio a profitable business. We spent a lot of money upgrading the studio to attract outside clients, but in hindsight, what Paul really needed was a space that was entirely his own. The studio was set up in a way that didn't make outsiders feel comfortable

– it felt more like Paul's personal space with his gold discs, equipment and Style Council branding everywhere. It was like renting a holiday cottage that wasn't set up for you.

Jo Ruocco: I loved going down the canteen for lunch break, because Paul's a vegetarian, so they made the most awesome cheese-melt sandwiches . . . and there was this old boy who worked in the canteen, I loved him to bits, he always made the perfect tea. In America, we would put a teabag in a cup with hot water and put it in the microwave. That's not how you make it. It was always a good time, full of laughs. Both Paul and Mick had great senses of humour.

We did a TV show out in Maidstone. At 7 a.m., we had to be on the show and that's freaking early. The night before, we were all at the hotel having a laugh. Paul's sister, Nicky, came up with the idea of messing with everyone's shoes, which were left out for polishing in the posh hotel. We swapped them all around. So when we got up really early for this call, for which we had very little sleep, you can imagine. We hear all the fuss and people going crazy and it was a nice way to start the day with a laugh. By the time we got to *Motormouth* show, it was no problem.

Jeremy Murray-Wakefield: One of my all-time favourite songs is on that album, and that's 'Changing of the Guard'. It has this incredible string part, written by John Mealing . . . it's really masterful the way the strings rise up on one side and go down on the other. A lot of people might think of that track as perhaps being overly sentimental, but I just loved it. I was left alone to finish off the mix on that song and it was one where I was actually in tears by the end of the mix, because I've always felt very strongly when you're mixing a track, you have to feel it. So if you're mixing a dance track, you should have the irresistible urge to get on your feet and be dancing around the studio. If you don't, then you should probably call somebody else in to do that. Similarly with that very sentimental track, I had had some sad moments in my life and, in the mix, I wanted what I was hearing to resonate with the pain that I had felt about mistakes I'd made in the past. It was lovely to get the opportunity to have that input on that track.

Jo Ruocco: One of the most fun moments I remember was being in the car with Paul and Mick. We were heading to Portobello Road to record 'Life at a Top People's Health Farm'. The whole setup was hilarious – Mick was on keys, I was on drums, Lady Ruth was on bass, Dee C. Lee was with us, and of course, Paul. The horn section was across in the pub, playing out the window, while we were on a café rooftop opposite. It was chaotic but so much fun ...

When you see Paul in his songs, you think he's very serious, he's very dramatic, but he can be very quiet and insular, too, but he's a true Gemini. He loves people.

Jeremy Murray-Wakefield: Paul wasn't happy with the initial mix of the *Confessions* album. That was an epic fail on my part. I was very young, and it was a massive learning point. It actually affected the course of my life in many ways, because he said, 'Look, I'm going to let you mix the album. Bring me in and play me the stuff when you've done it.' I'd been listening to what was in the charts and had researched what other producers were doing, listened to the sound and some of the steps other people were making and I built all of that into these first two or three mixes, and by the time it reached the third one, Paul was like 'Stop the tape!' ... There's a very awkward silence and he said, 'You need to stop trying to copy what other people do. I asked you to mix this because I trusted you, not all those other people. I can see over there on the shelf you got all those albums that you went out and bought. I'm not interested in those albums. I'm not interested in those artists. You have to learn what your own stamp is. What is the thing that you do?

You need to find your own way and build on that. Don't just go following what other people do.'

So then, as a pair, we mixed them collaboratively and that was great. My biggest takeaway from the whole experience was that, in life, Paul gave me the confidence to be myself, and I'd never had that. I had that beaten out of me at school. I was a very shy person. I was socially very, very awkward at that point in my life and just thought, *Oh, I'll just be quiet and do what I'm told.* That really doesn't help you in the long run. You need to be proud of who you are, and try and make a difference, and speak with your own mind, and with your own words. That was a massive lesson from that whole experience.

Jo Ruocco: We did some promo shows in Italy. We were in Milan at a big music festival. I was in the car with Paul, and all these people seeing the car with Paul Weller and he goes, 'I bet these are all your relatives.' It was funny.

We were meant to go on a world tour to promote *Confessions of a Pop Group*. Mick got unwell, so the tour was pulled. We were meant to go to Japan first as the album did really well there, it went platinum, and then we would work our way over to the USA. We were booked at Radio City Music Hall and that, to me, was wow. Playing with this really cool pop band in my homeland would have been very cool.

John Williams: The record company thinks that the artists are their chattel, whereas I was always on the side of the artist. For me it's the art. Without the artist, nothing can work in a record company. I've been told too many times, 'John, your problem with being in corporations is you're always on the side of the artist.' Which is ironic. I liked Paul, he's one of the great lyricists, songwriters, singers, since Lennon and McCartney . . .

The *Confessions of a Pop Group* album didn't do very well, charted fifteen, went silver, but all the other albums had gone gold and had done some business internationally. This one crapped out internationally. I say crapped out. I mean, Paul never really had a huge overseas audience except in Japan and Australia, maybe a few others. A bit like Paul Heaton, he's very English and/or British. Both men of the people. They speak for the common man, the man who was born with his arms tied behind his back. They're the supporter of the underdog. True socialists. That's why they're great spokesmen for their generations.

15 July 1988 – *1234* (EP featuring 'How She Threw It All Away', no. 41)

1988–89 – House music

Dean Rudland: By the time we got to the acid jazz dance scene at Dingwalls in 1988, Paul was going to those clubs. He was turning up on a Sunday. It was suddenly part of the same scene I was on, and it felt really cool. It also felt incredibly weird . . . he's not someone I really know . . . but he is always someone who says hello when you bump into him. Oddly, him and Jerry Dammers have an incredibly good memory for people they've met over a period of time.

Ernie McKone: I was a soul boy when I was young. I had an older brother and sister who were into soul music – my sister Vivianne McKone played as well. She used to write songs and play keyboards. I remember thinking, who's that guy on *Top of the Pops*? I'm sure he was doing kind of rock music a minute ago and this is The Style Council, obviously. I thought that sounds quite jazz-funky and I was into jazz funk. And a few years later my sister got the job as playing keyboards in The

Style Council . . . I went to see them a couple of times and that was my first encounter really with Paul . . . probably about '88. Then I got a band together with some mates called Push. We were on that rare groove scene that came around at that time, just slightly pre-acid jazz.

Jacko Peake: When we actually met Paul, we were supporting Curtis Mayfield as Push . . . me, Crispin Taylor and Ernie McKone, 1988 at the Forum in Kentish Town. This was a major gig for Push . . . Paul Weller and Dr Robert had come to see Curtis Mayfield because they absolutely adored Curtis. He was the godfather of soul as far as they were concerned. We'd done the gig, watched Curtis and we're backstage afterwards, and then Paul and Dr Robert burst into our little changing room full of lads, all smoking and drinking. 'That was just amazing.' He's so generous, Paul, with his love of music and inclusive attitude that he's got to all things musical.

Ernie McKone: I was like, *Oh, it's that guy that my sister's played with. He's cool, I like him.* He said, 'I like your band, and I'd like you to come to Solid Bond and do some recording.' So, we ended up recording a few tracks, one that he wrote called 'Waiting on a Connection'. We didn't put it out unfortunately, and I wish we had.

Jacko Peake: It was just amazing being in that environment and being in Solid Bond in Hyde Park, suddenly being thrown into this amazing creative space, getting to know Paul through that and seeing his energy and his enthusiasm for what we were doing.

Ernie McKone: Paul was brilliant, the way he recognized our groove and what we represented. He could see there was a new movement coming along which ended up being acid jazz. He was a great influence.

Paul Weller: I just loved that Chicago house music when I heard it, because I love the soulful thing in it. Soul had become really slick – Alexander O'Neal, all that sort of thing. It just sounded raw again, it sounded like they were made in someone's bedroom or something, on these drum machines and sequencers and whatever. That appealed to me. In a lot of those songs, [Joe Smooth's] 'Promised Land' and also some of the Ten City stuff, there was a kind of gospel thing to it. I could hear those influences. Especially in the piano style. I just love the rawness of it, and that it was really the opposite of what was happening production-wise in the eighties. And typical of me, right, when I get into something, it's just like, *Right, this is it. Everything else is shit. We're only doing this from now on.*

Mick Talbot: There was a lot of warmth to it. We met some of those people when they were on tour and they'd come out of Pentecostal gospel backgrounds, so it was like the true roots of soul that goes all the way back to someone like Ray Charles. So, it was a natural progression for us to get into that music and try and reflect the times with our new album.

Dee C. Lee: When house music came on the scene, it really did blow a lot of people away, us included. We're on it and we didn't mean it as a bandwagon thing. It just showed a different genre of music, and it was in our atmosphere anyway . . . it was fresh, it was new, and it really suited us. It was really what we were about. Beats with nice vocals.

Paul Weller: I was collecting at that time too. I used to go in all the shops and get loads of imports. But also in my mind, I was thinking, *Well, this is what a little mod would have done in 1963. He'd have just been buying a different sort of import, that's all.*

Mick Talbot: Paul and I could feel this dwindling audience, and we just said, let's just do this album, it'll be really different again. It'll be influenced by a lot of current house music that we're listening to, which we thought was the new way soul music was going. When we did that last album, *Modernism: A New Decade*, we expected that to come out early in 1990.

Brendan Lynch: They were totally, totally engrossed in that music. Also, into jazz as well. There would be a lot of Blue Note records being played, and there is a connection, it's still R&B, isn't it? All that stuff.

Stuart Deabill: Norman Jay was quite an influence on that final album. He was a DJ at High on Hope, where Paul and Mick went, and that gave them the idea, hearing all these new Chicago house records and influences to do the *Modernism* album that Polydor madly turned down.

Robert Howard: I shared a flat with a guy called Hector who was a DJ at the Wag Club but had previously been a DJ in northern soul clubs up in Derby. When we toured America, he gave me this list of records to go and get at this specific record shop in Chicago, '86. So I go and get them all and I start to listen . . . So, I got a bit of a head start in there, but Paul's then doing 'Promised Land' and things like that, with Brendan. I'm hanging around, helping with the technical shit. Actually, not many people know this, but Paul plays bass on 'Wait', he came in while I was doing it, because at this point, I think there was tension. It was coming towards the end of The Style Council, and I don't think he was very happy. In fact, I know he wasn't very happy, and he came down to the Townhouse. I was doing 'Wait', and he said, 'There's no bass on it.' I said, 'No, I haven't done it yet.' So, the Juno was there and he just played this bassline, which actually I think was very similar to something by Ten City, but it worked, it was perfect. So, I started hanging around a bit more when he was doing things, and I'd pick up this instrument or that instrument, or make small suggestions. I think, if he's honest at that point, although, I love some of that – 'Sure Is Sure' is a great tune, and there was some beautiful things on *Modernism* and Slam Slam – he wasn't really happy, personally or musically.

Dee C. Lee: Slam Slam was my band, as in I fronted it, but it was basically Paul and Robert doing the writing, and that came about because I'd had Natt, hadn't had Leah yet, and I'd lost a lot of confidence as a performer and Paul was like, 'Well, if you go under a pseudonym Slam Slam, you can do your music and you can sing.' Now, I didn't have the time for writing because I was still a new mum. I couldn't separate my brain any more from how I used to be able to do it because my kids were all consuming, like all mums feel. So, I found it hard to write and stuff. So, Paul and Robert were doing most of the writing . . . It was good while it lasted but then, yeah, it got a little bit too dance based, and I was just growing up then. I didn't really want to do the PAs and all that stuff, but it was good to know because at least people still like my voice and it just gave me an idea that, all right, if I do come back into this, when I'm ready . . . I have still got it and can still do it.

Alan McGee: When acid house happened, and Style Council were coming off the back end of their success, I ran into him. He will never remember this. I've never said anything to him. He was with Paolo Hewitt, who I'm friends with . . . Weller was obviously off his nut as well. I don't know, maybe not on E, but knowing Weller, probably pissed. And Weller was dancing with himself in a fucking mirror. Literally. So, he must have been fucking smashed. I was gone, man, but I remember that.

Eddie Piller: I met a guy called Gilles Peterson in 1987 and after a while we said, 'Let's set up a record label. What should we call it?' A DJ called Chris Bangs says, 'Why don't you call it Acid Jazz?' The whole scene came out of a very small club scene of 100-odd people who went to Dingwalls and the Wag Club. Paul and Mick used to come to the acid jazz clubs because Paul saw it as an extension of mod and what he was trying to do because we were playing early acid house, we were playing funk, soul, RnB, boogaloo, disco, but as mods . . . Then it was only a matter of months before he decided to make a Style Council record under a false name for Acid Jazz, which was King Truman.

Mick Talbot: That's full of mythology, and even the person behind it can't tell the story the same way twice, so you might have to leave that there.

Brendan Lynch: I had been working in studios as an assistant engineer . . . so I rang up Solid Bond. I targeted Paul because he always made great records, and it was always moving on and interesting. I really liked a lot of their stuff. I never thought I'd get it or even get a reply, but it was just good timing. Jeremy had literally left that week. They said to come in and Paul met me outside. We went and had coffee and that was it. This is September '88.

Jeremy Murray-Wakefield: My time working with Paul and The Style Council ended as randomly as it began. What happened was that one of the staff at Solid Bond, it turned out, had never filed any of my overtime sheets, and Nicky Weller, to her credit, the moment she found it, she sorted it out straight away. But that put me in the rather strange position of being a very young guy with a rather large sum of money in my bank account that I didn't know what to do with. So, like all irresponsible young people, I booked myself a holiday on a desert island, a luxury holiday. I was on this beach, it was in the Seychelles, and I was thinking, *This isn't like British weather, this is digital sunshine!* It really felt like really pure sunshine. There was the sounds of all the wildlife, and when I came back, I just felt the magic had gone for me . . . I knew I had to leave. I knew I had to forge a different path. Now, all my family and friends thought I was mad. But the one person who did get it was Paul's dad, John. He said 'Don't worry, sunshine! I totally get it. You're a young man. A studio is no place for a young person like yourself. I don't know how you do it. Locked away from daylight, day after day after day. That's mad. That's mental. You go, you do your travelling and meet people. That's how you'll grow. You learn more about the world through doing that.' He was absolutely right. I think he understood it better than I did at the time. I just knew that there was this force that was driving me on to do other things.

Brendan Lynch: We'd start each day and just play records. That's why it was so good working at that studio. It was really good fun, and because it was Paul's studio, it was his own place, so he could spend more time indulging and stuff like that. People would turn up all the time, DJs with records. It was a really, really creative space. Paul and Mick were doing various tracks all the time, so every day we'd come in and do something, I wasn't quite sure what it was for or what it was leading to. More ideas and being creative and trying new things. I can't actually remember the first song I worked on but it may have been the King Truman track.

Eddie Piller: There was a chap . . . nasty little man, an editor of a magazine. And he'd reviewed A Man called Adam and said, 'What a bunch of wankers. They're rubbish. They'll never be anything.' We then had the number one in the club chart so I wrote him a letter . . . told him exactly what I thought of him. So, then he called up David Munns at PolyGram, and said, 'You're not going to like this, but The Style Council are releasing a fake record under a false name with Acid Jazz.' . . . I was working for Polydor at the time as a consultant for their Black music record label called Urban . . . I'm in a meeting . . . The boss, David Munns, knocks on the window, points at me, 'Come here.' So, I go out, he gets me up against the window and he's a bit of a bruiser, Munns. He puts his elbow in my throat, and he goes, 'What the fuck have you done?' and I said, 'I don't know what you are talking about, boss.' And he goes, 'Clear your fucking desk,' and I said, 'What have I done?' He goes, 'You put out a record by The Style Council. You've interfered. I've been working on a settlement with The Style Council for two years and you've gone and put a record out. Clear your desk. You're sacked.' I said, 'But I haven't got a desk. I'm a consultant,' and he went, 'Get out of my fucking sight.'

Polydor sued us. They seized the records from our distribution company . . . We think maybe as many as 200 white labels, with photocopy press releases, got out. But here's the interesting thing. I was not aware that this was a collector's item until 2003. I'd given it no thought whatsoever because it's just another record. I'd released hundreds of records in Acid Jazz, and it was just another one of those records.

Dean Rudland: That was before I joined Acid Jazz. I think that was probably 1989. I didn't join until the summer of 1990 and there was one copy of the record left in the Acid Jazz stockroom when I arrived, which I grabbed.

10 February 1989 – 'Promised Land' (no. 27)

10 March 1989 - *The Singular Adventures of The Style Council Vol 1* (no. 3)

19 May 1989 – 'Long Hot Summer '89 Remix' (no. 48)

June 1989 – Live in Japan

Jacko Peake: I was living in Clapham in a short-life housing place down there and got a call one day. On the other end of the phone was Paul saying, 'Do you want to come to Japan with The Style Council?' I was like, 'Yes, there is only one answer.' I didn't realise what a difficult period it was for The Style Council . . .

Camelle Hinds: Paul got me to be musical director for the Japanese tour. I took on that mantle. It was a great experience, but I'd never do it again. Sixteen people touring Japan, that is a real nightmare for me, but I could understand the relevance of it. I learned a lot from it, as you do from things that you embark upon . . . Got paid handsomely for it, must say, for a week's work . . . But it was stress, and I don't do stress.

Mick Talbot: Camelle was good. We trusted him to do it. And it meant that we could get in a little bit later and do a bit of shopping.

Camelle Hinds: The rehearsals were no joke. Sometimes I couldn't sleep at night, because you got to be on it. People don't tend to realise, a bassist is not like a guitarist or keyboard player, you can lay down a chord; with a bassist, it's the melodic aspect. You have to remember all those riffs as well as everything else. It's not an easy job for a bassist. Paul would invite me around his house and tell me what he's intending and send me away with some tapes. I spent a month just absorbing what he wanted.

Jacko Peake: Steve White wasn't doing that tour. He was doing his Jazz Renegades thing. We had Richie Stevens on drums and a load of different people, a lot of different singers come up. Omar did it, Dr Robert was playing bass for a bit. We did the tour of Japan, which was great. Huge crowds.

Omar: I owe a lot to Paul for where I am now. The Style Council was my first professional gig . . . I was aware of Paul from The Jam. 'That's Entertainment', 'Eton Rifles', all the hits. But to actually get to work with him was when I was eighteen. He was about to go on tour in Japan and his bass player, Camelle Hinds, was doing some kind of seminar or something. I did my beatbox/a cappella thing. He said, 'Oh, Paul would love to hear that.' I went and did it for him. He said, 'Yeah. Come on tour.' I wouldn't say beatbox. It was more a cappella is what they call it. I got it from Bobby McFerrin . . . I was playing percussion and doing vocals as well, which ended up at the Royal Albert Hall.

Camelle Hinds: Paul had done a great version of the Joe Smooth song 'Promised Land'. He really absorbed the house thing there, but it wasn't really what Japan wanted from Paul at all. Bear in mind that Polydor kind of stiffed Paul at that time. And John was, like, beside himself. The way they treated him wasn't too good.

Guy Barker: I think we flew on the Monday, arrived on the Tuesday. Did a concert in Tokyo on the Wednesday. We did Yokohama or somewhere Thursday or somewhere else on the Friday and flew back straight away. It was in, then did three gigs and out. Omar was there. I remember that being really quite jolly and us all having a laugh . . . The dancing flower had just come out in Japan. It was when those ridiculous things that came out where it was a flower and you turned it on and it reacted to music. Nobody knew about them. There was also a teddy bear that you could buy, that you could speak into it, and it would repeat what you said. We were putting them outside members of the band's hotel doors, knocking on the door when they open. Teddy bear would swear at them. There was a lot of that. It was fun, but it was real hit and run.

4 July 1989 – Royal Albert Hall

Mick Talbot: We played the same set three weeks before in Japan, and we had such a great time, and everyone was open minded to it, and people really seemed to enjoy it. In a way that may have spoilt us or made us overconfident about going forward with it and doing it at the Albert Hall.

Camelle Hinds: It's funny, when I listen back to that Japan gig, I'm surprised, it's pretty good, actually. But the Royal Albert Hall . . . not.

Mick Talbot: Well, perhaps Japan was ready for more than Britain at the time.

Omar: Two hours of music that . . . nobody knew what it was! You could see it on the audience's face. They were all excited and all of a sudden, they're saying *What's this?* But that was the period that he was going through. He likes to experiment, people!

Jacko Peake: It was a massive mixture of music, and you could see that Paul was experimenting with ideas and musical directions and it was a big melting pot. Lots of different artists getting up there on that gig as well. And then that was the end of The Style Council.

Camelle Hinds: There was major transition in the music industry, it was morphing. That whole thing got caught up in the record company not wanting to make the right decisions with regards to the careers.

Kenny Wheeler: A neighbour of mine came to the Albert Hall. He was one of the best bass players in the country, Andy Brown, played with people like Barbara Dickson and Annie Lennox. He said to me after, 'I didn't come to see a load of people pushed to the front. I come to see Paul.' I've said to Paul about it since and he said, 'That's what was inside me at that time.'

Robert Howard: Paul asked me to play those gigs, and the Albert Hall was fun, I loved it. I mean, it's gone down a little bit, like they were tearing up programmes. They were booing a bit. This is what I mean about not giving your audience what they want. I totally respect that. It was such fun with an amazing band. I remember that Steve White wasn't playing, but Guy Barker and Jacko Peake was in it. Omar came and did something in the middle of it, some sort of beatbox thing, that completely flummoxed John Weller . . . 'What's going on there?' There was Marco, dancing with Dee. I did a couple of tunes . . . 'We didn't come to see you mate!' I just loved it. Paul only sang on about half the songs, as I recall. It was brilliant but I think you could see that there were one or two in the audience that didn't get what they expected.

Omar: On the setlist all it says is 'Omar song'. I think that is the a cappella thing . . . So, I just did a couple of songs doing it, but it's totally Bobby McFerrin's influence. I would never take the credit for that. And there's a little bit of Biz Markie at the end as well, when you tap the throat. So, yeah, just a little showstopper!

Jacko Peake: The thing that really moved me was when I first started working with The Style Council. I heard 'Changing of the Guard', and we played that on that very last tour and at that very last gig . . . Emotionally, that encapsulated so much of what Paul was about with the rest of the band.

Darren Fletcher: I thought it was going to be a greatest hits show when the adverts said 'Revue'. It certainly wasn't that. It was OK, and I recognised a few tunes, like 'Promised Land' and 'A Very Deep Sea' . . . 'Changing of the Guard' might have been on the setlist, but apart from that, it was all new stuff. To be fair, I don't remember anybody ripping their programme up.

David Rowe: I don't remember this hostile environment that people talk about. I think people, when they go to a gig like to hear stuff that they know, and they didn't get that. We were already into the dance scene and clubbing quite a bit so I could get the connection, but some people thought it was taking the piss. The Albert Hall probably wasn't the best venue, it's hard to create an atmosphere in there. It's not like a sweaty little box, is it?

Mick Talbot: What didn't help matters was that our greatest hits has just come out. We didn't really have control over that. Once we knew it was happening, we got involved in the artwork and what have you, but we couldn't stop that, contractually.

Even though The Style Council on paper only existed for six years, and then if you add the beginning of the end, we really were around for nearly seven. In those six years, there were four different MDs at Polydor, so it was a bit weird to try and get a bit of a relationship.

The last MD came in and immediately he wanted the greatest hits, and I think he had a look at the graph and thought, *The last two albums have taken a downward spiral*, and sometimes when they want to knock out the greatest hits, that can be the death knell for a band. So maybe things were looming, but we didn't really play ball, because I suppose there may have been a proportion of the audience that might have expected a greatest hits show, with *The Singular Adventures of The Style Council, Greatest Hits Vol. 1*.

I think we knew there weren't a volume two. That was quite an ironic title. So, we didn't play our hits, but we thought we were just being kind enough to let some of the audience hear our future hits. The thing is, all those tunes that people wanted to hear, if that's what they wanted to hear, they were all new at some point, you've got to move on. But I do think that it's grown, the mythology of that gig. Yeah, maybe some people were ripping up their programmes and that, and there was a bit of a funny atmosphere, but since then, a little bit like the *Confessions* album, even that gig has been reappraised.

Dee C. Lee: So again, that's what happens . . . You just do what you do, the best that you can, and then you deal with it from there. So yeah, it was a weird one, but I'm not ashamed of that. I don't think Paul is. In fact, none of us are. We did what we did, we enjoyed it. It's a shame that not everybody did as much as we did. But, you know, such is life.

Robert Howard: You've got to remember that The Jam audience could be quite scary, quite male, possibly, quite conservative, and I think he wanted to escape that. So, the biggest move was from there to The Style Council. That was the one that pissed a lot of people off, and that was so brave. So, Paul has just carried on doing that, carried on following that voice inside that says, *This is where I should be.* I think that's all part of this 'modernist philosophy' that encompasses almost everything in his world. New. Keep going forward. Don't get caught in nostalgia. Don't even look backwards. Although occasionally he will now, I think. But it's always being in the moment, always going with what's happening

Adrian Thrills: Interesting, isn't it? Because you'd think he's seen the music business from every aspect possible. As much as he's been a pretty consistent songwriter, commercially, there have been real lows and there'd been moments where he's gone probably out of fashion. The Jam fans are a more loyal and broad-minded bunch than they're often given credit for, but I think towards the end of The Style Council, he had somehow managed to alienate vast swathes of his audience.

1989 – *Modernism: A New Decade*, rejected album

John Williams: Polydor had an option album, which was the *Modernism* record, which never came out and this is the story, I guess, about how the record got turned down.

They had one more album to deliver. This is a long time ago, but I was not for dropping The Style Council. My opinion was that we should keep them, and, yes, so what, the advance is slightly higher? What used to happen is the advance would get bigger and bigger and bigger, and there came a stage where the record company, the accounts department, would do the sums and say, 'Well, just hang on a second, they only sold 30,000 albums, and we're paying a quarter million pounds for the record, which is going to sell less than that. Let's pass.' Right, my view was, well, he's one of the great artists of all time and of his generation, anyway, and you should keep him.

There was, of course, main characters in this. Maurice Oberstein, who was the chairman of PolyGram, and John Weller were at odds, and I got a phone call from Obi saying, 'I want you to ring up John Weller and drop The Style Council and to refuse to accept the album.' I said, 'No, I can't.' He said words to the effect of 'Do you still want a job here? If you can't do that, you're out of a job. You're the head of A&R. You've got to man up.'

Economics do come into it and you can't run a business with a whole bunch of artists who don't sell anything, that cost fortunes, so you can't do it. There has to be some pragmatism about it. But what's the back catalogue of The Jam and Style Council worth in the future? Zillions. It keeps on turning over good money, and the record companies pay out at poor royalty rates, so there's lots of income. Anyway, so I was the messenger. John Weller was apoplectic. I was in a very poor position.

Mick Talbot: We felt we had a good album, and we thought we would get a few singles out of it and go on tour. And the new MD . . . they'd become like buses. Four turned up at once . . . But the new one, that week, just didn't like the album and he just stopped it. Then the rug was pulled early, so we went out quite quietly really.

Nicky Weller: Yeah. It was a huge shock. Dad was probably thinking, *Shit, we've got to start from the bottom up again.*

Ann Weller: I won't tell you what John said when he came home that night. It shall be unrepeatable. It was just one of those things, wasn't it? I mean, I don't know. I wasn't worried. Not really. They'd made money by then. You never know from one day to the next what's going to happen.

Nicky Weller: Yeah, it was David Munns, which is really weird because in later years, when I went to work at Nordoff and Robbins Music Therapy, as a fundraising manager, he was our chairman. I was being introduced to him one day, and I was like, 'Oh, for God's sake, please don't hold it against me. My name's Weller, I'm a Weller.' He was like, 'Oh OK.' But he never held it against me. He was the one that turned down the album and it's like, what a big mistake you made there.

Nigel 'Spanner' Sweeney: Paul was out of a deal. How I heard about that I do not know. We're talking a long time ago, but I'm pretty damn sure 99.999 that I'd gone up to Nomis to collect something. It was terribly upsetting actually, because John Weller had an office there . . . He was literally stressed out to the high hill because his son hadn't got a record deal. He was visibly upset. 'What am I gonna do? They've dropped my son.' John was a lovely, lovely, lovely, lovely man. The thing is that he was crying because they'd just ditched his son. I don't know what happened at that point, whether John phoned Paul or Paul phoned John or Kenny was involved. I don't know. They rejected him.

John Williams: I had heard the album. I think it was sent recorded delivery overnight – saying 'that's the delivery' . . . *We'll give them that and they'll have to accept it* . . . Oberstein was angry about this and thought, *Well, no, you can't. We're not going to accept it. It's not technically correct*, or words to that effect. I wasn't mister popular with Paul and he was hurt, wounded, and you can't blame the poor chap.

Peter Button: I don't remember who told who what, but I do know that they rejected the album on artistic grounds. Paul had gone a bit experimental, which he does from time to time, and David Munns simply didn't like it and said, 'No, I'm not going to put it out. You're free to go.' I believe it was to be the last commitment album anyway. So, the agreement was due to run out and this was the last album that they were to have and they decided they wouldn't have it.

Paul Weller: I was naturally angry about it. Me old man said he'd had a call from David Munns, or Cunns, as I used to call him, saying that they didn't want the record. But musically, I don't know if it was for that reason. I think it was for a financial reason because I was tied into this deal where they had to pay us stupid amounts of money for each record. I think for them it was like, we've finished putting money into this and it was more of a financial thing. I was angry at the time, but then, after a while, it was like, *What the fuck, what does it matter?* It's good in a way, because it caused something else to happen.

Richard Ogden: When I heard David Munns had dropped him from Polydor, I couldn't believe it. Honestly, I couldn't believe it. I thought it was such a stupid thing to do. Bad thing. Just for the sake of the money, the deal, you know, and not trusting in the future of the artist.

Nigel 'Spanner' Sweeney: Paul would have said that album was the start of house. Nobody else did. I'm not saying I didn't. I'm gonna keep Switzerland on that. Who fucking knows what I thought at that time? It was a Paul Weller album. If I'm right, that record probably only had Paul singing on it twice? Even Paul, being as sensible he is, would go, well they're paying Paul Weller, but he's only singing twice on eleven or twelve tracks on an album. I'm not saying David Munns was right at that point, but they didn't see the vision of Paul.

Brendan Lynch: There's a track called 'Sure Is Sure', which I thought, up until that point, was the best thing I'd ever worked on. I really loved that. It's a really interesting song and Paul's singing on it is great.

Simon Halfon: The single 'Sure Is Sure' was done, but that never came out . . . I think that the photo session was done for the album with Lawrence Watson, but I don't think the artwork was done.

Brendan Lynch: It was a real shame that the *Modernism* album didn't come out because it was all finished. We put it all on tape, mixed it all, and I was really looking forward to the release. There's a song called 'Can You Still Love Me?', and 'That Spiritual Feeling' with the J. B. Horns. The whole James Brown thing was a really big thing at that time, and they all rolled in one day. They were all pretty old guys, but boy could they play, incredible. Fred Wesley, Maceo Parker, Pee Wee Ellis, Richard Griffith. It was great. Steve White wasn't around when I started working with Paul. Marco Nelson was always around. His band, Young Disciples, used to record at the studio as well. They'd be popping in and out. It was a bit like a youth club.

Mick Talbot: At the time, the biggest regret was the last album not coming out. I don't know if I'm deeply wounded that it didn't now, but at the time you're in the moment and you believe in what you're working on, and you put your best endeavours and efforts behind it and I actually think it got canned by Polydor for a very mealy-mouthed reason. I don't think that was about the quality of the album or the music. That went back to some personal thing. Each MD had different opinionated views and the last one through the door thought that he knew what a Style Council album was more than we did and that's very tricky. I don't know if there's any way forward from that. I'm pleased it saw the light of day ten years later, but I think it would have made more sense in the time and era it was recorded.

Lawrence Watson: It was strange stuff, especially to have your record label that you've made a fortune for, Polydor, saying no, we're parting here, we don't see it. They see this as the end of the road. Anybody with half a bit of nous would say, *No, he's a great songwriter*. That's not going to go away. There'll be different styles and trends going on or whatever and stuff but it's like, no, no, they didn't see it. It's like Columbia dropping Johnny Cash. Record labels, these buildings, they're built on the money these musicians have made for you. I had every confidence in Paul that there would be more songs coming along. There's no way they're going to keep this man down and you're not going to stop him from what he wants to do. Most musicians and good artists are out of time. They're doing something ahead of their time. Never satisfying the trends. He's just honouring his own artistic moments that are passing through his brain at the time and turning them into art.

John Williams: I think it caused them to rethink The Style Council. The record was rejected, and they decided it was probably best to break up the band. I loved Paul. He wasn't so much for my generation because I had Ray Davies and Pete Townshend, but I could understand what he was all about and he loved The Zombies, who I loved, and he loved Nick Drake, who I loved, so we have very similar musical tastes. Anyway, he was never to discover that, and I was *persona non grata* for years. I didn't try and repair our relationship at the time because I was gone myself four months later. A&R men are a bit like football managers. You're as good as your last win. I got a job back at Chrysalis, head of A&R, then I went to Sanctuary, where I became senior vice president of A&R. We were based in the Nomis building, the same as the Weller office, so I'd see Paul in the corridor and nod at him and he would nod back, but we never spoke. He knew exactly who I was.

I think it took Phil Bickley from Tonic who said to him eventually, 'Listen, John's a really great guy, he's a friend of mine,' and, then I was in Tonic one day and Paul came in and I was like his best friend. I love him. I think he's one of the greats, and I'm pleased with whatever happened that in the end he benefited. I'm sure he didn't think so at the time. Jokingly, I'd say I was responsible for his renaissance. He became an artist again, a real artist, and a genius one.

Mick Talbot: There wasn't really a day when we stopped going into Solid Bond, because there was a community there and I was working on four different albums, and they were all being done at Solid Bond, and the only one that didn't see the light of day was our one!

I was working on Dee's album; she had a group called Slam Slam which Dr Robert from The Blow Monkeys was producing. He was also in the studio doing his own stuff as well, which I was playing on, and the beginnings of the Young Disciples album was taking shape there. I played on nearly every track because I was involved with Femi Williams and Marco Nelson from the demo stage. So, all three of those acts got their album out, but we didn't.

Dennis Munday: Every album's got to have at least two or three big hit singles, and that LP clearly didn't. There was a decline. Perhaps it was inevitable because of the way that the band was structured and the way that Paul was running it. But if I'd have been there, I would have said, 'Look, it's crazy. Half a million is more than enough, and that gives you leeway. You should be able to sell half a million copies.' *Our Favourite Shop* certainly sold half a million worldwide. You're in the money, you're not getting in the red. But as the hits dried up, so did the album sales . . . I think the Orange album sold about 120,000 copies and *Confessions*, I think, sold 80,000 copies. By the time you get to *Modernism*, they're heavily in the red. So, it was a business decision. It's as simple as that. No A&R man would have picked it up. He'd have lost his job if the guy had picked it up.

Richard Ogden: That's why David Munns dropped him, because there was another album, another million quid. He went, 'Oh we're not picking up that.' They were options for record deals, they're not firm deals. It wasn't on me that things went wrong.

You have to let music stand on its own two feet, don't you?

You have to judge it for what it is, not what you want it to be. Fans are fickle people. They're fans and then they're not fans. What you have to have is a consistent level of quality music, whatever format or genre you happen to be wanting to work in. Look at David Bowie, how many genres did he create in? Did anybody like Tin Machine? No. Did it kill him forever? No. Paul Weller should be treated in the same way. I can say that because I wasn't there then.

Andy Macdonald: I would just have put it out but be realistic about it. It's a really good piece of work and it was something that needed to come out, and it stands the test of time. When do you value or evaluate something, in ten years, or thirty years, or fifty years?

David Quantick: You have this weird moment in history when both Pet Shop Boys and The Style Council are doing house records or doing Chicago, whatever it's called, and you think, we've come to this, where The Style Council and Pet Shop Boys are existing in the same space, and then, of course, fast forward thirty years later, you get Pet Shop Boys remixing Paul Weller, in the twenty-first century, which is just weird.

Ann Weller: Don't like house music, love. It's for the youngsters, innit. I used to call it bungalow music. No, it's not my thing. I like a song you can sing along to.

Mick Talbot: There was no big bang, but I think we wanted to honour a couple of charity things we had, so we technically did make it into the nineties. We officially did a press release like, March 1990, which would have been seven years after 'Speak Like a Child'.

Trevor Neal: Simon and I were invited to do a gig at the Dominion Theatre in February 1990. This was post-Style Council and before the whole solo launch. A gig in support of the ambulance workers who'd gone on strike. It was quite a big deal at the time. Me and Simon did a 'Swing your pants' thing and Paul Weller was on.

Darren Fletcher: If I remember rightly, I think it was a little bit of a disappointment. That's a shame . . . It fizzles out, bands come, bands go. Just move on.

Dylan Jones: The Style Council were better than The Jam. Deal with it . . . The music was great, they were funny, ironic and cool. It was another opportunity for Paul Weller to be dismissive of the industry, which I enjoyed. In their own way they were completely dismissive of the world that they were in. *We're going to do this. We're going to start an album with an instrumental. We're going to dress up and go boating.* It was playful and the image was good. But also, fundamentally, it always comes back to one thing, which is content, and the songs were great. It was a real joy to see him writing in different idioms and different genres. Just growing as a songwriter. They were terrific. They were a joy to watch. I still play those records. I mean, I still play Jam records, but I play Style Council records more often.

I think that the eighties is still a decade which people are patronising about . . . they still kind of treat it as though it's somehow less significant than the decades that surround it and I don't think that's true . . . Up until the eighties pop music was linear. One thing tended to follow another and, even though you had this big explosion in the sixties, a lot of the music that came out of it was very, very similar, even though there was a lot of talent that blossomed in the sixties, but in the eighties, driven principally by technology, you had this sort of kaleidoscopic amount of different types of music. And I think it's when music became atomised there was something for everyone, there were lots of little mini genres plus it was a very vibrant period for protest songs. People don't think of the eighties as being a decade of protest songs. The eighties is responsible for the most commercially successful protest song of all time, which was 'Do They Know It's Christmas?', the Band Aid record, plus you had 'Ghost Town', plus you had 'Free Nelson Mandela', plus you had Prince writing 'Sign of the Times'. You had all these extraordinary records, which were writing about the ills of society and societal changes, and they were very important.

Simon Halfon: This is a time where artists just got on with their stuff. There was no media training. There was no, 'Oh, you got to do this and go by this rulebook.' They just did what they did. They got on with it. Same with Paul's career. Do what you do and you get on with it and you believe in yourself. I think maybe that's gone a little bit now where everything has to be done by a marketing playbook.

Chris Catchpole: From splitting up The Jam to everything The Style Council did was Paul saying, *This is what I want to do. If you don't like it, fuck off.* He said to me that on reflection now, he'd be a bit less harsh with it and would try to take people with him a bit more. But his attitude then was like, *Well, this is what I want to do, if it's not for you, then listening is not compulsory.*

Paul wanted to leave The Jam and do something completely new, way before he even thought of calling Mick, but to this day, there are a lot of people out there who think that Mick's Yoko Ono.

Mick Talbot: I don't think Paul ever liked having to live up to what people thought he was, no one's that two dimensional, and I think he was keen to just have a laugh and sometimes people didn't get it, and people moaned about it being an in-joke and this, that and the other. But regardless of all the silly outfits and half puns or clumsy in-jokes, at the end of the day, it's the music that really counts. Whenever we made music we were serious about that. We did have quite a laugh, really, and a lot of that came from Paul. People sometimes say 'Oh, did you tell him to cheer up? Because he seemed like he was miserable before.' And that's so demeaning to him if you really knew him. I think it's all about if you're the right team, and people trust you . . . Paul's nothing like that caricature that the press may have you believe.

Nicky Weller: There was a little time when they weren't going out on the road and Paul was just working in studio, recording or whatever. Who would have known that the rest of his career was going to happen like it has? It's incredible, really. I think my dad even must have just thought it was all over.

1990 – Without a deal

Brendan Lynch: When Paul lost his contract with Polydor, he was still always coming into Solid Bond every day. He'd always come into the studio, usually four or five days a week. He would finish quite early, though, maybe half-six or something. That's his passion, isn't it? Just being around music. He'd come in and play the piano for an hour and listen to some records. It was that sort of thing. He was finding his way and wondering what to do next.

Kenny Wheeler: Paul was always working. He was always in the studio. He was always doing bits and pieces.

Dee C. Lee: He was very, very stressed and it was really hard trying to keep him occupied and say, 'Look at what we got, and you can take your time and think about what you want to do. You don't have to rush into anything.' But it was weird for him, more than I realised . . . well, it's weird for everybody when you got a kid but for him it was harder, I think.

Paul Weller: Totally lost. Because we got involved, as a lot of people did, with a whole eighties technological revolution that happened in studios. Digital recording, or the start of it, and we spent less and less time in the live area and more time in the control room with fucking drum boxes and sequencers and all that bullshit. Which is not bullshit. I take that back, because great things have come out of sequencers and drum machines. But we went totally that way and we stopped doing the live thing.

I wasn't writing songs in the same way that I used to, sitting down with a guitar or a piano. We used to go in every day, me and Mick, and just make it up as we went along. I got out of the habit, or the loop, of sitting down and writing, sheet of paper, guitar.

Dennis Munday: I never ever thought that Paul would give up. He was always going to come back. I think he lost his way with The Style Council. I think he was trying to get so far away from The Jam, he got away from himself. There was so much pressure on them that as soon as it started to wane . . . they weren't selling records, they weren't successful . . . I think there was tremendous pressure on him to reform The Jam because, if he'd have done that, Polydor would have picked it up, wiped out the arrears, but he didn't want to.

If you look at the last year or so where he stopped playing the guitar and one could say dancing on stage – loosely! – he still had the energy.

Martin Hopewell: From a live point of view, we were starting over again. The Jam broke into some markets around the rest of the world. Then The Style Council broke into some of the same markets, but also other ones and previous ones that were big didn't do so well. It was always this thing of pushing into the new areas. So, when Paul started solo, it was like history repeating itself, and you think, well, that really is it, because you get lucky, and you have The Jam and then The Style Council, but it can't happen again. Who has three different careers? Nobody.

Paul Weller: I was like, *I'm not sure anymore. I don't know how to do this*. So, it was a pragmatic reason that I went back on the road because we needed money, simple as that. We needed to earn some money. We didn't have a publishing deal, didn't have a record deal, didn't have a band or anything. So, it was just me old man saying, 'Look you've got to go back on the road, we need to earn some bread.'

Jacko Peake: I carried on working with Paul through The Paul Weller Movement. That was a really interesting time. I call it the dark years, really, where Paul was really struggling and wondering whether he should carry on and what he was doing. It was a big moment for Paul that I understood much more in later years. Steve White was the only constant in there and I learned a lot from Steve about the history of The Style Council, where Paul was at and what he was going through at that moment. We did some gigs at the end of 1990 and there weren't many people there. He was finding his way again and, he was really struggling, but because he's Paul, he just pushed his way forward. Relentlessly. Man of steel, he really is. He's got this tenacious grip on life and his creative output. I think he had moments where he thought that was it, he's not going to carry on anymore, but he pushed his way through. He got himself over the hump. I always remember The Paul Weller Movement as being a bit like a youth club. We had Max Beesley on vibes and percussion. He was eighteen. An extraordinary character. He's so full of energy.

Max Beesley: My mum was a jazz singer, and my dad's an actor and a brilliant jazz drummer. I grew up in Burnage, South Manchester, a very working-class area, but got into Chetham's School of Music as a chorister. I pursued percussion and piano before heading to the Guildhall in London. One night, I was playing with The Jazz Warriors, and after the gig, this guy came up to me – Steve White. 'Can you get to Solid Bond Studios on Friday? Someone I'm working with is looking for a keyboard player and percussionist.' I asked who it was, and he said, 'Paul Weller.' At the time, I had no idea who that was!

Steve invited me to a party at the studio on Thursday. Solid Bond was packed with people, and I loved the vibe. Then, outside by the kitchen, I saw this guy looking so cool, with a mod bowling T-shirt. He looked amazing, and I suddenly realised, *That's Paul Weller! Oh, The Style Council!* It all clicked. But I was shy, so I kept quiet.

Joe Beckett: It was an interesting time – a new era for Paul, where he was changing direction. I was playing percussion in clubs back then, doing gigs with people like Danny Rampling and Andy Weatherall during the early days of the house movement.

I actually got involved with Paul in a funny way. I was on tour with Spandau Ballet, and one of the sound crew invited me to a party at Solid Bond Studios. The sound system went wrong, and there were some bongos lying around, so I just started playing them – that was basically my audition! After that, I played on a few demos like 'New Thing', 'Kosmos' and 'Round and Round' and got to know Paul.

We'd hang out, go for a curry, and talk music. We had shared interests, especially funk and soul. I lent him some vinyl and thought I'd never see them again, but he gave back every single one in great condition. That really stuck with me.

Solid Bond was amazing. So many people came through – Dr Robert, Carleen Anderson, Young Disciples. We'd play five-a-side football and then go swimming down the road. Those were great memories. Then we started rehearsing for the tour. Paul tried out a few musicians, but it was Paul Francis who ended up on bass, and Max turned up too – larger than life, that guy. We got on really well and had a good laugh on tour.

Paul Francis: Steve White and I had been doing JTQ [James Taylor Quartet] and got on well musically. I don't remember the timeframe between me meeting Paul and that first audition. It was all slightly hush-hush. I knew there was something on the boil, but I wasn't quite sure what it was. I got the call to get down to Solid Bond. Steve didn't say anything about a band or tour. He said, 'Just come and have a play, and see what happens.' So, I picked up the bass, went in the room and Paul was there. I panicked. Inwardly. Paul started playing 'The Ghetto' by Donny Hathaway – there's a really fat groove on that tune – and I knew it really well. I sat there and started playing my bass and it all gelled together.

Joe Beckett: Paul was serious about the work. He knew exactly what he wanted and wasn't afraid to let us know if we weren't delivering. Rehearsals at Nomis were intense. I remember one time we all got a bollocking from Paul for not doing the backing vocals – he shouted over the mic, 'Where's the fucking backing vocals?' We all thought, *Oh, shit!* But that's how it was. He wanted it to be right, and honestly, that's how it should be.

Max Beesley: The next day, I went back to Solid Bond and met Paul's dad, John. Paul was in the main studio, sitting with his guitar by the grand piano.

I was such a young kid, man. Paul asked if I wanted to play a couple of things. He started playing on the acoustic and I listened to the chord changes and started playing along, keeping it simple. He said, 'Nice.' Paul went out after a bit, when he came back, he said, 'Go and see me dad, will ya?' I walked into John's office; he looked like this patriarchal king-like figure behind his big desk. He said, 'Paul wants you to do the gig. Going to be great. We'll give you a monkey a week, get you in all the gear, do the TVs – it's going to be fantastic.' I was eighteen, living on tuna and rice in Catford as a student with no money, and it felt unbelievable.

On Monday, I went to my college principal, Ian Horsborough, and explained the opportunity. I asked if I could come back if it didn't work out. He said, 'Absolutely, go for it.' That was it . . . my life was about to change.

Paul Francis: You always knew when John Weller was coming before he arrived. You could feel his presence in the building. He was an amazing character, a lovely guy. My dealings with him were mostly financial and a few small chats, but I've got nothing bad to say about John, man.

Jacko Peake: It was madness. We were just kids. Kenny Wheeler, the tour manager, had his hands full with us lot. There was so much chaos going on through that period. Paul was finding his feet again, and we were this bundle of young energy, facilitating any musical whim that Paul had. It really did cross a whole load of different styles – straight-ahead jazz sometimes, then quite hard-edged rock the next. It was such a broad musical palette, and it gave Paul the space to find his feet and a springboard for his solo career.

November 1990 – The Paul Weller Movement, first tour

Kenny Wheeler: It was a weird time really. We just started putting the dates together and Paul had a band that he wanted. We got some venues we wouldn't normally do. Different venues, smaller venues than we were used to. We just went out and done it. There was this thing about Paul that once he started playing again, he wanted to play. John was always the driving force, *We should be doing this, we should be doing that.*

Paul Francis: The Paul Weller Movement's first gig at Dingwalls was packed. It's such a small stage, and I remember looking around at Steve on drums and Max on vibes, Paul, juxtaposed against each other. In the sixties and seventies, a lot of the big bands had started in small clubs like the Marquee, and Dingwalls had that vibe. The energy was electric. I don't know how they squeezed us all on, but they did!

Joe Beckett: It was funny because it was an underground gig, all secretive, but when we got there, there were fifty scooters parked out front. All the mod mobiles parked up. So much for being 'underground'. That was a real experience, the crowd were really close.

Paul 'Smiler' Anderson: We went to that first gig at Dingwalls in November 1990, and loads of people were moaning, 'Why doesn't he play more Jam stuff?' A few of us went along as mods. We were amazed at what he did. It was brilliant.

Dean Rudland: That was the biggest event. I was working at Acid Jazz and we all got ourselves togged up in new gear, Duffer cardigans, whatever. It was a Shake & Fingerpop night. Norman Jay, Marco Nelson and Femi Willliams DJing, and that night the live band was Paul Weller Movement. Three hundred people or whatever. There's a story that's always told about the empty shows in those early days but they were hugely exciting.

Mark Baxter: It was incredible. I had a little stall down in Camden and I was meeting loads of guys who later become groups like Galliano, Acid Jazz, Gilles Peterson, the jazz thing, Dingwalls. Most of my peer group got a job, got married, had kids young and got a house, they were content like that, but I was always wanting to know if there's more out there. Following Paul took me on a journey. He would change so much. He was like a chameleon. People would go to gigs, and they'd be like, *Oh shit, my haircut's out of date*, but they're stuck with it for that gig! It was always moving, and I got into that massively. I love that side to him, really.

Paul Weller: That first tour, 1990, Paul Weller Movement. We did a European tour which was fucking shocking, man. Dreadful. Musically it was all over the shop because as the band leader, I didn't have a fucking clue. I was like a fish out of water. I'd lost touch with all of it. But it was fun as well. The fun probably outweighed the music. I can remember being in this Italian club and there were maybe 100 people, probably less, and we were playing this song, and I didn't know how to end it and nor did the rest of the band [*laughs*] so we just went round and round. I was like, *What the fuck are we doing, man?* I felt like an amateur again, and then we came back and did some English dates which were so poorly attended. I just thought, *Oh my God, I've got to start again*. Literally. Which I hated at the time. I just thought, *I've done all this work, and I've got to start again.*

Kenny Wheeler: Clubs again. It was the same job. You got to get in those places, and you play 'em, some of them are shitholes.

Some of them you don't want to sit down or walk across the floor. It brings you back down again. But the gigs were still good, and it was starting over again. Paul's writing was still good, and he was enjoying playing. So, my part is making sure you can help to the best of your ability. Making sure he's got everything he needs to do what he has to do.

Joe Beckett: The biggest thing I remember is the cards. John and Kenny playing twenty-ones, but it wasn't a pound in the middle, it was tenners and that game is over in minutes. We all got into playing cards and I done all right . . . Paul was a vegetarian, and I think he needed to eat more protein so was trying meat out. We'd be driving and would stop at a burger van for some greasy old burger. Not a luscious steak.

Max Beesley: I used to always forget a couple of tunes on the setlist. Just could not remember them on the live gigs. 'Ever Changing Moods' was one of the tracks. I just couldn't remember the chord changes. I used to get daggers off Paul.

Joe Beckett: We'd always start with 'Ever Changing Moods', 'Kosmos', 'Round and Round'. I always loved 'New Thing' as well. He played that to me when he wrote it in the studio and I was like, 'Oh yeah, this is really good.' It had that vibe and we had the horn section. Jacko, Damon Brown on trumpet, Chris Lawrence on trombone, Max on the vibes. Damon used to make me laugh because you'd be in a hotel, having a beer afterwards and then he'd disappear, go up to his room, but he's left his trumpet mouthpiece on the table. It's like, *God, he's done it again*. The most important thing, you know?

Damon Brown: Paul had a good ear for melody. I was having trouble at that time with my playing technically and Paul let me go after one tour. I remember he said, 'I don't think you're really into the music,' but I knew that he knew I wasn't cutting it, and I didn't feel bad about his decision. Just disappointed. I had some nice gigs, met some great musicians, and it was great to play with Paul. He then hired a great trumpet player called Gerard Presencer. Paul was not in a great mood at that time, I seem to remember.

Paul Francis: Back then, I was always a session guy, so I never really understood the pressure that was on the man at the front. It's a really big job. When I look back on that period, I can see the quiet moments when Paul didn't seem to respond, he had a lot of stuff on his mind . . . If you're at the front, you can experience ecstasy and anger, you can go through depression, but having said that, it doesn't matter where he was playing, he always delivered. It's a learning curve when you're working with someone like that. The professionalism is incredible to watch.

Shane Juson: My first solo gig was Coventry in November 1990. There weren't that many people there, but I loved it. I bought more tickets and organised a minibus trip down to Cardiff, and me and a mate went down to London as well. We met Paul twice in three days, which was fantastic. He was carrying his ironing board into the gig. How cool is that? He did 'Precious' for the first time solo, which blew my mind, just to hear that again was unbelievable. He did 'Tales from a Riverbank' and 'Pity Poor Alfie' as well on that tour and then he did 'It's a Very Deep Sea' on the piano. I remember some bloke in London shouting, 'Bring back Mick Talbot.'

Paul Francis: The first tour finished in December with two nights at the Town and Country Club in London and live on the BBC. By this point you knew what your job was. The engine room is running nicely, you just walk on and you play, and they happen to be recording it.

Neil Sheasby: That Town and Country gig was mad because the Council had only just split up really. Steve White was drumming for Paul. Mick got on stage and Dee got up. They did a cover of 'What's Going On?', Marvin Gaye, so there was a brief reuniting of the Council there.

Joe Beckett: That was my final gig with Paul. He got Max to play percussion and vibes on the second Paul Weller Movement tour. He changed the lineup, trying to find what was going to work. It was a hard time for Paul then, trying to get out and rediscover yourself and try new things.

Paul Francis: I think that Paul was having a few personal problems at the time. Then the musical direction changed, and he thought that I wasn't suitable. I came out of the acid jazz, soul thing, and he was going into a new area of music. It sounded great so I can see where he was going. I applaud him for doing that.

April 1991 – The Paul Weller Movement, second tour

Jon Abnett: I went to the gig at Subterania in London, April '91. Paul didn't come on stage until about eleven-thirty and we missed our train home. It's incredible to think it was just 200 people watching Paul Weller . . . with those early gigs, he didn't have enough songs, so he had to dig back into The Jam and Style Council catalogue to put a set together.

Brenda Taylor: Even when Paul came out on his own, I was still there. He was up in Aylesbury and there were a dozen people there, including me.

Steve 'Tufty' Carver: I distinctly remember going to Guildford Civic Hall with my brother Pete. It was probably one of them gaps where I hadn't seen Paul for a few years. We bought a £3.25 ticket. There were some people on the dancefloor, and I'm not joking, I could look at the microphone and just go, 'Paul, all right,' and he went, 'All right,' and it's just fucking hell, there's no way back from this. Fair credit to the guy, it was a long way down for a bit. I've never spoke to him about it, but a lot of people don't recover from that.

David Cracknell: I went to the infamous Newport gig with forty people. It was a big hall, and it wasn't full, but I do remember it was fantastic. It was one of those things where a flip of a coin, it could have gone either way and, fortunately, it went the right way.

Martin Hopewell: If you think about it, each time – with The Jam, with The Style Council, and with Paul's thing – we started at the bottom again and worked our way up. So, once more, starting off cautiously, and then suddenly, within a couple of years, you're back up there again. I think a lot of the venues we were playing were the same, because even in the nineties, I don't think there were that many arenas . . . We were playing places like Bridlington Spa and Blackpool Tower Ballroom again. Thankfully, not the Equestrian Centre in Braintree – I'm pleased to say that I don't think we had to do that.

Max Beesley: I was living my best life. We did the filmed gig at Brixton Academy. I've seen clips and I look like a complete tool, but the playing is all right. I've got away with it. As a man, I didn't have a clue. I used to wind Paul up and say, 'Brother, I'm eighteen. What are you, thirty-three?' He's fifteen years older than me. 'Wow, so you'll be fifty-five when I'm forty. That's horrendous.' It used to drive him nuts, man.

Neil Sheasby: On that tour, it felt like Paul really had the fire back. It was such a great time to see him, especially in those venues.

A few years earlier, with The Style Council's *Cost of Loving*, we had been to places like the NEC, but now it was back to being just a few rows away, reconnecting with the crowd. It was incredible hearing those solo tunes for the first time and then he'd throw in tracks like 'Tales from the Riverbank' or 'Precious'. Mind blowing to see him back on form.

Steve Cradock: I went to see Paul at Digbeth Institute. It was the day before Steve Marriott passed. There was only a few hundred people there, which was unbelievable. The comparison is interesting, because around that time we would go and see Steve play as part of either The DT's or Debt Collectors. He was doing covers, and it was that kind of audience, it was just a couple of hundred people, but this was Paul Weller. It was like 'what the fuck's going on?' But it changed thankfully.

David Cracknell: After Newport, I got a ticket for Brixton, I wanted to see how it had developed. No one was interested in going so I went on my own. That just tells you where he was at the time . . . You heard songs like 'Kosmos' and 'Into Tomorrow' for the first time. It was an amazing gig.

Paul Gomersall: I was sat in a truck outside with the recording equipment mixing it live. No overdubs. Sat with a screen to see the movements of the musicians. That's part of the charm. It didn't get remixed because of lack of funds at the time, but it sounded good anyway, thankfully. They probably never re-edited the video either.

John Harris: I was at university in Oxford, The Paul Weller Movement toured. This is the band with Henry Thomas from Rock School on bass. This is very early on. I got a T-shirt, styled like a football shirt with a number ten on the back. You hear stories in documentaries about how no one came, and they played to forty people in Newport. The Oxford Apollo was full, and it was great. What I loved about The Paul Weller Movement was that it was loud again with the guitar back at the forefront. I got off on that.

Max Beesley: Paul would say, 'Let's throw vibes in on this,' and we'd do a jazz number in the middle of this mental set that was such a cacophony and plethora of different tracks. You'd have the die-hard Jam and Style Council fans and what was great was his music covered so many elements that there was something for everyone in the shows. I think of playing 'Uh Huh Oh Yeh!', and the juxtapose with the Bobby Hutchinson track and then 'Precious', which we used to finish the set with. That was crazy audience participation. Lunatics. It used to kick off, certainly at the Barrowlands in Glasgow, where it's always been a good gig for Paul.

Neil Sheasby: I saw the Movement loads of times. He dismisses that in interviews, he glosses over that and says, 'I was lost, finding my feet.' But you talk to any Paul Weller fan that were at them gigs and they were really special affairs. You could tell he was reigniting with the audience. Finding his mojo again. That's when I first met him. Just as a fan outside Nottingham Trent Poly.

David Cracknell: He fell in love with guitars again, but not in The Jam way, this was with pedals and creating great sounds. Songs were going into jams at the end when you think they've finished. It was so experimental and different from what was going on at the time and so different from that last Style Council album.

Bobby Gillespie: I remember going to see The Paul Weller Movement in Brighton. It was great that he'd come back, and the guitar was more rock and roll. I think we'd been at Alan McGee's, and we were singing 'Weller, Weller' – just so happy to see him with a guitar in his hand, being aggressive. The band didn't have that aggression of The Jam – it was quite session-y and I think he was trying to feel his way back in. It wasn't a sold-out gig. Loads of guys, my age, with a girlfriend or their wives. It took him a while to build up again, get a big audience . . .

He started wearing longer hair and I remember him being in *i:D* looking really good, wearing very contemporary styles like Duffer St George. He was hanging out with people like Marco Nelson, who I later became great friends with, and Femi Williams, his friend – they became the Young Disciples. Weller had got into club and so he was into contemporary, funk and soul clubs and started to dress different style points.

I was watching all that from the distance. It was about the time that we started getting hits. I would say the first time I met him was 1991 on our tour . . . We had a good chat, and he was telling us he liked Primal Scream, and we were like, *Fucking hell, it's Paul Weller.*

Noel Gallagher: I went to see him in Manchester with Liam. I'd just joined Oasis and we're all huge Jam fans. He'd been out of the consciousness for a while. I don't remember the gig being this amazing fucking moment, but what I remember from the gig is him saying, like he always does, 'Gonna play something new for ya.' He played 'Into Tomorrow'. The minute that guitar riff comes in, me and Liam stood at the back going, 'Fucking hell.' It had everything that you would want in a Weller tune. It was up, defiant, soulful and it was fucking having it. Then the whole thing went from there.

7 May 1991 – 'Into Tomorrow' (no. 36)

Brendan Lynch: Paul had just started working on new material in 1990 and '91. Just before the Solid Bond Studios closed down, we started doing loads of demos. I remember doing 'Round and Round' which Dee sang on. I think even Mick played on a few of the demos. We did a song called 'Here's a New Thing'. That was earmarked as a single. I don't think Paul was at the start of the album. It was more that he was just doing tracks, thinking of them like singles.

Jacko Peake: We did a demo of a song called 'New Thing' at Solid Bond. Says it all really. Paul's whole vision was it's a new thing. He felt energised again. He felt in control. He felt like he wanted to do it.

That was when Paul said, 'Look, Jack, I'm afraid that I'm going to have to look for somebody else as I really need a saxophone player who can play flute as well.' I immediately said, 'I play flute.' I don't know why I said it – I only had a crappy old student model flute that didn't work at all. Every time I picked it up, it didn't work, so I always put it down again. He went, 'Oh, great. Problem solved then. Jack, I've got this track called "New Thing", and I'm going to be recording it in ten days. Just come down, bring your flute, and off we go.'

I went home, got the flute out of the case, and thought, *What am I going to do? What have I said?* I went to All Flutes Plus in Waterloo, who said it wasn't worth fixing. It was old and leaky, but he patched it up anyway and for ten days I practised at home, sweating, really bad. When we got to record at Solid Bond, Brendan Lynch was producing. The song came on the headphones, and it was like death by misadventure. It was terrible. There was a runner at the studio, and I said, 'Look, my lips have all seized up. You've got to go and get me some lip salve.' Sent him off down Edgware Road. I was trying to get my flute playing going, which was just crap, but the thing was, Brendan was quite patient. He said, 'It sounds all right, Jack. Can you just make it sound a bit more flash?' and I was thinking, *Why don't you ask a flute player?* I got away with it and about three or four bars got used on the actual track, but I think Paul knew all along that I was just completely bluffing it.

Brendan Lynch: Paul and I were doing demos in the back room around Christmas time. Young Disciples were in the main room. There was a really bad snowfall, and we couldn't get home so we just carried on working. We ended up doing the demo for 'Into Tomorrow' that night. It went really well. We eventually got a cab home, and I remember Paul getting out, looking back, shaking my hand and saying thanks. I could tell he got his mojo back that night.

Simon Fowler: We initially recorded our first album down at Solid Bond with Jimmy Miller. Brendan and Max were there at the time working on the Young Disciples – *Road to Freedom*. We became a little gang and Steve and Paul became very close.

Steve Cradock: I think we were the last band to record at Solid Bond. It closed quite soon after that. Jimmy came over from America and did a few tracks with the Real People. He did 'Movin' on Up' and 'Damaged' with Primal Scream, and then he was going to do 'Into Tomorrow' with Paul, but that didn't work. I think Paul picked him up from the railway station and he stunk of whisky! I don't think that's what Paul wanted or needed at the time. Whereas we went along with it, and he did a first version of our first album. That was the first time I met Brendan Lynch . . . and he'd show us what he's doing.

Damon Minchella: We used Paul's studio on the very first Ocean Colour Scene album, the one that no one bought at the time. He came in to say hello. So our guitarist, Steve Cradock was dribbling everywhere because he was a huge Jam fan, and then in the studio B, which is the back room, a guy called Brendan Lynch was finishing off *Road to Freedom*, the Young Disciples album, and I wasn't interested in what Paul was doing, but Brendan played me the track, which is with Carleen singing, Paul's playing guitar, Steve White's on drums and I was like, 'Oh, this is really good,' and Brendan said, 'Oh, yeah, it's quite Style Council-ly.' And I was like, 'Really? I must listen to The Style Council then.'

Steve Cradock: I bought Paul's scooter actually. It was a PX and he said he was getting rid of it. So, I bought that. I thought that was cool as a fan, but it didn't last long. I only had it for about a month. I took it back to Moseley in Birmingham and it got nicked.

Max Beesley: We were in the studio before we went out on the road. I remember recording two or three tracks with him. 'Into Tomorrow' was one of those – that was exciting. Full of energy . . . Paul shoved me into a little booth, between the live room and the control room. I got in on the tambourine and all the bits and pieces in there, because it was such a good sound.

Brendan Lynch: When we came to record the real version with the band, the guitar solo was never quite the same as that first time we played it. So eventually we just sampled ourselves. So, the solo off the record is from my eight-track demo. The tempo was pretty much the same, so it was easy to get it spot on.

Max Beesley: I've worked with some great solo artists since then, even written with some, and no one tops Paul for lyrics. He's got a very interesting approach to song structure. He's quite unformulated. I'm always like, 'Paul, why is that fucking six four bar in there? Why have you added half a bar there?' He'll say, 'Just go with it, Maxi.'

Robert Howard: Paul and I were living close to each other in west London. Our kids grew up together and we'd go on holiday together, so we were pretty close, and the guitars would come out in those relaxed moments . . . I do remember him falling out of love with playing the guitar at a certain point . . . that was part of the rediscovery that he had in the early nineties, through playing guitar again.

I was involved on 'Into Tomorrow'. Just rhythm guitar really, he didn't really need me, but I was honoured to play on it, and from then on, I started playing on a few more songs. It felt like the beginning of something new. I love that song. It wasn't like anything else that was going on. There was this stripped-back honesty to it.

Steve Cradock: Paul had a little playback at a studio called Comforts Place. As soon as he got to 'Into Tomorrow' – like all Jam fans, Style Council fans, Paul Weller fans, everyone there just went *Whoa, whoa.*

Max Beesley: We also recorded 'Kosmos', then went out and played it live and then back into the studio. It had a different vibe. He wanted vibraphone on it, and I then learned that he liked Bobby Hutchinson and some of the old American vibes players and so we incorporated that when we went out on the road with the Rhodes Hammond and the vibraphone. I had a set of congas as well at some point.

Robert Howard: I picked up a bass and played on 'Kosmos'. Somebody clocked it. It was just whatever was hanging about, you'd pick it up and play it. Every day, you could see that Paul was getting more inspired, like a child lost in music again. There were things going on in his personal life that were very difficult. I could see that, but he was allowing the music to flow and overtake him again. That was beginning to be reflected, and he did it the old-fashioned way, by playing live again. John telling him to get out there and play live again. That's all you can do.

Noel Gallagher: By his own admission, 'Into Tomorrow' was the spark that set it all off. It was a new thing for him, a new energy, and why he didn't get a record deal is beyond me. I don't know, but his songwriting in those years couldn't have been on a level with 'Wild Wood'. You're not telling me someone's sitting there fucking writing 'Wild Wood' and playing it to people, and they're going 'Don't hear it, mate.' Do you know what I mean? So, your talent, or your thing, will always dictate what you receive. I'm not saying he wasn't writing great songs. I don't know much about him in that period. I was too busy doing my own thing.

Eddie Piller: It was bizarre. Paul couldn't get any interest from record labels. He'd had a long-documented fight with Polydor over the end of The Style Council and couldn't really get signed afterwards. I think in the end they negotiated and were allowed to leave and so I came up with an idea to sign Paul. It was the peak of Acid Jazz and we were going to sign Paul. I'd agreed to deal with John. I went to Roger Ames at London Records, because they had the Brand New Heavies and I'd given them lots of hit records, and I said to Roger, 'I'm going to take Acid Jazz more professional, but I need to make it part of PolyGram. What I want is a label with Jamiroquai, The James Taylor Quartet, the Brand New Heavies, Paul Weller, Terry Callier. I want those five bands.' Roger Ames said, 'I'll do it, but I won't do it with Paul Weller.' I said, 'Why?' and he said, 'Because he's finished,' and I said, 'You're wrong.' So, I turned down it down. I wouldn't do a deal with anyone who thought that Paul's career was finished.

Dean Rudland: I do remember that there was that level of short-sighted thinking within the industry, and I don't know whether it was genius, or it was pig-headedness from John Weller, but I remember a figure that was being touted round that he was asking for and that kept on being rejected as too much money.

Paul Weller: 'No, he's finished, it's over.' So, the more I heard that, I was like: *Right, you fuckers, I'm finished yeah?*

Brendan Lynch: We were in the studio and there was a magazine article. 'Paul Weller. Where did it all go wrong?' and he read it and went, 'Well, that was a bit harsh.' I think that gives him a lot of motivation. He gets his motivation from people slagging him off.

Steve 'Tufty' Carver: John was going into record companies and they're offering quids for Paul, and he's going, 'This ain't fucking Tommy Tucker, this is Paul Weller.'

Peter Button: No record company was interested. I think they all knew that Munns had rejected The Style Council and assumed that he'd finished. So, Paul created his own label as the vehicle to control some rights for the record that we then licensed to the Japanese label, Pony Canyon. It was really a glorified white label just to put it out.

John Cohen: With hindsight it's mad, but not necessarily at the time. Munns was a good record executive. Did very well. He once travelled to Australia to see a band, INXS, saw them, came home and got a message as he landed saying, if you want to sign us, you better sign us now and he got straight back on the plane and went back to Australia.

Dean Rudland: I remember first hearing all the demos when Gilles was trying to sign it to Talkin' Loud, and they had a cassette of

'Kosmos', which for me stood out as the defining track of those early live shows – it was absolutely phenomenal. At the time, the industry just couldn't foresee what was about to happen. In fact, if you'd invested that advance money on any of Paul's contemporaries who were in a similar position – you'd have lost your money. It's very easy to laugh at those who passed on making deals after they see it become a massive success, but you have to look at it from the point of view of what else had happened. That said, I'm not sure anyone else at the time was presenting a set of demos quite as astounding as Paul's.

Nigel 'Spanner' Sweeney: Paul wrote a fucking genius song called 'Into Tomorrow', but he didn't have a record deal. To be honest, I didn't know what to do, but we set about releasing it as an independent single. There's me as the plugger, the press guy, Philip Hall, company called Hall or Nothing, he loved Weller, and there was a guy called Paul Dowling at Go! Discs, Andy Macdonald's label.

Paul Dowling: Spanner said that Paul Weller was having a few challenges. We went over to Solid Bond, and I met John, who was a fantastic guy. Loved him to bits. So protective of Paul . . . They wanted to release a single in the UK, but they were out of a deal. That was a tough period for Paul as an artist after so much success over the years.

Nigel 'Spanner' Sweeney: I said to Paul Dowling, 'Can you do it?' He said, 'Of course, but I'll have to ask for Andy Macdonald's permission.'

Paul Dowling: They played the single a couple of times and I'm like, 'Fuck yeah. We need to put a team together. We need to work out distribution. We need to get press on board.' Spanner would do the TV and radio; I would do the marketing and the sales side of it.

I went into Andy's office and said, 'Look, I'm in an unusual situation here. I'd like your opinion. Spanner's called me, introduced me to John and Paul Weller,' and, I could see Andy's eyes light up straight away, just on saying that. 'Paul, you have my attention.'

I told him what was happening, and I was expecting him to say, *Well, how do you feel about it? Is this something you really want to do?* But Andy just went, 'Fuck yeah. No questions, just fucking do it, but get me a copy of the album and get John to call me.'

Pete Mason: Paul Dowling brought in the twelve-inch single, put it on and my head was just, *Wow, he is back*. Then he said, 'We're thinking of signing him.' I was like, *Oh, this is insane.*

Paul Dowling: John and Paul had a very clear vision of what they wanted to do and how they wanted to take this forward. They were playing live in smaller venues. He put together a great band, Paul Weller Movement.

We put this plan together and during that six-week period up to release, it was getting great airplay. We were getting great press. Paul had a lot of fans in the media. From day one, they were all coming out, they all wanted to support Paul because he'd done so much great work for more than a decade. It was really well received, not only by the fans, but also by the media in general. I wouldn't say everybody, but in general, everyone embraced this project.

Simon Halfon: I moved to LA the end of 1990. The Paul Weller Movement had just done a handful of gigs to pick things up again. At that time, I had started working with George Michael and I'd been to Los Angeles on various trips for holidays and loved it . . . That was just ahead of 'Into Tomorrow' and so I designed that record sleeve in America.

Nick Knight did the photography on the single. Paul sent over a motif and the full mod target was reintroduced. 'Into

Tomorrow' was very much a guitar-based song, which Paul hadn't done really with The Style Council . . . it was him putting his hand in the air saying, *I'm back*. In those days the world felt like a much bigger place. It wasn't like you could send artwork to Dropbox, so it was great that he still wanted my artwork, even though I was 6,000 miles away.

Suggs: I got a pre-release of that from somebody that I know. They knew I was a fan, and my abiding memory was Jeff Barrett, who had Heavenly Records, came round my house and he went, 'What's that?' I said, 'It's a Paul Weller solo single.' He went, 'You're fucking joking me. Fucking play it to me now.' I mean, hats off, Paul was just doing clubs and all that, and released a little single and started to build it again.

Paul Dowling: Spanner did a great job. He got some great radio play, got TV appearances. Philip was getting great press. The single charted. Paul had a very, very clear vision on how he wanted to roll this out and he was absolutely spot on.

Nigel 'Spanner' Sweeney: It got played, written about, and ended up being a minor hit. It wasn't quite up there with the heights of The Style Council or The Jam days, but it was still great in its own right.

Tom Doyle: Gary Crowley played it on GLR. It sounded really modernist with that loop-based groove. It's such a driving tune. You can hear the rebirth for him in that track. It always sounds killer live – as soon as he starts playing that riff live, your head's going.

Gary Crowley: It was such an exciting record. It was exciting to say Paul Weller is back with something a little bit special. I was doing a Sunday afternoon show on GLR. Spanner called up and said, 'Jesus, wait until you hear this.' I couldn't wait to play it on the programme. I love a riff record. I always have done. That is a great riff record as far as I'm concerned.

Paul Weller: By '91, I got it together again. I think just by playing live and rehearsing loads, and then I was thrown a few lifelines. Jun Sato was one of them, because I couldn't get a deal over here.

Jun Sato: In 1990, I moved from Warner Music to Pony Canyon in Tokyo. Their deal with A&M records was about to end and we were trying to establish a nice roster of international acts with direct deals. The miracle was that I was watching a Saturday night television programme called *Beat UK* that introduces British music to Japan. The 'Into Tomorrow' video was shown. Now, because The Jam and Style Council were both on Polydor, I was automatically thinking, *Wow, lucky Polydor, man. Paul Weller's rocking again.*

Monday morning, I went to the office and Paul Weller's demo tape was sitting on my desk. Four or five tracks and I believe in this hugga-bugga stuff! Pony Canyon had lawyers in London, and I was very surprised that he was available. I had thought he was the Prince of Polydor Records. I told my superiors that I will make Pony Canyon happy with this demo tape and started dealing with my Woking dad, Mr John Weller!

Pony Canyon is a gigantic record company. A territorial major. And they wanted like Style Council 2. That's how conservative people think, right? The Style Council had been really popular in Japan. They were one of the few bands that played the sanctuary of the Sumo Stadium. They were always so cool, dressed cool, sounded cool, and the singer always looked angry!

John was a wonderful negotiator, but the numbers had to come from me, because the numbers are on my neck, right? If I pay too much, I'm dead.

Before that, I was dealing with America, and all these MBAs and Yale graduates, but John is a better negotiator. I really love his phrase of 'I'm a bricklayer. What do I know?' at the middle of negotiation. That's so cool and straight-on working class.

We did a three-album deal, and my job was to put him back on the map in Japan. Paul created a perfect trilogy. Those albums are masterpieces. My only regret is that I should have made my deal a seven-album deal.

13 May 1991 – *Tonight with Jonathan Ross*

Jonathan Ross: I don't like looking back at my early interviews because I'm so fucking inept in them. But you can remind me. Paul said he would always be a mod?

Paul 'Smiler' Anderson: 'I'll always be a mod. You can bury me a mod.'

Jonathan Ross: I can see that in his work and in his life. It's not just the superficialist fashion, although he's always looked amazing, but the original mods, the early British modernists, were into poetry and literature. They would be reading Colin Wilson and they were into jazz as well as they were into ska as well as they were into American R&B, Tamla Motown, Stax, all that stuff, so it didn't ever feel contradictory.

I never liked the mod haircut. He performed 'Tin Soldier' and something else. He's got the worst fucking haircut. He's got the same haircut Jim Carrey has in *Dumb and Dumber*. I never knew why the mods went with such a kind of unforgiving fringe.

Just after that first interview, I was putting petrol in my car on the Finchley Road, and there was a bloke in front of me doing the same. When he got out, I realised that it was Weller. Now, here's the difference between us. I was in my shitty grey, beaten-up Toyota Previa family car, the only one we had. He was in his family car, which was a black, stylish-looking Mercedes or similar, with a surfboard on top. He got out of the car to fill up, wearing a beret. Years later, I said, 'I saw you once driving and you had a surfboard. Did you go and have a surf?' He said, 'No, but it looked really good on the car roof.' I think that was a mod adornment.

September 1991 – Leah Weller born (second child with Dee C. Lee)

November–December 1991 – The Paul Weller Movement, third tour

Paul Weller: One lifeline was Jun Sato. He offered a very handsome deal to make a record for Pony Canyon. And then another offer came over from America, surprisingly, because I'd not been there for donkeys, saying will you come and play in LA? We ended up doing five nights in this small theatre. Don't know how. With The Style Council we only went to LA and New York and played there once. That inspired me to get my shit together and start writing again. But I only started writing again through playing live, through finding myself through playing live.

Jacko Peake: Just before the first Paul Weller album came out, we were on tour to Japan and America: Helen Turner was playing keyboards, Camelle Hinds, Zeke Manyika, Steve White, myself and Paul.

Zeke Manyika: I get the feeling that when he got this to this point, Paul wanted people he knew that he felt comfortable with. That was a real transition period – doing different music, free from a lot of obligations from record companies. He wanted that cosiness of people who understood how he worked, avoiding all the drama of getting to know people.

Camelle Hinds: What a band. I know magic when I hear and see it. Paul was still very fragile. We all jumped in and said, whatever it is, we're on board.

Helen Turner: Paul called me up as he wanted people he knew and trusted in the band. He was never one for doing mad long tours. That never happened. The longest was maybe a month. It was no Fleetwood Mac situation.

Zeke Manyika: Whitey was playing drums, so I played percussion – congas and the Moog, one of the old-school synthesisers. It's quite weird to think that record labels here were cold about him at that time . . . He was huge in Japan. Massive, massive places. Three, four, five thousand people, all sold out. The thing with Paul, even in America, the gigs were like two, three thousand venues. The gigs sold out. We got to play 'That's Entertainment' and 'Carnation' from The Jam. It was funny because some of the gigs were like going back in time. You'd turn up and people thought it was the seventies. Pogoing and stuff. It was bizarre.

Camelle Hinds: We absolutely blew America apart. That was a pinnacle for me – a band at the peak of professionalism . . . Over the next year, we became so tight as a band that it didn't matter who else was on the stage – it could have been Foo Fighters, Stevie Wonder, anyone. We knew we could hold our own. We had this unshakable confidence, like *Bring it on.*

Jeff Slate: The setlist was weird. Some Style Council tunes, some Jam tunes that were reinvented, like 'Man in the Corner Shop' with a jazzier feel . . . It was a little bit ramshackle. He didn't have his new look down. He was playing a Strat, which is unusual for Paul. He was great, but you could tell there was something very tentative about it. These were not sold-out gigs. In New York City he's got a name, he can fill a place and maybe they were sellouts, but they didn't feel like it . . .

Jacko Peake: We played Japan and then got a flight directly from Tokyo to LA. We'd been to the bar before the flight, as was the norm. Paul had a wicked look in his eye. He was up to some mischief. We're all three sheets to the wind, actually, ten sheets to the wind even. As the plane took off, Paul decided to go to the toilet. He gets up and gets thrown down, landing in a crumpled heap at the back of the plane. Flying economy, with hundreds watching. John Weller has got his head in his hands. Kenny's just sweating away going, 'What do we do about this?' Paul locked himself in the toilet; when he comes out, he is a bit lairy. We're trying to calm things down a little bit. A lot of people on the plane were pissed off, but a lot were finding it funny. Then a camp captain walked down the aisle, saying, 'Mr Weller, if you don't behave yourself, I'll manacle you to the seat in front.' The uproar was hilarious. Things calmed down, but when we got out the plane, I was thinking, we're all going to be thrown in a cell. We did the walk of shame through customs, heads down, no eye contact with any officials, relieved to make it into the States.

David Rowe: He'd taken sleeping tablets and loads of alcohol, and had a bit of a crazy turn on the flight. I don't know if that involved removing items of clothing. I think there was a time where he had to be restrained.

Brian had said, 'Do you fancy a trip to the US, Paul Weller Movement?' We flew out to LA. I remember that first night we went to an Italian restaurant, with the band. I don't know if he was a bit jet lagged or whatever, but Paul had a little T-shirt on and he was freezing cold. Jo had her Harrington jacket, so he put that on, and it came up to his elbows, but he still kept it on, which was quite funny. We then spent a whole week at the Ritz Carlton, lounging by the pool with Helen, Zeke, Camelle and Jacko.

Zeke Manyika: John was great fun to tour with. A bit too much drinking though. Too many White Russians and Black Russians, but I think that was all to do with too much flying.

Camelle Hinds: Paul is such a kind man. On the road, especially in Japan, fans would follow him with gifts – Gucci, Yamamoto and more. I'd go to his room in the hotel, and he'd give me clothes – like a polka-dot Giorgio Armani shirt. He'd take Jacko, Zeke and myself out to the West End shopping to get some proper gear for wearing on stage, leather jeans and stuff like that.

1992 – *Paul Weller* (no. 8), debut solo album

Paul Weller: The first record was completely slated, as I remember it. I like that record. 'Into Tomorrow' was the first single from that and my first solo single, and I fucking loved that. So did a lot of other people as well, including Noel Gallagher.

Pat Gilbert: Paul was only thirty-three at that point – the Jesus age – where you get crucified for your beliefs and he certainly had been. We take it for granted now that people in their thirties, forties and fifties can make credible music. Back then that wasn't the case. But he still looked great and was still evolving as a musician.

Dee C. Lee: He's a musician. You have to go with the flow, and that's what you have to take with Mr Weller. You don't have to like the music, but the fact that he does keep moving on and experimenting, that's really the sign of a true musician. I can assure you he gave up a lot of good family life to be as good as he is. I think he deserves it. To be a relatively successful musician you have to be quite selfish because it is a very all-consuming thing . . . You're eating your dinner, you've got a song, something in your head. You've got to get it down . . . so yeah, there's always a price to pay, I think.

Brendan Lynch: Paul was starting again and discovering a new direction. The influences harken back to the sixties and seventies, aiming to distance from the sterile sound of the eighties – with its massive snares and clicky-sounding bass drums. Hip-hop, acid jazz, UK soul, trip-hop, Blue Note, Joe Meek, Funkadelic were all influences with an emphasis on live performance. Responding to the spirit of the past without becoming its slave.

Paul actually played a lot of the instruments himself, which I persuaded him to credit on the album, as he was a bit reluctant at first. It's important to say that he was on a creative high point and finding his way as a solo artist. Really enjoying playing guitar again. The album was quite varied stylistically, and our working methods were experimental right from the start. We were using samplers and sequencers on that first album, but we wanted the technology always to take second place to the attitude of the songs.

Jacko Peake: That first Paul Weller album was basically Paul . . . on his own. We started recording at Comforts Place in East Grinstead in Surrey. It was a residential studio and Paul got me and Steve White to be there with him. It was such a pleasure to be asked but also just to hang out . . . have a laugh, be involved in every process. A lot of my input was just going, 'Oh yeah, that sounds great to me, what's for dinner?'

We'd start at ten in the morning and finish at two at night and it slowly got to the point where we were finishing later and later. We never quite managed to go around the twenty-four-hour clock. It was a really small core and a lovely vibe with Max Hayes engineering and Brendan Lynch producing.

Brendan Lynch: Max is very dedicated, talented and great at getting sounds. We had a strong working relationship. I was an engineer when I started with Paul, then he said, 'Why don't you just produce and forget about the engineering?' It was the best thing I've ever done. You can sit and listen to the song without having to worry about all the knob twiddling and the meters. Paul put his faith in me, and it really changed my life.

At that point, Paul wanted to play live with very natural sounds and would spend a lot of time setting up the sound as the band were playing. It might take us a whole day just to get it right, but the great thing was that when they played, that was pretty much the record. Sound didn't change.

Mick Talbot: Even when Paul had regrouped and got his new thing together, he said, 'Can you pop down Solid Bond? There's a demo of a song that we wrote together called "Strange Museum", and I want to put it on the first album, but I've forgotten the middle bit. Let's go through that again.' And so I contributed to that song.

Brendan Lynch: Solid Bond closed on 30 August 1991, and we started going to different places.

Peter Button: When Paul had the Solid Bond Studios in central London, he flirted around at starting to sign other artists and nothing had been really big. It was all good ideas and good intentions but a bit of a vanity project. I think the rents in central London were just getting extortionate and Paul or John's view was that we can't really justify the expense. We've been dropped by the major label. Paul had decided to break The Style Council and become a smaller operation, so they didn't need the overheads.

Brendan Lynch: We started recording at Comforts Place studio on 16 September. We also went to Black Barn . . .

Jacko Peake: Other people would come in. Marco Nelson, Carleen Anderson. Dr. Robert came in quite a bit, played a bit of bass. We also did things like 'Amongst Butterflies' at Black Barn – a very small residential studio in Ripley, near his hometown.

Brendan Lynch: That was the next important track. We were just trying to develop a sound and make something unique and special.

Paul Gomersall: Paul had wanted it to sound like an old record, which is quite hard to do when you've got all the modern technology. For the demo, he had played the guitar solo on a little pig-nose guitar amplifier, about the size of a cigarette packet, in the filing cabinet in the studio. He said that's where he got the best sound, so that's what we did on the final version.

Brendan Lynch: Sessions were really quick. A lot of people would do vocals at the end of the album recording process, but Paul would often do live vocals, playing the guitar or piano and singing at the same time – that saves you loads of time.

Jacko Peake: Brendan's input on that first album was enormous, really, when I think about it. The direction and the quirkiness of it, and sorting out Paul's ideas . . . which were quite disparate, into an album that made sense. There's a lot of different styles of music on that, and it's quite experimental in some respects.

Brendan Lynch: Some of those songs start with ideas from samples and then the samples might be discarded. It's a bit like a band playing their favourite song and then it morphs into something else, so they've got the groove. So yeah, sometimes it started with samples, sometimes I just add things. I was always collecting things and I just tried different things in various places, and we might use it or it might give you an idea for a different type of overdub. 'Kosmos', the '5, 4, 3, 2, 1', it's from one of those NASA space records. I think Paul brought that in. He was bringing lots of stuff, he had loads of ideas and has got a great ear. I really loved all that stuff and just tried to incorporate some of those ideas.

Pat Gilbert: The first time I ever interviewed Paul was just before his first solo album came out. He does take what you're asking him very seriously and he's very proud and protective about what he does, and quite rightly so. I remember thinking how silky his hair was. I'd never seen a man with such well-tended hair. He was very angular, but a bit reticent, grumpy and spiky.

Andy Macdonald: That first album was completely finished with Pony Canyon, the Japanese label. He's got such devoted fans over there, so it was an intelligent way to go. They revere him, really. There are Weller bars, like shrines to him. It was a really good place to start back and it's a really good record.

Jun Sato: The only battle that I had to take at Pony Canyon was with the people who wanted it to be Style Council. I played the demo, and they say, 'This is not Style Council,' and I have to say, 'He's not Style Council any more.' I wanted him to be as free as possible and for his fire to take us to new places.

After making the deal, we invited Paul to Tokyo for publicity, and a secret gig at the coolest club, Yellow. We did television, followed by a successful tour. The album went to number one in the international chart. I was giggling when I heard that London A&Rs were saying he's over. I wanted to tell all of them that *He's number one in Japan!*

Brendan Lynch: Paul took me on that trip. He did a little acoustic tour. I think he just took me because he's a really nice guy. He knew I'd absolutely love it and I did. It was brilliant.

Simon Halfon: Paul had a deal with Pony Canyon, before he had a deal anywhere else. So, the self-titled, debut album came out on CD-only in Japan first. We had good fun doing that cover. Nick Knight did a fantastic job capturing Paul and it was dipping into all those Beatle references and nicking stuff and hoping no one would notice. That was a good fun time.

Nick Knight: That album picture sleeve . . . blame Mr Halfon for how that looks, or credit Mr Halfon for how it looks. It was a slightly strange delivery of an image but what are you going to do? It's a square format and that photo of Paul does look better when it's that long line. Long, sleek and unbroken, and I think that's probably what Simon was trying to achieve with the album cover and decided fans would want to see that big and they'd probably put it on their wall.

You've gotta be able to be somebody to pull off that shirt though. It's not flashy. Cause he assumes it, so he looks great in it. I have the same shirt; I don't look great in it. His dad was always rather, 'What's that fucking shirt? You look . . .' I won't use the adjectives that we use because they're politically and totally incorrect now. But his dad would always give him a hard time for sure. But he got his sense of style from somewhere, probably from his dad in the end. Yeah, that shirt's amazing.

Lawrence Watson: Nick did the picture on the cover, and I had the internal ones alongside some more of Nick's. Paul really appreciates the image and art. I was fortunate to be able to get in there and document the time, and I loved Paul's ethos back then. He'd say, 'I don't care if I have to just go around playing in the pubs and stuff, as long as I'm playing, I don't care, just playing gives me satisfaction.' He didn't want to satisfy the beast of the record industry.

Nick Knight: I wasn't ever into the idea of doing loads and loads of different artists, so I wanted to find somebody who I respected and admired and who had a certain kind of innate sense of style so that you've got something incredible to photograph. I wish I'd had multiple lives but, in the end, you end up only working with a few people and Paul, for a long time, was one of the only artists I'd work with. You just didn't want to work with everybody.

I still play that album. I still listen to it now and it still makes me feel great. The way he puts everything together sonically, it's just so beautiful and so sharp. But it's what he is. People are very coherent to their art form . . . People tend to look like their art. Whether you're a painter or a singer, photographer. When somebody can hold one of your pictures or photographs or listen to one of your songs and it looks like you, that's when you know it's on track.

John Reed: I interviewed Paul in early '92, when the album was out in Japan and not out in the UK. He was clearly proud of it. He kept referring to it as British R&B . . . I think he had an idea of it as this concept, and I think it was him rediscovering the guitar.

Paul Du Noyer: It must have been a very tough time . . . there was quite a gap in my meetings and interviews with Paul, and I suppose that would have coincided with him going off the boil commercially. *Q* was quite a commercial magazine and Paul wasn't in the album charts at that stage for quite a while, so they wouldn't have been that interested in him. He did have a period in the semi-wilderness.

Alistair Lyon: I saw an *NME* advert for the Pony Canyon CD and sent off my cheque. Japan felt a world away then so getting that album six months before everyone else felt so special. It's still my most listened-to, favourite, most modernist album of all time.

Brendan Lynch: Paul always thought of a record as two sides. We weren't thinking CDs, it was very important. What was the next track or the first track, to set up that mood for the second listen, after you'd spinned over the vinyl . . . at the very end of the first half, the needle will stay on the record about a minute and if you listen carefully, you can hear Paul shout, 'Bring back vinyl!'

Nigel 'Spanner' Sweeney Go! Discs are a terribly important company in the independent world. They didn't have the politics of what Paul had been used to for the last number of years at Polydor.

Andy Macdonald: I'd met Paul very briefly on a CND march. Just said a quick hello. Didn't really get engaged in a conversation after that. I got a phone call from his dad, from John, who said, 'We're looking around.' I guess he was looking at small labels that he thought were decent homes. Because if you'd been treated badly and someone says, 'We're not going to put your work out,' Fuck that! That is bad manners beyond fucking belief, isn't it? 'I'm not going to put your record out.' Inexplicable.

John and Paul came in, and Paul's smoking five fags a minute! Probably his first time back in a record company. We had a good chat for a few hours, and he said, 'I'm going to go away and think about it' . . . He rang back the same day or the following day, 'I want to come in and see you, is that okay? He just came in and said, 'I really enjoyed being here yesterday. I think we could work well together, but I just want to let you know the things that work for me and things that don't. I'll do some press, but to be honest with you, I've been doing it since I was eighteen and it could be very repetitive and time consuming. So, I've got to be very selective about that and I just want to play live a lot.' He said, 'Here's what I do well and what I want to do. Are you up for it?' When someone knows their craft – studios, collaborators, sounds – there's no need to get over-involved in that stuff. What's an A&R guy going to do in there, apart from sit around and steal the oxygen in the studio?

Peter Button: I took over representing Paul when Polydor dropped The Style Council. I was relatively young, newly qualified and not particularly experienced so I brought back John Cohen when we got to the big negotiations with Andy Macdonald. John had more experience and considerably more gravitas than I did. Paul was out of contract and couldn't get a deal, and I found him a licensee who were willing to put it out in Japan, Pony Canyon, and then Andy Macdonald said he wanted to pick it up, so we were able to license the record to Go! Discs.

Paul Dowling: Andy was unique as a leader of a record label because he had a completely different perspective on how to work with artists. Very passionate about music. There was a culture that was quite unique. All the artists knew who everyone was in the company, which you never got at other larger companies . . . Towards the end of the day, Andy would always love to spark up, have a couple of spliffs, listen to new bands and tapes that had been sent in or that the A&R guys had recommended.

Andy Macdonald: To be honest, we did use to smoke a lot of weed. That's how we used to do it. But it opens the doors of perception. You can hear the fairy dust on the mixing desk. I think Paul said in an interview that I'd have a spliff on the go and would be playing football.

Paul Dowling: I used to wander in and fight my way through to Andy's desk. You could tell when he'd found something, this little glint in his eye. Go! Discs had a small roster, but so much success. Artists like Billy Bragg, Gabrielle, Travis, Beautiful South, Trash Can Sinatras and Paul. Billy was an important part of that and had delivered a great degree of success for the label.

Andy Macdonald: I was a huge fan, so it was a strange thing for me to sign a deal with Paul. I wandered around for three or four months going, *Fuck me, we signed Weller*. If you're a fan of someone, there's a bigger burden on you. When you know someone is that good, and they've meant that much in your life and the lives of millions of other people as well, you have to get it really right.

Record companies have this theory that you've just got to stick to what you're good at, which is bullshit, because if you've got something else inside you to come out, if it's film music or instrumental music, whatever it is, that's part of the process . . . A lot of journalists, there are some good ones, but some are dicks, right? And I think a lot of them were slighted, 'How dare you break up The Jam?' But that's his choice. It's his life to do what he wants to do and that's his artistic expression.

It came at a time when the label had good success, but we were a little bit low on energy . . . Paul came in and took everything up a couple of notches. That's partly because of the stature of the artist but he'd also ring me up regularly with music recommendations. It was like having an unpaid A&R guy out there. He'd bring tapes in and say, 'Listen to this lot, track four is amazing.' He really is a force of nature.

Pete Mason: It's like when a big soccer player comes to your team. I remember being really proud when we finally got product through, and it had the Go! Discs logo on it and Paul

Weller's name. That was a great feeling. It lifted everyone at the label.

3 August 1992 – 'Uh Huh Oh Yeh!' (no. 18)

Brendan Lynch: We used the Hot Rod sample, which is a B-side of a track . . . Just those amazing trombones which are on the bottom end, and it was just really fresh and exciting. It had a weird break, which was like a hip-hop thing, within a rockier track.

Jacko Peake: 'Uh Huh Oh Yeh!' was a lot of Brendan Lynch coming up with these samples. Most of that track was actually created in the studio rather than it being previously done by Paul . . . A lot of stuff we did on that first album was actually a result of just being together in a studio and fucking about, and making a noise. That song was quite constructed, in a way, with the samples and stuff, then the tenor solo I did on it just came out of a little riff that I'd play . . . you overblow it, and you get this double kind of thing going on, which I always thought was quite jazzy. I was thinking, *Oh, this is going to be too flash for Paul . . .*

Paul these days is very open to ideas. If he trusts you, and you're not wasting his time, or it's actually a valid thing to say, and you've thought about why. But back in the day it was less like that. You'd definitely have to have something worthwhile saying or doing before you presented it . . . he was trying to find himself.

Peter Gordon: 'Uh Huh Oh Yeh!' was released as the second single in August and the video was him going back to Woking and finding himself again. Says it in the lyrics. His Surrey upbringing is still a very important aspect of his life. I'm Surrey born and bred myself, and he would quite often feature things in videos or interviews.

Pippa Hall: The Go! Discs office felt really exciting. I was working regional press and radio for the first Paul Weller album. It took a time for national press get on board. Paul would just come into the office, say hello and make a cup of tea for everybody. He became part of the team. I wasn't a member of a band, but it felt like we were all in it together . . . I would have been twenty-one when I first met Paul, and we got the call from *Top of the Pops* for 'Uh Huh Oh Yeh!'

Jacko Peake: Paul hated *Top of the Pops*, but because it was the first album and promotion was needed, he acquiesced. We just had to mime with Paul doing live vocals, so the band was Paul, Steve White, Camelle and me . . . It was a long day, and we started drinking at lunchtime and, I mean, it was in the drinking days, and there was a bar open all day, and by the fourth run through . . . just so sick of having to turn up and stand on stage and mime, again, for the friggin' camera angles. We weren't even performing! Paul got it together on the last one . . . when we had to nail it.

Andy Macdonald: There was a really scathing one word review in the music press about that particular track, which we all just went like, *OK! There's a real perception thing that needs to be broken down here.*

Paul is someone who has a poetry about his lyrics. It only really matters if he's proud of the work himself, but when you put it out there it's going to get commented on and that can be very wounding. I see other people working in different artistic spheres, and it's like, how dare someone come in and fucking put their big clod-hopper boots all over something? It's been created and crafted for a reason.

Dean Rudland: That was a brilliant album, but for the record industry, it didn't necessarily prove those people wrong. I remember talking to Paul's plugger at the time, who said it had done all right, sold a couple of hundred thousand, but it wasn't a million seller. It's not like a Go! Discs Housemartins record.

Andy Lewis: I first met Paul Weller around this time . . . He got on the tube that I was on, our eyes met briefly, and we both checked out what we were wearing and it was like, *Oh, all right*, and then I had to get off . . . I was thinking, *Oh, my God, I've just seen Paul Weller, he has looked at what I'm wearing, and he deems it acceptable. This is a sign.*

Trevor Neal: That album has some great tracks on it. It was exciting and to me it was then like the third mod revival had begun. I was having a full midlife crisis, so it was perfect timing with the music. I ended up getting myself a Vespa and I had a bit more money, so I'd go into Covent Garden to kit myself out in mod clothing, and I felt I was back. I was riding into Soho on the scooter; finally I'm living the mod dream, age forty, however old it was.

Paul Moody: Modernism has always been about looking for something new, which applies the old rules to it. That's why it morphed into acid jazz, which became a phenomenon and Paul took a lot of that into his first solo album. That became a different kind of modernism.

David Lines: That first album has such a strong hook. Steve White said that if they played anything live, it should be that album – it's such a complete piece of work, full of diverse influences, jazzy, with space to breathe.

28 September 1992 – 'Above the Clouds' (no. 47)

Chris Bangs: I met Paul through Gilles Peterson while producing Galliano. We were recording at Joe's Garage in Clapham, an old bike repair workshop. Paul liked the production, mentioned that he'd almost finished his first album, and he asked if I'd like to come in to finish off.

There was a wonderful stone room, drums, fifty guitars, pianos, every instrument, Wurlitzers, you name it. He had a book of lyrics that he pulled out, saying, 'I've got a couple of ideas of lyrical stuff.' I got a record out of my bag and said, 'Well, I've brought a beat for you.' 'That'll do!' Paul is very 'Mr Snap Decision' . . .

He then worked out this middle eight, played it on acoustic piano and said, 'I've written the part, I'll go in and sing it,' and lit a cigarette. I said, 'What are you doing?' He said, 'Well, if I have a fag right before I go into my vocal, it makes it sound rougher.' He always wanted that grainy, coarse sound in his voice, which is one of the best bits in it.

Jamie Johnson: 'Above the Clouds' . . . There's a version of him doing it on a train carriage in a documentary. He's definitely drunk! He's drinking from a tinny, and he does this version of it, and it's fucking brilliant!

Steve Wheatley: 'Above the Clouds' is on the list for my funeral. I can't listen to it without thinking about a live gig because it's always punctuated at a certain point with the crowd's participation. Whenever I hear it, I always sing out that note at the appropriate point. Pavlovian dog.

Chris Bangs: It's such a simple little piece . . . he'd written it almost like a poem, so the music just literally worked around what he'd done rather than the other way around.

We did the mix down at Bucks Fizz's old studio, Comforts Place . . . it was actually Paul's birthday that day. We got a little bit silly. We'd been drinking down the pub all day, stayed up till silly o'clock, and finished off everything except the mix. We'd had oil, grass . . . Paul's most profound moment that he ever said to me was, 'Bangsy, do you know what makes a hit single?' 'No, mate.' He goes, 'You've got to be able to sing it in the bath!' There you go.

That song came from a very chance meeting and a casually thrown together thing, and at the time it was his least successful single ever! [*Laughs*]

Lawrence Watson: I did that single cover. We went out to San Francisco for a magazine shoot. I love my cinema and great cinematographers – it's a big influence on my photography, so I wanted to get Golden Gate Bridge in somehow. I found a cab driver, described a place, and said, 'This is the place in *Dirty Harry* where they find the body' . . . Paul was just scratching his head.

Carleen Anderson: I remember singing on that B-Side. We did 'Feelin' Alright'. The sleeve says a drunken night at Comforts Place? I mean, it might have been! That's what the boys did! They were hardcore, you know what I mean? They could go for a while, and I don't have that kind of constitution. My voice would never last, being drunk and singing.

Dylan White: Getting a song on the Radio 1 playlist was like trying to climb Mount Everest. That first Paul Weller album had quite a lukewarm reception. Poor old Spanner had struggled a bit with 'Above the Clouds' in particular. Now, in fairness to Spanner, I went to see Paul at the Royal Albert Hall that October and I did think the audience was quite old. It was the audience that had grown up with The Jam and The Style Council . . .

At this point, I had got a job as a plugger for Garry Blackburn at Anglo Plugging. He was doing Beautiful South and The La's at Go! Discs. We then started doing stuff for Alan McGee, Creation, and I got to do Ride, stuck my teeth in and got them a lot of radio play. So then Go! Discs wanted to get us involved with Paul. I don't think Spanner was very happy about it, but he was told, 'Thanks, but no thanks.'

Paul Dowling: When Andy did eventually sign Paul, he had already written most of *Wild Wood*. He was already focusing on the next album. Paul came into the office early and Andy was running late with a call. We were chewing the fat and Paul said, 'I've got a couple of demos I'm going to play Andy. Do you want to hear them?' I go, 'Fuck yeah.' I shut my door and he played me the song 'Wild Wood'. I was just like, oh my God, you've nailed it with this . . .

We had had a great deal of success with the Paul Weller album, but we knew what was to come. We knew what he had as a catalogue of new songs. He was such a prolific songwriter, and each album got stronger and stronger and better and better, and he was an absolute joy to work with.

1992 – Live dates

Neil Sheasby: I went to loads of gigs around that time. They played four nights on the bounce in London in June 1992. Small London gigs. Mean Fiddler, Town2, Clapham Grand and Subterania.

Shane Juson: I couldn't get a ticket for love nor money . . . I went down to the venue early and actually met Paul outside the gig. He said, 'Have a word with Dad.' John then got me on the guestlist, and I said, 'Can I be cheeky and ask to be added to all of the gigs?' He said, 'Yeah, no problem.' That's John. He was brilliant.

Subterania was a tiny place. I walked into the gig and John and Paul were at the bar. I bought him a drink. Paul had rum and Coke . . . The stage was only two foot high at the very most. Our knees were touching the stage. If you put your hand out, which I didn't, I must add, you could have touched him.

John Harris: Steve Lamacq recruited me to the *NME* and I managed to get a commission to review Paul Weller at Manchester Apollo. It was the first time I'd written professionally about him. I said that he's going to be the British Neil Young, which wasn't my line. That was a line I nicked from Iestyn George, who I worked with, who was another big Weller fan. That's not a bad thing to have in your first Paul Weller review.

He didn't really go anywhere near his back catalogue like he had with The Paul Weller Movement . . . by that point, he had the first solo album and the first stirrings of *Wild Wood*. He did play 'Man in the Corner Shop' and I've never seen anything like that . . . God, it was like being on a football terrace. It's some mark of his artistic bravery that he faced down audiences for that long and said, *I ain't playing Jam stuff. You've had that. This is what I'm doing now*.

When I went on the road with him in Ireland, writing a feature for the *NME*, I watched the gig with Ann, his mum, and she said, 'I wish he'd play a couple of the old things, "Going Underground" or something like that.' I was thinking, *Well, you're not the only one!*

Chas de Whalley: Alan Lewis, who had been the editor at *Sounds*, asked me to do a big retrospective interviewee-type thing for *Vox Magazine*. Very early in our conversation, Paul realised that I hadn't been following his career post The Jam and said,

'Oh, you haven't been listening to me then, have you?' A few months later, they offered me the opportunity to go to California, for a couple of dates. We flew into LA and drove up to San Francisco for the show up there, and my real memory is that me and the band and various members of the crew spent all day drinking black Russians in this bar. We started around two o'clock in the afternoon and went for a meal at eight o'clock, completely plastered. I was sitting in the meal completely catatonic. I did do an interview with Paul and John.

There used to be a joke that I used to have with the band's publicist, Philip Hall, because there used to be this weird thing where if somebody asked Paul to do something, he'd say, 'Ask Kenny,' so you'd ask Kenny and he would go, 'I better ask Paul,' and you get this circular thing.

Barry Pugatch: I had seen him at Berkeley Performance Center, a beautiful venue, and I'm there outside with my red Rickenbacker, hoping to get it signed . . . John Weller comes out, looks at me, says, 'You want Paul to sign this?' and takes me inside backstage. He hands Paul my guitar, and Paul starts to strum it. I am so excited. He autographs my Rickenbacker and then I'm like, 'Oh, so where are you guys going afterwards? Let me hang out with you' . . . So I'm at the bar at the Copley Plaza Hotel keeping my respectful distance. Send over a Kahlúa Sombrero to John Weller, because that's what he's drinking. Paul is chatting with Helen Turner and Steve White, and there's Dave Liddle. I'm trying not to be too much of a pest, but I'm pretty excited. Then they start handing my guitar around because I brought it up to the bar and everybody signs it. I'm thinking . . . *This is getting sweet.*

16 January 1993 – *Saturday Zoo*

Jonathan Ross: I always felt that, even if it doesn't work, TV should try and do something different, and *Saturday Zoo* was very much a failed experiment. Paul came on and did 'Bull-Rush' into 'Magic Bus', and I got up with him for 'Malice'. There's no stopping me. Shameless. To see him do an old Jam song, it is interesting, there is a certain resonance to it. I felt pleased to see him retake ownership of that early stuff.

David Quantick: I was working on *Saturday Zoo* and there was a bloke called Sean Rowley, who's gone on to do other things, DJing and stuff, who knew Paul. And he booked him on the show. They were great. But before that, unfortunately, Sean had been talking to Paul Weller about a review I'd done of the first solo album, which on the last line I'd written was 'Paul Weller is back . . . Almost.' I don't think Paul was very happy with that. Sean said, 'Paul Weller is back' and Weller goes 'Almost!' I think he was quite angry about the 'Almost'. But they were fantastic . . . It wasn't my taste. It sounded like Traffic.

Yolanda Charles: I was twenty-one and in an all-girl house band for the Jonathan Ross show. I was really miffed that it was an all-girl band, because I wanted to be taken seriously, and I kept getting put with the girls and I was like 'What do you mean? I'm not a girl . . . I'm a bass player! Why'd you keep putting me with girls?' . . .

I guess he'd seen me play when he was on. I was lucky, because usually the music we were playing wasn't all that great. A lot of the time it was idents, little bits of music. We had Candy Dulfer on so ended up playing 'Pick Up the Pieces' . . . That's the only time I ever really played anything vaguely funky on the whole show. We did thirteen episodes, but that particular one, Paul saw me playing something that had a bit of 'pocket' in it. I didn't speak to him . . . I had no idea that he'd checked out what I'd been playing . . . then got a call from his dad about coming and having a play. I then started working with Paul, which was the beginning of my so-called session career.

16 February 1993 – Brit Awards

Malcolm Gerrie: Paul and I had built a really nice relationship. When I got the gig for the Brits, I ran into him somewhere, probably in Ronnie Scotts, and he said, 'what the fuck you doing? I've heard you're doing the Brits, man, why are you doing that?'

I said, 'Because it's ghastly and awful and we're in the country that's produced the best contemporary music ever, in my view, better than America. They didn't have The Beatles or The Stones and I was literally begged three times by Rob Dickens, the chairman of Warners at the time, who was also chairman of the Brits committee, to take it over. I was horrified when he first came. I wouldn't have touched it with a barge pole. Sam Fox and Mick Fleetwood.'

Paul said, 'I thought that's what you would have done – told them to go fuck themselves', I explained that they'd given me complete freedom to do things my way. I wanted to shake things up – bring in collaborations and live performances – have some fun and mischief. Paul was really intrigued. I thought, *God, if I don't win over Paul, if Paul thinks I'm a schmuck for doing the Brits, then I'm fucked.*

Paul won a Brit award when I was producing it. I knew he wouldn't want to do it because it wasn't in his scheme of things to do something like the Brits. I remember talking to Clive about it and then ultimately, Paul. Paul rang me and he said, 'Malcolm, I don't want to let you down, but I've had an idea for who can pick up my Brit award, because I just can't do it, man, you know, I can't do it.' I said, 'It's cool, Paul. Don't sweat it.' And he said, 'What about me Dad?' I said, 'I love it. I love it, Paul. I just want to tip you off, though. The guy who would have been presenting the award to you is Iggy Pop.' Now, Iggy Pop and John Weller ... Probably the two most disparate figures you could ever put together in the universe. It was hilarious, man. It got a great reaction as well.

March 1993 – Pre-*Wild Wood* tour

Nick Heyward: I got to play with Paul in New York in '93. It was Teenage Fan Club, Catherine Wheel, Paul and me at a tiny little punk club in Buffalo. Paul had flown in on Concorde, which I was ribbing him about – 'You flew Concorde for a club in the middle of nowhere? That's cool, Paul.'

We wanted to do a song together – he suggested 'That's Entertainment'. Of course, I know and love that song, but I didn't know it off the top of my head ... So, we did 'Doctor Robert' by The Beatles ... I'm singing with fucking Paul Weller. Amazing. But then the mic was slowly sinking. In the end, it was like I disappeared, crouching down. My magic moment was ruined by the mic stand, but it was a moment, and I have gigged with Paul Weller for three minutes.

Camelle Hinds: My final performance with the Paul Weller band was on *Jay Leno*. Paul is one of the most generous people I've ever met. That man could not make the major contribution that he makes without morphing to keep going. That means leaving some things behind. I get that.

Jacko Peake: Those were the last live gigs that I did with Paul during that period. I fell in love with this girl . . . so I lived in San Francisco on and off, and was completely out of the London scene really. I did come back to record on *Wild Wood*, but I wasn't in the band per se then.

9 July 1993 – 'Sunflower' (no. 16)

Jun Sato: As soon as Go! Discs showed up on the horizon, we would just get sent the materials from them and I was happy with that. Of course, it's slightly sad feeling that Paul was not solely mine any more, but I'm happy that he's back in the UK scene and he had proved himself again for the third time. Those songs changed the tide of music. So, I think I'm lucky.

Dylan White: In early '93, Paul's perception at Radio 1 wasn't great. I had 'Sunflower' as the first single from *Wild Wood*. Garry was meeting with Paul and asked, 'What should I tell him?' I said, 'It's not going to be a walk in the park. This could be quite difficult.'

I took the song to a [radio] producer, Saira Hussain. I remember it crystal clear. I played her, 'Sunflower', and she went, 'That's fantastic. That is amazing.' She literally ran out the door and started telling people, 'This is brilliant, this is brilliant, this is brilliant.' I thought, *Wow, this might work*. Another key person was Lucy Armitage. These two young producers, both in their twenties, would pester to get it on the playlist, even putting notes on computer screens. 'Please play this'. They were crucial young adopters of the new Paul Weller.

Andy Macdonald: Music is important. It's one of the things that happens in any society that gets you closer to the gods. It's a beautiful expression of humanity, to be able to connect . . . It's one of the few things that can carry you through tragedy, elevate your spirit and inspire. For me, it's the most directional and impactful art form. If it's a pure expression, without people tampering or suggesting things that waste time or diminish it, it goes into the listener's ears pure, and it has so much more value because of that. That's always been the thing that I've tried to do with artists. Paul is the best that you could ever work with for that, because he knows what he's doing. He's confident.

9 July 1993 – *Later . . . with Jools Holland*

Mark Cooper: By the late eighties, music TV had ground to a halt. Shows like *The Tube* and *Old Grey Whistle Test* had stopped, leaving a void for live performance programmes. Paul talked to me about when he started doing his solo comeback and they went on *Top of the Pops* and had to mime. He swore that he'd never do that again . . . So Paul says that when *Later . . . with Jools Holland* came along, 'At last, here's a show that cares about music.'

The first time Paul came on, he was recording *Wild Wood* in 1993. We had a great chat on the phone, and I heard 'Sunflower', and was very excited. I'm not sure I'd heard 'Wild Wood' at that point and 'Has My Fire Really Gone Out?', clearly a meditation on those dark years and him questioning, *What do I have left?* Paul was very keen to do something new, to fit in with the show. There was a young singer-songwriter called Lena Fiagbe, and we agreed that he'd do a duet with her on Marvin Gaye's 'What's Going On' . . . it just felt like a statement, not only for Paul, but for *Later*, that here was this British guy who already was, and was clearly going to be a British great again, and back in his pomp.

Pete Paphides: I remember seeing him do 'Sunflower' on that *Later with Jools Holland* performance, I've watched it dozens and dozens of times. They're just on fire. Clearly he's a man with a point to prove.

6 September 1993 – *Wild Wood* (no. 2)

Andy Macdonald: Paul would occasionally ask me what I thought about a song. The first time, he had finished the majority of the songs for the *Wild Wood* album, and he gave me everything . . . Eight of them were absolutely brilliant. His songs tend to go from very good to legendary, the kind that last forever. There were two that I thought were really good, but one I wasn't sure about. I thought, *How the hell do I even broach this?* I was at home one evening, the phone rang: 'Andy. It's Paul. What do you reckon? Anyway, what I think is, I need another three songs. I've got one I've written already . . .' I was like, 'Excellent!'

It's a difficult thing to get some distance, to evaluate a body of work that you've created, but there's nobody in a better position to do it than the person it comes out of.

Lawrence Watson: Paul goes down to Oxford, to the Manor Studios and he said, 'Come down, stay and just document the recording.'

Richard Branson: I was twenty-one when we bought a seventeenth-century dilapidated manor in Oxfordshire and decided to turn it into a residential recording studio. We wanted to create a special place, outside of London, where artists could record their music in a setting where they could be inspired and create in the time and way they wanted to . . . and we had a lot of fun doing it! In London they had to record in the daytime but at the Manor they could record through the night, which most artists wanted to do. It became a sort of bohemian wonderland – guitars sprawled everywhere, and people gathered around the grand piano. Artists like Mike Oldfield lived there, while others came and went. There was always music playing and mischief brewing. It's incredible to look back and realise how much history was made there too. So many brilliant songs and albums: from Paul Weller to Mike Oldfield, Radiohead, The Cranberries, McCartney, Zappa, The Rolling Stones and INXS . . . the list goes on! There was a lot of talent and love in that Manor.

Brendan Lynch: The first session at the Manor was on 10 May 1993 . . . Everyone would live in the studio, and you'd have your own room, and it was really great because you get loads done. You didn't have to go home to your other life and your mind stayed focused as well.

Steve Cradock: The Manor was vast . . . A really posh stately home, big lake and outdoor swimming pool. The studio wasn't particularly huge, but it had an old feel to it, like how you'd imagine an old sixties studio really, and it was very 'womb-like' there. They had these huge, very loud speakers, and it was always very busy.

Brendan Lynch: *Wild Wood* was a more focused album with a cohesive sound, drawing influences from Lee Dorsey, Shuggie Otis, Nina Simone, Nick Drake, Traffic, Memphis soul, Spooky Tooth and Free. Paul made comments before we started recording, which I've written in my diary – folky, acoustic, earthy/powerful, right in your face (but not hard in a nasty modern way).

Tracks were recorded live with minimal processing – no click track, just natural sound. We spent time perfecting the set up for each song and the final record closely matched what we heard during live takes.

Jacko Peake: The change of attitude in how to record from the initial Paul Weller album to *Wild Wood* was massive. The first album was quite studied and thought about, whereas on *Wild Wood* a lot of the stuff was all one take. It was all really vibey and there was so much more confidence in the whole outlook, which allowed it to be more of a performance-based kind of album.

Brendan Lynch: 'Sunflower' was one of the first songs recorded and we got it in two or three takes. The sound of the intro inspired everyone, and the song set the tone for the rest of the album. Paul used to jam the riff to that a lot . . . and then Steve White used to play along, and it was just a bit of an instrumental for a long time. When we recorded it, I thought, *Wow, this is amazing*, because what I was hearing in the studio was the final record pretty much, apart from a few overdubs.

We'd reference demos to retain the songs' initial spirit, aiming to capture a moment in time, not worried about the odd mistake. The album was recorded on tape – which gave it that rounded sound with harmonic distortion. We used an SSL computer mix system and samples for added texture. The interludes were created with a sequencer. We got a great organic sound at the Manor – this wonderful rural, distraction-free setting – and the results sounded different to anything in the mainstream at the time.

Steve Cradock: I remember Paul calling me to go around his place to listen to 'The Weaver' and he had an acetate cut of it which had a different intro. I think it was acoustic intro with a harmonica on it. It sounded fucking great. I was shitting myself, so I swallowed a lump of hash, and by the time I got to his front door, I was tripping. It just became this really fucking surreal afternoon. Dee cooked a lovely Sunday roast, and Paul gave me a copy of the Small Faces album, the *Immediate* album.

Max Beesley: I got down there thinking I'd get to play all over the album. But most of it had been recorded. Marco from the

Young Disciples was playing bass, Steve had laid the drums, Mick had come in and done some keyboards, and Paul said, 'I've got this track for little Natt, "Moon on Your Pyjamas". Just put some whirly on it.'

Jacko Peake: On 'Holy Man', I stacked up baritone, tenor, alto, soprano to make a section, and Brendan Lynch was quite funny because I was forever trying to perfect things. I bunged it down in ten minutes and I went, 'Does that sound all right?' and he said, 'Yeah, that's it. That's brilliant, Jacko. Fantastic,' and I said, 'If you like the idea can I actually play it properly?' and he went, 'Well, you've just done that, it sounds brilliant. That was the whole thing.' So I was like, *Oh God, you're actually going to let that go?* But now I listen to it, and I think he was totally right. Paul knows me really well in that sense. He always throws me in the deep end. He won't let me hear a track, he'll just put me in the studio. He loves the raw, experimental, and explosive energy, not overly thought-out performances . . .

Steve Cradock: We've always recorded live, and around that time Paul definitely liked a direct sound. He didn't really like effects. He might have a wah-wah and that was it. For the intro on 'The Weaver', I came into the control room and played the first two chords, just through the amp. For the other elements, I was in the live room and also had some Boss pedals which I used.

Helen Turner: Paul and some others were staying at the Manor. I just turned up there when needed. Like playing organ on the song 'Wild Wood'.

Simon Fowler: Helen was far more refined than everybody else. It was really extraordinary that she was in Paul's band. I think everyone thought of her a bit like a schoolteacher . . . everyone was slightly frightened of her. Helen and Yolanda as well.

Steve Cradock: I've got a memory of it. Where we were living in Birmingham, it was speed and acid around that time and then the Manor days were pink champagne, speed and E.

Brendan Lynch: I think that's overblowing it a little bit. I don't remember the champagne!

Simon Fowler: Partying all the time? That's pretty much true, yeah. Paul actually had to pick me up off the floor basically when he said, 'Are you doing "The Weaver"?' because I was going to sing the backing vocals. It was about one in the morning, and I started whimpering away and suddenly this great bleeding Curtis Mayfield voice comes in at the side of me and it's Paul. I'm thinking, *What the hell am I doing on this?*

Mick Talbot: Paul got me to play Hammond on '5th Season'. There's something really special about being in a room, all of you playing together and the atmosphere that goes with that.

Steve Cradock: Even after a full day in the studio, they'd all be there in the lounge – Mick Talbot, Marco Nelson, Steve White – and it was just records. People playing different tunes. A lot of just enjoying themselves, having a spliff, and playing vinyl all night. That was great. It's still like being a kid, isn't it?

Lawrence Watson: I can't put into words what the magic is, but I suppose it's about finding a space that you're comfortable to create in. Residential studios help with that. You're there to make music, a lovely countryside location, away from the daily grind, and that focus helps . . .

Everyone's mojo was there. Paul would bring his kids down, Natty and Leah. I'd bring my lad down. Some kids from one of the canal boats down the bottom would come up to play. We'd have tea on the lawn, kicking the ball around. It was like documenting those perfect summer days in between recording a brilliant album.

Andy Macdonald: I went to the Manor a few times then, but just to make a cup of tea, roll a joint, drive back to London. It's a privilege to be invited along on something like that because it's a delicate balance in a studio. If the vibe's good, it can be fantastic. And if there's one thing that goes wrong, it can fuck everything up and suddenly the whole momentum can disappear. I remember Paul used to just get on with it, and then say, 'Come down. Check out where we are at.'

Robert Howard: I had moved out of London up to Oxfordshire and it just so happens that I was very close to the Manor . . . I played guitar on a couple of songs on *Wild Wood* – 'Country' and 'Has My Fire Really Gone Out?' . . . My memory of playing on those songs is that nothing was ever formal. If he was recording, he might ask me to play along on bass or guitar. 'Country' was just us two sitting opposite each other. A live take. Pretty much like we would do at home or backstage . . . He didn't really need me to play along, but he wanted to do as much as possible live. It was just mates playing along. How it should be.

At this point in my life, I'm still drinking, so there were times when I was staying over, for quite a few days sometimes! Very nice it was as well. It's a lovely place, you know, full-size snooker table. Now, I'm quite a keen snooker player, so after a few drinks, although I would sometimes lose quite a bit of money to John and Kenny on the tour bus playing cards, I would always make it up later playing snooker!

Brendan Lynch: Paul's really open to ideas. Anyone in the room who's got an idea, he'll try. We were messing about. Many things didn't work but a lot of them ended up on the record as well. He was writing stuff all the time, having new ideas. He'd call me up and say, 'Right, we're going to go in tomorrow. I've got another song' . . . once he gets the urge, we had to get it down . . . And all the songs just seemed to come out of nowhere really quickly and it was a very productive period.

Lawrence Watson: The cover for *Wild Wood* was one of those moments when the gods were with me. Sometimes the light works, but usually you have a rough idea of what you're shooting for. In that 125th of a second, you don't know if you caught the magic, but you know if the lighting's good or you're capturing a moment. If the photography gods are with you, something magical can happen.

The shot was taken at the studio doorway, with Paul silhouetted in the frame. He was just adding bass on a track, and it was a gorgeous sunny day. Through the darkness of that door frame, you could see the lush green of an English summer. I just rattled a roll on the Hasselblad, capturing this lovely silhouette, framed against the afternoon sun. Sometimes simplicity is the way to go.

Simon Halfon: From seeing that one shot, it was immediate that was going to be the cover. It was a fantastic, striking image. So that was a kind of no-brainer. Always great to work with Lawrence and always get the results with him. We all went from strength to strength. Paul would send me a fax with an idea for the next sleeve or whatever it is. We'd go back and forth as a nice collaborative endeavour. Paul had really hit his stride with *Wild Wood*. In many ways that is the definitive Paul Weller solo record. It felt like such a great, great, great album and then that rolled into *Stanley Road*, and everyone could tell he was on fire.

Andy Macdonald: *Wild Wood* is such a classic record. Listening back, there's nothing that you'd want to change – it's a beautiful expression of where Paul was at that time. Every single song works. When someone can create something like that, you want them to do it more.

This is where a good record company gets involved to help it hit as many people as possible who will really benefit from hearing it and who will respect what it is. There's a level where you can get too commercial and push things a little bit too far, but you don't want to leave anything on the table. You want to just reach as many people as you can.

I love the song 'Wild Wood' – the way it creeps in so gently is such a beautiful introduction.

Paul Weller: We used to play that live before it was even recorded, before it was even demoed. Might have been in a different style or something. It wasn't acoustic, as it turned out on the record anyway. I thought the reaction was really good the first time they heard it. I just thought melodically, it was really beautiful, and I did think it was special. Just finding the right vehicle for it really.

Brendan Lynch: I think 'Wild Wood' is my favourite song that I've done with Paul. It's a great performance and as close as we got to perfection. I don't think I changed anything on that one. Initially it was a bit faster, and the drum pattern was different. When we came to record it, Paul wanted to do it outside, which has quite a few problems. It was a windy day, and we put the mics out, but we were getting too much noise from the environment . . . We then took it inside and the drum pattern changed, and it was much more laid back on that final version . . . It has a handmade, rustic feel. During recording, we referenced an animation called *Pogles' Wood*, which was a childhood recollection.

The album's lyrics were becoming more introspective, and Paul wondered how fans would react. However, they were also growing older and experiencing the same concerns in life.

Tom Robinson: 'Wild Wood' is Paul at his finest. Out of nowhere. Just when you think you can write Paul Weller off . . . Yeah, come on. *He was quite good in the seventies and Style Council had its moments, but he's all washed up now* and he comes back, wham. Here you go. Take that. You can't write anybody off after they've written 'Wild Wood'.

Max Beesley: By his own admittance, he'll say, 'I was quite crazy at that point.' You can hear it in some of the songs and bits and pieces going on. He was a taskmaster in those days – if you got things wrong, you'd know about it.

He was a young man. He'd already been through two completely different nuances as a band leader and then switched it out again. Who knows what goes on in someone's mind when you're reaching that success and then you kill it, then you go again, get success and kill it? There were other things going on when he was doing *Wild Wood*, but I've always loved being around Paul. I'm very, very fond of him, and there was a softer edge on *Wild Wood*.

23 August 1993 – 'Wild Wood' (no. 14)

1 November 1993 – *The Weaver* (EP, no. 18)

1993–94 – 'Live Wood' tour

Martin Hopewell: It was weird, because looking at the characters involved, you'd think they couldn't organise a piss-up in a brewery. Yet somehow, it was like an SAS team – heading into different countries, putting shows together, and making it all happen. You'd think, *I have no idea how this is happening,* because it's not like the top-flight music business people that you get with the Pink Floyd tours and whatever.

You could be in the most beautiful part of the world with fantastic scenery and you'd find John downstairs with Kenny playing poker and robbing all the per diems off the crew before he could even pay them . . .

Those tours were really John and me sitting back and trying to work out what to do next, with John saying, 'We could slip a couple of gigs in there, couldn't we? How about we pop off and do this festival?' It was pushing all the time, just gig, gig, gig, with Paul having this work ethic, to just do it and have it. The expression *having it large*, that's Paul. He does not fuck about.

Paul Dowling: Paul always had a habit of surrounding himself with some of the best musicians that were available at the time. I used to go and see them rehearse sometimes, and even in rehearsal I'd be like, *Why are you rehearsing? This is just tight as fuck.*

Yolanda Charles: It was really tough for me at the beginning because I wasn't really from that British pop-rock background. I was coming from the funk, acid jazz territory . . . I wasn't mournful about not playing any Jam, because I'd never listened to it. I was more familiar with the more soulful stuff like 'Above the Clouds'; those tunes were right up my street.

As time went on, Paul's music started to get rockier, and I had to learn how to do that within his band. It was the best education. Paul would tell me about bands like Small Faces and Free. I'd never heard of these bands. I started listening to Andy Fraser's style of bass playing, which was so expressive . . . He used the whole neck, swooping around a lot, and that influenced my bass playing in Paul's band.

Steve Cradock: I was out somewhere, seeing a girl in London, when Paul phoned my dad at home. He was after a second guitar player, and asked if I could go and have an audition. Which, to be fair, I should have failed because I was shit on guitar at the time. I think, I only started becoming an all right guitar player when I had to learn Paul's songs . . . I quickly learned how musical Paul was with his chords.

Daniel Rachel: Ocean Colour Scene were on the downers at that point. Around the time that they were doing 'Do Yourself a Favour', their Stevie Wonder cover, and it'd all gone wrong. I lived with Simon all through the nineties. We were all on the dole. Steve wasn't because he had started playing with Paul, so he was bringing back money, which he felt really guilty about. He very wonderfully gave Simon a wad of cash.

Simon Fowler: We started to become a bit of a gang around that time with Paul and Ocean Colour Scene. Paul is exactly seven years older than me: 25 May . . . Paul's mother's maiden name is Craddock. The stars were aligned.

Daniel Rachel: Then Steve just said, 'Paul's coming round for tea.' Everybody wanted to be there . . . He came round to the upstairs flat, which was this really scuzzy, horrible place. Simon had a broken window in there for two years which he never fixed, and his room was scattered with clothes . . . Simon doesn't care about possessions. In fact, only one thing he cared about was Neil Young, *Decade* . . . He kept it in his drawer underneath his socks!

Paul had Levi's on that were ripped at the bottom, above the desert boots. It looked like he'd had a pair of scissors on them, so it had the dangles, the thread coming off them, and I thought that looked really good.

We had a little record player and Steve put on the P. P. Arnold *Kafunta* album and she was singing 'Eleanor Rigby' which isn't very good, and I was very quiet, I was always really shy, and I thought, *I need to say something*, so I said, 'It's great this, isn't it?' and Paul went, 'I think it's rubbish.' I just thought, *There's my lesson. Be honest* . . . I realised at that point, *Stop trying to impress him, just say what you really think*.

Steve Cradock: Paul came up a couple of times to Birmingham . . . played with us there. We did a version of 'Every Little Piece of My Heart'. He'd just come up to Birmingham to Moseley to hang out.

Daniel Rachel: We used to call Steve 'Little Paul' at that point. You know, like Frank Sidebottom, [*high pitched voice*] 'Little Frank'. So it was [*high pitched again*] 'Little Paul!', and Steve liked it, I think, [*laughs*] because whatever big Paul did, little Paul did [*laughs*].

Yolanda Charles: I remember when Steve had joined the band, and we got one of our first live reviews. Steve was older than me by maybe half a year or even a year. But in this article, they described Paul's new band as the young, bright-eyed Steve Cradock and session veteran Yolanda Charles! I was like, *You're making me sound like a freaking dame . . . Dame Yolanda!* It was funny. So, already, people had this perception that I'd been around for a while. I was actually very green.

Danny Eccleston: The first time I interviewed Paul Weller was for *The Guitar Magazine*. It's funny, I remember the negotiations around the interview. His team asked if I'd be putting Paul on the cover, but we couldn't. I had to say, 'We can't put Paul Weller on the cover because we've got a Paul McCartney interview'. The response from Paul was, 'Well, as long as it's Paul McCartney on the cover then that's okay.' Even now, there's not many people he'll defer to, but he will defer to Paul McCartney.

I went down to the Manor Studios . . . Paul showing me all these records that he was playing: Free's *Fire and Water*, a Grant Green jazz guitar album and Nick Drake's *Five Leaves*

Left. This was in the early days of the Nick Drake revival. I joked, 'Oh my God, Paul, you're a hippie!' He was holding his hands up that it really was the first time that he'd allowed some of this really hairy music across his transom. It was one of those moments where he was taking stock musically and allowing a load of new influences in to refresh his way forward.

John Harris: By then, there was a little clique of mods at the *NME* – me, Iestyn George and Paul Moody. Ted Kessler was around too. We were pushing to get Paul on the cover, in the teeth of an editor, Steve Sutherland, who didn't like Paul Weller at all. But then it happened, and I got the assignment from the features editor. 'Do you want to go on the road with Paul Weller?' Yes, I do. It was his first *NME* cover since '87.

Fair play to him – it was old-school journalism, like in *Almost Famous*. Back then, you'd go on the road for a proper stretch . . . I was on the bus. Welcomed into the fold. Paul's somewhat comedic tipple on that tour was Cointreau and Lucozade, which we were all encouraged to try. At one point I sat in Steve Cradock's room, smoking jazz cigarettes, listening to *Band of Gypsys* by Jimi Hendrix – with Paul there . . . My internal monologue is going, *I bet when you bought 'Strange Town' in Boots in Edinburgh, you didn't think this was gonna happen.*

Paul even made a tape for me . . . The track listing didn't cover all the tracks . . . I sang along to 'People Coming Out of the Rain' by Parliament for eight years before I finally identified it.

Ted Kessler: I was living in Ladbroke Grove at the time and I remember listening to *Wild Wood* at home one afternoon, I had to write about it for *NME*, and really loving it, and I thought, *God, he's really found his groove again* . . . It was a nice mix of the things I liked about both The Style Council and The Jam, although not sounding like either thing. The weight was off his shoulders, and it felt like he was free again.

Yolanda Charles: Paul surprised me – he knew more about the genre that I grew up with than I did. I had a narrow listening experience and he'd go shopping for records and clothes. He'd come back with CDs for me. 'I bought this for you, yeah. Didn't think you'd have this.' I didn't have any of it: Curtis Mayfield, my first Sly and the Family Stone album. That blew my mind, because it was just raw, rock music, but funky like James Brown, but more . . . attitude. He unintentionally (or maybe it was intentional) gave me an education. At twenty or twenty-one I still had a lot to absorb and what a person to learn from.

I remember sitting with Paul and the boys in a room, and I put Hendrix on. Probably 'Crosstown Traffic' and he said, 'I've got to switch it off.' I was like, 'Oh, what's up?' and he said, 'Sometimes, when I listen to music like this, I think that it will never be as good as this again. It feels like it's so special, that if I listen to it, it makes me feel, a little bit, that no one was ever going to make music as good as they did back then.'

Martin Hopewell: If you made the mistake of going into a bar with any of the Weller crew, then you probably were stuck there, and they might as well have held you down, put a funnel in your mouth and poured White Russians down it. You had no choice. 'Get it down, you fucking lightweight.' I'm in this bar with John and everyone's being reasonably well-behaved, but really knocking it back. Gradually, everybody else had left the bar. Paul had gone . . . There's just me and John in the bar. What he didn't know is I'd literally been tipping the White Russians into this plant pot . . . I had to help John get off his stool . . . ended up walking across the hotel lobby with John's arm wrapped around my neck, supporting him, trying to look as if we're just being pals in case there were any CCTV cameras watching us. Got him up to the corridor where his room was, in time to see another member of the Weller family flat on their back with their head and torso sticking out of their bedroom door into the corridor – being inched by an invisible force back into the room. As I come by with John draped round my shoulder, Paul has got this person's ankles and he's pulling them into the room. As I go past, he goes, 'What a fucking family.' At which point we tried to put John on his bed, and he bound straight up again, ready to start fighting anybody who just thrown him into his bed. It's like, 'OK, just go to sleep.' That was a typical 'don't ever go into a bar with a Weller'.

Steve Cradock: Paul was intense at that point. We'd rehearse for a tour for a week at a time and he was very driven, very professional, so it was intense. He had a point to prove but I don't think that was the number one driving thing though. He just wanted to be great. He wanted the songs to come over, he wanted to connect with people, with the crowd and he wanted to be fucking bang on.

Yolanda Charles: Because of my good technique, I could play without making it look like I was doing anything at all, and he wasn't having that! He wants to see you sweat, to make sure that you looked like you were putting everything into it. He'd come up to me, right in my face, and be like, 'Come on! Come on!' I'd be like, *Oh, my God! Help! Mum!* But being Caribbean, I was used to that kind of energy – growing up the banter used to flow, man. You couldn't be shy and quiet . . . I'd be like 'Yeah! All right then!' Stepping up, rising to it, but it was quite intimidating. He really egged you on to dig in and find more passion and commitment to the part and really give it. Don't just dial it in. Play it like you mean it or fuck off! I wanted to stay so I had to sweat and bleed.

Paul Weller: From '91 to '94, I was pretty much on the road. A lot of tours in America . . . maybe twice a year sometimes. It seemed like it was opening up to me. I don't know about hit records, but there was an audience there and I was playing all new stuff. And in America you get very, very generous audiences, that would just listen to the music and if they like it, they like it. They give it a chance. Unlike here at the time. So, I spent a tremendous amount of time on the road.

My son Nat was born in 1988, so for the first couple of years I was around, but '91 onwards was pretty flat out touring and then my daughter was born in '91, so I didn't see much of her really. Obviously, I'd be back in between some tours, but it wasn't particularly healthy for family life, because when you're out on the road you have to become someone else. I don't mean the character that's on stage, but to get through this touring thing, you have to be focused. So it wasn't great for my family. It wasn't good. I don't think it was beneficial for them . . . just the fact I wasn't around much.

1994 – Paul and Dee C. Lee split

Dee C. Lee: I've never courted the press. I know it's been to my detriment because maybe I could sell more records, but my music has to just do it off its own back. Every year that goes by it's harder and harder without selling your soul to the devil a little bit, to get any attention. You have to do that. I was never prepared to do that much. But then that in itself worked in my favour when I needed the privacy at a time that was very, very heartbreaking for me and it would be heartbreaking for anybody. Anybody's marriage breaking up is incredibly heartbreaking and especially when there's kids involved. So yeah, it was not a very nice time for either of us. But in my defence, I didn't care how he was feeling at the time because I was far too heartbroken.

For Paul, the balance between music and family life just didn't seem to work . . . and it took a little while for us to realise that this is not going to happen . . . because in my mind the kids come first. You know, and in his mind the kids come first, but he was finding it difficult to do this and to do the writing. What I do remember is that he always said that he was too happy, and he wasn't writing . . . I'm like, 'How can anybody be too happy? Let's just enjoy it, man' . . . That should have been a little flag to me for what was going to come and, without going into too much detail, it just deteriorated and went from bad to worse to the point where it was definitely for everybody's sanity, especially mine, to do that. It's not good for kids to be around unhappiness . . . It's better to try and salvage whatever you've got left, and I'm glad that we did that because we actually do have a relatively good friendship now, which is how we started off and that's how it should be.

It eventually all came out. But I do believe that John and Ann might have had something to do with keeping the press away because they had quite a good relationship, and I think it was Piers Morgan who was head of whatever at that time. But I do remember Ann Weller saying to them, please keep them away from Dee because she's already really, really upset, and I'm really very private and I couldn't have dealt with that. They weren't in my face the way they are with people now, but I think it's because they know that we've never courted them.

28 March 1994 – 'Hung Up' (no. 11)

Dylan White: Radio 1 had changed at this point. Matthew Bannister had become the new broom and the old guard, broadcasters like Simon Bates, were barmed off out the door. It was the start of this new breed. Britpop was starting to come through. 'Sunflower' and 'Wild Wood' had done well. We were definitely on the move now, and we get to 'Hung Up' . . .

Brendan Lynch: We recorded 'Hung Up' in February 1994 after the album was released. Paul, Steve White and Yolanda Charles. At the time, I thought it could have been better but now it's one of my favourites.

Paul would also encourage me to do dub versions of songs – as mental as possible! They were really fun – you'd let your hair down and go a bit crazy. That 'Kosmos' remix on the B-side was picked up by Andrew Weatherall. He'd finished his DJ set each night. That's how I ended up working with Primal Scream, because they heard that track.

Simon Halfon: For me, 'Hung Up' has everything . . . I recently saw a clip of Paul, Steve Cradock, Yolanda Charles and Steve White performing it – just the four of them – and they absolutely knocked it out of the park. I also really love the sleeve. It has that *Sgt Pepper*-like wash over that great Lawrence Watson photo, with minimal and simple typography. It's a standout design.

25 June 1994 – Glastonbury

Steve Cradock: In the lead up to Glastonbury, we did this tour supporting Herbert Grönemeyer in Germany. In hindsight it was a fucking genius thing to do. They were playing like big auditoriums and he was this hateful . . . not as a person, right. But his music was shite and just this strange eighties-sounding German rock-pop nonsense. And I was thinking, *What the fuck are we doing playing here?* . . . But when we got to Glastonbury, we felt in a position where it gave us strength. If we wouldn't have done that, we'd have gone from the normal-size gig straight onto the stage at Glastonbury, and I think that would have been a lot more pressure.

Helen Turner: Glastonbury '94, I think, was one of the best gigs we've ever done in one place. It was almost perfect. The way we were doing 'Kosmos', as the sun was going down, really was something. It couldn't have been a better day and the transition to evening was magical.

Yolanda Charles: We did 'Foot of the Mountain', and it was never really a fully fledged song. It was more like a jam with a couple of sections that Paul would cue. It was never fixed. It was one of the first times I experienced being in the headlights, with everyone hanging on your every note. We didn't pre-plan it much. It came from a soundcheck jam. Paul already had the song idea, the basis of it . . . It reflected the personalities and characters in the band. He didn't tell me what to play, what basslines to play. Steve was a free agent, and we evolved the tuning to something specific to the musicians on that stage. I didn't realise how much I'd learned from that experience because what he did with that song, and how we played, it is what I do with my band now. Every night is different. Paul watched that evolve.

Helen Turner: That performance of 'Foot of the Mountain' was mighty, wasn't it? I think it's the heaviest thing we'd ever done, at least when I was there. Songs often evolve in a live setting, which probably applies to many bands. Something starts from a soundcheck idea.

Yolanda Charles: We built that familiarity, getting used to each other's body language. Paul and Steve developed a relationship where they were reading each other without doing anything . . . almost telepathic.

Noel Gallagher: Back then, Glastonbury backstage was literally one tent, and a few white plastic chairs kicked over in a corner. We were sat in the damp, drinking fucking lager at two in the afternoon, and someone told me Weller had mentioned Oasis in an interview – something like, 'Who was you looking forward to seeing?' I'd had enough to drink to go and find him. I just walked up and said, 'All right. Pleased to meet you.' Within twenty minutes, he asked where I was living, gave me his phone number and said, 'Bell us when you get back.'

I got back home. I'd sobered up and thought, *I've got his number . . . should I?* Nowadays you'd just send a text, and if they didn't reply, whatever. But this was 1994 – pre-everything. So I called this number . . . Of course, he picked up. I don't think he even said hello! He just went, 'Who is it?' and I was like, 'Oh, is that Paul?' 'Yeah. Who's that?' I was like, 'It's Noel Gallagher, from Oasis.'

He was living in a mews house, in Maida Vale actually, where we would both end up living. So I went round to his house and by the end of the night, we were going to start a supergroup. He'd written down the setlist. We were going to open with 'Dead End Street' by The Kinks – just covers! The irony of it all is, he was renting this mews house that was owned by Adam Clayton from U2 . . . who he fucking hates!

16 July 1994 – Phoenix Festival

Paul Moody: Phoenix Festival was a phenomenal performance – a perfect moment. Paul would probably remember it: beautiful skies over the Midlands, everything seemed to coalesce. Why did it happen then? I'm not sure, but Paul was so central to that entire movement.

I remember Noel Gallagher saying he could recite every lyric of every Jam B-side, and there are probably a hundred thousand people who could do that. All of those people were suddenly back in the mix – forming bands, getting into the mainstream. That's when it gets exciting: when articulate music – you could say working-class music, something that relates to people on the street – is actually being played on the radio. That's when real change happens.

Pat Gilbert: There was a *NME* do at the Royal Festival Hall in that early summer of 1994, in those brief few months between 'Parklife' exploding and Oasis breaking big. It was interesting, because Weller was there with Paolo and Marco Nelson and a few others, all dressed up in their corduroy shoes and acid jazz finery, and they seemed completely separate from everything else. It was that real working-class mod outsider thing that hung over from The Style Council days. I remember one of them looking over at Blur and muttering, '*Fucking student music*', or something to that effect! You have to remember that even at that point Weller was still being treated with suspicion by the music press – and vice versa. And that didn't change for at least another year or so.

Dylan White: By '94, Blur and Oasis were openly saying how much they love Paul Weller, which triggered a whole new wave of interest . . . it reignited his presence for young people. There was a famous *NME* cover, with the Modfather headline – I think it was with Damon Albarn or Noel Gallagher – where they raved about him.

He headlined the Phoenix Festival, which was a big moment. I remember Steve Lamacq interviewing Paul on the *Evening Session*, banging on and on about Oasis and Blur. If I remember rightly, Paul wasn't too keen to talk about them, saying, 'They're just young bands coming through, I don't wanna talk about them.' But that's where the younger audience came in – kids who clearly weren't around for The Jam or even The Style Council.

Graham Coxon: All our influences came to the fore in the music that we wanted to make at that point and that involved all sorts of stuff from The Jam, The Beatles, Pink Floyd and all the rest of it. That mid to late sixties stuff, a little bit of that punk and post-punk stuff mixed in. I hope it was obvious to Paul that he was influencing us or had been an influence or a major part of our musical upbringing. It was all there, and the scene was set for him to get back in it in a way.

Richard Hawley: This is something I wanted to say to you about Paul, but I guess about me and you could include Noel in that and Jarvis and a few of the white working-class musicians . . . where we're from and who we are. Those things are completely inseparable. You couldn't become who we've become without those things being so closely interwoven that create such quite fierce individuals, and I don't mean fierce and aggressive, but fiercely unafraid to be yourself. That working-class environment, and geographically as well, couldn't have possibly thrown up anything else. It was very specific to where we are and the time as well . . . the viewpoint, the eye, the beginning of the telescope is where we're from: Woking in Surrey for him and deep South Yorkshire for me. That perspective informs so much of who you are and what you are.

Damon Minchella: The mid-nineties was really like the mid-sixties. Mainstream music was genuinely good, and the cool stuff was on daytime radio. It was a mix of disparate bands making the records they wanted to make and, for some reason, Radio 1 played it all. Mainstream music at the time was cool, unlike before or after, when it rarely was.

Noel Gallagher: All the main players in those groups – Oasis, Pulp, Blur – were Jam fans. We all came through at the same time, and I remember him saying, 'It's the first time I've met a load of people in the music business I've got anything in common with.' We were all working-class lads, playing guitars, and into The Beatles and The Kinks. I think he saw a bit of himself in us, and it inspired him.

Weller was playing the G-Mex and we happened to be in town on a night off. We said to Weller, 'We'll go on before you.' We were all up for it . . . We were number one in the charts at the time.

Weller said, 'Oh Dad, gonna get Oasis on to support us tonight.' 'Oh right. Who are they now?' 'They're from Manchester.' He's like, 'What? A local band. Fifty quid. The local band fee is fifty quid.' I think somebody tapped him on the shoulder and said, 'They might be worth a bit more than fifty quid!'

He was always trying to get you to play cards.

Bill Wheeler: I've sat in when Dad took me, and I don't know what the notes were, but there was a lot of them, and normally a couple of people went away rather upset, but if Dad won, that probably meant we were going to go to Disneyland! So, thank you very much to whoever.

Noel Gallagher: I never did. Fuck that . . . John would always try and get you involved in the card game. And he'd always say to me, 'Fucking hell, son. Crack a smile. Crack a smile, son. Are you joining us?' 'Like fuck. I'm not playing cards with you lot. I'll play snap if you want.'

He was a top dude. He was fiercely fucking loyal to Paul . . . and his mum was a force of nature too. A fierce family. Do not fuck about with them, that's for sure!

Yolanda Charles: To be quite honest, it was a bit of a dodgy time for me. We did pretty much everything in a few days and had to break the recording to headline the Phoenix Festival, where Paul and I had a confrontation, that he instigated, and I decided I had to leave after that. But I did have to go back to the studio and do some more, even with me having decided I was leaving! . . . I was feeling awful about not being able to just throw my bass down . . . well, place it gently, and leave! As soon as I finished the take and we came out for a break and I was done for the day, I said, 'Paul, I'm not coming back, mate.' So that *Stanley Road* experience is tinged with a sense of departure – I left at the start of the recording of the album. That's why I'm only on three tracks.

Robert Howard: I had played with Paul quite a bit on his first album, and *Wild Wood* and then on *Stanley Road*. He was always sacking his bass players! I was in Japan, doing some gigs with The Blow Monkeys or maybe solo gigs . . . It wasn't Yolanda, it was someone else who was playing, and they weren't happy. I think it was Steve White that actually suggested to Paul 'Get Robert.' So he sends me a fax when we get back to England with all the chords and all the bits and pieces, and he just says at the end, 'I know you'll be all right, you've got a good feel' . . . I was like, *Fucking hell, how am I going to learn all these songs?* I'd never played bass with people live before, and I loved it, because first of all, you're playing with one of the great drummers of all time, when Steve did a drum fill, I just took a little break and came back in afterwards because they were so good . . . At this point, things were really beginning to happen. I remember playing 'Changingman' live, and no one had ever heard it before. Instantly you could see: *Wow.*

24 October 1994 – 'Out of the Sinking' (no. 20; February 1996 LP version reissue, no. 16)

Damon Minchella: The first track I played on was a version of The Beatles, 'Sexy Sadie', for the B-side of 'Out of the Sinking'. I've gone down to the Manor. He said, 'Alright Damon, come down you cunt,' in his sort of nice way . . . So we did.

1994 – Dr. Robert, *Realms of Gold*

Robert Howard: Paul and I had both been to Japan a lot and had success there. And at this point, Pony Canyon offered me the best deal I could get, which gave me enough to go and record the album *Realms of Gold.* I went to this studio in Leamington Spa, and Paul very kindly came down for two days, stayed in a hotel, and played on loads of stuff. He picked up a bass, played piano and did some backing vocals. He ended up all over the album. The song, 'Have No Roots', was just me and Paul. He really brought something special to it. He really liked that one. He's a really good bass player. I think that's what Paul started out on, with one of those Hofner, Paul McCartney-type bass, and nailed it on the first take. We also jammed on other things . . . Paul joined in with 'Red Balloon', Tim Hardin, and we did 'Life's a Gas', Marc Bolan . . . I remember making up a tape and putting Nick Drake, 'River Man', on which then became a big tune for him with the whole Nick Drake experience. There were times when we would just sit, play two acoustics without saying much. That sounds romantic, but really, it's the musical connection that is the real bond.

Rhoda Dakar: I'm credited as 'Rhoda the roadie' on that album . . . Neither of them could drive manual vehicles and they needed a van to take the kit and the drummer and bass player from London to the studio. I'd go, hang out a bit, and because it was in Leamington Spa, I could drive back to Leicester and pick stuff up the next day . . . I was listening to the recording, enjoying it, and Robert said, 'Come and sing on it.' I remember being mortified at the thought of standing round the microphones, me, Robert and Paul, singing backing vocals. Nobody is ever going to mistake me for a backing singer – I don't have that kind of voice. I was so nervous, I could barely sing, so I just did, 'Oooo, oooo, oooo.' They managed to get away with it, cut out all the high frequencies.

October 1994 – John Weller's heart bypass

Nicky Weller: So, 1994, we moved into our flat in Sutherland Avenue and the reason I'm saying that is because Dad stayed with us once we come out of his angiogram. He hadn't had a heart attack, but he had collapsed. All his arteries were furred up and stuff.

Ann Weller: I think it was all to do with cigarette smoking and drinking all the years.

Nicky Weller: But it started as a bypass and then ended up as a triple bypass. So it was more serious than he thought, really.

Kenny Wheeler: It was fucking terrible. It broke my heart. He had the bypass done, and it was dreadful. We was away on the road, as it had already been set, and John was saying, 'Go and get it done.' It was hard for me because I didn't have anybody. Everything me and John had done together.

Nicky Weller: He was a little shit when he had to go into hospital. Me and [partner] Russell were with him in London when he got told he was having it and we had to hide his passport because he reckoned he was off to Japan the next day on tour and I was like, 'You fucking well ain't,' and he's like, 'I am.' So, we took all his clothes away from him in the hospital and hid his passport. He was literally standing there in a little gown, and Mum was like, 'Don't you fucking let him get on the plane.' I was like, 'Mum, don't worry about it. He's not going anywhere.'

Ann Weller: He was there in his knickers.

Kenny Wheeler: I think we were in Osaka, when he had it done, and he was in hospital, and he sat and pulled all the wires out. It was terrifying. He weren't the most patient person in the world. He just wanted to be out on the road. I remember Ann telling me that he said, 'Can you pack me a bag?' 'Why?' 'Well, I'm going away tomorrow for a month.'

Martin Hopewell: I went to visit him after the op and it was the only time I ever saw him with his usually immaculate teddy-boy quiff out of place.

Nicky Weller: Literally when he had his triple bypass, he stopped, he never smoked and he never drunk another drop, just like that, literally overnight. It was amazing, actually.

Ann Weller: I couldn't believe that he did it.

Nicky Weller: Then he was back out on the road again, weren't he? Quite quickly, actually. It's amazing, to be honest with you. He had his triple bypass, and he was fine, and then Mum had just come back to ours to stay the night and then we all got a phone call to say he's gone back into surgery because he'd fucking bled. He was a haemophiliac, my dad, and he bled, and it was horrendous. So, we had to go back up there, and they opened him all up again. He was out of it for about three days. He thought someone was building a Mercedes car in the bed next to him!

24 April 1995 – 'The Changingman' (no. 7)

Ric Blaxill: Paul's catalogue is incredible, but 'The Changingman' is such an incredible song. The lyrics get me every time. No matter what stage you're at in life, that song can hold a different meaning. It meant an incredible amount to me at one point. The sincerity and depth are brilliant. You don't want to go too deep on this because he's clearly getting this stuff out of his soul.

Brendan Lynch: 'Changingman' was demoed at Nomis studio. Paul was also rehearsing in the same building and would pop up from time to time during breaks to add another verse or guitar part. I was really chuffed to get a co-writer credit on that song.

Lawrence Watson: A friend of mine, Pedro Romhanyi, shot the video. I was there shooting cutaway imagery, something called cross-processing, which isn't as easy to do with film so much. It involved putting transparency film through a colour-negative bath, giving you those really vibrant colours. Pedro wanted to recreate that on the moving imagery.

Graham Coxon: He looks so freaking great. I was going out with Jo Johnson from Huggy Bear at that time and we were watching 'The Changingman' video going, 'Fucking hell. Paul looks bloody great. Look at his fucking hair' . . . when my mum used to cut my hair when I was thirteen, fourteen, I'd always be saying, 'Can you cut it like this Paul Weller picture?'

15 May 1995 – *Stanley Road* (no. 1)

Paul Weller: Fame is too fake for me, man. I don't like it. I can't live up to that. Whatever people's expectations of that is, it's not me at all. I couldn't care less about it. If people like me because of my songs, my music, then great, fantastic. But that's it, that's it for me. Or if you like the pair of shoes I'm wearing in that particular photograph that's fine, because I've done that myself. But beyond that, I couldn't care less about any of that at all. And it just brings other problems with it. So false and so fake, for instance, like *Stanley Road*, when you're flavour of the month and all that, and everyone's laughing at your jokes and it's all funny. It's just bollocks. And really I just want everyone to fuck off and leave me alone and let me just play my music and leave it at that.

Ann Weller: I think he loves his music, but doesn't want all the faff that goes with it.

Nicky Weller: He's never been great with that level of fame. It was because it was bonkers, weren't it? Around that time. Don't forget, that was kind of the start of Britpop and all that shit, as well and lots of drinking and lots of Noel Gallaghers and hanging out with them lot. So that wasn't great either.

Dee C. Lee: That was a particularly hard time for me, and not because I wasn't happy for Paul's success, but in order to get that success he had to basically destroy a really good setup. But you know, like I said, prices to pay and it depends what's important to you.

Jun Sato: I was so happy that I let Paul do what he wanted to do, because I knew, almost superstition, that he would take me somewhere like *Stanley Road*. It helped me a lot when the gentleman in Oasis kept raising Paul Weller. Those things count, and Japanese people like that. Someone respecting someone.

Andy Macdonald: There was so much good work from Paul in that period, it's phenomenal, really. I'd sit there and think, *Who else compares?* The Beatles had this huge global thing – thirteen albums in seven years before splitting. But out of the UK, who else is challenging that? It's brilliant that someone has something to say and keeps expressing themselves in really poetic and beautiful ways.

Brendan Lynch: Those three albums – *Paul Weller*, *Wild Wood* and *Stanley Road* – feel like one record to me because we never stopped working, even in between them.

I was with him all the time and I just couldn't figure out when he had time to write. Later, I realised he worked late at night, when everyone's asleep and he's on his own. I'd be thinking, *He's got a new song, when did he do that? I saw him two days ago.*

He was always doing demos, often three or four before we recorded them properly. The first demo would be done quickly on my little eight-track machine – bang it down, try a few overdubs and that's it. The next version would be more refined, maybe adjusting arrangements, and then the next would be closer to where we would end up. By the time we went into the studio, we were ready. Paul would play some of them live, which made a huge difference, especially on *Stanley Road*.

Paul Weller: Once I got my shit together and my muse came back from '92 to '95, I was just always writing. I was writing loads on the road; I was writing loads at home. So, by the time we finished the first solo album, which came out in '92, I think that was all in the can. A lot of stuff that became *Wild Wood*. Maybe a couple of things that ended up later on *Stanley Road*. I was just constantly writing all the time.

Brendan Lynch: We went all out and pushed everything as far as we could go. Paul said, 'This is shit or bust!' The working process was the same as before with several demos before final recordings but we'd record straight after touring, so the band were super tight. At the start we'd be laying down the backing tracks with drums, bass, probably a keyboard player, and maybe Steve Cradock would come along on *Stanley Road* . . . then everyone would go home, and we'd carry on with the overdubs, either with additional musicians or Paul actually played a lot of stuff.

Mick Talbot: I bumped into Paul at Nomis and played on demos for a couple of other tracks that are on there, but I didn't end up on the final versions. They got someone called Steve Winwood to play on it. They had to settle for someone like that. I think Marco Nelson was playing bass on the track and he told me that Steve Winwood said, 'I like what the fella's doing on the demo, so I'm playing that.' It was nice to hear that I had some sort of subliminal influence on someone that great.

Brendan Lynch: Steve Winwood came down and played piano, Hammond and Wurlitzer on 'Woodcutter's Son' and piano on 'Pink on White Walls'. He said, 'How are we going to do this?' and I said, 'Well, we're all going to play together.' He said, 'What? The whole band? Do you always do it like that? Wow, that must save a lot of time.' I'm thinking, *He was in Traffic and the Spencer Davis Group, that's how they used to do it. They'd all play together.* Obviously later in his career, he'd been doing it differently, starting with the drum, or whatever process they used.

Ted Cockle: I had the pleasure of working with Winwood for a period of time doing Spencer Davis, Blind Faith, Traffic, solo. I don't think there's many artists, like him and Paul, with such incredible incarnations. This is something with artists, and Paul shares it in a different way, is that they do not understand why their public likes particular songs of theirs. They just don't comprehend. Winwood is more excited about the choral group song that he's just created in the Cotswolds, as he is about 'Valerie', 'Higher Love' or anything else. And Paul's the same. You're telling me that you like 'Malice'? You're telling me that, but I'm telling you that I could give you forty other songs, you know. If Paul was to put his greatest hits together and you actually asked him, separate to fucking any sales, what would you think were your best songs that you wrote in each period? He doesn't see it. I mean, he's happy with it. He likes it but he just doesn't comprehend the perception of himself.

Carleen Anderson: I love the atmosphere of a residential studio. It's less 'laboratory' type. You're creating in an atmosphere of nature, and it was a lot of fun. I learned a lot about recording and producing in that atmosphere.

With 'Wings of Speed', Paul preferred to record vocals together, all at once. It worked because it kept us in sync, allowing us to work by ear. I'm from the school of organic – everything is done in the moment, all at the same time, and that's your lot, you don't get to go back and fix it.

Mick Talbot: 'Wings of Speed' was a weird session because I played that on a church organ, but we wanted to record it live. They ran a cable about a quarter of a mile long, down this hill, to a little chapel in Oxford near the Manor. I'm on the other end of a tin of baked beans, getting contact from mission control. It was cold and Dave Liddle set up this temporary fire to try and warm me up. I had a duffel coat and mittens on, playing this bellows organ in a little chapel. We got the take, and it worked.

Most of the tracks had been done so we then had a listen back, and a bit of a drink and something to eat, a few hours went by, and then it got to nearly midnight and Paul went to Brendan, 'Oh, I forgot that other thing. I want Mick on that other thing.' That other thing was 'Pebbles on a beach' – 'Broken Stones'. That was a very last-minute thing. I said, 'I could have done with you telling me that three hours before we started drinking.'

Brendan Lynch: It actually started off as a guitar track and then Paul said, 'Let's try a Wurlitzer'. He literally sat down, played the intro and first verse and then said to Steve White, play this sort of beat, and we had the track in the next ten minutes. Really quick.

Simon Halfon: I was friends with Mary McCartney, whose father, as you probably remember, was the bass player in Wings. In the past, he'd a connection with Peter Blake so she had his number. I reached out to see if he'd meet with Paul and myself. I was living in LA, but was often in the UK, so we arranged a chat. We were thrilled. We didn't think it would go anywhere, but were pleased to have met him. We were talking and he said, 'I'd love to do the cover if you want.'

He came up with the genius idea of a painting of the younger Paul holding a picture of himself as he is today, surrounded by a collage of influences that we gave Peter – John Lennon, Georgie Best, New York, the Small Faces – all the different things that we loved. He did an exceptional job.

The record speaks for itself – *Wild Wood* sold 100,000 to 200,000 copies in the UK, and *Stanley Road* sold a couple of million.

Suggs: George Best was on the cover of *Stanley Road*, and originally it was going to be Peter Osgood, King of Stamford Bridge, and then somebody along the way said, 'It would be more universal if you put George Best on'.

Andy Macdonald: With *Stanley Road*, as a record company you prepare your marketing plans to reach people – through live events, press, TV ads – but that album was always outstripping your expectations, driven by word of mouth. It was always ahead of the game of what we could do.

Nicky Weller: Every week someone would nick the Stanley Road signs at both ends of the road. The council stopped putting signs up for a while and then they sussed it out so that no one could actually nick them in the end.

John Cohen: The classic moment with *Stanley Road* was when the record company wanted to do TV advertising. The album had reached a certain status but hadn't sold massively yet. Back then, TV-advertised albums came with reduced royalties for sales linked to the campaign – it was quite draconian.

I negotiated the best deal ever for a television advertised record, keeping the reduced royalty rate to only a limited number of records for a very short period, before reverting to the full rate. John grudgingly agreed to that. It was brilliant.

Peter Button: That TV campaign has to be one of the most successful of all time. Sales went from 30,000 to 40,000 up to 300,000 in just a few weeks. It was just massively successful. Perfectly timed, it was also perhaps the most lucrative one from an artist's point of view.

John Cohen: It's the only album I've ever put on my wall – a triple platinum disc in this case.

Pete Mason: We'd try to keep on top of it as much as you can, but thousands of CDs would be sold in a week; 40,000 records would be going out. We were being distributed through PolyGram at the time, so they had all the tools to get it all done. We weren't producing from a little office at this point, but you'd still come close to going out of stock, and that's the last thing you wanted to do. The record was so successful, that the record plant and cassette manufacturers were just trying to keep up with the demand.

Andy Macdonald: I do ask myself whether we could have done more overseas. Paul performs well in the States. He can go and play to 7,000–8,000 fans in LA and New York. There won't be an empty seat. We licensed the album internationally, so you never quite know how it's going to go. You're reliant on the goodwill of strangers, really. Your Dutch record company have got their own priorities. The French record company have got their own French priorities. There's always give and take. People have asked me before, whether it is too British a sensibility. I wouldn't have a coherent answer for you on that, really.

Dylan White: When we got to *Stanley Road* things are moving along even more ... By this point, we were on the Radio 1 A-list all the time.

Gary Crowley: Dylan said, 'Paul wants to come in to do a track-by-track exclusive interview.' There was great anticipation for this. I want to say he walked into the studio, but I think he was poured into the studio. As soon as I saw him, I thought, *Fuck*, because we'd been trailing this for such a long time. He uttered those immortal lines, 'Knobbly, let's not do the interview, let's just play the music, eh?' Oh, great. That's all you want to hear as a presenter. I'm like, *What are you, nuts?* I remember my producer Jim looking at me and Dylan looking at the floor, not wanting to catch my eye.

I think we got away with it, and actually I've got a memory of coming home and him calling me, at about half-eleven or twelve ... sobered up a little bit, and he was like, 'I'm sorry, I was out of order.'

It's funny in a way really, because I can remember in the early eighties we would meet for a drink every now and then with Paolo and Simon. That was the little gang that would meet at the Barley Mow, just off Oxford Street . . . but then Paul would abstain. It's weird when you think about him. I mean, he's been playing in working men's clubs since he was fourteen, fifteen, so beer has always been around. Alcohol was always around. I can't talk for him, but I'm guessing that he'd have a drink or two to steady the nerves or maybe afterwards. And we all know that can get out of control. So, the excess and the work blended into each other. But not to the extent where it was all the time. Paul was a good one for going, 'Right, that's it,' and then he wouldn't drink for a few months or something, so he could switch it off.

To experience that level of success again in the nineties must mess with your head. Thankfully, he's come through that. He could be a little bit tetchy at that time. Listen, he still can. Again, that's one of the things that I love about him. He's still got sharp teeth.

Alan McGee: Me and Bobby went to that listening party . . . and I'd just come out of rehab. I was in their dressing room and Paul was there. I don't think Oasis knew how much I was into Weller. I came in, and I looked good. I had a Paul Smith Crombie on and he looked at me and I thought, *Fuck, this could go either way, man. I'm effectively a record company rep. He probably thinks I'm a cunt.* And Weller goes, 'All right, boss?' Amazing. I was like, 'All right!' . . . I was nice to him, but I could barely talk to him.

Pete Mason: He was gaining a new audience. His fanbase had grown up and people were telling their kids – 'This is the guy I listened to when I was a kid, you should get into some of his stuff.' It all really exploded.

Pat Gilbert: We talk about Britpop, Oasis and Blur, but there were other things happening, like, Weller's renaissance . . . All those people who had been influenced by the sixties were coming back, and oh my God, it was like the sun was shining every day. Every new record that everyone was putting out was brilliant and everyone looked really cool. They got rid of all that horrible grunge stuff with people with ripped jeans and goatee beards.

Lee Cogswell: *Stanley Road* was the first Paul Weller album that I heard. I was thirteen, had got a guitar and music started to mean something to me. I got into Paul Weller, and Ocean Colour Scene, and all that kind of scene. Those records were on repeat, and I was trying to work out how to play every one of the songs.

Steve Brookes: 'Time Passes' from *Stanley Road* always breaks my heart . . . I know Paul's not a sentimental person, but I think it was about the fracture of his marriage with Dee C. Lee . . . Paul and I had reconnected in the early nineties. I was approached by Barry Neal to do an interview for his *Boys About Town* fanzine . . . and then he said, 'Paolo Hewitt's now got wind of it and wants to know if he can film it for a documentary.' I had nothing to lose so I was in that *Highlights and Hang Ups* film. I think it's one of the best Weller films because John's on it as well, and there's some classic bits when he was talking about something and he said, 'Ah, that's crap. No, it's not *crap*. Yeah, it is crap.' It was just quintessentially John.

David Quantick: I know *Stanley Road* is considered to be a masterpiece, but I honestly think there's better ones. There was a perception that Paul Weller had got a bit above himself with The Style Council later on, which I think is wrong. If he'd been an indie artist doing weird, strange, sprawling concept albums, people would have loved it, but because he was working with black music and he was commercially successful, people dumped on him, which led to the bizarre situation that when Britpop came along, he was making, in my opinion, the worst records of his career, the most conservative ones. People were really happy because he sounded like the people he was influencing then, or at least he dressed like them. The Modfather and all that stuff.

John Harris: On Paul Weller's part the legwork had been done before Britpop. The first solo album came out in '92 and *Wild Wood* came out in '93. All of that was building and things were being put in place long before Britpop came along. It just so happened that generation of musicians were born in the late sixties and early seventies and so The Jam were a big thing for them. Paul was held in great reverence by those musicians. Noel Gallagher and Graham Coxon are good examples of this. Inevitably, they were going to strike up friendships and play with each other. *Stanley Road* is a very vivid part of the Britpop moment. I'm not sure that it's a Britpop record, but everybody was once again talking about The Beatles, the Who, Small Faces and punk rock to some degree.

Ted Kessler: I reviewed *Stanley Road* in *NME*, and I think I gave it a fair hearing, although it's not my favourite piece of Paul Weller work. I felt it was a bit complacent and cosy . . . I think I said, 'Old Fart Blues . . . He needs a kick up the arse'. I was trying to be encouraging, saying that Weller is always at his best when he's embracing new influences, and I just felt like he was embracing the cosy stuff.

I got a phone call from Paul's PR, Pippa, who said, 'I've got some bad news. Paul's not happy about the review.' She said, 'I've got to read you a message from him: "You tell that Ted Kessler, if he wants to give me a kick up the arse, he's welcome to get on a train to Woking and try."' I wasn't going to have a fight with Paul Weller. I know he can beat me up, but it's ridiculous . . . I was mortified. I really didn't want to fall out with

Paul Weller. That wasn't the point of this exercise, working for *NME*. It was the opposite. I wanted to meet him one day.

Danny Eccleston: I have friends among music journalists who were called by Paul Weller and asked to have a fight. In the nineties, that wasn't uncommon. He found it hard to understand why someone would write something about him that they would not have said to his face . . . A lot of music writing in the old-school weeklies was fairly on the edge back then – regularly tipping over into ridicule and abuse. That alienated Paul from the music press for quite a long time.

David Quantick: He did threaten to beat me up once . . . Just as I finally got to sleep, my phone rang and it was Paul Weller, and he said he wanted a word. 'That thing you wrote . . . You compared me to Duran Duran.' My mind is racing at this point. 'I'm nothing like Duran Duran.' And then I remembered that I'd done a funny thing in *Mojo*. A completely innocuous article about bands who changed their image, like The Beatles . . . Duran Duran were in it and that was just because they'd been New Romantics and had then gone a bit moody with Nile Rodgers, and of course, Paul Weller, because you can't deny that Paul Weller has changed his image . . . He then said that we should meet up and talk. I replied, 'All right, where?' and he said, 'Regent's Park.' This was the point where I realised what he meant was that he wanted to have a fight with me! It fizzled out, but I was a bit alarmed at the time.

Pippa Hall: Paul would say, 'Pippa, can you get them on the phone?' and I'd say, 'Do you think that's a good idea?' I would advise against it and Paul would say, 'I don't care.' I mean he's a grown man and can do what he wants. I've always said if you can't dine out on your story of Paul Weller wanting to beat you up then it's a missed opportunity!

Paul Weller: Some of them definitely deserved a fucking slap, man. I don't mind if you don't like my record. That's fair. I don't expect people to like my record. But just don't make it personal because then you take it to another level.

Brendan Lynch: The bullets just bounced off him. But he just carried on doing the same thing, artistically, which is to just be totally engrossed in music and be creative and write songs and get in the studio and not go and sit on a yacht for four weeks, you know what I mean?

Paul Weller: Because one record is successful, 'Let's do it again.' I'm not into that. I don't think it's destructive. I just think I'm not going to go down that road. I'm not going to get into this thing where you keep making the same fucking record over and over. I don't care about being the biggest artist on the planet and playing to millions of people in one show and all that crap. It doesn't interest me. Because also, when you get to those levels, your freedom gets curtailed a little bit as well. It's easier to fall into the trap of just replicating what you did before because it sold well last time, 'Let's do it again.' It's easy to lose that spirit of trying to do something different next time. Experiment a little bit. You get pushed into this little, tight sort of framework. So, I've always kicked against that, I suppose. And whatever people think I am in those sort of times, I'm not. And I'm not doing it for those reasons. Of course, it's nice if you sell records and all that, but especially now at my age, I couldn't give a fuck really. I just want to make what I want to make. And obviously I hope people like it, and it makes a difference to their lives possibly. Some tracks might do, and in a good way, positive way. But beyond that I'm not interested. None of the other trappings interest me. I've got a great lifestyle. I'm very, very lucky. I've always made good money, and I've lived how I wanted to live. And I haven't really got a boss, especially not any more. No one breathing down my neck about 'Can you do this? Can we . . .' I'm in a very fortunate position, and so I'm more than happy with what I've got with that, I don't wish for anything else. All I want is a bit more time to be able to keep doing what I'm doing.

Dylan Jones: Wanting success is deemed to be one of the pivotal motivators of being an entertainer. When you shun that, or when you publicly decry it or say you're not interested in this level of fame in the way that George Michael or Paul McCartney did for a while . . . it's not done in a kind of mean-spirited way, it's done in a very particular way. I think you ultimately have to admire Paul for that. In fact, I don't even think you have to admire it, you just have to accept it.

When Paul became a solo artist and had to get back on the road to make money to re-establish himself, he got back to a level of fame that he probably hadn't achieved since the early eighties. I think a lot of cynics would say, 'Well, you should be happy with that,' but after you've experienced extraordinary fame, I think some people have a huge issue with it. Take Mark Knopfler, he could be responsible for probably the biggest touring band in the world if he only reformed Dire Straits, but he has no interest in doing that. And you know what? Why should he?

I think it calls into question critical acclaim and popularity and I think that one of the things that Paul certainly has is a very good radar, not just for external bullshit, but also to temper his inclination to wander off in particular directions or pursue particular directions. He's a very harsh critic of his own work and his own motivations.

10 July 1995 – 'You Do Something to Me' (no. 9)

Brendan Lynch: To be completely honest, 'You Do Something to Me' was a song that wasn't top of the list. At one point we weren't even sure if it was going to be on the album, and Carleen Anderson was going to do her version for her LP. It was earmarked for Carleen, but her manager didn't like it. That's how I remember it. Paul did a few more demos and it started to come together.

Paul Weller: I was trying to get a few different singers to do it. When I first wrote it, I thought maybe Joe Cocker. I don't know why I thought Joe Cocker, but I either didn't get it to him or he never got back. Carleen was one who was going to do it. I put it out to a few people. Didn't happen. And then I grew to love it after a while. When I first wrote it, I thought it's a really good song but is it a bit middle of the road? Am I stepping into that MOR territory with this tune? But luckily for me, or luckily that Brendan or whoever it may be, said, 'That's fucking great. It's got to be on the record.' Once we cut it and finished it, I thought *oh yeah, that's on the record definitely.*

Yolanda Charles: 'You Do Something to Me' is such a beautiful song. I can't take any credit for it. Paul demoed most of the bass part so there was a guide bass on the track, and I just played the bass the way I play. I made it my own, but he wrote the part. I probably did the ghost in the accompanying melody. We were in the Manor, which was always nice, because you're together, you get a chance to play, hang, eat, joke, socialise, walk if you want, or just be quiet and have a room to disappear.

Paul didn't work us too hard. The atmosphere was as usual – sometimes intense, other times more relaxed, 'Hey, man, just take a chill pill. Go and do some meditating or something' We were very efficient and got what we needed to get done, done.

Joe Connor: Paul lives very much in the now and does whatever he wants to do. He can't write that music without having a real mainline into human emotion. All the great musical storytellers like Joni Mitchell, Bruce Springsteen, John Lennon, Paul Weller, all have this mainline into human emotion and what it means or feels like to be a human and have experiences. He can take super complex emotions and deliver it in a single line. Take 'You Do Something to Me' – he's summed up the whole human experience of love in one line.

Max Beesley: Paul wasn't sure about that track at one point. He was like, 'I don't know' . . . We've had a chat about it recently and he said, 'It's amazing that it comes around and becomes so many people's favourite tune.'

Carleen Anderson: That one is like tops for me. It's a thing that I can't relate to as a story, but to hear Weller tell that story . . . as my brother, my experience with him was him being kind, but that's a whole different kind of thing to being that kind of sensitive. That song is a completely different thing for Paul.

Pete Mason: I remember 'A Year Late', the B-side from 'You Do Something to Me', and saying to Paul that I think it's the closest anyone's come to Nick Drake – that really iconic folky sound . . . the lyrics are just beautiful. I don't know what it's about really; I'd love to find out that. I remember him telling me that Helen, the keyboard player, had arranged the strings for that.

Sarah Jane Morris: Paul and I had kept in touch, and I was in awe of him – not just a great songwriter but an incredible singer with such a unique voice. A couple of years after the Red Wedge tour, I was pregnant with my son, and wanted to start to collect some good songs for my solo career . . . I asked Paul if he could write me a song, and he sent me this beautiful demo of him singing and playing guitar. At that point, it was called 'Leaves Around the Door'.

What is interesting is when we were on that Red Wedge tour, I can remember being with Richard and sitting behind Paul and Dee C. Lee, and, I have no idea whether their relationship was already happening before this tour, we witnessed a kiss and we remember thinking, *My God, they're together*, and being so excited about this, thinking that this romance started there, but I have no idea of its history. Then this new song was obviously about the end of their relationship. Paul released it later as the B-side of 'You Do Something to Me'. His version is called 'A Year Late'.

Sonja Phillips: The video shoot for 'You Do Something to Me' was funny. I had been a runner on 'Changingman' . . . At the time, I was starting to direct and showed Paul my work – beautiful fisheye lenses, fields and sunflowers. He likely thought, *Looks nice, and she'll be cheap because she hasn't done anything before.*

Two months later, he called, 'Ah, yeah, it's Paul, do you reckon you could do that video? I've got 500 quid.' And I was like, 'Not sure if I can do it for 500 quid, but let me introduce you to my production company.' We came to an arrangement, and he turned up with three boxes of Beatles VHS tapes, saying 'This is everything that The Beatles has ever shot. Watch every single one, follow it. Look at all the fisheye lens, look at all the way it's shot. That's what I want' . . . He'd collected every single performance, taped off the TV – that is someone that really is a massive fan of them. So I spent two days watching every single Beatles video, film, everything that they'd done, and then I got an idea.

Simon Halfon: You'd have to get up pretty early in the morning to catch Paul out on The Beatles, to ask him any sort of Beatle question that he wouldn't have an answer to or know the reference point or whatever it is. He's a dyed-in-the-wool Beatles nut, definitely.

Sonja Phillips: I wrote a treatment that Paul liked. I wanted the video to feel really intimate, smiley and happy, which is just not really what Paul does. We'd just walk around Woking and Stanley Road, and we created a beautiful day for the four of them. Made it feel really naturalistic, and everyone was happy and I think it shows in the video, but we really wanted to feel Beatlesy and real and homemade and authentic. He even went topless at one point, didn't he? I think any opportunity. The first time I ever met him, when I was a runner, I was a hip-hop girl . . . I didn't really know The Jam at that point. I was about twenty-one and I was like, 'Who's the bloke with this bloody top off wandering around posing?' They were like, 'Oh, that's Paul Weller,' and I'm like, 'Who?'

Paul has a blokey persona. I remember seeing his dad, John, later and he went, 'You're that bird that done the video,' and I'm like, 'Yes, that's right, John. I'm the director of the video.' Paul's quite like that as well. But actually, when you look at his songs and the way he writes, he's got this beautiful, poetic heart and soul. You probably have to peel through a few more layers than most people have to get that 'You Do Something to Me' side of Paul. He's really hard and really soft at the same time. He's a very complex character, but from what I remember he knows what he wants, and he really pushes to get there and he won't take any crap from anyone – he's brilliant.

18 September 1995 – 'Broken Stones' (no. 20)

Sonja Phillips: Paul wanted the 'Broken Stones' video to be quite literal, so it had to feature a stony beach. The first time was a disaster. Five days before Reading, we drove all the way to get to this stoney beach, but Paul, Steve Cradock, all of those guys, they were in no state to work after a gig the night before . . . No one could even really stand up.

Then they decided they were going to take all the instruments down to the beach, so all the roadies had got to the back of the van. This was five in the morning. Kenny Wheeler was saying, 'I'm not doing it. We've got five days until Reading. The instruments will be full of salt. They won't work . . .' and drunk Paul, Paolo and James Brown, who used to run *Loaded*, was in the van going, 'Don't worry, it'll be fine.' Kenny's like, 'It's not going to be fine' and he just started walking down the street and Paul's like, 'Don't worry, we'll do it another day.' And I'm like, 'This is going to cost you money.' 'How much money?' 'It's going to cost you five grand.' 'Well no, we'll do it now.' And then Kenny kept walking, so eventually they decided they weren't going to do it, and Kenny was worth more than five grand . . .

[Years later] I was going to LA and I was at Gatwick Airport. I saw Paul walking up the stairs and, 'Oh my God. Paul . . . Where are you off to?' and he's like, 'Oh, easyJet have some really cheap deals to Egypt.' I just walked away going, 'Oh my God, you haven't changed. I love it. You love a bargain. Paul . . .'

Conor O'Brien: One of my favourite memories of my musical development is trying to learn 'Broken Stones' when I was twelve or thirteen and then writing my own version. Paul had a huge impact on me. *Stanley Road* came out and it was one of those albums that just appeared as I was learning my fourth guitar chord. I was instantly sucked into it.

Robert Howard: I couldn't keep up with Paul to be honest, when he was on it. But I had a good go, you know! . . . It got out of hand sometimes, because at the Manor there was a couple of times when we were worse for wear and it got a bit edgy . . . both our fathers were boxers, I think it got a bit heated and we were face to face, going to fight and all that, and I remember Marco was there, little Marco, and he stood between us with a poker from the fireplace saying, 'Don't make me use this!' And of course it was ridiculous and the next morning it was all over. Kisses and cuddles . . .

I was immature; there was part of me that was a little bit competitive as well, I think, when I think back to it. And in the end, I felt like I had to move away a little bit . . . it's like, *Can I grow in the shade of this great big tree?* I was getting sort of tagged a little bit as a kind of Weller acolyte, which is fine, but I needed to go and find myself a bit more.

1995–96 – *Stanley Road* tour

Damon Minchella: I joined Paul's band for the *Stanley Road* Tour. 1995. I was actually twenty-five or twenty-six, but I looked about eleven. We were very young. Yolanda had finished the tour and Paul had come up to our studio to do some guitar on 'The Circle'. It was a Friday, and he said, 'What are you doing Monday?' I said, 'I don't know, something with you, probably?' He said, 'Come down to the studios, you're going to audition for the band.' He gave me a setlist with seventy-two songs on it. I didn't go to bed for forty-eight hours . . . When I got there on the Monday he said, 'Which ten did you learn?' I said, 'What do you mean? I learned all seventy-two,' and he was like, 'Fuck me, that's amazing. Can you play them, though?' and being cocky, I said, 'Yeah, just pick one.' I played through it and he's like, 'All right, you're in the band.'

Simon Fowler: We were all chuffed when Damon and Steve were in his band. Paul always used to imagine that I had an issue, but we were flattered. Also, we thought it couldn't do anything but good for us. Some of that magic was falling on our shoulders as well. It wasn't just dandruff!

Damon Minchella: We rehearsed for three weeks and then we did the whole *Stanley Road* tour, which lasted about a year. We were then fitting Ocean Colour Scene's gigs in and around it because *Moseley Shoals* had just gone massive. Me and Steve then didn't play with Paul from '96 to some point in '97 because we just couldn't fit it in. Much to Paul's chagrin, we'd be headlining festivals and he'd be second on the bill. In the end, we said, 'Let's get our agents together so whenever you want to book some shows, your agent speaks to ours, and we'll do likewise. We'll fit around it.' He was like, 'It will never fucking work.' Within a year, that's what we were doing, because it had to work. The chemistry between me, Steve, Whitey and Weller was the same as the chemistry between me, Steve, Oscar and Simon in Ocean Colour Scene. That level of trust where we could just go on stage or in the studio, and be like, *This is working. We don't need to discuss it. Let's just get on with it.*

Helen Turner: The longer the band was together, the quicker we actually learned things. You get that osmosis thing going on. We did learn a lot very quickly. My time in the band then came to an end in early 1996. Paul just wanted to slim the band down, I suppose. Do more himself, possibly, and see how it went on. He's not a bad keys player himself.

4 December 1995 – The Smokin Mojo Filters, 'Come Together' (no. 19)

Andy Macdonald: A really imaginative marketing guy that worked for us, a scouser called Tony Crean, he came up with the War Child connection and had the idea for putting *The Help Album* together. He's a maverick genius.

Pippa Hall: The *Help* album kicked in . . . I will never forget that day I spent in Abbey Road Studio 2. We had to go in on a Monday morning, get it all recorded and get it in the shops by Saturday. Paul's version of 'Come Together' was the big song because *Stanley Road* had been such a massive success.

Brendan Lynch: That was a mad day. So many people there. We mixed the track at the end of the day and it was like a cheese and wine party with so many people in the control room I could hardly hear them through the speakers.

Pippa Hall: I picked up a ringing phone and it was Paul McCartney, 'Is Paul there?' I was thinking, *Oh my God!*, and I had to run down the hall going 'Paul, Paul – Paul McCartney's on the phone.' Both of us were like giddy teenagers. Him even more than me. You knew that kind of environment was never going to happen again. That was a moment in time that I will never forget!

Brendan Lynch: We didn't know McCartney was turning up. Some gear turned up, and the roadie said, 'I've got Paul's gear for you,' and I said, 'Paul's gear is already here.' It was Paul McCartney's. So, the roadie brought it all in and then Macca turned up himself and we were in Studio 2, which is The Beatles studio, so he's back at Abbey Road. He went over to this window at the side of the control room, pulled a screen down that nobody knew was there and said, 'Ringo got caught behind that one day. He couldn't get out.' Then he said to me, 'What you want me to do?' We'd already put down the track, because Paul wanted it down before Macca came along and so the bass was already done. I said, 'Why don't you play a bit of Wurlitzer?' He goes, 'All right.' We went downstairs and he had a beautiful Wurlitzer. I'd never seen one like it. He said, 'Yeah, when the band split up, we all had choices about what instruments we could take, so I took that one.'

Pippa Hall: Lawrence Watson was taking photographs of that day. There's a brilliant picture of Paul Weller stood next to Paul McCartney, who is leaning over my head to shake hands with Noel, who was sat next to some of the Ocean Colour Scene boys. I'm going, *This is never going to happen again . . .*

Johnny Depp and Kate Moss had arrived. Johnny was very excited because he can play the guitar. I'll always remember the dulcet tones of Kate Moss going 'Johnny, Johnny, Johnny!' I was thinking, *Leave him alone love, he just wants to play with his new friends.*

Danny Eccleston: It's a great version of 'Come Together', for a great cause. It was one of those real moments in British pop music . . . because The Beatles had been written out of the picture – the eighties weren't kind to them . . . They were too tarred with the brush of being your mum's favourite pop group. But that didn't mean anything to Paul Weller or Noel Gallagher . . . The whole Beatles revival was at least partly to do with what Noel Gallagher and Paul Weller were doing in the nineties.

16 December 1995 – *Jack Dee's Saturday Night*

Jack Dee: The first time I met Paul, he did my Saturday night TV show at a theatre in Wimbledon. Paul played 'Stanley Road' on the piano, looking so cool. I mean, I wish I was as cool as Paul Weller. I wish I'd been as slim as him and as talented. Frankly, I was very in awe of meeting him. He's quite shy. He's not an extrovert, which I should have expected, really. It doesn't necessarily mean that because someone gets on stage, he is going to be a great extrovert. I had a beer with him, in his dressing room afterwards, just chatting. You do pinch yourself because this is someone that I've really admired for a long time.

February 1996 – *Later Presents . . . Paul Weller*

Mark Cooper: Such a great moment for Paul, and for us as a production team ... Paul was in his prime with his great band and for that special he had Carleen Anderson and her cousin Jhelisa, on backing vocals. It had a wonderful soulful, gospel energy, harking back to the backing singers on Joe Cocker's *Mad Dogs & Englishmen* in the early seventies or the Stones – that lovely call-and-response feel. Jools and his band were involved, with Rico Rodriguez adding trombone on 'Broken Stones'.

We did three specials with him over the years and that first one has that *Stanley Road* energy that was extraordinary. It balanced intimate acoustic moments, like 'Wild Wood', with powerful performances on songs like 'The Changingman'. The band are really strutting. If 'Sunflower' in '93 marked his comeback, this was him reaching the heights of The Jam at their peak. Paul had found out who he is.

16 March 1996 – Tyson v. Bruno

Simon Halfon: By 1996, I felt that I'd run my course with Los Angeles. I had a really good time, but London felt like it was swinging again, and I wanted to come back. Before I came home, we had a fun trip to Vegas: myself, Paul, Kenny Wheeler and John Weller. I'd been working with Paul for thirteen years at this point and he knew I was a trusted friend. They didn't want to fly, so we got this stretch limo for the six-plus hour drive . . . At the time, I had just put together *Fire and Skill*, a Jam tribute album . . . the first people that I asked to do the track was the Beastie Boys. They were the only band that turned around and said, 'Yeah, great, we'll do it,' without saying, 'What's the deal? How much will we get?' They did a version of 'Start!' I picked it up two weeks later, just before this trip. We played the cassette endlessly in the limo. He absolutely loved it.

We stayed at the MGM Grand, which was inundated with Brits to see the Bruno v. Tyson fight. The crowd was deafening: 'Bruno! Bruno!' Although he only lasted about twenty-three seconds. It was a great trip.

A week later, back to London, his nibs turned up at my flat with a gift – his beautiful sunburst Rickenbacker in its flight case. It's taken pride of place in this room ever since. Not that I can play a note on it, but Rickenbackers have always enthralled me, since seeing The Beatles as a kid. Having one of Paul's played Rickenbackers was a lovely welcome-home gift.

1996 – Robert Wyatt / Gallery Studio

Jamie Johnson: I'd started working at Gallery Studio in Chertsey, owned by Phil Manzanera, the guitarist with Roxy Music . . . Just after *Stanley Road,* Paul Weller came down to try the studio for a few days, just doing some demos. He said it reminded him of the Manor in Oxfordshire, which he loved, but it had just closed down. A few months after that we started recording *Shleep* with Robert Wyatt. We told him that Paul had been in, and I think he'd always been a little bit of a fan, so he wrote a little note and asked us to give it to Paul when he next came in . . . The original idea was for one song, but [Paul] heard all the demos and ended up playing on lots. Robert even did a version of The Style Council's 'The Whole Point of No Return' – an amazing, completely different version. Charles and I provided the background 'oohs'!

Charles Rees: That's when Paul really taught me something important: if you think you're going a little too far on something, you might be wrong. You might need to go huge and go a hell of a lot further on it. Louder. More of it. Cut it. Just don't be afraid. We did a session with Robert Wyatt, and I ran out of fader room. I needed to turn it up, and Paul said, 'No, just make it louder.' I was thinking, *What? This is just daft* . . . but then it clicked. *Oh my God, it's amazing. I see exactly what he wants*. It was meant to sound harsh. Ever since then, when I think I've known how to do something, there's always that little question mark where maybe we could do this better, or just make more of a point. I've worked with some other people and they're reluctant to do that. They always mix within the boundary.

May 1996 – Dylan Weller born (third child, first with Lucy Halperin)

2 August 1996 – *The White Room*

John Reed: Paul was on *The White Room* again in 1996. They filmed at Ealing studios, on the same road as the *Record Collector* offices. *Heavy Soul* wasn't out yet, but I heard that Paul was on, and although we were meant to be on the guestlist, we weren't. We climbed through a toilet window. Like you do. My partner in crime, Pat Gilbert, said, 'If you meet Weller later on, don't leave me behind . . .'

I'd had a few to drink, and after the show I wandered through this maze, up the stairwell, searching for his dressing room, passing Suede's which was full of alcohol. Piles of bottles still left. Eventually, somebody directed me to an annex behind the main block, and as often happened, he spotted me before I spotted him. 'Hello, John. How's it going? All right . . . Ah, journalists – they never bring the beers in.' I went, 'Wait there,' and trotted off back up the stairs to get two crates of beers from the dressing room.

We had a lovely moment, sitting opposite each other on these work surfaces in the kitchen. He then said, 'You're a good writer, I'm a good musician. We're both doing what we're doing.' I thought, *I'll take that, Mister Weller*.

Then we got on their big coach, and, like an idiot, I said, 'Well, I only live around the corner. Why don't we go back? We can have a listen to some music' . . . Paul was with Samantha at the time – they came inside with two or three of Ocean Colour Scene . . . I only lived in a two-bedroom flat, and my girlfriend was asleep in the bedroom. We were having the walls decorated and it was all a bit of a mess. We played records till about 4 a.m., including the Graham Bond Organisation.

A proof of my Paul Weller book was on the table. I remember Steve or Simon reading bits aloud. Paul didn't support the book outright but didn't have a problem with it . . . I did quite well in terms of royalty payments . . . he was somehow annoyed about that . . .

Fast forward a couple of years and I was running Sequel, a little label at Castle Communications. One day Vicky, the receptionist, said, 'Paul's on the phone.' I didn't click who it was so said, 'Paul who?' and he went, 'Paul Weller, ya cunt, the bloke you wrote a book about.'

5 August 1996 – 'Peacock Suit' (no. 5)

Ric Blaxill: When I took over *Top of the Pops*, I was flexible about miming or singing live. I'm cool either way. For pop bands with great choreography, it's better to focus on performance than struggle to sing while dancing – it's a TV show, not a gig. Then I read an interview when Paul said he'd never do *Top of the Pops* because you couldn't play live. I didn't think he'd even consider doing it. I got in contact with his management immediately and said, 'If that's the only issue, he's welcome with open arms and I'll make it happen live. He can do two songs, a new single and something from his back catalogue. They asked if I was being serious because no one had played live on *Top of the Pops* for about fifty years. Yeah, completely serious.

Brendan Lynch: We played 'Peacock Suit' and 'Changingman'. That was a bit of a special one.

Daniel Rachel: I asked Paul about 'Peacock Suit' when I wrote *Isle of Noises*. He explained the line, 'I'm Narcissus in a puddle', as 'a combination of Greek mythology and classic ideas put on to a high street'. Wow! That's so Paul, isn't it? A clever idea . . . I mean, Paul's read, hasn't he? He goes and looks at art and he understands art, enjoys art, gets inspiration from it, maybe in the same way as somebody like Martin Scorsese does, but he can always filter his ideas into an accessible 'street' way.

Ric Blaxill: No one had done two songs on *Top of the Pops* back-to-back either. That led on to Prince and Ramones doing that later on. It was such a buzz having Paul Weller on *Top of the Pops* playing live. A real moment for the audience.

17–18 August 1996 – V Festival

Richard Branson: It was incredible. The whole festival was just so nerve-wracking and exciting, as it was our first ever festival. We didn't know exactly what we were doing but we said screw it, let's do it, and it turned into a brilliant festival that brought people a lot of joy. It was wonderful when Noel Gallagher got up on stage with Paul. We witnessed something wonderful that night.

Tim Burgess: I remember playing V Festival in 1996. The first one. We were doing that without Rob [Collins], our keyboard player, who had died. It was only the second gig that we did after Knebworth. Paul was the first person that I saw when we walked backstage, and he came up and gave me a big brother hug . . . It felt like he was watching out for us at that time – putting an arm around the band. We then did a benefit at the Brixton Academy – he came along and played. I think Noel joined him as well, and the Manics. That was quite a decent evening. I went out on the piss with him, but I can't remember a fucking thing. That's the headline. The small print is, it was me, Weller, Mani, James Dean Bradfield. It was 1996. Everyone was on it. Paul came on and played 'Can't Get Out of Bed' and 'Sproston Green' with us. I don't think any of us knew what key we were supposed to be in. So, we're playing songs in various keys, no one knowing exactly what to do, but smiling all the way through it.

August 1996 – Sale of Go! Discs

Paul Weller: Go! Discs were brilliant. They were just like a breath of fresh air, man. A great little team with a real family vibe there. They were brilliant and I loved working with all of them. It was so sad when it all went. I was really disappointed. Not in Andy. I was just disappointed when it all fell apart, when they were taken back over by PolyGram. That was really sad. It was like we just felt comfortable and have had success with *Wild Wood* and *Stanley Road* and then it was all just kind of gone again.

Andy Macdonald: The sale of Go! Discs to PolyGram really wasn't something that I wanted to happen. Not least because it was working out brilliantly. It was a lot of fun and we were selling lots of records. The roster was fantastic. But you learn things as you go along. I had initially done eleven months through Rough Trade and Pinnacle as a completely independent label. We then did a deal with Chrysalis that lasted for three years. They were great, they helped us build up. And then did a deal with PolyGram – I had cut the deal with them after four years of doing it – and it's a little bit more serious. There's more money on the table for us to go and make more records.

We knew a little bit more about what we were doing then, I guess. It was a strange contrast in the sense that we kept fifty-one percent, sold them a minority share. And after five years, after seven years, after nine years, then you'd sit round a table. And I was always like, 'No, no, we want to carry on, but we

(above & right) Confessions of a Pop Group, Shepperton Studios, Surrey, 1988. Mick and Paul with a heavily pregnant Dee.
(Lawrence Watson)

(below) Paul Weller Movement, Brixton Academy, 20 April 1991.
(Justin Thomas/IconicPix)

(top, above) The Manor, early/mid '90s. *(Brendan Lynch Archive)*

(left) The Manor, Spring 1993, *Wild Wood* sessions. *(Lawrence Watson)*

Paul, John and Ann Weller.
(Lawrence Watson)

Kenny Wheeler and John Weller. The infamous card school continues … Guildford Civic Hall, 12 March 1994.
(Lawrence Watson)

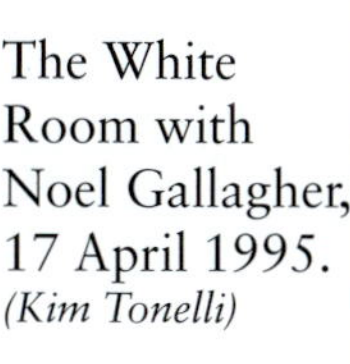

The White Room with Noel Gallagher, 17 April 1995.
(Kim Tonelli)

(above) War Child recording for 'Help' at Abbey Road Studios on 4 September 1995, including Paul McCartney, Noel Gallagher and Paul. *(Lawrence Watson)*

(left) Brendan Lynch, Dave Liddle, Helen Turner and Paul, mid '90s. *(Lawrence Watson)*

(below) Eurockéennes de Belfort Festival, July 1995. *(Kim Tonelli)*

Photoshoot for *Mojo Collections*, Summer 2001. *(Lawrence Watson)*

(above) The 100 Club, 20 May 2014, *More Modern Classics* launch gig. *(Derek D'Souza)*

(right) Brit Awards, Outstanding Contribution to Music, 14 February 2006. *(Dave Hogan/Getty Images)*

Backstage at Danforth Music Hall in Toronto, 10 October 2017. *(Andy Crofts)*

Breakfast on the way to Chicago, 12 October 2017 (*A Kind Revolution* US tour). Tom Van Heel, Paul, Kenny, Bill Wheeler and Mark Carr. *(Andy Crofts)*

Rehearsal for the *Other Aspects*, Royal Festival Hall concerts, October 2018. Paul with arranger and conductor, Hannah Peel, Phil Veacock (on sax) and the London Metropolitan Orchestra. *(Andy Crofts)*

(above & left) Black Barn Studio, Ripley, 22 February 2019. *(Dean Chalkley, Camera Press London)*

(below) Paul at the piano in Black Barn, 16 March 2022. *(Derek D'Souza)*

(right) Author and podcaster, Dan Jennings, gatecrashing Paul's photoshoot for *Find El Dorado*, March 2025. *(Dean Chalkley, Camera Press London)*

(below) Paul, Black Barn Studio garden, Ripley, March 2025. *(Dean Chalkley, Camera Press London)*

want to own it. We want to get the other shares back.' So the mechanism that was in place was that we had the final right to outbid Universal, as it became, by paying an extra fifteen percent on top, but critically, they could value the company. So, the reason that we lost control of the company was that they put a very high valuation on it. I was running around speaking to various people, bearded billionaires who've set up rocket ships and stuff. Everything to try and find backing in this new venture, but we couldn't quite get anyone to back us that far.

In the end, Universal, as it became, priced us out of our own label, which was just awful.

Pippa Hall: It was a sad time . . . Go! Discs was a cool little label and if you were PolyGram you would want to have a lot of these people on your roster. You keep the ones that make money. It felt like they binned the ones that didn't and that's not how a good record company builds up their roster, is it? Things take a bit of time.

Andy Macdonald: Heartbreaking. I'm not an easy crier, but I was in floods, man, for like the rest of that evening. I pretty much set up Independiente the following day. The best way to get round it, is just to keep doing it. Do something different, and off you go. But I was really keen to keep working with Paul, so he did a deal where I sort of A&R'd because then he at least had the same freedom and team around him. It wasn't the case of switching over so someone new could come and go, *Right, you've got to do dance music now, mate!*

Paul Weller: Andy's a great fella. He's just a beautiful guy and he got paid a lot of money when they bought him out, or whatever they did, took over Go! Discs. Bless him, man. He gave everyone considerable money from that as well. Me included. He shared it out to all the staff. But it was a great team, and I really missed that family thing, and that connection we all had. I loved that. It's very rare to find that, and you can never plan for those things. They just happen at that moment. That was really sad when that all went. And all of a sudden, I was put on Island. Just moved over to this other lot, who I had no connection with, didn't really like. The MD was a complete tosser as well. And I didn't like any of them. And so, it's like, *Fucking hell. We've got to start again, finding a home.*

31 December 1996 into 1 January 1997 – *Hootenanny*

Mark Cooper: Paul came on *Hootenanny* at the end of '96. I think he was a bit dubious about coming on, but he did Billy Preston's 'Will It Go Round in Circles'. The energy coming off Paul and the Rhythm and Blues Orchestra was extraordinary. He really found that primal energy that he's always had, that drove The Jam when I first saw them at the Whisky and it felt like that energy is back in a different form and Jools's orchestra really captured that, and matched it, even though Paul was on with some people he was probably quite unsure about musically and culturally. Paul and Mick Hucknall singing together! Yeah, exactly! I'm very proud of that. Both great singers and, of course, both socialists, but in many other ways, you'd say, not necessarily kindred spirits.

23 June 1997 – *Heavy Soul* (no. 2)

Paul Weller: It started off well and then I ran out of ideas towards the end of it. So that was a real struggle. I finished them in the end, but there's a few things on there that are just like pfff . . .

'Peacock', I loved. 'Up in Suzes' Room', great. 'I Should Have Been There to Inspire You'. 'Mermaids', that's a good tune. 'Science', that's great man. Well, those ones are good, and the rest are shit. I don't know what's up with the rest of it. My memories of it were that I was too involved in getting fucked up. Whether it be coke, definitely drink, always drink. A lot of coke involved. None of which is conducive to making good music, I don't think. So, it was a bit of a fucking laborious record to make and not only because I was always off my head. I don't think it was just that. But maybe we'd all just had enough. We'd had those three solo albums leading up to it, which each one I thought got better and better. We were all pretty much the same team, working on the records prior to that. Maybe we'd all just burnt out. I could have made it with someone else. Maybe it was one of those ones. You get into a pattern after a while. You can't help it. It's just human nature.

Marc Marot: The first thing to say is that I didn't sign Paul to Island Records. It was really an inheritance when Go! Discs closed. Various talents were effectively given to me from the roster, with Paul being one of them, which of course, I was very happy about . . .

I got on with Paul and John Weller really well. A lot of people said that John was a tough guy and very difficult to work with but, in fact, I had an immediate bond with both of them. It was a productive relationship.

Any artist with credibility should have been proud to be on Island, when you look at our history, but also if you look at our current history at that time . . . Polly Harvey, Pulp, Nine Inch Nails, NWA and all the things that we did . . . So I would have felt that he would be quite comfortable in that roster. It's not like he was joining the 'Barbie Girl' roster.

Brendan Lynch: The Manor had closed down, so we had to find somewhere else. We tried Ridge Farm, and Wool Hall was really nice. Wasn't quite the same as the Manor, but it was good.

Steve Cradock: I went down there and smoked a spliff with Richard Branson. He was fucking great, man. I think he was trying to sign Paul. He was trying to poach him.

Charles Rees: Paul was using Van Morrison's studio in Beckington. The Wool Hall. He did a lot of *Heavy Soul* there, but he needed somewhere else and came to Gallery.

Jamie Johnson: In that first stint for *Heavy Soul*, everyone was in the room together, which is like a Motown thing, I guess, or goes back to the beginning of recording. Things like Abbey Road. Paul wanted to capture all the guitars in one take, since they were in the same room. You're really going for the drums and the bass and then maybe you overdub guitars, but actually we weren't separating stuff that much.

Brendan Lynch: We realised that we wanted to do that album live. Vocals, guitar, bass, drums. It was very important that the vocals were part of the live thing, and it wasn't just a backing band.

Jamie Johnson: Paul's singing and playing with screens set up so his vocals don't bleed into the drum mics too much. But everything is captured. On 'Mermaids', you can really hear that everything was there.

John Harris: *Heavy Soul* is much misunderstood. I think a lot of the people who were spoiling for a fight, who wanted to get him for *Stanley Road* being a big success, had their chance. That record did get unfairly criticised. He was in quite a sort of taut, angry mood then. You can hear that in tracks like 'Brushed', it's very ferocious. That's as much like The Jam as he'd sounded for years. 'Science' is a bit like that. That does sound like someone who's really wound up. In the lyrics, he's telling people what he's not. I mean, it's like a big fuck off, isn't it? – lines like 'I have no solutions' from 'Peacock Suit'.

John Reed: *Heavy Soul* was definitely an album that I laboured with at the time . . . This is true of a lot of artists, but Paul is someone who, if ninety-nine people say, 'Great track,' whatever, right; one person says, 'I don't like it,' he remembers that. When I was at *Record Collector*, Weller would be around in that orbit, and we'd chat. He asked me what I thought of 'Peacock Suit', and I made a comment that wasn't overtly positive . . . Fast forward months, maybe a year later, I bumped into him, and we were chatting, and he went 'You don't like "Peacock Suit", do you?'

Keith Cameron: I met Paul for an interview at some live session at MTV. He was trying to give up the booze . . . and this tells you a lot about their relationship . . . his dad was there, in the distance, dangling a bottle of red wine, and I said, 'How's that working out, the giving up the booze?' He said, 'It would be a lot easier if it wasn't for that cunt over there!'

Chris Catchpole: I think *Heavy Soul* has been written off as a kind of lost weekend, the cocaine and divorce record. It is angry and it is stormy. The title track is really good. Some of it is, by his own admission, off the ball a little bit, but the fiery moments on that record really do stand out. He said himself that his head was fucked up at that point and it really does come across.

Jamie Johnson: We did a new version of 'Everything Has a Price to Pay' for the film soundtrack to *Face* with Robert Carlyle. That '97 version came out as a B-side to 'Mermaids'. That was just Paul and Matt Deighton. They had started hanging out. Paul had seen the film's intro and was talking about how long the song had to be to fit this intro. They were sat opposite each other in the studio with a sound screen thing between them and did it in a few takes. I kept saying, 'Should we check that one against time?' He went, 'No, I think it's about right.' It was then synced up with the film and it finishes at the perfect point in the scene – the way he did it to time was unbelievable.

Matt Deighton: I'd just fallen out with the record label for a pretty good reason and was like, right, well, I won't be doing Mother Earth, I won't be doing solo stuff, I'm not going to be doing anything, and then I got a call from Paul going, 'Do you want to come join me at Wool Hall, we're recording in Somerset?' Then he said, 'I've got these shows to do.' It was perfect because I wasn't doing anything.

Pippa Hall: Go! Discs had been eaten up by the bigger PolyGram thing. I was losing my job. Jane Wilkes had worked at Go! Discs in A&R and then started doing press for Polydor. We decided to set up our own business – Monkey Business PR – Jane brought her bands with her, Cast, Monaco, which was Peter Hook's band, and Silver Sun. I spoke to Beautiful South, and managed to keep hold of them, and then we spoke to Paul. 'Look, come on, come on. We've done *Stanley Road* together. Come on, you know you need me. Let's do this' . . . He said, 'Yeah, come on, I'm going with you.' So that's how we started Monkey Business, with five really good bands and artists.

Marc Marot: I didn't know anything about *Heavy Soul* until it was delivered because Paul was already in the process of recording it by the time he joined us. I didn't feel the need to interfere with somebody as brilliant as him . . . I felt like he needed to feel comfortable, feel like he wasn't being watched, feel like there was nobody looking over his shoulder and he needed to just get on and do what he did. But also, the two records preceding *Heavy Soul* were so brilliant that there was no need to fuck with it.

Andy Macdonald: Somehow someone in our marketing department had missed the memo that the rules had been changed to only allow three postcards, because it's seen as being an extra 'freebie' inducement, which it isn't really . . . *Heavy Soul*, the best record of that week, came out and sold enough to go to number one, but there were maybe fifteen or twenty thousand sales disqualified, because there was one extra postcard attached to it. I can remember thinking, *Oh Christ! Fucking hell. How the hell did that happen?*

Marc Marot: And do you know what, this speaks volumes about Paul. He came into the office the following day, and just said, 'Don't worry about it. Eyes on the prize, let's keep pushing forward.' He let everyone off the hook, which is a proper grown-up way to behave, because it's not badly intentioned, it's just a really, I wouldn't say unforgivable, it's like a major error.

Paul Weller: We had five postcards instead of four or something. But I mean, it wasn't my idea to put postcards in every album anyway. What the fuck? Who needs a postcard? I wasn't upset by it. Not at all. I'd lost interest in a lot of it by that time.

Up until *Stanley Road*, we were still on Go! Discs and I loved being there. It was a real family and that all changed, when they were bought out. I then got shoved to fucking Island where I did a couple of records with them, or one record with them, and then it was with someone else. So, it had all changed for me. I think if it had been at Go! Discs and we had the same team, it might have been a different prospect, but who knows.

Marc Marot: It was the only mistake that I felt we made in all the years that I ran Island. But what a mistake to make . . . In the history of Paul, it's probably a very minor one, but it robbed him of a number one album, and I felt terrible guilt, I can't begin to tell you, but Paul and John Weller, who was a heavy soul [*laughs*], never punished us.

28 July 1997 – 'Brushed' (no. 14)

Brendan Lynch: 'Brushed' was a really good single. It felt more like a remix vibe. That was really a thing that I like doing. Messing about with the arrangement or changing the ending or getting a really good intro. You've got to have a great intro on a single. It was really lovely for Paul to give me a co-writing credit on that one. He would do that right from the first album.

Charles Rees: Paul must have known Beatles techniques. That must have influenced him somewhat ... Think about 'Tomorrow Never Knows' – they broke all the rules for that one and I think pop music came out of that. That's a studio tool.

28 Sept 1997 – 'Friday Street' (A *Heavy Soul* EP) (no. 21)

1997 – *Heavy Soul* tour

Matt Deighton: My first gig with Paul was in Wales ... We had very intense, amazing rehearsals. I doubt if they're any different now, where he'd do a gig, really, in a rehearsal room, there'd be no difference ... You're either playing it, which means full on, or we're having a cup of tea and a cigarette ...

People don't really appreciate how clever he is on the guitar. They know he's good but he's real clever, he'll come up with chords. There's one on 'As You Lean into the Light' . . . I'd never played it before. It wasn't really a chord. It was two strings held down on a really weird bit of the neck and I said, 'What chord is it?' He went, 'I haven't got a clue. I don't know. It's just there and then it goes there.' . . . No boundaries on it.

Steve Cradock: Damon and I had to step back as we just didn't have time to play in Paul's band and in Ocean Colour Scene. That sound was great with Matt Deighton, Yolanda had come back for a bit and then Ernie McKone came in.

Yolanda Charles: Going back to play in the Paul Weller band was interesting. I wasn't the same person I was at twenty-three. Paul and I had a couple of little clashes . . . One day, he said we'd had a shit gig and I protested about his accusation. I was tired of stuff like that. I was not putting up with it. He said, 'I'm paying you enough, you should be playing better,' and all that. I said, 'Well, I actually had a good gig. I think maybe you had a shit gig . . .' My God, the bus went silent! Everyone was like, *Gulp!*, waiting for some fireworks . . . It worked, because after that he spoke to me and said, 'I really respect the way you stood up to me on the bus.'

He was one of the few artists I worked with who was the boss that would actually phone me directly, 'All right, yeah, it's Paul . . .' A lot of artists I wouldn't even meet; in fact, one artist I met on stage at soundcheck . . . of the first gig! Paul was much more approachable. I liked the fact that I could actually speak my mind with him, but he was rare. Most of the time I was just a session 'Yes person'. Like everyone else.

Keith Cameron: I interviewed Paul before a gig at Aston Villa Leisure Centre . . . I got an insight into the kind of mania of some Weller fans, because there was all these people who followed him back to the hotel . . . it was a bit frightening for me. God knows what it would be like for him. He was going out and meeting them and chatting to them in the hotel lobby and everything. I remember sitting with Steve White saying, 'It blows my mind, that people are this devoted and obsessed.' And he said, 'Yeah, there's a bloke who just came up to me earlier today, pulled up his trousers and showed me his Weller tattoos. He had one on each calf . . . "What do you think of that then?" . . . "You know, it's like, it's your leg."'

Keiko Egawa: Paul went to Japan again in 1997, so did I. *Heavy Soul* tour. I met Paul again and John Weller was there, and he was telling me that he'd had a heart bypass . . . He didn't show me the scar, but he was saying, 'Oh gosh, I think I'm not doing a tour any more . . . I'm getting a bit old and I want to spend more time with my missus.'

10 November 1997 – Paris arrest

Yolanda Charles: Ah yes, Paris . . . I had stayed in London for a day longer, so I arrived straight at the venue for soundcheck from the train. It was like someone had died. I asked, 'What's going on?' and they said, 'Paul and Matt got arrested.' And I was just, 'Whoa, whoa! What? Why? What happened?' They said, 'Well, they got arrested for trashing the hotel.'

Matt Deighton: Oh blimey. Yeah, it's terrible really. I'm not proud of that . . . It was accidental. It was started at the bar a little bit and then we went upstairs, and we hadn't checked into the rooms and my bag swung round and knocked a picture off the hallway wall, completely by accident. Then Paul accidentally bashed something over as well and then the whole thing happened.

Kenny Wheeler had fallen asleep at the bar . . . And it was a bit, you know, let's see if anyone can stop us. I don't know. Not to excuse it, but we were laughing our heads off a lot in a drunken, merry, mad, anarchic way, but it ended up really bad . . .

That weekend France had passed a bill that if there were more than two or more people in a disturbance, it would be seen as a riot. Which explained why there were ten or twelve riot police down in the concierge bit . . . and we got put away for a bit . . . Thankfully, no one was hurt.

I'd heard so much about these things happening . . . I thought Paul had gone through it before, so I said, 'You've been in a cell before haven't ya?' He said, 'No.' My heart sank at that point . . . John had to come out. He wasn't supposed to come out for a couple of days, and he had some appointments he had to keep. He didn't want that to happen. I was surprised I wasn't sacked there and then.

Yolanda Charles: I was like, 'Are you serious? Is it like the 1970s?' . . . I got there when everyone was wondering whether this gig was going to happen. It might get cancelled because they hadn't been released and then, at the last minute, they appear . . . The door flings open, everyone goes 'Wahay!' Paul and Matt go 'Wheyyy! I'm free!' It was all like, '*Oh, well done. Oh, man, that's mental!*' Everybody gradually leaves to go and get ready for the gig. It was just me and a couple of the band, and Paul and Matt, and . . . then Paul comes up to me and gives me a big hug and said, 'Oh, Yo! It was terrible, man.' I was like 'You wimp!' Never mind about coming in cheering like he's escaped from Alcatraz. He wanted his mum! It was lovely that he did give me a cuddle, because it must have been a bit of a shitty experience.

Matt Deighton: After that room breakage stuff, we met Noel and Liam up in Scotland for T in the Park and they all went, 'Oh, hang on to your belongings. Here's Matt. Hold onto the chairs, here he is.' Not a good reputation.

Nicky Weller: I don't think Paul and I were bestest mates around the *Heavy Soul* time.

Ann Weller: Mickey Mouse would fall out with Paul.

Paul Fitzgibbon: I saw Max Beesley introduce Paul Weller at the Palladium. He introduced Weller onto the stage doing a Brucey spoof impression.

Max Beesley: My dad used to open his act with Bruce . . . I used to mimic Bruce on the tour bus and Weller used to laugh his arse off at it. Then John, Kenny or Paul came up with the idea, saying put the syrup on, get the moustache on, get the jacket, bring him on as Bruce. I mean, the balls I had to do that.

24 November 1997 – 'Mermaids' (no. 30)

April 1998 – Carleen Anderson, *Blessed Burden*

Carleen Anderson: During that period, I went on some full UK tours with Paul. It overlapped with us doing my album *Blessed Burden*, so I was able to open up the show with some of my tunes, and Paul would play on my show and then I would come out on his show.

Marco Nelson suggested to cover 'Maybe I'm Amazed' by Paul McCartney. I wasn't sure but then Paul piped in, 'Yeah, you should.' I'm very much a storyteller, and it's a song about a person who is loved, and they are amazed that they're loved, but they recognise that they're loved . . . I had no clue of what that was like. When we were in the studio, I'm recording, I've got my herbal liquorice tea and I'm nearly in tears, because I can't feel it . . . Paul could hear that I was near breaking point and said, 'What you drinking?' I was like, 'My tea, my herbal tea, my liquorice tea.' 'Have a little bit of this.' A little bit of this was a whole bottle of Captain Morgan. I'm telling you these guys were hardcore. Hardcore. We ain't in the night-time yet. He put a bit in there and my tea just evaporated and then I was gone . . . [sings] 'Maybe I'm amazed . . .' I was definitely gone!

1998 – Tour

Ernie McKone: Galliano had finished, and I got the call to play with Carleen Anderson . . . We had two tours supporting them. On the third tour, Yolanda was thinking of not doing it. I knew Paul, I had been watching his show every night for a couple of tours, so I guess from his point of view, it was an easy option to ask if I wanted to come and do his show . . .

I remember doing Victoria Park. That was a big gig on a very hot day. Noel opened up for us. It was at that point that I realised just how big Paul was and how besotted people were by him . . . I walked out, and as far as I could see, there were people.

Noel Gallagher: Paul would always do this fucking thing where he wouldn't say to you before the gig, 'Do you want to get up and do "Woodcutter's Son"?' In between the gig and the encore, when you're rat arsed, he'd then say, 'You getting up? . . . You fucking getting up or what?' . . . A huge gig. Of course he did the thing. 'Get up and do this tune.' He gave me one of his guitars and I got up, but I was so drunk I couldn't play. I just turned the volume right down and I was giving it the big 'un on stage and Weller's going, 'Go on, my son! Fucking yes, mate!' We're in this restroom afterwards and the sound man, Ange, said, 'Were you fucking playing there or what? ... I kept turning it up on the desk! ... There's nothing coming out of it!' I was too drunk – all I could do was dance! I couldn't even do that well.

There was a tight little firm. There was his band, Ocean Colour Scene, the Primals and us, and we all hung out together. We'd all go to each other's gigs and have a fucking great time and get up to all sorts of petty crimes. They were great days.

Aziz Ibrahim: In all honesty, I have never met or worked with an artist like him and I've had the privilege of being in The Stone Roses. I met Paul through Steve White, because I was in that band The Players, which was Mick Talbot, Steve White, Damon Minchella and myself ... Steve walked in with Paul Weller, who said, 'All right Aziz, nice to meet ya,' and then goes on to say, 'You wrote fucking "My Star", didn't ya?' ... That's how our relationship started, just based on him listening to music. Obviously, he was interested in what Ian Brown's output was going to be after the demise of the Roses and this was the first single. *Melody Maker* and *NME* hid most of my contribution. I've still got the magazines because they angered me ... They used to write things like Ian played everything, and he did this all by himself. I broke me back playing the bass, the drums, the guitars, writing the music ... and that's how the press treat ya. Whenever people ask me about Paul, I always say, he's the nicest, most intelligent, most musical person I have ever met. And a real friend. Somebody that you can trust, that has your back, and that stands up for you.

Steve Cradock: I went round to Paul's house when he was living in Send ... He just handed me one of his Jam guitars and said,

'Happy Birthday'. I was just like, 'What the fuck? Wow.' It was the one with XITS on it. I did use it live for a little bit with Ocean Colour Scene ... I'd be too nervous these days but, yeah, what a gift.

26 October 1998 – 'Brand New Start' (no. 16)

Brendan Lynch: I remember the first time that I heard 'Brand New Start'. Paul played the demo in the car. I loved that track, and it was another one where the whole thing was pretty much finished by Paul on his own. I had bought him this little cassette player that you could record songs on quite easily. Just demos. This is before iPhones and all that, and maybe you could do one overdub on it. He might have written it over Christmas and maybe recorded it at a studio that The Charlatans were working at. But my memory is very hazy on that.

15 December 1998 – *Modern Classics* (no. 7)

Paul Lester: I spent two or three days with Paul for an early *Uncut* magazine cover story – in London at the PR company and down at Black Barn Studios ... 13,000 words long, which was massive, and it needed lots of input from the man himself.

When I turned up, Weller was really urging Pippa to respond to Caroline Sullivan's very negative review in the *Guardian* of his concert at Victoria Park ... the fact that he cared enough and that he knew the name of the journalist suggests someone that really closely scrutinises things ... Someone that's not so critical will just go in and make the same record over and over again. And that's quite evidently not what Weller is about at all.

Pippa Hall: I always got on with Paul Lester but he could be quite a contentious chap. They always got on really well and I think that's why he got a lot of stuff from Paul that was a little bit more surprising, and Paul hadn't really talked about before. As I say, it was a difficult time for him.

Paul Lester: I did ask him whether he'd ever had an off-the-road moment and he talked about having a bit of a freak out when he was sixteen and dropped a tab of acid on the train. He never seemed to be one of those Ian Curtis types or a tortured soul, heavy soul, but he must have experienced some of that stuff. Our conversations were mostly about music, but to get a sense of where he was at musically, you want to delve a little bit into his personal life because that will impact on the things he's writing and what he has to say. The personal informs the musical.

I made a very unhealthy attempt to dig into the whole area of Weller's sexuality. That was embarrassing. He also bristled when I mentioned Gill Price, his girlfriend from The Jam days, and rightly so, because he probably thought, *Well, once we've started, where will it lead?* . . . he didn't like some of the lines of enquiry at the end. As the music journalist, you always worried that you haven't got enough material, so I suggested trawling through a set of photographs of him through the years and asking him to commentate on all the changing haircuts. He didn't go for that one at all!

March 2000 – Jesamine Weller born (fourth child, first with Samantha Stock)

10 April 2000 – *Heliocentric* (no. 2)

Marc Marot: When it came to Paul's next album, I'd left Island Records for my own reasons. As much as I would have loved to have stayed and supervised because that would have been an opportunity to get it right this time. I'd heard tracks by that stage. I knew he was in the right direction. I was quite confident.

Paul Weller: Painful. We kept switching studios, we went to different places, and I don't understand the technical side of this, but it was recorded on different formats as well. So, it just became difficult at the end to mix because it was on different formats, they had to transfer them and blah, blah, blah. I think, really, if I'm really honest, I'd lost fucking interest by that time. I should have just stopped for a bit. I think, on *Heavy Soul* and *Heliocentric*, I was looking to recapture that spirit we had at the Manor on *Stanley Road* and *Wild Wood*, and of course it's impossible. They're just things that happen, and there's a moment in time and that's it. It was impossible to recreate those moments. So, I think the time had gone for all that.

Jamie Johnson: Paul phoned up wanting to do some new demos to start this new album. That was in Jacobs in Farnham, not far away from Chertsey . . . Steve White on drums. Damon has come in on bass, and Steve Cradock is playing guitar – both from Ocean Colour Scene. They liked a laugh and a party as well! Paul said, 'Bring Charles as well.' Aziz Ibrahim came down and played guitar on some demos too.

Aziz Ibrahim: I mean, let's get things straight . . . I'm not his musician, I'm not his band, right? He knew that our relationship was different, and he made a conscious decision, because he let it slip. He was the guy that used to get drunk, and I didn't. So, I remember everything! We were at the studio and Paul was contemplating whether I was going to play with him or not. I could hear him going, 'Nah. No, it's not going to work.' Because we want to keep it a friendship . . . I respect that and I'm thankful that that's how we've kept it.

Chris Difford: Paul came down to my studio Heliocentric with his team to record for a month . . . Chaos, in a good way, [but] we said, look, you can't really record after ten at night because we need to get the kids to bed and all that stuff. But they didn't hear that. So quite frequently they'd be recording till three or four in the morning, which is absolutely fine, they booked the place out. We had some very funny times.

Damon Minchella: Paul actually set fire to Chris's bedroom.

Chris Difford: We live in a small village and the fire brigade came, but it was like four blokes who had been in bed who were being called to the fire. It was like *Trumpton*. They came flying down the drive in a fire engine just to find five stoned guys standing out in the field.

Steve Cradock: I was woken up by fire engine alarm sirens going off. Everyone was going, 'Get out of your rooms, the kitchen's on fire!' This big fat chef is sweating at whatever time in the morning, black smoke coming out of the kitchen, and he turns round to me and goes, 'I've really gone and fucked it up this time.' Fucking brilliant.

Charles Rees: Around that time is when Paul got Black Barn and asked if I would look after this place.

Roger Nowell: It used to be a commercial studio before Paul bought it. There's a lot of people recorded here, like the Manics and people like that. It's just a good vibe innit.

Paul Weller: I think it was built in the eighties. It was still old school enough to be a proper studio with a live room. As opposed to a lot of places now that are just for mixing and not necessarily for a band. There's so few of those studios left. A lot of them are closed down, especially the ones in London. So, it's just nice to have this live space. I think that surprises a lot of people, not me and my band, but other people who've come here to work. It's like, oh wow, this is how a studio can be, because they're used to those smaller places now.

Jamie Johnson: For that album, we had strings from Robert Kirby, Nick Drake's arranger. They recorded that in another place, maybe at Angel Studios, but he came in for the day. He was quite a character. He liked to party as well! He came in to hear the songs and just to hang out and then they must have recorded all those string arrangements afterwards.

Steve Cradock: That reminds me, on the first UK tour that I did with Paul, we were staying in Solihull, where I grew up . . . my mate Des got his Ford Zephyr out and we took Paul on a little pilgrimage to Nick Drake's burial place in Tanworth-in-Arden.

Dylan White: The singles on *Heliocentric* were more difficult, 'He's the Keeper' and 'Sweet Pea'. We struggled with Radio 1. It was getting trickier. They weren't such obvious bangers, shall we say.

Steve Cradock: 'Frightened' is an amazing tune. He played that to us, actually, the night I did the vocal with Liam of 'Carnation' . . . Liam got the vocal down, I thought Paul might turn up, but Liam didn't know, and he was shitting himself. 'What do you think that fucking Weller's going to think?' It was different to see Liam, in that kind of artistic state maybe. Paul came in, listened to our track and then he sat down and played us 'Frightened'. Just him on a Wurlitzer electric piano and me and Liam were sat down on the floor just listening to Paul and it was just like, *Fucking wow*.

Neil Jones: The image on the front is as cool as fuck ... You've got the amazing Robert Kirby strings on there. One of my favourite songs that Paul's ever written, just a work of art, is the song 'Frightened' . . . the way it's opening yourself up to everyone and saying I can really struggle sometimes, but I can find my way in the end. I love the beauty in that.

Simon Halfon: 'Frightened' should have been a single. I said that from the get-go. That's up there with 'You Do Something to Me' in the ballad department.

Pippa Hall: He used to laugh a little bit about what he was wearing on the cover of that record.

Julian Broad: The background to that picture was the studio wall at the Ragged School . . . Paul loved the band Free . . . He referenced an album, *Fire and Water*, which was shot very low on the ground. That was our starting point and inspiration.

My overarching vibe of Paul is that he's just kept his life really simple. He drives himself to his shoots, doesn't have a flash car. When we were doing *Heliocentric*, he had a camper van. If he wants to get his haircut, he'll go and get his haircut. It's not a drama. He won't get a stylist to go and do it . . . He's authentic.

Ted Kessler: I actually think he was trying to do the stuff he ended up doing a decade or so later, but I think his head, and I don't think the band, were quite good enough for it. You could tell that he was reaching for something different, to test himself around then. He was trying to get out of whatever he'd got stuck into in the Britpop era. The slightly more cosy thing. That's what I liked about *Heliocentric*. He was looking for something different.

Brendan Lynch: That was the final album that I produced with Paul. You make a record that you're happy with and you think, *Oh, I've got a formula now, let's go*. And then you try it on the next project and it doesn't work because there's so many factors that are involved in making that particular record, the one you liked. Things are always changing, people change, everything's changing all the time, so you got to move on. I did produce a track on one of his later albums, the double album, *22 Dreams*. We'd had twelve years. Life changes and different things. We didn't fall out or anything. I still contact him now and again. Nothing lasts forever.

2000 – *Heliocentric* tour

Christopher Holland: I remember there was one *Hootenanny* when Paul said, 'Nice playing and nice jacket, man.' I was so pleased that he complimented me on my jacket. It wasn't long after that I got a call from him for the *Heliocentric* tour … Working with Paul wasn't a retainer, but almost every day there seemed to be something happening, you'd be asked to be somewhere, Abbey Road or some radio thing or some TV thing. They just seemed to be like that for that year that I was playing with him.

Edgar Jones: Our paths didn't cross until I auditioned to play bass for him. I was in-between Johnny Marr and the Healers and St Etienne … Moving from Johnny to Paul felt like leaving *Coronation Street* to join *EastEnders* … You just go in and play and you hope that they're going to be nodding rather than shaking heads. There were some slight nods, so better than nothing . . .

Paul brought his cousin in, Mark, to play guitar, who was a lovely guy, and it was all going great. We were getting towards a week before we went on the road and then the strangest things just started happening. I think it was nerves. He was getting his guitar from the tech, banging it out of tune so much during one song he must have been quantumly affecting the strings with his nervousness because I've just never seen anyone pull a guitar out of tune so much in real life. So, Steve Cradock was brought in last minute to save the day.

Simon O'Brien: I was up close and personal to it for the best part of twelve months. My friend, Brendan, knew I was a big Paul Weller fan. He was doing full-time security. I was privileged to get a job with them. I was blessed to be at the side when he's playing the piano to 'Frightened'.

I always considered myself a part of the band because that's the way I was treated from John, God bless his soul, and Ann, Kenny. I was treated like a family member. The connection starts as soon as you get on the bus, everyone's on and people are doing whatever they're doing, you know, John and Kenny are playing cards, Paul is sat talking with Steve, Ed is at the back, strumming his guitar. Chrissy Holland sitting quietly. It was a privilege.

Edgar Jones: The main thing with Kenny was watching his relationship with Steve Cradock really. It was like a cartoon . . . They were always trying to, I dunno, punch each other's heads in.

John was amazing . . . During the soundcheck of the first show proper . . . he called me over to the side of the stage . . . 'I got you your first week's wages, here's the cheque.' I look at him and said, 'Er, John, this is actually for double the amount you said.' He went, 'Yeah it's great innit?'

Christopher Holland: *Heliocentric* had some great songs: 'Frightened', and 'Dust and Rocks' was great. Yeah, it was really powerful . . . with the sort of weird Moog bits and all that stuff . . . I remember 'Picking Up Sticks' when Paul would get off stage and we'd stand on the side and Steve would go into a drum solo and literally your hair is tingling on the back of your neck.

Edgar Jones: Paul was trying to veer off in an elegant direction, especially with getting Robert Kirby into the arrangements . . . [Paul] prances round like an antelope but an antelope with boxing gloves on.

Christopher Holland: Particularly because there was a lot of drinking going all the time when I was there in the band. That must have been quite tiring. I couldn't keep up.

Martin Hopewell: The insanity carried on exactly the same with John and Paul and Kenny and that crowd . . . the V Festival booked Paul and it was like a co-headlining thing with Richard Ashcroft, who'd just come out of The Verve. Big festival, thousands and thousands of people out there and Paul went on and did a blistering set . . . at the end of it they were running out of time . . . You've got Richard Ashcroft's people jumping up and down looking at their watches. At which point Paul decides to invite Noel Gallagher up to appear, right? So Noel walks out there and the crowd go, 'Waaaahh! Hooray!' But in the meantime, on the side of the stage there's this massive ruckus going on because Richard Ashcroft's people do not want this to happen . . . this stage manager comes rushing on with his headphones on, blah, blah in Paul's ear, and pulls them off the stage . . . Then coming down the ramp back towards the dressing rooms again, Noel was asking Paul, 'So what was the problem there?' and he said, 'Well, we're overrunning . . . The promoters would have had to pay extra money if they overran their curfew,' and Noel came out with this classic line, he was dead serious. 'Well, I've got my credit card, have you got yours? Whatever it is we'll pay it.'

1 May 2000 – 'He's the Keeper'

21 August 2000 – 'Sweet Pea, My Sweet Pea' (no. 44)

2001 – Paul Weller signs to Independiente

Alan McGee: I did try to sign Weller. I forgot about that! I'd sold twenty-three million Oasis, *What's the Story*, so we were awash with cash . . . That year I went in and said, 'How much have I got to spend?' and they went, eight million. I was like, *Oh fuck, amazing*. They said, 'Who do you want to sign?' I went, 'Number one, Neil Young. Number two, Paul Weller . . .' So Neil Young was tied up with us. I got a meeting with John Weller and I actually offered Paul two million to sign to Creation . . . I'm not going to say what it went for, but it was a lot more than two million and he went back to Andy Macdonald.

Pete Mason: When Go! Discs came to an end, Andy just wanted to get straight back in there again, and started the company called Independiente. Andy needed someone to do the manufacturing side and took me across as production manager.

Peter Button: I think it was always Andy's intention to try to keep Paul. Andy was obviously a big fan. Go! Discs/Island continued to exercise the options that they had for the recordings . . .

Independiente started to pay for records that were going to be released by Island. Very complicated and the sign of a madman – a sign of a real fan I think. Andy really wanted to have Paul on his own label. The Independiente deal was financially a very good deal for Paul and probably not a very good deal for Andy.

2001 – Acoustic tour

Martin Hopewell: It's the early 2000s. John was getting older, and he wasn't liking the idea of jumping on planes to go off and do foreign shows. So, there wasn't the same sort of push there, I guess. We ended up in a situation, I don't think it's unfair to say, where the forays outside of the UK were anywhere that you could get to without too many hours on a coach. So, a lot in northern Europe. Paul started doing his solo acoustic stuff, which was a blistering idea because it meant that you could go off and play in similar capacities to what we've been doing, a thousand or two thousand, but just with Paul and a guitar . . . It sounds weird, it's just a guy with an acoustic guitar, but they were really powerful.

Andy Macdonald: Paul came in and said, 'I'm just going to take an acoustic guitar out there. Just me. I want to sit really close to an audience.' I went to see him over in the Horticultural Halls in Brussels . . . That discovery of when the songs are really stripped down like that, incredible . . . Most songwriters could look back at things that they'd change, or they'll have a certain association with that period of their lives and stuff, but to be really comfortable with everything that you've done, predominantly, is remarkable.

Paul Weller: Kenny thought that was the best tour, because there weren't so many people for him to have to look after. So, him, and me old man, and me were just on the piss the whole time. Them two would be playing cards the whole time. That's probably why they liked it. And Kenny didn't have to fret about a band. 'Be down here at five o'clock' or at ten o'clock.

Kenny Wheeler: We went out on tour with just Paul, John and myself, with one front of house, Ange Jones, Clive Sparkman was doing Paul's guitars, and we had a merchandiser. That was it and we went out on the road. We started playing small dates in Belgium and then Germany. The venues were anything from 500 to 1,500 . . . It was funny because we'd tell the venues that we'd need someone to do the lights, and then I'd get there and the guy would say, 'I've done this, I've done that,' lots of complicated lighting, and I'd say, 'No, no, it's one light down on him and when he comes on, you put it on, and when he leaves the stage, you turn it off.'

Paul Weller: It was a whole year. Fucking went everywhere. It helped me see that it's just these are all my songs and whatever framework they're performed in, stripped down, bang, whatever, they're still my songs and so, if nothing else, it helped me get over that thing of putting these things in compartments.

Steve Cradock: It was a game changer. I went to the Wolverhampton show . . . I remember him playing 'English Rose' and there was these two big old skinheads crying their eyes out.

Kenny Wheeler: Over the year it just progressed, and the venues started getting bigger and we started going abroad to the States, Canada and Japan with it.

Charles Rees: That was a lovely period to see Paul on his own, and then Steve White joined at times as well. Just the two of them go off to do these shows. He was starting to play The Jam and Style Council songs again. That was a big time.

Steve Ellis: One of my best pals, Mark . . . He's phoned me up talking about the fact that he's going to see Paul Weller. I couldn't tell him that Paul had already phoned me to ask if I fancied getting up to do a couple of numbers . . . I looked down to the crowd and there was my mate Mark. I just pointed at him and burst out laughing. He still mentions it to this day.

Keith Cameron: I went up to Newcastle to do a review of that tour and got to have a quick hello beforehand . . . He played 'Science' that night and dedicated it to me. I almost fell over at this point . . . I made a joke in the review about a rare lapse in taste from Weller dedicating a song to a journalist.

Mark Cooper: There was another *Later Presents*, which was Paul playing solo acoustic guitar which is a great show. Noel came out and they did 'That's Entertainment' together. Jools comes out at the end and they do 'Town Called Malice' . . . I don't think anybody had really seen him like that, before or since.

Noel Gallagher: I just happened to be around, and Paul said, 'Do you want to get up and do something?' and I said, 'Oh, fuck it. I'll come on tour . . . but don't announce it.' That was great, it was great seeing people's faces . . . T in the Park, I was up there hanging out and he was doing his acoustic thing . . . Ten minutes before he goes on stage, he says, 'Do you want to do "Town Called Malice"?' and I was like 'Er . . .'

You know the first line 'Stop dreaming of a quiet life because it's the one . . .' What are the rest? Nobody fucking knows! . . . I don't know the fucking chords . . . I fucking had to get somebody's fucking phone and be like, fucking hell, in a little room, 'Oh . . . the chords, there . . .'

Later on, one of the best nights we had was with High Flying Birds, at the end of one world tour, he got up and did 'Pretty Green' and 'Town Called Malice' with us. In the lead up to that gig, we were in America rehearsing the tunes. And it's only when I had the words in front of me for 'Town Called Malice', that I realised what that song means. I mean, the words are fucking astonishing. They really are. You're going, 'Is that what it says?' You know, 'To either cut down on beer or the kids' new gear'. I'm like, 'What?' Who mentions beer in a song anyway? Apart from The Wurzels or some shit. It's only when you see these words written down and you're singing them, that you go, 'Fuck!' That is an astonishing song. It really fucking is. I know he's in awe of McCartney and all that, but he needn't be, because he's written some fucking great words. When you read them, it's just like, 'You can fucking come up with that?' It's unbelievable. And he's a guy that, by his own admission, is not well read. He hates books, so where this all comes from is, well, it's got to be somewhere within him.

Kenny Wheeler: He was playing in the tent that could hold 8,000 people . . . There was over 10,000 people in there, and twenty minutes later the police are saying, 'Get him on stage, we can't get any more people in here' . . . Afterwards, I said, 'You should have played the main stage,' and he just said to me, 'You fucking get a guitar and walk out front in front of 50,000 people, with just you and a fucking guitar!'

Paul Weller: It was a lot of fun. It's funny, because I can't even imagine doing that ever again. I can't imagine getting up with my guitar or going on tour on me own and fucking doing that. I've done similar things since then. I did a little thing with Gem one time, I think an American tour. That was fun. I've done a similar thing in more recent years with me and Cradock. We went out together. That was good fun. But generally speaking, it doesn't interest me one bit. Because I'm not a good enough guitar player to really hold a song. I'm okay if I'm just singing the song I've written, but no one's going to come and see me to look at what I'm playing . . . because I'm just playing the chords.

Stuart Deabill: Gem Archer joined them on some of the 'Days of Speed' tour later on and said, by the end of it, he was glad to get back to Oasis because Paul and his crew absolutely ruined him. That's got to be great: go back to Oasis for a rest.

October 2001 – *Days of Speed* (no. 3)

Pete Mason: One of the specs for the *Days of Speed* album was to make it feel as if you were there, so it feels like you're at a gig. Paul phoned me up at Independiente and said, 'I'm going to go out on an acoustic tour, but I'm going to record it. I'll get Kenny to get you the tapes as we're doing them, have a listen for the best versions.' That's what happened.

We've all been waiting to hear him do 'That's Entertainment' and all of sudden I've got sixty copies of it from different shows, and I've got to pick one of them . . . That's the other thing about Paul. He can break his songs down to acoustic versions and they still sound insane. That's how good a songwriter he is.

Andy Macdonald: That album again was one of those that just kept racing ahead. I think the idea was just put it out and let it find listeners, and it kept going. Sold half a million copies. It's a proper work of art, isn't it? . . . I think future generations will just keep finding that stuff.

Pippa Hall: *Days of Speed* was Pete Mason. That was his record. It was an amazing body of work and, well done, Paul, but Pete put everything into that record. It is a brilliant thing. Paul was comfortable looking back then. It seemed like he had proven himself. He started to play some of the old tunes from his past lives.

December 2001 – Jools Holland, 'Will It Go Round in Circles'

Sam Brown: We did 'Will It Go Round in Circles' around that time for a Jools Holland album. It's a great rock-soul track. One of the first times I met Paul was on a Jools gig, at Shepherd's Bush Empire. Eddi Reader was on the gig, and it must have been a Christmassy thing because she had the most incredible outfit on, which was a negligee with fairy lights sewn into it underneath. She started up her battery pack, and boom, she was like a Christmas tree. I remember going down to soundcheck, eating a pear. Paul looked across at me and said, 'Nice pear,' and off he went. I think they were the first words he ever said to me!

28 July 2002 – 'The Route of Kings', Hyde Park

Matt Askem: I had only made a few films when I first met Paul . . . The Hyde Park show was created around the *Illumination* album and put together in quite a hurry . . . I didn't really meet Paul until the day of the film, so there was no kind of collaborative process. It was more like, right, there's a bunch of cameras, go and capture it . . .

I've reflected on some of those films that I did for Paul and some of them are just too busy . . . And I think Paul deserves something a bit more timeless in reflection. I was trying at that time to deliver an energy into Paul's work that frankly he does all by himself. The Hyde Park film particularly is a fast-cut piece of work, and it could have done with being a bit more laboured. I was very much of that MTV generation where everything had to have a pace and a momentum.

Bill Wheeler: Out of me and my brother, I was the one that always went into work more with dad, from memory, so I was always about here or there. He'd do itineraries in a book, which tells you what is going on for the whole tour. You'd class it as a book of lies, because you can write whatever you wanted to in the start of that, and then two days in, it could all be bullshit because everything is changing. But there was a period where we got a computer at home, and he's not the best typist, neither am I, but he would give me his handwritten notes and get me to type them up. So, I started doing itineraries, then going out on summer shows in 2002. That was, really, my way into it, and he must have squared it away with Nicky, Paul's sister. She used to do the merch, and he asked if it would 'be alright if Bill came out doing stuff'. I started doing T-shirts with Nicky, and I've always been about ever since then.

2 September 2002 – 'It's Written in the Stars' (no. 7)

16 September 2002 – *Illumination* (no. 1)

Paul Weller: It's easy to say fucking thirty years later, man. I wouldn't wittingly put a shit record out. I mean, I've made shit records, but I didn't mean to. At the time I wasn't thinking, I'll make a shit record. It's just the way they turn out sometimes, and you don't know that until it's all put together and it's the finished thing and either you go, *Wow*, or you go, *Oh, dear*. By that time it's too fucking late.

Damon Minchella: I toured with Paul for about a year before we did any proper recordings . . . Paul would always do lots of demoing and it got to the stage where the four of us – Paul, Whitey, me and Cradock – would do the demos . . . by the time you got into the studio, you'd played the songs loads. It became a really easy process. It was just a case of Paul being sober enough and not too grumpy to enjoy it, because at that stage, he was getting quite heavily into booze. There were certain times of the day where it was going to work and certain times of the day when it wouldn't.

Pippa Hall: *Illumination* . . . It felt like a different sound. Another number one album. 'Peacock Suit' remains his highest selling ever solo single release, number five, but 'Written in the Stars', which is Simon Dine's sound, got to number seven.

Aziz Ibrahim: We did two tracks for the *Illumination* album, 'Spring (At Last)', an instrumental, and 'All Good Books'. Paul and I discussed religion a lot – believe it or not. Me trying to be a practising Muslim, which is very hard in the rock and roll industry when you got one woman sat on one lap . . . and they're trying to force champagne down your throat. I'm not sure of his Christian heritage, but me being a Muslim was a constant discussion. He is often approaching those themes in his lyrics and I seemed to be one of those people that triggered his thoughts on those subjects.

Pete Mason: That's when he started to work with Simon Dine, 'It's Written in the Stars'. I love that single. I love 'One x One' as well from that album, with Noel Gallagher on drums. Funny enough, Simon Dine was an A&R man at Go! Discs when I joined and then he left and was doing the Noonday Underground thing, and that's where Paul really thought to get Simon in to work with him.

Kevin Metcalfe: It helps to have a connection between you and an artist as that mastering expert. The artist wants his record to sound as best as it can. I'd never met Paul until he came in to master *Illumination*, but he was a lovely chap. I already knew Simon Dine, he used to come in and cut records for Go! Discs. He always wanted to use little samples, which I wasn't keen on so much.

Sean Alexander: I was looking after the gallery at Great Western Studios for the day. There are lots of painters, artists, designers and sculptors, and I was head down on the desk dealing with a few customers, when this voice said, 'I like this. I'll have this. Who made it?' and plonked down a picture of John Lennon. I looked up and it was Paul Weller. It was actually my work, and he asked if I'd ever done any album sleeves. I hadn't but loved the idea.

He phoned me up a little while later and came to the studio with his designer, Simon Halfon. They liked my *Focus* series – blurred photographs reproduced in primary colours and wood. We collaborated on an album sleeve – starting with a teaser poster: a blurred portrait of Paul for 'It's Written in the Stars'. Fly posters appeared all over town. That was a real buzz. My pieces at the time always used to have rounded corners. Simon decided to do rounded corners on the record sleeve.

Pete Mason: It was a pain in the arse to do. Paul was very particular about the artwork, he was always about making sure we got the vinyl right . . . Also, if you go back to really old records like Frank Sinatra, there's a thick coating of gloss on the sleeves back then. He wanted that finish on a lot of the albums and, of course, the manufacturing had moved on, so trying to replicate that was difficult. We got as close as we could, but it still wasn't perfect for him. He really did spend a lot of time and involvement in how the record would look. That was just as important to him.

Paul Weller: Absolutely. Well, I'm only still thinking in twelve-by-twelve vinyl terms. That little stamp thing, no, or even a CD to be honest with you. So, it's really important to me, but only that vinyl is important really, regardless of whatever you sell or don't sell these days. That is the art form, for me anyway.

John Reed: *Illumination* is a really interesting record, though it's not sequenced in a way that plays to the crowd. That is one criticism I have of some of his records. Paul sometimes puts the best tracks, in my view, at the end, while most records are judged on the first few songs.

Sean Alexander: The album playback was at a secret location, organised by the record company. I found it all a bit overwhelming and wanted to sit in the shadows and take it all in. Paul saw me and came over, 'How you doing, mate? Come and have a drink.' I'm then sat between Paul and Noel Gallagher, having a beer as they're bitching about all the record company executives. I said, 'Who's that lot over there?' He said, 'Well, those cunts over there, they're record company cunts, and those over there, they're from the press. They're a proper bunch of cunts.' It was brilliant . . . the three of us just sat there like three boys having a little cheeky laugh at the disco.

Damon Minchella: I think Paul found it really hard to write the songs for *Illumination*. That's one of the reasons why we ended up doing the covers album next. I think it was Steve White's idea. We were all pissed after a gig, and Whitey was like, 'Just do that fucking covers album you've been banging on about for years,' and Paul was like, 'OK, let's fucking do it.'

October 2002 – Live at Braehead

Matt Askem: It was after the Braehead film that Paul and I really started to get on . . . I think Paul's lighting designer at that time was of an age in an era that wasn't right for him. There were lots of oil patterns and all kinds of stuff going on in the background. The band are all lit in really prime colours and you couldn't really see what was going on. I didn't have enough budget and enough leverage to change all of that. I was trying to cut around some of the backgrounds that were going on . . . it's a bit too busy.

He smacked himself right on the mic and cut his lip. I was quite shocked. He said afterwards, 'What do you want? Blood?'

I remember the crowd getting pretty angry as well. Some of my cameramen in the crowd, just getting properly thrown about, people being stabbed in the audience and all sorts of stuff. It was one of those nights where it wasn't just Paul that was angry.

18 November 2002 – 'Leafy Mysteries' (no. 23)

24 July 2003 – Paul Weller signs with V2

Andy Macdonald: That was at the end of our contract. The last records with Independiente. I'm not sure exactly how or why. You know what they say about the music business, 'If you can remember what was going on, you weren't doing it properly!' What a pleasure and a privilege to work with someone like that, though.

Peter Button: I don't think there was a falling out. I think it got to the stage where Paul was ready for a change. I really have absolutely no recollection of there being animosity between Paul and Andy . . . I think it may have been that the albums hadn't done as well as Andy had hoped, they hadn't been doing as well as *Stanley Road*, and I think Andy thought it was too expensive.

Craig McLean: I interviewed Paul for the *Word* magazine article at that point and it was really a crossroads point for Paul. He said on more than one occasion, 'the records sell fucking niche', as he puts it, he was very sanguine about that, stoutly unbothered, and you get that kind of thing from artists all the time, but he meant it . . .

Peter Button: I don't even know that Paul necessarily knows this, but I think Andy wanted us to accept a much lower fee in advance for the next album and exercise of the option. I think John Weller's view was business is business and, by then, I had indicated that V2 were keen, and I think we thought, *OK, well, we can get the advance that we want from V2 who are as naive now as Andy was six years ago*, or whatever it was. I think Andy may have been a little upset that we went for the money rather than what he might have considered would have been appropriate loyalty as he had paid a lot of money for two albums prior to that, or even three, that I don't think had done awfully well.

Craig McLean: I mean, you wouldn't mess with his dad in any capacity, whether it was in the pub or a boardroom . . . I was glad I was on the inside, shall we say, on that trip, because if I'd been on the outside, he would have scared the shit out of me.

Richard Branson: It was an innovative time for music – with the launch of Napster, iTunes and the iPod. It was a time of change and disruption – that's always good for creativity. V2 was an attempt to recreate Virgin Records. We heard Paul had parted ways with his label, and we knew he would be a great fit for V2. His hair, his style, his music. I'd gotten to know him when he recorded his *Wild Wood* album at the Manor in 1993, which is a beautiful album, so it felt good to reunite. We didn't know each other enormously well but I loved watching him play. We were thrilled when he decided to join us at V2 just a few months after leaving his old label.

Dylan White: Paul went from Independiente to one of Richard Branson's companies on Virgin, V2. That's when John Weller rang up. 'Well, they want me to use in-house. They've given me all this money. So I better go along with it.'

Pippa Hall: I'd been working with him since 1992, had a great relationship, knew exactly what his foibles are and all that kind of stuff. The labels at that time didn't see it like that ... you sign to a bigger label like V2 then everything goes back in-house ... It was dark, sad times. I was devastated, but it's just business isn't it? Polly took over and that was bye from us.

Peter Button: I was very involved in going out to and finding Branson. I knew that they were very keen ... John was involved in that deal, but he was beginning to be less able, and I think he realised that ... you don't have a dog and bark yourself. They had me on board and I might as well do what I am good at.

Tony Harlow: I remember John's negotiating style. He was a really unique and amazing person. If you were prepared to lose some money at cards and could stand up after twelve white Russians, you could do business with him. Brilliant. Such good, amazing stories. He spanned that experience, from talking about standing in the rubble of a bomb site, right the way through the eighties record business, and I don't think he changed or compromised that much.

John wasn't the kind of manager who came in with the music. Paul popped in and out, which was a lovely part of it. He'd stop for a drink on a Friday night. He'd bring the music in. Obviously, you didn't fuck with the music Paul Weller brought in. I think at that time John was maybe stepping back a little bit. But it wasn't noticeable because he just didn't do that bit, with us at least.

Nicky Weller: We did a mad tour in Germany. That was all fine but after that I think me and Paul started to notice a change in Dad, and I think that's when he got diagnosed with dementia. It was a good few years of being on the road before I realised the severity of it, really.

Paul Weller: He had his heart op around about '94 and he was never really quite the same after that. He got a little bit better, but his health wasn't great thereafter. He just loved the road so much. He loved being out on the road. He should have really turned it in then. He could have had a better quality of life in terms of health. Spent more time with my mum, but he didn't. He just loved being on the road. He loved that life. More than me, definitely.

Kenny Wheeler: I think John done a few more tours after the acoustic tours . . . all of a sudden, he wasn't coming out all of the time. It was hard, I used to miss him on the road. He then had a driver who used to bring him up to places for a few days and then he'd go home. Sometimes I used to follow him home, just to make sure he got home all right.

14 June 2004 – 'The Bottle' (no. 13)

30 August 2004 – 'Wishing on a Star' (no. 11)

14 September 2004 – *Studio 150* (no. 2)

Polly Birkbeck: I was head of press at V2 Records when Paul signed, so I automatically got to work with him. To be honest, I didn't really like much on V2, apart from Grandaddy, so signing Paul felt incredible – a proper legend. If you look at the photo of the signing, I'm wearing an Alexander McQueen dress, dressed up on purpose, and I'm grinning like a lunatic, standing next to Paul Weller – me and nine blokes.

The first thing was his covers album, *Studio 150*. I was quite nervous when they said I was going to be working with him. That sounds a bit mad now, but I thought, *I better do a good job here because he's Paul Weller*. He used to laugh at me because I'd get tongue tied. I've worked with Paul ever since. I've always been a fan, loving The Jam and The Style Council. I taped The Jam off the radio and bought their records, although I swapped my 'Eton Rifles' single for a pair of snakeskin stilettos.

Richard Engler: The roster of V2 was phenomenal – Underworld, Stereophonics, Elbow and then we signed Paul Weller . . . As a kid, The Jam, Buzzcocks and The Clash were my bands. I joined The Jam fan club, got the badges, posters and letters from Nicky; the first 'punk' album I ever bought was *In the City* . . . Fast forward to 2004, I'd had a couple of meetings with Paul . . . Then he popped in and walked by my desk, 'All right, Rich.' My life was complete. *Paul knows my name.*

I had been head of marketing at Atlantic, EMI . . . they're big corporations, and V2 was the best of both worlds: an indie record label with loads of money to spend on both signings and marketing . . . The first record we put out was *Studio 150*. That had a difficult gestation period, but was still a great record. The impression I got is it helped Paul move on to his next stage of his career.

Polly Birkbeck: We had a famous open bar at V2. You could have a drink in the morning. It was like our café. It was quite near where Paul lived, so he'd come to the offices to hang out and have a drink in the bar. Everyone used to say, 'Is it true you've got a bar there that's open all day?' Probably, in retrospect, a bit detrimental to getting things done.

Claire Moon: I was the senior marketing manager and looked after Paul, Stereophonics and a couple of other bands . . . The great thing creatively about working for V2 was that it was a very indie-spirited record label, but it had major label money. You could afford to run your campaigns properly, but you really cared about your artists and your roster . . . I had the craziest first day ever. The head of marketing said, 'Hey, this is a curveball. You're going to go to Heathrow and pick up Carla Bruni in a car and drive her down to Black Barn, where you'll meet Paul Weller, because you're going to be looking after him.'

Richard Engler: Carla Bruni was rock royalty; she'd been partners with Mick Jagger and Eric Clapton. She wasn't yet wife to the president of France, but she was a big deal . . . She's huge in France, Paul's huge in the UK, maybe we could swap a bit of the old fan base . . . Maybe there'll even be a bit of chemistry between them, who knows?

It was just a little bit frosty . . . They had a go at a couple of tunes, and it just didn't really work out. I think they only spent a couple of hours in there . . .

As we came to leave, Carla is already out in the car and I hear John Weller's voice coming through the playback, 'Who is this French bird, anyway?'

Damon Minchella: That relentless pressure to come up with a whole bunch of new songs is tough, which is why Steve White told Paul, 'Just do the fucking covers album'. Paul loved it – it let him play and record whatever he wants without overthinking if the songs were good enough or how they compared to the back catalogue. If people don't like it, then it's a bunch of covers. There's your get out.

Benjamin Herman: I got a phone call from Paul. He'd got my number from Candy Dulfer, the Dutch saxophone player . . . I talked to Paul and went over and met everybody and started doing some work on some horn arrangements. There were a bunch of other Dutch musicians involved, the sound technician, Joeri Saal, and a real string arranger called Willem Friede.

Paul likes Amsterdam. It's a place that he could just walk around and not be bothered too much by people. He had a couple of favourite hangouts, and Studio 150 was five minutes' walk from those places, all based around Leidseplein.

Joeri Saal: I think the first recordings were also going, 'Let's see how it goes, and if it goes all right then that's good but if not, then we'll just get somebody else in.' I think the first track we did was 'Wishing on a Star' . . . That was interesting because Damon was the bass player on the basic cut of that. He's a great player, but he played maybe a little bit safe, and on the first take was 180 degrees the other end. Heavy stuff. Quite a different approach, and for me that was really like, 'All right, something's happening here.'

Steve Cradock: Damon was over there more than me. I came over just for one session . . . and it was Turkish pizzas and beer, and of course shitloads of spliffs.

Benjamin Herman: That's Amsterdam for you. But to be clear, there was no daytime drinking or smoking during recordings – only hangovers. You can't get a whole bunch of people over here and expect them not to sample the local products.

Joeri Saal: Don't forget the cheesy sausage of Cafe Chaos. That was a special kind of sausage where they put some cheese inside the sausage and then they heat it up a little bit. That was a famous combo that Paul had every day.

Benjamin Herman: That was back in the day when all of us enjoyed our drinks, but I was surprised by how the sessions would stop by 8 p.m. or earlier. I was used to studio days running from 11 a.m. until 4 a.m. Paul was very efficient and very fast. Have an idea, try it and move on. With my own projects, we'd always get into rows before we even tried something out. With Paul, it was different . . . I was totally blown away because Paul had ideas all the time – throwing suggestions at the musicians or Joeri, behind the mixing board.

Roger Nowell: *Studio 150* was when I became Paul's roadie. For five years, I hardly went home . . . I'd drive the gear to Amsterdam, stay for the sessions, then drive it back. It was pretty messy but a good old time . . . we had to be out of the studio by a certain time. So, then we'd be off to a restaurant or a bar until the early hours in the morning.

Lawrence Watson: It got messy [*laughs*]. I've got to plead the fifth here, haven't I? Kenny was the one trying to make sure that we went to bed on time . . . Kids let loose in the sweet shop in Amsterdam, and a hell of a lot of sweets to consume . . . I think Kenny was a shepherd and they needed a lot of shepherding at some points!

Roger Nowell: Steve White setting himself on fire. We're in a bar and Whitey's leant against a candle. Paul said, 'You're on fire, mate.' Steve went, 'Thanks, man.' 'No, mate, you are. You're on fire.' His jacket had gone up.

Benjamin Herman: It was such an incredible thing that Paul came to Holland to record and asked some local musicians to join in, because it lifted the scene. Straight away everyone stepped up and it was a big boost for everybody involved. Also, for Joeri, the sound technician . . . because of his work with Paul, he got noticed by other people and got a lot more people trusting him to mix their records.

Joeri Saal: I was especially proud when he told me the title of the album. Named after our studio. That was super.

Danny Thompson: I was sitting at home and the phone rang. 'Hello Dan, it's Paul Weller here. I just want to say that I've listened to your playing on the Five Blind Boys of Alabama albums and I'm just phoning to say I really love what you do' . . . Then months later, he asked me to do some recording. I played on the Tim Hardin song, 'Don't Make Promises', and Sister Sledge, 'Thinking of You'. Paul is totally without prejudice.

Paul Weller: We have this phrase in the studio now called 'Serve the Song'. That came from Danny Thompson. It means put your fucking ego outside or leave it in the car or whatever, and then come in and listen to this tune and to what the person is trying to put over and what they're trying to reflect within this music. Don't go 'Yeah, I'm the fucking best bass player in the world, and this is how I'm going to do it.'

Danny Thompson: Paul's a phenomenal artist . . . his energy, his output, and it's not cosmetic. It's not to be a hit and it's not manipulated to reach a certain market . . . He's totally honest. What you see is what you get, and I can relate to that one million per cent . . . it's a responsibility for me if I'm asked to go and play something, and I obviously want to do a good job. And the important thing I've always said is to serve the song and not what you want to do, not be clever.

Eliza Carthy: I'll be very honest with you, whilst I was aware of The Style Council and The Jam when I was a teenager, aside from a brief obsession with Rage Against the Machine, Red Hot Chili Peppers and Queen, I largely spent my time with my nose in a book learning traditional songs.

It wasn't really until I signed to Warner Brothers, and they suggested 'Wild Wood' to me as a song to cover on the

Cigarettes and Angels album that I really went, *Oh, hang on a minute, I've been missing something here.* That started a journey to a really lovely friendship. Paul asked me to be on *Studio 150* and I went to the studio. We were being very polite and nervous, and I had some ideas and I suggested them to the producer and the producer was like, 'No thanks, we don't need you to sing with Mr Weller, love. We don't want your folky tones all over this. Just sit down and get the fiddle out and we'll see what's happening.'

I put the headphones on and the track started and Paul's voice came into my head. I was just like, *Bloody hell. How have I not been listening to this man for my entire life? This is absolutely amazing.* That started off loads of things.

Sam Brown: I remember our session because Carleen Anderson was on it, and she's just amazing, and Claudia Fontaine who has very sadly died since . . . Paul knew exactly what he wanted, and the sound he wanted, and had booked the right people to get the sound that he wanted.

Carleen Anderson: Sessions with Paul were never planned. It was always random. It's like family, like when your brother calls you up and says, 'I need you.' 'When?' 'Now!' Paul's been fortunate to have some really good singers over the years. I love the whole thing of being called up at the last minute and going 'Can I hear it first?' 'No, just come on down.'

Sam Brown: The defining thing about him as a musical person is his feel, it's the ability to pick up a guitar and lay down a feel. All the great people have that. Steve Marriott. Pete Townshend. David Gilmore. Eric Clapton. Jeff Beck. It's not just about what they're playing technically. It's about it being concrete. They make music tangible, and they make you feel it.

Kevin Metcalfe: I was in Latimer Road, which is basically Notting Hill. Paul lived nearby and would pop in . . . He knows what he wants out of a record. He's got a vision of what it should be. He does let people get involved in them and put their brush-strokes on it. Paul's done that in a few cases with Noel Gallagher and a few other artists on collaborations.

Jack Dee: We were creating my sitcom *Lead Balloon*, and I heard the song 'One Way Road'. I always knew the theme was going to come in at the end of each episode . . . that little bit of clarinet at the top of the song attracted me and the fact that it was Paul Weller singing was, I thought, well, that's just kind of icing on the cake . . . It just worked so well, tonally and lyrically as well . . . It's Noel Gallagher's song but I'm sure it was Weller's idea to just slide it in with that bit.

Peter Button: John came in to see me when Paul did the album that was all covers. *Studio 150*, and he said, 'Er, have you seen this?' and it was the royalty statement. He said, 'There's no fucking money for *Studio 150*. Where's the advance? Where's the advance?' I said, 'Well, it's an album of covers. Paul hasn't fulfilled the commitment yet. That's why you'*ve not got the money*.' He said, 'What you fucking talking about? The album's out.' 'Yes, but he hasn't written any of them.' 'What does that fucking matter?' This was his lack of understanding of the industry, but it shows his loyalty to his son. 'My fucking son records their songs, he should fucking get some money from it, otherwise no one would make any money from it.'

John Cohen: John's language was always very fruity, and an unauthorised biography was written about Paul. It clearly referred to John, quoting him many times, but the word fuck was always in it, or fucking. John brought in the book to me and slammed it down on my desk and said, 'Have you seen this?' I said, 'Yeah, I have.' He said, 'I don't fucking talk like that.' I treasure that moment.

Richard Engler: Working with Paul meant figuring out how you engage his core fan base quickly to give the whole thing a momentum, and then how do you break through to a wider audience? We had data that showed his last few records had all performed similarly, with hardcore fans who bought the album on release day. The challenge was to cover those fans but also ensure that a bigger audience gets to hear the music . . . We made use of the superfans' enthusiasm to shine a light on the release and then made sure ads are in the right places, plugging to radio and TV, and giving those guys access to Paul . . . A couple of singles got airplay, and it was well received. People who understood music understood partly what the purpose of the record was: helping Paul get to the next stage, recognising songs that had influenced him . . . and that set him on the next path.

14 September 2004 – A live selection from *Studio 150*

Matt Askem: We were filming a show at Riverside Studios, Hammersmith for TV and a DVD film. I'd voiced some of my concerns about lighting and his production . . . Paul and I used to talk quite honestly about some of those things. Because it was *Studio 150*, it was fitting to do it in a studio. Paul and I met in Soho for breakfast one morning and he cited this old black and white Nina Simone film that he loved. She was playing on a circular stage in the round and it was surrounded by audience on tiered seating, very well dressed . . . 'That's what I'm after. I want an audience that looks presentable.' That film was much more collaborative. I had a steer from him as to what he liked . . . It was just more measured and about the musicianship rather than trying to give it a style.

Louise Marshall: That was the first time that I worked with Paul. It was actually the week of my wedding. Sadly, Sam Brown wasn't able to do a gig, so she asked me to fill in. The beautiful thing was to work with Carleen Anderson and Jocelyn Brown . . . We got to sing 'All Along the Watchtower' . . . Wow, that was BV heaven to be with Paul.

Benjamin Herman: After *150* came out, there was a tour planned . . . and then Paul lost his voice. So, the whole thing was cancelled, and he paid everyone from his own pocket . . . I've never heard of that before. Usually, if something gets cancelled due to health reasons and postponed, it's like, *Sorry, guys, you'll get your fee the next time.*

Damon Minchella: I left Ocean Colour Scene in 2004. We'd done an acoustic tour in Ireland, and I was on the bus and just thought, *I can't bear it any more*. So, I just went up to the bus driver, said, 'Just stop the bus. I'm getting off.' That was it. Just left them to it. Paul phoned me two days later. He's like, 'I fucking heard what's fucking going on. Does that mean you'll leave my band?' I said, 'No, Paul, it doesn't.' He's like, 'Well, that's fucking all right then. Shall I have a word with Cradock and let him know?' I said, 'Yeah, please do' . . . and I carried on with Weller for another three years.

15 November 2004 – 'Thinking of You' (no. 18)

14 March 2005 – 'Early Morning Rain / Come Together' (no. 40)

April 2005 – Stevie Mac Weller born (fifth child, second with Samantha Stock)

2005 – Live

Martin Hopewell: I had twenty-eight years working with the Wellers. It would have been nice to have made it to thirty and a nice round number . . . we're talking about the sad bit about how the whole thing ground to a halt with me, and this is something I've got to be very careful how I talk about it. But look, the reality is, it wasn't that much later that John died, and it became very clear to me that he wasn't well. It got to the point where, oh God, this is horrible, but the memory was starting to go. I was finding that John would forget stuff that we'd agreed to do.

There was a festival, Benicàssim, in Spain, that Paul was due to play and John had no recollection of having agreed to it and got quite angry about it. We had a meeting at the agency with myself, John and Paul and a guy from the record company . . . the problem was, I was trying to talk to Paul about it, but John didn't like the idea of that, he felt that you were going over his head if you went and spoke to Paul directly. So that didn't work. Eventually, I had to down tools and stop because I couldn't do my job and commit promoters to lots and lots of money booking halls and doing advertising campaigns and stuff like that, if there was a very strong chance that the show wasn't going to happen.

I miss John so much. I still have dreams about him. He was a really important figure in my life and I loved him to bits. It's really very, very sad, but there you go.

Kenny Wheeler: I remember one day, coming in and John was sat at his desk in the office at Black Barn, and he went to me. 'What did we used to do here?' I said, 'Well, you used to organise everything here, John. We still do.' You just used to carry on . . . It was never sort of like, *Oh, it's all down to you there.* It was never like that, it just went on.

18 July 2005 – 'From the Floorboards Up' (no. 6)

Tony Harlow: We were thrilled when Paul delivered 'Floorboards' because we were like, *Oh, wow, this is the record.* We'd been needing that kind of visceral energy for a while from Paul. I guess *As Is Now* probably is a record where you look at it and say he was trying to make a statement about being super relevant in that generation of people with really strong guitar records: Bloc Party, Libertines, that type of thing. But then we were also thrilled with *Studio 150*. We were just happy to be in business with one of the greatest artists in UK music history, if not the greatest.

26 Sept 2005 – 'Come On / Let's Go' (no. 15)

11 October 2005 – *As Is Now* (no. 4)

Noel Gallagher: Paul would go through periods where he'd say that he'd had enough, 'That's it for me, next year,' and we'd all be like 'Really?' I don't know where his head was at because, fucking hell, I mean, if no one is ever going to retire, it's going to be him.

Roger Nowell: *As Is Now* was a completely different thing. We spent a lot of time at Music Bank rehearsing songs and then went to Wheeler End and recorded them more in a live-type thing and we brought Joeri over from Amsterdam.

Damon Minchella: It was full of Oasis equipment everywhere. You'd have to move their fucking stupid guitars and drum kits out the way to actually do anything. Noel's 87,000 guitars would be everywhere.

Benjamin Herman: They were Paul's own songs. It was very inspiring to see how he developed his songs; he did that during the tours as well. Paul would sit in the front of the bus with his guitar, playing all day with a notepad, and when we'd get to the hotel, he'd run straight to his room and continue to finish what he thought up in the bus. I saw a couple of songs evolve that way just from things he would pick up, conversations from people in the bus or something he saw on the road or some thoughts.

Steve Cradock: 'Floorboards Up' – there's a bit of a grittiness . . . I think he found his love for the Feelgood vibe and the Telecaster again.

Benjamin Herman: That was one of the tunes he wrote on the bus.

Jacko Peake: I remember one day he grabbed Steve White and Damon Minchella into a room just to play it through. 'We've got to do this. Come. We've got to do this now!' and off they went, and then it was a thing that we played live after that.

Paul Weller: *As Is Now* was the last time we used multi-track. We started off, got a few days in, and we ran out of tape. You couldn't get it because Ampex got into financial difficulties. So, we were fucked! I had to send Charlie off to university to learn about Pro Tools!

Charles Rees: We started that in RAK Studios and they stopped manufacturing tape, so the cost started to skyrocket. We were using digital then anyway, but tape's just better and if you're in a great studio like RAK then you go analogue. It's just not worth it now, for instance, we end up having to send the tracks to people now. When we did that in the past, you'd have to stick it on an aeroplane and send it somewhere and you're thinking it's going to be X-rayed. Who would do that now?

Paul Moody: I did the interviews for the *As Is Now* documentary with Lawrence and Stuart Watson . . . During the recording of it, I went down to Wheeler End, Alvin Lee's old place. Paul would be in the studio, permanently wearing shades with the military green jacket on at the time, brilliant look, John Lennon inspired, I guess. He'd be in the vocal booth delivering this incredible vocal on 'Paper Smile' or 'Blink and You've Missed It'.

There was such a spirit in the band at that point and the sessions in Amsterdam were similarly nuts. Very much party central and that went into the music. The gigs around that time and the camaraderie in that band was very strong. I was only there for three or four days but it was a regular pattern. They'd go to Studio 150, which was also where they recorded the previous album. They would record for two or three hours and then all troop around to the pub on the corner for cheese and sausages. It was like a daily ritual and then they would have a couple of drinks, and it would evolve into something else. I know there was a lot of problems. Maybe Paul personally wasn't feeling his best there. But it's a brilliant record.

Jacko Peake: I was involved and touring with Paul again, with a Dutch horn section. Benjamin Herman – amazing alto player. Jan van Duikeren on trumpet and Louk Boudesteijn on trombone. I was the tenor player. I also did a little bit of horn stuff on the album.

Damon Minchella: Some of those songs were quite old, like 'Blink and You'll Miss It' had been around since '92, but they never got the version he liked. We carried on the same way, so we demoed them for about three weeks . . . We'd just keep playing through them and by the time we hit the studio, we were relatively well-oiled . . . and at times a little too well-oiled.

Jacko Peake: Alcohol has always been a big part. We used to joke, me and the Dutch guys a week before rehearsal started, 'We'd better get in training', training meant going to the pub every night. Get your tolerance levels up.

John Lewis: The first time I met Paul Weller, I was working at *Time Out* . . . he was shaking my hand going, 'All right, you fucking hate me at *Time Out*, don't you? . . . Fucking things you've written about me . . . Not you, but your fucking colleagues. I wanted to come down there and firebomb the building.' Quite an introduction, isn't it? Pleased to meet you too.

It was interesting to watch him before a gig. There were always rituals. Apparently, he always vomits before he goes on stage. He has that sense of nervousness that he's open about. He did drink a lot as well around that time . . . I'm not sure if he still has that sense of nerves now.

Paul Du Noyer: I interviewed him in Amsterdam; he'd just finished the song 'From the Floorboards Up' and was playing that to me. He then took me on a pub crawl. I gather from other journalists who were around at the same time that he did this with everybody. It was as if he was putting you to a test . . . I'd never drunk as much as I did on that day, and evening, and night, and I don't know how I ever found my way back to the hotel without falling into a canal.

Ted Kessler: I was working at *Q*, and the first meeting was actually right by where I grew up in Edgware Road, and it was coincidence, but he asked me to meet him by the bus stop near Marble Arch. I met him by the bus stop, which is weird enough, but when I was an eleven-year-old kid, dressed like Paul Weller, walking down the Edgware Road, I'd be walking up and down past this bus stop, and then Paul Weller gets off the bus, at that same bus stop where I used to walk around. It's eleven in the morning, so we go to a shisha cafe, and we sit there and he's puffing away on his shisha. I'm trying to do this interview. It's not great. I think he's more thoughtful now as an interviewee. He thinks more about the answer. But then he was more quick sentences. He wouldn't overanalyse himself. He did this interview and invited me down to Black Barn, 'I'll play you some of the record, and we'll have a bit of a drink.'

Four days later we go down to Ripley and we're approaching the end of his drinking days here. He was quite into it. Fucking hell. It was six or seven hours of really intense drinking, one where if your glass is empty or you finished a bottle of whatever it is you're drinking, something else is in your hand, straight away. Then after about three hours of listening to the music and him dancing around the studio, we went to the pub, had a couple of drinks in there. That was the weirdest thing. Going to the pub with Paul Weller. Sitting in his local in Ripley, and just chatting. It doesn't really compute, does it? And then we go and have a curry with the rest of his people who work in the studio, absolutely wankered. Then we get in a car with his guitar tech, Roger. Lovely Roger. 'Let's drive to the K West in Shepherd's Bush and have a nightcap!' It's like eight in the evening. We're driving, all the windows are down and he's just singing. He's obsessed by the song Razorblade, by The Strokes. He keeps playing it over and over again in this car as we're zooming over the Westway. It's been burned into my mind. It's one of those wonderful evenings. And then I get to the K West, it's like 'Two gin and tonics!' And I'm like, 'Fuck. I can't do this anymore.'

Tim Burgess: We were in LA for an Oasis gig and the after-show party . . . Paul was playing the next night at the Wiltern, and he said, come and sing a song with us. I was wondering whether it was going to be 'Shout to the Top', probably hoping for 'My Ever Changing Moods' . . . 'No we're going to do one of yours, man' . . . 'We All Need Love'. Him and Steve Cradock learned my song . . .

Weller said that I once had the best haircut in pop. I said 'When?' And he goes, 'I don't know, 1990?' I'm then playing with my hair, thinking, *Right, OK, well, how is it now?*

Pete Paphides: Paul's son Natt was doing work experience at V2. You'd never guess he was Paul's son – he was an emo goth kid. He looked amazing – magnificent make-up, dyed black hair straightened with tongs. I couldn't work out why this intern was hanging around, lingering a bit too long in the room where our interview was happening. Eventually Paul said, 'Oh Pete, that's my son, Natt,' and I just started laughing because I thought it was so hilarious that he looked like Marilyn Manson's younger brother. It was wonderful. The rapport between them was lovely and warm and tender – a lovely father–son moment.

I wrote the piece and mentioned how I was trying not to laugh, so it was a little bit irreverent, and I was really quite worried whether I might have overstepped the line. Paul's PR called and said, 'Paul wants to speak to you – is it all right if I give him your number?' You really don't want one of your heroes to be pissed off with you . . . he infamously offered David Quantick out and suggested they sort it out like men.

Paul actually rang for two reasons. First of all, he thought the feature was funny . . . and secondly, he really liked the CD I had made him and wanted to know what a couple of songs were. Weeks later, I was at a friend's house on a kids' playdate and my phone rang. 'All right, Pete. It's Paul Weller . . .' 'I know!' 'Listen, I've been thinking about those CDs you made for me and that. I'm doing this gig at Ally Pally in a couple of weeks' time and I was wondering if you wanted to DJ at the gig.' I was a bit shocked, and so I paused . . . I think he took my pause as like I was thinking about it or something because at that point, he felt the need to say, 'Obviously I'll pay you.' 'You don't need to pay me and of course I'll do it' . . .

Two days later, Paul called again. 'All right, Peter, I've got this cheque I've made out to you. Where'd you want me to send it?' Doesn't that say a lot about him?

5 December 2005 – 'Here's the Good News' (no. 21)

15 February 2006 – Brit Awards

Declan O'Rourke: My record was coming out and one of the A&R team at V2 told me, off the cuff, that they had given Paul my record and that he really liked it and that he loved one song in particular – 'Galileo'. I didn't believe it, I just thought they were pouring smoke into my pocket . . . So, the record came out and I was in Dublin in a bar on a Sunday with a few of my friends, playing songs in the corner. My phone rang. It was hard to hear, but it was this very thick London accent. 'Who is it, sorry?' And he's like, 'It's Paul, Paul Weller here.' I was like, *Holy shit*. He was just calling to say hi and I love your record.

A few months later they were going to give Paul the Brits Lifetime Achievement award. He was performing too and wanted to do a warm-up at the 100 Club in Oxford Street, which is a cool little venue, and he invited me to open that show.

Damon Minchella: What sticks in my mind about that Brits performance is the song, 'Come On / Let's Go'. It's got a really tricky bass part. Paul was amazed that I came up with that because it's really hard to play. What he doesn't know is I semi-nicked it off a Red Hot Chili Peppers song. Just changed it. You wouldn't know but I know. Flea might be able to tell slightly, but anyway, it's really fucking hard to play. Paul would have this running joke when he'd always count it in slightly too fast. If you watch the TV footage, just before it starts, he comes up to me, 'I'm going to catch you out.' Bearing in mind this is going out live on the Brits and he counts it in so fast. Yeah, but I can play even faster than you can fucking count it.

October 2006 – *Into Tomorrow* documentary

Stuart Watts: Having the opportunity of making a documentary on Paul blew my mind. I was quite nervous meeting him because I did idolise him . . . he was very collaborative . . . very open. He immediately got into talking about how we could make this documentary, what sort of documentaries he liked and mentioned *The Kid Stays in the Picture* and Robert Evans telling his own story. I thought, well, it fits perfectly with Paul telling his own story. He reflected on everything. I was somebody who was just a fan listening to the music; I wasn't aware of the times after The Style Council or the loss of confidence. Those are quite personal things and once Paul was telling me those, or other members of the band or whoever we interviewed, it became richer and richer. I remember one quote, which really resonated with me, and it was, 'It's my religion . . . music . . . it's my faith.' It really struck me when I heard him say that. This was a person who lives music and everything else around him sort of pales slightly. And that if you're going to follow that religion, that faith, as he's done, it's going to be a rollercoaster, isn't it? Things are going to fall by the wayside. It's not necessarily a normal arc in life. Not many people are so driven or so passionate about one thing. Other things come into your life, and you let them happen. Where this is just so . . . so central to Paul's being, really.

I said I'd finished it. The record company saw it, and Ted Cockle saw it, who was overseeing the project, and he said, 'Well, I think we need to show Paul the documentary.' So we arranged for a time and a date, somewhere off Oxford Street. Very nervous. Paul's gonna walk in and watch what I've been doing for the last six months. He sat down, and off we went. It got to the end, and I thought my heart rate had gone up double by this time. He just sat back, and I can remember it to this day, and he just went, 'Excellent, Stu.' Little round of applause. And he just got up and he's gone. Well done. Thanks. Bang.

6 November 2006 – 'Wild Blue Yonder' (no. 22)

Noel Gallagher: Look, this sums him up in a nutshell. I was having a party at my house. Quite a few people there. Loads of birds and someone wanted to put 'Shout to the Top' on and they were going to me, 'Oh, do you think he'll go mad?' and I was like, 'I don't fucking know. What's he gonna do, smash the gaff up?' Somebody went over to him, 'Excuse me, Paul. Would you mind if we played "Shout to the Top"?' He got up and said to me, 'Fucking come and dance to it, man!' We got up and had a dance off to it!

Anyway, a few hours later, as the party was calming down . . . 'Oh, play us a tune!' and I forgot to hide the guitars. Usually when I get people around, I hide them for that very reason, that they want me to play 'Masterplan' at five o'clock in the morning, when you're drunk and you can't play it! . . . I can't remember what I played, some fucking Oasis tune. Then I hand the guitar to Weller, he plays them a new song! 'Wild Blue Yonder'. He was still writing it. I was going, what's this one? I think it's a new one! At least have a go at fucking 'Town Called Malice'. Come on, man! This is what we've got to put up with!

31 December 2006 into 1 January 2007 – *Hootenanny*

Mark Cooper: By 2006, *Hootenanny* had evolved into this huge TV show with a full audience and loads of musical guests. Paul was on this show along with Amy Winehouse and Seasick Steve. Paul had done the Electric Proms with Amy a bit earlier on that autumn and had come up with Dinah Washington's version of 'Don't Go to Strangers'. Paul starts it off. He's in a little V formation with Jools, both on keyboards and Amy comes in between them with her verse. You see Paul and Jools just look at each other – it's just magic – just incredible.

It's very sad about what happened to Amy, but they both got on, as certain kind of London voices. They just got each other, I think, musically. And you can really feel that it's such a vulnerable vocal at the same time, from both of them, and such a poignant song . . . probably the biggest thing we've done with Paul in terms of that sort of take-up of people recurring. And it's understandable, because every time you watch it, it touches you.

2 July 2007 – 'This Old Town' (no. 39)

Graham Coxon: There was a song I did called 'You and I', which is a bit Jammy with that propelling chuggy-chuggy rhythm guitar playing of Paul's . . . That's how and why I play like I do, because of how he approached rhythm playing, and I think he just recognised it. I was in the studio with Steve Lamacq when the call came through . . . 'Do you want to meet up?' . . . I was flipping very happy.

We got together and he sent me over the 'This Old Town' thing . . . He said, 'I've got this chorus, why don't you come up with a verse to it?' . . . we recorded it live with Zak [Starkey] and that flipping beautiful maniac of a bass player, Mani . . . I remember after one take, right at the end, Zak going, 'Did you notice I did one of my old man's fills?' It was like Abbey Road at the end, just before it kicks off. I was like, *Yeah, this is great. I'm playing with an almost Beatle, Paul Weller, a Stone Rose. This is pretty cool.*

10 August 2007 – Universal announces purchase of V2

Polly Birkbeck: V2 scaled down, and so I got let go, but they let me take the acts I was working on with me, Paul being one. Then a year later, V2 went tits up.

Peter Button: V2 had record company options and when that deal finished the label was being run by Universal. At that stage, we went on to single album deals ... Claire or I would phone up a record company executive and say, 'Might you be interested?' 'Yes, we'd like to sign for four or five albums.' But Paul is only doing a one-album deal. Paul hates being tied down and feeling obliged to record an album ... virtually every time he delivers an album, he will say, 'I don't want to do another one. That's it, I'm finished.' And before the album is even released, he's been in the studio, recorded another one and I'm ready to shop that deal ...

6 September 2007 – *Suburban 100*

John Wilson: I had the huge privilege of editing Paul's anthology of lyrics, *Suburban 100*. Random House wanted him to write a memoir, but he insisted on a poetry-style anthology with no pictures or extras ... We went for songs that stand up as poetry or could be enjoyed on the page ... I'd note his thoughts, suggest ideas and we added brief annotations for each lyric – sort of observations or memories about where he was or what inspired the song.

Jeff Slate: That's the great thing about his songs, you can pull out the *Suburban 100* and look at them and be like, there's some poetry going on here, this is pretty cool, or you can take the records, and they're just remarkable in so many ways.

John Wilson: The earliest lyric in *Suburban 100* is 'Tube Station'. I was arguing with Paul for earlier lyrics like 'In the City' to show the full development. If I edited now, I'd insist on including it – that's him at seventeen years old, projecting himself and it's the aspiration and all of that idea. Some of those lyrics on the first album may have been a bit crude and naive but they tell a story as well. 'I know I come from Woking and you'll say I'm a fraud/But my heart is in the city where it belongs'.

September 2007 – 'Are You Trying to Be Lonely?' (no. 31)

Andy Lewis: My mobile phone rang in the middle of the night, and it's like, *what the fuck?* It was a number that I didn't know so I thought it was an emergency. I answered the phone. 'Hello? Yeah, this is Paul.' 'Paul? Paul?' 'Paul Weller, I've just been playing that CD of yours with that song on it. It's brilliant. I love it. Got to do something with this song. I've got some words and everything,' and he just starts gabbling away. 'Ah, you try to be lonely' 'Okay. Brilliant. Well, that's nice, Paul. Let's talk about this later.' I hung up and half an hour later the phone rings again. 'I've given your number to Charles at Black Barn. You got to come over, we gotta do this song. We gotta do this song.' Fair enough. Anyway, the following day I get a phone call from Charles at Black Barn Studios, and we set up a session where we go in and do this song.

26 October 2007 – Live in Greenspace, Valencia, Spain

Richard Hawley: Paul must have clocked my solo music really early on, man. He'd nod to me or say, 'All right!' and I'd think, *Why's he saying hello to me?* I couldn't get my head around it at first.

I remember arriving at the hotel after a long journey. It was really hot and I was at reception checking in. Shez [Sheridan] tapped me on the shoulder and said, 'Rich – incoming.' I see Weller and Cradock striding purposefully through this big dining area. They were walking across with quite some speed, kind of chucking chairs out of the way to get to where we were. Because of my childhood and the whole mods and rockers thing, I was thinking, *Fuck, there's gonna be a fight* . . . I dropped my arms by my sides, as taught by my uncle Eric, a boxer, and his best friend, Brendan Ingle.

I piss myself laughing now just thinking, *You stupid fucker, Hawley*, it's so ridiculous, but it was their intent to get over this room. Paul eventually got to me, and he just threw his arms around me, and he goes, 'Fucking love you, man. Your music.' That night, I played and Paul stood leaning on this flight case watching the whole set. That was unsettling. Now I wouldn't give a shit, but back then it was like, *Fucking hell, it's Weller.* Over time, we've become really solid pals, someone I know I could rely on if the shit hits the fan, and vice versa.

That night we ended up in Paul's room. We lifted the bed against the wall and danced the tango – completely pissed.

2008 – Paul Weller signs for Island Records

Tony Harlow: V2 was a complicated partnership. What David and I, along with Andy Gershon in America, were tasked with doing was to get the business profitable and sellable. I think we did that, and we made a lot of exciting music. We were partnered with a big bank in America. They went into a crisis and their financial structuring required certain things, and that was just the time when it had to happen, which was a real tragic thing for a lot of amazing people who I worked with.

Ted Cockle: I was running Island. We were in a great place, we'd got Amy Winehouse, Florence and the Machine, Mumford and Sons. So I was trusted, and I could be indulged in some things, to do things that I loved. I don't think I'm talking shit, but Paul turns up and there's a bloke running the company who is respectful, knows what he's about.

So that was 2008. You'd have discussions, conversations about what they were making but I was astute enough, clever enough, stupid enough to know that you wouldn't be having that conversation with him. This is when I'm saying I'm sketchy. I think we're in the deal, and you knew what you were getting, and he was up for it. I mean, the barnet was as crazy as you could imagine in those years. I always remember the one picture. It was like on the Greenwich Tunnel or something, and the barnet was completely bonkers all over the shop and everything was fucking madness.

Claire Moon: Paul was at V2 for a while before it was bought and absorbed by Universal, which is how he ended up back at Island Records for *22 Dreams* ... During the V2 years, John wasn't very involved, which is a shame. Hence Paul and I becoming close during that time. A lot of people were using me as a conduit to reach him, so he eventually said, 'You may as well just come and work for me.' That's literally how the conversation went . . .

I didn't actually work with John a huge amount because when I came to work for Paul, John was healthy, but he maybe was declining . . . I think what I learned from him, really, is that this is just a big family. I know that sounds really corny, but it is. His love for Paul and Paul's love for him, was just incredible to watch . . .

As for the cards . . . I did get rinsed, mainly by Kenny and John together as like a tag team.

25 May 2008 – Paul Weller's fiftieth birthday

Paul Moody: Paul turned 50 in 2008 and felt that he had to change for himself and break out of that straitjacket with the band. The album, *22 Dreams*, reached a broader audience than the hardcore . . . it was a key moment. There was a gig at Hammersmith Odeon on his fiftieth birthday and then a big party afterwards with Roger Daltrey, Peter Blake and Ian McLagan from the Faces, Martin Freeman, Bobby Gillespie, all there.

Eddie Piller: I was backstage chatting to Roger Daltrey, when he said, 'Excuse me, I think I've got to go on stage,' and casually walked out to sing 'Magic Bus'. Then Paul's mum, the lovely Ann, said, 'Ed, when Paul comes off stage for a fag halfway through the set, go out and sing "Happy Birthday".' Kenny Wheeler goes, 'If you do that, I can guarantee to you, he'll come on stage and punch you. You're not to do it.' Ann is going, 'If you don't do it, you're never coming to see my son's band again' . . . Paul comes off for a fag, I sneak on the other side of the stage, grab the microphone and say, 'It's somebody special's birthday today!' and led 6,000 people in 'Happy Birthday'. Paul kicked me up the arse.

2 June 2008 – *22 Dreams* (no. 1)

Charles Rees: Black Barn Studio originally was good for some things and not others. Great for demos, but if we wanted to get some really good drum sounds, we just didn't quite have the equipment then to make it solid. You have to learn to trust in a studio and now that Paul's spent years investing in the studio, it was just getting better and better. By the time we went full on digital and purchased some decent mics, decent pre-amps and all that stuff, then Paul was like, 'Yeah, this is really good.'

We recorded a song called 'Have You Made Up Your Mind' and I don't even think there was going to be an album then. It was a strange time. Paul may have found it hard to write at that time and so Simon Dine got brought back in and that meant we could have some days where we didn't need full on musicians here. We had samples. That was helpful and gave Paul back some creativity.

Paul Weller: Don't get me wrong. They're all great musicians, but, as a band, we were in a rut back then, and something had to happen, something had to change. We probably could have carried on playing live and doing really well, because we were a good live band. But the records . . . There were some good tunes here and there, but they were all just sounding a bit ploddy and a bit like going through it, to me anyway, I don't know how the others feel about that.

I just thought, *I can't make any more fucking records like this, something's got to change here.* Then I had a year off from touring, in which I made *22 Dreams*. There wasn't really a core band and that was good really, for me, because it meant I got different folk in. There was no preconception of what we're going to do and how this song goes. It just all unfolded as we went along. The more we made, the more it became apparent where else we could go with it.

Steve Cradock: He was going to have a year off after *As Is Now* and then he phoned up and said, 'Do you fancy just coming in and jamming in the studio?' I got here about two in the afternoon, and he was putting the guitar part down to 'Have You Made Up Your Mind', and by 2 o'clock the next morning the track was finished. That's always fun. That creation thing in front of your eyes. It's such a buzz to be around to see that happen.

Charles Rees: Paul was reflecting on his songwriting. He wanted something else. He's a bit tired of 'just the band'. He also really got into the studio as a tool. That's what changed it. Most things up to then had been done with a band live or you start a song with a few people in the studio, live, and then you do a few overdubs. Then you may embellish it more with an orchestra. Bear in mind that, I think, he'd done the same thing up until *Illumination*, until Simon Dine got involved. When he got involved, the palette of sounds changed. He helped Paul to discover new ways to write music, or at least to be inspired to write differently.

Paul Weller: It was mental. It was a wonderful, beautiful thing, but it was all booze-fuelled. Making *22 Dreams*, we did it over the course of a year. It was just fucking party central down here. Not drugs anymore, but drink. So, every day was just a massive piss up and celebration of, I don't know, life, I suppose. But that record came out of that. I always had a plan. But the record made itself; it just kept unfolding. It was sprawling and beautiful. I mean, there were two camps on the road: there was me and Cradock, the fucking nutters; and then there was Damon, the bass player, and Stevie . . . Whitey who were the more sensible, sober people. So, it was a little bit of a divisional thing going on, because we'd drive the other two fucking mad, blasting music out as loud as possible on the piss. But I enjoyed it anyway.

Damon Minchella: There was no falling out. It would have been harder for Steve White because he'd been with Weller at that stage for thirty years or something ridiculous . . . It just felt like the right time to move on. Paul does from time to time. It wasn't like we were sacked or anything. I remember Paul phoned up Whitey to say, 'Are you two going to come back and play?' and Whitey was like, 'I'd have to speak to Damon, but I think I can speak on his behalf and definitely on my behalf, that it's probably time for you to explore other options.' Paul was like, 'Yeah, I think you're probably right. Let's do that.' Even after that, Paul phones Whitey pretty much every week and he's always asking, 'How's Damon getting on, what's he doing?' Whitey would say, 'Paul, you know full well what he's doing . . . he's playing with Richard Ashcroft.'

Steve Brookes: He's not a sentimental person. If a lineup needs to be changed or something has to be changed, then he won't cling to it through sentimentality. He makes decisions and they're acted on. He doesn't dither.

Roger Nowell: *22 Dreams* was the first album fully down at Black Barn. Up until that point, he'd use this studio more for demoing, because back in those days, record companies would pay you to go to the Manor or Studio 150 or whatever. I think that's when the business started changing. Paul was out of a record deal at the time, so he had a free rein, and no pressure on him, so could just go down when he wanted. I'd pick him up in London and bring him down. He'd come with four chords and at the end of the day, it was a song. We spent weeks, months down here doing *22 Dreams*.

Tony Harlow: We have to be very clear. Paul Weller is a genius. He doesn't need any help from record company people. Paul made lots of music and he would play it to you generously. He knows what he's doing, he knows where his head's at. What was interesting in that period was talking to him about things like records that were exciting and collaborating. He was in a bit of an Alice Coltrane phase, and we would talk about how strange it was that people thought that Alice Coltrane is now more interesting than John Coltrane and things like that. We made *22 Dreams* and when the companies were exchanged, I went straight to Ted Cockle, who's a good mate, and gave him the cassette. I knew he would get on with Paul and fully respect it. I said, 'There's this record, it's fucking amazing.' That was the last record in the deal.

Ted Cockle: We worked out the record deal and Paul wants to shed his skin. Suddenly we were in the most indulgent double-album craziness, madness of *22 Dreams*. I remember the reviews when it came out, everyone's like, *It was delicate*. It didn't feel fucking delicate to me when that arrived. It felt like a fucking stream of chaos and consciousness. I've been around for the arrival of enough albums and that felt angular and completely fucking sprawling and it's a complete spirit of adventure.

Charles Rees: The regulars were Paul, Steve Cradock and Simon Dine. We'd push as far as possible before bringing in other musicians. Often, we'd handle the drums, or use samples to start it off, then guests would come in – even Steve White, who played beautifully on 'Cold Moments'. His style was perfect for that song, but it needed a little bit more ferocity than some of the songs. Just by chance working with other drummers on the album opened his mind. However fantastic Steve's sound is, I think we'd moved on, even then.

Steve Cradock: Steve came down to play on 'Cold Moments'. I think Paul and I were quite badly behaved. Looking back. We'd go to the pub and not come back here. We were lying in the middle of the road, looking at daytime stars or some bollocks. We were pissed up and it was a cold but fresh day and we just thought it'd be good to lie down and see it from a different direction. But then we looked up and there was a policeman there. And then Ann Weller turned up, which is even more scary than the old bill. 'What have we fucking done?' Whitey was annoyed. Rightfully so. He had been sat waiting all day. It's not cool, is it? There was a lot of chaos then, but through that came a lot of interesting ways of what the album is.

Ted Cockle: At that time, most people on the firm would say, you don't need to be around Paul after ten-thirty at night. You'd go to the Indian in Ripley. That was where things would continue and that was where that went on. Listen, I'm not a drinker . . . Even by then, I was over ten years in the industry and you're never going to be their mate. We got on and get on very well, but I'm not that person . . . We'd be at Black Barn, do the session. He'll make me a cup of tea beautifully. We'll have a biscuit. Then we'll let him off into the night.

Jamie Johnson: He's got an incredible constitution. For *22 Dreams,* his drinking was coming to a head. It used to amaze me how you could see the others falling by the wayside during the day. They would be on the couch, sleeping, but Paul still had the same energy and drive at the end of the day, and annoyingly, would still pick up on things, you think, *How can you be* *picking up on that little detail?* He's still pushing against the edge of something, to try and capture something amazing.

There were chaotic points during the end of those *22 Dreams* sessions. You can hear it in its music and drive. It's given him another kick – relentless and passionate.

Pat Gilbert: At the time, I knew *22 Dreams* was a really good album, but I didn't realise how important it was going to be historically. It was a crazy time. After the vindication of his solo years and becoming massive again with *Stanley Road*, he'd enjoyed boozing and travelling – more than he had ever done. That was towards the end of that thing.

We had three interview sessions for a *Mojo* cover story – one in an Italian restaurant, one at Black Barn and one where he was supporting The Rifles at the Town and Country Club. We were just pissed the whole time.

John Lewis: Some of the tracks on *22 Dreams* are co-credited to Simon Dine and Paul Weller – likewise the subsequent two albums. At this point Simon was presenting ideas or Paul was presenting fragments of an idea to Simon . . . Paul at his best is slightly outside of his comfort zone and with those different collaborators, different guests, different musicians moving in multiple genres all the time.

Steve Brookes: I played on a song called 'One Bright Star'. Paul phoned me one day and said, 'Have you got a Spanish guitar? Could you bring it over?' He'd never asked me to play on anything before, so it was nice to get the call.

Barrie Cadogan: Paul asked if we wanted to play on the title track . . . but it felt weird playing along to a drum loop that were already there. We found it quite hard. A good friend of ours, Tony Pritchard, came with us and to Tony's credit, he just said, 'Why don't you just cut one live?' It was done in a day.

Noel Gallagher: That album was another gear shift. I remember going down to Black Barn and we were doing 'Echoes Round the Sun', or what became it. He started playing us these tracks. After about ten you're going, 'How many fucking songs are on this record?' . . . it was chaotic, and mad, and disjointed, and funny, and fucking brilliant. I was with Gem. We're driving home going, 'Fucking hell, that is a record an eighteen-year-old would make.' He had a load of fucking ideas. It was so up, and joyous. I reckon it's up there with his best albums.

It's amazing. Really fucking is. 'Push It Along' is the stand-out one, the chord changes are mad, and the singing is wild. It was a gear shift going into hyperdrive for that thing.

Steve Cradock: Paul was ripping up the rule book totally. You'd come in one day and he'd say, 'You're going to play Moog. Dine's going to play the mellotron, and I'm going to do something else' and I'm like, 'Well what key's it in?' He said, 'I'm not telling you.' I think that was '111', which is just mental, isn't it? And then we'd mix it straight after, we'd have a channel each and we'd be thinking we're Lee 'Scratch' Perry over a B-side. But it was liberating, it was fun, and we were making crazy sounds. A lot of people really like that album, which is great because it could have gone the other way really.

Charles Rees: It probably was the album that changed it for Paul, studio wise, once and for all. There were no rules after that. You didn't have to just do this type of album or make sure that everything was as live as it could be. You could do songs, music, like '111' or 'God'.

Aziz Ibrahim: That wasn't my idea!

Charles Rees: In order to do that track we had to audition different people to read the words for 'God'. Paul had a go at first, Cradock had a go. Roger Nowell. Yeah. 'Ee bah gum! Aye! God!' You can imagine it. Sorry, Roger! But, yeah, that was funny.

Roger Nowell: I'm sure it was me right down until Aziz come in. Paul's brief with me is like, 'Read this, but just read it as yourself. Don't try and act it or do anything, just be you.'

Aziz Ibrahim: I'll tell you the story straight from the horse's mouth, now. I rang him up and he says, 'I'm just in the studio, we're working, why don't you come over?' I went to the studio, with a guitar on my back, hoping to play a little sneaky one. I walk in, and we always talk religion, so he presents me with this piece of paper with these lyrics on it and says, 'What do you think of that?'

This guy is a prolific and legendary songwriter and he's asking me, what do I think of these lyrics? I said 'I agree with what you're saying, and I agree about your approach, and your opinion, I think, very valid, very honest. That's my two penn'orth if you want it?' and he says 'Good. Now get in that room and read this out!' So that's how that came about. I went in this live room. Got this sheet of paper. I've only just had a little glance through it.

Now, little did I know that there was already a Steve Cradock, Chopper version of it on there. It's a one take thing. I come back in the control room, and he's sat there at the mixing desk, with his hands on two faders. One has got my voice on it, and the other has Chopper's voice on it. So he's going Steve . . . Aziz . . . Steve . . . Aziz. He's pulling these faders up and down. Then he turns around to me and says, 'Yeah, God's definitely a Manc!' [*laughs*]. Imagine if my own Muslim community knew what I'd done, blasphemy on this record! But thank God the two cultures don't meet. I don't think anybody in the mosque bought that album, otherwise, there'd have been a jihad on my arse!

Charles Rees: There were plenty of late nights, and we were trying different things. When we did the demo for the song '22 Dreams', I remember coming back, we'd all had a few to drink, recording over Paul's drums that he'd just played, putting it down. Paul didn't seem to mind. We carried on overdubbing.

Jamie Johnson: Oh, blimey! I used to feel bad for the neighbours. We used to listen to that so loud at three in the morning, the doors wide open and you'd go outside for a fag. It's just countryside, there's nothing to stop it. It must be going for miles. They probably don't mind.

There was quite a bit of tension at the time with the Pro Tools and working differently. It was always at two or three in the morning so everyone's always a bit tired and slightly drunk. There's a sense that it's quicker and easier to edit something on the screen rather than play it through and do the edits on a fader like you would have with tape, but sometimes it makes the creative process a bit duller. Everyone's looking at this box in the corner of the room, because it's all happening there, on this screen, rather than what you used to do, which is happening in the room.

Tim Shepard: I was brought in to do the cover right at the start . . . I went down to listen to the demos, very early stages, sat and listened to about ninety minutes' worth of stuff, just quietly, him sitting next to me at the desk and then he asked me, 'So do you feel it?' . . . 'Absolutely I do. I think this is brilliant.' I went to Black Barn regularly over the year, so that cover is a collage that captures the landscape around the studio, which is a walk that he goes on to clear his head.

I didn't show Paul anything until very, very close to it being finished, he loved it, and he only had one comment, and it was interesting. He said that he felt he wanted to live there in this space . . . He could really feel like he could walk through these gates on the front of the picture and enter into this space ... But he asked me if I could put a religious symbol, like a crucifix as a blessing as you go through the gates. I had a little crucifix at home. Took a picture of that, stuck it on and you can see if you look closely there's a little cross on the gate.

Lawrence Watson: For the album inlay, we'd sit down with the imagery and revisit contact sheets. He knows he's going to have to live with those images for the rest of his life ... on 22 *Dreams* the hair is a bit long. That's probably one of the times that I think the hair could have been trimmed a bit on the sides.

Ted Cockle: The chart position is something that is rooted in the spirit of every artist ... He's cool enough, but in his heart of hearts, there won't be anything nicer to him still than to say he's got a number one album. It's a major fuel for Paul.

David Quantick: The first thing that came into my head with that album was that it sounds like someone barging about in an attic with a dim bulb looking for things. It's very clattery.

Jeff Slate: The best artists, the people that we love the most, the Dylans and the Lennons and Tom Petty. Paul Weller. They don't care what we want from them. There's ego in what they do. They want to sell records, but they also balance that with a big helping of 'I don't give a fuck!'

Tony Harlow: It was, kind of, ahead of all shuffle culture. It was Paul Weller doing music he liked, in all sorts of genres and completely freed from the context of 'this album must sound like this'. That record was an explosion of colour ... Amazing.

Paul Weller: 22 *Dreams* was a very pivotal moment for me really, in terms of making records, how to make a record, how you go about it. Almost like how I felt back at that start of The Style

Council where we didn't have a band, then got different people in, and that changes things, everyone brings something else different to it. It was a great record, I think as well. But it's an important record . . . because it just showed that there ain't really any rules. You just make it up as you go along, as we all do in life anyway. But there's something, sometimes, really beautiful about that, and unexpected that happens as well. So that was important, and I think that outlook has probably endured since.

May–July 2008 – Tour

Andy Lewis: The first gig where I played bass in Paul Weller's band was at the Roundhouse in March of 2008 for a Crisis charity gig. We went to the studio, we were there all day and spent most of the time drinking tea, chatting, mucking around listening to music, having the fun and then we went in and did some work, and it was a twenty-minute rehearsal for a half-hour show. Paul said, 'Oh, don't bother rehearsing that, it'd be fine.'

We then played a little place in Oxford as the first on the *22 Dreams* tour. It's the first time that I'd played at that level of anticipation and excitement, everybody who was there was dead keen to see what was going on. There was a sense that the new band was finding our feet a little bit, but at the same time everybody involved in it wanted it to be good, and everybody else in the band did as well.

I wasn't even worried about whether the fans were going to accept me. It was more like, can I do this? It's a really amazing thing to discover that actually you can, and that someone who you've admired for a very long time is not only giving you the chance to do something but has absolute confidence in your ability to do it. It's an incredible thing. It's not that I didn't care what the fans thought, it's just if I thought about it for a moment, I'd have locked myself in a cupboard and refused to do it. It was a hard enough job thinking, the last person who played bass on this song live was Bruce Foxton or Camelle Hinds or Yolanda Charles or Damon Minchella. I wouldn't have done it, if I'd thought about what the fans were going to think.

Steve Pilgrim: I'd just landed in the south of France with my wife on holiday, our first abroad since we've been married and Paul was like, 'Oh, I've got this thing happening, can you make it down next week?' and I just said, 'I'm really sorry, Paul, I've just landed. I don't think I can get back,' and he's like, 'Oh, no problem, no problem at all.' Beep. Phone went dead. I didn't hear from him for another twelve months . . . 'Can you come down to Black Barn and have a jam on some stuff?'

Andy Crofts: In one of my random texts to Paul over the years, I did say . . . 'I know you got a bass player, but if you need someone else . . .' A year later or so, I get a call from Paul, saying, 'I'm looking for a keyboard player for the band, are you interested?' and I was like 'Yeah!' Then went and got my keyboard book out!

Andy Lewis: There were a few people who just weren't having it. The sort of people who don't like change in any way, shape or form, feel quite resentful if they're being asked to stretch their minds a little bit. They're the kind of people who maybe had been left behind by The Style Council but came back in when it became more fashionable to like Weller again. People who go, 'It's my favourite Weller song. "Pebbles on the Beach" or "Hanging on a Wire". I love that one.' There's that mentality. I wasn't worried about it.

Steve Pilgrim: I remember early on when I joined, there was quite a lot of heckling about Whitey coming to the stage directed at me. Definitely some voices that weren't happy about the shift, and there are some that still aren't happy. But there's also been a lot of people who say now is the best band that Paul's ever had. As a unit, we work like a machine, and I'm really proud with how we work as a band and how we all sit in each other's pockets and fill the spaces and allow spaces for others . . . I'm happy that I'm still part of it.

Andy Crofts: I think the first night I ever played officially was Oxford. Bricked it a bit . . . everybody who loves Weller knows everybody in the band. There was a lot of strange faces that night, *What's going on?* A complete turnaround in the band apart from Cradock. There was a weird vibe, but it was good. It did what he wanted it to do.

Pete Paphides: *22 Dreams* was a special time for me because I got a glimmer into the process at the beginning of its creation. It was an exciting time to be a fan of his, and I really wanted to write something about him, just to mark that point in the tour. The opportunity came on the last night of the UK tour when they played at Leicester De Montfort Hall. It was a brilliant gig. Natt joined him on stage for a bit. Paul looked really proud to see him on stage with him.

We all piled into the tour bus afterwards. Everyone started drinking hard and quick, straight away. There was a real atmosphere of euphoria on the bus because it had been the last night, the tour had gone well. The album got to number one. He was fifty years old now. He was really at a creative and commercial zenith with a record that was really uncompromising and brilliant and imaginative. The great thing was, what did we listen to on the way back? . . . We listened to *22 Dreams* [*laughs*]. He had a bottle of beer in one hand. He was punching the air, singing along to one of the songs. Maybe that sounds naff but there was a real purity about it. He's like this generally

– like someone who has won a competition to be the lead singer in Paul Weller's band for a day and he just happens to be Paul Weller. He hasn't lost that.

I managed to get my interview, whilst everyone's spirits were getting higher and higher and suddenly, we were in West London. But he's drunk and he's already turned to me and uttered the immortal words 'Pete, have you ever been to Kebab Machine?' 'No, I haven't.' 'You've never been to Kebab Machine?' 'What is it?' He says, 'A kebab shop. But it's better than all the other kebabs.'

His idea is that the tour bus, and everyone on it, should park outside Kebab Machine while Paul gets two kebabs. One for me and one for him. Tour manager is like, 'Fuck that. The band need to sleep ... But if you want to get a kebab then, bottom line is there's going to be a car waiting for you to take you to *Later* at nine o'clock tomorrow morning.' It's already two in the morning. So we roll out and Paul orders two kebabs. While he's waiting for his kebab, a bunch of Roger Waters fans, who've been to see him at the O2, recognise him and he's immediately posing. Suddenly he's life and soul of the party, posing for photographs with these Roger Waters fans that look like they've just tumbled out of David and Sam Cameron's house.

He insists on ordering my kebab as well, and then the guy goes, 'How many chilies do you want on your kebab?' He says something ridiculous, like ten or something. But he then, in this weird drunken logic, specifies the amount I have to have on my kebab. Three less than his. We get into the cab, and go back, but not too far away. One good thing about Paul is he asks you a lot of questions about yourself. It's untypical of a lot of musicians, especially well-known ones. He says, 'How many kids you got then Pete?' 'Two.' 'You going to have any more?' 'No, I don't think we can, really, because in terms of trying to do our day jobs and stuff, two is about the maximum really.' He said

'Oh, you should. You won't regret it. I'd just keep on having kids for the rest of my life if I could.' Anyway, he gets out of the cab, and I see him through the window, opening his front door. Then I get to my house and the taxi driver goes, 'What are you going to do about your luggage?' I said, 'I haven't got any luggage. I've just got this shoulder bag.' There's a massive suitcase, maybe a guitar or something in the boot. He's just left all his luggage, three weeks of touring, in the cab. So, I take it into my house and take care of it. That really expensive looking leather jacket he was wearing at the time, that was there as well. Caitlin and I are taking the kids to school the following morning, the car has already come to pick up Paul's luggage and I'm saying to Caitlin, 'I've got to watch *Later* tonight, because God knows what state him and his band are going to be in.'

At that moment, the phone rings and it's Paul. I can hear music blaring out in the background. 'What'd you think about that kebab last night?' I didn't really know what he was expecting me to say, it's a kebab, but I said 'Yeah, it was okay.' 'You know what? I think that is the best kebab I've ever had in my life. I can still taste it now.' It was like he'd never had a hangover in his life. He's sounded completely delighted and happy. I tuned in that night to watch him on *Later*. It was a really good performance. No apparent downside.

Mark Cooper: Paul had taken a huge leap forward and reinvented himself in terms of production. The spread of songs on that record are incredible. He was reborn. On Friday nights, BBC Four had started to create programmes for real music lovers. We were building somewhere for people to come and doing a lot of sessions. David Byrne, Youssou N'Dour, John Cale. We did a special with Paul at Television Centre. Eliza Carthy came and played on 'Wild Wood' and 'Where'er Ye Go', and then Graham Coxon and some other guests.

Barrie Cadogan: It was fairly short notice. Paul said, 'we're filming a TV special, would you come and play the song?' I remember getting a cab down to Shepherd's Bush and playing the song. I had red trousers on. My favourite colour. I got away with them then! It's always great to play with people you like playing with and you like the song. But those types of things, a fair amount of it is just winging it. Sometimes you get a chance to run through something at sound check, sometimes you don't, so you just get up and do your best. It's a lot of fun but you're flying on the seat of your pants a bit.

Eliza Carthy: It was so weird to be playing 'Wild Wood' and not be singing it as well. What an honour. Paul was so lovely that day. I was wearing a knockoff silk, cow print wraparound dress. I was about eleven weeks pregnant but hadn't announced it yet and I was already starting to show. I'm desperately trying to be glamorous, walk into the studio for soundcheck and Paul came up to me, threw his arms around me, gave me a massive cuddle and stood back and went, 'Corr, you've got a body on you, girl. How's your dad?' It was one of the loveliest things that anyone's ever said to me. It made me feel completely at ease straight away. Just lovely. The whole gig was amazing.

The after party was the weirdest thing. It was an invited audience of competition winners, so it was all Weller heads in the audience. All mods. All with the haircut. All Wellends, it was amazing. We went to the BBC bar and Phill Jupitus was there, Robbie Coltrane and people like that – all there to see Paul. But the other thing that was happening in the BBC bar that night was the last night of *Strictly Come Dancing*. It was this combination of glittered up bloody ballroom dancers and mods. The mods on one side and Jodie Kidd in a spray-on diamanté gown and Bruce Forsyth over there. I wasn't drinking because I was pregnant and I was just looking around, going, *This has got to be one of the strangest nights of my life.*

Souad Massi – 'Let Me Be in Peace' (One Take Version)

Souad Massi: Paul knew my work and music which amazed me. He asked if he could do a new arrangement of my song 'Ghir Enta' which he did as 'One Bright Star' and invited me to work together to make a song at his studio.

He gave me a paper and pen and asked me to write a song on the spot – improvisation music. I was surprised, so I told him 'I need time.' He told me, 'Okay, 1 hour, 2 hours.' *[Laughs]*

It was the first time I've done anything that quickly. It was a big opportunity for me, and I wrote a song called 'Let Me Be in Peace' – about children suffering in the world. I started with the words, and I told him the meaning of the song and improvised on piano.

He asked me 'do you want to drink? Something to smoke?' I told him I don't smoke. I drink only water. So, he told me I'm not a rock and roll star [*laughs*].

Paul gave me valuable advice: don't take a lot of attention to the words. The most important thing is that you are real when you sing, people feel it. Now when I write, I work with that idea.

Dot Allison – 'Love's Got me Crazy'

Dot Allison: Paul texted me completely out of the blue. 'Hi it's Paul Weller, I'm with Bobby Gillespie. I hope you don't mind; he says you're good. Should we write a song together?' I said to my mum, 'I think somebody's winding me up.' I was really shocked and really blown away and excited and slightly nervous because I'm quite shy. I wanted to do it and then thought, oh, God, don't embarrass myself.

He had a song called 'Love's Got Me Crazy', that he wanted to continue working on and he'd like to co-write on it to help complete it. We ended up nailing a few ideas via text, working on the bones of it.

Once we had a direction, we met at Black Barn to finish and record it. It was lovely – he even wrote me a letter and sent it with an explanation of the plans for the collaboration.

I learnt a lot from Paul about songwriting, because he was searching for perfection in one line that we were not entirely sure about. We ended up rewriting the last line and improving it. It was important that the word scanned with the melody and I was thinking of songs like 'That's Entertainment' – it makes total sense. Seeing how it all locked into the chorus was a real learning curve for me and something I've carried forward.

Paul was doing a lot of writing at the time, and the song found a home on my album.

June 2008 – *Mojo* Award, Outstanding Contribution to Music

Claire Moon: Paul is really humble. While he might say, 'I don't care about awards,' I think they mean something to him. I often get emailed about awards. 'We'd like to present Paul with a Brit' or, 'Paul's been nominated for an award.' I'll tell him, all excited, and he'll just go, 'What, me?' Why'd they want to give it to me?' I'm like, 'Because you're Paul Weller!'

Graham Coxon: I remember presenting Paul with the *Mojo* Outstanding Contribution to Music award. At the time, he was sporting a man bag that he was quite proud of.

It's a crazy thing giving Paul an award because I've been a huge admirer from such a young age. Always keeping my eye on his progression musically.

When I presented the award, I probably bowed. Paul is very self-effacing and seems startled by any kind of love, or admiration.

Richard Hawley: It was an awards thing, that celeby-shite, which Paul and I loathe . . . I remember Paul saying, 'Rich, don't get excited about awards – if you hang around long enough, mate, they give you one anyway . . .'

One thing I've noticed, if Paul likes you, it's dead on. There's no side to him. He'll just talk to you one to one. No bullshit. I have seen what he can be like if he doesn't like somebody and it's fucking funny.

We did a radio show once together . . . the first question he was asked was, 'Has anyone ever said to you [*sings*] Weller-Weller-Weller Ooo . . . Tell me more, Tell me more . . .' Paul just shut up. Completely zipped up and didn't reply to anything else. There was about a minute's silence on radio. It felt like an eternity . . . I was in the other room crying with laughter because he was so brutal.

Paul means business. He's not around for the benefit of pleasing people. He is with his music and his art, but he's deadly serious about what he's doing.

26 May 2008 – 'Have You Made Up Your Mind' / 'Echoes Round the Sun' (no. 19)

25 August 2008 – 'All I Wanna Do (Is Be with You)' / 'Push It Along' (no. 29)

3 November 2008 – 'Sea Spray' / '22 Dreams' (no. 59)

2008 – *22 Dreams* World Tour – Japan, Australia, USA, Europe & UK

Bill Wheeler: The actual thing from going from merch to tour manager . . . I got taken to America and Japan selling T-shirts, which is bonkers. Dad and John had been a team for so long, when John started to take a step back or just couldn't be there all the time, Dad was then kind of on his own. It's a fucking lot . . . six-, seven-piece band it could be sometimes . . . maybe ten to twelve crew. That's a lot of people. I got taken out because he just needed another pair of hands. And then I just got more and more responsibility, and then Dad couldn't travel certain places.

My first tour on my own was Japan, which sounds daunting, but Japan's a great place to tour because they do a lot of it for you. You send everything over and they're so organised over there, there's never a problem. I got nervous before, because I was also the youngest person on the whole thing. Got all these crew guys who have been with Paul for a very long time . . .

Everyone was drinking then, and I had way too many on the plane and had to get put back in my seat. I'm meant to be the one in charge! When I look back on it, it's really fucking embarrassing to be honest. I'm putting it down to nerves!

Andy Lewis: I think a lot of people there really didn't know what to expect from those live gigs, and of course, Paul turned up full of aggression to prove himself as a new contemporary, innovative artist, pushing the frontiers of what he could get away with, in terms of popularity. Most of the people there were really up for it, because we played enough of the hits. We played 'Speak Like a Child', which had been a hit down there and a few other things that they knew, but most of the people that were there were just caught up in the excitement of having him there. He really went for it as well. I remember by the time we got to Brisbane, he'd actually lost his voice and so some of the shows had to be rescheduled, which was a bit of a tough ask because we were on a really tight schedule. We went straight from the final gig to the airport and then off to America.

This is how it was on the *22 Dreams* tour. Paul had made a decision that he was going to push the boundary in every direction. He felt comfortable having a band that could rock out for The Jam with 'Eton Rifles', could be soulful enough to cover Style Council things and were flexible and hip enough for what he wanted to do, to cope with the new material, which was big, it was a lot to take on board.

22 April 2009 – John Weller dies from pneumonia

Paul Weller: I can't remember what year it was, but he would be all right for a bit on the tour then he'd have to go home because he caught a chest infection or would be ill. But being on the road, late nights, being up all-night drinking, it's not good, not if you're not 100% it ain't. Well, it's not good for anyone. So, he was still continuing that lifestyle really, when possibly he should have been at home putting his feet up or being with my mum. But what could I do? It was hard for me to say to him you're sacked, or you should really turn this in, mate. How am I going to say that to him? 'As my dad, I think you should really fucking turn this in, mate, and go home?' But I also knew how much he loved it as well. So, it's very, very difficult. But, in life, you pay your money, and you take your choice, and that was his decision. He had an amazing life. I mean, he died at seventy-seven. Okay, well, he could have gone for another ten years and been eighty-seven. You know, well, what the fuck? You know what I mean? What difference does that make? So, he lived his life how he wanted to live it, and I think that's fair enough. Whether he made the best decisions at times is another matter, but that applies to all of us.

Jun Sato: Very sad, because he's one of the few managers that really, really protected the artist. It's not about the 24 per cent cut that American managers care about. He really cared about his son, which was pretty beautiful. I did visit his cemetery. There was a bench that Paul set up, in Ripley, but I told Paul later, I couldn't sit on that bench because it was like sitting on John's head!

Kenny Wheeler: I was thinking about him the other day, just talking about John. When we got married, he drove Pat to the church, silly things like that . . . He was great that way. When we done the gigs in Paris, and the fans come over on the buses, one bus driver drove off and left two young girls over there. Went off with their passports on this bus. John got hold of them, got in touch with their families, told them they was all right. Put 'em in a hotel overnight and made arrangements for 'em to get home. He cared about the fans, and it went right the way through from day one. That's why I used to get told off! John, he weren't a big man, but he filled a room, I'll tell you that. He was my mate.

Dee C. Lee: I'm still very close with Paul's family. John had very much become the dad that I didn't have. We were very, very close and he's very, very, very dearly missed. But my God, he was such a good man and such a funny man. Losing John caused a major shift in dynamics in the family, as you can imagine, because he really was the backbone. But for quite a while he was becoming weaker and weaker, so it wasn't a great time. Paul and I weren't together . . . but we still very much had a lot of family commitments. So, we'd still be there for each other for, like if I had a funeral or something, Paul would just turn up for me . . .

It was a very, very sad time to be honest and it took a little while for us all to adapt and find our feet. John was a very, very big part of our lives. That's Paul's dad but he was also my father-in-law. I really had a lot of love. We were very, very close as a family and that's probably more than anything what I miss because it was one thing when you have a partner but when you have families that actually intertwine and love each other and get on, it's a very rare thing. When Paul and I split up, it wasn't just heartbreaking for Paul and I, we broke a lot of other people's hearts too within the family.

Martin Hopewell: I'm the ex-public school university chap with the little briefcase and the jacket and everything else, and John was like a lovely mixture of Del Boy and Ronnie Barker in *Open All Hours*. You wouldn't have thought that we'd have got on, but we really did. John didn't have any time for nonsense. Neither did Paul. Absolutely you don't fuck about and really, if your name wasn't Weller, then you didn't really count as anything. You were very disposable.

I'm probably wrong, but I always thought I was like an honorary Weller in a funny sort of way. I'd call up to speak to John at home. Ann would answer the phone and go, 'John . . . it's your only friend!' When John died and I sent some flowers. I put, 'From your only friend,' and probably people looked at that and thought, *You arrogant little tosser*, but that was the joke . . .

The thing for John was getting out on the road, sampling the bars and the restaurants and stuff like that, looking after Paul. Every night, he'd be on this little flight case on the side of the stage, sitting there with his leather jacket and his white hair all swept back and everything.

I mean, loved him. He was an absolutely smashing bloke. I have a huge debt of gratitude to not just Paul, but to John as well. Because so much stuff that happened to me wouldn't have happened if it hadn't been for their loyalty.

Bill Wheeler: John was a very genuine, down to earth person. My dad loved John to the bone. He felt a lot of gratitude because he went from potentially being security, to being given this ridiculous fucking opportunity. My dad has forever been grateful to the Wellers. It's hard to explain because it was just like a group of mates travelling around the world, having a laugh. John was the manager, and dad did the job he needed to do. But then they would just sit in a room and play cards together. Once the gig was done, they'd sit at a bar together and just chat.

John was really good to me – as a kid and when I got older and was doing the merch. He liked the fact that I used to bring all the cash at the end of the night! He was happy to see me coming.

Same for Ann Weller. She's a lovely lady that I get on really, really well with as well. She misses John loads. It's always had a family element to it. It's tight. Paul and the Wellers. They're very down to earth, loyal people.

Bruce Foxton: John was just unbelievable. Nothing but praise to say about John. The whole package. If it hadn't been for John, we wouldn't have been anywhere.

Sam Molnar: His funeral was a sad occasion, but there was loads of people there and it was a lovely turnout, beautiful service. At the hotel afterwards, I'm sure Nicky won't mind me saying it, but we got asked to leave because it got a bit rowdy. I phoned her the following day and said, 'Your dad would have loved that.'

Ted Kessler: I was writing my book *My Old Man, Tales of our Fathers* and asked Paul if he'd talk about John. This was after his passing. I went down to Ripley. It was quite fresh in his mind and it's really beautiful what he said about his dad. He sent me a photo of him and John, and said, 'Pissed in some airport somewhere!' John was quite badly ill for a couple of years, and I think it really affected Paul. I think the book was a nice outlet for him to say something about that period.

Richard Hawley: That was another thing with me and Paul. We lost our dads at a similar time, and we were both very close to our fathers.

Another side of Paul, which people don't know or aren't aware of, is that he's incredibly kind and an immensely sensitive human being to others. There's been occasions on a personal level that he's helped me out immensely. Emotionally over certain things, and vice versa. That's the nature of when you truly love somebody as an artist and as a person as well. You're always there, to help them out, and over the years we've become extremely close.

David Quantick: The two big freedom moments in Paul Weller's life are when The Jam split up and, less nicely, when his dad died, and I don't mean that cruelly, but when John Weller died at the end of a very long career, looking after Paul Weller, Weller just seemed to change. He gave up drinking and became experimental again. It could be a complete coincidence, it could just be nonsense that I'm talking, but I think a big traumatic event like that either knocks you down completely or you make a fresh start.

January 2010 – *Keb Darge & Paul Weller Present . . . Lost and Found*

Keb Darge: This is not a silly story. This is true. I first met Paul in a urinal comparing each other's penises! I used to do a stall at Camden Market. Nicky was in a stall opposite, and we got pally. She asked me to DJ at her birthday party. I goes for a piss and then Paul comes into the toilet. 'Great tunes, man! . . . Do you deal in records? There's a few I'm after. Can you help me?' 'All right. Nae bother.' And from then on, it was every fucking week he was phoning up, 'Can you get me one of these . . . ?'

We did a compilation called *Lost and Found* and I'll give him his due. I was up in Scotland; I get a phone call from the cunt. He says 'I've just seen the sleeve. It's not right.' 'What's wrong with it, Paul?' 'Well, it's got my name at the top in big writing, and your name in smaller writing, Keb. I'm telling them to change that' and he fucking did, got them to put my name on top, above his. . . .

We went to Europe DJing together. We're at the train station coming back through Belgium. Tickets booked and Paul's like, 'Do us a favour, take my records home. I'm off to Amsterdam.' I thought, *For fuck's sake, Paul* . . . We were DJing in Belgium,

I thought, *He's going a bit hard here. Christ, he's going to die. God almighty.* I was looking after him, DJing, then goes back to the hotel and I put him in his room and I goes to my room to go to sleep and think, *Thank fuck he's asleep now. I'll get a decent sleep. Don't have to worry about him any more.* Fucking eight in the morning. Bang on my door. 'Come on, Keb. The bar's open!' . . . I did think at one point, *Christ, I'm going to be the one that's going to fucking have to say to all the world, Paul died in his toilet surrounded by his own vomit and pee.*

12 April 2010 – 'No Tears to Cry' / 'Wake Up the Nation' (no. 26)

19 April 2010 – *Wake Up the Nation* (no. 2)

Craig McLean: I interviewed Paul for the *Telegraph*, just ahead of the release of *Wake Up the Nation.* We spoke a lot about his dad. God knows how that must have hit him, given how close they'd been as a family and as a working relationship. The man hours they must have spent together just defies tabulation . . . He was telling me how what happened with his dad deepened his faith. I don't think any of us would ever have thought that he would be a man of any kind of faith . . . I don't think he was talking about it in a real Christian sense per se, maybe just more in a general spiritual sense . . .

The flip of that is the fact that he's in a new relationship now as well with Hannah. He'd split with Sam a year and a half previously, so obviously a time of huge tumult in his life and at that point he's nearly fifty-two. A lot going on in his life.

Paul Weller: I love that thing of getting here in the morning and having a very, very loose, raw idea, and it doesn't feel like it's going anywhere. Then suddenly, within a matter of hours, by the afternoon or evening, you play it back and it's like, ah, OK, there's a track forming here, the song's forming here. I always think that's fascinating. There's something magical about that. All of a sudden it turns and changes and you've got something very real, and something's come alive, and you don't really know how that happened. It's just flipped and there's something there. I don't know if you really want to understand why or how that happens because it will spoil it. I don't know if there is any way of explaining it either. It's the same with gigs, because you can play five gigs in a row and they'll all be good, but one will be great. And you don't know why that is. No idea why. Something just clicks, something in the room. You become one with the audience, they become one with you. You can't plan for that, and you can't really explain how that happens.

Charles Rees: The actual creation of the album, because of Simon Dine and samples, was a continuation of *22 Dreams*, but I would say a lot harder. Everything about it seemed even more intense and more focused. I absolutely loved making that album.

Terry Edwards: That album was largely, if not entirely, co-written with Simon Dine . . . He was a neighbour of mine, lived down the road and shared a house with someone I knew. As happens when you've been doing this for a while, people go, 'We need a saxophone on this. I know . . . Terry!' . . . I played baritone on the song 'Wake Up the Nation' and flugelhorn on 'Grasp & Still Connect'. I was replacing samples on the tune that was in there. Simon's way of working was sampling things, taking sounds and putting things together. He's not a songwriter in the truest sense. He's always taken bits and pieces and been a bit of a magpie in a certain way . . . some of the drum samples, they're very much that sixties feel.

Bev Bevan: Paul called me out of the blue to ask if I'd play on the *Wake Up the Nation* album. I don't even know where he got my number from, but he said, 'I'm such a massive Move fan, man. I love The Move and The Who, but I got to tell you, you're not my first choice.' I laughed and said, 'OK.' He said, 'No, I wanted Keith Moon, but he's been dead twenty years.' I know you can play like Mooney, so I want you to do that.'

Bruce Foxton: Playing on that album was another step of having our renewed friendship ... We'd had a disagreement in the nineties about The Jam's merchandise ... it was a complete waste of time and cost our friendship a lot at the time. Did a bit of damage. It was a while before Paul and I got to speak to each other again and move on. My first wife, Pat, had cancer and we were in Israel for treatment . . . he called us while we were in Tel Aviv, just to wish us all the best with my wife's treatment. That meant so much as well that he took the time out and gradually it just made you realise that life's too short. It's classic. This is crazy. Why have we not spoken for so long? We moved on. Now, I don't see him every day of the week, but we're friends, simple as that. I played on a couple of his tracks, on his various albums. He's played on a couple of our albums . . .

I went down to Black Barn to record. I've never seen so many people in the control room. I think they'd heard that I was coming in to play on one of Paul's tracks and they just wanted to see and hear it so it was like a mini gig almost. It was already pressure enough because I wanted to do a good job on Paul's album and then you've got this huge crowd of people there, expecting magic and the spark. Hopefully they got what they came for, but that was the most awkward bit. It's a bit, *Fucking hell, I've got an audience now as well. Paul better like it.*

Steve Hinders: 'Fast Car, Slow Traffic' is the one he and Bruce collaborated on. What a song. Wow, that's Bruce and Paul right there. That's the closest The Jam are ever going to get to being back together. That is so cool by me.

Ted Cockle: *22 Dreams* was mental – a very esoteric, sprawling spirit of adventure going off. And then a couple of years later, we go straight in to *Wake up the Nation*. The fucking madness of that. Exciting, obstinate, esoteric. Fuck you. He was nicely on form.

Steve Cradock: I went down a few times during that album recording and the mixing sounded bonkers. I don't know when Charles stopped smoking weed, but whenever I heard anything back the production sounded messy.

Andy Lewis: That was the last album Paul made as a drinker. After that album, he knocked it on the head and I tell you what, musically, it got so much better. You didn't have that horrible, 'Which Paul are we going to get today?' moment . . . it meant that all the rubbish that goes with it, the paranoia of drunkenness and stuff like that, goes out the window. You can concentrate on the job in hand and actually develop a relationship which isn't based on either backslapping bonhomie or physical violence. You could get back to what it's all about, which is the music and the clothes and being a little gang of people that are into the same thing.

Paul Moody: We all get to that point in your life when it's like, *Hang on, I don't think this is a good idea*. You either have a health scare or you just come to the realisation. The beauty of that is I think that the creativity is stronger than ever. The booze gets in the way of the muse. He can now wake up with a clear head and go into Black Barn, and suddenly the ideas are flowing, and he hasn't got that four-day hangover that he might have had during those albums.

Chris Catchpole: Simon Dine had an important role on that record. Paul was going in cold and working on loops and samples. To think at that point in your career, where you're used to sitting down with acoustic guitars and writing songs very successfully for forty years, to throw all of that out the window and try a completely new way of working, I think it's amazing. *Wake up the Nation* is right up there. It's a great record – angry, eccentric, and overflowing with ideas. It's mad – one of the oddest records he's ever made.

May 2010 – Five nights at the Royal Albert Hall

Andy Crofts: I attempted to wear this suit jacket that was a bit tight, and I was going through a fat Elvis period at the time, so I was struggling. I looked like a fat crow! We'd been pestering Paul to play something like 'In the City' and it came to the point where he just said, 'You can sing "Art School",' and I was like, yeah, of course I'll sing 'Art School' but in the back of my head I was like, the fans ain't going to care if I'm singing it.

Bruce Foxton: I was really very proud to have performed with Paul at the Albert Hall . . . The hardest part about that show was, I had my own dressing room at the Albert Hall, which I couldn't believe, but there's a bottle of red wine in there as a hospitality, and it was so hard to not have a drink before I went on . . . I could have a little taste and maybe . . . no, no, no. That was difficult, but, yeah, it was really emotional for me as well. I could see the family and my mates . . . A moment I'll never forget.

Steve Cradock: I realised what an amazing bass sound Bruce Foxton had . . . I never saw The Jam live, but he's just got . . . I don't even know how to describe it. It's fucking loud. There's loads of bass and there's loads of treble. I've never heard a bass guitar like it since. I'd imagine it's similar to the way that John Entwhistle had his. I guess it's a three-piece thing, that has to be the guitar just doing chordal things, doesn't it? Then you've got this beautiful thing that plays the riffs, the intros. It's a bit of a muso thing to go on about really, but that's how good he was as a bass player. It was nice to see that they were friendly enough to play with each other and the way it went down was just incredible. 'Fast Car, Slow Traffic'. I think that's a fucking great tune that is. It was nice that he was playing something new and then they did 'Eton Rifles' and 'Butterfly Collector'. It was fucking incredible.

Steve Brookes: Yeah, I was at that one. Everyone got excited that it was all going to get going again.

Andy Lewis: Some people said to me, 'Didn't you get the hump when Bruce came on?' No, absolutely not. Because he played on the record and also, more importantly, it's the closest I'll ever get to seeing The Jam. Even more significantly to be part of that, playing in the same band as all of them, because I think when he took over on the bass, I played the piano on one song, guitar on another, and Hammond on another. It was a really fun thing to be doing. It just felt so good.

Richard Hawley: Paul played at the Albert Hall and invited me to go down. It was when the smoking ban came in, so me, Paul and Hannah went into the bogs . . . Open the window, in we go. Hannah asked me to play my song 'For Your Lover, Give Some Time'. They both loved that song. They were courting then, and that song became something fairly important for them. We were having a fag in the bogs, and I sang them that song.

July 2010 – Paul gives up alcohol

Paul Weller: When I stopped drinking, it was like my body just said, 'You've finished now, had your time, you've done.' And that was it. I'm not saying it was that easy, but that's what spurred me on. There was this internal voice, whatever you want to call that.

Do you know what? And I really don't want to go on about this because it's so boring. But when I stopped drinking and got sober, I immediately felt more comfortable in myself. People say booze releases your demons, but I don't know if a lot of the demons are actually in the bottle. A lot of the things I used to worry about, or think about, when I was drinking, stopped like that. They vanished. It's just like they weren't important, and I don't even think about them any more. Why am I telling you this? Because that's what made me realise, from that time especially, I just felt immediately more comfortable in myself really. Obviously, that's getting older, and old age as well does that if you're lucky, I suppose.

Claire Moon: He massively has strong willpower . . . and literally didn't touch a drop again . . . I was then imagining that we'd be a dry tour . . . But that's not the case – there's alcohol backstage and he's happy for the band and anyone else to drink around him . . . He doesn't feel tempted by seeing beer or wine or vodka in a fridge, in a dressing room. He's just done with it. He started really looking after himself physically as well. He works out a lot. He eats pretty healthily. So I think it was just a massive turning point in his life.

Steve Cradock: It was just time for him to stop the bevs. I think it's incredible for anyone who gives up booze, not just Paul but anyone who goes and deals with what they're going through . . . I think that's brave and it's not an easy thing for anyone.

Noel Gallagher: I've seen Paul at his highest, and I've seen him when he's been going through a lot of fucking shit, and vice versa . . . I think out of all that lot, there's only me still drinking and doing that thing . . . it's the only profession, that I'm aware of, where you're required to party as much as you can. And we certainly did that, but we used to have the best nights in, talking shit about music. And you get up the next day and be like, 'What the fuck were we going on about last night!'

I'm glad he doesn't drink any more, because from an outsider, and from his mate who loves him, everything has improved. In the way he looks, and his life, and his music, and his outlook on everything.

Paul Weller: It took a long time; I was fifty-two when I stopped, so I had a good thirty-five years of it. But once I made the decision, I wouldn't say it was easy . . . but it becomes easier once you just think *that is it*. Something internally, whether you want to say something higher than yourself or whatever it is inside you, that just said to me, *You've got to stop, mate*. This is time to stop. And that was it. It took a good two years to get used to it, to being out on the road, being sober, being on stage, totally sober.

I wouldn't go on lagging, but I'd always have a hangover from the night before, and you'd have a few drinks just to make you feel better, feel like human again. And then off you go and it's just round and round and round and round, for fucking weeks on end. But, you know, I can't go, I wish I'd done it ten years earlier, or twenty years, because I didn't. But the last fifteen years have been worth it, to have a different frame of mind and sobriety and to see things clearly. Become a nicer person, a better person, and have more empathy for people, more respect for what's around me. So, yeah, I could have stopped earlier, but I didn't. But I did in the end, and that's the main thing for me, I ain't never really looked back since then. Not really.

Tom Van Heel: For years, my mum would say, 'Just ring up the barn and go down for a bit of work experience.' I thought, *You can't just ring up Paul's studio and show up.* But evidently you can! . . . I spent the day pulling up cables, filling up the skip, making tea, and holding up massive soundproofing that they were putting in. Paul was signing some stuff and went, 'Who's this? The new teaboy?' Steve Pilgrim came down that week to record an album and I ended up playing piano on one of the tracks and went home buzzing, 'Mum, you're not going to believe what happened.'

24 September 2010 – Paul and Hannah get married in Italy

January 2012 – John-Paul and Bowie Weller born (sixth and seventh children, first with Hannah Weller)

19 March 2012 – *Sonik Kicks* (no. 1)

Paul Weller: People ask me what it is that keeps me creating new material and pushing forward. It's probably a variety of reasons really. The main one is that I think it's what musicians are supposed to be doing – it's part of the job description. You make records and go on tour. That's probably an old school way of looking at it, but that's still what I think that's what it's about. Just keep pushing it, pushing it and pushing it and just putting it out, as opposed to a lot of younger artists who will make an album and then not make another one for five, seven years or something. I don't understand that. I often think, *What do you do in those in between years? What do they do?*

Jon 'Mojo' Mills: That modern psychedelic period was just great. A lot of his older fans probably thought, *What the hell's going on here?*, which made it great. It would be very easy when you're over forty to just settle back and do what the people want.

Andy Crofts: I played a few bits on *Sonik Kicks* – did some backing vocals and played the farfisa. A classic 60s organ sound. I also did string arrangements on 'The Attic' and 'Be Happy Children' and even got to do a music video for that and for 'Dragonfly'. I've always got my camera to film bits and bobs, and I think he liked what he saw. I had done this little video, just for myself, of a girl holding a balloon in black and white, an artist thing with a bit of classical music on top and he really loved that. 'You should do a video for me.' I'd never done a music video before and I was a bit out of my depth, because I don't know the technical side of things, I know the artistic side. I did two videos on a very basic camera, and he liked them.

Graham Coxon: That time was still slightly chaotic. There was quite a lot of people knocking about in the studio. It was extremely creative and mad and at some point, one of Paul's friends gave me this jazz cigarette. I started to have a little smoke and it knocked me really bloody sidewards, 'What the hell was that? What sort of jazz cigarette was this?' And he went, 'I dunno, it's just the usual.' I'm not used to that sort of thing.

Paul was starting to put on these demos, and they sounded like the most insane music I'd ever heard . . . the old Jam track, 'Pop Art Poem', you know how mad and weird that is and stupid and interesting, a lot of these demos he was playing were like that. He had this song where he kept saying, 'She's cool, she's cool, she's cool,' and then there was loads of echo on it. I'd just had this jazz cigarette, and I'd never heard anything so out there. This is insane music. Then I'm like, 'Quick, quick, quick, get me on the drums,' and I'd rush in and bash about on the drums, and it was rubbish. Paul was like, 'What in the fuck are you doing?' I said, 'Dunno, just wanted to play the drums to it.'

Aziz Ibrahim: I actually sat down and wanted to write something for him, and I wrote 'By the Waters'. I introduced him to my secret weapon . . . a baritone acoustic . . . I put it in a weird open tuning and made up these chords. He just picked up a piece of paper and started writing. It was as simple as that. Came up with those lyrics for 'By the Waters'. *Come down beside the water sit and rest.* We were both saying how good it would be to have an orchestra and have the arrangements off centre and really left field.

Sean O'Hagan: Paul said he would love to work with me on these songs and I remember saying, 'So what happens now? Do I contact your manager?' And he goes, 'No, no, where are you?' I said, 'Peckham.' He said, 'I'll just pop there.' The next day he was down. He's just happy to go wherever the music takes him. When we met, we spoke about the two songs that I arranged on *Sonik Kicks* and we put some work in there, ideas, and then we just started to talk about music in general. We had this great couple of hours where we were literally playing and trading tracks, which was fantastic. We were going deep into Tropicalia and French soundtrack, Italian, bit of psych folk, we were all over the place. He kept on doing it, by text, for a few months afterwards, 'Just heard this. Have you heard that?' It was lovely. It was such a nice musical friendship that I thought I'd never have.

Andy Lewis: As an album it was made with a lot of feeling as much as it was made with Stan Kybert splicing things up on his Pro Tools rig that he and everybody else barely knew how to make work. There are some incredibly tender, emotional moments in there. 'Study in Blue' as this dub thing is wonderful. 'Dangerous Age', when I first heard the demo for that, I thought, oh yeah, this is going to be a bit special.

It's funny because it was that period where Paul was talking about discovering Bowie for the first time and getting into Bowie. He was making a big deal of the fact. It was interesting to discover that Bowie had been a big influence, throughout most of Paul's career. It wasn't something that he made a big deal of. It was just something we were talking about one day and he said, 'Well, yeah, of course I listened to Bowie. Everybody did.' But I think it's the difference between hearing it and understanding it and getting it. It was that wonderful moment where you could tell that everything that Paul was trying to do was to push things forward a little bit.

Boy George: Paul's a Gemini like me. You're always like, oh, I hate it, I love it, I hate it, I love it. I remember, when Paul got into Bowie, that was like, never going to happen. And then it was like, *Oh, my God, he's got it. He's finally got it.* And it was so beautiful. Because I'm a massive Bowie fan. I was like, *Oh my God, I can hear some Bowie in here*, and then I spoke to him about it and he was like, 'Yeah, no, totally. I hated him, but I didn't get it.' I'm always worried about anyone that doesn't get Bowie. So that was a saving grace.

Julian Broad: The album packaging and the visual aspect of his records from then on was changing gear . . . I work with a great set builder called Andy Tomlinson and came up with an idea of using different coloured fluorescent lights . . . Paul arrived, with various outfits, and we're playing with the light levels and the contrast . . . On one of the pictures of him, he'd moved slightly, and my initial thing was to discard that image because it was movement. Completely by accident. We looked at it and he said, 'That's the one.' That was five frames into the shoot. Boom!

Daniel Rachel: I saw him at the Roundhouse when he came out and played the whole of *Sonik Kicks*, start to finish. It had only come out that day, so nobody knew it. Then he went off for an interval, came back out . . . So, I'm thinking *Well, Paul's going to come out and do 'Eton Rifles'*. Of course he didn't. He did stranger songs like 'Porcelain Gods' and lesser-known album tracks for the whole of the second half . . . It was the point when lots of bands were reforming to do a classic album live, like Echo & the Bunnymen, Ocean Colour Scene.

Ted Cockle: I was with Paul at Island for the most contrary years of his career. In those shows, he was literally throwing a bone to the audience. *I am here to wind you up completely . . . I'm fucking playing exactly what I want to, and you can all fuck off as much as you want to.*

Paul Weller: I suppose I need to just shake things up a little bit, say with *Sonik Kicks*. I was so sick of hearing all these bands out playing their classic album from, fucking, twenty years ago, thirty years ago, whatever. I just thought, *I'll play my classic album, my new one!* Which is a nice idea. In reality there were certain times, certain nights, I'd just think it's either really brave or it's really fucking stupid, because it was quite a hard album for people to hear, first time anyway, I guess. Not for me, but most people I suppose. And to expect people to listen to it like that. I suppose my head's also sort of back in the seventies, I would say, like with The Jam for instance . . . you made a record, you put the record out but then you go and tour that record, right. And not only do you want to play these new songs to people, but people want to hear these new songs as well. Well, of course we don't live in that time any more.

People, generally speaking, like to hear what they're familiar with or what they grew up on or what they loved when they were fourteen or wherever, which is fair enough, I understand that to some degree, but that is definitely more prevalent now than ever, that people like what they remember, what's special to them, and least likely to want to hear the new stuff . . . I think it's just a question of just letting people know that's not going to happen. We're not going down that fucking heritage, nostalgia bullshit route.

Chris Catchpole: There was a line of perplexed looking blokes of a certain age stood at the back going what the fuck is this?

Sean O'Hagan: I popped along to one of those shows and he brought out a string quartet and played those tracks on stage. That was a brave thing to do. I wonder what people thought. *What's going on here?*

Steve Cradock: Wow. Starting with the tune 'Green' which I like as a production thing but it's not really a fucking opener. What do people who saw it think? Imagine someone who saw that on Sunday night, when you didn't know that album and it was played in full. How did it go down? Were they ripping up programmes?

Andy Crofts: That was hard. Paul said he wanted to play the album . . . 'Let's learn it like the record,' and no one had ever heard it! That was heavy going, but it was fun. Looking back, the challenges like that are what keep you fresh, and on your toes, you can't be complacent. That was hard work, but it really was beneficial, made us better as a band as well.

Steve Cradock: We probably had a three-week rehearsal for that. It was so difficult to learn how to play that album from my point of view, it's just fucking, because it had musically gone into this sort of electro kraut rock. It was definitely into another scene and so it was hard to depict what guitars were.

Andy Lewis: Those shows are the epitome of my time in the band and certainly it's my favourite period of Paul's career, partly because the ambition of taking it out and doing it and playing the whole thing from beginning to end, that had all sorts of musical and technical challenges.

Pete Paphides: Around the time of *Sonik Kicks* and *Wake Up the Nation*, Paul started talking about bands like Broadcast, Pram and the Boards of Canada from that scene. That's what I want him to be doing, and you'd see it start to seep into his work. Even in recent interviews, he's mentioned J Hus and Dave. He seems to have made a pact with himself – a true modernist, in his view, has a duty to assimilate a certain ethos that he sees coming through in new music – that reflects the aesthetic rigour of the original modernist outlook.

18 June 2012 – 'Birthday' – (One day download in honour of Sir Paul McCartney's 70th birthday)

2012 – Jools Holland, 'September in the Rain'

Dave Swift: Paul came to Jools's studio to record 'September in the Rain' for the *Golden Age of Song* LP . . . I knew his voice from The Jam, The Style Council and everything else, but suddenly I was hearing a jazz crooner . . . He's got this beautiful vibrato and this rich velvet sound. I love when people reinvent themselves.

Phil Veacock: I'd been asked to do the horn arrangements on that tune, but I didn't really know quite what he wanted, so I'd done a Nelson Riddle, Sinatra kind of version. It was a nice arrangement. Paul came and recorded it, but later that day he phoned me up and said, 'I really liked your arrangement but it's not at all what I wanted to do with that song. Can we do it again?' He said, he'd been listening to a sax player called Lynn Hope, someone I'd never heard of. He's a very obscure 1950s saxophone player, who converted to Islam, and he was famous for wearing a turban on stage, even though he wasn't a Sikh. His sound was unusual. Paul gave me the only CD of Lynn Hope in existence, as far as I can tell.

Paul also said, 'I want it to be more French.' [*Laughs*] So I brought in Geraint Watkins, a fantastic piano player and singer, who also plays accordion. He does a lot of work with Nick Lowe. We recorded this new version in one take and that take is on the album. You can hear me shouting out chords to the rhythm section at the end because we hadn't properly gone through it. You can also hear Jools's brother Chris arriving late for the session. It reminds me of those old Motown recordings where you can hear things like people using the water fountain outside.

2012 – 'Bankbusted Nuclear Detergent Blues'

Graham Coxon: Oh, my God! 'Bankbusted Nuclear Detergent Blues', that studio session was crazy. We just felt so free and inspired – not having to work within a framework to just be improvising around some Beat poet.

Charles Rees: The men in white coats – Paul, Graham Coxon, Michael Horovitz, Damon Albarn and Andy Crofts. Damon knew Michael, and he needed a bit of encouragement to just do something. Damon wanted to put it on vinyl, so Paul invited them to Black Barn. They thought it would be a great thing to improvise everything apart from the poetry, which he manipulated as we were going.

Graham Coxon: Michael's words which are pretty funny. Some of the things he says in that beautiful, fragile way that he has, mixed with the mischievousness of that creativity really tickled us all. That kind of humour is right up Weller's street . . . With Paul, whether it was driven by Stella or tea driven, it's always stupid humour going on. We're basically 90 per cent melancholy, so at some point, you need to get some humour in there, otherwise, we'll just fucking kill ourselves.

Charles Rees: That first piece was fifty-five minutes long. Recorded live. Damon on the piano in the live room, wearing one of the Black Barn Corporation lab coats . . . Paul was on synthesisers in the control room. We had it pumping through the big speakers, and it was insane. We all got told off by Michael for misbehaving. We started to enjoy ourselves a little bit too much and found it funny. 'It's not funny. It's not funny.'

Graham Coxon: We then performed it live at Teenage Cancer Trust . . . It was fun, but intimidating, improvising over poetry at the Royal Albert Hall . . . We then played 'Tender' with Noel, and Paul Weller was on the drums. It was odd because I was suddenly singing this 'oh, my baby' thing that I'd written half asleep one morning, and Noel was harmonising with me and I just thought, *That's flipping nice.* I mean, I would have rather done the drums, maybe, but Paul managed it. He did all right.

November 2012 – *Mastertapes*, Radio 4

John Wilson: At the end of 2012, Paul came on my Radio 4 *Mastertapes* programme to talk about the inspiration behind *The Gift*. He was talking about that final Jam album and the way it was recorded and played a version of 'Just Who Is the 5 O'Clock Hero?' He was trying to remember the chords. He had been working it out in the days before. We'd been chatting on the phone about which songs he might be able to play, because he said, 'I haven't played any of those songs apart from "Town Called Malice" in years.' He tried to work out '5 O'Clock Hero', which it turns out has got the most ludicrously complex chord structure, the amount of chords in that song and the amount of lyrics. He tried to play it, and the song fell apart twice. The audience were laughing. And in the edit, my producer Paul Kobrak came to it and phoned me up and he just went, 'What are we going to do about that bit?' I said, 'Well, you keep it in there.' He said, 'You can't keep it. He's getting it all wrong. The audience are laughing.' I phoned Paul and said, 'We got this thing, when you got it wrong. Do you mind that being in?' and he went, 'What do you mean?' I said, 'Well, getting it wrong' . . . He went, 'Well, that's the whole point, isn't it? It's so complex. It was such a long time ago.' I just thought that's fantastic.

Daniel Ash: I met him backstage at the Roundhouse *Sonik Kicks* gig and then got to go to the *Mastertapes* recording and even asked a question.

John Wilson: Daniel asked a question, 'Do you ever have writer's block and how do you deal with it?' and Paul talks about how you work through it, and you've just got to relax and you've got to trust yourself, and the words will come at some point and the muse will return. Then later on I said to Paul, let's have another song and he said, 'No, I want to hear his song,' and Daniel was sitting in the audience and Paul handed him his Gibson J-45 guitar and said, 'Go on, play me one of your songs.'

Daniel Ash: He was like, 'I've got to go to the toilet. Dan, will you play a song?' . . . He didn't go to the toilet! He sat on the stage and watched me nervously play through a song that I probably forgot every word to . . . I got through it and it was unreal.

John Wilson: I think it says a lot about Paul Weller; it's that thing that goes back to those early days of The Style Council and The Jam and how supportive he was of other bands and artists.

20 April 2013 – 'Flame-Out!' / 'The Olde Original' (Record Store Day Single)

Charles Rees: I'd say 'Flame Out' was a one-off really. We were between albums. Let's just put it out as it is. As it started, it morphed into the song 'White Sky' later on. It was like something that Paul planted. He's done this before with Ocean Colour Scene, when he gave them a track called 'For Dancers Only'. They did the song, and then later he extended it and changed the lyrics, and it became 'This Old Town' with Graham Coxon. It morphed into something harder, heavier. In that period, I can't remember there being any album leftovers. 'Flame Out' was definitely not a leftover. Same with 'The Olde Original'. It was more of an immediate concept.

April 2014 – Paul and Hannah Weller win privacy damages over *Daily Mail* photos

Polly Birkbeck: Sometimes I've had to deal with the tabloids and send them packing. When he had the twins, they kind of wanted to know more . . . but I don't really have much trouble with that side of things. The interviews he does do, he won't get someone that's going to ask him something as banal as that. There's the one thing when we do photo shoots . . . Often they say, 'Oh, can he hold a guitar?' 'No.' That's the one thing we always veto immediately.

Claire Moon: Paul is the least showbiz person ever. The court case was a peculiar experience – I had to testify as part of Paul's team. They were completely right: the press shouldn't photograph your children without your permission. Thankfully, we won the case.

There's an unwritten rule . . . if you court the press with your children on a red carpet going to premieres, you're kind of fair game . . . Paul doesn't do that. Maybe occasionally with his older children, like Nathaniel, when it's been something appropriate like fashion but certainly not with the younger ones. They shouldn't have been fair game. Paul avoids celebrity culture.

19 April 2014 – 'Brand New Toy' – (Record Store Day Single)

Joe Connor: I started to make music videos for bands . . . One of the people was Andy Crofts, singer of the Moons. He said, 'Do you reckon we could make some music videos together?' Three music videos where all we had was fifty quid and a packet of crisps. I remember Andy saying, 'I showed Paul your music videos and he loves them. He'd love to meet you,' and I was like, 'Who the fuck is Paul?' I just thought he meant his mate Paul. He's like, 'Paul Weller.' I was like, 'Why are you showing my films to Paul Weller? How do you know Paul Weller?' He's like, 'Oh, I'm in Paul Weller's band' and I was like, 'Sorry, what?'

Ben Gordelier: 'Brand New Toy' was a favourite because that was so different. Me and Paul both had the exact same idea at the same time. That was a moment. A backwardsy drum-beat thing.

Joe Connor: They sent me the track 'Brand New Toy' and said, 'Come up with some ideas.' I always try and get past the obvious first-base concepts and explore something more fun or a bit deeper . . . At one point, I thought about a massive bouncy castle with everyone playing on it – but then realised, I can't put Paul Weller on a bouncy castle! . . . I don't want to be the guy that Paul goes, 'You made me look like an idiot.' The idea for the kaleidoscope came from thinking about toys and something playful . . . I built a thirty-foot kaleidoscope – a triangle of mirrors – with Paul at one end. We pushed a camera through it on a techno-crane to create an amazing visual trick.

8 October 2014 – *Real Stars Are Rare* launch

Phil Bickley: I've been in the clothes business for the best part of thirty years, but Paul's more into clothes than I am. He's got a really good eye for quality, and finish, and the story behind things. I know other people like that, but Paul's basically an upside-down triangle, his shape. Those people, they've got straight, broad shoulders and a thin waist. That, for a male, that's the perfect shape. That's why when he sticks something on, it looks good. He knows what he likes and he wears them well.

Real Stars Are Rare started from a conversation that just grew over time. I couldn't even put a timeframe on it – it might have been a year, maybe two – but Paul and I kept talking about clothes, what we were into, and what we could do. It wasn't some big strategic idea; it was more like, 'That'd be cool. We could make that.' Paul would always come in with sketches, constantly scribbling down ideas and drawings. He'd say, 'What do you reckon of something like that?' From there, I reached out to some of my contacts in the clothing business to figure out how we could actually make it happen. Bit by bit, we pulled together a network of factories, and before we knew it, this thing had a life of its own. It was like, 'Well, we may as well make some clothes then, eh!'

When we launched, the response was incredible. I'm fairly sure that first week was still our best week ever for my business, even after nearly twenty-five years.

18 May 2015 – *Saturns Pattern* (no. 2)

Nicky Weller: After my dad died, Paul and I had a little time where we didn't speak to each other. It was a few years, where we wasn't really getting on, because of his drinking.

There was also a point where me and my partner, Russ, had enough of this country. We were going to sell up and move to LA. We'd been out there for three months, found an amazing place that we were going to buy. We came back, and within two weeks my whole world went pear-shaped. I found a lump. The doctor said it was just a cyst, but I got it checked and it was grade-three breast cancer. I was straight in for an op, straight on chemo. Russ looked after me all the way through my breast cancer.

I said to Russ, 'You had better let me brother know.' Paul had just had twins with Hannah, his new wife, and life's too short, right? My brother wanted to come to one of my chemo things . . . I was in there plugged up and all the nurses are saying to him, 'Ooh, do you want some tea? Do you want biscuits?' What the fuck? I'm having chemo. He's just here for the beer. Do you know what I mean? But they were all running around him. Then after my chemo that day, I actually collapsed, and him and Russ had to carry me out to the car, and he was just fuck . . . He didn't come again! I think it was a bit of an eye opener for him. He put special thanks to the Royal Surrey County Hospital on the *Saturns Pattern* album cover and added some of the nurses on the guestlist for Guildford and they all came. They were a fantastic lot.

Ted Cockle: My professional opinion is that across *22 Dreams, Wake Up the Nation, Sonik Kicks*, it was esoteric. Paul was up for the fucking rumble with his own fans by not doing anything that they wanted. But what I would say about him, is it's never contrived . . .

After *Sonik Kicks,* there was a pickup for Island, but we needed to look again at the size of the advance. Paul wouldn't know what it's worth at all, but the moment that you question it – and I've had Rod Stewart recently and he's the same, he's got no idea about it – but the moment that you question their value, that's a fucking red rag to them. I can't remember exactly, but I'm sure Warner came in and offered him a better advance.

Miles Leonard: I was aware that he had been on an album-by-album deal. We certainly had a meeting of minds. Paul very much knows what type of record he's going to make. But he just needed or wanted a label that could support his creative vision as much as possible.

Claire Moon: Miles Leonard, who ran Parlophone, approached Paul directly, so we went to see him. We weren't massively happy with how things were going at Universal at the time, and Parlophone's legacy with The Beatles and Bowie held a lot of draw for Paul. Back then, Paul and I would go in together from the offset – to assess if we could work with these people, if they shared our creative vision, and if they'd do right by us.

Miles Leonard: For my first meet with Paul, we just talked about music and artists that we admired. We also talked about artists on our roster, some of which he was brilliantly dismissive about. I was talking about how we cared and looked after our artists, even through difficult times. A label shows its true colours when things aren't going so well . . .

I wanted to talk to Paul about how we were here to support his creative vision and offer feedback or critique if he wanted that, but I knew I had to earn that trust . . . All I could really give was to show the support we've given other artists, allowing them to be as creative as they wanted. We talked about some other artists, but he said, 'I don't want to fucking talk about Coldplay,' which is just brilliant. He's very strong with his vision. He's very direct and very honest, and he's incredibly loyal with it.

Paul Weller: *Saturns Pattern* was just a silly album title that I thought up and I didn't even realise that Saturn, the planet, actually does have a pattern. Sometimes it's just whatever comes to me at the time really, and then you find other meanings in those things afterwards. There's not so much conscious thought put into them.

Josh McClorey: The Strypes first came over to London in mid-2012 and then Paul found out about us . . . he was doing a live performance in Studio One in Abbey Road for Channel 4, and we got asked to support . . . I was seventeen at the time, playing in that room and getting that support from Paul was wicked.

Paul's amazing in the studio – he never stops from when he goes in to when he leaves. The vibe is always up and fun. He drinks a million cups of tea and smokes a million fags. He doesn't really like to get stuck. Even in his life, I think if something doesn't feel right, he moves on to the next thing . . . Getting other people in the studio helps that situation so there's new energy coming into the room all the time. He's the puppeteer making everything happen.

Andy Crofts: We were recording 'Going My Way' and there was this gap. It was my turn to do my bit, and I went '*with me, ooh, ooh*' that big outro bit. Then I layered up with harmonies and it became this lovely thing that they put a beat to. That was accidental. When we sing like that all around the piano, it sounds amazing. You really hear the harmonies. It's always a special moment.

Tom Van Heel: 'Long Time' is a great song. Paul had these chords, and we played the song from start to finish. Bill Wheeler, Kenny's son, was on guitar, Paul was on guitar, I was on drums. Charles Rees is on bass on that one. Do you remember those whisk-o-lait things that you put in your coffee and spin around. He's like, I've got this idea, and he played it on his guitar. Brrrrr brrrr brrrr . . . I was like, 'This is far out, man.'

Bill Wheeler: I like the more energetic, rocky songs that Paul does so to be on one that he still plays now is great . . . 'Long Time' was done in two takes as well. That was basically Paul working me like a puppet . . . I haven't been invited to perform live. My fee is way too high!

Steve Brookes: I played guitar on 'These City Streets'. I'd done a bit on the demo, and Paul liked it. When they came to cut it, he couldn't quite get that feel from what I'd done, so he gave me a ring. Typical of Paul at the time. He asked, 'You free this afternoon? Can you come down and play what you did on "City Streets" again?'

Steve Cradock: That was just me, Steve Brookes and Paul all playing three electric guitars which could have been a fucking car crash. But we kind of arranged it and it was one of them things where it was a live take. It's quite a long track, so you have to noodle in a way, and it just happened in that instant. It's not really planned but you watch what people are playing and keep out the way.

Roger Nowell: I got a credit on *Saturns Pattern*: 'Head Roadie . . . Sorry, tech!' Paul's like, 'What's all this tech business? You're a roadie, aren't you?' It's an American thing.

Claire Moon: Paul is never A&R'd these days. Nobody is saying, *I think you need another mix on this track or need to add horns on that track*. That would never happen. That's just out of respect for Paul. It comes back to sharing that creative vision, but most record labels these days are honoured to have an artist like Paul with them . . . he's not just going to churn out something that they can't work with. It's going to be great. It's just that we don't quite know what direction it's going to go in yet.

Julian Broad: We did the photoshoot for the inside of that album at Sunbeam Studios in Notting Hill. I worked with a really great set builder called Ciaran Beale . . . we used some light to create that psychedelic blue flare with him which felt quite *Saturns Pattern-y*, I guess.

Paul always has a strong idea about what he wants to wear. He had a lot of changes for that session. There was one where he's holding a cigarette, and he wanted a classy Bailey-esque black and white of him. He loves a fag! He makes it look so cool, doesn't he?

Miles Leonard: The Beatles are obviously a huge influence on Paul and so I was also coming to the table with what I hoped was an ace card up my sleeve – having that wonderful Parlophone logo on the centre of your record . . . He knows that classic logo, it couldn't be any more quintessentially British . . . the finished copies of *Saturns Pattern* came in, I had quite a moment, being able to show him and seeing his face and having something within that classic, historic, label and roster.

Paul Baines: Claire told me . . . he got quite emotional when he took the record out of the sleeve, it was like, whoa, that's many years of his life coming together in his first record with that label on. Then when Paul turned sixty, the head of our creative team in Parlophone, a guy called Rich Welland . . . came up with the great idea of doing a painting of the sixties classic Parlophone label, but with 'Paul Weller' on it.

Stuart Deabill: Around that time, I was working with a band called The Spitfires who used Black Barn and recorded a couple of bits. The lead singer, Billy, was working for me up in London. We were on a job one day and Paul pulled up in front of us in his mini. He parks like he plays guitar – angular. He comes straight in front of us and just left it and walked out. I said, 'Look there's a fiver, go and get some coffees.'

Billy Sullivan : I followed Paul in and didn't really know what to say then. I would have been about nineteen, twenty. He could see that I was awkwardly standing in the queue looking at him, and could probably see my brain going 'what do I say, what do I say?' So he said, 'Hello mate.' I said something about his jacket, and he went, 'Yes, nice innit.' I said, 'I'm in a band called The Spitfires. We've used Black Barn before, thank you for letting us use it' and he's like, 'Oh, nice one, nice one.'

Stuart Deabill: Paul then offered the band two gigs on his next tour to support him. That was bizarre. He was in Costa with one of his kids, so I went in and said 'thank-you'.

Billy Sullivan: He was having a coffee and then he come back a couple of minutes later and went, we should do some gigs together in the future. Two months later we got an email. We couldn't believe that one of the gigs was in my hometown, Watford, and especially at that time, because no one played Watford. We've got one venue, the Coliseum, and they only used it for people like Weller.

Stuart Deabill: The whole set up was fantastic. It was a really good launching pad for the band to get a bigger audience.

Polly Birkbeck: I think the thing that comes to mind about *Saturns Pattern* is it's the only time, and we still make jokes about it in the meetings now, where Paul did a performance for *The One Show*. He never, ever, ever wanted to do it, but he did it for that album. I don't think he enjoyed it at all. It wasn't a bad performance, but totally out of his comfort zone.

Miles Leonard: Oh my God, we had *The One Show* offered to us. We'd done it a few weeks before, could have been with Noel, it was certainly somebody who Paul would have respected, and had seen quite a significant spike in album sales, so I asked Paul if he would go on it. Sometimes you've got to make that call. I said, 'Look, there's no interview, so you're not sat on the sofa having a dreadful conversation where they're going to show some old clips and want to talk to you about The Jam', which I know would just have been hell for him, and for all of us quite frankly! I said, 'You're performing outside the studio, in the courtyard. Just perform your song and that's it.'

We persuaded him to do it. I think he probably still hated every moment of it, and it actually only moved the dial slightly, but look, you've got to try these things. I then got to have the conversation afterwards with Paul going, 'Okay, you persuaded me to do this. What the fuck did it actually do for my record?' 'Not as much as we hoped!' 'Well, why the fuck did I do it then?' But that's just part of the relationship, those sorts of conversations.

28 June 2015 – Glastonbury Festival

Andy Lewis: We played Glastonbury on that tour, 2015. We arrived in a bus, drove onto the site, got off the bus, went backstage on these raised platforms of duckboards so that we didn't get our expensive shoes dirty. We were backstage for about twenty minutes while the stage was set and then we went on, played our show, came off, had a towel down, got back on the bus and drove to our next gig . . . I barely qualified for a Glastonbury campaign medal on that occasion.

Every festival gig we ever did, Paul was comparing it to Glastonbury 1994. He had been on just before the sun went down – it was the high point of his comeback and it was the festival show that every other festival show was judged by, even twenty-odd years later . . . I think it's really funny that for someone who doesn't really like looking back, he kept comparing himself to something that he could never get again, without thinking that what he was doing was every bit as good and the music that he was making was every bit as interesting and innovative and forward looking.

26 June–27 September 2015 – *About the Young Idea*, The Jam exhibition at Somerset House

Nicky Weller: We had wanted to do an exhibition on The Jam for a good twelve or eighteen months and we couldn't find anywhere in London that was suitable. My brother had started up Real Stars Are Rare, his clothing thing, and the PR bloke was based in Somerset House. I didn't think we had a hope in hell's chance of getting into Somerset House because they were a real posh lot. We went there. Me, Den, my business partner, and my partner, Russell, three of us. We did this pitch and a week later we heard that we got the gig. We'd been to my mum's garage, pulled out my dad's bags, videos and cuttings and photographs and everything you can possibly imagine. Den had all the records and the drum kit he bought from Rick Buckler, guitars and all that stuff. But he didn't have that personal collection, my brother's schoolbooks, which we found.

Den Davis: Paul was blown away that they were still there. His imagery as a fourteen-year-old drawing four people with 'The Jam' on the drumhead . . . he knew what he wanted . . . I also had my archive, but going through their family stuff was incredible. Ann pulled out a quarter-inch tape and just chucked it on the floor. It was 'Blueberry Rock' – the first demo they ever recorded. We had all these tapes, and we spent a couple of days in Abbey Road, remastering them. All the old demos which are still unreleased. Paul agreed that we could play them at the exhibition, so people had headphones and they could listen. When the exhibition opened, Paul came along – he ended up coming seven times – and loved it.

Nicky Weller: Across from my mum in Ripley is my brother's recording studio. We cleared his shed out for him and found his exercise books. They had geography or maths on the front, but there wasn't a scrap of work in there, it was just poetry, doodles, stories, songs.

It was a combination of our own personal items that we'd saved over the years. My brother's shed, my mum's garage, clearing through stuff. Quite incredible, really, what you find that's never been uncovered.

John Wilson: Paul is reluctant to look back because there's always so much more to do in the future, but I phoned and asked if he would walk around the exhibition with me for *Front Row* before it opened. It was the only press that he did. He had no preconceptions and didn't know what was in it. Nicky had told him they had got some great stuff, but that was it ... There were some lovely moments, like finding the comic strips that he used to write as a kid. His mum, Ann, had kept all his school reports and they were on show. He took great pride that they were OK. You often hear about Paul Weller leaving school with no qualifications and hating it. Academic failure. Actually, that's not true ... He said, 'Look, good grades. Bs and Cs and an A for English and Art.'

Ann Weller: I'm a little bit of a magpie ain't I? I come from a generation that don't throw nothing away, love. In the war you didn't have anything, so you kept everything ... I think what's so nice is a lot of Paul's fans all bring their kids to things.

Shane Juson: I burst into tears on the train just going there. Then I burst into tears as I walked around the corner, and it said *The Jam* above the building. I had to walk across the Somerset

House Plaza thing in tears. Then I got inside, and I was in the first room which was the Bingley Hall room, and I was on the video. I burst into tears there. I was in there for an hour and a half, just in the first room. Sobbing in the corner.

I went into the next room and there was this girl crying. I said, 'Are you all right?' She said, 'No. No one understands.' I said, 'I do.' I'm bursting into tears, and we were having a hug.

Bruce Foxton: I was there with Paul, and we get on great. Rick said he had a book signing to go to, but it would have been an ideal opportunity because we're not going to have a go at anyone. It would just be lovely for the fans to see that photograph of the three of us together again, just chatting, no mention of gigging or anything else. That was an ideal moment. I'd have loved it. I'm sure Paul would. Rick seems to avoid it somehow, which is a shame.

David Pottinger: Martin Freeman turned up, and I remember he turned a few heads because he looked immaculate. Weller was at that one as well, so it was a real big occasion . . . The whole thing was lovely because it was a celebration of the band and the people who the band has touched. Seeing the cool little doodles in the schoolbooks and stuff . . .

2015 – *About the Young Idea* documentary

Bob Smeaton: I remember going into Woolworths in 1977, and there was a track playing . . . I thought, *Fucking hell. What's this?* I went up to the girl on the counter, 'What's this record?' 'It's The Jam, "In the City".' It was the first ever punk-rock record I bought . . .

Fast forward to 2015 and a mate of mine, Gary Crowley, asked if I'd like to make a documentary about The Jam. I told him that it would never happen because Weller will not do it, he'll just say fuck off, but Gary said Paul was possibly up for doing it if I was going to do it, because Paul's a massive fan of The Beatles and I'd done *The Beatles Anthology*.

Me, Gary Crowley and Nicky Weller go and meet Paul in Queen's Park in northwest London. I thought, *Shit, what do you wear when you go to meet Paul Weller?* I cannot turn up looking like I'm not into the music . . . The day I went to see Paul, it's the first time I'd ever had to dress to go and meet a rock star and I've met some pretty big stars . . . So, I had this old pair of trousers that looked like Levi's Sta-Prest. But they weren't. They weren't even Brutus Sta-Prest. So, I put these on, and I had a pair of desert boots, I put those on, and I had this Fred Perry-esque T-shirt, which I put on, and I thought, *Right, I'm gonna meet Weller. I'm looking the part.* I goes up, knocks on his door, thinking, *Fucking hell. I hope he thinks I look cool. Paul doesn't stand for any bullshit.* So, he opens the door, and he was wearing a pair of cut-off jeans, a wife-beater vest and a pair of flip-flops and he says, 'It's nice to see you dressed for the occasion.' I said, 'You obviously didn't.' I thought I'd blown it!

I was there to tell him my vision but all he wanted to talk about was The Beatles . . . We're there for half an hour, and Paul's making the tea, and I'm thinking, *When are we going to talk about The Jam?* . . . I says, 'Paul, it's your story.' He says, 'It's not my story, mate, it's yours.' . . . From that moment on, he was great and right behind the project. Paul watched it on telly when it went out on Sky Arts. I was dreading him saying it was a heap of shit. He said, 'Loved it mate. Fucking great.' That's all he said, and that was enough for me.

2015 – US tour

Conor O'Brien: I was on *Jools Holland* in 2010, playing the title track from my first album and Paul was directly across the room watching it. Paul told my manager that he was digging the tunes, which blew my mind. Pretty weird, surreal . . . Five years later, he invited us to tour with him on the west coast in America. Paul introduced himself to me on the first night and was super cool and made us feel really welcome and then gave me his Villagers record to sign. *This is the wrong way around. This shouldn't be happening.*

Peter Watts: *Uncut* wanted a cover story with Paul, so I joined him in San Francisco . . . the iconic Fillmore West . . . I talked to Paul before he went on and he was shaking and I was like, 'You're really nervous.' He said that he still gets nervous before every single show, from the very first time he played in a school hall to now.

Paul Weller: From the time I wake up – there's the anxiety and the nerves and adrenaline and all that stuff. It's not as bad as it used to be, but it's still pretty bad. The hour or so before I go on stage is normally pretty bad. Thinking about all the things that could go wrong, which they can't really. But I've always been like that. It used to be way worse. Sometimes I used to be physically sick before I go on and all that sort of thing, so I'm not that bad now! But the anxiety, I suppose, just because every night you've got to go out and prove yourself again, you've got all those people who paid their money and they've come to see something special and you want to deliver that but there's still that little voice in there saying, *Are you going to be able to do it? Can you still do it?* And all those insecurities come out of that when you're nervous I think.

Often when people say to me, 'What's your favourite gig?' It's like, 'Well, last night,' mainly because I can't remember the rest of 'em! But whatever's fresh in your head. But I think there's a lot of truth in that. Whether it's true or not, it's not a bad thing to have in life really, to think well, whatever you've done previous, in the last forty years or last forty minutes, whatever, doesn't matter. It's what you're going to do tonight, that's where you're going to prove yourself, and see what you can do with this thing. And that's a good thing, I think.

I know a few of my friends who . . . I won't name names, but who are musicians. But they never get nervous. And I just think, *Are you nervous?* Whenever I see them before they go on, and they're like, *Hmmm.* I just think that's so fucking weird. I don't understand that.

Billy Bragg: I go to America a lot . . . When I used to go in the early days, people would always talk to me about Paul, particularly in California. There's a very strong mod vibe over there. It's a pity Paul didn't engage with the Americans more, but then again, without wishing to be offensive, there is something quintessentially English about the way he works and the way he is as a person. Not in his music. His music is a much broader palette than that. But, *This is me and take me as I am. This is what I do.* You don't feel he wants you to love him. He wants you to hear him, he wants you to appreciate him, but he ain't going to pander to where he thinks you are. He's going to forge his own path. There's a line in 'In the City' . . . 'You better listen now/You've said your bit'. That sums up Paul's attitude right there at the beginning and it's still there now. He's the governor.

Peter Watts: He played me a demo of 'The Cranes Are Back'. It was absolutely stunning . . . I remember listening to it and saying to Paul, 'Wow, this has a real Philly soul vibe,' as in, that classic

Philadelphia soul sound, but Paul misheard me and said, 'Oh yeah, it's just that silly soul thing' . . . To this day, it still plays on my mind that he might think I was dismissing this beautiful piece of music as 'silly soul' when, in fact, I was in awe of it.

I knew Paul had stopped drinking – that wasn't a shock to me. What did surprise me, though, was when he admitted he'd had a problem with alcohol . . . I was taken aback by his honesty. Either he told me, or someone else told me that he wasn't a particularly nice drunk. It didn't bring out the best side of him always. I think that's something that he was aware of . . .

I remember he went jogging when we were there. I'd love to have seen Paul Weller jogging around the hills of San Francisco. That was an eye opener. That's not rock and roll.

He's always been very open, and if there's something he doesn't want to talk about, I don't think he's ever refused to answer. He's the kind of person who, when asked a question, gives a response. He said something like, 'Oh, just write what you want. Just don't make me look like a prick.' I thought he'd be a bit more controlling over things.

31 December 2015 into 1 January 2016 – *Hootenanny*

Andy Lewis: *Hootenanny* 2015 was the last time I played with the Paul Weller Band. That was a lot of fun. It's recorded in the middle of the afternoon. You're about twenty-three days away from Christmas when it's recorded. You're having to come on like it's New Year's Eve, and the production company ply you with cheap booze, and amp up the festivities by having all these stilt walkers and Victorian policemen and people dressed as clocks. It's absolute madness. Jeff Beck was on the bill. At the end of the gig, I gave him a hand with his amplifier, loading it back into his Land Rover.

In 2016, I found out that I wasn't going to be in the Paul Weller band anymore. It's funny, when you think I was in the band for longer than The Jam had a record deal. That's a statistic that I can be proud of. I think the only reason that I wasn't in the band was for reasons of economy. He got so used to the nucleus of people that he had around him doing the next album, *A Kind Revolution*, and I think that rather than wasting time, rehearsing, he just wanted to go out and play it. So fair enough.

It was a funny old time, because on the one hand you think, okay, I'm doing all these incredible new things, working with all sorts of wonderful people, but at the same time, there's a big, empty hole in your life because you're not in the Paul Weller Band anymore.

He finds different people that he wants to work with, and that's what he does.

2016 – Africa Express Live

Seckou Keita: I did a tour in 2016 with Africa Express, organised by Damon Albarn . . . It happened that Paul Weller was also part of that bill . . . They asked me. 'Do you mind joining this song called "Wild Wood"?' and then I said 'Oh, OK, how does that go?' Then I heard it, it's beautiful, wow! To me it was new, it felt like it had been written the same year, not twenty-odd years ago. Then I'm on stage playing on it. Paul's there, and I do my part, the usual Seckou Keita approach to the music and the style of it. I happened to take a photo, put it on my social media and then I had all these relatives and close friends that said. 'Oh, my God, you and Paul Weller!' I was like 'Who's Paul Weller?' [*Laughs*] I became a new follower, a friend and also a fan. We had a chat and exchanged phone numbers and talked about making music together in the future.

16 December 2016 – Concert for Corbyn

Billy Bragg: Music may no longer dominate youth culture as it once did, but it still has the ability to bring people together, as it did with Red Wedge, during the miners' strike, and for other issues and causes. Paul is still tuned into that because he did a gig for Corbyn in 2016. I was so pleased to see that because that's the Paul Weller I know. I know he has not lost it because I hear it in his music. It's just whether he's willing to stick his head over the parapet. Paul is still a writer driven by conscience. Corbyn's not an easy thing to support. The way he was portrayed and messed around by the press, means it's quite a divisive thing to come out and support him. Paul doing that was a nod to anyone who's still watching those principles that he had back in the day. He's still willing to step up when it counts.

Kathryn Williams: One of my best friends was Jeremy Hardy, who was close with Jeremy. Through Jeremy, I knew Corbyn was a good person, always on the right side of history. A lot of my friends thought I was an idiot for getting involved politically, but I was happy to be there, and I got to see Robert Wyatt . . . Paul was supporting Robert, and I reached out and told him that I thought it was brilliant.

John Lewis: I've tried to piece together what I think Paul Weller's political journey has been, because he became very apolitical after Red Wedge and got completely sick of the whole thing. There have been glimmers where he's been sparked by Islamic fundamentalist terrorism or where he's written about Russian activity or something like that. He was one of that generation who was quite enthused by Corbyn but, at the same time, there's always a scepticism about grand narratives and politicians who think they know everything. I'm sure he's very, very sound politically, but I'm wary of asking people too much about their political opinions because I don't think it's very fruitful.

February 2017 – Live

Tom Van Heel: My parents moved out to Spain, and I'd been knocking about at Black Barn. I definitely didn't consider myself as part of the band . . . My dad said, 'Look, you've got until June to get a job.' I was like, *Shit, OK, I'm going to move out to Spain and open a beach bar.* I got on the plane and I landed and I turned my phone back on and a text came through and it was from Paul. 'All right, Tom, are you up for playing some keys on this tour coming up in February?'

Then you get sent a list of songs and it all becomes a bit real. OK, I've got to lock myself away for about a month now . . . I was presented with seventy songs . . . A trail of these sheets in my flat. They went from the kitchen through the bedrooms, in the bathroom, right around to my bedroom. I sent Andy a video. 'How am I going to remember all of this?'

March 2017 – Stone Foundation, *Street Rituals*

Neil Jones: I got a message to say, 'Your number has been passed on to Paul. He's going to ring you today.' We just started talking about music. He told me how much he loved the band's sound and then he said, 'I've got the makings of something here that I'd like you to have a look at.' It was the opening bars of a song that eventually became 'The Limit of a Man' . . . 'Would you like to try and co-write it with me?' I was like, 'Yeah man, me and Sheas will get our heads around it and I'll get it back to you.'

Neil Sheasby: We finished the recording of 'Limit of a Man' and were having a playback, when Paul's mum Ann comes into the studio. She cocks one ear onto the speakers, listening intently, and lets the song play. When it finishes, she says, 'Paul, play that again,' and he's shuffling around as a son would do when his parents are in, mildly embarrassed. We play the track again and she says, 'Paul. Do you know who that reminds me of? You don't know? The bloody Style Council!' like it was a band he wasn't in. And he goes, 'Yeah all right, Mum . . .' and when she shuffled out he said, 'Fucking hell, at least she never said the Thompson Twins!' . . .

Paul and I went up to the Nest for a coffee and he said, 'What's your plan for this then, Sheas? What are you going to do?' I said, 'I don't know, Paul. Probably put a four-track EP out.' He said, 'It's a bit good for that, though innit mate, why don't we make an album? Go away and write another batch of four or five tunes and come back. I've got no touring plans, we'll put something in the diary and we'll do it again, because I've really enjoyed the last couple of days.'

Steve Trigg: I'd worked with Stone Foundation on and off and had stood in on various occasions for a few gigs. They said, 'We're moving up a level across the board. We're just about to go into the studio with Paul. Do you want to be involved?' 'Let me think about that for a minute. How much do I have to pay you?' . . .

He's got no airs and graces. He's not pretentious, he's not the great rock star, he's busy making you a cup of tea or taking a run down to the chip shop to get some food the same as everybody else does. But you do find yourself having a sneaky look over your shoulder and thinking, *Fuck that's Paul Weller*, you can't help yourself.

Neil Sheasby: When we turned up to the first session, I had a Music Man StingRay bass, and he looked at it a bit suspicious – 'You sure about that?' I said, 'Wait till I plug it in because it makes a great noise.' We'd done the session and were getting on famously and at the end he's going, 'Fucking hell, man. That bass sounds great' . . .

We go back for the next session, and I turn up with a Fender Precision. He said, 'Fucking hell, Sheas, where's the Music Man StingRay?' . . . the trust rod in the neck had bent, so I sadly had to get rid of it. I said, 'It's you, innit? You fucking cursed it, didn't you? You mod gyppo bastard.'

We all got hauled into Clare's office at one point when he wasn't there just to rebook and stuff and she goes . . . 'Which one of you called him a mod gyppo bastard?' I was like two steps backwards, keeping my head down as they all look at me, and she goes, 'He loved that. It's really funny.'

Neil Jones: We had started writing 'Your Balloon Is Rising' very early on when me and Sheas started writing together. Probably 1998. We could never get it quite right. Fast forward to the *Street Ritual* sessions, and a weird moment where me and Sheas simultaneously looked at each other and said, 'Can you remember that song, "Your Balloon Is Rising"?' and I think it was because we were both thinking that we could hear Paul singing that chorus.

Neil Sheasby: We both thought maybe it's something we could ask Paul to sing. It would be a missed opportunity if we didn't try to get him to do a vocal. He recorded that song in one take.

March 2017 – *Jawbone* (film soundtrack)

Mark Baxter: The *Jawbone* film was written by my mate Johnny Harris . . . I was at a Paul Weller Q&A gig at Maida Vale and someone asked what he wanted to do next and he said, 'I'd love to score an arthouse film.' The minute he finished, I found his manager, Claire, and gave her the script. She was like 'Oh Bax, we get inundated with this stuff . . .' I said, 'Paul will get that.' It's about boxing and drinking and has so many layers. It's much deeper than just a boxing film. Paul read it immediately said, 'I'm in . . .'

Claire Moon: Paul really enjoyed that project. He had a lot of creative freedom to design and create the music how he wanted, which isn't typical when you come to score in a film.

Charles Rees: That first draft was given to Paul in 2012, and he loved it. He said, 'Two days in the studio, let's create a twenty-minute piece with segments and we'll join them up.' I had an iPhone Brian Eno App that we used on that whole piece of music – Paul pressing buttons to change the moods. We built it over two days and then sent it to Johnny.

Miles Leonard: We would talk about the record that he was delivering, and sure, with *Jawbone*, nobody was under the impression that that was nothing really more than what it was, a soundtrack, and that there probably wasn't going to be those radio tracks on there. As long as we were all fully aware of where we see the album and what its intention is and what it's there for, what it relates to, what it supports, then we're all very clear . . . artists need to sometimes create a piece of music that gives them the impetus to go on, then come back and do something perhaps more commercial.

19 May 2017 – *A Kind Revolution* (no. 5)

Charles Rees: *A Kind Revolution* was a continuation. There was definitely a vibe where Stan [Jan 'Stan' Kybert] and Paul were working really well together, and Stan was even generating more sounds of the music himself. It was back to playing in the live room and a real confidence in the band.

P. P. Arnold: The first time I met Paul was through Steve Cradock and Ocean Colour Scene. I did a jam with him at some festival in north London. He gave me a song, 'Shoot the Dove', back in the nineties . . . I so appreciate his support as I'm always going through such hard times struggling, trying to do this and do that . . . I don't really get to hang that much, but whenever we're together, we have a good time. We did 'Woo Sé Mama' with Madeline Bell.

Jamie Johnson: I went up to Louth to record Robert Wyatt's parts for 'She Moves with the Fayre' in his front room. Paul had just said, 'Do your thing on it. Wyattise this section of the song!'

Charles Rees: How Paul creates music can be really simple and really quick. I love those little snippets, little grooves that he puts down. He did it with 'She Moves with the Fayre'. He sung this little riff into his phone, I was listening to that on my headphones and put it on the kick drum and recorded the rhythm that he was playing. That was the beat for the song, just off his phone, I played it, Stan recorded it, and we looped it – all just from one little idea.

Phil Veacock: I find there are little corners of Weller songs that get in your head and stick there – then something will happen, and it will spring into your head. Little phrases. 'Long, Long Road' is one of those. I love that one.

With 'Nova', he said he wanted that Mott the Hoople, grunty, rock sax. A mixture of the baritone and the tenor really does that. On the song, 'Hopper', his instruction was to bring as many saxophones as I had. It did change quite a lot in the studio. Paul is very good at taking what you give him and then moulding it, if it's not quite there, he's very good at turning it a little bit to make it exactly what he wants.

John Lewis: Boy George was a guest singer on 'One Tear' and I said to Paul that it would be really interesting if Boy George sang that whole song and he's said, 'Yeah, I know that's the kind of thing we would have done in The Style Council days, but I can't really do it now. I can't really have an album with Paul Weller on the cover and me not singing every song,' which I think is a pity in a way. I like that 'anything goes' experimental air that The Style Council had. Back then he wanted to achieve other things, move with a more modular format, using session musicians a lot more.

Miles Leonard: I love the fact that there was not even a hint of why that might be seen as quite strange. Now, look, purely on the face of it, it's like 'Oh, Boy George is on the new Paul Weller record?' Anyone may think of P. P. Arnold or that Noel Gallagher is coming down. But you know what? Paul would just recognise the great vocal talent of George, and that's why he'd want him on there, because the vocal would work brilliantly.

Boy George: We've talked about writing together so much, and we definitely will do it at some point. I really would love to do that because I think I'm a lot better at collaborating now than I used to be. I definitely used to be a bit controlling in the studio, which I'm sure Paul is as well. There's mutual respect. So, I feel like it would be fun. Working on 'One Tear' was amazing. It's the funny thing that happens when you're going to work with someone you respect. You get a fear of, shit, it's the wrong key. I don't know if I can do it. And then when you step on the mic, suddenly it's another world, and when I did that track, I catastrophised for weeks and days before. And then I went into the studio and I was like, easy. It was just great, it was like, quick, vibey. It just works, and I love it.

Josh McClorey: It was pretty wild being on a track with Paul and Boy George, that's something I would never have thought I'd end up doing in my life . . . I'd be lying if I said I wasn't really nervous because you want to do a good job. It's great that he loves my guitar playing, but he's fucking playing guitar and then Steve's playing guitar and it's like, what the fuck am I doing here? So, there's that impostor syndrome that I definitely had at the beginning of it where it's like, what's the point in me being here when Chopper exists? You have to get past that.

Noel Gallagher: That song, 'The Impossible Idea', was my title, but he shortened it. My title was quite flowery and a bit long. It was like 'The Blah, Blah, Blah, Blah, The Impossible Something' and he went, 'Let's just call it "The Impossible Idea".' I was like, 'Alright mate, it's your tune!'

We've sat man-on-man playing guitar. More often than not, that doesn't happen. I remember going down to the studio once. I had a few ideas on the way, and he fucking hated them all! I was going, 'Oh, I've got something,' and he's going 'Hmm . . . no.' 'Another thing, on the Mellotron . . .' 'No' . . . He was saying, 'Well, I was thinking about this . . .' and I was like 'Nah.' 'Well, I've got another thing. It's called . . .' I was like 'Nah'. We've had more days like that than we have of 'Fucking hell! Amazing!'

I had posters of this guy on my wall when I was a fucking teenager at school, right? So, it'd be like sitting down, across a table, with fucking McCartney and saying, 'Let's write a song.' It'd be just like 'Fucking hell!' You'd quickly realise what a shit kicker you are . . . To describe it to people who don't know what it's like is difficult, because most people, and rightly so, think that when you write a song, you go 'Okay, today we're going to write a song about this, and it's going to go like this.' Well, that's not what happens at all.

But then we have had some great days too. When we wrote that song for The Monkees, 'The Birth of an Accidental Hipster' . . . That is a mad, mad tune, right? We wrote that together in his studio . . . we were like, 'What are we going do with it?'

Then a week later some guy called me and said, 'The Monkees are getting back together.' They were asking people to write songs for them and I was like, 'No!' Then as I put the phone down, I went, *Oh, hang on a minute!* They fucking loved it!

Billy Bragg: You can see Paul trying to freshen up the way he makes records. *OK, I've done it that way. What's another way to do this? How do we do this another way?* . . . With his earlier solo albums, he's building up his confidence and his style, but I think since 2000, he's been on an interesting journey. Sometimes I get where he's coming from. Other times he's gone off in the bushes somewhere and I can hear him thrashing about over there and then I think, *Oh, I don't know where he's going*, and then for me, he's suddenly back on the track in front of me, singing about Hopper's paintings.

Paul Moody: I felt *A Kind Revolution* and *Saturns Pattern* were a reconnection of him and his audience's core musical values. Just as they are with all of us, from the teenage years, you've got a core musical set of values which for Paul are soul and funk and classic sixties pop, The Creation and The Who and The Kinks. So sometimes it's just natural to go back to the well, back to the original sources and you do feel as though those are the ones that hit the fans the most, because on some level this is pure classic Paul songs.

Miles Leonard: I remember sitting with Paul at Black Barn to listen to each album. For that one, I talked to him a lot about the production – saying it was brilliant, sonically, how it was, and what he delivered. He eventually said, 'Forget about production. What do you think of the songwriting, what do you think of the songs?'

Steve 'Tufty' Carver: On the album notes for *A Kind Revolution*, Paul called us the Legendary Carver Brothers. I can't tell you what that meant to me. I texted him straight away. That's forty years. He's remembered the legendary Carver brothers.

July 2017 – Nova Weller born (eighth child, third with Hannah Weller)

August 2017 – *Mother Ethiopia* EP

Steve Trigg (The General): Paul had an idea that he wanted to do this. You can tell from the title where his brain was at. We had a discussion on what it was going to come out like, people like Fela Kuti, that's where we're going with it. That kind of feel. To be honest, I wasn't massively familiar with a lot of his stuff. I knew of him, and had heard some of it, so I did what I always do when I'm faced with that kind of challenge, I soak everything up. I downloaded everything I could find and put it on continual loop and listened over and over. It's about trying to get inside somebody's head and understand where that's coming from. We went into the studio and recorded everything as a stream of consciousness. Paul took the bits he liked and then created the EP.

John Lewis: One of the questions I asked Paul, was that he's never really done much reggae. He's embraced so many different types of music, bossa nova, funk, hip hop, touches of Indian music, the *Mother Ethiopia* EP. I know he's a reggae fan, but he's never really tried it. He just said, 'It's just too hard to play.'

January 2018 – Nia Wyn, 'Turnstiles'

Nia Wyn: I did a session at Black Barn. I was super nervous. He picked me up from the train station in his car and he'd said, go through this entrance to Woking, don't go round the back because I don't want you to have to see how rundown it is! . . . I had the bare bones of a song that I wanted to work on with him. He said that I had a really unique voice, and he was really into it. I was feeling optimistic about this because I know that he's passionate about supporting young artists. He's not the kind of guy that's gone up the ladder and cut the rope behind him. He's one of those people that invests in the next generation to do music and he's really on board with that. People take his recommendations as gospel. I think sometimes working with other people really does push you to go against your normal habits and it can be really for the greater good. The song that we created, 'Turnstiles', it is personal but it's also a soul love song that a lot of people can relate to.

February–March 2018 – *A Kind Revolution* tour

Josh McClorey: The Strypes supported Paul on the tour for *A Kind Revolution*. Arenas across the UK including the O2 . . . A lot of people just don't fucking bother with the support act, which I get; they want to see who they paid to see. But his fans came in early, appreciated us, and even bought merch and vinyl.

That was quite near the end of our band . . . Before we broke up, I called Paul for advice. Me and Evan, the drummer, had been in a band together in our heads since we were five or six. Even though we felt like it had run its course and wanted to stop, it was still a hard decision. You wonder if you should stay in something because it's easy or should you move on? . . . He said, 'The only thing you can do is the thing that makes you happy. If you want to go and make new music and do something else, then you have to do that. You can't just stay in something because it's comfortable.'

April 2018 – Steve Ellis – *Boom! Bang! Twang!*

Steve Ellis: The Black Barn Crew are all like-minded people, there's no egos abounding, everybody gets on, you should have a good time and make music, which is what it is supposed to be about, for God's sake. I hadn't made an album for a few years. Paul said, 'Why don't you do your album here?' Paul's my mate. I don't speak to him all the time. I don't drive him mad. I'm always there for him. One day I says to him, 'It was fucking weird the other day.' He says, 'Why?' I said, 'I was standing at the sink washing up and I don't know why, I'm thinking about you, and then you rang me up.' What I like about Paul is he's black and white. We've never had a bad word in what must be over thirty years.

August 2018, Stone Foundation – *Everybody, Anyone*

Kathryn Williams: Stone Foundation were looking for someone to do a shared vocal. I'd been doing something in Scotland, so I travelled all the way down to Black Barn on the hottest day of the year to sing that song 'Don't Walk Away'.

That was really the first time I properly met Paul. I was so boiling hot, it was ridiculous because I'd driven seven hours without stopping for a wee. So the first thing I was thinking was, 'What do I say to everyone?' But the first thing I actually said was, 'Hi Paul, where's your toilet?' I was so desperate.

That broke the ice, and then he made me a cup of tea. I thought, *Oh, that's nice*, and then we got to work on the song. I've got a picture, the only one I have of me and Paul from that day. It was so hot, Paul's got no top on, and he's got his arm around me. The photo cuts off at waist height, and I've got a shirt on. When I showed my husband, he said, 'Well, it looks like he's got no top on and you've got no trousers on.' So that's not going on social media – it just looks ridiculous. That's just for me. Maybe I should have taken my top off just to be polite.

5 September 2018 – *GQ* Men of the Year, Songwriter of the Year

Dylan Jones: I'd been trying to get Paul to the *GQ* Men of the Year awards forever, for twenty years. There were three people I really wanted there: David Bowie, Van Morrison, and Paul . . . Bowie came in 2002 at the Natural History Museum. Van came in 2014 . . . and Paul came to the Tate Modern in 2018.

Trust me, when you're in a room with Paul Weller, you're

not the best dressed person in the room. He takes it to obsessional heights and it's kind of extraordinary, and I take my hat off to him. He really cares. It's genuine . . . Lots of people still don't understand it. Journalists didn't really understand it in the eighties. They thought it was an affectation, but it's a real thing. He is a well-dressed man. When he starts talking about something with such an attention to detail, and the minutiae of a shoe or the stitching on something, I'm like, whoah, that's even too much information for me.

People loved having him in the room. You can judge when you walk around the Men of the Year awards. There'd be over a hundred really, really, really, really famous people there every year. A-listers, big people and people are walking around going, 'That's Paul Weller. That's Paul Weller. Fuck. That's Paul Weller.' And it was, it was Paul Weller.

14 September 2018 – *True Meanings* (no. 2)

Paul Weller: I love 'Gravity' so much as a song, I thought it's so beautiful, and I don't say that in an arrogant way, I genuinely thought it was a great song. But I could never put it on any of the albums around that time. It just wouldn't fit, it just seemed so at odds with the rest of it. So, I thought, well, maybe try and write an album that's similar to that, then I would have a home for it, or find a place for it. Which is what I did with *True Meanings*, which is another record I really love as well.

John Wilson: He played 'Gravity' on Radio 4 for *Mastertapes* back in 2012 as a work in progress. 'Here's a new song. I'll just try this one.' He was more or less finished, but he hadn't recorded it and he was putting it out there. He's not precious like that . . . Paul has always had a great voice that suits different styles. I go back to 'Thick as Thieves' and 'Setting Sons' and 'Sound Affects' a lot because it's where I came in, and his voice at that time was astonishing. He's a young man at the time, and it's got a character and a depth. When we were kids, he seemed not just like a big brother, older and wiser, he had this depth and authority. A lot of that was in the voice. I think technically he's probably tuning his voice better now. He's using it in a different way, more as an instrument.

Miles Leonard: I'd tend to go to the studio when they're three-quarters of the way through an album to sit with Paul and have a listen. *True Meanings* was slightly more folk rock, acoustic, sonically it was different in terms of his performance vocally, and of the band. I think it's one of his greatest albums. Definitely my favourite of the three key ones that we worked on at Parlophone. 'Gravity' reminds me of 'Tales from the Riverbank' in a sense, or 'English Rose'. His voice on that is like velvet. 'Soul Searchers' makes a real statement at the start of the record. Slightly more stripped back. Lyrically there's that idea of coming of age and understanding vulnerability in life.

Conor O'Brien: Paul told me he was writing a more philosophical, acoustic-based album and asked if I wanted to collaborate on a song. He sent me a phone recording of him playing a riff and mumbling non-words, just to convey the melody. A second voice memo was a little bit more developed, but still without actual words – just sounds. I played the riff into the computer, looped it and the words for 'The Soul Searchers' came very quickly. His chords suggested to me that it was a song for somebody who's searching for something deeper inside or maybe an authenticity. That was the starting point and then the rhythm of the song suggested the rest of the words.

There wasn't any pressure. I've listened to Paul's music since I started making music, and his work has always been part of my writing foundation. He's a central figure in that. When I was younger, I used a lot of his songs as blueprints. So, when it came to collaboration there was no sense of having to fit into someone else's mould. I'm just going to write music that feels good to me, and it clicked. The only change he made was to the title – I had called it 'The Searching Soul', and he thought 'The Soul Searchers' was better. Then I discovered the band The Soul Searchers, a funky soul band from the late sixties, early seventies, and really got into them for a while.

I added string samples, drum samples and bass guitar to the track and sent it to Paul. A couple of months later, he sent me back a version with my string samples replaced by real players and your man from The Zombies, Rod Argent, playing Hammond organ, which was wild.

Rod Argent: Paul sent me a few demos and said, 'I'd love you to play a bit of an organ solo at the end.' Then I had a lovely morning at Black Barn. I wandered over to the organ, oh my God, it's in the key of B, which is not a great key for keyboard. I just hoped I wouldn't make a pig's ear of it! . . . Paul also fancied me playing a bit of Mellotron on 'White Horses'. I ended up playing a bit of piano on the end of it too.

Noel Gallagher: One of my favourite tunes he's ever written is 'White Horses'. Did I play on that? Please tell me I didn't, because I have no recollection of that. Did I? No, surely not. [*Laughs*] Oh, I did. That's why I love it so much! . . . When I saw the gig at the Royal Festival Hall, it was the best I'd ever seen him, and he was doing Jam songs with the strings and all that, 'Boy About Town', and it was just brilliant.

Hannah Peel: Paul was looking for somebody to score. He sent 'Aspects' from *True Meanings* as a bit of a test. At that time, I was playing my violin a lot, so I layered up the string arrangement on there, built this quartet, just out of my violin, and sent that back to Paul who loved it and asked if I could do more?

I wasn't aware of the themes of the overall album . . . I don't usually know the process behind it, and I guess our conversations are always so present. They're not about what has been happening, they're always just about, *how do we do that? What do we do? What's the ideas? Let's go do them.*

Paul's always amazing with music and with having a chat to as well. He's one for gossip, that's for sure! 'Why aren't you married yet? Why aren't you doing this?' He also thought I was about twenty-four or twenty-five and when I told him my actual age, he was like, 'No. What? I can't believe it!' He probably thought he was getting a young prodigy, and he wasn't!

Barrie Cadogan: Paul could easily play loads of instruments himself on his albums, but I guess he's always going to do what's best for the music. That goes above the ego . . .

I did the track 'Old Castles'. I don't know if the original idea was something more acoustic, but I played something more electric mellow. They seemed to like it. I did a few takes, and thought I was working it out, and they were like, 'Great, we've got it.' And I was like, 'Hang on, I don't know what I'm doing yet' . . . Sometimes there's good stuff that comes out when you're not thinking about it too much. There's no red-light fever because we didn't think we were recording.

Phil Veacock: That was quite different from things I've done in the past. He was using the brass section more as a texture or a colour rather than us playing specific lines.

Danny Thompson: Nowadays the business has people recording in your dining room and sending in the track to America or Austria or somewhere. Whatever happened to being in a room together, making music and singing and having a cup of tea? That is what the Black Barn is about . . . the quality that comes out of there is so fantastic because it's real. It's people sitting in the same room, breathing the same oxygen and making this beautiful music together, led by Paul. It's like being back in the garage again. Real music making, and long may it continue.

Can I just say, because the tide is running out and I'm running out of time as well, and a few health issues . . . I would dearly love my last notes, recording wise, to be with Paul . . . You go in the studio, and you're given the freedom to express yourself within his poetry, and that's a great compliment.

Tom Doyle: Paul tends to write late at night – the life of a touring musician, who's been doing it forty-odd years – they do tend to switch on later. I'd get a lot of late-night texts with voice memos and rough ideas, and we batted a few of them forward and back.

Paul Weller: That's when I write them, that's when I mainly write them. I'm able to record a lot of stuff on my phone, so I can be anywhere and put an idea down. When I'm on the road, I always carry a notepad and write stuff down. And it's me strumming aimlessly on a guitar at home, sometimes on a piano. I guess it hasn't changed too much from that point of view. I think probably what's different is, whereas back in the day if a song didn't come together quickly in my head, I would probably abandon it, lose interest in it . . . now even if it doesn't go anywhere eventually, I'll try and see it through because I've learned that sometimes you start on something and you just think, it's never going to work, you should abandon it, leave it, but then I've seen other songs where I thought that, and then we have gone through that process, we've gone through that wall, and all of a sudden this thing that you didn't think was going to work is fucking brilliant, and it has worked. I guess that's patience, I suppose, is it? You know what I mean? Being a bit more patient, letting things develop.

Tom Doyle: The song 'Movin' On' started with Paul's opening riff, the one that runs through the verse. As soon as me and Anth heard that, we're like, *Yes, we know what we're doing with this.* Most of what we do leans into psychedelic soul or that late sixties trippy vibe. We're big fans of Jimmy Webb and that late sixties, early seventies style.

We worked on the instrumental, going back and forth with Paul. Then, while I went over to New York on a Q magazine trip, I was just off the plane, went to the dressing room, and he started blasting it out. Surreal. Steve Cradock popping in going, 'What's that sound?' The next day the band were on *The Late Show, Stephen Colbert*. It was funny because the smoking ban is everywhere, but certain musicians just don't give a fuck. I could smell he was smoking in his dressing room, so I stuck my head around the door, I said, 'I've come in here for a smoke' and he pulled out of his bag the lyrics to 'Movin' On'. I don't know if he'd written them earlier or overnight, but he said, 'Have a look at that as a writer.' You can tell that there's a universal aspect to that song as well as a personal aspect to it.

Sheema Mukherjee: I first met Paul when I was in Imagined Village. He did a version of 'John Barleycorn' on our first album and a couple of live shows with us early on. With *True Meanings*, Paul was looking for a sitar player for the song 'Books' . . . His lyrics were on scraps of paper, and he got me to play along in one section and do a solo in another and gave me complete freedom to improvise . . .

He was going to Rishikesh fairly soon after and wanted to know what I thought of it. I knew it was this terrible tourist trap now. It's the place where The Beatles went and so everybody heads for that, and I don't think he liked it as much as he thought he would. I spoke to him about it afterwards and he was saying how it's just full of people . . .

He also asked if I could do a prayer at the end of 'Books'. It's a Sanskrit saying: 'May all people have hope, happiness and freedom' . . . We put it to music – it's just one line, a phrase that sums up the whole song.

Paul Baines: The cover photo shoot was by an amazing person, Nicole Nodland. It was the first time working with Paul, and he loved her work. When we met up at the studio for the session, Paul – who's done a million photo shoots – came prepared. He knows how to pack his suits, so everything comes out immaculate. He always brings more than enough to wear, rather than just a couple of T-shirts and a pair of jeans . . .

The shot that made the cover stood out immediately, though there were so many amazing images. Did we leave the cigarette in Paul's hand on the album cover? We may have had to retouch it off . . . None of us are going to say to Paul, 'Put that out.'

Nicole Nodland: It was 2019, two weeks after my brain surgery. I was out of the hospital and photographing Paul for the album cover. I was just trying my best at that point, wanting to create something fresh and not pastiche. He was so gentle, charismatic and wonderful.

He mentioned Prince, and we talked a bit about it, since I'd been Prince's first in-house photographer at Paisley Park. There's definitely a connection with Paul and Prince. They would have gotten along like a house on fire because you couldn't put Prince in a box. He'd do jazz, then funk, then hip hop, then rap, then he'd do soul – he created his own genre.

Prince taught me to stay authentic, to focus on what you're doing without worrying about the critics. Just be true and free, and Paul has that same thing.

I knew Paul's music – The Jam, The Style Council, 'You're the best thing that's ever happened' – at that time I had a little bit of a crush on him . . .

Paul just turned up for the shoot. No entourage. Just him, his suitcase and his beautiful face and hair. He's content, he's peaceful. He gives you peaceful vibes. His children came and helped steam his clothes, which was funny.

I don't understand how he knew after the brain surgery, but he would gently take my hand and walk me across the street. You think of Paul as a bit of a geezer, but he is a gentleman. I felt safe. I felt secure, and he trusted me. He said, 'You do what you want. You're Nicole fucking Nodland' . . . Thank you, Paul. Because you brought me out of St Mary's Hospital and gave me the incentive to save my life.

Miles Leonard: I was incredibly privileged and proud to be working with that record and releasing that album. I know for a lot of people it was like. 'OK. This could be pretty difficult' . . . We had incredible support from Radio 2 and *Later . . . With Jools*, and print was not what it was. It was hard to really try and get the records moving . . . because it's this soporific album, but it was so beautiful.

2018–19, *Other Aspects – Live at the Royal Festival Hall* (no. 10)

Hannah Peel: Paul said, 'Do you want to do the concerts at Royal Festival Hall?' I said, 'Yeah, great! . . . but I'm not conducting, I'm not a conductor.' I'd never have done it, maybe in sessions, but not ever on stage. Paul's very persuasive.

Joe Connor: I'd always wanted to create a film that caught someone like Paul in a situation that he was uncomfortable in. He'd never done anything like that before, where he'd stripped his music down. He worked with an orchestra and Hannah, who is an incredible artist. The symbiosis between a rock band with classical players and a classical knowledge was something that Paul had not really done a lot of. I'm sure he'd done it in a studio, but there's something about doing it live in front of people, and it created an inherent drama that I leaned into. I thought, *I'm going to explore this more.*

That's why the film became episodic, with three songs followed by a glimpse into the creation, then three more songs and more of the creative process. It became a richer project for it.

Miles Leonard: Annoyingly, Paul is the sharpest dressed person I've ever seen. I remember he came on with this pink and purple rugby top on and I was thinking, *You know what, if I wear that I'm going to look like a rugby player. Why is it you wear it, and you look like the coolest person on the fucking planet?* I then went out and actually bought one, and I just looked like a rugby player.

John Wilson: Paul talked to me about resetting 'Private Hell' for those shows. He felt quite uncomfortable about that lyric because it is so bleak and it's got such cynical, but amazing, couplets in it . . . That woman with the sadness and the floating down the high street in the Valium haze, and the kids aren't writing letters because they've gone off and they don't need her any more, and she's lonely and her husband just doesn't care. Projecting himself into a world that was so different to the life he was living. That is astonishing. I was quite surprised, in a way, that Paul said he felt very uncomfortable singing it.

Charles Rees: Listen to the way he sings 'English Rose' back in The Jam and listen to the way he sings it now. It's such a difference. His voice is huge now, whereas back then there was almost a sense of . . . I was going to say, innocence. But maybe a bit of naivety or something in the vocal cords, not in the lyrics or anything like that. But the way he sings it now, it's not just the smoking [*laughs*], it really comes down to using that muscle and getting stronger. His voice is ten times bigger than it was thirty, forty years ago, it's developed so much.

Miles Leonard: On the front cover of that *Other Aspects* album, he reminds me of Burt Bacharach, George Martin in those studios. You see him across that piano, and Paul just looks cool as fuck. What we captured there was quite stunning. I really hope people go back to live albums. They can always struggle to be noticed and find their place, but I think over time people discover that they like old live albums which went, maybe, unnoticed at the time and see that as a very special live recording.

Joe Connor: To see my documentary film on the big screen was amazing. I have this feeling of elation and beauty about it that the music seems to translate more because you've gone on this journey with them rather than just watching a concert straight from beginning to end . . . you feel like you've gone on this journey with this character.

One of the things that I've heard him talk about is that he doesn't necessarily think about the mechanics of how he's doing what he's doing. I think Jacko or it might be Mick in my *Wild Wood* documentary says it's like a carpenter. He's just making a chair. And to Paul Weller, just making songs, and he doesn't really know how he's making them or why he's making them, and he's not really thinking too much about it . . . he puts himself in these positions as ways to kind of keep himself creatively stimulated, so he's not just doing the same thing over and over again, but he's coming across new challenges and new ways of doing it.

17 December 2018 – *Q* Awards, Best Act in the World Today

Noel Gallagher: Paul is always saying, 'Fucking Bono . . . your mate!' I remember once, I was going off on holiday to Bono's in the south of France . . . So, as I'm packing the fucking thing to go, he calls me, 'All right, mate. What are you up to this afternoon?' I'm like 'I'm just out the door, I'm just off on holiday.' 'Oh, right, where are you going?' 'I'm going to the south of France.' 'All right, where are you staying?' 'I'm staying at Bono's.' He went, 'Ha, ha! Yes, mate! Where you staying?' and I was like, 'I'm staying at Bono's.' He went, 'Yeah, fucking go on, mate. Give us a shout when you get back.'

So, we're down the south of France. We go out for dinner one night, me and Bono and his missus, and his kids and my kids, and wouldn't you fucking know it, Elton John is in there. And I know Weller hasn't got a lot of time for these people, right . . . So I said to both of them, 'I never do this but can the three of us get a selfie, because I want to send it to somebody?' I knew it would fucking do his head in. We take a picture, I'm in the middle of Bono and Elton John! I've got my arms around them, and I sent it to him saying, 'Having a great time. Wish you were here!' And literally, as I fucking sent the thing, crying laughing, the fucking thing came back, and it was him. Just sent me a text: 'You've gone too far.'

So fast forward to 2018. We're at some Q awards ceremony. Bono's there presenting me with an award. Weller's there, because he's won summat. I know we're all going to be there.

So I'm fucking . . . *right!* . . . I'm like a pathetic child getting high off the awkward scene that I'm going to cause . . . Me and Bono are with the photographers, and I know that Weller's getting the next award. I can see Weller is walking up the fucking thing, and it couldn't be more fucking perfect.

The thing about Bono is he fucking loves Paul Weller. He loves him. He's always saying to me 'Why don't you get Paul to . . .' And I'm like, 'Bono. You don't get it. He fucking hates everyone!' 'No, no, The Jam and that . . .' I was like, 'No, you don't get it. He fucking don't like U2. He hates it.'

So, Weller comes walking up, and I grab Weller. 'Get in here! Way-hay!' Fuck! Brilliantly, the photographer kept on shooting. I've got a picture of the three of us, I'm in the middle, Weller's trying to get out of the picture, and I've got my arms round him. I've got it in my house. It's the fucking best picture! . . .

A week later, I'm round at the shops in Maida Vale, and there's a guy around there who knows us both. 'All right, Noel. I believe you had a good day at the fucking Q Awards. Paul was telling me he met Bono,' and I was like, 'Was he now?' and he said, 'Yeah, he said he's a lovely bloke!' I said, 'Did he now? Fucking hell, that's interesting!' He went, 'Yeah, said he was a lovely man.' 'Well, fucking hell, let's get him on the phone now, shall we?' And I was like, 'So, I believe Bono's a lovely man.' 'Yeah, he's all right. Yeah. He's all right.' I was like, 'Yes, he is all right. I've been telling you for the last fucking thirty years that he's all right!'

May 2019 – Suggs: *Love Letters to London*, Radio 4

Suggs: Paul is very serious but equally has got a great sense of humour, when you get to know him. He is not interested in exposing that in interviews is he? Doesn't like doing telly and all that, but he is actually a very humorous guy. Another thing about him, he's very interested in other people. He's constantly at it with people. It's exhausting. He wants to talk to the geezer who is doing the tea, the fucking van driver, my son-in-law, whoever . . .

I was doing a show on Radio 4, *Love Letters to London*, all about different parts of London. I wanted to do Soho, and I was thinking about him, '"A" Bomb in Wardour Street', and I knew that he'd done the clubs, Maximum R&B and all that. So, I asked him to come on to talk about his earliest memories of Soho and do a song. I was talking about doing 'Piccadilly Palare' by Morrissey. He said, 'You can fuck that right off.' [*Laughs*] I knew straight away what the answer to that was. Then he said, there's this really obscure song by The Kinks called 'Nobody's Fool', which was the theme tune to *Budgie*, a TV series when we were kids. It's a really nice song. He came around my house. We started to rehearse and look, I hate it but I'm not really very professional, but he really is. He's going, 'Let's not let down Uncle Ray. Let's keep rehearsing, Suggsy, till we get this right.'

January 2020 – *In Another Room* (limited edition EP)

Tom Van Heel: The *Another Room* EP . . . even I haven't got it on vinyl [*laughs*]. That is a total 'coming down for a cup of tea' moment. I went into the studio, and I could hear birds tweeting and thought, what's going on here? It was really far out, man. The day was getting later and later, and it was getting darker and darker and they're messing about with echoes ... doof doof ... and all these birds tweeting. I played a bit, and the prayer bowl was sitting next to me on the filing cabinet. I was like, 'Should we just try that?' It was one of them ones where you could literally do anything, throw anything on it. I've got some mad demos of that. I've got this CD, and it's just got three minutes of Paul's footsteps.

Being at the Barn is never the same, it's always exciting and it makes you want to play.

Jon 'Mojo' Mills: Paul started dropping me texts and emails and he's cropped up in the *Shindig* mag numerous times. I got him sorted out with Ghost Box Records. He made his really avant-garde musique concrète single, which was just bizarre. But he wants to make music and his fans clearly absolutely detest it but he just doesn't care. It's obviously a mega collectible now. We did that and then I do a Soho radio show, so we had him in to cut live to a lathe for a disc that got sold for thousands of pounds for charity.

3 July 2020 – *On Sunset* (no. 1)

Miles Leonard: Parlophone went through a real change after I left. I can't sit here and attribute that just to me leaving, I think labels have zeitgeist moments ... When Paul left the label, it didn't ultimately surprise me. I'm not sure that people after me had that same feeling, strategy or vision for Paul that I had. I was always there, somebody fighting that corner of how important it was to have Paul on the label. I had a measure of success that was sometimes very different to the people that ran the company. It doesn't matter if you're selling ten thousand albums, if you're making a record that's really important, that has a place . . . I always fought for the importance of having someone like Paul on our label, and the fact that that in turn may bring younger artists to our label who see an artist of that calibre.

But I was very pleased that he then went to Polydor. It was brilliant that he went back to his old stable, his old home. They really missed a trick letting him go in the first place.

Claire Moon: Returning to the original home of Polydor was never part of a strategy. It's a nice story for industry press, but it was never about, *Let's go back*. It's more about who's running a company and whether can we work with them. It's always about the people for us. A lot of our team are out-of-house. Polly for press, Karen manages TV, Joe takes care of radio. They're independent people who've been with us for years so we move as a team . . . I spoke to Tom March, who was running Polydor, and said, 'Do you want to have a chat?' He said, yes, cleared his diary and that's how that came about . . . which leads us on to *On Sunset*.

Paul Weller: A lot of *On Sunset* was done live. A lot of live takes. And then we embellished them, adding strings and whatever.

Mick Talbot: I was down at Black Barn to record The Style Council documentary and Paul said, 'There may be a couple of tracks on my current album that I need a Hammond on.' Paul ordered a curry, which we sat down and ate, and then all the film crew had gone and he went 'Oh wait . . . these tracks.' So, I got home a bit later than I expected. I said to my wife, 'I played on a couple of Paul's new songs. I suppose if they hear it back and it works, I might end up on the new album.' Then when *On Sunset* come out, it turned out those two tracks were three tracks, and somehow I'd nodded off for one of them! But I'm on it. 'Baptiste', 'Village' and 'Walkin''.

Paul Weller: A lot of the time there's elements of me in it, and there's elements of my own experiences that are in the songs. But beyond that I visualise or invent the rest. Going back to the visualisation of musical words, I just saw this guy striding down probably in Greenwich Village, that's probably where the title comes from, I don't know why Greenwich Village, I've not spent time there anyway! But it could be anywhere, right? Could be Portobello Road, someone just striding down the road, sunshine, and then it's a great day. They've got no worries, 'Fuck everything, man. I'm just feeling good!' And I love that image. So that's where that song comes from. But I'm not saying it isn't connected with the fact that I definitely feel comfortable in my skin as well. I think it's something tied in with that as well, you know.

Ben Taylor (Magic Mod): Track number three, 'Old Father Tyme', there's actually a magician in that song . . . I was in the studio, and Paul was doing this song, when Stan said, 'We need some claps in that,' and Paul goes, 'Magic, come on.' A while later he texted me a picture of the back of the album, before it came out. I had tears of joy in my eyes. Under the credits: 'Magic Mod. Claps!' That's it, mate. To be on an album from my hero. No matter what else happens, that is it.

Phil Veacock: I was going around, 'I'm on the number one album.' It's the first time that ever happened. I was made up. My favourite song is the actual 'On Sunset' track. I said to Andy Ross who was playing the flute that I wanted it to sound like that Randy Crawford song called 'Rio de Janeiro Blue' . . . I love the sectional stuff, the way it blended with the Staves' backing vocals . . . I also got very fanboy excited about the fact that there's a bit on 'Equanimity' where Jimmy Lea from Slade does the little violin solo and then a few bars later, I basically duet with him . . .

Paul gives great directions. On the song 'Walkin'' he said, 'I want a post horn sound on it. I want this to sound like The James Last Orchestra going on holiday to New Orleans. Can you make it sound like that?' I was at my mother-in-law's for Sunday lunch just before we did the session, and noticed that hanging on her wall was a great big, old antique post horn. I said, 'Sheila. is that actually a thing or is that a fake one?' She said, 'No, it's a genuine antique post horn. It's quite valuable.' She very nicely allowed me to borrow it, and Chris Storr played it on the track . . . with Alastair White and John Firkle holding it up because it's so long.

Hannah Peel: For the orchestration Paul just said, 'Go for it! We want big summer fun' . . . I'd heard the demos, half mixes, in the studio, and for me it felt like a Beach Boys vibe. That classic sound where all the strings are doing the same melody at once.

Max Beesley: 'Maxi . . . I'm in LA, do you want to do a bit on a video? It'd only be an hour . . . Come on, it'll be all right. None of that pissing about.' I was late, six o'clock, and the guy's running around with the rep, 'We're going to lose the light.' 'It's going to be all right, man. Where would you like me?' He went, 'Over there. Paul's going to drive over.' We were just laughing because he was looking at me and I'm like, 'How are you doing?' It was just great to be a part of it with him. It was just another step in reconnecting and embracing what we can together in these short lives that we have.

Nicole Nodland: I was shooting the stills on the video. *Hell yeah, I'm coming.* That's my second home. I know LA inside and out. I spent three days just shooting behind the scenes. I got to meet his son and the son's boyfriend, who directed the video, and it was incredible.

Danny Eccleston: When I interviewed Paul for *On Sunset*, I was lucky enough to become one of those people that he'd text for a while with music recommendations. He'd go, 'I've just heard this, it's amazing, check it out' and you'd be drawn into this relationship where you wanted to share things you'd heard with him. One thing he insisted I listen to was an amazing 1969 jazz album by Andrew Hill, *Lift Every Voice*, on Blue Note. It's a jazz record but it's also got a choir with a gospel vibe. Weller really loves gospel music. I remember thinking anyone who can talk about The Small Faces and also talk about Andrew Hill has the kind of musical world that a *Mojo* reader would appreciate.

When I interviewed him around *On Sunset*, I also asked him how he could sing and chew gum at the same time. How does he manage it without swallowing it? He looked at me and just said, 'lots of practice'.

John Lewis: Every time you meet Paul Weller, he always asks 'What are you listening to at the moment?' There was a genuine sense of curiosity where he wants to know. He's not just being polite, and quite often, the next time you'll interview him, he'll remember, *oh, yeah, I listened to that Shabaka Hutchings album. I really liked it,* or *I listened to the Ezra Collective thing. I thought that was a bit shit.* He follows up on the things that you'll mention to him, which is quite weird.

A lot of people of a certain age, just stop listening to new stuff, get into your comfort zone and only listen to things that you like. Don't really have any interest in finding new vistas. But Paul Weller always seems to be interested in that. He's not somebody who just wants to retreat into the past. He's always interested in hearing new stuff that comes out. He checks out new classical albums, London jazz, folk records, and things from Brazil and Spain.

When I wrote the biog for *On Sunset*, he had just come back from India and was listening to a lot of Indian music. Both my parents come from India and I know a bit about Indian music and remember recommending a few things that he might be interested in. He was genuinely interested in writing down things that I was saying. There is a curiosity which is rare with a lot of musicians.

Will Hodgkinson: He's got an account at Rough Trade for a lot of money every month, a few hundred quid every month. They do a list of recommendations and he'll say, 'Yeah give it a punt on that.' Every month he's buying a load of records which is brilliant because he's supporting young artists for a start and supporting the shop which is really important. I think it's for someone who's kind of, so embedded in a certain, aesthetic which is associated with the sixties. It's really great that he's really interested in stuff. Often it surprises me. Like, I think he's just going to say guitar bands and then he'd come up with some like Nigerian band he'd be listening to.

Polly Birkbeck: He is so enthusiastic about new stuff and always saying, 'Have you heard this?' He actively seeks out things and is ready to hear different things. People whose taste he likes recommend things to him. I played him a remix of something yesterday, and he said, 'I really like that, see if that guy wants to remix something.'

Chris Catchpole: It's an incredible privilege to have someone like Paul think to text you or recommend a record. It never gets any less weird. It happens a lot. During Covid I would get texts talking about music. I think that's down to his character, that if he meets someone and he gets on with them, he's just like a mate. There's no other musician even close that I've had anything like that with. Johnny Marr's very nice but I wouldn't expect to wake up in the night and see that he got a text at quarter to one in the morning. 'Have you heard this?' Sylvia Patterson and I were talking about it, name me another pop star that wouldn't think twice of doing something like that because there's just no ego there whatsoever.

He has a genuine hunger for discovering music. His antenna is always up and he hasn't lost that enthusiasm. He still has a teenager's attitude towards finding new music, something most people lose by their thirties. His passion is incredible. I once asked Noel Gallagher where he gets his music from, and he said, 'All my music recommendations come from Paul, I don't know what fucking weird pirate radio stations he's listening to, where he's fucking finding all this stuff constantly, but he's constantly hungry for it.' I think that attitude is how Paul approaches making his own music, always looking for something new, something different. First and foremost, he's a music fan.

Paul Weller: I don't know if I'm ahead of the curve. I just think I'm still a fan of music in general. Any blinkers I've had in my life, when it comes to music, have long since fallen away. I'm really open to listening to anything, whether I like it or not. A lot of it's word of mouth. Music like Villagers or Lucy Rose, I probably saw on TV shows, or we did *Later* with them, or something like that; with Declan O'Rourke, we were both on the same label, so that's when I heard 'Galileo' and his first album. It's like how we used to share music – taking a bus to your mate's house, with a couple of albums under your arm, saying, 'You've got to hear this record!' Or lending records at school. Now we just send tracks digital, but it's still the same ideas. There's a lot of that with me and my mates texting each other tracks, 'You've got to hear this!'

Richard Hawley: Paul is like a sponge. He listens to everything and soaks it up. There's two ways to go about keeping your individuality, I think. Weller's way is a bit like Dylan where everything is fair game, I don't mean in terms of him stealing ideas, but Paul is a genuine music lover, and he just reminds me of an old scientist or an old adventurer in *Boy's Own* books or something, like *Journey to the Centre of the Earth*, Jules Verne. He's not fakery in any way, shape or form. He's genuinely interested in the next move, the next thing, the things that are happening now, and his enthusiasm for it is just unwavering. But also he's like me, he looks back as well into the past of music, and his enthusiasm for that is remarkable. He hasn't become tired or jaded in any way.

Steve Pilgrim: The only thing that I don't understand and can't get my head around is what lights the fire in Paul to drive his creativity. What is it that still, at his age, is so relentless and so seeking about his nature and his character? What is it that keeps him looking out? Pete Paphides said to me, 'He's always got his antenna up, hasn't he?'

Hannah Peel: The amount of material Paul has is insane. Whenever you go into the studio, there's always a list at the back, of all the tracks. There's always way more than an album. I guess that's what makes his music so good, because you're overwriting and then you get the best pick of the bunch.

Boy George: What I like about Paul is he's as prolific as I am. There's that impulse that he just can't stop recording. Whenever I get told I do too much, I go, 'Look at Paul Weller, he's fucking put four albums out in five minutes.' I do use him as a bit of an example when people say I do too much. I definitely enjoy making the thing. The physical act of doing music, making a piece of art is what I actually enjoy, because you've got no control over the reactions. You've got no control over where someone thinks it's good or bad. I had this funny phone call with Paul. I was doing something with Mikey Craig from Culture Club and we'd had this row, and he'd really annoyed me. And I got back to my house, and I was raging and Paul called me randomly, 'How are you?' And I said, 'I've just had this massive row with Mikey.' And Paul goes to me, 'Yeah, democracy in rock 'n' roll, it's a fucking disaster.' He goes, 'Somebody has to be in charge.' And I think he's right, to a certain degree. I just think Gemini's don't like compromise. We find that word quite difficult. I think all musicians think they're the only ones that can do it right. Particularly Gemini. It's instinctual. Creativity is just this thing that drives us, and we can't really understand what it is.

31 October 2020 – *Long Hot Summers: The Story of The Style Council*, Sky TV documentary

Eddie Piller: For many years, Paul didn't like talking about what he's done. Even today, he doesn't like looking backwards. It's about moving forwards. He's never really been one to talk about his past and yet, in the last three or four years, I detect that he's very happy within himself because he's now talking about it. I asked for years to be able to write a Style Council documentary and he said no. And then he lets Crowley do it. How dare he?! However, the point being, Paul is now much more comfortable in his own skin, so he can look backwards and maybe analyse his decisions.

Mark Baxter: The Jam documentary had gone down a storm, with the biggest ratings Sky Arts ever had on a Saturday night. The company that made the film discovered I knew Paul quite well and said they wanted to immediately do a follow up on The Style Council. I was a huge fan of that band. I knew Paul well enough to think, *He won't do that because he wants to keep going forward. Doing The Jam one must have been difficult for him.* I asked him, and he said, 'No, I'm not doing it. Not interested.' Everyone thought it was a disaster, but I said, 'Give it a couple of years.'

Then on his sixtieth birthday, I got invited to a little lunch with a few pals, and after a cheeky red wine, I said, 'Paul, going back to The Style Council again . . .' and a little bit reluctantly, he went, 'Ah blimey, ah, might do, might do, maybe . . .' That was the best that I was going to get. I went away, thinking, *That'll do!* and called everyone, saying, 'Paul said yes!' – which wasn't true. But they started working on it, and with Sky Arts and a private investor, we found the funding for all the archive material. We got Paul, Mick, Dee and Steve, and you could tell they loved that time. They enjoyed being around that music and those albums.

Lee Cogswell: I had created documentaries on *A Kind Revolution* and *True Meanings*, so I got to know Paul quite well. When he was ready for a Style Council documentary, I put myself forward as wanting to direct it and luckily, Paul supported the idea.

Mark Baxter: We got Gary Crowley to do the interviews and people like Boy George, Billy Bragg, Martin Freeman and Julian Jules to talk about their connections to the band.

Mick Talbot: It was shot late summer, 2019, about a year before it transmitted. I'm surprised that the cat didn't get out the bag with that surprise at the end. How did we keep it a secret?

Lee Cogswell: When we were planning the film, Bax and I discussed getting Paul and Mick together in a room, but we didn't even consider asking them to perform – we might have been pushing our luck there. Before one of the meetings with Paul, we debated whether to bring it up, not wanting to risk putting him off. As soon as we sat down for coffee, though, the first thing Paul said was, 'I know what we should do. We're going to get the band back together.'

Mark Baxter: His manager, Claire, wasn't sure if he really meant it. Was it going to happen? We had no idea what the song was. We never found out why Paul wanted to do 'It's a Very Deep Sea'. We were just told, 'This is the time. We're doing it. Everyone's going to be there.' We turned up, let the cameras roll, and I was like a kid in a sweet shop.

Dee C. Lee: Paul said, 'You don't have to answer anything or do anything that you don't want.' I said, 'No, I don't mind. I'll come and do the documentary. I'd love to do it.' When we were filming, he said, 'Next time you come down, we're going to do a little thing. Nobody's meant to know but we're going to do "It's a Very Deep Sea".' I couldn't remember it as it had been ages, so I had to go find it.

Mick Talbot: It was Paul's idea. He's a very forward-thinking person and not overly sentimental or nostalgic – he doesn't like to trade on his past. But I think he felt it might be good to do. We all still get on, and it would be nice to do a track. I think he sees 'A Very Deep Sea' as one of his best songs, maybe an overlooked one.

Paul mentioned it just prior to me getting to Black Barn for the first day of filming. He sent me a little demo – less than a minute, of him mucking about with it, on his phone. I listened and suggested we change the key. He went, 'Well, next time you're down here, Dee and Steve will be here. I thought we could all do it.'

There was no real pressure, but at the same time, that first day was so great because you're reliving seven years of your life and that can wash you out a bit. It's quite intense and deep scrutiny.

The next day, with Steve and Dee, we didn't even play the song all the way through before recording. We started playing, got less than a minute in, and Paul stopped us. I thought something was wrong, but he said, 'It's sounding good. We might as well just do it. Start taping.'

Dee C. Lee: Paul used to perform that song, and I would just follow his lead and do these jazz scat things around his vocal. So, we brought that back and, all these years later, there's a lot more that I could have done with the track. And we just did it, and just how we are, we just gel together so easily that it didn't take long. We literally rehearsed it a couple of times, mainly for camera angles, and we still have the thing that we've always had where we might not have rehearsed it, but we can just look at each other and we all know where he's going to go and what he's going to do.

Mick Talbot: I like that. It was an honest performance and spontaneous. That was always the way with The Style Council, and it completed the circle in a way.

Dee C. Lee: It is a very special thing that we have. But I'm telling you, I've always had it with Steve, with Mick and with Paul. We have a connection of the thing that when we're on stage together, Paul can just change it up. He can decide to extend, he can do anything. He'll just look at us and he'll go one way, and we'll just follow him. That's how it used to be. And it just went exactly the same way when we did that. And it was nice.

I don't know if you notice, but there's a bit where we both come into the vocal together and we look at each other because we both have to come in with the 'ohhhh diving' . . . and we do this thing and it's like I'm looking at him and he's winding me up, like he's going to now. I'm hanging on, and we almost laugh as we hit it, but it worked. It was quite special.

Claire Mahoney: When The Style Council split up, Paul said, 'We've made some really good music, but people won't get it for many years to come.' He was so right. He has this sixth sense about music. Back then, we didn't get it – but look at us now. It's incredible, the diversity of the music. The documentary did an excellent job of showing that. And then that last scene – none of us knew about – it just blew people away. Even now, that brings tears to my eyes watching it.

Lee Cogswell: Having that secret, we were quietly confident that that was going to please a lot of Style Council fans. I remember on the night of it playing, as soon as the film finished, my phone just started and didn't stop for about three days, which was lovely.

Chris Catchpole: I think with that documentary, Paul was surprised and quite touched by how much love there was out there, because there was a period in the nineties where they were looked on as the shit bit of his career. He was touched by people like Martin Freeman saying, 'The Style Council were my Beatles.'

Karen McBride: It was so beautiful. I cried. The Style Council holds so many memories for me in so many different ways.

Brenda Taylor: The documentary meant the world. 'A Very Deep Sea' was always one of my favourites. It makes you tingle, and I love the fact that you could see they still love and respect each other. People go on and have different lives, break up, make up, but I still think there's that love, definitely.

Mick Talbot: We had a semi-lockdown situation when it aired. There was a screening for around thirty principal people that worked on it. A small cinema in the back of a hotel in the West End. That was quite emotional. You just think, *Who was that boy and what was he thinking?*

Dee C. Lee: It's good that people still love what we did, we're grateful for that, but I'm glad because, without sounding big-headed, we did make some really good music. I was really so proud to have been a part of something that progressive and making music with people like that and still having them as all part of my life now.

Noel Gallagher: I love The Style Council . . . My interest in them had waned a bit towards the end as, I dare say, a lot of people's interest had waned towards the end. But up until about '87. Again, the first five years! Fuck! I mean, I'll argue with anybody . . . It's as good as anything that he's ever done. Anything. And that's not looking back on it, I felt it at the time, I had all those records, all those EPs. I didn't quite understand what the fuck they were going on about! 'The Cappuccino Kid' and all that! It's a known fact that you couldn't get a cappuccino in Manchester till 2018! My mum's Irish . . . 'What's a cappuccino?' It's like 'You don't know what a fucking cappuccino is?' I thought they were great, particularly the singles. The first year, eighteen months, those singles are fucking amazing. Quite dodgy videos as well, it's got to be said!

November 2020 – *On Sunset Remixes*

Gwenno Saunders: Paul really liked our records. We've been in touch, and he's been so supportive. I remember he was down in Cornwall and he asked, 'How do you say thank you or goodnight in Cornish?'

During the pandemic, Paul asked me to remix one of his songs, and that was a real godsend. Those kinds of things really kept me going. It was a way of collaborating remotely. I love remixing people's work because I'm such an introvert. It's a nice way to connect with other musicians without having to jam in a room.

I got sent the drums and bass and other elements, and we went back and forth, mostly focusing on vocals. I'd reversed all the vocals, and I liked that because I'd always wondered what Paul Weller would sound like not singing in English. His voice is so distinctive, and with remixing, you get to know someone's voice deeply. You're constantly listening to their vocals, and I just really enjoyed it.

Seckou Keita: We'd been trying to work together for a while but never found the right time. During lockdown, Paul sent me his vocal from 'Rockets' and said, 'Go on, do something with it.' I didn't even know it was a remix!

At home in my cellar studio, I built something around Paul's voice without knowing the original track – which turned out to be a good thing. Amazingly, I did it in one go. Paul texted me, 'Wow! This is different. This is beautiful.' Then he said 'Who's singing there, by the way? That's a beautiful voice.' I said, 'Yeah, it was me!' And he really loved it. Adding my kora, vocals, and the strings made it a really emotional journey – and only then did I realise it was a remix!

Christophe Vaillant: I knew Andy Crofts from The Moons, and one day he told me, 'I gave your album to Paul, and he liked it.' Later, I saw my music on Paul's *Uncut* magazine playlist – incredible! Paul then invited us to play with him and asked me to do a remix. During the pandemic, I quickly put one together. The pressure was huge. I picked 'On Sunset' and asked for the vocals and strings. Andy played Moog on the track, so I kept that too. Paul just said, 'Do what you do,' and loved the result.

February 2021 – Declan O'Rourke – *Arrivals*

Declan O'Rourke: For about a year, I'd been thinking I'd like to work with a producer. I didn't want to go to some name or hot producer. I wanted someone who gets my music, someone I admire. I remember that *True Meanings* had just come in the post on vinyl, and I stuck it on while getting my son ready for creche. I thought, *Jesus, that sounds good – really comfortable.* You can hear how relaxed he is. I thought, *How many fucking hours has he spent in the studio*? I'd love to be a fly on the wall.

While listening to that record, all those thoughts came together – maybe Paul's the guy. But would he say 'Yes', or 'Fuck off'? Before I chickened out, I sent him a text: 'Have you ever produced anyone before?' He replied straight away, 'Let me hear some stuff. I'm honoured and would love to be involved if I feel I can help.' From that point, I felt rewarded. I believe the universe listens.

I went into Black Barn, having sent him thirteen songs, live recordings from gigs. Paul steered me toward the more intimate songs. I asked if we should aim for radio. He said, 'Fuck knows what gets on radio anyway. I just think we try to make a great record.' That's fucking music to my ears. That was license to indulge in the place I inhabit. His impact was huge.

Between sessions he said, 'Write me another song.' I loved the challenge. A week later, I sent him 'Painter's Light' which made it on the album. I thought it would just be me and guitar, but he added subtle textures – little brushstrokes. They worked. It was a stroke of genius.

14 May 2021 – *Fat Pop (Volume 1)* (no. 1)

Charles Rees: The week before lockdown, Paul was down here, and on the Monday, they were talking about going on tour. 'Can't wait for this. This is going to be mental!' By the Thursday, it was like, 'Fuck this, I'll just have to do another album. That's it. Fuck it.'

Danny Eccleston: Steve Cradock said as soon as lockdown was announced, he immediately started worrying about Weller because he knew that he would find it exasperating, beyond all other human beings, to be shackled in such a way. Weller does have the advantage of having his own studio that he can leg it down to. There was a lot of music making.

Ted Cockle: During lockdown, I was speaking to him at the end, 'You fucking all right, Paul? You not being on the road?' 'It's all right, son, I've got two albums done.' . . . I was around Tom Jones for a very long time, who's still a mate, and he'd made a record. I was at Hypnosis and Lindsay Buckingham at seventy-three had made a record. Chrissie Hynde had just done a Dylan covers album and something else. See why those fuckers survive? Because under the most intense circumstances, all they do is create. That lot were just fucking cracking on and creating. That is why they're incredible people.

Ted Kessler: Of course that's what he's going to do is, he's going to go into the studio and make music, isn't he? There were a lot of people that you could worry about. I think Paul Weller can always satisfy himself creatively and he's got the space to do it . . .

I think he's always been a victim of depression or anger. That is definitely part of his character. You can tell that he's a moody man. The rate of mortality, that is also why he's always been in a race against time, hasn't he? Even in The Jam, it was always like, everything's in a rush, which is why he creates so much. He's in a rush to beat the last bell, and he's aware of it. I'm amazed he still smokes. For a man in his mid-sixties who's so scared of death to still be a chain smoker is incredible.

Paul Weller: On a nice day it's wonderful to be down here among all this greenery and space. So just to get out of London is part of it, but at the end of the day it's about the work as well. We get a great sound here and it's always got a good vibe here. Everyone I've ever spoken to or ever worked with here have always loved it and loved the vibe here. And that's kind of unexplainable sometimes, whatever that is. But it just feels comfortable here. It's far enough away from London, and yet it's only an hour down the road. And I like that as well, the fact that I'm not too far from home.

Charles Rees: I was living here during lockdown, in Paul's bubble when he was here. We had to send things out for the band to play to. They couldn't come here. Ben was always sending us drum takes.

Ben Gordelier: I did 'Still Glides the Stream' at home. It was just nice to be trusted enough to record it. I did do a few different takes, different ideas, and Paul picked his favourite. It would just be him doing a beatboxing down the phone at me sometimes. Which is nice [*laughs*].

Andy Crofts: I did 'Shades of Blue' in my little studio in my back garden. It's the first time I've ever done that. I did the bass and some backing vocals on that. In general, we don't like to work like that, but that was the situation at the time, so we had to deal with it. It worked, but it's not something we'd want to do often. We like to put the magic in the room.

Tom Doyle: We sent over the music for 'Glad Times'. It was quite long and meandering, pretty much the same chords all the way through. It ebbed and flowed. Paul started putting ideas down on it and they were sounding brilliant, man, but the structure of it wasn't clear, I think that's one of the reasons why it didn't end up on *On Sunset*.

Paul Weller: It took me two or three years to get the song together on top of it. I really believed in the backing track and what it sounded like, but I just couldn't find the right vehicle for it. They're the things that I would now keep pursuing even if I can't get it at the time. I think, I'm not going to totally disown that, or ditch it or whatever. I'll keep chipping away and come back to it. Back in the day, I'd have just lost it.

Tom Doyle: Paul then said, I think we need to finish this together, so we did two days, all of us together down at the barn. That was really interesting, because they've got their team, with Stan, Paul and Charles, and so a couple of interlopers coming in, you're not quite sure how this is going to work, but it worked immediately.

Paul Weller: It was worth doing, because I think it's a good song and it's lovely to play live as well. But I suppose while I'm writing, not always, but I'm writing a lot of things that we can all relate to, because we're all going through the same things as well, you know, with our relationships, with our . . . 'Am I a good person? Am I a good father? Am I a good partner?'

Whatever it may be, we are all feeling those things, aren't we? Do you know what I mean? Unless you're a dickhead or something!

But it's good to acknowledge those things, I think ... And I'm saying this as me, as a punter as well, it's good to hear those things in a song, because you think, *Other people feel like that as well, it's not just me then*, you know what I mean? Other people are questioning themselves, so it's important to let people know that.

Noel Gallagher: When I first ever met Paul, in '94, he didn't offer me any advice, but he did say something to me which has stuck with me for years and it might be the best, most practical bit of advice I've ever had. He just said, 'When it's not there ... don't chase it. Just let it go, and let it find you.' At the time, in 1994, every time I went to the fucking toilet, I was writing a song that became famous! So, it didn't apply then. But as I got older and that thing, when you're young and powerful, dissipates, and leaves you a little bit. Your instinct is to try and chase it. I always hark back to that. That's what I do now if things are not working ... He's the same. He'll have a song which is twelve years old on his new record. There'll be an idea, that didn't work, but there was something about it that you were interested in ... Park it for a bit. Some songs have taken me eight years to finish off, but, if it's got something of value in it and it's good enough, it will come back to. I've made a lot of records. He's made a lot of records, and we've seen it all. Although we're still learning, I'd like to think. I'm calm with it now. I would imagine he is too, he's a lot calmer than he was.

Steve Cradock: Songs would be sent down the line and so I played on a few. I played on 'Shades of Blue', the tune that Leah sings. Really like that tune and I really like my playing on that as well. We did a co-write called 'Still Glides the Stream'. Paul asked if I had any lyrics. I think there might have been a few chords. The middle eight wasn't written, but I just saw it in a bookshop. Two books on display and it was *The Man Who Never Was* and *Still Glides the Stream*. And it's just when something takes you, isn't it? I just wrote the first verse and the middle eight and gave it to him and then he turned it into that beautiful melody.

Jacko Peake: So what happened was I heard *True Meanings* and was blown away because I've always loved the folk element of what Paul's done. That was an amazing collection of things, especially 'Aspects' and 'Gravity', and then I heard, *On Sunset* and it felt like Paul is in a place that is so calm and so creative. I got in touch with Paul to congratulate him on the album and that's all I wanted to do, but he said to me, 'This is just amazing, Jacko, because yesterday I was thinking of you. I've got this track called "Shoobie Do" and there's a couple of tracks on this new thing I'm doing called *Fat Pop* that I'd love you to do.'

I've got this little studio at home now, so I was well prepared to do the virtual recording thing. I did a bit of flute on what became 'Testify' and on 'Still Glides the Stream'. Sent it to Paul. I was waiting for the call. Has he got it? Has he heard it? Does he like it? Is it going to be any good? My missus who's one of my biggest critics, said, 'I think you'll be fine, Jack, don't worry. Sounds all right to me.' Paul just went, 'It sounds brilliant, mate.'

Charles Rees: In the end, we didn't really like doing it remotely to be honest. Most of the drums that Ben did, when everybody was released from their own self imprisonment, we got him down to do in the studio. We felt after a time that we needed the physical human being in the room. You can't beat that.

Hannah Peel: We did the orchestra for *Fat Pop* in the summer of 2020. That was the first time I'd seen more than two people, in my garden. I was really freaked out about it because it felt so weird. When I got there, Paul gave me a big hug and I went 'Why are you hugging me? If I have something, I don't want to give it to you, no!'

Fiona Cruickshank: Studios opened up with very strict social distancing and limits on capacity, and all these new rules. *Fat Pop* was done in a socially distanced way, and it was like learning again how to record. It felt like the gang was back together. It was such a nice day, just seeing everyone. I remember Paul coming in and going for a big hug and at that time, everyone was being weird, touching elbows, and I was just like, 'Oh, you're hugging, good,' and he was like, 'Oh, sorry, I should have checked. It's a minefield now.' Seeing everyone again was like going back to school. *Yay, Hannah's here and Stan's here, we're all together, let's do this.* We know where we are, we know what we're doing, and everyone's relaxed and knows their role.

Steve Trigg: It's been a really interesting experience to watch or hear how tracks evolve because I've been lucky enough to get early-stage demos. They're quite skeletal. It's like watching an artist, Van Gogh or somebody, layering things up to create an image that they've got internally, but also being able to move where their target and their goal is. As a thing develops, it takes on a life of its own and things that you thought you might want to do, you're no longer going to do. There'll be a track with two or three little guitar notes that weren't on there previously and it changes it, makes it different, it transcends where it was. You wonder what sort of brain listens to that and goes, well, that just needs three notes?

Paul Weller: Well, I think that's because some people I know, some other musicians I know, who are guitarists or a drummer whatever, they will listen to something and go, 'Great drums on that, brilliant drums' or 'Great guitar riff on that'. But I've always listened to a record, I've always listened to the whole thing, the whole piece. I love everything. I'm hearing the bass, I'm hearing what the drums are doing, the guitar, the vocal. I'm hearing the whole thing. I'm trying to see the whole picture, hearing the whole picture! So I think it's probably come from that. Obviously, you've got to have a good song to start up with, if you're lucky. But immediately, if it's a good song and it excites me and inspires me, I will almost immediately hear other things as well. How the beat could be possibly. Could have strings on it. Strings would be nice. I could hear a piano there, whatever it may be. I'm seeing the whole picture. Not just listening to my bit, which a lot of musicians do. They'll say 'No, no, no!' Fuck off! Yes, you do! I know you do! But I don't do that, right. I listen to the whole thing. I'm hearing and seeing the whole thing.

Jacko Peake: Paul and I have touched on the subject of, how can I put it, the benefit of an older age and the creative process. The idea that there are some benefits of getting on a bit, and it is the fact that you can actually know what you want a little bit more and your decision making is better. That's what Paul and I have chatted about a little bit, in the sense, isn't it great? Does this actually exist, this idea that you actually improve with age?

Pat Gilbert: I had a text with a sound file attached. August or early September, not long after *On Sunset*, and it was a song called 'Cosmic Fringes'. It was really great. Paul said, 'You've got to hear the album.' Hold on . . . another album? I thought he must have mistyped it.

Alex Borg: Andy Crofts had showed my artwork to Paul . . . He had the title *Fat Pop (Volume 1)* and knew where he was going with it. He knew what he wanted. Bright and vibrant.

I was nervous. It's not every day you get to meet Paul Weller. The night before I had a very surreal dream that Paul and I were starting up an ice-cream business, we were having quite a heated debate over the name of what the venture should be!

We arrived at Black Barn. It's a lovely leafy, quiet, picturesque place. Paul was in bed after recording late. They had to go and wake him up. The place is a sensory overload – memorabilia, jukeboxes, gold records everywhere – it was overwhelming.

I brought a box of sixties records, thinking it might inspire something, but Paul already had a direction in mind. We listened to four songs on the big speakers . . . There was one track with a string arrangement in it and I really love strings, since I was a kid, things like *The Planets*, Gustav Holst. There's something about it that gets under my skin, and this track, I could feel myself going and I thought, *Christ, hold it together man. You're not going to blub in front of Weller.*

Afterward, my head was spinning with ideas. I locked myself away for two weeks creating designs, anxious about whether Paul would like them. When Andy Crofts later messaged me saying they loved what I'd done, it was a huge relief. I returned to Black Barn to finalise designs with Paul, which was nerve-wracking and fun.

Danny Eccleston: His idea initially with *Fat Pop* was that he would release all the tracks as singles. It's typical of Weller to have a plan like that. Then it was pointed out to him that people didn't really do singles anymore, which made him quite cross.

Polly Birkbeck: There was talk of that. Somebody said, they all sound like singles. The record industry doesn't really have that now. It's all impact tracks, impact dates, instant grats and all this jargon that's used now. It's hideous. Hideous. 'Instant grats'. Urgh. Another word for teaser. Instant gratification. I hate it.

Danny Eccleston: They have the qualities of singles. So, while *On Sunset* and *True Meanings* are both really great records, they're shaped conceptually to have an arc and to work as albums. This record is full of these spiky, urgent, pithy postcards from lockdown.

Pete Paphides: It's like his 'most tunes' album. It's just tune after tune after tune. He seems to have found a source of low-hanging, melodic fruit that no one else had noticed prior to now and has come back with a very full and tasty basket . . . There's a real positivity and brio and optimism and energy to their execution.

John Wilson: Paul will say you really are only as good as your last work. That's what's driven him on in the last few years.

Steve Ellis: *Fat Pop*'s a really good album. I'm not praising him anymore, otherwise I'll be getting a phone call. Top geezer. Top bloke. Much misunderstood. He's not a grouchy, miserable old git . . . Very far from it. His biggest fault? Chelsea.

Neil Sheasby: When are we going to have a ceremonial burning of that Chelsea flag that's in the studio? It's in every picture and every video. I don't think Paul even really likes football. I think he likes the nostalgic idea of Osgood, Bonetti and Charlie Cooke in that era. That needs to come down.

Pat Gilbert: He's got CFC tattooed near his knob. He showed me and Polly in the street.

Paul Weller: Still Chelsea, man. Fuckin' right, mate! But that was the first team my dad took me to see. First division team. So again, those things stay with you, I suppose. They were a great team at that time, this was late sixties, 1968. Osgood and Charlie Cooke, Peter Bonetti and Chopper Harris and Alan Hudson. All them cats, man. Charlie Cooke was a great winger,

Scottish fella. Brilliant. They were the first team I ever saw, and they've remained my team.

I've been in recent years, but not often. Couple of times. I'm always cautious about saying I'm a Chelsea fan because I know there'd be other football heads that'll be going, 'Well, where were you then? Well, how come you . . .' So, listen, I'm a casual observer at times, but if someone said, 'Who's your team?' It's always been Chelsea.

I've only really got back into football recently because one of my sons is mad for it at the moment. Bowie plays in a team, so I've got the interest in football reactivated through his involvement.

2021 – Paul Weller with Jules Buckley & the BBC Symphony Orchestra, *An Orchestrated Songbook* (no. 4)

Craig McLean: I did a joint Zoom interview for the *Radio Times* with Paul and Jules Buckley ahead of the Barbican concert. Zoom was not the best medium to be talking to Paul Weller because it gives him a distance that he recedes into. Luckily, Jules Buckley is one of the loveliest men in the world and is a very affable and gregarious and impassioned person. I think he geed Paul along a wee bit in that joint interview . . . I think that brought a new dimension to Weller as a new awareness of his own back catalogue. Hearing it from Jules's perception – this Berlin-based orchestral arranger, what songs would he glom on to with a view to making something special and magical of them.

Steve Cradock: The Jules Buckley gig at the Barbican during lockdown was mental. It looked amazing but it was just strange playing with those people. I don't know how they fucking count music. They don't count like us lot. They don't work the same hours as us lot.

It was like an out of body experience. Just how am I meant to play on it, and I just tried my best to keep in with Jules. It was different to the *Other Aspects* experience. Because we play as a group on that. It's us backed by a thing. But then to have no drummer or no metronome and everything's floating and it was mental. Insane. I was just thinking this is going to be easy ... And we went to the first day rehearsal at the BBC Maida Vale and it was just fucking mental ... I felt like I was drowning and trying to swim and there's nothing to keep the one on. We'd be rehearsing a tune and just everyone walks out because it's dinner time. It's just like, *What the fuck?* Like half-way through a tune. It's such another world. They're on the clock, but we were on their clock. That's weird.

Boy George: Paul just asked me, and when he said, 'You're the Best Thing', that again was so terrifying. I said, 'Oh, my God, I can't sing that song.' It's such a beautiful song and he does it so well. I was like, woah, but I feel like when you're performing something like that, you've just got to let go of it and try and be as emotional as you can and respect the writing. I got sent a rough track. I had it at home, so I was able to sing it and sing it and then we had a rehearsal in the afternoon and then go and do it. It was just magical.

November 2021 – UK tour

Bill Wheeler: I am extremely fortunate to work with Paul, because he looked after me – and my dad – throughout the lockdown ...

We ended up moving European tours about four times,

because we were desperate – Paul was desperate – to go out and play. Everything was sold out, and we didn't want to upset people who had paid. There was no real guidance, so we had to rely on gut instinct. In hindsight, we should've just cancelled everything, but no one could have known . . .

Trying to grapple with everything was hard, especially while seeing friends struggle. The government did absolutely fuck all. They helped out venues, which was fair enough, but the actual people that keep it going . . . they did fuck all for them.

Jacko Peake: I got called in to join the live band for that first tour after the lockdowns. There was Paul, Steve and me, who are the old guard, and then you've got these young 'uns.

Josh McClorey: Something happened and then Crofty couldn't do the tour and so Paul called and asked if I'd played bass.

Andy Crofts: I'm not going to lie. I'm very gutted not to be there for that tour. I'm still part of the band. I've been told I'm welcome back with open arms, which made me very happy, because, naturally, I thought, *That's it.*

Tom Van Heel: That first rehearsal made me laugh. Seeing people come through the door at the Barn, the smiles on their face. It was like . . . Freeeedom! The boys are back in the gang. Made me laugh. Hugs everywhere. Everybody was buzzing.

Paul Weller: I really missed that, and I feel there's a different mood at the gigs since that time. Whether it's because you just appreciate it more maybe. I've noticed it personally, since we've started back up again, that there seems to be more of a joy there, more of an enthusiasm for it. Including us as well, both sides of the stage. That's exactly the sort of thing that I remind myself of when I'm sitting in some grotty little dressing room prior to a show, and I'm moaning about it. I remind myself of that. Just think, *Hang on, you missed this, and one day you will miss this when you don't do it any more.* So, I try and appreciate it now even more.

When we first started back, we added an acoustic set on top, which was about half-an-hour long. It was just getting too long and sprawling. We were doing more of the *True Meanings* songs in that little set, but we couldn't make it work, man. It just felt it was fucking going on forever. The set was like two and a half, nearly three hours or something. It was too much for me, I think two hours is long enough personally. I find the same with films these days. They're all like three hours, three and a half hours. What was wrong with an hour and a half? That was good. You could say all you need to say. What's wrong with three minutes or three and a half minutes for a song? Ray Davies made it work for him all right, man.

Roger Nowell: Early doors of touring with Paul, there used to be a lot of staying up drinking and doing whatever. These days it tends to be a cup of tea and bed. The younger guys now don't seem to be as keen to have it like we did.

Tom Van Heel: That Beatles film – *Get Back* – came out while we were on that tour . . . seven hours long, so every day we would do the next episode and it's the quietest the bus has ever been. We sat there for two, three hours wherever it was, and we were just glued to the screen.

Paul Weller: Imagine what the album would have been like if they all got back together in '95, whenever the *Anthology* was, with 'Free as a Bird' and 'Real Love'. They're great tunes, man, and when I hear them all play together, there's still that chemistry there. I will always be a fan. Always. Look how much they created in that relatively short space of time. Recording career was like, I don't know, eight years or something like that. I mean, there's so many songs, so many records, which I think is a wonderful thing. And I think it's really sad, with, say like . . . someone like Amy Winehouse, who was a brilliant, brilliant artist, but she's only left two records in the world. I mean it's a shame that she left this world anyway, obviously it's better if she'd have carried on. That's so little music to leave behind in the world. I think that's why it's important to try and create as much as you can really, put as much as you can out, not just for the sake of it, not shit obviously. It's got to be good. But that's what we do. That's what we're supposed to be doing. If you're a writer, then you write books, don't you? If you're a playwright, you write plays. I mean, you make films if you're a director, whatever it is. But do lots of it.

25 September 2021 – 'Going to a Go-Go'

Tom Van Heel: It was cool to be on Jack White's label. We did 'Road Runner' for the Third Man Record release [B-side]. Paul normally suggests the covers. To be honest with you, most of the time I have to lie and go, 'Oh, yeah, I love that tune.' I've never heard it before in my life. I just don't want to look like an idiot in front of everybody else. I have to go listen and learn it. That's what you get for being fresh legs and the youngest. 'What Does It Take?', Junior Walker. I didn't know it [*laughs*]. But, actually, that's my favourite one on the record.

24 March 2022 – Teenage Cancer Trust concert, Royal Albert Hall

Craig Hassall: I arrived for my new job as CEO of the Royal Albert Hall during the week of Teenage Cancer Trust 2022.

The first concert was Ed Sheeran and then I saw Paul Weller, and then The Who with Liam Gallagher supporting.

Roger Daltrey was the artistic director of Teenage Cancer Trust ... Apart from Roger Daltrey, Paul Weller is the most well-known personality of the whole TCT history. He's been there so many times and so when you see Paul perform at TCT, he's not just a hired gun, he's there passionately because he believes in the cause. You'll see him give the most incredible concert. Looking at the archive of the Royal Albert Hall, at this point Paul has done forty-six performances since 1984. That's pretty amazing. Seven with The Style Council, twenty-four as a solo headliner since '92, fourteen with Teenage Cancer Trust – that's almost every year since 2000.

Andy Crofts: It's just lovely to be back ... It feels like I'm back with the family and I'm more than happy ... First, it's a bit of fun, the first lockdown, you're like, *Oh, this is a bit loopy. Everyone's going mad*, and then it gets to the point where things start to ease off. But because of my partner Tara's medical condition, it didn't ease off for us. It started to weigh down on our minds, that the rest of the world is trying to carry on and we're not. It mentally took it out of me, and then seeing the band go off on tour without me, that was tough. Obviously, I'm happy for them, and Josh did an amazing job on the bass, I love him to bits, but your mind plays tricks on you. All that time off, and I was just going, 'Maybe I'm not good enough to play any more. Maybe it's been too long ...'

Royal Albert Hall, Teenage Cancer Trust, supporting Madness ... Suggs popped into the studio yesterday. We were hanging out. I hadn't met him before, so it was quite a big thing for me. Paul and Suggs are good pals from back in the day ... It's a little bit of a warmup for the tour in an odd way . . . After all that time off, you get a bit rusty, nervous and that, so it's good to kill some butterflies.

Eddie Piller: Paul phoned about three years ago, just before lockdown. He goes, 'Right, me, you and Suggs are going to go out for a ride and have scooters.' Then I saw Suggs and I said, 'Oh, Paul wants to go out for a ride as soon as this lockdown thing's over,' and he goes, 'He hasn't passed his test yet, has he?'

Paul phoned me up in tears of joy about a year ago, going. 'Eddie, you're not going to believe it.' 'What?' 'I've passed my scooter test.' At the age of what, sixty-three? . . . Well done, Grandad. I passed mine at the age of seventeen, thanks to Paul Weller, funnily enough, because I would never have been a mod otherwise. I would never have got a scooter

Suggs: I found my old Vespa in a garage in Whitstable. I'd forgotten where it was. I sent Paul a picture, 'You'll never guess what I've just found,' and he sent me a picture of this really elaborate Lambretta. Mine was just some shabby old Vespa. Again, it's just aesthetic innit? The mod thing, whatever you call it, the whole point of a scooter was you didn't get yourself greasy and dirty and all that. They've took to me as some sort of surrogate mod because, for sure, I always like clothes, and I like to look after how I looked, and all my band did.

I've been out shopping with Paul a couple of times. There's a photograph of me and him at Red Wedge, he's wearing cut-down jeans. I was laughing about that, but I had this T-shirt. It was a very old vintage Japanese T-shirt. I went, 'I loved that.' So, I went to meet him for a coffee, and he took me to a shop where they're still making these flipping T-shirts, but they were 300 quid a pop. Right. He's loading 'em up like that. I'm going, 'No, I'm all right. I'll see you outside, Paul!' I totally dig that enthusiasm for your aesthetic.

March–April 2022 – UK tour

Steve Pilgrim: It's been one heck of a ride from the start to the finish. I've been in the band a long time now . . . Just a million blessings and all of those Instagram clichés. I think Chopper's the longest-serving band member now. Steve White was longest-serving member for Paul for a long time. But I think Steve Cradock has knocked him off that top slot . . . We were thinking about putting a leaderboard up of how many years you've lasted in the band.

Steve Cradock: Why has it lasted so long? I think that I don't have an ego musically. If a song doesn't need a guitar, then I would sit out. Paul and I have been through a lot together, I guess. But that wouldn't allow that either. I don't know. I'm arsed, I turn up early and I put a lot in. I think my attitude's good for work and my attitude's good for music. So, it must be them two things. I love the man and he's a genius. Incredible brain, he's funny as fuck, man, and he's an incredible singer and the way he uses his words, he's just very unusual from anybody else I know. He's a one-off.

Paul Weller: Steve's an incredible person and an incredible musician. And the reason why we're still playing together, I think anyway, is because we're both able to adapt and to see that whatever you do today, I might not want tomorrow. I might want something else. So you have to be a little bit adaptable and then be able to go along with that mode of thinking as well, which not all musicians are happy with.

As long as they are able to rise to what I'm trying to get to . . . but some people might not want to do that or don't know how to do that, and that's fine as well. But if you can adapt, like with Cradock, then they'll have a future.

March 2022 – Stone Foundation, *Outside Looking In*

Neil Sheasby: Writing new music was the thing that we could do in lockdown since we couldn't gig. Under the guise, we were allowed into the studio, and Paul let us use Black Barn. We utilised the time and recorded another record. You can't keep Paul off a record – he played on a few bits – just because he enjoys hanging out. If we're in the studio, he'll text and say *I'll pop down tomorrow*, and then show up. 'Sheas, Sheas, I can hear a bit of piano on this . . . maybe a bit of guitar.' I'm like, 'Be my guest!' I'm not going to tell Paul Weller that he can't play on our record.

20 June 2022 – Suggs and Weller, 'Ooh Do U Fink U R'

Suggs: We were texting during the lockdown, and Paul said, 'Have you got any lyrics? I'm writing a new album.' It turned out that I did – 'Ooh Do U Fink U R'. At first, I thought it was a bit of a joke, but we fleshed it out, and it turned out great. Originally, the title was going to include 'Sunshine', but Paul said, 'Nah, that's too Oasis – Sunshinnnnnnnnnne' . . .

I remember wanting to add a middle eight. I had this idea inspired by that bit in 'Under Pressure' by Queen and David Bowie – the song was rubbish apart from that bit Bowie did late in the song . . . Paul went, 'No, fuck that off.' That was as close as I got!

We were working on another song, and it was getting a bit stuck. I said, 'Paul, look mate, it's only music,' and there was just a silence on the phone, and he went, 'No, it fucking ain't, Suggs.' It was a great reminder because I'd been through this nothingness of lockdown, starting to lose perspective. To be reminded of how important music is to us in this country.

June 2022 – UK tour

Andy Crofts: When Covid hit, my girlfriend, at the time, got very sick. Her kidneys were affected, and she was hospitalised, so it was pretty bad. We've got two kids and not a lot of help, and I was starting to become the person I feared the most or hated the most. I was starting to become . . . unreliable. I wasn't letting anyone down yet, but it was starting, and I was starting to get a bit worried because, I was in this horrible situation where I didn't know which way to turn.

Jake Fletcher: The first time I met Paul, I had so many questions I wanted to ask him, and he just kept asking about me! . . . How I joined the Paul Weller band was quite bizarre really. I was supposed to be covering for Steve Cradock with The Specials in Norway and Holland, but I'd just moved house, and bits of my life were scattered around everywhere and I couldn't find my passport. Couldn't go to Norway. Felt really bad. I'd let everyone down. And then got a text from Steve Pilgrim, 'I've heard that you're free. You're going to get a call in a minute.' Then Paul rang, 'Hi, Jake. Can you get down here as soon as possible? We need a bass player . . . Like now! We've got a gig in a couple of days.' I then had thirty-eight songs to learn.

Ben Gordelier: Jake turned up and he'd learnt thirty songs, and he didn't have one sheet of paper. He had no notes at all. Just a pair of headphones and his phone and a little bass with rubber strings on it.

Jake Fletcher: My first gig was the Hop Farm in Kent. There were a few nerves, but that's not always a bad thing. I do remember . . . when Paul introduced the band, he got to me and said, 'On bass guitar we've got Jake . . . er . . .' and forgot my second name. I just shouted, 'It doesn't matter what my second name is, just get it done with!' It was initially a run of eight outdoor shows over the weekends of that summer and by the last one, Paul took me aside and said, 'I think you're doing really well. I hope you've enjoyed it. Do you want to carry on doing the next gigs that are coming up?' It was never a weird, secret masons like initiation ceremony. It's just like, *Right, you're doing it now.* I feel like I'm going to wake up at some point and it won't have ever really happened.

Andy Crofts: In the end it was kind of my decision, and it was the Weller team as well, saying, if you can't do it, we're gonna have to get someone else. It was that kind of vibe. We haven't fallen out, we're still friends, everything's still cool. It's just, unfortunately, I'm not in the Weller world anymore. I'm really sad about it still, because that was my life for fourteen or fifteen years. Having done so many amazing things. The band was 100 per cent. So to come out of that world, for the reason it did, was a real wake up call for me. It made me realise a lot of things. I had to go through a self-discovery. I don't want to get too deep in it, but I had a lot of mental problems about it all because I felt like I stopped at a time I didn't want to stop, and suddenly happened to be released back into the real world. It made me realise . . . who am I? I know I've contributed to the Weller stuff and, I did my 100 per cent best on everything I ever did with him. But I come out of it thinking, *Well, who am I now?* I'm slowly building it back up again now to make my own record. But it did knock me for six.

September 2022 – Steve Pilgrim – 'Beautiful Blue'

Steve Pilgrim: *Beautiful Blue* was the longest time I've ever spent making a record. It feels like the biggest opportunity I've had, really, having Paul produce it. It's a really big deal for me, and I wanted it to be right. Paul has been heavily involved. It would have started back in 2019, I'd said to Paul, in rehearsals or down on a session, 'I'm working on this thing, but I'm just struggling with the last few songs.' I wasn't implying to him, *would you write?* I was just telling him where I was at, and then I got this message off him in the middle of the night. It was just a voice note. He often works like that – he'll send demos he records quietly in the early hours – these little sketches. A little doodle, a vocal and acoustic thing. I guess he just thought, this is in keeping with what Steve does. Then we got talking and I asked whether he'd be involved with the record more broadly, and he was keen. We recorded the record in a matter of days. Paul's very fast, and I like to work fast as well. It was great. The bulk of the album happened in the first forty-eight hours. It's like Beatles pace of recording.

28 October 2022 – *Will of the People* (boxset, no. 15)

John Wilson: Paul got in touch, 'I've got this album compilation – remixes, rarities, things I've been working with in the studio over the years. Would you write the liner notes?' . . .

Writing it was daunting because I'm a big fan of the liner notes from the sixties, like Dylan or Dusty, a lot of the jazz albums . . . sometimes quite strange and impressionistic, capturing a sense of the music rather than just giving a straight biographical résumé. I approached it with the idea of Paul himself being an artist, which I firmly believe he's a true artist in many senses of the word. What came to mind when I wrote the analogy is that so many of these songs are sketches, and he is working in the studio in the same way that a painter would. Like masterpieces, great paintings often have multiple preparatory sketches. Paul's doing that in these demos. Working very quickly, creating something which, in its imperfection, is so beautiful and so immediate.

I know Paul takes inspiration from painters very often. We've talked about art a lot. We went to see a Hockney exhibition together a few years ago at the Tate. It was brilliant going around with Paul, seeing what he was getting off on, especially the stuff in the seventies when Hockney was working so quickly – cutting up photographs, experimenting and pushing himself on. Then you get right up to the recent work and he's working on an iPad – as prolific and experimental as he ever was. Paul saw a kindred spirit there. What I wrote is pretty pretentious, but I don't think it's too far wide of the mark.

Johnny Chandler: There had been lots of releases – singles, remixes and extra material – since the *Fly on the Wall* boxset. Paul loved the idea of a follow up and was very involved in the whole process. He went through everything and was coming up with ideas for it – even the cover, where he sketched out what he was thinking. Paul curated it and wanted to include certain things, and with the track-listing flow, he had the input on that. That was his vision.

John Wilson: The cover image pays tribute to Klaus Voormann's work on *Revolver*, with those beautiful ink-drawn portraits of the band with the hair spilling down, but that waterfall cascade of hand-cut images of The Beatles. The design has a similar effect – almost like an eye, with a scene from afar with around a hundred faces.

Polly Birkbeck: We do get lots of really ridiculous press requests where if they knew anything about him, they'd know that the answer's going to be no. I've definitely had *Hello!* magazine in the past . . . He did used to sometimes say rude things about other people, but he doesn't really do that any more. Like when he said, 'I'd rather eat my own shit than listen to James Blunt.' A completely throwaway comment. James Blunt's press officer, Barbara Charone, rang me up and had a go at me about that. I was like, 'I didn't say it!'

There was the one in *Record Collector*, when he was talking about *Will of the People*. The Robert Smith comment that went viral. Was it the f-word that made it really bad? It would have been fine to call him 'fat cunt' but not a 'fucking fat cunt'.

Oh, my God, there was also when Paul showed Pat Gilbert his tattoo. I was like, 'What are you doing? Why are you showing a journalist your Chelsea tattoo?'

Luckily now Paul is in a position where he can pick and choose who interviews him so you're in a safe area.

2023 – Live

Paul Weller: During the lockdown when we couldn't play, there'd be times I'd think, *Do you know what? I really fucking miss playing 'Shout to the Top'*, and would think back to what it sounds like when we used to play it live, or whatever old song it might be. I actually thought *You know what? I really love playing them songs.* I've proved whatever I need to prove to myself with that anyway but most of the old tunes we do play, I really enjoy playing them, and I miss when we don't play them. I love playing 'Shout to the Top' and I love 'My Ever Changing Moods'. There's some things I've been doing for a long time as well but I really love playing them tunes, man. And that's really what it's about. What turns you on yourself. You've got to get something from it, man. You have to get a buzz. And if you don't really connect with the songs necessarily or lyrically, whatever, but at least you're connecting because you know the crowd are really loving this song. I get off on that as well, with what it does for people and what it means to them. I love that . . . Getting older as well, I suppose, I've just grown to appreciate what these songs mean to people. Every time I think, *I'm not playing fucking 'Wild Wood' any more or 'Changingman'*, and we might drop it for a night or two, but then I miss doing that because I miss that vibe, that feeling I get from how people feel when they hear certain songs.

That tour in southern Europe – all of us, me included – we all said it's the best tour we've ever done . . . regardless of whatever I've done in my last forty-odd years. It was just the best tour ever, man. And the best band I've ever played with. I don't know how long those things last for, but we were all at the top of our game, and there was so much communication between us, and the audience as well. It was just incredible. You think after all that time you're still hitting a personal best, and that's pretty incredible, right? That doesn't always happen. It normally goes the other way.

Robert Howard: I live near Granada, in the foothills of the Sierra Nevada, up in the mountains, and I knew that Paul was playing about a four- or five-hour drive . . . I hadn't seen Paul for a few years – last time was at a Stone Foundation gig. It was so lovely to walk in and hear his sound . . .

The thing about Paul that I've always loved was that he doesn't necessarily give the audience what they want. There were new songs that I didn't recognise. That's a real strength . . . I understand it myself. You're either a museum piece or a nostalgia act, or you're somebody that still feels alive. There's something dangerous and exciting about playing songs that people haven't heard before. It's a thrill, but it can be anxiety-inducing too. I understand why some bands play that same set every night. That's OK. But someone like Paul is far too fidgety and alive to want to just do that. I admire that.

Paul Weller: I'm in a very fortunate position that I can pretty much do what I want musically. I haven't got anyone breathing down my neck saying we need a record by next week, or an album out next month. I can pick and choose when I do that, but I think it took me a long, long time to earn that. That's only really come about in the last ten years or so. And if I'd have listened to a lot of other people, whether they be company people, fans or just people generally, I wouldn't necessarily be in this position. You have to stick with your vision of what you think it should be and then hope for the best. And you just do that to the best of your ability. So, not to say to ignore all advice, but some of it's shit, man. And you have to really follow your heart and do what you think is right.

There was a thing a few years ago where they were talking about heritage acts. I am not fucking going down that road, mate! I'm not a fucking heritage act, whatever that's supposed to mean, like bullshit fucking term. I had to fight my own little fight, in a sense, to get through all that stuff and I probably lost a certain amount of audience along the way during this last ten or so years. The ones who just wanted to hear The Jam stuff, they've gone now. I guess they go and see Bruce's band or other people or whatever. I don't mind, whatever they want to do, whatever makes them happy. But it's been worth it, because now I proved myself, that if you just plough through that bullshit and you follow your programme of what you think it should be, eventually you'll get there. You will definitely get there. But it's easy to get sidetracked by people who say, 'Maybe you should do this, or could do that, or make it like the old record.' Just follow your vision, if you've still got one.

Robert Howard: I love the whole thing about being a musician and doing what we do, especially in the world that we're in at the moment. It feels like, ultimately, a good thing to do. I was thinking that when I was watching Paul, I was looking around the crowd and there was a real euphoria . . . The best moment is when a musician and an audience just become one, and it's not about the band up on stage. They have a word for it in Spain called *duende*, which is when the magic enters the room – at a certain point, people lose themselves, and that happens to the musicians, as well, that are on stage . . .

Paul's a very special dude. He's very funny, and he's an incredible, incredible songwriter. Unparalleled in the journey that he's taken. I'm more than happy to speak in his honour, because he's been very influential on me, especially when I was emotionally open as a teenager . . . Listen, he can be a right difficult bugger! He really can be. But I think we've all grown up, and that was partly me as well. Insecurity, competitiveness, all that . . . more than partly me! So I love the guy. Love him.

Noel Gallagher: Paul is still one fucking billion per cent into the craft and I am too . . . we've got a fucking lot in common, which is, I guess, why we've been friends such a long time. I remember, when I first met him, somebody saying, 'Oh, he'll fall out with you eventually. He falls out with everyone.' We've never fallen out.

The one thing that we don't share is the output. He fucking gets them out, you know. The tours are so long now that if I make one album every fucking five years, I'm all right.

24 May 2024 – *66* (no. 4)

Paul Weller: I mean, what else is there? Metaphorically, existentially, you have to just keep going, don't you?

There wasn't anything left after *Fat Pop*. It was the usual thing with most albums where I'll demo one or two songs here, and then they evolve into something more. One or two become three or four, like cells multiplying, and soon there are six or seven songs – and you think, we've got over half an album. You just follow that trail.

As we went along, I had quite a few songs and they were all quite eclectic. Not all of them ended up on the album, but as they increase with more songs and more ideas, and then suddenly you've got an album.

I wanted to call it *66* because that's the age I'd be when it comes out. It amused me that I've even got this far down the road with it all. I was also influenced by Adele – she names her albums *19* and *25* and whatever, so I thought, I'll have some of that.

Charles Rees: The creation of *66* felt like the start of something different with people who weren't normally involved in the album-making process. Paul had a few really good ideas of who to work with, who to bring on board and one of those is Jacko Peake. Bringing him back into the fold really changed some of the songs that Paul writes. He's writing songs with that space in mind. *66* is a much more sensitive album. I'm amazed at how beautiful some of these songs are.

Paul Weller: I had twenty-odd songs or more, and I just couldn't really make it hang together. It didn't sound like an album. It was too eclectic, but not in the same way that *22 Dreams* was. It just didn't work. It was too uneven and unbalanced, so I've whittled it down to twelve tracks. The others are going to be bonus tracks and an EP later.

I don't know if there's any sort of central themes on it. There's a little bit of melancholia and resignation on it, but I wasn't conscious of any themes. There are quite a few songs where I haven't written the words – Noel wrote for one, Bobby Gillespie, Erland Cooper. There's a song with Dr Robert and two with Suggs, so that was nice.

I didn't have so much to say myself, I guess, and anything I did was put into the other songs. I was quite happy to farm out the lyrics to other people and ask if they had any ideas. Originally, I considered doing a duets record, but I couldn't really think how to go about doing that. This is as close as I could get, in a way – letting someone else write the words.

Noel Gallagher: I didn't know that, lyrically, he didn't have many songs. Cos his lyrics are amazing to me. I think he's one of the most underrated lyricists ever. If I could write lyrics like that, I'd give up music and be a fucking poet. I thought I was special, and he was there going, 'You know what this tune needs? It fucking needs NG!' but now you're telling me he's farming it out to fucking any Tom, Dick and Harry!

Suggs: Paul asked if I had any more lyrics. I'd written this song called 'Ship of Fools'. It was sort of autobiographical and partly about my band.

Paul Weller: Suggs sent me the words and they worked with this tune I had. I know what the words meant to Suggs, but I thought they were about Boris Johnson and his Tory cronies. All these idiots leading us into the abyss. But it could be applied on a world stage as well, all these headcases.

Suggs: Everything can be whatever you want it to be, but certainly Paul took it that way and I suddenly can see there's a whole new direction for the song. That wasn't my intention though. It's a very amorphic thing innit. 'Ship of Fools' could apply to pretty much fucking everything. But Paul took it in that world of greedy people that he didn't want to necessarily appreciate, and I totally dug that . . . Paul took the whole ship analogy and then took it a bit further, adding the idea of swimming to the shore. It's a very poignant song and I like it a lot.

Will Hodgkinson: It's a really interesting album because it's quite reflective. I wrote a book on seventies singalong pop called *Imperfect Harmony*, a kind of social history, taking it seriously. And I said that 'Ship of Fools' reminded me of that early seventies sound, people like Cook and Greenway and Tony McCauley, that novelty pop-sing-song thing where it's very cheerful melody that mums and dads and kids and grannies like. I told Paul that it reminded me of a song that a guy from The Creation wrote, thinking that'd be a nice thing, and he went, 'Don't mention "Grandad"!'

Max Beesley: I went down, and we spent two days just playing vibes, with Paul playing guitar. Then Jacko came down, which was beautiful for us to be together again.

Paul Weller: I thought it was different enough to be an album opener. Normally we start with a fast tune, like a live set, but I thought it'd be nice to do something different. I don't know if I've ever opened with an acoustic song before, but I like the mood on this one.

Suggs: We initially discussed it being a duet like our previous song. I felt I could have joined in. Then we agreed that we didn't want to end up as the working-class Everly Brothers. I couldn't see a concert with me and him standing together for a whole concert. One track is fine, so I totally understood that it'd be better if he just sang it.

Paul Weller: 'Flying Fish' was probably the first song of the album that we started work on. It's quite electronic sounding, and at one time I was thinking the whole album was going to be like that. I thought that was the blueprint for how the record was going to go, and it changed. It didn't happen that way.

Christophe Vaillant: Paul sent me the song and said, 'I need some synthesisers.' I have a few old synths here in my house . . . Moogs and Oberheim and all this stuff together. Every synthesiser has a specific sound. I use these instruments very often in my own music.

Paul Weller: With the wonders of modern science, you can just send stuff off to people and they send it back and it's brilliant, really. Christophe put some synths on it for us.

Noel Gallagher: I think the best way that we work is if he's got something and he sends it to me, or if I've got something and I send it to him. I find it very difficult to sit opposite someone.

Paul Weller: It was great. I just sent Noel the backing track, and said, 'You ain't got any ideas for this have you?' and twenty minutes later he sent the lyrics back! It was definitely no longer than that. They just all worked. I sang the melody on the track I sent him, and he just wrote to that. He didn't sing it. He just sent me the words and they scanned.

Noel Gallagher: Only songwriters will know what we're talking about here. It's bizarre for people to think that 'Live Forever' was written in under forty minutes . . . but these things do happen . . . Not often . . . I sent the lyrics back through and he called me and said, 'You just fucking wrote them now?' I still, to this day, don't think he believes me . . . he's like, 'No. You fucking had them lying around.' And I was like, 'No, I've just done it now. Fucking hell!'

Between the two of us, we came up with the title. 'Have you got a title?' and I was like . . . 'Fuck. I don't know . . . "Jumble Queen"?' The next thing, he's playing it on a gig in Stockholm or somewhere! That goes back to the 'Instant Karma', John Lennon thing. It's like, write it, do it, get it out.

Paul Weller: There wasn't too much of a brief on the album, but I did say less is more. I wanted to be able to hear all the instruments and have a sense of space, especially on 'Nothing'. Generally, we lost a lot of stuff to create that space.

Jun Sato: I saw Paul on the 2024 tour in Japan and they were already testing the 66 songs, and his daughter was singing, and Paul's proud about his grandson, so backstage was like a different family travelling band, different from the cards and Black Russian days, but it was still a travelling band. I was thinking, *Wow, this is modern age Mad Dogs and Englishmen!* He was very kind and relaxed, and he seemed very happy . . .

He played the song 'Nothing' at the Tokyo show before the album was released and I was thinking, *Wow, he came this far and he's not pretending that he's a young man.* It's not like the band Kiss, talking about one thousand girls when they're in their seventies. The Weller songs are so real.

Paul Weller: Suggs sent me this beautiful poem, 'Nothing', which is the bulk of the lyrics. I naturally thought it was his. I was like, *Wow. I like that.* I had some music I thought it would work on, but it was also the words.

The poem came from his friend called Chalky, who I've never met. I spoke to him on the phone, and he lives in a caravan on the south coast somewhere. I think his poem was about him and Suggs when they were kids growing up together, but by that time, I'd already fitted these words to my tune, and then Suggs wrote some words for the chorus part. I spoke to

Chalky, and asked if it was OK to use the lyrics, which he was very, very happy about. Happy to see his words come to life. It's a nice little story, man. He's not a professional writer. He's not poet or songwriter. He's just a fella who wrote this heartfelt poem . . .

Andrew 'Chalky' Chalk: I just sat down and wrote this poetry to try and explain to myself the odd uniqueness that our friendship has, not so much why it's lasted, but what it was, because what it was then, it must still be now. It's about how everything else goes on in life and there are events, and we move on and we're this and that and the other. But, because we started with nothing and we shared nothing to begin with . . . that's what our friendship was built on. So, in a way, there was nothing that could ever get in the way of that friendship continuing.

Paul Weller: I could take it on many levels, right? I could think about me and my family, how we started off with fuck all, and then where we got to. And for Suggs and Chalky it's a different experience. I immediately connected with the words. I thought they were not only simple and beautiful, but I read my own meaning into it, as we all do with all songs. It's not always important what the writer intends. It's what you get from it, I think that's the most important thing.

Andrew 'Chalky' Chalk: They've caught the whole essence of what I could say and Suggsy added this lovely nostalgia to the chorus. There was a whiff, a wind, melancholy looking back and I thought that was really nice. Paul's song was a throwback to that gentle summer, almost like Style Council feeling about it.

Paul Weller: Christophe knew that I liked his stuff – Le SuperHomard – and then he did a remix of 'On Sunset', the actual track, which was great as well. I'm just a fan of what he does, and he's got that sort of French Gallic sense of melody and sense of chords and harmony. You can hear it in the music, but I don't know how to explain it because I don't really know what they do, but it's a very definite sort of sound to it. I wish I knew what it was because I would do it myself, but I don't know. I said about trying some writing, so he sent me a few backing tracks, maybe half a dozen.

Christophe Vaillant: I'm playing piano, acoustic guitars, basses and percussion, I think. Everything except the drums and the strings in fact.

Paul Weller I was bathing my kid, my daughter, playing that backing track for what became 'My Best Friend's Coat', as soon as I heard it, straight away I could hear the melody, and I could hear almost like the first verse. It came really quickly. I could see the whole picture. I was trying to imagine that it was a French lyric that I'm now translating into English. I don't know why, but that's what I thought. A little brief in my head in a way. I was trying to work in that very dramatic thing that was in a lot of French music, the obvious things like Brel, Édith Piaf and all that.

Hannah Peel: That's the first time I've been in Abbey Road. First time I've worked with the Britten Sinfonia as well. I think it's quite important to find a lot of players that are on your wavelength ... It was about finding that balance between the contemporary classical and the classical, and who would be really good at playing this type of music, which crosses a lot of genres, but is essentially soul and pop and rock.

Paul Weller: Well, they're amazing players. I don't know much about them, but I thought they were incredible. Abbey Road was amazing, man. Expensive day out, but worth it . . . We did quite a few tracks – five or six tunes there. The sound was incredible. Number two studio. We did two three-hour sessions, like old-school thing as well. Little break in between and all that, and we even finished before we're supposed to as well.

Robert Howard: I was working with Miles Copeland, who runs his own label, Wonderful Sound. He often has ideas and gave me this little loop, which just had these two chords. I worked on that and wrote a lyric for 'Rise Up Singing' during lockdown. It was about what we lost in lockdown: that communal spirit.

Paul Weller: Robert had the backing track, and I added some stuff to it over here because he's based in Spain and it eventually did come out, but not like anyone noticed. It just fizzled out, really, and I thought it was too good just to let it go.

Robert Howard: It didn't really get across, and I think Paul felt that the song was stronger than that and it deserved it better. So, he went away, and he put beautiful strings on it – recorded at Abbey Road and the whole thing just came up a whole level.

Paul Weller: Leah did backing vocals on it, and Marco, who is Charles's son and my godson, is on it as well. He was here getting a sound together for me and just played that little wah-wah thing. I was like, 'Yeah, we'll have that.' If it works, man, it works. You haven't got to think about it too long.

Robert Howard: Paul's always searching – we all are as writers, not to repeat ourselves . . . There is a kind of gentleness and melancholy to the album that I haven't heard before. And also, in the way Paul sings now, I think he's got new things coming through. There's a new power there. There's a new force in the voice that comes from being older and letting go of certain things, I think.

Richard Hawley: Paul sent me the first version demo of 'I Woke Up' on the phone. He hadn't finished the lyrics. It just had the 'I woke up and everything had changed' bit.

Paul Weller: There's not any metaphorical meaning to that song. It's one of those songs that people will read whatever they want into it or take whatever they want from it. For me, it was just a little story. Waking up and everything's entirely changed, but not because that's what I went through or that's what I felt. I don't know why. I just wrote it and hoped for the best, but I knew it was a good song. I like the melody and I like the words as well. They're intriguing. I don't know what they mean. I have no idea. Probably don't mean anything.

The only thing I said to Steve Brookes, and maybe to Hannah as well, is that, kind of, any reference at all would be Bach. That was the only reference I could hear, like a baroque thing as well. I don't study that stuff. It's just what I cop and what I hear, and I think, *That's nice. I like that.*

I knew that Richard Hawley could play slide guitar, so we sent that song up to him in Sheffield . . . on a truck, and then he sent it back. He's a brilliant guitarist. We've been trying to work together for ages and ages. We keep talking about writing a song together, which will happen maybe one day, but I knew he had a pedal steel and he could play it. Good enough reason, innit . . .

Richard Hawley: I remember on that song I had quite a few comments about the final mix. That was really funny, he just texted me back – 'It's done, Cunt!'

Paul Weller: Abbey Road is a special day out for us and it's a day out for the boys, isn't it? It's a Beatle studio. It's number two. So, yeah, we're all going to be there. But with 'My Best Friend's Coat' and 'A Glimpse of You', Hannah used what Christophe had put down. He put down his own strings, but on a machine. So she worked to his blueprint and just expanded it, made it bigger.

Hannah Peel: I think it's the horns that come in and the trombones, they just always gonna give a bit of Bond, aren't they? No matter what.

Paul Weller: 'Sleepy Hollow' would have started with me just playing those chords on guitar, putting something on my phone, sing la-la-la, and a melody, or maybe even singing 'Sleepy Hollow', even though I didn't even know what it means, and I still don't. That's just the first thing I've started singing. The first thing that come into my head and I was intending on changing them because I thought, *I don't know what that means at all*, but I couldn't think of anything else and I kept going back to this sleepy hollow motif thing. It ends up in my mind as being like a little kind of lullaby for my kids, or for kids in general. Just a little gentle song. Beyond that, I had no idea. But I just love the mood of it and the warmth of it.

Tom Doyle: Sometimes I get 2 a.m. texts from Paul. We were in a period of sending ideas back and forth. One night, he sent me two: one was thirty seconds long, the other was eight and a half minutes. That ended up being the basis of 'In Full Flight'.

Paul Weller: 'In Full Flight' was another one of those that I had for quite some time and I couldn't find my way into the song, even though I thought there's something good in this. Tom and Anth from White Label just sent me their backing track, which wasn't massively different from what it ended up like.

Tom Doyle: Another thing cool thing was when Paul said, 'I can hear a mad choir on this.' I said, 'Yeah, we can do a mad choir, man.'

Paul Weller: I think the older one gets, the harder it is to find new things to write about because your experiences don't come as quickly as they do when you're younger. As you live longer, you think, *I've done that, been through that, seen how that's* *going to turn out*, and you're not getting these revelations every week. So, it's inevitable that you end up writing about the same subjects, me included. I don't think there's any way around that.

Musically there's always something to say, but lyrically maybe there's not. I don't mind farming it out to other people to see what they come up with. It's still creative, it's still part of the process and keeps things moving. That's fine with me.

Bobby Gillespie: I was just sitting at home one night and got a text from Paul. He said, 'Would you consider writing some lyrics for a piece of music that I've got?' and I went, 'All right, send it over.' So, he sent me a backing track over. I listened to it a couple times and the lyrics just came out. I thought, he's a spiritual guy. He's a searcher, he's a questing artist, but he's on a spiritual search as well.

Paul Weller: I just sent Bobby a bit of a backing track. Quite a rough skeletal one, with me singing the melody, so we had a phrasing to write to. Then we built it back up from that. I wanted really loud, old school, shouty BVs [for 'Soul Wandering']. I'd sung with Louise a few times with Jools. I wanted something strong and loud and just singing out and Louise and Sumudu were great.

Louise Marshall: Paul gave us the freedom to be able to do what we do best. He works very quickly because he's got things to do. Brilliant.

Sumudu Jayatilaka: We had this amazing moment where he had to sing his part so that we could match his rhythm and his phrasing first. I got to hear him and watch him do his thing in seconds to just nail it. Just beautiful. I am not one of these people who takes it for granted. When you're watching Paul Weller do that, I know that means something.

Bobby Gillespie: My mum messaged me the other week saying Paul's on *Jools*. I turned it on and he's doing the song. Unbelievable.

Charles Rees: 'Burn Out' could be my favourite Paul Weller song.

Ben Gordelier: There were three of us, after a day of recording or rehearsing. It was me, Crofty and Paul – very late – at least two in the morning . . . Charles is dribbling, and he needs to go to bed and wants to turn the computer off. 'Let's take a quick idea down'. It might have been a quick play around for a minute or two and then press record.

Paul Weller: We didn't even do two takes. We did a little half bit. And I just showed the others what the chord structure was and then the next take was the one we ended up using. So, it was all spontaneous. And when we just chopped it up and edited it, there it was.

Andy Crofts: I didn't know that song was going to be on the album, which was a lovely surprise. What we'd normally do, was we'd rehearse all day, have dinner, and then we'd go in and just play around a bit, jam some ideas down and stuff, and that was one of them ones. Paul would have a bit of an idea, and we'd just go around it a few times and then press record so he doesn't forget it. Sometimes when you record an idea you just know when there's a good vibe there and there's some magic. So obviously he felt the same. He kept my original bass line, which was improvised. We learned it on the spot. It wasn't like I did it in my head for a few weeks and then nailed it. I just went in with the band and just went down with it, and it sounds great.

Paul Weller: That song was just something that was knocking about, to be honest with you. It had been finished for some time, maybe even in 2021, and I wasn't really sure what to do with it. It had a filmic quality about it and I thought maybe it could get on TV or a film or something like that. Wasn't really thinking of it as an album track at the time. But then when we got to the end of this album, I thought it'd be a good closer. It's got a big finale . . . not end of days, but end of an era thing. Erland wrote the words and there's a lot of references, in my mind anyway, to the lockdown. I can hear a lot of that in it. 'This inner circle is bored of you and me. There's no more detailing . . .' all of that. We have seen that whole thing of when, whatever Tory twat it was, who said that I should retrain? I shouldn't possibly think about retraining. What on earth could I do? It was pathetic. Anyway, that's what those lines mean to me.

It is fairly bleak, but it just felt right as an album closer. To be honest, I don't think it's appropriate at this time with the way the world is at the moment to end on a joyful, happy song. It wouldn't seem right. It is a bleak time, if we're really fucking honest. So, I guess for me that reflects that a little bit.

Steve Cradock: We played it live on the last tour, but Paul said it was a bit too miserable. But I like the darkness of it and the fact that nothing moved. There wasn't the middle-eights and the pre choruses and the decoders at the end. It was just this fucking fog. The intensity, and dynamic, is the only thing that really moves in that song.

Paul Weller: When we finish an album, yes, there's a sense of achievement, but it's often overridden by a sense of fear. You've been around it all this time – sometimes years – and towards the end, it becomes even more intense as you try to finish things. You are so close to it – know what's good, you're not sure about other bits – and then you've got to play it to other people. That's nerve wracking.

We think it's good, but we don't know what others will think. So, it's a very intense feeling that first time you play it to someone. However good you feel about it, you still never know.

It's also very different when you have other people in the room. It's one thing to have the band or me and Charles, because we'll hear things and think, *We'll fix that later.* But when you're playing it to other people for the first time, you hear it differently as well. I don't know why that is, but you look at people and think, *What do they like about it, what don't they like?*

In the end, you just do your best and what you believe in, and then you put it out into the world and hope other people relate to it or like it.

2024 – Live

Paul Weller: I don't get tired of playing music to people, because that is just a brilliant, fantastic, fascinating thing. The only thing that I do tire of is the travelling and hanging about and all that. That's just part and parcel of it. That's what you have to go through to get to the good bit. Sometimes when I'm sitting in a hotel room or on a plane or a bus or whatever, I think, *What am I doing? I could be at home watching TV with my daughter*, or whatever, and then you get on stage, and for those two hours or whatever it is, there's nowhere else you should be. You're exactly where you should be. So it's always that weird dichotomy or whatever you want to call it. And the little magical two-hour bit at the end of the day is really what you want and that's what you're after, that's what you're looking for.

18 October 2024 – *Supplement: 66* EP

Kathryn Williams: "Paul said, 'Oh, we should write a song together,' and I was like, 'I'd love to.' Inside, I was thinking, *Oh my God. Oh my God.* He gave me a title and suggested we write something based on that idea. I went down an absolute rabbit hole, diving into *National Geographic* and writing about twenty pages of lyrics. I put a melody to it, went into my studio, laid down a track, added backing vocals, Mellotron, double bass — basically, I made a whole song in a week because I was so overexcited.

I sent it to Paul, and he replied, 'Well, this is really great, but I haven't done anything.' I'd been so thrilled that Paul Weller asked me to write a song with him that I didn't actually write *with* him – I wrote a song *at* him. I said, 'I'm really sorry I've written a song at you. Could we please start again?'

Paul found it amusing, probably because I was trying to show I was a hard worker who could get things done. Even now, my butt is clenching with the embarrassment of it.

We started again properly. Paul jammed a track and sent me different versions, and I began writing lyrics and ideas. Going back and forth, slowly building the song that way – which is the way it should be done *[laughs]*.

2024 – *Blitz*

Claire Moon: I was at Black Barn when I got an email from one of the producers that we'd worked with on *Jawbone*, introducing me to a lady called Nina [Gold]. An hour later she phoned me, I don't know who she is, and she said, 'I want to talk to you about the new Steve McQueen film called *Blitz*.' I'm like, 'Do you want Paul to score it?' and she's like, 'No.' I said, 'Oh, like opening credits . . .' and she's like, 'No, stop!'

At this point, I had the phone under my chin, googled her and realised she's an Oscar-winning casting agent who worked on *Harry Potter* and *Star Wars*. She's a big deal and incredibly lovely. Then she said, 'No, we want him to appear in the film.' I asked, 'What, as a cameo?' She said, 'No, it's a supporting role that Steve had written, with Paul's likeness and voice in mind, so we've come to you first.'

I hope Paul doesn't mind, but I did say to her, 'I need to be honest with you – I don't think he can act.' I knew that's the first thing Paul would say. She replied, 'We know, we've watched videos, and he definitely can't act!' That's how the process began.

The next stage was Paul and Steve McQueen meeting for coffee. They're big mutual fans of each other and got on. Steve reassured Paul, saying, 'If it doesn't work, I won't make you look foolish. You won't be in the film if it's not great, and we'll help you through the process.'

Steve McQueen: I landed on the idea of Paul quite early in the writing process. His face was of that era – he reminded me of a Samuel Beckett or Sam Shepard type, with those lines, that posture and presence. There's an authenticity to him as a Londoner that made me think he'd be amazing for the role. I figured, if he can write and perform his own songs, then he can act.

At first, I don't think Paul realised his potential, but we paired him with an acting coach and he just blossomed. He was amazing. His role isn't large but it's extremely important. If the audience doesn't feel the depth of him in that role, there's no payoff. I'm so pleased he said yes. Paul's a worker – so he works at it, and he nailed it.

What was especially beautiful was seeing Paul work with Saoirse Ronan, who plays Rita, and Elliott Heffernan, the nine-year-old who plays her son. You had Paul at sixty-six, Saoirse at twenty-nine, and Elliott at nine, and they loved collaborating with each other. Paul is a talented genius as a musician. He knows where to come in and come out. There's a collaborative thing innately in him. If you don't have that authenticity and appreciation of each other as a family, then it doesn't work.

Claire Moon: I explained my conversation with Nina to Paul, and his immediate reaction was like, 'Really?' – which is classic Paul whenever something unusual comes up. Then he said, 'Oh, I don't know if I can pull it off, Moonie.' I'm like, 'Well, I think they're going to help you if you want to do it. Let's just take it step by step. Let's do the meeting with Steve first, see how you feel after that. Let's do the next camera thing, see how you feel after that.'

He wasn't pressured into committing right away. We were well into the process before any contracts came into play. In the end, he spent about seventeen or eighteen days on the shoot.

Steve McQueen: Paul's minimalism and real heart were key. If he feels something, it's going to come out. He's not pretending; it's authentic emotion. He's like a fine wine; there's a real depth in him and I imagine with his music as well. This is a guy who's had number one albums over five decades. Ridiculous. Who does that? He's a real auteur. His art connects with people across generations – it can't just be the people who bought his records fifty years ago, but new audiences as well.

I'm very grateful that he was in this picture, showing another dimension of his artistry. He's an artist through and through. If Bob Dylan can act, if others can, why not Paul Weller?

Claire Moon: The best thing about it was him having his haircut.

Steve McQueen: Could you imagine cutting Paul Weller's hair? I was like, *Bloody hell. Was he going to want it? Is he going to be OK with it?* Apparently Paul's team were saying, 'I hope he keeps it like that.' It was a really good short back and sides.

Classic. He looked perfect. It was like The Style Council days, wasn't it? You've had those similar images of him as a young person with that kind of haircut.

Claire Moon: I really wanted to go with him from the offset. And he was like, 'No, I'm not going to be that person that turns up with an entourage.' He felt very much like everyone else were actors, and he was a musician. He didn't want to be like a rock star with an entourage. Not that that's ever his attitude, but he didn't want that to be how he was perceived. He did quite a lot of it on his own, and then by the time it came to the Waterloo East outdoor shots, I was like, 'Please let me come, I'm dying to see you do it.' He was more comfortable by then.

Steve McQueen: It's cool but it's also weird. You do a double take though, don't you? *It's Paul Weller* . . . move on. Paul's such a beautiful man and he's an artist and I think that first and foremost, an artist is an artist is an artist. You don't stay relevant for fifty years without evolving. I hope others and myself follow in his footsteps in the way of taking risks. I wouldn't even call it taking risks: as an artist there's a compulsion to work through things. If you stay still, you know what happens? Nothing. You have to move forward. Sometimes we do put limits on ourselves, but I feel that as this door has opened for him, I'm hoping more will, because he ain't done yet, that's for sure.

July 2025 – *Find El Dorado* & beyond . . .

Tony Harlow: I spoke to Claire, and she said, 'Are you interested?' and I was like, 'Of course.' We shook hands and it was as simple as that. Paul came in for a meeting with the team at Parlophone, and obviously whenever anybody meets Paul

Weller, apart from falling over themselves to get into the room, they love him because he's so direct. He played a couple of songs from the covers record and everyone was like, 'Yeah, we're in for that.' It did feel like this is a battery recharge, then he'll have a look and see what it is. But they're brilliant. The only thing I'd say about it is, if I looked at *Studio 150*, probably the covers were relatively mainstream. 'Wishing On a Star' and things. With this one he's really dug into the record collection. There are some surprises for fans and a really incredible creation that's going to excite people and cause them to go, 'I can't believe that song is that great.' His ability to switch from being an artist to a fan and find those things that are just more exciting is part of what you get on this record and it's really special.

Pete Paphides: *Studio 150* was recorded during a pretty hedonistic time, whereas this has been very lovingly and carefully put together. You can really hear the work. It's a very, very carefully and lovingly crafted album. Everyone's put so much into it. This was the first record Steve Cradock's produced for Paul and he really sweated over it. He took it really seriously and carried that weight very conscientiously. It's a real testament to the almost psychic bond those two have now. They've been working together for decades, and I think there will always be a part of Steve that was a fan – and at some level, his life has been building up to this.

Steve Cradock: Paul wanted to do an acoustic-based covers album just because he thinks it would be nice to have in his canon of albums. He doesn't want to promote or tour it; it's just a bit of fun. He had the songs already. They were tracks that friends had played him over the years, and he'd kept them earmarked. He sent me the A-side and B-side, in the running order he was hoping for.

I did simple versions at home, either on piano or acoustic. I'd try to orchestrate and arrange it to see if it was in the right key and had the right arrangement. Most of those versions ended up being the backing tracks. I added bass, drums, and strings to a few. We've got some guest artists too: Declan does a duet, Amelia Coburn sings a verse, and John McCusker plays on some tracks.

I tried to make it sound like a relaxed, unpolished record rather than a big production. I didn't know most of the songs, so it was good being turned on to new music. Paul's always looking for new stuff. I think he found Amelia Coburn while Googling himself and saw her version of 'Tube Station'.

Paul Weller: They're quite obscure songs. Some will be known to some people. A few folky, sort of old obscure folk songs. It was a way of making a record, for me to still make music and without any pressure really . . . and not to go out and tour it. I just need a year off touring. That's really it. There's a lot of tunes I want to cover and it's a good way of me still being creative and making the records, but I ain't got to think about writing because it's very consuming.

When you're writing and making a record, it just fills my head fucking twenty-four/seven pretty much. It's so consuming, and I just don't want that at the moment. I just need to clear everything. I don't want to think about writing or making records for some time.

It's really hard to balance the two things, man – the music and family. It's hard to get the right balance. I mean, I kind of do all right, but it'd be nice to have a period of time when I don't have that.

I don't want to write for a while as well. I just want to switch the machine off for a little bit. But beyond this year, man, I ain't got a clue what's going to happen. I don't know.

You can only make plans up to a point and then you have to see how things go, how things pan out.

I've been doing a bit of writing with other people, and I've enjoyed that. Not for me, for them. I've done a tune with Maverick Sabre and Liam Bailey. A really good reggae tune. Me and Cradock have done a couple things with him. Hopefully going to do something with Amelia Coburn as well, the little folk singer. So, I'm just enjoying that. I still want to make music. I just don't have the intention of making an album for a while. If it happens, it happens, and if I don't do it then that's what it is as well.

Steve Cradock: I think it's the right time to stop for a while and then to try something different because it's been going up like that for a few years now, which is extraordinary. I don't know how, but I thought the last tour in the UK at the end of 2024 was a pinnacle and if you carried on repeating it, that's all you do. And Paul's not about that.

Paul Weller: I don't think it's possible. I don't think it's humanly, physically possible. So, I think it was good to leave it. Last year, the last thing we did, apart from the Gaza show, was Hammersmith Odeon, we did two nights which were fucking amazing. That's a good place to leave it for a bit. Because those peaks, they last for a while, but they don't last forever and once you get to that certain peak, the only other way is down. So rather get to a stage where you all hate each other and hate being on the road, and *I got play that fucking song again tonight*. It's a good place to leave it and then come back some other time and be fresh and optimistic with it.

Tony Harlow: Everyone wants to meet and be near Paul Weller, because he's genius. There are some artists who are like that for me, but you might not do their record because what they're doing now isn't amazing. With Paul Weller, he constantly makes music you want to hear. Even if it's a covers record – he'll have picked more interesting songs, thought about the arrangements in a cleverer way.

I think the reason he's got such longevity is because he never looks back. The nearest equivalent is Dylan. I can imagine Paul writing *Modern Times* or *Time Out of Mind* in another ten or fifteen years and speaking better than anyone to those dark kinds of concepts. He's like Dylan – always listening, always hearing, always trying to find new young musicians to be excited about. So, the music's always exciting and relevant.

The other thing is – he's an amazing singer. No one would have thought from 'In the City' that he'd become the person who'd sing 'pebbles on a beach'. His voice changes and matures all the time. It's always exciting. People will always sign Paul Weller because he's always making it brilliant music.

Dylan Jones: Most great artists, even the ones we deeply admire, don't typically make their best work in the latter part of their careers. As much as I love people like Brian Wilson and The Who, you can pick any great artist that we all love and revere, it's unlikely that they're going to make their very best work thirty or forty or fifty years after they first appeared. Artists seem to have a narrative arc – a seven-year period in which they are imperious – perhaps based on the professional lifespan of The Beatles.

It's important to acknowledge that Paul Weller's an exception to have bucked that post-war, seventy-year trend. The records he's made in recent years have been extraordinary. Anyone who knows or cares about his work would agree with me.

Paul Weller: I don't get the impostor thing, man. Because, fucking hell, I've had to work for it all. But sometimes on a nice sunny day when I'm walking here, back and forward, up and down from the house to the studio, I still have to pinch myself. Just think, *Fucking hell, this is mine now.* It's not like I haven't worked for anything I've got. But I still can't get over how lucky I am, really. Because I don't think I'm that talented, really. I'm not doing this as any false-modesty bullshit either. Because I don't like any of that. But it's not like I'm a fucking genius or something. I mean, I'm just good at being me, I suppose. I don't know where I stand against contemporaries or whatever. I have no idea any more about that. Don't care either. So you can only try and be the best version of yourself, can't you? But I think I've worked hard for it. But a tremendous amount of luck involved as well. I'm very lucky to be here. I'm lucky to be alive, man, to be honest!

You have to count your blessings. I think it's important to recognise what you've done and your achievements, but don't dwell too much on it and be grateful. Be humble as well. Not just in music, but in life, I think it's important to learn that. If there's anything I'd ever try and instil in my kids, it's that. Be grateful and be humble for all the good things you get in life.

The cast

The voices that shape this story

Adrian Thrills	Early champion of The Jam, creator of *48 Thrills* fanzine. Later wrote for *NME* maintaining a connection with Weller through The Jam, The Style Council and his solo career.
Alan McGee	Founder of Creation Records and a lifelong Paul Weller fan, who credits The Jam as a major influence on his career.
Alex Borg	Pop artist who designed the artwork for Paul Weller's *Fat Pop (Volume One)* album. He is also a bassist and producer for the band Moonlight Parade.
Alistair Lyon	Never doubting Paul Weller fan since 1983.
Andrew 'Chalky' Chalk	Friend of Suggs who wrote a poem called 'Nothing' that became a Paul Weller song on the album 66. Passed away in December 2024.
Andy Crofts	Multi-talented musician in Paul Weller's band from 2008–2022, founder of the Moons, and creator of the Paul Weller documentary *One*.
Andy Lewis	Musician and producer who played bass in Paul Weller's band from 2008–2016 and co-wrote 'Are You Trying to Be Lonely?' with Paul.

Andy McDonald	Founder of Go! Discs and Independiente record labels. He signed Paul Weller to Go! Discs, releasing the albums *Paul Weller*, *Wild Wood* and *Stanley Road*, and continued to work with him on Independiente with *Days of Speed* and *Illumination*.
Andy Miller	Paul Weller fan since The Jam days.
Andy Rosen	Punk photographer known for his iconic images of The Jam, including the *Setting Sons* album back cover and the final live shots of the band.
Ann Weller	Beloved mum of Paul and Nicky Weller, Ann was a vital source of support throughout his career. From ironing suits and running The Jam's fan club to providing a stable home, she helped lay the foundation for his success. Ann sadly passed away in July 2025.
Annajoy David	Co-founder of Red Wedge, a cultural and political movement that engaged young people in politics. Annajoy collaborated with Paul Weller on Red Wedge and other projects.
Anthony Harty	Bass player who toured with The Style Council from 1983 to 1985. He later won a Grammy Award for his work with Lee 'Scratch' Perry.
Ashley Slater	Grammy-nominated trombonist, singer-songwriter, and producer who played on The Style Council's 'The Lodgers' single and *The Cost of Loving* album.
Aziz Ibrahim	Guitarist and songwriter known for his work with the Stone Roses and Ian Brown. He collaborated with Paul Weller on the *Illumination* and *Sonik Kicks* albums and provided the voice of 'God' on *22 Dreams*.

Barbara Snow	Trumpet player with The Style Council in their early days. Playing on the first tour and on studio recordings of 'A Gospel', 'Headstart for Happiness', 'Me Ship Came In' and 'Dropping Bombs on the White House.'
Barrie Cadogan	Guitarist and singer-songwriter, known for fronting Little Barrie. Cadogan has supported Paul Weller and played with him live and on record for the *22 Dreams*, *Wake Up The Nation* and *True Meanings* albums.
Barry Cain	Music journalist and publisher, known for his early coverage of Punk with *Record Mirror* and his close relationship with The Jam. He received a 'Special thanks' credit on *The Modern World* album. Later launched *Flexipop* magazine, which featured Paul Weller on multiple occasions.
Barry Pugatch	Founder and frontman of All Mod Cons, a tribute band dedicated to the music of The Jam. He has met Paul Weller and jammed with him.
Ben Gordelier	Drummer, percussionist and producer who has played live with Paul Weller since 2012, touring extensively and contributing to albums such as *Sonik Kicks*, *Saturns Pattern*, and *On Sunset*.
Ben Taylor	The Magic Mod Rock 'n' Roll Magician and Paul Weller fan and friend. Credited with 'Claps' on the song 'Old Father Tyme' from the *On Sunset* album.
Benjamin Herman	Dutch saxophonist and bandleader. He played saxophone and flute on Paul Weller's *Studio 150* and *As Is Now* albums, also contributing to the horn arrangements on former.

Bev Bevan	Celebrated drummer with the Move, Electric Light Orchestra (ELO) and Black Sabbath. He played on 'Moonshine' and the title track for Paul Weller's *Wake Up the Nation* album.
Bill Smith	Art director and designer who created The Jam's iconic logo and designed many of their album covers while at Polydor Records (1976-1978) and later at Bill Smith Studio.
Bill Wheeler	Tour manager for Paul Weller, a role he took on after his father, Kenny Wheeler.
Billy Bragg	Singer-songwriter and activist. He supported The Style Council on tour in 1984 and co-founded the Red Wedge movement with Paul Weller.
Billy Chapman	Saxophonist in Animal Nightlife (admired by Paul Weller), which led to his involvement with The Style Council. He played on tour and on tracks from *Café Bleu* and *Our Favourite Shop*.
Billy Sullivan	Singer-songwriter and musician, frontman of the Mod-influenced band The Spitfires. A lifelong Weller fan, he supported Paul Weller on tour.
Bob Manton	Songwriter and musician, a founding member of the Mod-influenced band Purple Hearts, who supported The Jam on tour.
Bobby Gillespie	Frontman of Primal Scream, who collaborated with Paul Weller on tracks 'Big Brass Buttons' and 'Soul Wandering' and cites Weller as a major influence.
Boy George	Singer-songwriter and frontman of Culture Club, who collaborated with Paul Weller on 'One Tear' from *A Kind Revolution* and

performed 'You're the Best Thing' with Weller at the Barbican.

Brenda Taylor — A longtime Paul Weller fan, known as one of the 'Mad Nurses' alongside Karen McBride.

Brendan Lynch — Record producer. Engineered The Style Council's *Modernism* album. Produced Paul Weller's self-titled debut, *Wild Wood*, *Stanley Road*, *Heavy Soul* and *Heliocentric*. He also created remixes for Paul Weller, including 'Kosmos SX Dub 2000,' and for artists like Oasis and Massive Attack.

Bruce Foxton — Bassist for The Jam, known for his distinctive and melodic bass lines integral to the band's signature sound. He later joined Stiff Little Fingers, reconnected with Paul Weller in the '00s and played on the *Wake up the Nation* album.

Bruno Gallone — Songwriter and musician, founder of the Mod-influenced band Reaction, who supported The Jam at the Hammersmith Palais in 1981.

Camelle Hinds — Member of the Brit funk band Central Line. Bass player for The Style Council (from 1985) and Paul Weller's early solo band. He co-wrote 'Sure is Sure' with Paul Weller for the *Modernism* album.

Carleen Anderson — Singer, songwriter, and musician. Performed with Paul Weller live and on record. Singing on songs, such as 'Wings of Speed' and 'All Good Books.' Weller co-produced her album *Blessed Burden*.

Cat Santos — Designer at Fifth Column T-Shirts (1979-2017), a company known for its iconic punk rock designs who hand-printed t-shirts for bands like The Jam and The Clash.

Charles Rees — Studio manager and engineer at Black Barn Studios, Paul Weller's HQ, since 1999. Rees has played a key role in the sound of numerous Weller albums and is known for his technical expertise and close working relationship with Weller.

Chris Bangs — Producer and DJ, a pioneer of Acid Jazz. Bangs co-produced Paul Weller's single 'Above The Clouds'.

Chris Bostock — Musician and songwriter with Joe Boxers and Dave Stewart. Playing bass on 'The Paris Match' and double bass on 'Here's One That Got Away' for The Style Council's *Café Bleu*.

Chris Catchpole — Digital Editor at *Mojo* and co-writer of *The New Cue*. A Paul Weller fan who has interviewed him on multiple occasions.

Chris De Whalley — *Sounds* magazine writer (1976-1978) who provided early coverage of The Jam. He later worked in A&R at CBS Records.

Chris Difford — Lyricist and founding member of Squeeze, whose career has intersected with Paul Weller's. Weller's 2000 *Heliocentric* album was recorded at, and named after, Difford's studio in Rye.

Chris Free — Songwriter and musician, known for being one half of A Craze, who were signed to Paul Weller's Respond label. He released the single 'Wearing Your Jumper' and now performs as The Sound Of Pop Art.

Chris Green — Writer and director of *The Pebble and the Boy*, a film inspired by Paul Weller and mod culture.

Chris Parry — A&R executive who signed The Jam to Polydor in 1977 and co-produced their first three albums. He later founded Fiction Records, signing the Cure.

Chris Pope — Songwriter and musician, a founding member of The Chords, a Mod-influenced band who supported The Jam on tour.

Christophe Vaillant — French musician and producer who co-wrote and played on tracks for Paul Weller's *66* album and opened for Weller on his European tour.

Christopher Holland — Keyboardist, singer, and songwriter. He played keys for Paul Weller on the *Heliocentric* tour and is a member of Jools Holland's Rhythm and Blues Orchestra.

Claire Mahoney — Journalist and editor of *Detail Magazine*, a publication focused on Mod culture. Mahoney is the author of *Welsh Mod* and a longtime fan of Paul Weller.

Claire Moon — Paul Weller's manager. She began working with Weller at V2 Records where she worked in marketing and has now managed his career for nearly twenty years.

Conor O'Brien — Award-winning musician and songwriter behind Villagers, praised by Paul Weller. O'Brien remixed 'She Moves with the Fayre' for the deluxe *A Kind Revolution* LP and collaborated with Weller on 'The Soul Searchers' on *True Meanings*. He has also toured with him.

Conny Jude — Created illustrations for The Jam's *This is the Modern World* album inlay.

Craig Hassall — Chief Executive of the Royal Albert Hall (2017-2023), a long-time Paul Weller fan who brought Weller to the venue for performances.

Craig McLean — Music journalist and editor. He conducted in-depth interviews with Paul Weller, pro-

	viding unique insights into his creative process and personal life, particularly during the *Illumination/Studio 150* era.
Damon Brown	Trumpet player who toured as part of The Paul Weller Movement in 1990.
Damon Minchella	Bass player for Ocean Colour Scene and the Paul Weller Band (up to 2007). He now plays with Richard Ashcroft and is a Dr. of music.
Daniel Ash	(AKA Teenage Waitress). Singer-songwriter and musician, who has supported Paul Weller on tour.
Daniel Rachel	Award-winning author known for his books on British music and culture, including *Walls Come Tumbling Down: The Music and Politics of Rock Against Racism, 2 Tone and Red Wedge*.
Danny Eccleston	Senior editor of *Mojo* magazine and a Paul Weller enthusiast, who collaborated with Weller on a guest-edited issue of the magazine.
Danny Thompson	Legendary double bassist and founding member of Pentangle. Thompson played on Paul Weller's *Studio 150* and *True Meanings* albums, along with what he called his final recording, 'So Quietly' on the *Supplement 66* EP.
Darren Fletcher	Singer and frontman of The Style Councillors, a tribute band dedicated to the music of The Style Council.
Dave Rowe	Lifelong Paul Weller fan who, with his partner Jo, sold merchandise for The Style Council and Paul Weller.
Dave Swift	Double bass player for Jools Holland and His Rhythm & Blues Orchestra. He has collaborated with Paul Weller.

David Cracknell	Former political editor of the *Sunday Times*. Cracknell's appreciation for Weller began with The Jam and deepened through The Style Council, whose political lyrics resonated with him. Happened to play piano on Gabrielle's 'Why,' featuring Weller.
David Lines	Author of *The Modfather: My Life With Paul Weller*, a memoir about a lifelong fan's journey with Paul Weller's music.
David Pottinger	Modernist writer and co-founder of *Move On Up*. Pottinger interviewed Paul Weller for *About The Young Idea*.
David Quantick	Writer and music journalist who wrote for *NME* and won an Emmy for his work on *Veep*. He has reviewed The Jam, The Style Council and Paul Weller's solo work.
David F. Ross	Scottish author whose debut novel, *The Last Days of Disco*, was inspired by The Jam's *Setting Sons*.
Dean Rudland	Acid Jazz General Manager, with a lifelong passion for Paul Weller's music.
Dean Standerwick	Paul Weller fan since The Jam days.
Debsey Wykes	Musician and singer, known as a member of the band Dolly Mixture who supported The Jam in 1980 and signed to Paul Weller's Respond Records.
Declan O'Rourke	Award-winning Irish singer-songwriter, known for his emotionally raw and affecting music, including his 2021 album *Arrivals*, produced by Paul Weller. A testament to O'Rourke's songwriting talent, Weller has publicly stated that he wishes he had written O'Rourke's song 'Galileo.'
Dee C. Lee	Singer and songwriter, best known for her integral role in The Style Council. She and

	Weller were married for a time and have two children together. She has also had a successful solo career, including the hit single 'See the Day,' and continues to make music.
Den Davis	Superfan and collector with a vast collection of Jam vinyl and memorabilia. Davis created the 'Jam Tapes Collection' of live recordings with Paul Weller's approval and shares his collection through exhibitions, often in collaboration with Nicky Weller.
Dennis Munday	Former Polydor A&R executive who worked closely with The Jam and The Style Council, playing a key role in their success.
Derek D'Souza	Photographer of The Jam (1979-1982), capturing live images 'in the crowd.' His work is included in the National Portrait Gallery.
Dot Allison	Scottish singer-songwriter known for her work with One Dove and her acclaimed solo albums. She collaborated with Paul Weller on 'Love's Got Me Crazy' for her 2007 album *Room 7 1/2*.
Dylan Jones	Award-winning journalist and author, known for his work in music and fashion and for curating *Magic: A Journal of Song*, a book providing insights into Paul Weller's songwriting.
Dylan White	Multi-award-winning plugger who worked with Paul Weller, helping to promote his solo music to a wider audience.
Eddie Pillar	Acid Jazz Records boss, DJ, and writer, known for his deep knowledge of mod culture and his early love of The Jam. He featured in the music video for 'Solid Bond in Your Heart', is the man behind the infa-

	mous King Truman shelved record and even played records at Weller's fiftieth birthday party.
Edgar Jones	Musician, singer, and songwriter (the Stairs, solo). He played bass in Paul Weller's live band around the *Heliocentric* era.
Eliza Carthy	English folk musician, singer-songwriter, and fiddle player. Carthy covered Paul Weller's 'Wild Wood' and played on his *Studio 150* album.
Ernie McKone	Bass player and music producer. McKone toured with Paul Weller during the *Heavy Soul* era.
Fiona Cruickshank	Award-winning engineer, producer, and mixer. She engineered the strings for Paul Weller's *On Sunset* and *Fat Pop*.
Gary Crowley	Broadcaster, DJ, and journalist. A longtime fan of The Jam, Crowley interviewed Paul Weller early in his career and has maintained a friendship with him.
Gered Mankowitz	Photographer who captured iconic images of rock stars, including The Rolling Stones and Jimi Hendrix. Mankowitz photographed The Jam for the cover of *This Is The Modern World*.
Graham Coxon	Guitarist for Blur and solo artist. He collaborated with Paul Weller on songs 'This Old Town' (2007), 'Black River' (2008), 'Dragonfly' (2012), and the Jazz-Folk-Rock-Poetry SuperJam, 'Bankbusted Nuclear Detergent Blues' with Weller, Michael Horovitz, and Damon Albarn.
Guy Barker	Award-winning composer, band leader, trumpet player, and arranger. Guy played trumpet on The Style Council's 'Money

	Go Round,' 'The Lodgers,' 'Fairy Tales,' and trumpet & flugelhorn on 'Walking the Night.' He also toured with the band.
Gwenno Saunders	Singer-songwriter and musician known for her unique blend of synth-pop and vocals in Cornish and Welsh. She remixed Paul Weller's 'Old Father Tyme.'
Hannah Peel	Award-winning composer and musician. She has arranged strings for Paul Weller's albums from *True Meanings* onwards. She also conducted the *Other Aspects: Live at the Royal Festival Hall* shows.
Helen Jones	Paul Weller fan since The Jam days.
Helen Turner	Keyboardist and Honorary Councillor for The Style Council, and later a member of Paul Weller's solo band during the *Wild Wood* and *Stanley Road* era.
Hilary Robertson	Saxophonist and Honorary Councillor of The Style Council. Played live with the band in 1983 and on 'A Gospel' and 'Headstart for Happiness' from the *Café Bleu* album, and the single version of 'My Ever Changing Moods'.
Ian Snowball	Author of many books relating to Paul Weller, The Jam and The Style Council, including *Paul Weller: Sounds from the Studio* and co-author of *Thick as Thieves* and *Soul Deep*.
Ian Stone	Award-winning stand-up comedian and author of *To Be Someone*, a memoir about his teenage obsession with The Jam.
Jack Dee	Award-winning comedian and actor, a longtime Paul Weller fan who hosted him on his TV show and used 'One Way Road' as the theme for his sitcom *Lead Balloon*.

Jacko Peake — Saxophonist and flautist, a long-time collaborator with Paul Weller, known for his contributions to Weller's albums and live performances across different eras of his career.

Jake Fletcher — Bassist and backing vocalist in Paul Weller's band since June 2022. Played on the 66 album and *Supplement* 66 EP.

Jamie Johnson — Producer and sound engineer who contributed to albums from *Heavy Soul* through to *A Kind Revolution*. He recorded and mixed Paul Weller's Mercury-nominated album *Wake Up The Nation*.

Jamie Telford — Keyboard player who toured with The Jam at the end of their career.

Jaye Ella-Ruth — Singer who performed with The Style Council in 1984 and sang lead vocals on the Brand New Heavies' debut album.

Jeff Shadbolt — Musician and founding member of Purple Hearts, a Mod-influenced band who supported The Jam and recorded tracks produced by Paul Weller.

Jeff Slate — New York-based musician and journalist, a lifelong Paul Weller fan with an extensive bootleg collection, who has interviewed Weller multiple times.

Jeremy Murray-Wakefield — The Style Council sound engineer known as 'Jezar'. He was a junior assistant for Peter Wilson on *Our Favourite Shop* and was promoted to Chief Engineer for *The Cost of Loving* and *Confessions of a Pop Group* albums.

Jill Furmanovsky — Award-winning music photographer, known for her images of iconic musicians, including The Jam and Paul Weller. She is the founder of Rockarchive.com.

Jill Webb	Blogger and Jam enthusiast from Hull, co-creator of *The Jam Scrapbook*.
Jim Cook	Former Head of A&R at Polydor Records (1975–1984), who signed The Jam. He left Polydor during the first year of The Style Council.
Joanne Ruocco	Drummer and percussionist, known as Little Jo, who played with The Style Council from *Confessions of a Pop Group* LP.
Joe Beckett	Percussionist who toured as part of The Paul Weller Movement in 1990 and played on demos for tracks like 'Kosmos' and 'Round and Round'.
Joe Connor	Award-winning film director, screenwriter and musician. He directed the *Wild Wood* documentary and *May Love Travel with You*, a film about Paul Weller's Royal Festival Hall live shows, and recorded an album at Weller's Black Barn studio.
Joeri Saal	Recording engineer at Studio 150 in Amsterdam, where Paul Weller recorded *Studio 150* and parts of *As Is Now*.
John Cohen	Partner at Clintons law firm who represented The Jam and Paul Weller during the 1970s and 1980s.
John Harris	Music journalist and author. A longtime Paul Weller fan, he has interviewed Weller multiple times and written liner notes for The Jam's box sets, including the 40th-anniversary edition of *1977 and The Jam: The Studio Recordings*.
John Lewis	Writer, editor and journalist who has interviewed Paul Weller multiple times for publications like *Time Out* and Uncut, providing insightful commentary on Weller's career.

John Mealing — Composer and arranger who provided string and horn arrangements for The Style Council, including on the hit single 'Shout to the Top.'

John Reed — A music journalist and author of *Paul Weller: My Ever Changing Moods*. He wrote for *Record Collector* magazine and has written sleeve notes for several of Weller's releases.

John Williams — Music industry executive who was Director of A&R for Polydor Records between 1987 and 1989, where he worked with The Style Council.

John Wilson — Radio broadcaster and journalist. Has conducted many in-depth interviews with Weller, including for Radio 4 specials, the *Suburban 100* book, the *These Three* podcast, and documentaries about *True Meanings* and *On Sunset*.

Johnny Chandler — Former Head of A&R at Universal Music Catalogue. Involved in reissuing Paul Weller's back catalogue, *including Fly on the Wall* and *Will of the People*.

Jon Abnett — Author and designer, known for his work on The Jam's box sets and his book *From the Floorboards Up*, documenting Paul Weller's solo career live.

Jon Mills — Founder and editor-in-chief of *Shindig!* magazine, a publication dedicated to 1960s music and culture. A fan of Paul Weller since childhood, he has interviewed him for *Shindig!*.

Jonathan Ross — Broadcaster and talk show host, a longtime fan of Paul Weller's music. He has hosted Weller on many of his TV and Radio shows over the years.

Josh McClorey	Songwriter, guitarist and musician, known for the Strypes. He has collaborated with Paul Weller on multiple occasions, supporting him on tour and playing on tracks like 'Long Time,' 'Woo Se Mama,' and 'Soul Wandering.'
Julian Broad	Photographer who shot images of Paul Weller for album covers and inlays for *Heliocentric, Sonik Kicks* and *Saturns Pattern.*
Jun Sato	International A&R, Pony Canyon Inc., Japan (1990–2002). Sato signed Paul Weller to Pony Canyon in 1991, providing him with a three-album deal and launching his solo career in Japan.
Junior Giscombe	Grammy Award-winning singer known for 'Mama Used to Say.' Giscombe collaborated with Paul Weller on 'Soul Deep' and toured with The Style Council. He was also a key figure in the Red Wedge movement.
Karen McBride	A longtime Paul Weller fan, known as one of the 'Mad Nurses' alongside Brenda Taylor.
Kathryn Williams	Singer-songwriter and author. Co-wrote 'So Quietly' with Paul Weller for the *Supplement* 66 EP
Keb Darge	Scottish DJ and music producer known for his expertise in Northern soul, funk, rockabilly and garage music. He collaborated with Paul Weller on the compilation album *Lost & Found: Real R'n'B & Soul.*
Keiko Egawa	A Japanese superfan who has attended hundreds of Paul Weller concerts over forty years, including sixty-nine Jam gigs. She is known for her long-standing dedication to his music and her friendships with the Weller family.

Keith Cameron	Music journalist for *Sounds, NME*, and *Mojo* who has interviewed Paul Weller multiple times, offering insightful perspectives on his career.
Kenny Wheeler	Tour manager for Paul Weller since The Jam, Kenny has been a key part of Weller's touring operation for over forty years.
Kevin Metcalfe	Sound mastering engineer, with a career spanning nearly fifty years. He mastered music for artists including David Bowie, Adele, U2, Queen, ELO, Depeche Mode and Paul Weller (*Illumination, Studio 150, As Is Now* and *Catch Flame* albums).
Kevin Miller	Bass player and Honorary Councillor of The Style Council, playing bass on the *Groovin'* EP in 'You're The Best Thing', 'Big Boss Groove' and 'Shout to the Top'.
Lawrence Watson	Photographer who did The Style Council's *Confessions* LP cover. He captured key moments in Weller's solo career, including the *Wild Wood* album cover and imagery for *Modern Classics* and *As is Now*.
Lee Cogswell	Filmmaker and director, known for his documentaries on Paul Weller and The Style Council.
Lenny Henry	One of Britain's best-known and most celebrated comedians, as well as a writer, radio DJ, TV presenter and award-winning actor. Performed with The Style Council on *Saturday Night Live* and for 'The Stand Up Comic Instructions' on The Style Council's *Our Favourite Shop* album.
Louise Marshall	Singer and vocalist in Jools Holland's live band. Performed live with Paul on Hootenanny and for the *Studio 150* album launch/

	DVD. Sang backing vocals on 'Soul Wandering' and 'Jumble Queen' for the *66* album.
Lucy Hooberman	Filmmaker who produced the Red Wedge documentary *Days Like These* and The Style Council's film, *JerUSAlem*.
Malcolm Gerrie	Influential British television producer, behind *The Tube* and *The White Room*, which showcased Paul Weller's talent and featured memorable live performances.
Marc Marot	Managing Director of Island Records from 1990 to 2000, who oversaw the release of the *Heavy Soul* album.
Mark Baxter	Writer and filmmaker who runs MonoMedia Films with Lee Cogswell and has produced documentaries on Paul Weller.
Mark Cooper	Music journalist and television producer, best known as showrunner and co-creator of *Later... with Jools Holland*. The influential music programme has featured Paul Weller more than any other artist.
Martin Hopewell	Booking agent for Paul Weller from 1977 through to *Studio 150*, spanning The Jam, The Style Council and his solo career. Hopewell worked at Cowbell and later at World Service (Primary Talent).
Martin Speake	Saxophonist who toured with The Style Council on their 'Council Meetings Part 2' tour in 1984
Martyn Goddard	Photographer who documented The Jam from 1977 to 1980, creating iconic images for their album covers (*In the City, Sound Affects*) and seven singles.
Matt Askem	Film director who captured Paul Weller's live performances for DVD releases of

	Route Of Kings, Hyde Park (2002), *Live at Braehead Arena* (2002) and *Studio 150* (2004).
Matt Deighton	Singer-songwriter and guitarist. Frontman for the 90s acid jazz band Mother Earth. Deighton was a guitarist in Paul Weller's band during the *Heavy Soul* tour (1997-1999).
Max Beesley	Actor and musician. Beesley played keys and vibes in The Paul Weller Movement live band and on early solo tracks. Has recently collaborated on Weller's 2024 album, *66*.
Mick Talbot	Keyboardist and founding member of The Style Council. Talbot's musical journey began in various bands before joining Paul Weller to form The Style Council. He is known for his keyboard skills, his contributions to the band's sound and his encyclopaedic knowledge of music.
Miles Leonard	Chairman of Parlophone Records, 2008–2017. Signed Paul Weller and supported his creative vision during the release of *Saturns Pattern, A Kind Revolution*, and *True Meanings*.
Neil Jones	Musician and songwriter, a founding member of Stone Foundation and frequent collaborator with Paul Weller.
Neil Sheasby	AKA Brother Sheas. Bass player and songwriter, a founding member of Stone Foundation and frequent collaborator with Paul Weller.
Neil Tinnings	AKA Twink. Photographer who documented The Jam on tour in 1981. His images also appear on *The Gift* album cover.

Nia Wyn	Welsh soul artist and producer with a talent for raw and powerful storytelling. She collaborated with Paul Weller on her song 'Turnstiles' and has supported him on tour.
Nick Heyward	Singer-songwriter (Haircut 100) and a lifelong fan of The Jam. He shared a stage with Weller in Buffalo, New York, and his songwriting has been a significant inspiration.
Nick Knight	Influential fashion photographer, awarded an OBE for his services to the arts. Knight's work includes photographing Paul Weller, including The Style Council and his debut solo album cover.
Nicky Weller	Paul Weller's sister, a music industry veteran who managed The Jam and Style Council fan clubs and curates exhibitions celebrating his music.
Nicole Nodland	Photographer who shot the cover for Paul Weller's *True Meanings* LP and worked with him on *Other Aspects*, *On Sunset*, and 66.
Nigel Sweeney	AKA Spanner. Music industry figure and top TV and radio plugger, including for The Jam, The Style Council and Paul Weller solo.
Noel Gallagher	Songwriter and musician, best known as a founding member of Oasis. Gallagher is a longtime friend and collaborator of Paul Weller, having co-written songs like 'Echoes Round The Sun' and 'Jumble Queen' with him.
Olly Ball	Photographer known for creating the iconic album cover for The Style Council's *Our Favourite Shop*.
Omar Lyefook	Pioneer of UK soul music known for 'There's Nothing Like This'. Omar toured with The Style Council in 1989 and collab-

orated with Paul Weller on his 2025 album, *Brighter The Days*.

P.P. Arnold — London's First Lady of Soul, known for her work with Ike and Tina Turner and The Rolling Stones. Arnold collaborated with Paul Weller on 'Woo Sé Mama' for *A Kind Revolution* and on her own *The New Adventures Of...* album.

Pat Gilbert — Author, broadcaster and veteran MOJO writer. Has interviewed Weller many times and wrote sleeve notes for The Jam and Style Council box sets, as well as other official Weller projects.

Paul Anderson — AKA Smiler. Author and DJ, known for his book *Mods: The New Religion*, a key work on Mod culture. Paul Weller is a fan of his work and suggested the idea for his book *Scorcha!*.

Paul Baines — Senior Marketing Manager at Parlophone Records, who oversaw the marketing campaigns for *Saturns Pattern*, *A Kind Revolution* and *True Meanings*.

Paul Barry — Songwriter and musician, known for writing hit singles for Cher and Enrique Iglesias. His band, the Questions, supported The Jam and The Style Council on various tours and signed to Paul Weller's Respond Records.

Paul Dowling — Director of Marketing at Go Discs! (1990–1993), who helped launch Weller's solo career with the independent release of 'Into Tomorrow' which led to Weller's signing for the label.

Paul DuNoyer — Author, editor and music journalist. He was a founding editor of *Mojo* magazine and has interviewed numerous iconic musicians, including Paul McCartney and Paul Weller.

Paul Fitzgibbon	Paul Weller fan since The Jam days.
Paul Francis	Bass player who was part of The Paul Weller Movement in 1990, marking the start of Weller's solo career.
Paul Gomersall	Studio engineer who mixed 'Into Tomorrow' and the *Live at Brixton Academy* concert recording.
Paul Lester	Editor of *Record Collector* magazine. He has interviewed Weller extensively, including a notable 13,000-word *Uncut* cover story in 1998.
Paul Moody	A longtime Paul Weller fan who discovered The Jam as a teenager. He is a rock 'n' roll writer (*NME, Q, Another Man, Uncut*) and musician (*Regular Fries, The Studio 68!*), and interviewed Paul Weller for *NME* around the time of *Stanley Road*.
Paul Weller	Iconic British singer-songwriter and musician whose five-decade career has spanned The Jam, The Style Council and a successful solo career. Known as the 'Modfather,' he is celebrated for his authenticity, ever-evolving style and commitment to pushing creative boundaries. A four-time Brit Award winner, he has also received the Ivor Novello Lifetime Achievement Award, *Mojo* Outstanding Contribution to Music award and the *NME* Godlike Genius Award.
Pete Mason	Exec producer of Weller's *Days of Speed* album. He worked for Go! Discs and Independiente, and with artists like The La's and John Martyn.
Pete Paphides	Music journalist, broadcaster and author of *Broken Greek*, known for his insightful writing on music and his memorable kebab-fuelled encounter with Paul Weller.

	Wrote the liner notes for 2025's *Find El Dorado* album.
Peter Anderson	Photographer known for his iconic images of musicians, including Madonna and Iggy Pop. He is also recognized for his work with Paul Weller and The Style Council, capturing key images during their early years.
Peter Button	Partner at Clintons law firm, who has handled the majority of Paul Weller's legal work since the split of The Style Council.
Peter Gordon	Radio broadcaster from Surrey and longtime Weller fan, who has interviewed him on several occasions. A strong advocate for recognizing Weller's legacy in Woking, he unveiled The Jam tribute sculpture in 2012.
Peter Watts	Journalist and author, who has written for *Uncut*, the *Guardian* and *Sunday Times*, and has written a book about the history of Denmark Street: *London's Street Of Sound*. Interviewed Weller on many occasions including on tour in the US.
Peter Wilson	Polydor producer who took over from Vic Smith towards the end of The Jam's career including their final album *The Gift*. Produced the early Style Council singles, and the first two albums, *Café Bleu* and *Our Favourite Shop*.
Phil Bickley	Fashion entrepreneur and owner of Tonic, who collaborated with Paul Weller on the Real Stars Are Rare clothing line.
Phil Veacock	Saxophonist and arranger with Jools Holland's Rhythm and Blues Orchestra. Veacock has multiple credits with Paul Weller, arranging and performing on albums from 2017's *A Kind Revolution* to 2021's *Fat Pop*.

Pippa Hall	Music publicist who joined Go! Discs in 1990 and rose to Head of Press, promoting Paul Weller's albums *Wild Wood* and Stanley Road. After Go! Discs, she co-founded Monkey Business PR and worked with Paul up to his move to V2 in 2004.
Polly Birkbeck	Paul Weller's PR representative. Has been managing his press and media relations since 2004.
Rhoda Dakar	Two Tone singer and activist, known as a member of the Bodysnatchers. Dakar chaired the Red Wedge steering committee and collaborated with Paul Weller on Dr Robert's *Realms of Gold* album. She remained connected to Weller, supporting his early solo career and later recording at Black Barn Studios.
Ric Blaxill	Radio executive and former *Top of the Pops* producer, who brought Weller back to the show for a memorable double live performance.
Richard Engler	Marketing Director at V2 Records from 1997 to 2005. Worked with Weller on *Studio 150*. The Jam Fan Club Member from 1977.
Richard Hawley	Singer-songwriter and guitarist. Richard played lap steel guitar on Paul Weller's track 'I Woke Up' from the album 66.
Richard Houghton	Author of *The Jam – The Day I Was There*, a book chronicling the band's history through the experiences of over three hundred fans.
Richard Ogden	Head of International Marketing at Polydor Records, who promoted The Style Council overseas, before becoming Managing Director. He was responsible for Weller's new million-pound contract following the success of *Our Favourite Shop*.

Rick Buckler	The Jam drummer. A founding member of the band who played a key role in their energetic live performances and iconic sound. Passed away in February 2025.
Robert Howard	AKA Dr Robert. Singer, songwriter and musician, best known as the frontman of The Blow Monkeys. He collaborated with Paul Weller on his early solo albums and on the Monks Road Social track 'Rise Up Singing.'
Rod Argent	Composer and musician, known for his work with the Zombies and Argent. Weller has often named Zombies' *Odessey and Oracle* as his favourite album. Rod guested on Weller's 2018 album, *True Meanings*, playing Hammond organ on 'The Soul Searchers' and Mellotron and piano on 'White Horses'.
Roger Armstrong	Music industry veteran and a founder of the original Chiswick Records in 1975, who first met Weller while running a record stall in Soho Market.
Roger Nowell	Head roadie/guitar tech for Paul Weller since 1999. He also played on 'Andromeda' and 'Around the Lake'. Bass player for the post-punk band Skeletal Family who have recorded at Black Barn Studios.
Roger Pilling	A friend of Paul Weller since their school days in Sheerwater, Pilling has known Weller since age thirteen.
Russell Hastings	Frontman of From The Jam, performing The Jam's music alongside Bruce Foxton.
Sam Brown	Singer-songwriter known for her hit 'Stop' and performances with Jools Holland. Contributed backing vocals to Paul Weller's *Studio 150* album.

Sam Molnar	A longtime friend of Paul Weller, known as 'Sammy Carpet.' He organised Wake Up Woking, a charity event featuring Paul Weller, and conceived of The Wild Wood Garden at Woking Hospice.
Samudu Jayatilaka	Singer-songwriter and member of Jools Holland's live band. Sang backing vocals on Paul Weller's *66* album, specifically on 'Soul Wandering' and 'Jumble Queen.'
Sarah-Jane Morris	Singer-songwriter and actress known for her diverse musical style and powerful vocals. She was part of the Communards and the Red Wedge tour. Weller gifted her the song 'Leaves Around the Door' which she recorded live.
Sean Alexander	Artist and graphic designer who created the album artwork for Paul Weller's *Illumination* and related singles.
Sean O'Hagen	Frontman of The High Llamas, who arranged strings on Weller's *Sonik Kicks* album in 'Sleep of the Serene' and 'By the Waters'
Seckou Keita	Senegalese kora master, praise singer, pioneer, composer and drummer. Played with Weller as part of Africa Express and remixed 'Rockets' for the *On Sunset Remix* EP.
Shane Juson	Superfan of Paul Weller since 1979, known for his dedication to The Jam and his emotional connection to Weller's music. You'll usually find Shane down the front row of gigs.
Shaun Hand	Author of *Pop Art Poems: The Music of The Jam*, known for his detailed analysis of The Jam's music.

Sheema Mukherjee	Sitar player and composer. Contributed sitar and a Sanskrit prayer to the track 'Books' on Weller's *True Meanings* album, which she also performed live with him at London's Royal Festival Hall.
Simon Fowler	Lead singer and songwriter for Ocean Colour Scene. He has a long-standing connection with Weller, with OCS supporting him on tour and both artists performing on each other's records.
Simon Halfon	Graphic designer known for his iconic artwork for The Style Council and Paul Weller solo, creating designs for marketing, single and album covers for over twenty years.
Simon Napier-Bell	Music industry veteran, songwriter, and author. Owned NOMIS Studios, where The Style Council and Paul Weller rehearsed, and John Weller rented an office.
Simon O'Brien	A longtime Paul Weller and Style Council fan who went from attending gigs in his teens to working as part of Weller's tour security in 2000.
Sodge Adams	Director of Fifth Column T-Shirts (1976-2017), a company known for its iconic punk rock designs who hand-printed t-shirts for bands like The Jam and The Clash.
Sonja Phillips	Award-winning filmmaker and director. Created iconic music videos for Paul Weller: 'Broken Stones' and 'You Do Something to Me.'
Souad Massi	Franco-Algerian singer-songwriter. Paul Weller cited her as an inspiration and collaborated with her on the song 'Let Me Be In Peace.'

Steve Barron	Film director who created music promo videos for The Jam ('Strange Town,' 'When You're Young' 'Going Underground' and 'Dreams of Children'), Michael Jackson ('Billie Jean'), and A-ha ('Take On Me').
Steve Brookes	Singer-songwriter and guitarist, a founding member of The Jam alongside Paul Weller. Brookes left the band in 1975 before their rise to fame. Known for his long-standing friendship and collaborations with Paul Weller.
Steve Carver	AKA Tufty. Friend and fan, known for his close ties to The Jam since 1976. Tufty was in the inner circle from the days of Punk and witnessed their rise to fame. He's also fucking hilarious.
Steve Cradock	Guitarist for Ocean Colour Scene and the longest serving member of Paul Weller's band. Cradock joined Weller's band in the 1990s and has been a key collaborator ever since.
Steve Ellis	Singer known for his work with The Love Affair and for his long-standing friendship and musical collaborations with Paul Weller, who produced his 2018 album *Boom! Bang! Twang!*.
Steve Hinders	US-based Jam fan and collector, co-creator of *The Jam Scrapbook* with Jill Webb.
Steve McQueen	Acclaimed British film director and visual artist (knighted in 2022). A longtime admirer of Weller's work, McQueen cast him in a key role for his 2024 film, *Blitz*, recognizing his authenticity and presence.
Steve Nichol	Multi-instrumentalist and songwriter, known for his work with Loose Ends and for playing brass and keys with The Jam during their final year, contributing to *The Gift* album and touring with the band.

Steve Pilgrim	Drummer, singer and songwriter. Member of the Paul Weller Band since 2008. Pilgrim has contributed to numerous Weller albums and tours and is also a solo artist, with his album *Beautiful Blue* produced by Paul Weller.
Steve Rapport	Rock photographer who captured iconic images of The Jam, The Style Council and the Red Wedge movement.
Steve Sidelnyk	Drummer, percussionist, and programmer. Honorary member of The Style Council live and on record. He has worked with artists including Madonna, The Rolling Stones and REM.
Steve Trigg	AKA The General. Trumpet player and arranger. A key member of Stone Foundation since 2016, he has also arranged and recorded horns on Weller's *On Sunset*, *Fat Pop* and *66* albums, as well as *Mother Ethiopia* EP.
Steve Wheatley	Dedicated Paul Weller fan and creator of *Love Weller Live*, celebrating the live music experience.
Stewart Prosser	Brass musician and arranger. The Style Council Honorary Councillor from 1984 for the Council Meeting live tour and remained with the band until the end of 1985. He played trumpet on 'Big Boss Groove', 'Walls Come Tumbling Down' and 'Heartbreakers', and flugelhorn on 'A Man of Great Promise'.
Stuart Deabill	Author and Paul Weller fan, co-author of *Thick as Thieves: Personal Situations with The Jam* and *Soul Deep: Adventures with The Style Council*, and the upcoming *Decade – Paul Weller: Nineties* coffee table book with Nicky Weller.

Stuart Watts	Filmmaker who directed *Paul Weller: Into Tomorrow* (2007), a career-spanning documentary from The Jam to The Style Council to the solo years.
Suggs	Singer and songwriter, best known as the frontman of Madness. He is a longtime friend of Paul Weller and collaborated with him on their duet 'Ooh Do U Fink U R' and co-wrote two songs on 66.
Ted Cockle	Music industry executive, former President of Island Records. Compiled the *Hit Parade* boxset and signed Paul Weller to Island for a trilogy of albums: *22 Dreams*, *Wake up the Nation* and *Sonik Kicks*.
Ted Kessler	Writer and editor who has interviewed Paul Weller multiple times, navigating a complex relationship to become a trusted voice on Weller's music. He also devised *My Old Man: Tales of Our Fathers*, which featured Weller.
Terry Edwards	Multi-instrumentalist and founding member of the Higsons. Played on Weller's *Wake Up The Nation* album (Baritone Sax on the title track and Flugelhorn on 'Grasp & Still Connect').
Tim Burgess	Singer and songwriter, best known as the frontman of the Charlatans. Longtime Paul Weller fan, who collaborated with Weller on the track 'Spinning Out'.
Tim Parsons	Legendary concert promoter and former music mogul, who co-founded Midland Concert Promotions (MCP) in 1978. Worked with The Jam and The Style Council, as well as U2 and Oasis.
Tim Shepard	Artist and photographer who created the album artwork for Weller's *22 Dreams*.

Tony Harlow	UK CEO of the V2 record label for *Studio 150* and *As is Now*. Chairman & CEO of Warner Music UK since 2019.
Tom Doyle	Acclaimed music journalist, author and contributor to *Mojo* and *Q*. As part of music duo, White Label, Doyle has collaborated with Weller on remixes and co-writes, including 'Movin' On' (*True Meanings*), 'Glad Times' (*Fat Pop*), and 'In Full Flight' (*66*).
Tom Robinson	New wave bandleader 1977–79, part-time performer on 1986 Red Wedge tour.
Tom Sheehan	Photographer who captured key moments in Weller's career, from The Jam to solo. Author of *Aim High: Paul Weller in Photographs 1978–2015*, a book charting his photographic history of Weller.
Tom Van Heel	Keys player in the Paul Weller band, contributing to albums from *Saturns Pattern* onwards. Van Heel, a longtime Weller fan from Woking, joined the band after a chance encounter at Black Barn Studios.
Tracie Young	Sang backing vocals on The Jam's final single, 'Beat Surrender,' and The Style Council's 'Speak Like a Child.' She then launched her solo career on Weller's Respond label with hits like 'The House That Jack Built' and 'Give It Some Emotion.'
Trevor Neil	Comedian and actor (*Trevor and Simon*) and long-time Paul Weller fan, who performs The Jam covers in his band.
Vic Coppersmith-Heaven	Worked with The Jam as sound engineer and record producer from their *In the City* debut in 1977, through to 1980's *Sound Affects*, along with singles such as 'Going Underground' and 'Start!'.

Virginia Turbett	British rock music and social reportage photographer known for her images of bands, fans and street culture, including The Jam, The Clash and Prince.
Will Hodgkinson	Music journalist and author, chief rock and pop critic for *The Times* and a contributor to *Mojo*. He has interviewed Paul Weller multiple times – including a *Mojo* cover story for the album *66*.
Yolanda Charles	Bassist and bandleader. Yolanda played with Weller from the *Wild Wood* tour through the *Heavy Soul* period.
Zeke Manyika	Drummer and percussionist, known for his work with Orange Juice and for collaborating with Weller on The Style Council early singles and in The Paul Weller Movement live band.

Author acknowledgements

Dancing through the Fire is an oral history, conceived as a definitive exploration of Paul Weller's remarkable five-decade career in music. My aim was to create an intimate and unprecedented portrait of the man behind the music, tracing his journey from the incendiary spark of The Jam to the sophisticated sounds of The Style Council and the ever-evolving landscape of his solo artistry. This chorus of voices – bandmates, collaborators, record company personnel, friends, family, fans and more – offers a unique perspective on his enduring influence and the creative forces that have shaped his life.

This oral history owes its existence to my *Desperately Seeking Paul* podcast and the vibrant community that surrounded it. Thank you to every listener; your enthusiasm, social media shares, and constant mentions to Paul Weller himself were essential in building the trust and momentum that led to this book.

My sincere thanks to every guest who shared their stories, with a special call-out to **Stuart Deabill** and **Mark Baxter**, who agreed to be interviewed before it was even out in the world. They showed a faith that I'm not entirely convinced I even had myself.

Gratitude is also due to the writers, broadcasters and passionate fans whose articles, interviews, books and documentaries were invaluable throughout my research.

As this book project took shape, I sought guidance from author **Daniel Rachel**, who generously shared his time and wisdom, patiently listening to my anxieties and offering invaluable advice over pints of Guinness at the Hope and Anchor. His analogy of an oral history as a play, a room filled with characters whose interwoven stories unfold like a conversation, profoundly shaped my approach. It is this spirit of shared storytelling that I hope resonates within these pages of *Dancing through the Fire*, where each voice, carefully placed within the larger narrative arc, contributes to a vibrant and compelling whole.

Of course, the reality is that these people (sadly) weren't all together in one room having a conversation. Instead, over the past five years I have interviewed over 250 people about The Jam, The Style Council and Paul Weller. Every conversation has been meticulously transcribed, a task made possible by the dedicated efforts of several individuals, especially **Ian Traynor, Gary Fairhead and Janice Bartholomew**. I extend my sincere gratitude to them.

Many interviewees, including **Steve Cradock** and **Vic Coppersmith-Heaven**, generously shared their stories exclusively for these pages, and I am deeply grateful for their time, insights and trust. The book benefits greatly from their inclusion.

There are many people who I have spoken to on multiple occasions – *I have another query* – cross referencing stories and fact-checking places and timings as best anyone could remember. Particular thanks to **Nicky Weller, Mick Talbot** and **Claire Moon**. I'm sure at times I was annoying with my volume of queries, but the book is so much better for their support. They also served as conduits for other interviews, introducing me to people on my hit list. Tracking down people who had gone off the radar was one of the most time-consuming elements of this project, so these introductions were a huge help.

I was fortunate to find a literary agent, **Tim Bates** at Peters Fraser & Dunlop. From our first conversation, Tim's guidance and unwavering support have been instrumental. He wisely advised me that this book should be more than just a companion to the podcast, envisioning a broader scope and a richer narrative. Tim's expertise in shaping my initial vision and proposal into a viable project has been invaluable, as has his role in securing the perfect publishing partner in Little, Brown. Thanks to Publishing Director, **Andreas Campomar**, who believed in this project from the outset and helped me shape it into the book I hoped it could be.

I am immensely grateful to **Pat Gilbert**, whose extensive experience as a music writer and deep appreciation for Paul Weller's career and music, proved invaluable. His expert guidance was crucial in organising the wealth of material and balancing the multitude of voices, ensuring a cohesive and compelling narrative.

During the process of bringing this book to life, we sadly lost two individuals who contributed to its narrative. **Andrew 'Chalky' Chalk**, whose poignant poem inspired the evocative lyrics of 'Nothing' on the *66* album, and **Rick Buckler**, the powerhouse drummer of The Jam. Their contributions enrich these pages greatly.

The recollections gathered in this oral history span decades of memories and sometimes present variations in chronology and perspective, a natural consequence of time and individual interpretation. While I've diligently strived for factual accuracy and a clear timeline, some discrepancies may remain. All interviews have been condensed and edited for clarity and readability.

This book, woven from the voices of those who have journeyed alongside Paul Weller, would not have been possible without the generosity and openness of so many individuals. To each person who contributed their time, memories, and insights, I offer my heartfelt gratitude. It is your collective voice that brings this story to life. I hope I've done your stories justice.

To my wife, **Kate Fontana**, thank you for being my rock

throughout this long, long road. Your early editing – meticulously tracking changes and offering crucial suggestions on what to keep, cut, and move – was essential. Combined with your unwavering support, patience with my obsessive late-night writing or podcast sessions, and willingness to listen (or at least pretend to) as I endlessly talked about this project and all things Weller – have been invaluable. This book wouldn't exist without you, and it's as much a testament to your love and understanding as it is to the music of Paul Weller.

To my children, **Henry** and **Freddie . . .** Your enthusiasm for this project, thoughtful inquiries about my progress, and wholehearted belief in me were a constant source of motivation. The laughter and love you bring to my life, particularly at the end of a long day, made the challenges of writing this book infinitely easier. I am immensely proud of both of you and hope that this book, a product of passion and perseverance, inspires you to pursue your own dreams with the same enthusiasm.

To my mum, **Jan,** thank you for always nurturing my passions, even when they involved driving me to the hospital radio station at the crack of dawn in my teens. You've been there through the ups and downs, offering encouragement every step of the way.

To my nana and grandad, **Pat and Bob**, though you're sadly no longer with us, your love and support remain a constant source of strength. You always championed my pursuits, from my early days in radio and I know that you would have loved seeing this book out in the world. It is dedicated to your memory.

Special thanks to everyone at Paul Weller HQ. **Claire Moon,** your trust in granting me access to Paul and his world has been essential to capturing the true essence of this story. **Charles Rees,** the Wizard of Black Barn, thank you for sharing your expertise. Your contributions have added an invaluable dimension to this book.

To **Nicky Weller**, Paul's sister, thank you for your candour, warmth, and hilariously vivid recollections. Your personal insights added a unique layer of intimacy and understanding that made this story so much richer.

To **Ann Weller**, Paul and Nicky's mum, thank you for sharing your memories and insights, offering a unique and personal perspective on Paul's life and the environment that nurtured his creativity. Your interview for the 100th episode of the podcast was a true highlight, and your presence within these pages is deeply valued. As I completed the final edit of this book in July 2025, the sad news came through that Ann had passed away peacefully, surrounded by her family. I hope these pages stand as a small tribute to her memory.

To **John Weller**, Paul's dad and longtime manager, whose unwavering belief in his son's talent and tireless dedication to his career are woven into the very fabric of this story, thank you. Though John passed away in 2009, his presence is deeply felt throughout this book. The countless stories and memories shared by interviewees, reflecting his spirit, drive, and profound love for Paul, paint a vivid portrait of a remarkable man who played a vital role in shaping his son's success. While I'm saddened that John's own perspective couldn't be included, I'm grateful that I missed out on card school as part of this project.

Finally, to **Paul Weller** – thank you. Your music has been a constant companion, a source of solace, joy and inspiration, for more than half my life. It's a testament to the power of music how the songs we discover at pivotal moments can resonate so deeply and stay with us forever, shaping who we become. Your music has done that for me, and this book is, in many ways, a reflection of that profound connection. Thank you for not only allowing me to tell this story but for also planting the seed that made it possible. It has been a true honour and a privilege.